Auditing today

Auditing today

SIXTH EDITION

EMILE WOOLF FCA, FCCA, FInstM, MAE, FIIA
Partner, Kingston Smith, Chartered Accountants
Chairman, EW.FACT plc Accountancy Colleges

 Prentice Hall
FINANCIAL TIMES

An imprint of Pearson Education
Harlow, England • London • New York • Boston • San Francisco • Toronto
Sydney • Tokyo • Singapore • Hong Kong • Seoul • Taipei • New Delhi
Cape Town • Madrid • Mexico City • Amsterdam • Munich • Paris • Milan

Pearson Education Limited
Edinburgh Gate
Harlow
Essex CM20 2JE
England

and Associated Companies throughout the world

Visit us on the World Wide Web at:
http://www.pearsoned.co.uk

First published 1978
by Prentice Hall
© Prentice Hall Europe 1997

Typeset in 9½/12 pt Sabon
by Mathematical Composition Setters Ltd, Salisbury, Wiltshire

Printed and bound by CPI Antony Rowe, Eastbourne

Library of Congress Cataloging-in-Publication Data

Woolf, Emile.
    Auditing today / Emile Woolf. – 6th ed.
      p. cm.
    Includes index.
    ISBN 0-13-589466-2 (pb : alk. paper)
    1. Auditing. I. Title.
    HF5667.W65 1997
    657'.45–dc20
                                       96-34646
                                              CIP

British Library Cataloguing in Publication Data

A catalogue record for this book is available from the British Library

ISBN 0-13-589466-2 (pbk)

Transferred to digital print on demand, 2006

Contents

Preface and acknowledgements

If *Auditing today* is to live up to its title (rather than risk being referred to as *Auditing yesterday*!) each edition must capture significant developments at the technical, legal and professional levels. This will in turn reflect changes in the commercial environment in which auditors work.

Eighteen years have passed since I was persuaded to produce a comprehensive text that would serve the needs of practitioners and students alike. Although the broad thrust of its content has altered almost beyond recognition, certain themes persist, notably:

► the underlying importance to society of a group of professionals whose *raison d'être* is independently to authenticate financial accounts and reports produced by others;

► the dangers implicit in accepting such responsibility in an increasingly litigious world;

► the need for objective standards against which financial performance, and the audit thereof, can reliably be assessed by all those with a legitimate interest in such matters.

The sixth edition reflects these developments and concerns, first, by excising all material that, although once in the forefront of the profession's thinking, has since been overtaken by events that give rise to new issues and new problems; and, second, by incorporating both text and commentary on the important new developments that have surfaced since the fifth edition was published in 1994.

High on this list is, of course, the 1995 translation into full Auditing Standards of the APB drafts that appeared a year earlier. Although these incorporate much of the subject matter covered by earlier guidelines, they are strengthened by the fact that they carry mandatory status rather than being mere indications of good practice. Many smaller firms will face a difficult period of adapting their methods and their files to the new SASs, particularly the more technically challenging ones on materiality, risk assessment and sampling.

At the legislative level the most important new development addressed in this edition is the release of many hundreds of thousand companies from the statutory audit requirement altogether, under the government's banner of removing unnecessary burdens on small businesses. The effect has been to abolish not only the audit for these companies, but also the nest-egg of recurring fees for the small firms that hitherto carried out this work.

Since this enactment in late 1994 some 1,500 such firms have so far renounced their audit registration: that they have continued to add value to their clients' activities by providing non-mandatory services is a credit to their own innovative and entrepreneurial abilities.

Parliament may well raise the thresholds for exemption still higher, of course, and it is quite possible that companies with turnover between £90,000 and £350,000 now requiring the controversial 'Accountants' Report' will be freed from the need for professional input altogether by the time the seventh edition is under way.

This edition addresses crucial case law developments in the area of auditors' liability, culminating in the December 1995 judgment in *ADT* v *BDO Binder Hamlyn* (now subject to appeal) that left the present and former partners in that firm facing an uninsured damages award of many millions of pounds. I have, in this context, summarized the profession's case for legislative reform in an area of law in which the cards are so manifestly stacked against it. Unless this is recognized by government and translated into statute, many firms will follow the North American trend of classifying auditing as an activity whose risks outweigh its benefits, and will simply decline to undertake it – a development that will hardly be in any sector's interests.

To facilitate ease of reference each chapter now commences with a brief summary of subject matter content. Students and lecturers alike will welcome the addition of review questions and exercises and outline answers to a selection at the end of the text; this will, I feel sure, enhance the value of the text for those preparing for professional and university examinations, and I am grateful to Graeme Reid at the University of Hull for preparing this assessment material.

The whole text has, of course, been comprehensively updated to reflect developments in information technology, relevant financial reporting standards and ethical guidance; and I am, as ever, indebted to my fellow professionals at Kingston Smith, notably Janice Riches, David Masterson and Adrian Houstoun for their invaluable assistance in producing a text that, I am confident, my readers will regard as a worthy successor to past editions under this title.

Emile Woolf

1

The past and the present

1.1 What is auditing?

Audit is a Latin word, meaning 'he hears'. Our word *audit* is derived in this way since, in ancient times, the accounts of an estate, domain or manor were checked by having them called out to those in authority by those who had compiled them.

In its modern sense, an audit is a process (carried out by suitably qualified auditors) whereby the accounts of business entities, including limited companies, charities, trusts and professional firms, are subjected to scrutiny in such detail as will enable the auditors to form an opinion as to their truth and fairness. This opinion is then embodied in an 'audit report', addressed to those parties who commissioned the audit, or to whom the auditors are responsible under statute.

1.2   The development of auditing

1.2.1   Early economic growth

It is common these days for auditors to be regarded in an unflattering light. In many situations they will be thought of by management, particularly in the case of smaller companies, strictly as 'overheads' – a necessary evil, imposed by statute and unlikely to result in any tangible benefit. Should a misfortune occur, however, such as fraud by a member of the client's staff, the auditor is usually viewed as the scapegoat, and becomes the legitimate target for accusations and charges, often ill-founded and ill-advised, which may nevertheless require him to defend his position in a court of law. This latter situation, particularly in the USA, has now reached epidemic proportions (although there are, at last, indications of sanity being restored).

In the early days of auditing the prime qualification for the position of auditor was reputation. A man known for his integrity and independence of mind would be sought for this honoured position, the matter of technical ability being entirely secondary; consequently his function, in those days, was never confused with that of accountant. However, as accountancy gradually became more complex and concerned with technicalities, auditors found themselves out of their depth and, in turn, became increasingly dependent upon the expertise provided by accountants. Eventually the audit function itself became totally dominated by the accountancy profession. It is for this reason that the descriptions 'auditing profession' and 'accountancy profession' are today used synonymously. Herein lies the root of many of the problems which the profession now faces.

Auditing, in some form, has existed for as long as men have been required to account for their transactions; but auditing, as we understand it now, has its roots some three hundred years ago, in the first division of interests between those engaged in a business undertaking (the entrepreneurs) and those who made the finance available without necessarily becoming directly involved in day-to-day management.

The sixteenth and seventeenth centuries witnessed a great expansion in exploration and international trade, involving Europe in dealings with the East and the Americas. The adventurers who undertook these exploits rarely possessed the necessary financial means, and they consequently depended heavily on outside backing from wealthy merchants, bankers and even royalty, as in the case of Christopher Columbus. In England, Queen Elizabeth I gave active assistance to a number of such foreign ventures.

It became a common feature in the coffee-houses of the City of London for information on prospective undertakings (often in remote corners of the globe) to be circulated, and syndicates were formed with a view to providing the necessary funds. Information of this nature was usually embodied in a 'prospectus' which, as the word suggests, described the venture's prospects of success, and to which syndicate members and other 'backers' were required to append their names. As might be expected, prospectus details were often painted in terms more glowing than the circumstances justified, and several massive frauds – such as the infamous South Sea Bubble – gradually drew attention to the need for some form of control. That particular venture involved royalty and ministers of the Crown (including the Lord Chancellor) in a monumental fraud whose ostensible purpose was to secure a very large part of the national debt on the illusory fortunes of the South Sea Company, formed specially for the purpose of trading on the lucrative shores of South America and the South Sea Islands.

Another prospectus issued towards the end of the eighteenth century proclaimed a project 'for the purpose of extracting silver from lead'. Others were 'for supplying London with sea-coal'; 'for trading in hair'; 'for transmuting quicksilver into a malleable fine metal'; 'for carrying on trade in the river Oroonoko'; 'for salt-works in Holy Island'; and 'for importing a large number of jackasses from Spain' (though, it seems, there was no shortage of them in England!). One villain even had the effrontery to offer a prospectus 'for a special purpose, nobody to know what it is' – unbelievably, he cleared no less than £2,000 in the course of a single morning in the coffee-house and then, wisely, made himself scarce. Such was the fever.

This situation led to the development of a body of legislation whose aim was the protection of investors against unscrupulous attempts by promoters to divest them of their funds, culminating in our most recent companies, insolvency and investor protection legislation, notably the *Financial Services Act 1986*, the *Insolvency Act 1986* and the *Companies Act 1989*.

1.2.2 The birth of limited liability

Before the eighteenth century the concept of limited liability was unknown, all participants in a venture (whether as active or sleeping partners) being fully liable, jointly and severally, for the full amount of the debts of the enterprise. Two major factors combined, however, to alter this situation:

1. Outside assistance was needed on an unprecedented scale to finance increasingly ambitious projects, and the full liability of non-active backers would have entailed prohibitive risks for them. The scientific inventiveness of the eighteenth and nineteenth centuries led to the Industrial Revolution, and the realization of its fruits required an economic investment (and consequent risk) of vast dimensions.

2. Successive waves of land enclosures laid the foundations of a 'landlord economy'. This increased the hazards of enterprise and initiative owing to the ability of the new landowners to demand higher rents from entrepreneurs, with the threat of foreclosure if they failed to comply.

The new situation created new problems which, in turn, called for new solutions. The immense impetus of the Industrial Revolution in this country is attributable to the relative ease with which these solutions were found, and the result is the entre-preneurial society as we know it today.

Every student of elementary economics is aware that, for production to take place, three factors – land, labour and capital – are needed. In nineteenth-century Britain, these requirements were largely met by two main expedients. The first was to dispossess (albeit by Act of Parliament) the commons of their land, which had the dual effect of (1) making the land available for new industries, and (2) providing the labour – a workforce of men, women and children, dispossessed by successive *Enclosure Acts* and thus forced to work in the locations and appalling conditions imposed upon them. The financial and psychological consequences of depriving so many self-reliant men and women of the use of the land are still with us; even Sir Francis Bacon complained that enclosures 'bred a decay of people, and by consequence a decay of towns, churches, tithes and the like'.

The second expedient, designed to facilitate the provision of capital on the scale needed for the new age of industry, was the establishment of the limited liability ('joint stock' in the early days) company. Under the rules of limited liability no participator can be called upon to settle debts of the undertaking over and above the amount of capital he has already agreed to subscribe (measured in 'shares'). In this way, therefore, shareholders were able precisely to quantify the extent of risk which their investment entailed.

As the practical advantages of this split between the 'operators' and 'owners' of enterprises were experienced, the incorporation of limited liability companies (these days misleadingly abbreviated to 'limited companies') grew apace, and it became clear that legislation was needed for the following purposes:

1. Effectively to protect the interests of the non-active shareholders from the extravagance, inefficiency, ineptitude and, in some cases, deceit of the active stewards (who, in time, came to be known as 'directors').
2. To force the stewards to account for the results of all transactions undertaken by them on the company's behalf during their period of stewardship – hence the phrase 'stewardship accounting'.

1.2.3   Emergence of the auditor

A series of *Companies Acts*, commencing in 1844, gradually developed to meet the need for stewards to account for their transactions, and in time incorporated requirements that the stewardship accounts should be subjected to examination by independent experts – the auditors – who would then report (normally annually) the results of their findings to the shareholders who had appointed them.

It is a relatively recent requirement that auditors should have a recognized qualification as a mark of their competence: before 1948, auditors required no external professional qualification. Subsequent *Companies Acts* have, however, moved steadily towards such a stipulation, so that, in effect, all auditors must now be professionally qualified.

Apart from the intrinsic interest which lies in tracing the roots of the auditing profession, it is, paradoxically, becoming clear that a return to the earliest conception of the auditor's role is the next step forward. Progress in auditing has been measured during the post-war decades in terms of the development of new and advanced audit methods and techniques. This is quite natural and should continue, since such abilities are needed in the business environment of today; but this form of progress should no longer be pursued at the expense of developing the auditor's more 'intuitive' skills, a lack of which has become alarmingly evident of late, and such skills can only flourish in a situation of true independence – of which more in due course.

When company and case law first gave prominence to the audit function there was no defined limitation to audit responsibility – all investors, whether shareholders or creditors, were entitled to look upon the auditor as the guardian of their various interests. As time went on, case law gave more precise definition to this growth in accountability, but throughout the nineteenth century there was little to suggest that audit responsibility should be confined to shareholders.

Case judgments ranged wide and free over such matters as investment losses, recklessly optimistic prospectuses, negligently worded audit reports, determination of distributable profits, non-detection of cash and stock thefts, unjustifiable reliance on third-party certificates, management frauds and window-dressed financial statements, to select but a few. These early judgments were necessarily and genuinely creative, in that the age-old principles of English law, based chiefly on the concept of what is reasonable, were brought to bear on the particular situations facing the courts, and the precedents thus established were reliably followed for a hundred years or more.

1.2.4 Present confusion over accountability

The present view that the auditors are responsible mainly to shareholders was given its first major impetus in the *Companies Act 1929* which, for the first time, required the published financial statements of all public companies to include a profit and loss account – an account whose bottom line is the most obvious focus of shareholders' attention. The years which followed saw attempts by auditors to reduce their level of responsibility towards outside interests, but with no more than partial success.

This drive has resulted in the recent tendency of auditors to settle claims out of court, the cost of so doing invariably falling on insurance cover. Although understandable, this form of protection has immense disadvantages, not least in that the lack of development of case law has left the question of auditors' liability to third parties in a confused state.

The professional risks related to accountancy and auditing work do not disappear with insurance: indeed, those risks are potentially heavier when the business environment in which auditors practise is itself subject to economic upheaval – and this is the very situation which has typified the period in question. The satisfactory identification and quantification of such risks during this time of rapid change has been rendered more than usually difficult by the tendency to insure and settle rather than to employ the traditional institutions of law.

This, in turn, carries the penalty that auditors are seeking protection from liability which, in all probability, the English courts would not have laid at their door had they been given the opportunity so to decide. There is thus a tendency to insure against risks both real and imagined, and pay ever-increasing premiums merely to gain a level of comfort that exists in the psychological realm alone – for in the real world the measure of liability at any point in time can be determined only by decided cases, of which there are relatively few these days. This has naturally led the profession to call for a formula, preferably with statutory backing, for establishing a ceiling on the amount of negligence claims.

The profession's reluctance to defend itself in court with as much vigour as may be warranted, i.e. the tendency to settle in order to protect 'the name' (or for any other reason), leaves insurers in as much doubt as everyone else on the determination of liability for negligence, and the only adjustable variable in an equation filled with an increasing number of unknowns is, of course, the premium.

In recent years firms have had to face far greater readiness on the part of clients and third parties to hold auditors liable for their financial losses suffered following alleged reliance on financial statements. No individual firm can be criticized, however, for not wishing to become a test case. There are obvious advantages in settling claims before costs mount and energies are sapped.

1.3   The current scene

1.3.1   Development of the professional bodies

Following developments already described, it became clear that the work of accounting and auditing was far too important to be left to the inept efforts of persons who possessed no suitable training or experience in these fields. A number of nationally based professional bodies were established in the latter half of the nineteenth century, commencing with the Institute of Chartered Accountants of Scotland. The Institute of Chartered Accountants in England and Wales (ICAEW), whose centenary was celebrated in 1980, and its counterpart in Ireland were set up shortly afterwards. Three other eminent accounting bodies – the Chartered Association of Certified Accountants (CACA), the Chartered Institute of Management Accountants (CIMA) and the Chartered Institute of Public Finance and Accountancy (CIPFA) – also possess royal charters.

Each body has its own specialist expertise in the fields in which it operates, and is independently governed by a council of elected members with the support of a full-time secretariat. Although their specialisms vary, there have been powerful attempts to effect a total integration of the accountancy profession, but this has so far failed to win the necessary support from memberships of the bodies concerned.

The ICA and CACA memberships provide the full range of professional work, both in public practice and as directors and employees in commerce and industry. Approximately half of the chartered membership, and a much smaller proportion of the certified membership, is involved in public practice in the capacity of accountants and auditors. It would, however, be wrong to think of professional practice as narrowly confined, and the following table roughly indicates the range of assignments normally undertaken for company clients. Although the major source of fee income for most such practices often relates to audit work (usually accounting for between 40 and 70 per cent of total fee income) this will vary depending on the nature of the practice. Some, for example, specialize in liquidation work; others in taxation consultancy.

Table 1.1 Category of assignment

Category of assignment	Outline nature of work
Auditing	– Independent examination of records and draft accounts produced by clients
Accountancy	– Writing up books of account from source documents provided – Preparing final accounts and other useful information from books, e.g. statements of cash flows, detailed management accounts
Taxation	– Providing advice on the most beneficial method of organizing clients' affairs from the tax point of view – Preparing tax computations from accounts adjusted for tax purposes – Dealing with tax assessments levied on clients, including tax appeals – Handling all correspondence with the Inland Revenue and other taxation authorities – Dealing with Customs & Excise officials over VAT
Share registration	– Maintaining registers of shareholders, debenture holders, directors' shareholdings, charges and other statutory books
Management consultancy	Providing advice on: – Systems of general internal control – Devising costing systems – Recording and assessing divisional operating results – Budgets and forecasts – Design of documentation – Internal and operational audit – New accounting records – Computer systems – Recruitment of management personnel
Financial consultancy	Providing advice on: – Optimum avenues of investment – Raising finance in the short, medium and long term; preparing the associated reports and schedules – Client company's profitability and liquidity, and monitoring at regular intervals – Key financial decisions arising in the course of trading – Establishing optimum levels of readily realizable assets such as stocks, debtors and investments – Bank presentations
Investigations	– Alleged fraud – Under the *Companies Act 1985*, at the instigation of Department of Trade

(*continued*)

Table 1.1   (*continued*)

Category of assignment	Outline nature of work
	– Prospectus reports and other work in connection with new issues of shares or debentures – Valuation work: purchase of business; share in partnership; shares in limited company (minority or majority holdings); takeovers, mergers, amalgamations, reconstructions, absorptions – 'Back duty' tax investigations – Prospective loans to third party
Liquidations and receiverships*	– Realizing the best return on the assets of a company being wound up, as expeditiously as possible, in order to settle the claims of its creditors, and for the benefit of its shareholders – Acting as receiver for the debenture holders and/or other creditors of a company being wound up or defaulting on the terms of its debenture trust deed or finance agreements – Acting as administrator or administrative receiver under the *Insolvency Act 1986*
Trusteeship	– Acting in a fiduciary capacity as trustee, in accordance with the terms of trust deed, in the exclusive interests of beneficiaries
Miscellaneous	– Preparing or certifying claims for subsidy, grant or rebate for submission to the appropriate grant authority – Compiling reports for submission to government departments, containing figures relating to quotes, levies, subscriptions or tenders; or for statistical purposes; or confirming solvency – Preparing reports on profit forecasts in bid situations, in accordance with the City Code on Takeovers and Mergers – Providing advice on establishing staff pension schemes – Specialized assignments, e.g. international investigation work

Note: *Most of this work is limited to holders of insolvency practitioner licences.

1.3.2   Private audits and statutory audits

As a natural outcome of developments already described, the practice of auditing today can conveniently be split into two main areas, which we may respectively label 'private' and 'statutory'. A private audit is one undertaken at the behest of an interested party (e.g. a sole trader) or parties (e.g. partners in a partnership), even though there is no legal obligation that an audit be carried out. A statutory audit, on the other hand, arises under the *Companies Act 1985*, which prescribes that every company not eligible for exemption by reference to size and other specific criteria shall have its accounts audited annually by a professionally qualified auditor.

In the case of private audits the scope of the audit may be determined as narrowly or as broadly as the client wishes; but statutory audits have their scope largely determined by the governing legislation, which the directors, shareholders, or even the auditors, of the client company have no authority to vary in any way.

The term 'private' audit in this context should not be confused with that relating to private companies, a term that embraces all companies other than public companies. Under the *Companies Act 1985* a public company is one limited by shares, the memorandum of which states that it is to be a public company and which has been registered as such. As a public company, its name will end with the words 'public limited company' or with the letters 'plc'. This category of company must have at least two members and have a minimum issued share capital of £50,000.

The requirements for a public company, which alone may raise money from the public, are more stringent than those for a private company. In particular, the special requirements for public companies concern:

1. The minimum amount which must be paid up on all its issued shares.
2. The issue of shares for a non-cash consideration.
3. The procedure to be followed when a deficit of 50 per cent or more of its called-up share capital has occurred.
4. The calculation of distributable profit.

Before private companies may become public they are required to comply with a number of formalities. Apart from those related to the definition of a public company (given above), these formalities include the filing with the Registrar of a balance sheet made up to a date not more than seven months before the company's application (and on which the auditors have given an unqualified opinion), and of a statement by the auditors that the company's assets at the balance sheet date were at least equal to its share capital and undistributable reserves.

If an existing public company wishes to achieve private company status, it will have to pass a special resolution to that effect. One has in mind particularly those existing public companies which are wholly-owned subsidiaries, and where it is not necessary to have public company status.

1.3.3 Statutory audits – the legal relationships involved

It has been established for nearly a century that a limited company has a separate corporate identity ('legal personality') irrespective of what befalls its promoters, officers and shareholders. A company is therefore able to enter into contracts and business relationships in its own right. This important principle was established in law by the case of *Saloman* v. *Saloman & Co. Ltd* in 1897. In practical terms, this is done through the agency of its officers.

Despite the fact that the appointment of an auditor is a statutory requirement, the relationship between company and auditor is governed by contract, and it is important to understand that this contract is between the auditor and the company (not its shareholders, directors or any officers). The reason is that, under the law of contract, valuable consideration must move from the contracting parties, regardless of who benefits from the consideration. Figure 1.1 sets out the legal position. It is seen that shareholders, directors and other officers and employees of a company stand in a third-party relationship to the company's auditor, i.e. outside of contract. It is important to appreciate this since it has important implications for the question of the auditor's liability in law.

In relation to the consideration provided by the auditor, i.e. the performance of his statutory duties and the issue of his report to the members, it should be remembered that this work must be performed with that nebulous but vital quality, 'reasonable care and skill'. Any charge of dereliction of duty or negligence will invariably be judged in the courts by reference to that criterion, even though what constitutes 'reasonable' is subject to change in step with changes in legislation and standards of professional work in general.

1.3.4 The distinction between auditing and accountancy

Strictly speaking, an audit can commence only once the necessary accounting work has been completed. In practice, however, especially in the case of small companies, the distinction between audit and accountancy work is not clearly appreciated. This confusion usually arises because of the limited book-keeping and accounting capabilities of those involved in running small businesses, and it is always tempting to 'leave things to the auditor' to complete. It should be clearly understood, however, that in such a case the preparation, or completion, of the accounts is not part of the audit.

Thus, although many practising accountants readily undertake both accounting and audit work (as well as handling all the client's tax affairs), these tasks are respectively undertaken with 'different hats on'. It would, however, be quite wrong to infer from this that accounts preparation work provides no audit assurance. It is now generally

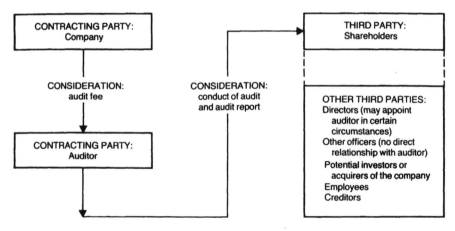

Figure 1.1 The legal relationships

accepted that the assurance derived by the auditor from preparing accounts contributes significantly to the overall assurance required, thus allowing for reduced testing in other areas.

1.4 The general advantages of an audit

There are many inherent advantages in having accounts audited, even where there is no statutory requirement for this to be done. If, by way of example, we take the case of the independent audit of a business partnership, the following advantages may readily be cited:

1. Disputes between partners may largely be avoided, especially where complicated profit-sharing arrangements subsist.
2. The admission of a new partner is facilitated if sets of past audited accounts are available for examination.
3. Any partnership change (e.g. death or retirement, or alteration of profit-sharing ratios) will have to be reflected in the accounts, and sometimes the partnership assets, including goodwill, are revalued at such a time. Since such revaluations directly affect the respective shares of each partner, it is advantageous to have the post-change accounts independently audited.
4. Applications to banks and other outside parties for the purpose of raising finance are greatly enhanced if supported by audited accounts.
5. Audited accounts (albeit adjusted for tax purposes) submitted to the Inland Revenue carry greater authority than accounts which have not been audited.
6. The presence of a qualified auditor is useful because of the variety of other capacities in which he is able to assist. Indeed, a number of partnership deeds incorporate a provision for the auditor to act as arbitrator in the event of dispute on specified issues.

1.5 The qualities required of an auditor

1.5.1 Living up to expectations

Although the audit is predominantly concerned with a client organization's accounts (and hence its underlying accounting records and documentation), the auditor needs to maintain the widest possible view of the client's circumstances. Each individual business transaction takes place within a broader context, and the skilled auditor maintains, at one and the same time, a view which includes seemingly insignificant details and their place in relation to the mainstream of the client's business activity. It could justifiably be said, albeit loosely, that the auditor should audit the *client*, not just its accounts.

A balance sheet is, after all, simply a 'financial photograph', seemingly motionless, frozen in time, with almost a tinge of inevitability about it; yet that photograph might be taken with wide or narrow-angle lens; it might be 'touched up' for effect, dramatized, distorted; it might be explicit, or merely suggestive, leaving the important message to be discerned by the perceptive and experienced interpreter. It is the task of the auditor to consider and to report on the impression conveyed by the accounts, by that financial photograph. Successive *Companies Acts* have searched for a formulation which most effectively sums up the impression that accounts ought to convey. Before 1948 the accounts were required to present a view that was 'true and correct', but it was later concluded that 'correct' stressed precision and accuracy which, although important, were largely covered by the word 'true'; and should be subsidiary to the need for 'fairness'. For this reason the 1948 Act introduced the phrase 'true and fair' in this context.

We thus have a statutory formulation which, although stated as an objective require-ment, involves, by its nature, a good deal of subjective assessment in its interpretation in particular circumstances. This imposes a great burden on the auditing profession since, although there will be few dissident voices when the business is flourishing and the accounts contain little that is controversial, this subjectivity is easily transmuted into deception when 'things go wrong', or when, with hindsight, subsequent events cast a different light on the matters portrayed in the audited accounts. The tenets of few professions enshrine concepts like truth and fairness, and it is no easy matter to live up to such elevated principles; indeed it is unfortunate that the phrase 'true and fair' is bandied about in such a mechanical way, so that the real significance of the words is sometimes lost.

It is clear that before expressing his own opinion on accounts, the individual auditor needs to consider far more than merely whether each and every individual transaction is accurately reflected therein. It is quite conceivable, for instance, that a set of accounts might 'accurately' be prepared from the records of a concern on the verge of bankruptcy, and yet give no hint of the impending disaster. The auditor of those accounts has a clear duty to 'spell it out' in terms which cannot reasonably be misconstrued by interested parties.

1.5.2 Professional ethics

All worthy professional bodies impose a code of conduct on those who practise as members in the public eye. The ideal such code is one which lays down no more than the essential requisites that need to be observed in the course of daily professional life, so that the service to clients remains flexible and unhampered by petty restriction, and yet is seen to be in accordance with the highest standard of conduct at all times.

The ethics codes operated by the major accountancy bodies do, by and large, allow their members that degree of freedom which is compatible with the mature attitudes which the majority, as men and women of undisputed integrity, display: yet periodic challenges to these high standards lend greater urgency to the question of ethics.

The matters that traditionally fall within the scope of professional conduct guidelines for chartered accountants in public practice are specified in the *New Guide to Professional Ethics* issued in March 1992, and subsequently updated. Its contents are wide-ranging, and any member found to be disregarding the rules laid down, whether in letter or spirit, runs the risk of disciplinary action and the severe consequences that may follow – from reprimand (with disclosure of their name and that of their firm) and payment of costs, to exclusion from membership. The latter will, in practical terms, often entail the loss of livelihood, and such instances are, fortunately, comparatively rare. The *New Guide* has taken on special importance in the context of audit regulations following the *Companies Act 1989* since the Regulations, with which all registered auditors must comply, incorporate the whole of the sections of the *New Guide* applicable to auditors. The *New Guide* covers the following subject matter:

1. Professional independence.
2. The need to observe confidentiality.
3. Rules on advertising and publicity, including literature produced by members or their firms such as house journals and recruitment brochures.
4. Descriptions and designatory letters.
5. Exchange of correspondence with any former incumbent before accepting engagements for professional work.
6. Determination of fees.
7. Participation in multi-discipline practices.
8. Participation in organizations providing general and management consultancy, data processing and company registrar services.

In view of its regulatory and practical significance, every auditor should maintain an ongoing familiarity with prevailing ethical requirements.

The *New Guide* of the ICAEW begins by setting out the 'Fundamental Principles' applicable to the conduct of every qualified accountant.

The section on 'Independence' deals, in the audit context, with threats to objectivity posed by:

► undue dependence on a single audit client,
► overdue fees.
► litigation,
► external pressures or influences,
► family and other personal relationships,
► beneficial interests in shares (and other investments) and trusts,
► trustee investments in audit clients,
► voting on audit appointments,
► loans to or from clients,
► receipt of hospitality or goods and services on preferential terms,
► provision of other services to audit clients.

Rather than simply prohibit every conceivable potentially compromising situation the *New Guide* prescribes review procedures within audit firms, involving partners other than the assignment partner. Sole practitioners are required for this purpose to set up arrangements with another firm.

The *New Guide* also prescribes procedures to be followed by accountants on any change of a professional appointment. Prior to accepting nomination to act in any capacity of a recurring nature it is necessary to write to the existing (or previous) holder of the office in question, requesting such information as that holder considers relevant to the appointee's decision whether or not to act. On receipt of such a request the previous holder must respond either by stating that there is no such relevant information, or he must provide it – after, of course, seeking his (former) client's permission to discuss his affairs with the nominated appointee. If such permission is not granted, the appointee cannot accept nomination.

1.5.3 Audit committees as an aid to independence

The appointment of an audit committee is an important development intended to 'create space' between auditors and the directors of the companies they audit. Following the American example, it is now a Stock Exchange requirement that listed companies appoint an independent audit committee, whose members are mainly non-executive officers of the company. It is their function to view the company's position in a detached and dispassionate light, and to liaise effectively between the main board and the external auditors.

The need to appoint audit committees was lent substantial impetus by the Cadbury Committee's Report in 1992 on recommendations for enhancing corporate responsibility and audit effectiveness.

The Cadbury Committee's emphasis is that all publicly quoted companies must appoint a suitable number of non-executive independent directors who should play a keen part in monitoring corporate activity and the exercise of the stewardship functions of the executive management.

The Cadbury Committee also recommended that financial reporting should incorporate a clear statement of management's statutory responsibilities and how these are to be distinguished from those of external auditors. The directors' statement should include reference to their belief that the company is a going concern, the steps they have taken to affirm that status, and the circumstances that could threaten it. This statement should fall within the scope of the external auditors.

The Cadbury Committee made it clear that independent directors should not allow themselves to become mere 'rubber-stamping' objects, but that they should exercise their free-thinking faculties intelligently and objectively and be prepared to speak out against any actions of the executive directors with which they did not concur. Auditors should have unencumbered access to independent directors (whether or not the latter have been formally constituted as an audit committee). It is also suggested that audit independence would be enhanced by periodic rotation of the audit partners responsible for the audit in question. Other noteworthy suggestions include:

1. Granting auditors immunity from action when they report suspected management fraud to the authorities.

2. Requiring directors to report on the adequacy of their company's internal controls.

3. A compulsory audit review of the published interim reports, which may be extended to include balance sheets and cash flow statements.

The Cadbury Committee's recommendations were wholly unsurprising, coming as they did in the wake of a spate of spectacular financial scandals: Guinness, Barlow Clowes, Ferranti, BCCI, Maxwell, Polly Peck, to name but a few. Whether their implementation will prove to be effective must necessarily await the next cyclical economic downturn, which is always conducive to fraud and misconduct, particularly in relation to financial reporting issues. If previous experience is any guide, however, it will take far more than Cadbury's exhortations to directors to behave more responsibly to effect a substantive culture change in corporate conduct. It may, for example, also require more effective sanctions against delinquent directors, including longer prison terms.

Since the form and function of the audit committee are matters for continuing development, it would be misleading to attempt too close a definition. The following activities have, however, been associated with its appointment:

1. Formally and regularly to review the financial results shown by both management accounts and those presented to shareholders.

2. To make recommendations for the improvement of management control.

3. To ensure that there are adequate procedures for reviewing 'rights' circulars, interim statements, forecasts and other financial information before distribution to shareholders.

4. To assist external auditors in obtaining all the information they require and in resolving difficulties experienced by them in pursuing their independent examination.

5. To deal with any material reservations of the auditors regarding the company's management, its records and its final accounts, including the manner in which significant items are presented therein.

6. To facilitate a satisfactory working relationship between the management and auditors, and between the internal and external audit functions.

7. To be responsible for the appointment of auditors, as well as fixing their remuneration.

8. To be available for consultation with the auditors at all times, if necessary without the presence of management.

9. To discuss regularly and review the procedures employed by the auditors.

10. To be concerned with all matters relating to the disclosure by the accounts of a true and fair view for the benefit of all users.

It is clear that the independence of external auditors may be undermined, either mildly or severely, in a variety of ways and that a similar variety of remedies have been put forward. While these and other proposals continue to be debated it is important to grasp the fact that without his independence the auditor is like an ornament: his effect is cosmetic only. The condensed history, related in the early part of this chapter, demonstrated how the need for a totally disinterested review first arose, and this need has in no way diminished with the passage of time.

It is now equally common for listed companies to appoint remuneration committees, composed chiefly of non-executive directors, whose functions include:

▶ approval of the terms of new or changed directors' contracts,

▶ determination of executive pay, including bonuses and share options,

▶ approval of employees' share options.

1.6 Professional publications

1.6.1 Official pronouncements

All the major professional accounting bodies have an established publishing tradition. Much of the dynamic growth and development of accounting theory can undoubtedly be attributed to the works published under the auspices of these bodies over several decades. Since independent auditing of UK companies, as considered in this text, is traditionally practised by members of the Institutes of Chartered Accountants and, to a lesser extent, by members of the Chartered Association of Certified Accountants, most auditing pronouncements stem from these sources and from the Auditing Practices Board, formed in April 1991.

Although many official pronouncements appear to relate to matters outside the strict confines of auditing, such has been the extension in the 'realm of concern' of the auditor during the 1980s and 1990s that virtually every development tends to have an auditing dimension. It is therefore important to acknowledge the formal recommendations of the professional bodies as contributing in large measure to the codification of contemporary auditing practice and procedures. The specific recommendations and guidance statements issued by the Chartered Institutes and the Chartered Association of Certified Accountants to their members have, over many years, constituted some of the most authoritative indicators of best practice in the world.

One of the most prolific sources of such material was the ICAEW series entitled Statements on Auditing, although these have largely been replaced by standards and guidelines issued by the Auditing Practices Committee (APC) and its successor the Auditing Practices Board (APB). Of the original Statements on Auditing the following are still relevant:

▶ Verification of debtor balances: confirmation by direct communication (June 1967).

▶ The ascertainment and confirmation of contingent liabilities arising from pending legal matters (August 1970).

▶ Guidance for auditors on the implications of goods sold subject to reservation of title (December 1977).

▶ Auditors' reports on friendly societies' accounts (August 1978).

The official journal of the ICAEW, published monthly, is *Accountancy*, which is recognized all over the world as authoritative, indeed indispensable, reading for all those who require to be well informed and up-to-date on matters of contemporary interest and practice.

The pronouncements of the Accounting Standards Board (ASB), in the form of financial reporting exposure drafts (FREDs) and financial reporting standards (FRSs), comprise another important official source. Once recommended accounting treatment has been published as an exposure draft, constructive comment is invited from interested parties. After a suitable period of 'exposure' the ASB will consider submissions before issuing the definitive accounting standard, with which compliance then becomes mandatory.

Following recommendations by a committee chaired by Sir Ron Dearing, a Financial Reporting Council (FRC) has replaced the Accounting Standards Committee (ASC) as the UK's principal standard-setting body, and it issues standards in its own name for mandatory application by UK companies.

The FRC presides over the ASB (which takes direct and immediate responsibility for the issue of FREDs and FRSs) and a Review Panel with powers of monitoring compliance, primarily by listed companies and other public-interest entities. The FRC has also spawned an Urgent Issues Task Force (UITF) which makes pronouncements on best reporting practice in areas not fully or adequately covered by the ASC's Statements of Standard Accounting Practice (SSAPs) or the ASB's own FRSs.

All of the activities of the FRC and its subordinate rule-making entities carry statutory force following the *Companies Act 1989*, as now incorporated in the *Companies Act 1985*, the principal Act.

There have been several instances of perceived transgression from both the letter and the spirit of standards and UITF pronouncements, resulting in the directors and, in some cases, the auditors of the companies concerned being taken severely to task prior to capitulation and, if warranted, the reissue in amended form of the offending financial statements.

1.6.2 Published auditing standards

Background

The most important development in authoritative auditing sources was the publication in June 1980, by the Auditing Practices Committee (APC), of the first three auditing standards. The APC had a somewhat chequered career, spanning one of the most difficult periods in the profession's 125-year history. These early problems arose primarily from the country's economic malaise during the 1970s and its inevitable effect on corporate conduct and performance, as manifested in dozens of Department of Trade inspectors' reports. Many of these described in graphic terms the difference between the actual contribution made by auditors and public expectation of their role. It thus became clear that the work of auditors must be based on altogether more rigorous standards of objectivity and vigilance, especially when external pressures – arising from fluctuating exchange rates, international competition, and high inflation and interest rates – had the combined effect of severely squeezing normal commercial returns.

The initial concept of the standards was undoubtedly given impetus by the persistent public reproaches suffered by auditors during the 1970s, usually at the hands of Department of Trade inspectors (one of whom is in every case, ironically, a chartered accountant) in their reports on failed companies, suspected fraud, instances where there was evidence to suggest that business was not being conducted for the benefit of the shareholders, or simply that the latter were not receiving the information to which they were reasonably entitled. These reports certainly caused the profession and the general public to look again at the role that auditors were expected to play in the regulation of corporate conduct and the competence with which they were seen to be doing so.

The three initial standards were respectively entitled 'The Operational Standard', 'The Audit Report' and 'Qualifications in Audit Reports'. The latter two were revised and combined in a single standard in 1989. The first covered such matters as audit planning, documentation, examination of evidence, internal control evaluation, and other procedures which together provide a reasonable basis for reaching an opinion on the financial accounts as a whole.

Auditing Practice Board pronouncements

The guidelines issued originally by the APC have been systematically replaced by Statements of Auditing Standards (SASs) issued by the APB. At the time of writing, the APB has issued the following SASs:

Auditing standards

► **Introduction**
   SAS 010   The Scope and Authority of APB Pronouncements

► **Responsibilities**
   SAS 100   Objective and General Principles Governing an Audit of Financial Statements
   SAS 110   Fraud and Error
   SAS 120   Consideration of Law and Regulations
   SAS 130   The Going Concern Basis in Financial Statements
   SAS 140   Engagement Letters
   SAS 150   Subsequent Events
   SAS 160   Other Information in Documents Containing Audited Financial Statements

► **Planning, Controlling and Recording**
   SAS 200   Planning
   SAS 210   Knowledge of the Business
   SAS 220   Materiality and the Audit

SAS   230   Working Papers
SAS   240   Quality Control for Audit Work

▶ **Accounting Systems and Internal Control**
SAS   300   Accounting and Internal Control Systems and Audit Risk Assessments

▶ **Evidence**
SAS   400   Audit Evidence
SAS   410   Analytical Procedures
SAS   420   Audit of Accounting Estimates
SAS   430   Audit Sampling
SAS   440   Management Representations
SAS   450   Opening Balances and Comparatives
SAS   460   Related Parties
SAS   470   Overall Review of Financial Statements

▶ **Using the Work of Others**
SAS   500   Considering the work of Internal Audit
SAS   510   The Relationship between Principal Auditors and other Auditors
SAS   520   Using the work of an Expert

▶ **Reporting**
SAS   600   Auditors' Reports on Financial Statements
SAS   610   Reports to Directors or Management
SAS   620   The Auditors' Right and Duty to Report to Regulators in the Financial Sector

---

There is an important difference between the structural approaches adopted by the APC and APB respectively. Whereas the APC based all published guidance on only two standards, the APB has adopted a structure in which Statements of Auditing Standards (SASs) cover essential principles and procedures, compliance with which is mandatory (and which are printed in bold type in the published statements), and explanatory material designed to assist in interpretation and application (the equivalent of APC guidelines).

The APC reporting standards required auditors to provide reasons for qualifications in their reports and, where relevant and practicable, to quantify their effect on the accounts. Even the form of qualifications to be used was provided, and two main categories of circumstances requiring qualification were identified. These were (1) uncertainty, which prevents the auditor from reaching an opinion; and (2) disagreement, where the auditor's view conflicts with that of management, as given in the financial statements. A further subdivision relates to the importance of the matters involved: if fundamental, the auditor should either disclaim responsibility or express an adverse opinion. If material (but not fundamental), a true and fair opinion would be given 'subject to' the uncertainty, or 'except' for the disagreement.

The whole of the APC text on reporting standards has, however, been superseded by SAS 600. The SAS requires a lengthier and more explanatory type of report than has hitherto been issued, and this came into effect in respect of all financial statements relating to periods ending on or after 30 September 1993.

Whereas the APC reports required 'subject to' qualifications for matters of material uncertainty, SAS 600 abandons these completely. If the nature of an inherent uncertainty is adequately explained in the financial statements, then there is no need to qualify the report since a true and fair view (which includes the explanation of uncertainty) is given – although added emphasis may be warranted. If the uncertainty is *not* properly explained, however, a disagreement-type report ('except for' the failure, etc.) could be given.

Systems-based origins

The systems-based approach to audit work was a natural response to the increasing post-war demands of business revival which manifested in greater centralization of business units, a rising tide of takeovers and mergers, and the commensurate ability of data-processing technology to cope with the recording of the greatly increased number of transactions involved. The systems-based approach emerged in the late 1950s with the production by a few major firms (with the obvious help of their US counterparts) of the first yes/no-type internal control questionnaires (ICQs), and these have formed the documentary cornerstone of all that has been thought of as 'modern' auditing for more than forty years.

The essence of the systems-based rationale may be expressed thus. The accounting system produces the records, and its strengths (or control features) therefore determine the reliability of those records. The latter, in turn, are summarized in the form of the final accounts, upon which the auditor is required to express his statutory opinion. Every system will, by definition, incorporate a certain measure of consistency, regularity, intelligent delineation of tasks and procedures, etc., in other words it will possess those ingredients which stand at the opposite pole to randomness, and which, both individually and collectively, have a self-checking effect. Why, then, the argument runs, should the auditor not exploit this self-checking element to the full, once he has evaluated its influence and extent? Why not, in a nutshell, see the external audit as complementary to the self-audit features of the system, and hence concentrate audit work almost exclusively on the system's known deficiencies?

As an exercise in logic the argument is faultless. Thirty years of field tests, though, have shown that its translation into practice is another matter entirely. 'Practice' in this context means the imposition of time constraints, the use of inexperienced audit staff, and clients who regard the audit as an overhead without a benefit—the real world, in fact. The great void between the systems review and the audit opinion may therefore be only ineffectively bridged, and to some extent this is due to the inadequate development of specialized techniques required for the purpose (for example, the selection, albeit at random, of thirty items for examination from a population of many thousands, requires to be justified before it passes muster as a 'substantive test'). Tests conducted in systems-based audits may well lead to unreliable conclusions – in turn embodied in unjustified audit opinions – although this could be caused by a lack of conceptual grasp at the sampling level.

The systems-based approach has, over forty years of dominance, become an end in itself rather than merely a means to an end. Consequently, operational audit attitudes risk becoming distinctly mechanical, especially where large-scale audits are concerned. Page after page of standard pre-printed documentation in the form of checklists, index sheets, questionnaires, evaluation summaries, flow diagrams, etc., are meticulously compiled by dutiful junior members of the audit staff, on the basis of which an inspired decision is reached on, say, how many returned cheques should be compared with their stubs.

In the dark old pre-system days, test-checking was pretty haphazard, it is true; but what is the net gain achieved by today's so-called scientific approach, apart from the erection of a massive technical superstructure? The systems approach, logically, must be right; implementation, however, seems to be the problem, possibly because the scientific approach demands scientific application disciplines if conclusions are to be valid.

It is easy to be lured into the highways and byways of standard working schedules and remain buried under them for days or weeks on end. In this way the auditor's primary asset – his intuitive skill – becomes blunted by the dead weight of its less effective substitute: paper, paper, paper. How easy, in turn, to forget that it is the client that we should be auditing, not just his records. It is for this reason that the new SASs' re-emphasis of the need to search for evidence, in whatever guise it may be found, is so relevant.

Let it be said on the positive side: the reminder that evidence is, after all, what auditing is all about has (1) served to release smaller practices from the shackles of borrowed ideas, and has encouraged them to develop the intuitive skills without which all investigative work is a fatuous charade – for evidence is where you find it; and (2) prompted the large firms to move away from the exclusivity of the systems-based ritual, rationalize intelligently their approach to sample sizes and selection techniques, and instil in the minds of their professional staff the principle that audit satisfaction is reached by reference to an inner guide, not an outer questionnaire or checklist – these latter being audit aids, not audit ends.

1.6.3 Other pronouncements and publications

Apart from the pronouncements already listed, students preparing for professional auditing examinations may refer to other appropriate sources, such as the research results and field-test findings of universities, government departments and other institutions, performed on an ad hoc basis.

The professional accountancy press should be mentioned as the prime continuing means whereby most accountants keep abreast of day-to-day developments. This, of course, is extensive, but the considerable quantity of material which is published regularly should not deter serious students from maintaining a keen interest in these developments – they do, after all, constitute a major source of examination questions, and involve the professional world which, it is hoped, aspiring members will inhabit (and from which they will derive their livelihood) once the examinations are safely out of the way. Each of the main professional bodies publishes its own monthly journal, and students should read regularly the journals issued by the body whose examinations they intend to sit, as well as any other reading which may be recommended as useful.

Reading newspapers and periodicals efficiently is an art. It is essential to be selective and, ideally, to maintain files in which useful articles are kept in subject order. It should be remembered that items of news and current interest (such as a new exposure draft, or the heavily qualified audit report of a major public company) will invariably be featured in several journals at the same time; the study of one such report is all that is needed, provided it is comprehensive. Nevertheless, apart from essential reading, the extent of further reading depends upon the availability of time. Most publications listed are available at special rates for students.

1.6.4 The structure of a professional firm

Like all business entities, accountancy firms have a structured management. The partners will generally delegate decisions of routine management to the managing or senior partner, who reports to the full partnership at regularly convened meetings, usually monthly. The partnership secretary, reporting to the senior or managing partner, takes responsibility for administration, including preparation of agenda papers and minutes of meetings, accounting and management records, time records, word processing, microfilming, printing, photocopying, binding, post, fax and communications generally.

The salaries paid to those involved in these activities form part of the firm's overheads. By contrast, the professional staff and partners maintain accurate time records to ensure that all time assigned to client affairs is properly billed at the appropriate hourly rates, determined in turn by reference to salaries. In this way the firm aims to obtain full recovery of the direct salary costs of professional staff as well as overheads. The difference between these costs and the fees represents partnership profits, shared between equity partners in their profit-sharing ratios.

The professional staff are subdivided both laterally (into departments) and vertically (into seniority grades). Usual departmental divisions might be audit, taxation, liquidations, accounts preparation services and any other assignment category undertaken by the firm on a regularly recurring basis.

Partners take ultimate responsibility for the service given to those clients for which each of them is designated 'assignment partner', but the detailed management of each assignment is the work of managers, who in turn take charge of the work of teams of seniors and juniors within the broad departmental areas.

To ensure the efficient and profitable running of the firm, certain key features must be emphasized:

► Communication of progress on assignments.

► Communication of problem areas.

- Supervision of work.
- Planning of work and its allocation to appropriate staff members.
- Quality control, including evidence of work completed.

Needless to say, technical training and updating must be a feature of quality control, and this will take the form of in-house bulletins, seminars, and the provision of an up-to-date technical library and data bank.

1.6.5 The future of auditing

In this précis of the forces currently at work affecting and moulding the framework of professional auditing practice we have noted the following:

- The enforcement through statutory backing of the accounting standards setting process.
- The issue of SASs by the APB.
- The Cadbury initiatives on corporate governance.
- The acknowledged importance of the public interest and renewed public expectations as to the assurance provided by auditors in the wake of many publicized scandals.

In the context of meeting public criticism by narrowing the so-called expectations gap, the APB have published consultation papers on the future development of auditing. Their suggestions include:

- The acceptance by auditors of wider responsibilities than those currently dictated by statute or case law; in particular, by altering their focus from past to future performance of client entities.
- Acceptance of responsibility to a wider range of interest groups, although ill-defined and without explaining the limits of such responsibility.
- Evaluation by auditors of directors' performance and stewardship.
- The assessment of a company's future prospects and risks.
- Responding to regulators' demands for 'monitoring basic ethical standards of corporate behaviour'.
- Reporting on summaries of directors' principal assumptions and judgements made when preparing the financial statements.
- Meetings between auditors and small shareholder-elected 'panels' to discuss issues arising from the audit.

The consultation paper recognizes the need to rationalize the potential liability of auditors under the present legal system before extending their roles and responsibilities. What it does not address is the key issue of the exposure to litigation from all the third parties embraced by a widening of audit accountability.

A flurry of law-reforming zeal follows every scandal-tainted wave of collapses –

whether induced by ineptitude, delinquency or just plain daylight robbery. We are told that higher standards of stewardship and audit need to be legislated, yet every misdemeanour committed was already against the law; and every failed audit was condemned by reference to current laws and standards.

The sensible issues to focus on are therefore the enhancement and enforcement of the laws and standards we already have. Audit regulation has given the professional bodies more clout over the activities of their membership than ever before. We need prompt disciplinary hearings, widely publicized findings, the suspension of audit registrations and financial penalties that really hurt.

Review questions

*1.   Having regard to the fact that the auditor is usually proposed by the directors, works closely with them and negotiates the fees with the directors, can it not be stated that the auditor has a contractual relationship with the directors?

*2.   What are the advantages of an audit? Explain briefly the difference between a private audit and a statutory audit.

3.   It has been stated that an auditor is only as independent as the directors of the company being audited allow him to be. If this statement is taken to be true, and having regard to the practice in the UK of providing extensive non-audit services, discuss what steps may be taken to minimize the effect of this.

4.   It can be readily argued that the concept of independence is a 'state of mind', the qualities for which are acquired over time by an auditor. Given that this is the case, discuss why it is necessary to have so many rules and regulations governing this area.

Exercises

1.   You are the training partner in a multinational firm of chartered accountants that is required as part of the introductory week for new trainees to explain to them the purpose of working papers in accounts preparation and, more especially, those used on an audit assignment. The students have a little knowledge on the subject of auditing but needless to say, being junior trainees, not a lot.

   You are required to prepare a handout which seeks to explain why an auditor needs to prepare accurate working papers, the contents that are required of such papers and the criteria by which the adequacy of the papers is judged.

2.   You have been asked to attend the Annual General Meeting of your firm's largest plc client. The partner in charge has had advance warning that one of the largest shareholders is intending to ask some awkward questions. The two most difficult ones are the following:

   (a) Why are the shareholders in General Meeting required to pass the resolution to re-appoint the auditor when this appears to be a foregone conclusion? The auditor has already been asked by the directors, has accepted in advance and there are no alternatives offered.

(b) How can it be justified to state that the auditor is independent? The connections that are necessarily built up between the auditor and the company are such that audit and consultancy fees are predetermined and the auditor would be a fool to indicate that the audit report was not going to be signed since this would mean a loss of income.

The partner requires a fully referenced memorandum that he can photocopy and distribute to the meeting if necessary which fully addresses these two points. The memorandum should include appropriate references to audit regulations and the *Companies Acts*.

2

The approach to audit work

THIS CHAPTER DEALS WITH:

▷ the purpose and content of the letter of engagement;

▷ the chronological phases through which an audit develops;

▷ the importance of recording audit evidence.

2.1 Before engagement – ethical clearance

Before accepting an appointment to act as auditor, members of the professional accountancy bodies are required, under strict ethical rules, to communicate with the previous holder of office to seek information which could influence their decision as to whether or not they may properly accept appointment. The existing auditor or adviser has no responsibility for that decision, and there is no 'professional clearance' which he or she can give or withhold. This applies regardless of whether the existing auditor is a member of the same professional body. This duty to communicate should be explained to the prospective new client, from whom authority to do so should be sought. If authority is not given, the appointment should not be accepted; nor should it be accepted if the existing auditor is refused permission to discuss the client's affairs with the proposed new auditor. Normally such communication takes place without difficulty, but if every reasonable attempt to get in touch with the existing auditor is unsuccessful, the prospective successor should send a final letter by recorded delivery stating that unless he receives a reply within a specified time, he will assume that there are no matters of which the existing auditor is aware that should be be brought to his attention.

2.2   Letters of engagement

Since the task of the auditor today is at once more onerous and more complex than ever before, it is essential that both client and auditor should be 'of one mind' as to the work that the auditor is undertaking and their respective responsibilities. It is therefore the practice of professional firms to issue letters to their clients at the time of being engaged in which they set out in clear terms the following items:

1. What they understand the engagement to involve.

2. Respective responsibilities of directors and auditors.

3. The way in which they would normally set about the work, including the assistance and co-operation which they would expect from the client.

4. The basis on which fees would be calculated.

   In connection with (3) above, the letter should cover the scope of the engagement and state that the nature and extent of the audit procedures will vary according to the auditor's assessment of the company's accounting systems and, where the auditor wishes to place reliance on it, the internal control system.

   An individual firm would normally standardize the form of engagement letters to be issued by it in differing circumstances. It is normal practice to send a copy together with the letter, requesting that it should be signed by the client as an acknowledgement of agreement as to terms, and returned immediately to the auditor for the latter's records.

   In March 1995, the APB issued Statement of Auditing Standards no. 140 – 'Engagement letters', which establishes standards and provides guidance to auditors on the contents of audit engagement letters. The Statement of Auditing Standards stresses, *inter alia*, that:

1. The functions of the auditor are quite distinct from the provision of accountancy, tax and other services.

2. It is not the main purpose of the audit to discover defalcations, irregularities and errors in the client's records, and the audit should not be relied upon for this purpose. The SAS correctly relates the auditor's responsibility under this head to the materiality of the defalcation, etc. in relation to the 'true and fair' requirement for the financial statements being audited.

(The question of how effective the partial disclaimer in (2) might prove to be in practice is dealt with in detail in Chapter 10.)

   In the case of statutory audits, the letter should set out the requirements imposed by statute, which cannot be varied by either client or auditor, with particular reference to the significance of the audit report.

   Engagement letters relating to non-statutory assignments, e.g. work requested by sole traders, partnerships or unincorporated associations (such as social clubs), which usually require no more than the preparation of accounts and tax returns, should delineate the work involved as specifically as possible, since any subsequent dispute or negligence charge, possibly leading to litigation, would be decided largely on the question of (a) the scope, and (b) the depth of work, as defined at the time of engagement. Many court cases might have been avoided had closer attention been paid to this matter, and in most of these cases the courts took the view that the onus was on the accountant, as the professional party to the contract, to take the necessary steps *ab initio* in order to avoid a misunderstanding as to the work, and hence the responsibilities, undertaken. With statutory engagements, however, there is less risk of the relationship between client and auditor being misconstrued by the client since so much of this relationship is governed by legislation.

A well-drafted engagement letter will, for example, serve to clarify for the client's benefit the respective responsibilities of directors and auditors, as summarized in Table 2.1.

Despite the caveat previously mentioned regarding errors, irregularities and defalcations, it is important not to give the impression that no responsibility for these is assumed. The auditor should undertake to exercise that degree of care and competence required by the circumstances, but in the context of an investigation designed to enable him to express an opinion, rather than one specifically directed to the discovery of fraud and errors. The engagement letter should set out the directors' statutory responsibilities for ensuring that proper accounting records are maintained and that annual accounts showing a true and fair view are prepared. The letter should mention the directors' duty to ensure that there is a proper system of internal control – by far the best method of preventing irregularities. The reader is referred to Chapter 10 for a full consideration of the auditor's responsibility for fraud detection.

Ignorance of other services available sometimes leads to the client (especially smaller enterprises) failing to ask for help which the auditor (in his capacity as accountant) could provide if so requested. Where it is appropriate, and is not likely to result in a conflict of interest and consequent loss of independence, the opportunity may be taken in the engagement letter to mention any services, other than auditing, which are available.

Table 2.1 Summary of directors' and auditors' responsibilities

Directors	Auditors
Devise/implement internal controls	
Maintain proper accounting records	Report lapses only
Prepare annual financial statements	
Ensure accounts give 'true and fair' view	Opinion to members
Ensure accounts comply with *Companies Act*	Opinion to members
Lay accounts before members	
File accounts with Registrar	
Act throughout in fiduciary capacity	Act in independent reporting capacity

It should always be borne in mind that the letter of engagement would be looked upon by the courts as *prima facie* evidence of the essential contractual arrangements which subsist between auditor and client. The following is a specimen of a typical letter of engagement, appropriate to a company client, which incorporates the matters explained above. It is based on the example given in the Statement of Auditing Standards no. 140 and incorporates all the points emphasized in the Statement concerning content and form.

Specimen letter of engagement for a company client

> Warrington Smith & Co.
> Chartered/Certified Accountants
> 29 Corporation Street
> Watford
> Herts
>
> The Directors   Date
> Boxwood Timber Co. Ltd
> Ivy Lane
> Berkhamsted
> Herts
>
> Gentlemen:
>
> The purpose of this letter is to set out the basis on which we (are to) act as auditors of the company (and its subsidiaries) and the respective areas of responsibility of the directors and of ourselves.
>
> ### I.   Responsibilities of directors and auditors
>
> 1.1   As directors of the above company, you are responsible for maintaining proper accounting records and for preparing financial statements which give a true and fair view and have been prepared in accordance with the Companies Act 1985 (or other relevant legislation). You are also responsible for making available to us, as and when required, all the company's accounting records and all other relevant records and related information, including minutes of all management and shareholders' meetings.
>
> 1.2   We have a statutory responsibility to report to the members whether in our opinion the financial statements give a true and fair view and whether they have been properly prepared in accordance with the Companies Act 1985 (or other relevant legislation). In arriving at our opinion, we are required to consider the

following matters, and to report on any in respect of which we are not satisfied:

(a) whether proper accounting records have been kept by the company and proper returns adequate for our audit have been received from branches not visited by us;

(b) whether the company's balance sheet and profit and loss account are in agreement with the accounting records and returns;

(c) whether we have obtained all the information and explanations which we think necessary for the purposes of our audit; and

(d) whether the information in the directors' report is consistent with the audited financial statements.

In addition, there are certain other matters which, according to the circumstances, may need to be dealt with in our report. For example, where the financial statements do not give details of directors' remuneration or of their transactions with the company, the Companies Act requires us to disclose such matters in our report.

1.3 We have a professional responsibility to report if the financial statements do not comply in any material respect with applicable accounting standards, unless in our opinion the non-compliance is justified in the circumstances. In determining whether or not the departure is justified we consider:

(a) whether the departure is required in order for the financial statements to give a true and fair view; and

(b) whether adequate disclosure has been made concerning the departure.

1.4 Our professional responsibilities also include:

▶ including in our report a description of the directors' responsibilities for the financial statements where the financial statements or accompanying information do not include such a description; and

▶ considering whether other information in documents containing audited financial statements is consistent with those financial statements.

2   Scope of audit

2.1 Our audit will be conducted in accordance with the Auditing Standards issued by the Auditing Practices Board, and will include such tests of transactions and of the existence, ownership and valuation of assets and liabilities as we consider necessary. We shall obtain an understanding of the accounting and internal control systems in order to assess their adequacy as a basis for the preparation of the financial statements and to establish whether proper accounting records have been maintained by the company. We shall expect to obtain such appropriate evidence as we consider sufficient to enable us to draw reasonable conclusions therefrom.

2.2 The nature and extent of our procedures will vary according to our assessment of the company's accounting system and, where we wish to place reliance on it, the internal control system, and may cover any aspect of the business's operations that we consider appropriate. Our audit is not designed to identify all significant weaknesses in the company's systems but, if such weaknesses come to our notice during the course of our audit which we think should be brought to your attention, we shall report them to you. Any such report may not be provided to third parties without our prior written consent. Such consent will be granted only on the basis that such reports are not prepared with the interests of anyone other than the company in mind and that we accept no duty or responsibility to any other party as concerns the reports.

2.3   As part of our normal audit procedures, we may request you to provide written confirmation of certain oral representations which we have received from you during the course of the audit on matters having a material effect on the financial statements. In connection with representations and the supply of information to us generally, we draw your attention to section 389A of the Companies Act 1985 under which it is an offence for an officer of the company to mislead the auditors.

2.4   In order to assist us with the examination of your financial statements, we shall request sight of all documents or statements, including the chairman's statement, operating and financial review and the directors' report, which are due to be issued with the financial statements. We are also entitled to attend all general meetings of the company and to receive notice of all such meetings.

2.5   The responsibility for safeguarding the assets of the company and for the prevention and detection of fraud, error and non-compliance with law or regulations rests with yourselves. However, we shall endeavour to plan our audit so that we have a reasonable expectation of detecting material misstatements in the financial statements or accounting records (including those resulting from fraud, error or non-compliance with law or regulations), but our examination should not be relied upon to disclose all such material misstatements or frauds, errors or instances of non-compliance as may exist.

2.6   We shall not be treated as having notice, for the purposes of our audit responsibilities, of information provided to members of our firm other than those engaged on the audit (for example information provided in connection with accounting, taxation and other services).

2.7   Once we have issued our report we have no further direct responsibility in relation to the financial statements for that financial year. However, we expect that you will inform us of any material event occurring between the date of our report and that of the Annual General Meeting which may affect the financial statements.

3   Other services

You have requested that we provide other services in respect of .... The terms under which we provide these other services are dealt with in a separate letter. We will also agree in a separate letter of engagement the provision of any services relating to investment business advice as defined by the Financial Services Act 1986.

4   Fees

Our fees are computed on the basis of the time spent on your affairs by the partners and our staff and on the levels of skill and responsibility involved. Unless otherwise agreed, our fees will be billed at appropriate intervals during the course of the year and will be due on presentation.

5   Applicable law

This [engagement letter] shall be governed by, and construed in accordance with, [English] law. The Courts of [England] shall have exclusive jurisdiction in relation to any claim, dispute or difference concerning the [engagement letter] and any matter arising from it. Each party irrevocably waives any right it may have to object to an action being brought in those Courts, to claim that the action has been brought in an inconvenient forum, or to claim that those Courts do not have jurisdiction.

6   Agreement of terms

Once it has been agreed, this letter will remain effective, from one audit appointment to another, until it is replaced. We shall be grateful if you could confirm in writing your agreement to these terms by signing and returning the enclosed copy of this letter, or let us know if they are not in accordance with your understanding of our terms of engagement.

Yours faithfully

WARRINGTON SMITH & CO.

2.3   Opinions and certificates

Before discussing the detailed approach to audit work it is important to establish a true perspective on what an audit is designed to achieve. The number of individual transactions undertaken by the majority of business concerns in the course of a financial year makes any exhaustive check virtually impossible. From a practical point of view, therefore, the auditor's aim is limited to the expression of an opinion (as opposed to a guarantee, certificate or absolute assurance) on the view presented by the accounts of the entity which he has audited. Companies legislation is quite clear on this point, using the words 'in his opinion' in several references to the auditor's duties.

For this reason the word 'certificate' should be avoided in this context since there is obviously a very great difference between certifying the correctness of figures presented and merely expressing an opinion on them. The only situations in which it is appropriate for an auditor or accountant to use the word 'certificate' arise when:

1. As auditor he has checked that a submission has been accurately drawn up, in a form prescribed for a particular purpose, such as when claiming an investment grant.
2. He has, as accountant to a non-statutory entity such as sole trader or partnership, prepared a set of final accounts from underlying records and information supplied for the purpose, and is hence in a position to certify that the accounts are in accordance therewith, notwithstanding the fact that no audit has been carried out.

It should not be imagined that the general requirement for the auditor simply to provide an opinion rather than a certificate in any way lightens his burden. On the contrary, apart from the fact that a professional opinion has inevitably to be expressed on the basis of a less than exhaustive enquiry, the very vagueness of the phrase 'true and fair' imposes particular risks. Furthermore, the question of whether or not the audit work which has preceded the expression of opinion satisfies current standards of requisite care and skill can never be answered with certainty: the unavoidable element of personal judgement which the auditor is forced to exercise in determining the extent of audit tests plays far too great a part. Exposure to potential liability therefore accompanies every audit assignment and cases of liability which have arisen in the past are often attributable to the failure, in the opinion of the court, of the auditor to execute a sufficiently deep or extensive examination in the particular circumstances pertaining.

2.4   The chronology of an audit

Although all audits will have precisely the same objective, namely to report to the interested parties on the results of the audit investigation undertaken within the context of the engagement, it is nevertheless true that the detailed manner in which the audit is conducted will depend largely upon the size and circumstances of the client concerned.

For the audit objective to be achieved, a systematic approach to the task is essential and, although all aspects of audit work are closely interrelated, it is convenient to distinguish the essential phases through which the audit develops.

A full appreciation of the chronology of audit procedures requires subdivision of audit stages, distinguishing the audit objective applicable at each point from the means or techniques whereby those objectives would normally be achieved in practice. Figure 2.1 assumes the following:

1. That the audit is being conducted for a new client company for the first time, i.e. that there is no pre-existing accumulation of information built up in the files from previous audits.

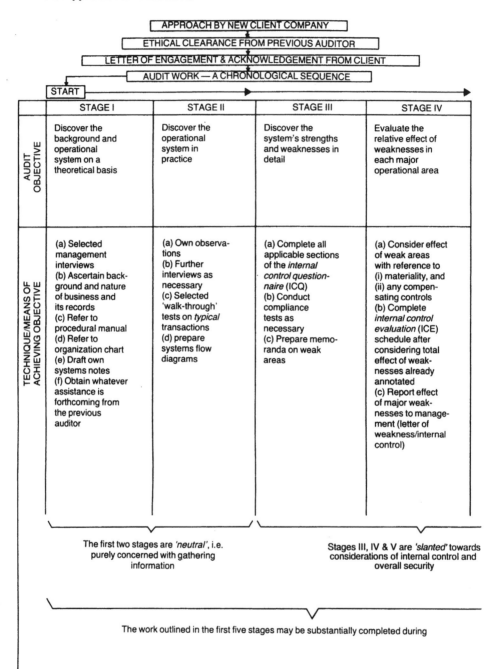

Figure 2.1   The chronology of a systems-based audit

STAGE V	STAGE VI	STAGE VII	STAGE VIII
Confirm the reliability of the records as a basis for preparation of final accounts	Ensure that the draft financial statements are in agreement with the underlying records	Form an opinion as to whether the accounts as presented give a *true* and *fair* view, and comply with statutory and other requirements	Express opinion in the audit report to members
(a) Prepare detailed *audit programme,* specifying (i) nature of substantive tests (ii) extent of substantive tests of transactions and balances (b) Execute audit programme *N.B.* (i) Sample sizes should ensure that tests are *representative* (ii) Consider the use of statistical sampling methods when warranted by volume of homogeneous transactions (iii) Depth testing techniques should be used on the sample selected, wherever appropriate	Prepare own (or check client's) detailed year-end schedules: (a) P & L account schedules, summarizing individual items by cross-reference to the records; and (b) Balance sheet schedules, reconciling the movement of each item from previous balance sheet position to current balance sheet position, suitably cross-referenced to summary schedules on file	(a) Obtain letter of representation from chief executive (b) Complete verification of assets and liabilities (c) Execute balance sheet audit programme: (i) make comparisons with previous periods (ii) inter-firm comparisons (iii) compare trends and ratios with those of other clients in same type of business (iv) consider effect of – changes in accounting policy – post–balance sheet events (d) Use checklists to cover all disclosure requirements (e) Post-audit review of files, audit programme and accounts by independent partners	(a) Refer to special checklist covering the technical content of the auditors' report and possible clerical errors (b) Review draft contents of directors' report (c) Consider the need for qualification (d) Refer any qualification to independent partners (e) Draft final formulation of audit report for inclusion in the published accounts

interim audit visits

Most of this work can be executed at the final audit stage only

Figure 2.1   *Continued*

2. That the client organization is sufficiently large and complex to require the extensive use of all the usual techniques applicable at each stage of the audit, and employs conventional internal control systems in major operational areas.

3. That the company is of a size which would cause the auditor reasonably to expect that controls in force are basically satisfactory, and hence that a systems-based audit (see below) is justified.

The function of Figure 2.1 is to provide an expanded outline covering all auditing procedures; there is virtually nothing which takes place during the audit which cannot be related to the procedures described in the diagram. This is of enormous practical value during routine audit work since the ability to relate the detailed procedures to an overall plan always adds a new dimension to audit work, particularly for the clerks engaged thereon.

The following points arising from Figure 2.1 should be specifically noted:

1. Although the execution of the audit programme takes place at stage V, this excludes such work on the verification of assets and liabilities that can be concluded only when the balance sheet has been prepared at the close of the period.

2. The first two stages are objective, being concerned with fact-gathering; as such, they are not especially audit-oriented: indeed, the information compiled could equally be used by Organization and Methods personnel. However, whereas the latter would then proceed to use the data with considerations of *efficiency* uppermost, the auditor's work during stages III–V is predominantly concerned with the efficacy of *internal control*.

2.5   Audit planning

We have seen that whilst all audits have the same objective, the way in which the audit is conducted will vary depending on the type, size and circumstances of the particular client.

In order to conduct an audit effectively and efficiently, the work needs to be properly planned and controlled. Variations in clients' circumstances should be recognized and reflected in the audit testing.

In March 1995 the APB issued a Statement of Auditing Standards (SAS) on the subject of planning (no. 200). Its key points may be summarized as follows:

1. Planning is necessary for all assignments. The SAS differentiates between the 'overall audit plan' (an overview) and the 'audit programme' (detailed tests and procedures).

2. The audit plan should be documented. Typical contents include:

   (a) knowledge of the entity's business,

   (b) risk and materiality,

   (c) nature, timing and extent of audit procedures,

   (d) co-ordination, direction, supervision and review.

3. The initial audit planning will be based on the auditor's knowledge of circumstances at an early point in time. During the course of the audit, circumstances may change so there must be scope for review and, if appropriate, amendment to the documented audit plan. This may involve the recalculation of materiality. Any changes should be recorded and explained.

4. Practitioners dealing with smaller audit clients will be relieved that the same degree of documentation is not necessarily required for all audits, regardless of size.

5. For recurring audit assignments, many aspects of the planning for the following year can best be dealt with at the conclusion of the current year's audit, whilst any difficulties experienced are fresh in the minds of the audit team.

6. It is common for current-year audit files to devote a separate section to all the aspects of planning. This should demonstrate compliance with the SAS.

7. The auditor should be satisfied at the planning stage that he will not compromise his independence. Points to consider may include:

   (a) undue time pressure on reporting deadlines,

   (b) availability of audit staff,

   (c) fee pressure or outstanding fees,

   (d) restrictions in the availability of financial information or accounting records,

   (e) changes in the relationship between the auditors and the client's senior management.

8. The use of standard audit planning records is encouraged, together with an accompanying planning memorandum detailing specific points of reference and/or action. This should of course be signed as approved by the audit partner at the planning stage.

It is essential to document the audit planning process as this will assist in the briefing of audit assistants to ensure that they understand the entity's business and any audit areas with significant risk. Most firms will use a pre-printed checklist to document the approach and planning processes.

The SAS on planning (see extract below) recommends that the following areas are considered, and these could form part of any checklist.

12. Matters for auditors to consider in developing the overall audit plan may include:

   Knowledge of the entity's business

   ▶ general economic factors and industry conditions affecting the entity's business;

   ▶ important characteristics of the entity, its business, principal business strategies, its financial performance and its reporting requirements, including changes since the previous audit;

   ▶ the operating style and control consciousness of directors and management; and

   ▶ the auditors' cumulative knowledge of the accounting and internal control systems and any expected changes in the period.

   Further guidance on these matters is given in SAS 210 'Knowledge of the business'.

Risk and materiality

▶ the setting of materiality for audit planning purposes;

▶ the expected assessments of risks of error and the identification of significant audit areas;

▶ any indication, including the experience of past years, that misstatements that could have a material affect on the financial statements might arise because of fraud or for any other reason; and

▶ the identification of complex accounting areas including those involving accounting estimates.

Nature, timing and extent of procedures

▶ the relative emphasis expected to be placed on tests of control and substantive procedures;

▶ the effect on the audit of the use of information technology by the entity or the auditors;

▶ the work of any internal audit function and its expected effect on external audit procedures;

▶ procedures which need to be carried out at or before the year end; and

▶ the timing of significant phases of the preparation of the financial statements.

Co-ordination, direction, supervision and review

▶ the involvement of other auditors, including other officers of the same firm, in the audit of components, for example subsidiary undertakings, branches and divisions;

▶ the involvement of, and communications with, experts, other third parties and internal auditors;

▶ the number of locations; and

▶ staffing requirements.

Other matters

▶ any regulatory requirements arising from the decision to retain the engagement;

▶ the possibility that the going concern basis may be inappropriate;

▶ the terms of the engagement and any statutory responsibilities; and

▶ the nature and timing of reports or other communication with the entity that are expected under the engagement.

The APB have issued specific Statements of Auditing Standards on some of these matters as follows:

1. SAS 210 – Knowledge of the business

Under this SAS, the auditors are required to obtain a knowledge of the business of the entity to be audited sufficient to enable them to identify and understand the events, transactions and practices that may have a significant effect on the financial statements or the audit thereof. The auditors should use this information to assess risks and identify problems, plan an effective audit and subsequently evaluate audit evidence gained from the audit work undertaken. It is important that the audit team are provided with a detailed knowledge of the business to enable it to carry out the audit work effectively.

The Appendix to the SAS includes the following list of matters to consider in relation to understanding the business:

Appendix

Matters to Consider in Relation to Knowledge of the Business

This list is provided for illustrative purposes only. It is not exhaustive, nor is it intended that all matters listed will be relevant to every engagement.

General economic factors

▶ General level of economic activity (for example recession, growth).

▶ Interest rates and availability of financing.

▶ Inflation.

▶ Government policies

   – monetary

   – fiscal

   – taxation – corporate and other

   – financial incentives (for example government aid programmes)

   – tariffs, trade restrictions.

▶ Foreign currency rates and controls.

The industry – conditions affecting the client's business

▶ The market and competition.

▶ Cyclical or seasonal activity.

▶ Changes in product technology.

▶ Business risk (for example, high technology, high fashion, ease of entry for competition).

▶ Declining or expanding operations.

▶ Adverse conditions, (for example, declining demand, excess capacity, serious price competition).

▶ Key ratios and operating statistics.

▶ Specific accounting practices and problems.

▶ Environmental requirements and problems.

▶ Regulatory framework.

▶ Specific or unique practices (for example, relating to labour contracts, financing methods, accounting methods).

The entity

Directors, management and ownership

▶ Corporate structure – private, public, government (including any recent or planned changes).

▶ Beneficial owners, important stakeholders and related parties (local, foreign, business reputation and experience) and any impact on the entity's transactions.

▶ The relationships between owners, directors and management.

▶ Attitudes and policies of owners.

▶ Capital structure (including any recent or planned changes).

▶ Organizational structure.

▶ Group structure.

▶ Subsidiaries' audit arrangements.

▶ Directors' objectives, philosophy, strategic plans.

▶ Acquisitions, mergers or disposals of business activities (planned or recently executed).

▶ Sources and methods of financing (current, historical).

▶ Board of directors

  – composition

  – business reputation and experience of individuals

  – independence from and control over operating management

  – frequency of meetings

  – existence and membership of audit committee and scope of its activities

  – existence of policy on corporate conduct

  – changes in professional advisers (for example, lawyers).

▶ Operating management

  – experience and reputation

  – turnover

  – key financial personnel and their status in the organization

  – staffing of accounting department

  – incentive or bonus plans as part of remuneration (for example, based on profit)

- use of forecasts and budgets
- pressures on management (for example over-extended, dominance by one individual, support for share price, unreasonable deadlines for announcing results)
- management information systems.

► Internal audit function (existence, quality).

► Attitude to internal control environment.

The entity's business – products, markets, suppliers, expenses, operations

► Nature of business(es) (for example manufacturer, wholesaler, financial services, import/export).

► Location of production facilities, warehouses, offices.

► Employment (for example, by location, supply, wage levels, union contracts, pension commitments, government regulation).

► Products or services and markets (for example major customers and contracts, terms of payment, profit margins, market share, competitors, exports, pricing policies, reputation of products, warranties, order book, trends, marketing strategy and objectives, manufacturing processes).

► Important suppliers of goods and services (for example long-term contracts, stability of supply, terms of payment, imports, methods of delivery such as 'just-in-time').

► Stocks (for example locations, quantities).

► Franchises, licences, patents.

► Important expense categories.

► Research and development.

► Foreign currency assets, liabilities and transactions by currency, hedging.

► Legislation and regulations that significantly affect the entity.

► Information systems – current, plans to change.

► Debt structure, including covenants and restrictions.

Financial performance – factors concerning the entity's financial condition and profitability

► Accounting policies.

► Earnings and cash flow trends and forecasts.

► Leasing and other financial commitments.

► Availability of lines of credit.

► Off balance sheet finance issues.

▶ Foreign exchange and interest rate exposures.

▶ Comparison with industry trends.

Reporting environment – external influences which affect the directors in the preparation of the financial statements

▶ Legislation.

▶ Regulatory environment and requirements.

▶ Taxation.

▶ Accounting requirements.

▶ Measurement and disclosure issues peculiar to the business.

▶ Audit reporting requirements.

▶ Users of the financial statements.

2. SAS 220 – Materiality and the audit

This SAS requires that:

(a) Auditors should consider materiality and its relationship with audit risk when conducting an audit.

(b) Auditors should consider materiality when determining the nature, timing and extent of audit procedures.

(c) In evaluating whether the financial statements give a true and fair view, auditors should assess the aggregate of uncorrected misstatements.

Materiality is defined from the point of view of the addressee of the auditor's report, in the context of whether an omission or misstatement would reasonably influence his decisions.

The SAS acknowledges that materiality cannot be calculated using a precise mathematical formula as it is too subjective.

Auditors should assess materiality at the audit planning stage so as to direct audit procedures for the different areas within the financial statements.

3. SAS 300 – Accounting and internal control systems and audit risks assessments

This SAS provides guidance on audit risk and its components:

▶ inherent risk,

▶ control risk,

▶ detection risk,

and on the auditor's approach to obtaining an understanding of the accounting and internal control systems.

The three components of audit risk should be separately considered at the planning stage when the audit procedures are designed. This enables efforts to be targeted towards areas of materiality and to reduce overall audit risk.

In addition to the above, the planning process should:

1. Establish a 'materiality factor' for the assignment.

2. Establish whether a compliance or substantive testing approach is appropriate, i.e. whether or not a system of internal control exists on which the auditors can rely.

3. Set out the audit programme of tests to be undertaken.

4. Establish initial sample sizes for testing.

5. Set staff allocations and a fee budget.

6. Involve the briefing of audit assistants. It is good practice for this briefing process to be evidenced, perhaps by the assistant signing an appropriate section of the planning checklist.

2.6   The systems-based audit

The systematic approach to audit work depicted in Figure 2.1 has come to be known as the systems-based audit. The name correctly incorporates the principle that the nature and depth of audit tests should take into account the extent to which the system of internal control in operation 'audits itself'. It is for this reason that such a large proportion of the work described in the diagram relates to the ascertainment and evaluation of the system prior to the planning and execution of the audit programme itself. This contrasts favourably with the haphazard approach which traditionally prevailed until the 1960s when the mushrooming of large groups of companies and conglomerates forced upon auditors the realization that a far more scientific approach to their work was essential; that is, if they were to justify the relatively small number of audit tests carried out in relation to the enormous volume of transactions falling within the period under review.

However, no universal change in approach takes place overnight. Inevitably the larger international firms pioneer new audit methods; this involves careful research, planning and long periods of field-testing if the charge of negligence is to be avoided. Many smaller audit firms, caught under the combined pressures of generally raised standards, professional recommendations and legal case decisions, are eventually forced to follow suit. Relics of the old regime still persist, however. A colleague once related to me the scarcely credible story of two student trainees who proudly described how they had 'vouched' no fewer than one million sales invoice copies. They were obliged to execute this singularly unadventurous and unrewarding feat (which occupied them for a fortnight) due to an ancient instruction in their audit programme, to check the sales figures for three months from the copy documents to the sales day book.

It is possible that, at one time, three months' checking of this nature might have been appropriate, but clearly no one had taken the trouble to review the testing depth specified by the now archaic programme. Apparently our two stalwarts, who could barely have remained fully conscious during this task, discovered only one solitary 'error': it was noticed, by the clerk whose function it was to enter 'vouching ticks' in the day book, that one entry which should have been vouched (he could tell this from the numbering sequence) remained unticked. The other clerk, whose function it was to 'bash' each document with a rubber 'audit' stamp, paged back through the file to see whether it had been inadvertently missed – but no, the invoice was undoubtedly missing.

Feeling that their unremitting labours had proved worthwhile after all, they then reported this matter to the chief accountant. He had clearly summed up the calibre of the audit staff, for his response was promptly to instruct his secretary to produce a replica of the missing item, correct in every detail, which he duly passed back to the terrible twins for insertion in the file, in its proper place. It seems that the duplicate was then dutifully bashed, and its counterpart entry 'vouched', thus allowing the headlong rush to continue on its way to completion.

This anecdote demonstrates the futile nature of blind audit testing, consideration having been given neither to the number of invoices which it might have been appropriate to vouch, nor to the way in which the recording of sales related to other associated entries in, say, the stores records or remittances received. For all its apparently extensive coverage, the test was exceptionally shallow, being confined to one 'horizontal plane' of entries, all of an identical nature.

It is also clear that the clerks were concerned only with outer appearances: they were completely satisfied once a duplicate voucher was placed on the file. It apparently did not occur to them that there might, conceivably, have been more serious implications behind the missing item, such as deliberate suppression of part(s) of the invoice set, perhaps to conceal missing goods, or a variety of other possibilities on which one can but speculate without knowing the mechanics of the particular system.

This totally haphazard approach, amounting to little more than guesswork, is sometimes euphemistically termed 'judgement' sampling, thereby suggesting that the auditor has carefully weighed up the circumstances and conditions in which the records are created, and then exercised his judgement in determining the requisite volume of testing. No doubt this is true in a number of cases, but all too often judgement amounts to little more than an excuse for testing 'the same number as last year'. In any event, it is difficult to see how judgement of this variety can ever be an effective substitute for a scientific approach to sample testing which, although it too may involve a good deal of judgement, is nevertheless based upon the mathematical laws of probability. The scientific method, employing statistical sampling techniques, is not always appropriate – for example when items within the population being tested are not homogeneous, or where the population sizes are relatively small – but it has the advantage of quantifying the risk that the characteristics of the sample are not representative of those in the population, and generally forces the auditor to exercise his judgement in a constructive way.

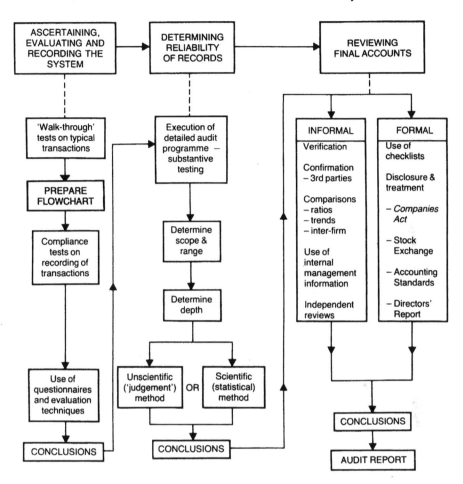

Figure 2.2 The incidence of audit testing

Whatever method is used for determining sample sizes, it is imperative that random selection techniques should be employed during the examination process itself, otherwise personal bias may affect the selection of individual items, thereby invalidating the sampling exercise and resulting in incorrect inferences being drawn concerning the population. Although the use by auditors of statistical and other sampling techniques is discussed in detail in Chapter 5, it may be useful to illustrate this section by highlighting in Figure 2.2 the testing stages included in the previous 'chronology' figure, as they would feature in the context of a systems-based audit.

2.6.1 The end-results alternative

The vast majority of businesses in the UK incorporate systems of internal control which are either rudimentary (due to the limited number of staff employed), or are dominated by proprietary directors. The application of the systems-based audit philosophy in such situations is rarely possible, and the auditor's prime concern should rather be to establish the following:

1.　That all the transactions of the business have been accurately and completely recorded.
2.　That the transactions recorded were undertaken on behalf of the business itself, rather than any individual or related party.

In pursuing these objectives the auditor of a small business will inevitably be forced to rely heavily on the representations and assurances of the owners of the business, and such evidence as exists in support of these representations will rarely arise from its system of internal control. It is far more likely that corroboration will be found in ratio analysis, comparisons with previous periods, comparisons with other businesses in the same trade and general 'market intelligence' – all of which is encompassed in the term 'analytical review' – not to mention that all-important (perhaps *the* most important) indicator of all, the auditor's personal assessment of the character, trustworthiness and general credibility of the directors themselves.

In practice, particularly where the auditor is familiar with the business situation as a result of many years' experience, audit work will concentrate heavily on pursuing the first of the above objectives, entailing extensive checking of the records and of the schedules supporting the figures in the final accounts – a procedure often referred to as an 'end-results' audit. In the circumstances of small businesses this approach is more practical than attempting a systems-based audit.

It is rare for small companies to employ qualified accounting staff, and the auditor, in an accounting capacity, will often take on the accounts preparation work. A reasonable degree of audit assurance may, however, be derived from this work, although this will relate to book-keeping accuracy, and will of itself provide no assurance of the completeness and accuracy of source documents, nor of the accuracy of stock values provided by the directors. It is therefore never a valid substitute for an audit.

2.7　Audit classifications

As has been pointed out above, the quantity, range and depth of audit work undertaken in any given set of circumstances will depend upon the auditor's own assessment of the system which produces, in the first place, the records which he is required to audit. Since both the complexity and dependability of systems are almost infinitely variable, the length of time taken to conduct an audit, and the number and level of audit personnel required to do so, are equally variable. It is nevertheless possible to draw up the following broad classifications:

Complete or final	Usually applies to smaller concerns, where the volume of transactions and complexity of records does not require the auditor's attendance

more than once in each year. This visit normally takes place as soon as possible after the business's financial year-end and continues until it has been completed and the audit report signed. In some cases, for mutual convenience, the records may even be transported to the auditor's own offices for audit purposes.

Interim and final
In the case of larger clients the auditor will often find it necessary to proceed with the audit on an interim basis, in view of the volume of testing which it is necessary for him and his staff to undertake in order to reach an opinion on the reliability of the records. Interim audits, always arranged with the co-operation of the client, may be biannual, quarterly, or even monthly, depending upon the volume of audit work considered necessary. Interim audits possess the advantage of leaving the final stage of the audit relatively free for the verification of the year-end accounts; the assessment of the system and most detailed checking of underlying records and documents having already been carried out.

Continuous
Where the system of internal control operated by a large company displays certain fundamental and material weaknesses, the auditor will be obliged to check a higher proportion of transactions than would otherwise be necessary and, in exceptional circumstances, members of the audit team may be required to execute checking work continuously throughout the period to which the accounts relate.

2.8 Audit files and working papers

Nothing enhances the efficiency with which an audit may be conducted more than the careful compilation and maintenance of audit files and 'working papers'. From the very beginning of an audit the files should be built up systematically, and technicians involved on audit assignments should be constantly reminded of the importance of (1) recording everything of consequence that arises during their investigative work, and (2) ensuring that audit papers are kept in an orderly fashion at all times. This is essential as working papers form the basis record of audit evidence on which the audit opinion is based. Working papers must be signed and dated both by the preparer and the reviewer as a record of when and by whom the audit procedures were undertaken and reviewed.

Whenever it is possible and appropriate, brief notes should be taken during interviews with company officials, subsequently amplified and then placed in the relevant section of the audit file. All queries arising during the conduct of the audit should be resolved as soon as possible, the answers being entered alongside the related queries on schedules specially pre-printed for the purpose.

Each firm will design the full range of pre-printed documentation required to support its audit procedures, and completeness of files is usually ensured by use of the standardized index or 'front sheet'. The key points and comments in Statement of

Auditing Standards no. 230 – 'Working papers', issued in March 1995, are summarized as follows:

1. Working papers form the basic record of audit evidence on which the audit opinion is based.

2. The SAS does not prescribe any particular layout of working papers, and this is left to the auditors' judgement.

3. 'Permanent' files contain information of continuing importance as distinct from 'current' audit files, which contain information relating primarily to the audit of a single period.

4. It is essential that the working papers are signed and dated both by the preparer and the reviewer as a record of when and by whom the audit work has been undertaken and reviewed.

5. There is no specified period for which audit working papers must be retained. However, once destroyed, the working papers cannot be recreated. For this reason auditors should consider the likelihood of requiring future retrieval and hence whether working papers should be microfilmed before destruction.

6. If the client's nominal ledger is effectively part and parcel of the accounts preparation working papers and spreadsheets on the audit file, they must not be destroyed until after the time limit for retention of proper accounting records has elapsed.

7. Most firms regard the reviewer's notes and the proper clearance thereof as a vital part of the evidence to support their opinion.

Some of the practical applications to consider include:

I. Audit file retention

There are no formal pronouncements on the length of time that auditors are obliged to retain their files.

Audit files constitute evidence of the most fundamental order in the event of any negligence action and, following the *Latent Damage Act 1986*, the time limit on claims could be up to 15 years from the date of the alleged damage. Cases involving alleged fraud or other criminal acts by a partner or employee of the firm, although rare, are not subject to time limits and indefinite retention on microfilm is therefore sensible.

There is no statutory rule governing retention of audit files, although to the extent that such files hold client records they are subject to the same retention periods specified by the *Companies Act 1985* for accounting records, namely three and six years for private and public companies respectively. These considerations would, of course, apply equally to audits for former and current clients.

SAS 230 stipulates no retention periods, rather it appears to give dispensation from retention – but only in respect of the audit review notes to the extent that the issues identified have been properly addressed and evidenced elsewhere on file.

2. Ownership of working papers

The ownership of working papers may become relevant in cases where the relationship between the practitioner and the client has broken down and the client and/or successor firm are seeking copies of the auditors' working papers.

There is therefore every good reason to resist requests that serve only to provide potential adversaries with ammunition. So far as ownership is concerned, your audit files and working papers are your firm's property and need not be passed to your successor.

3. Client wishes to see your papers

Assume that the auditor is about to qualify the accounts of an audit client on the grounds that stock values are materially overstated and has discussed his reservations in detail with the client, but the client demands to see the detailed working papers. The fact that the auditor has confidentiality over his working papers means that there is no obligation to reveal audit working papers to clients. Indeed, there are many matters normally included in such papers, such as remuneration records or comments on the competence or conduct of directors and senior management, which should under no circumstances be revealed to anyone outside the senior audit team.

There may, however, be good reasons in the circumstances cited to let the client have sight of the working papers relating exclusively to the stock values. There may be complex technical issues relating to the valuation methods used that the client may believe the auditor has not adequately grasped, and going through the relevant working papers could help to resolve such doubts.

It is also possible that the client does not appreciate the statutory and professional requirements governing reductions to net realisable values, and the auditors' relevant calculations could help to demonstrate to the client why the auditor contends that the stock value is materially overstated.

Many firms also design and standardize supplementary audit aids such as:

1. Certificate of directors' emoluments, including fees, commissions, bonuses, pensions, expense allowances and benefits in kind.
2. Detailed report on attendance at stocktaking.
3. Audit completion checklists.
4. Calling over sheets.
5. Checklists for:
   - *Companies Act* requirements;
   - Statements of standard accounting practice and financial reporting standards (particularly noting dates from when operative);
   - Stock Exchange requirements for listed companies;
   - content of the Directors' Report;
   - other statutes and regulations, e.g. building societies, friendly and provident societies, solicitors, pension funds, charities;

➤ Securities and Exchange Commission (SEC) requirements for subsidiaries of US parent companies;

➤ the audit report.

Although the subject of the audit report is dealt with extensively in Chapter 7, in order to illustrate the checklist technique, an audit report checklist is reproduced below.

Audit Report Checklist

Technical content	Yes	No	N/A*	Initial
(a) Have all the explanations and information necessary for the purposes of the audit been obtained − with particular reference to certificates and confirmations from third parties, including subsidiary auditors?				
(b) Have proper accounting records been kept and proper returns received from any branches not visited?				
(c) Are the accounts in agreement with the accounting records and returns?				
(d) Do the accounts give not only a *true* but also a *fair* view of the results and cash flows (where required) for the period and the state of affairs at the accounting date?				
(e) Do the accounts comply with the requirements of the *Companies Act 1985*?				
(f) Are we satisfied that any audit qualification is not material in determining whether, under sec. 271, CA 1985, any dividends paid or proposed are permitted? If not, have we made the required written statement to that effect?				
(g) Are details of the following items included in the audit report to the extent that they are not properly disclosed in the accounts?				
− Directors' emoluments, pensions, and compensation for loss of office.				
− Emoluments of highest paid director (other than chairman).				

*Not applicable

	Yes	No	N/A*	Initial
– Directors' emoluments waived.				
– The number of directors whose emoluments fall within specified statutory bands.				
– Loans and quasi-loans to officers.				
– Details of contracts and other transactions with directors, covered by CA 1985.				
(h) Do the accounts or accompanying information (for example, the directors' report) include an adequate description of the directors' relevant responsibilities?				
(i) If answer to (h) is 'no', does the audit report include a description of these responsibilities?				
(j) Does the audit report give details of the respective responsibilities of directors and auditors?				
(k) Does the audit report state the basis of the auditor's opinions?				
(l) Where appropriate, do the group accounts show a true and fair view of the group position and comply with the requirements of the *Companies Act 1985*?				
(m) Where appropriate, does the audit report include any qualifications contained in the reports of auditors of subsidiary and associated companies to the extent that the qualifications are material in the context of the group accounts as a whole?				
(n) Have questionnaires sent to subsidiary auditors been duly completed and returned to our satisfaction?				
(o) Does the audit report refer, in appropriate terms, to all significant departures from accounting standards?				
(p) Have the accounts been approved and signed by the directors before the audit report is signed?				
(q) Have all outstanding queries been satisfactorily resolved?				

	Yes	No	N/A*	Initial
(r) Does the report satisfy the requirements of the Audit Report – Statement of Auditing Standards?				
(s) Do the accounts include a cash flow statement which complies with FRS1?				
(t) If answer to (s) is 'no', does the reporting entity satisfy one of the exemptions set out in FRS1?				
(u) Have we examined the directors' report as required by the *Companies Act 1985*, and if so are we satisfied that it is consistent with financial statements? If not, have we disclosed lack of consistency in our report?				
Possible clerical errors				
(a) Does the audit report refer to the correct accounting date and period?				
(b) Does the report state correctly whether the company has made a profit or a loss for the period?[†]				
(c) Are the references in the report to the page numbers in the accounts correct? (It is essential that the report covers only the information required to be given by the *Companies Act* and accounting standards and not any additional non-statutory information.)				
(d) Is the audit report correctly addressed?				
(e) Has a partner, not in any way involved with the audit in question,				
– independently read the draft audit report and approved its technical content and the suitability of the wording relating to any departures from an 'unqualified' opinion?				
– reviewed *this* checklist?				

[†] To avoid the danger of this error, many firms prefer to use the word 'results', instead of referring to a profit or a loss, especially since the accounts may show an operating profit and a final loss; a pre-tax profit and a post-tax loss; a profit *before* extraordinary items, and a loss *after* extraordinary items; etc.

2.9 Financial reporting – accounting standards and the myth of objectivity

Perhaps it is appropriate to conclude the chapter on the audit approach by reminding ourselves that no matter how meticulously financial accounts are prepared and audited, no matter how many accounting standards are enforced, total objectivity in accounting is probably an idealist's dream. Even if it were practicable for the auditor to examine in detail every single shred of documentary evidence relating to the transactions of a large company throughout its financial year, it would still not be possible to certify more than the arithmetical and book-keeping accuracy. Accounting, as opposed to book-keeping, involves the exercise of judgement, and there is thus every chance that two auditors, of equal skill and experience, will view a particular circumstance differently, even at a fundamental level.

Views, which some may regard as cynical, have been expressed suggesting that modern accounting, being necessarily complex, may all too easily be manipulated subjectively in pursuit of unworthy motives. Managements facing financial difficulties may be tempted to present their accounts in ways that seek to hide the problems they face, and the auditor, as guardian of the interests of shareholders and (indirectly) other outsiders, has the clear duty to insist that appropriate amendments be made, or else to qualify his own report explicitly.

There are accounting areas which despite accounting standards designed to cover them, are unavoidably susceptible to a variety of interpretations (and hence presentations), such as the treatment of deferred taxation, depreciation, research and development expenditure, goodwill, leasing, government grants, extraordinary items, post-balance sheet events, prior-year adjustments, foreign currency translation, unrealized capital surpluses, and many others. The work of the Accounting Standards Board is aimed at the standardization, or at least the narrowing of the range, of the accounting treatments of the above and other, equally contentious, issues.

In times of severe business stress it is all too easy to succumb to the temptation of what may be called expediency accounting – or not admitting that there is a conflict in the first place – for it is, after all, not a difficult matter to work out a plausible justification for adopting the accounting treatment which produces the result desired. It is this manipulative trait inherent in accountancy which constitutes the real challenge to the drafters of both company law and accounting standards. It is a challenge which has so far not been faced squarely. Standards that prescribe a uniform accounting treatment are obviously useful but they do not remove the subjectivity that may enshroud a decision which will have a significant effect on the way in which a company's results are presented.

The ASB with FRS 5, 'Reporting the substance of transactions', requires that, generally, the economic substance of transactions (rather than their legal construction) shall determine the appropriate accounting presentation. The standard was prompted by the fashion in 'off balance sheet finance', mainly through the use of controlled non-subsidiary companies – a device designed to enhance the group's apparent gearing. A number of similarly contrived situations, invariably carrying the support of legal advice, have become popular in recent years, including the financing of the company's stocks by suppliers, ownership being transferred only on a sale to an outside party; meanwhile, neither the stocks nor the liability appears in the accounts, and the finance costs are included as cost of sales.

It is quite impossible that accounting standards could ever completely remove subjectivity, and this limitation on what can be achieved through prescribed standards should be clearly understood and acknowledged. As new exposure drafts and consequent standards appear on the scene it would be foolish to expect them to provide a resolution of all the anomalies which have hitherto arisen. No standard will tell us precisely the period over which expenditure on a fixed asset should be charged against profits, since no standard can take unpredictable factors, such as obsolescence, into account; it is difficult enough for an individual management to come to terms with the unknown. In any case, the ASB is hampered by having to work from a number of accounting models that lack a cohesive, consensus-backed conceptual framework. In such circumstances expediency is unavoidable.

Although progress in the standardization of accounting treatment is both desirable and possible, we should not imagine that such progress is ever likely to reduce the level of vigilance and the degree of care which the auditor is expected to exercise. The resolution of this paradox is linked with the profession's own future in this age of 'public accountability', and it depends very much on a different kind of standard altogether: a standard of genuine independence of the audit function in a way which will effectively preclude its involvement with 'expediency accounting'. For too long the profession has had to defend itself against charges of complicity in cases where accounts, although on the face of it prepared in accordance with legal requirements and accounting conventions, have nevertheless been embarrassingly exposed as little short of a deception imposed upon their users. *Recte numerare*[1] indeed!

Review questions

*1.   It is recognized that the final result of the audit work is a report to the shareholders of the company. Auditors do however, in some circumstances, issue certificates and in the USA the audit report is referred to as a certificate. What is the difference between the certificate and a report and why should an auditor be very careful what terminology is used?

*2.   To what extent do you consider that the auditor is entitled to rely on certificates from third parties when performing his audit?

3.   'The use of "Tick Lists" or "Checklists" is becoming more prevalent in the audit files in use today. It is readily argued that these prevent an important item being overlooked and causes the auditor to look from different angles when performing his work. It can also, however, be stated that the lists merely add weight to the audit file and the person filling out the columns need never really do any work.'
      Discuss the above statement.

[1] *Recte numerare* is the ICAEW motto – it means 'to count correctly'.

4. SAS 230 – Working Papers – sets out procedures with which the auditor should comply when conducting an audit. To what extent do you consider that this standard applies when auditing a small, owner managed limited company?

Exercises

1. You have just been appointed the auditor of a local chemical company which supplies weedkillers to farmers. They have, during the past year, successfully won overseas contracts in the face of heavy competition from the multinational chemical companies. Some of these contracts have gone to the states comprising the old USSR.

   There now appear to be two areas of concern to the company:

   (a) The European body which controls the safety testing of the products being sold has indicated that there may be a health hazard arising from using the weedkillers.

   (b) Due to the unstable nature of the economies of the states to whom the sales have been made there have been little or no funds received in respect of the high sales volume.

   In what areas of the audit do the above matters have an impact and how should the auditor vouch and document his findings?

2. 'The main object of the auditor's working papers is to record and demonstrate the steps that have been taken in order to arrive at the opinion that has been given on the accounts being audited.'

   Is the above statement true having regard to the current auditing climate?

3

Systems-based auditing

THIS CHAPTER DEALS WITH:

▷ the definition of internal control systems;

▷ why the auditor is interested in the operations of accounting and internal control systems;

▷ the practical application of internal control and how to record and evaluate its operation.

3.1 The importance of internal control in systems-based audits

From Chapter 2 it will be clear that the strengths and weaknesses in the system under review will strongly influence the volume of audit work necessary in relation to each area of operation. The interplay between strengths and weaknesses will, of course, be evaluated by reference to (1) their materiality in relation to the system (and, ultimately, the accounts) as a whole, and (2) the existence of related 'compensating controls' which minimize (if not eliminate) the effect of identified weaknesses.

This chapter should, however, be read and understood within the context of the systems-based audit. It was pointed out in section 2.6 that the alternative 'end-results' approach may be applicable to many audits, especially of those businesses whose controls are rudimentary. In such cases auditors will concentrate their efforts on 'substantive' testing of the records, examination of all available supportive evidence, and analytical reviews of final accounts.

In view of the importance of the system of internal control as the basis for determining the extent of the audit tests, it is worth considering the principles of control more closely. The Statement of Auditing Standards no. 300 – 'Accounting and internal control systems and audit risk assessments' defines the internal control systems as:

> 'Internal Control Systems' comprises the control environment and control procedures. It includes all the policies and procedures (internal controls) adopted by the directors and management of an entity to assist in achieving their objective of ensuring, as far as practicable, the orderly and efficient conduct of its business, including adherence to internal policies, the safeguarding of assets, the prevention and detection of fraud and error, the accuracy and completeness of the accounting records, and the timely preparation of reliable financial information. Internal controls may be incorporated within computerised accounting systems. However, the internal control system extends beyond those matters which relate directly to the accounting system.

The striking thing about the definition is its all-embracing nature, and it is clear that internal control is concerned with the controls operative in every area of corporate activity, as well as with the way in which individual controls interrelate.

For all of its practical importance in the context of the 'systems-based' audit, examination and evaluation of internal control systems can mistakenly become an audit objective in its own right, whereas it should more correctly be viewed as a means to an end. The main end is to obtain sufficient appropriate audit evidence to be able to draw reasonable conclusions on which to base the audit opinion. Reliance on a client's system of internal control is only one method of obtaining audit evidence, and in the case of many companies the auditor will have to rely to a greater extent on substantive testing.

3.2 The company's organization

Before analysing the above definition of internal control systems in relation to its practical applications, it is worth setting out the broad subdivisions into which most client entities are organized. It is a mistake to identify the audit function with the client company's accounts department exclusively; the latter is certainly at the core of the recording function, but every thorough audit examination will extend beyond the records, into the various departments whose activities are being recorded. The auditor should therefore be reasonably familiar with all major departmental functions, as set out in Table 3.1.

Many companies produce, and keep up to date, charts that depict the organizational hierarchy in linear terms. These have the advantage of indicating most departmental functions as well as identifying the personnel responsible for executing them. The charts cannot act as an effective substitute for explicit procedural manuals and/or functional flow diagrams, but they do perform an important role in identifying two other significant, but less obvious, 'flows':

1. The flow of authority and the dissemination of instruction downwards through all internal channels of communication.

2. The flow of information (which is (a) adequate, (b) sufficiently detailed and explicit, (c) accurate, and (d) up to date) in an upward direction, as part of a routine management information system.

Table 3.1   Major departmental functions

Main departments	Subdepartmental functions
Accounts	Ledgers
	Invoicing
	Computerized data processing
	Cashiers
	Credit control
	Budgets
	Taxation
	Divisional accounting
	Product costing/pricing
	Preparation of interim and final accounts
Personnel	Employee files
	Staff welfare including pensions
	Trade union relations
	Staff recruitment and reviews
	Interdepartmental liaison
Wages	Time recording
	Time work ⎫
	Piece work ⎬ Collation and calculation
	Overtime ⎭
	Payroll preparation
	Departmental analysis
	Staff loan repayments
Sales	Customer relations
	Advertising
	Technical
	Market research
	After-sales servicing/guarantees
	Filing/documentation
	Analysis/statistics
	Internal liaison
Buying	Ordering
	Supplier records
	Production/sales liaison
	Purchases control/optimum reorder quantities

continued

Table 3.1 *Continued*

Main departments	Subdepartmental functions
Production	Inspection/quality control
	Production scheduling
	Plant maintenance
	Production records
	Plant registers
	Work in progress costings
Warehouse	Stock recording
	Despatch/issues control
	Goods inwards control
	Requisition/reordering

Notes:

(a) although the above subdivisions are typical, many companies will adapt the allocation of functions to suit their particular requirements. For example, many will have a separate department to deal with costing, budgets and pricing — these are included in the accounts department in the table.

(b) The table is by no means exhaustive and could easily have been extended to include those departments that deal with:

 — Estates, i.e. development, buying, selling and leasing

 — Vehicles and transport fleet management

 — Research and development

 — Organization and methods

 — Overseas liaison

 — Internal and management audit

(c) Data processing is often a service supplied to the other departments listed, but nevertheless requires to be controlled in its own right.

The significant feature of these two flows is their mutual interdependence: the management decisions which result in the downward flow cannot be reached on any reliable basis other than that of the upward flow of information.

Organization charts may be prepared on any practical basis but, apart from the 'master chart', which encompasses the entire framework from the board of directors downwards, most charts will portray the relationships specific to a particular area of corporate activity. The three charts shown in Figures 3.1–3.3 relate to the following:

1. Production.
2. Accounting and office services.
3. Internal audit.

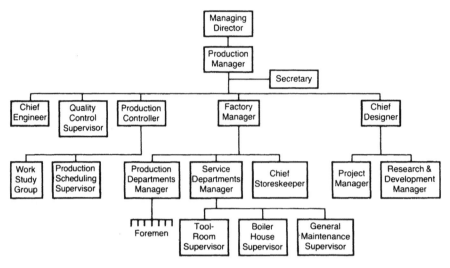

Figure 3.1   Production

It will be readily appreciated from the charts that these may be adapted to be either more or less informative, depending upon the needs of the user. For example, the chart on accounting and office services may be criticized in its present form in that it identifies the senior and supervisory personnel and names the functions for which they are responsible, but gives us no idea of the number of staff involved within each subsidiary area. This information, which could easily be provided, would act as an additional control feature, in that:

1. It would force a management decision to be taken on the optimum staff complement required in each section and, as such, would assist budgetary control over salaries.

2. It could be used as an internal check on the payroll itself, since the full departmental establishment would be known.

It is clearly of vital importance for the auditor to have up-to-date copies of all organization charts on file, and to familiarize himself with the channels of responsibility and communication as displayed. The charts also provide the auditor with an indication of probable weak links in the organizational chain. For example, both the chief accountant and the production manager (see first two charts) are responsible for no fewer than five subdivisions, whereas a useful management rule-of-thumb suggests that four should be the maximum. It may well be that the executive concerned can cope satisfactorily, but this requires close investigation. In the case of the second chart, much will depend upon the nature of the office manager's responsibilities; it may be more appropriate, for example, for him to report to the company secretary rather than to the chief accountant. A well-drafted chart will focus the attention on such potential problem areas and available options.

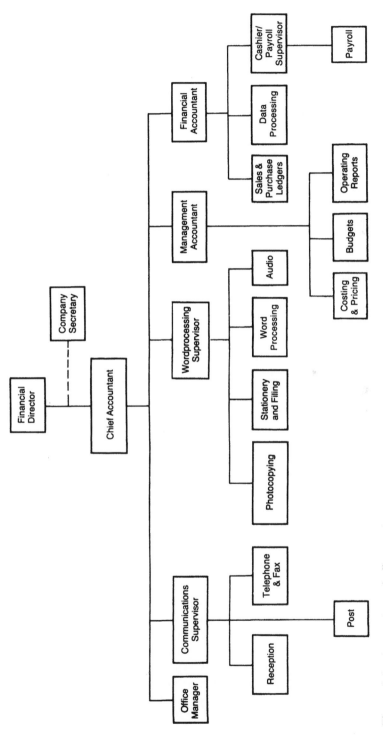

Figure 3.2   Accounting and office services

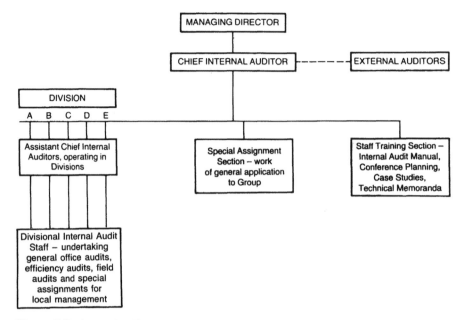

Figure 3.3 Internal audit

3.3 The essential features of internal control

The detailed nature of the controls operative within any commercial organization will depend upon the following:

1. The nature and size of the business conducted.
2. The number of administrative staff employed.
3. The materiality of transactions concerned.
4. The importance placed upon internal controls by the organization's own management.
5. The management style of the entity, particularly the trust placed in the integrity and honesty of the key personnel, and the latters' ability to supervise and control their own subordinate staff.

Although the auditor is deeply concerned with the existence and quality of all significant control features, he should never give management the impression that the audit function itself acts as a substitute for effective management control. The responsibilities of management in this direction are paramount and are based upon statutory requirements derived, as we have seen, from the principle of stewardship. The presence of the auditor should never, therefore, lull the management into attitudes of complacency. The precise nature of the relationship between a company's auditor and its directors should be made apparent to the latter from the wording of the engagement letter, discussed in Chapter 2.

Despite the many variations in internal control which will be manifest in different situations, all internal control systems will possess one inviolable principle: that of separation of functions. This does not mean the haphazard allocation of clerical duties, but rather the rational recognition that all commercial transactions in practice entail three fundamental elements:

1. *Authorization* – the initiation of contractual obligations on the company's behalf.
2. *Custody* – the handling of assets involved in the transaction.
3. *Recording* – the creation of documentary evidence of the transaction and its entry in the accounting records.

It should be noted that (a) adequate *management supervision* over all three aspects of activity is essential at all times, and (b) in a well-organized business the adequacy of internal control will be evidenced in a clear and up-to-date *plan of the organization*. The essence of internal control lies in the separation of the three functions of authorization, custody and recording. It is, of course, the responsibility of management to devise and establish the plan of the organization, and to supervise its day-to-day operation.

The separation of these three functions represents the objective of control in any departmental context. For example with regard to wages, the authorization function relates to the hiring of staff and should reside with the departmental head concerned, in conjunction with the personnel department; the terms of employment, once agreed, will be held on file in the personnel department. The custody function, i.e. the handling of the wages involved, should have played no part in the recording function, i.e. the creation of the time records and the payroll.

A second example may be seen in relation to sales. Authorization in this context means ascertaining the following information from the appropriate sources, before accepting the order:

1. The customer's credit rating and present account balance.
2. Whether the goods are in stock and delivery requirements can be met.

The sales staff involved in these tasks should play no part in handling the goods ordered, i.e. the custody function (warehouse staff), nor in creating the invoices, delivery notes and related accounting entries, i.e. the recording function (accounting staff).

The validity of the concept of control through separation is evident at both the level of the company itself and the level of the individual department. For example, within a warehouse (custodianship function) the subfunctions of stores recording, authority for release and admission of goods, and handling should be separated.

In its broadest sense, as suggested by the definition in section 3.1 above, internal control extends beyond the mere allocation of clerical duties to include the quality of management supervision itself. It is indeed difficult to envisage any organizational matter which falls outside the realm of internal control: budgets, cash requirement projections, cost and variance analysis, as examples of internal monitoring controls, all fall within its scope, as do arrangements for inspection of goods on arrival from suppliers to ensure that they match the description, quality and quantity ordered.

In March 1995 the APB issued a Statement of Auditing Standards no. 300 – 'Accounting and internal control systems and audit risk assessments'. This SAS sets out standards for auditors on assessing audit risk and obtaining an understanding of accounting and internal control systems. Its key points may be summarized as follows:

1. Audit risk, i.e. that an inappropriate audit opinion is given, has three components:

    (a) inherent risk,

    (b) control risk,

    (c) detection risk.

2. Detection risk incorporates audit sampling risk, which is covered by SAS 430.

3. Central to the SAS is that the auditor should have an understanding of the accounting and internal control systems of the client. Clearly, the auditor should maintain notes, documents, flowcharts, etc. on the permanent audit file detailing the control procedures operated by management.

4. In order to assess the adequacy of the controls, and therefore the extent to which reliance can be placed on them, it is common for an auditor to carry out 'walk-through' tests, i.e. to check whether what happens in practice is consistent with what is supposed to happen.

5. The three components of audit risk should be separately considered at the planning stage when the audit procedures are designed. This enables efforts to be targeted towards areas of materiality and so reduce overall audit risk.

6. In the case of small, owner-managed businesses, there may be little scope for segregation of duties so that control risk can be significantly influenced by management override of internal controls. In such circumstances the audit evidence may have to be obtained entirely from substantive procedures. The auditors' planning record should allow for this eventuality, together with a documentation of their reasons.

7. The SAS does not permit, whatever the perceived (low) level of inherent and control risk, an audit to be conducted without applying substantive procedures to material balances and transactions. However, these procedures may in certain circumstances be limited to analytical procedures.

8. In extreme cases, if the auditor derives no confidence from the system of internal control and also considers audit risk to be high due to the state of the records, he may have no option other than to undertake a 100 per cent check of transactions and balances as recorded. Before undertaking such an exhaustive and time-consuming vouching audit it would, however, be sensible to suggest that the client's own staff undertake remedial work on the records and, until this is completed, discontinue further audit work.

9. Letters of weakness, or management letters, are often written following a review of internal controls.

10. A checklist within the planning documents may be useful to ensure that all components of audit risk are adequately covered.

11. It is not necessary to complete detailed flowcharts and questionnaires on every audit assignment; for smaller clients with uncomplicated transactions, a straightforward list of the books and records maintained will be sufficient.

12. Where it is clear that reliance on controls to reduce substantive testing would not be worthwhile, a detailed assessment of these controls and control risk is not necessary.

3.4 Internal check

That aspect of internal control which is exclusively concerned with the prevention and early detection of errors and fraud is usually referred to as 'internal check', and this will therefore involve the arrangement of book-keeping and other clerical duties in such a way as to ensure:

1. That no single task is executed from its beginning to its conclusion by only one person.

2. That the work of each clerk engaged upon a task is subject to an independent check in the course of another's duties.

The latter need not involve pure duplication of effort, but might be achieved incidentally (yet intentionally) within the course of another clerical function. For example, the independent listing of all remittances received from debtors in a cash diary when the mail is opened may act as a control over a number of subsequent clerical tasks, including the daily lodgement shown on the bank paying-in slip.

Instances of internal check will abound in most well-organized businesses, but the following two adequately illustrate its operation, with special reference to the separation of the three key functions.

Example 1

The wages office of an industrial company employing a large number of staff (who are paid in cash, based on hours worked) may employ a system which involves the following separate clerical tasks:

1. Collection and sorting of time cards.

2. Calculation and listing of standard hours and overtime hours worked, by reference to time cards.

3. Calculation of gross pay by reference to records supplied by personnel department.

4. Production of payroll on computer, i.e. entry of gross pay, deductions, calculations of net pay, and cumulative cast and cross-cast.

5. Sample double check payroll, i.e. gross pay, deductions.

6. Submission of payroll to signatory in order to obtain wages cheque.

7. Visit to bank to obtain cash for wages.

8. Insertion of cash in envelopes by reference to duplicate pay slips.

9. Payment of wages against signed receipt from each employee.

10. Returning receipt signatures and unclaimed wages to cashier's department for special action (e.g. rebanking, locking in safe, or posting to absent employees, etc.).

If we assume that four members of staff (Thomas, Fred, Patrick and William) are employed in the wages department, and that a computer is used, then one way of allocating the above tasks is as follows:

1. Thomas
2. Thomas
3. Fred
4. Patrick
5. William
6. William
7. Thomas
8. Fred and William
9. Fred and Thomas
10. Fred and Thomas

The above arrangement is by no means the only one which achieves a satisfactory check within the existing constraints, although any variation of the suggested allocation should nevertheless ensure that tasks 8, 9 and 10 are performed by two members of staff, and that whoever is responsible for the creation of the payroll itself should play no further significant role in the wages procedures. This is the recording function and, as such, should be carefully separated from functions of authorization (e.g. approving overtime claims) and custody (e.g. collecting the wages cash from the bank).

Apart from the separation of duties as indicated above, certain overall wages controls will also normally operate, such as the independent retention by the chief accountant of an 'establishment roll' with which the payroll may be compared. Provided it is rigorously kept up to date, thus taking into account the names of new staff and leavers (supplied weekly by the personnel – not wages – department), the establishment roll acts as a useful control over payroll accuracy prior to the signing of the wages cheque, and may go a long way towards the elimination of 'dummy' names.

Example 2

A large retail store may employ a system which is designed to ensure that:

1. No member of its sales staff handles cash.

2. The cashiers have no contact with customers other than to take cash or issue receipts.

Sales staff would issue the customer with a detailed docket describing the goods, and extending the price. The salesperson packages the goods with distinctive wrapping while the customer pays the amount shown in the docket to the cashier, who in turn provides a receipt. On seeing the receipt the salesperson then releases the wrapped goods to the customer.

Such a system would also provide an independent check over the cashier if the salesperson retains copies of the dockets (which he would normally have to do for commission purposes). The daily list of dockets represents the cash which should be in the till. The till should be kept locked, with only the manager of the shop having a key.

3.5 Practical applications of internal control

The ICAEW Statement on Internal Control (U4), now superseded by the Statement of Auditing Standards 'Accounting and internal control systems and audit risk assessment', describes the practical application of internal control in the following areas:

- ► General financial arrangements,
- ► Cash and cheques (received and paid),
- ► Wages and salaries,
- ► Purchases and trade creditors,
- ► Sales and trade debtors,
- ► Stocks and work in progress,
- ► Fixed assets and investments.

The following is a summary of the internal control considerations appropriate to each of the above activities, and is taken from Appendix 1 to Statement U4 which, although officially superseded, is still relevant since the APB Statement of Auditing Standards provides no comparable examples. An updated version of U4 would now refer to electronic point-of-sale terminals and the controls they afford over cash takings and stocks. The advances of information technology should thus be taken into account when reading the following sections. The principles of control outlined are, however, as relevant as ever.

General financial arrangements

(a) Devising an appropriate and properly integrated system of accounts and records.

(b) Determining the form of general financial supervision and control by management, using such means as budgetary control, regular interim accounts of suitable frequency, and special reports.

(c) Ensuring that adequate precautions are taken to safeguard (and if necessary to duplicate and store separately) important records.

(d) Engaging, training and allocating to specific duties management and staff competent to fulfil their responsibilities; arranging for rotation of duties as necessary; and deputing responsibilities during staff absences.

Cash and cheques received (including cash and bank balances)

Receipts by post and cash sales

Considerations involved in dealing with cash and cheques received by post include:

(a) Instituting safeguards to minimize the risk of interception of mail between its receipt and opening.

(b) Wherever possible, appointing a responsible person, independent of the cashier, to open, or supervise the opening of, mail.

(c) Ensuring that cash and cheques received are (i) adequately protected (for instance, by the restrictive crossing of all cheques, money orders and the like on first handling), and (ii) properly accounted for (for instance, by the preparation of post-lists of moneys received for independent comparison with subsequent records and book entries).

In establishing an adequate system of control over cash sales and collections it should be decided:

(a) Who is to be authorized to receive cash and cash articles (i.e. whether such items are to be received only by cashiers or may be accepted by sales assistants, travellers, roundsmen, or others).

(b) How sales and the receipt of cash and cash articles are to be evidenced, and what checks may usefully be adopted as regards such transactions (for instance, by the use of serially numbered receipt forms or counterfoils, or cash registers incorporating sealed till rolls).

Custody and control of money received

(a) The appointment of suitable persons to be responsible at different stages for the collection and handling of money received, with clearly defined responsibilities.

(b) How, by whom, and with what frequency cash offices and registers are to be cleared.

(c) What arrangements are to be made for agreeing cash collections with cash and sales records (preferably this should be carried out by a person independent of the receiving cashier or employee).

(d) According to the nature of the business, what arrangements are to be made for dealing with, recording and investigating any cash shortages or surpluses.

Recording

(a) Who is to be responsible for maintaining records of money received.

(b) What practicable limitations may be put on the duties and responsibilities of the receiving cashier particularly as regards dealing with such matters as other books of account, other funds, securities and negotiable instruments, sales invoices, credit notes and cash payments.

(c) Who is to perform the receiving cashier's functions during his absence at lunch, on holiday, or through sickness.

(d) In what circumstances, if any, receipts are to be given, whether copies are to be retained; the serial numbering of receipt books and forms; how their issue and use are to be controlled; what arrangements are to be made, and who is to be responsible, for checking receipt counterfoils against (i) cash records and (ii) bank paying-in slips; and how alterations to receipts are to be authorized and evidenced.

Payments into bank

(a) How frequently payments are to be made into the bank (preferably daily).

(b) Who is to make up the bank paying-in slips (preferably this should be done by a person independent of the receiving and recording cashier) and whether there is to be any independent check of paying-in slips against post-lists, receipt counterfoils and cash book entries.

(c) Who is to make payments into the bank (preferably not the person responsible for preparing paying-in slips).

(d) Whether all receipts are to be banked intact; if not, how disbursements are to be controlled.

Cash balances

Questions to be decided in connection with the control of cash balances include:

(a) What amounts are to be retained as cash floats at cash desks and registers, and whether payments out of cash received are to be permitted.

(b) What restrictions are to be imposed as to access to cash registers and offices.

(c) Rules regarding the size of cash floats to meet expenses, and their methods of reimbursement.

(d) The frequency with which cash floats are to be checked by independent officials.

(e) What arrangements are to be made for safeguarding cash left on the premises outside business hours.

(f) Whether any special insurance arrangements (such as fidelity guarantee and cash insurance) are judged desirable having regard to the nature of the business, the sums handled, and the length of time they are kept on the premises.

(g) What additional independent checks on cash may usefully be operated (for instance, by periodic surprise cash count).

(h) What arrangements are to be made for the control of funds held in trust for employees, both those which are the legal responsibility of the company and, as necessary, those which are held by nominated employees independent of the company's authority (for instance, sick funds or holiday clubs).

Cheque and cash payments

The arrangements for controlling payments will depend to a great extent on the nature of business transacted, the volume of payments involved, and the size of the company.

Cheque payments

Amongst the points to be decided in settling the system for payments by cheque are the following:

(a) What procedure is to be adopted for controlling the supply and issue of cheques for use, and who is to be responsible for their safe-keeping.

(b) Who is to be responsible for preparing cheques and traders' credit lists.

(c) What documents are to be used as authorization for preparing cheques and traders' credit lists, rules as to their presentation to cheque signatories as evidence in support of payment, and the steps to be taken to ensure that payment cannot be made twice on the strength of the same document.

(d) The names, number and status of persons authorized to sign cheques; limitations as to their authority; the minimum number of signatories required for each cheque; if only one signatory is required, whether additional independent authorization of payments is desirable; if more than one signatory is required, how it is to be ensured that those concerned will operate effective independent scrutiny (for instance, by prohibiting the signing by any signatory of blank cheques in advance); limitations, if any, as to the amount permissible to be drawn on one signature; whether cheques drawn in favour of persons signing are to be prohibited.

(e) Safeguards to be adopted if cheques are signed mechanically or carry printed signatures.

(f) The extent to which cheques issued should be restrictively crossed; and the circumstances, if any, in which blank or bearer cheques may be issued.

(g) Arrangements for the prompt despatch of signed cheques and precautions against interception.

(h) Arrangements for obtaining paid cheques; whether they are to be regarded as sufficient evidence of payment or whether receipts are to be required; and the procedure to be followed in dealing with paid cheques returned as regards examination and preservation.

(i) The arrangements to be made to ensure that payments are made within discount periods.

Cash payments

Factors to be considered include the following:

(a) Nomination of a responsible person to authorize expenditure, the means of indicating such authorization and the documentation to be presented and preserved as evidence.

(b) Arrangements to ensure that the vouchers supporting payments cannot be presented for payment twice.

(c) Whether any limit is to be imposed as regards amounts disbursed in respect of individual payments.

(d) Rules as to cash advances to employees and officials, IOUs, and the cashing of cheques.

Wages and salaries

(a) Who may authorize the engagement and discharge of employees.

(b) Who may authorize general and individual changes in rates of pay.

(c) How notifications of changes in personnel and rates of pay are to be recorded and controlled to prevent irregularities and errors in the preparation and payment of wages and salaries.

(d) How deductions from employees' pay other than for income tax and national insurance are to be authorized.

(e) What arrangements are to be made for recording hours worked (in the case of hourly paid workers) or work done (in the case of pieceworkers), and for ensuring that the records are subject to scrutiny and approval by an appropriate official before being passed to the wages department; special supervision and control arrangements may be desirable where overtime working is material.

(f) Whether advances of pay are to be permitted; if so, who may authorize them, what limitations are to be imposed, how they are to be notified to and dealt with by wages and salaries departments, and how they are to be recovered.

(g) How holiday pay is to be dealt with.

(h) Who is to deal with pay queries.

Preparation of payroll

The procedure for preparing the payroll should be clearly established. Principal matters for consideration include the following:

(a) What records are to be used as bases for the compilation of the payroll and how they are to be authorized.

(b) Who is to be responsible (i) for preparing pay sheets, (ii) for checking them, and (iii) for approving them (preferably separate persons), and by what means individual responsibility at each stage is to be indicated.

(c) What procedures are to be laid down for notifying and dealing with non-routine circumstances such as an employee's absence from work, or employees leaving at short notice in the middle of a pay period.

Payment of wages and salaries

Where employees are paid in cash the following matters are amongst those that require decision:

(a) What arrangements are to be made to provide the requisite cash for paying out (e.g. by encashment of a cheque for the total amount of net wages) and what steps are to be taken to safeguard such moneys during collection and transit and until distribution;

(b) What safeguards against irregularities are to be adopted (e.g. by arranging for pay packets to be filed by persons other than those responsible for preparing pay sheets, providing them with the exact amount of cash required, and forbidding their access to other cash), and what particulars are to be given to the payees.

(c) Who is to pay cash wages over to employees (preferably a person independent of those engaged in the preparation of pay sheets and pay packets); how payees' identities are to be verified; what officials are to be in attendance; and how distribution is to be recorded (e.g. by recipient's signature or by checking off names on the pay list).

(d) What arrangements are to be made for dealing with unclaimed wages.

Where wages and salaries are paid by cheque or bank transfer the matters to be decided include:

(a) Which persons are (i) to prepare, and (ii) to sign cheques and bank transfer lists (preferably these persons should be independent of each other and of those responsible for preparing pay sheets).

(b) Whether a separate wages and salaries bank account is to be maintained, what amounts are to be transferred to it from time to time (preferably on due dates the net amount required to meet pay cheques and transfers), and who is to be responsible for its regular reconciliation (preferably someone independent of those responsible for maintaining pay records).

Additional checks on pay arrangements

In addition to the routine arrangements and day-to-day checks referred to above, use may be made, as judged desirable, of a number of independent overall checks on wages and salaries. Amongst those available may be listed the following:

(a) The maintenance, separate from wages and salaries departments, of employees' records, with which pay lists may be compared as necessary.

(b) The preparation of reconciliations to explain changes in total pay and deductions between one pay day and the next.

(c) Surprise counts of cash held by wages and salaries departments.

(d) The comparison of actual pay totals with independently prepared figures such as budget estimates or standard costs and investigation of variances.

(e) The agreement of gross earnings and total tax deducted for the year to 5 April with PAYE returns to the Inland Revenue.

Purchases and trade creditors

The three separate functions into which accounting controls may be divided clearly appear in the considerations involved in purchase procedures. They are buying ('authorization'), receipt of goods ('custody'), and accounting ('recording').

Buying

Factors to be considered include:

(a) The procedure to be followed when issuing requisitions for additions to and replacements of stocks, and the persons to be responsible for such requisitions.

(b) The preparation and authorization of purchase orders (including procedures for authorizing acceptance where tenders have been submitted or prices quoted).

(c) The institution of checks for the safe-keeping of order forms and safeguarding their use.

(d) As regards capital items, any special arrangements as to authorizations required (for a fuller description of this aspect see the section dealing with fixed assets below).

Goods inwards

Factors to be considered include:

(a) Arrangements for examining goods inwards as to quantity, quality and condition, and for evidencing such examination.

(b) The appointment of a person responsible for accepting goods, and procedure for recording and evidencing their arrival and acceptance.

(c) The procedure to be instituted for checking goods inwards records against authorized purchase orders.

Accounting

Factors to be considered include:

(a) The appointment of persons so far as possible separately responsible for:

   (i) checking suppliers' invoices

   (ii) recording purchases and purchase returns

   (iii) maintaining suppliers' ledger accounts or similar records

   (iv) checking suppliers' statements

   (v) authorizing payment.

(b) Arrangements to ensure that before accounts are paid:

   (i) the goods concerned have been received, accord with the purchase order, are properly priced and correctly invoiced

   (ii) the expenditure has been properly allocated, and

   (iii) payment has been duly authorized by the official responsible.

(c) The establishment of appropriate procedures in connection with purchase returns, special credits and other adjustments.

(d) Arrangements to ensure that liabilities relating to goods received during an accounting period are properly brought into the accounts of the period concerned (i.e. cut-off procedures).

(e) The establishment of arrangements to deal with purchases from companies or branches forming part of the same group.

(f) Arrangements to deal with purchases made from employees under special terms.

(g) Regular independent checking of suppliers' accounts against current statements, or direct verification with suppliers.

(h) The institution of a purchases control account and its regular checking by an independent official against suppliers' balances.

Sales and trade debtors

The separation of authorization, custodianship and recording functions described above in respect of purchase and trade creditors applies similarly to sales and trade debtors.

Sales

Considerations include the following:

(a) What arrangements are to be made to ensure that goods are sold at their correct prices, and to deal with and check exchanges, discounts and special reductions including those in connection with cash sales.

(b) Who is to be responsible for, and how control is to be maintained over, the granting of credit terms to customers.

(c) Who is to be responsible for accepting customers' orders, and what procedure is to be adopted for issuing production orders and despatch notes.

(d) Who is to be responsible for the preparation of invoices and credit notes and what controls are to be instituted to prevent errors and irregularities (for instance, how selling prices are to be ascertained and authorized, how the issue of credit notes is to be controlled and checked, what checks there should be on the prices, quantities, extensions and totals shown on invoices and credit notes, and how such documents in blank or completed are to be protected against loss or misuse).

(e) What special controls are to be exercised over the despatch of goods free of charge or on special terms.

Goods outwards

Factors to be considered include:

(a) Who may authorize the despatch of goods and how such authority is to be evidenced.

(b) What arrangements are to be made to examine and record goods outwards (preferably this should be done by a person who has no access to stocks and has no accounting or invoicing duties).

(c) The procedure to be instituted for agreeing goods outwards records with customers' orders, despatch notes and invoices.

Accounting

So far as possible sales ledger staff should have no access to cash, cash books or stocks, and should not be responsible for invoicing and other duties normally assigned to sales staff. The following are amongst matters which should be considered:

(a) The appointment of persons as far as possible separately responsible for:

   (i)   recording sales and sales returns

   (ii) maintaining customers' accounts

   (iii) preparing debtors' statements.

(b) The establishment of appropriate control procedures in connection with sales returns, price adjustments and similar matters.

(c) Arrangements to ensure that goods despatched but not invoiced (or vice versa) during an accounting period are properly dealt with in the accounts of the period concerned (i.e. cut-off procedures).

(d) The establishment of arrangements to deal with sales to companies or branches forming part of the same group.

(e) What procedures are to be adopted for the preparation, checking and despatch of debtors' statements and for ensuring that they are not subject to interference before despatch.

(f) How discounts granted and special terms are to be authorized and evidenced.

(g) Who is to deal with customers' queries arising in connection with statements.

(h) What procedure is to be adopted for reviewing and following up overdue accounts.

(i) Who is to authorize the writing off of bad debts, and how such authority is to be evidenced.

(j) The institution of a sales control account and its regular checking preferably by an independent official against customers' balances on the sales ledger.

Stocks (including work in progress)

Amongst the main considerations may be listed the following:

(a) What arrangements are to be made for receiving, checking and recording goods inwards.

(b) Who is to be responsible for the safeguarding of stocks and what precautions are to be taken against theft, misuse and deterioration.

(c) What arrangements are to be made for controlling (through maximum and minimum stock limits) and recording stocks (e.g. by stock ledgers, independent control accounts and continuous stock records such as bin cards); who is to be responsible for keeping stock records (preferably persons who have no access to stocks and are not responsible for sales and purchase records); and what procedure is to be followed as to the periodic reconciliation of stock records with the financial accounts.

(d) How movements of stock out of store (or from one process or department to another) are to be authorized, evidenced and recorded, and what steps are to be taken to guard against irregularities.

(e) What arrangements are to be made for dealing with and accounting for returnable containers (both suppliers' and own).

(f) What arrangements are to be made for dealing with and maintaining accounting control over company stocks held by others (for instance, goods in warehouse, on consignment or in course of processing) and goods belonging to others held by the company (e.g. how withdrawals are to be authorized and evidenced, and how goods belonging to others are to be distinguished from own goods).

(g) What persons are to be responsible for physically checking stocks, at what intervals such checks are to be carried out, and what procedures are to be followed (for instance, if continuous stocktaking procedures are in use, arrangements should ensure that all categories of stock are counted at appropriate intervals normally at least once a year; counts should preferably be conducted by persons independent of storekeepers; how stock counts are to be recorded and evidenced; and what cut-off procedures are to be operated to ensure that stocks are adjusted to take proper account of year-end sales and purchases invoiced).

(h) What bases are to be adopted for computing the amount at which stocks are to be stated in the accounts.

(i) What arrangements are to be made for the periodic review of the condition of stocks, how damaged, slow-moving and obsolete stocks are to be dealt with and how write-offs are to be authorized.

(j) What steps are to be taken to control and account for scrap and waste, and receipts from the disposal of such items.

Fixed assets and investments

Fixed assets

Some of the principal matters to be decided in connection with controls relating to fixed assets are as follows:

(a) Who is to authorize capital expenditure and how such authorization is to be evidenced.

(b) Who is to authorize the sale, scrapping or transfer of fixed assets, how such authorization is to be evidenced, and what arrangements are to be made for controlling and dealing with receipts from disposals.

(c) Who is to maintain accounting records in respect of fixed assets and how it is to be ensured that the proper accounting distinction is observed between capital and revenue expenditure.

(d) What arrangements are to be made for keeping plant and property registers and how frequently they are to be agreed with the relevant accounts and physically verified.

(e) What arrangements are to be made to ensure that fixed assets are properly maintained and applied in the service of the company (e.g. by periodic physical checks as to their location, operation and condition).

(f) Where fixed assets are transferred between branches or members of the same group, what arrangements in respect of pricing, depreciation and accounting are to be made.

(g) How depreciation rates are to be authorized and evidenced, and which persons are to be responsible for carrying out and checking the necessary calculations.

Investments

Arrangements for dealing with investments will involve, *inter alia*, determining:

(a) Who is to be responsible for authorizing purchases and sales of investments, and how such authorizations are to be evidenced (those responsible should preferably have no concern with cash or the custody of documents of title).

(b) What arrangements should be made for maintaining a detailed investment register; and who should be responsible for agreeing it periodically with the investment control account and physically verifying the documents of title.

(c) What arrangements are to be made for checking contract notes against authorized purchase or sale instructions and for ensuring that charges are correctly calculated; for dealing with share transfers; and for ensuring that share certificates are duly received or delivered and that bonuses, rights, capital repayments and dividends or interest are received and properly accounted for.

3.6   Internal audit as a control factor

It will have been observed from the definition of internal control given in section 3.1 that its scope is wide enough to include the control provided by internal audit, although not specifically mentioned. The objectives of internal and external auditing are similar, except that the internal auditors are employees of the company and are responsible to its management. They consequently lack the independence with which the external auditor's position is (or should be) endowed.

With the growth in size and complexity of many companies in recent years, the importance of the internal audit has correspondingly increased so that it is today a major factor in establishing the quality of a company's internal control, and its development has made a considerable contribution to contemporary audit practice. The Institute of Internal Auditors is an independent professional body well established on both sides of the Atlantic, and the importance of the role which its members are able to play within the commercial and industrial sphere has gained wide recognition.

Obviously, only large organizations have both the need and the means to support a full scale internal audit department (see Figure 3.3) but where such departments do operate, the statutory auditor will pay particular attention to their activities since these will have a direct bearing on the scope and depth of work required to be performed by external audit.

3.6.1   Assessment of internal audit

An assessment of the quality and effectiveness of internal audit in practice is necessary since internal auditors often cover a wide variety of assignments, not all of which will necessarily relate to the accounting areas in which the external auditor is specially interested. For example, it is common for internal audit to undertake the extensive and continuous task of setting management goals and monitoring its performance, i.e. one aspect of what is usually termed the 'operational audit', and the fruits of work at this level of responsibility will only marginally concern the external auditor. There is also a good deal to be said, incidentally, in favour of internal audit responsibility at 'audit committee' level (see section 1.5.3).

In so far as internal audit work does relate to the functional efficacy of internal control systems, its usual scope in this context may be conveniently classified into four main interlocking capacities: (1) advisory; (2) executive (or implementative); (3) reporting; (4) routine testing. It is therefore necessary for the external auditor to discover the effectiveness of the internal audit operation in each of these capacities before deciding how far to reduce the volume of his own transactional tests in important areas.

The following are a few of the more important questions which would need to be asked and answered in relation to the four capacities:

1. *Advisory role*:
   (a) To what extent is the internal audit department required to recommend improvements in the system currently in operation?

    (b) If so requested, to which level of management are the recommendations directed?

    (c) Are such recommendations made as a matter of course, or in response to specific instructions?

    (d) What evidence is there that such recommendations have in the past been ignored/acknowledged/read/studied/partially implemented/wholly implemented?

2. *Executive role*:

    (a) What part is the internal audit department expected to play in implementing its own proposals?

    (b) To what extent is it involved in the planning and phasing in of new systems, e.g. new computer applications?

    (c) Is it required to monitor the functioning and output of systems recently instituted?

3. *Reporting role*:

    (a) What is the department's brief with regard to management reports? In particular are, say, monthly reports on routine matters required, or are reports prepared only when special matters are under investigation?

    (b) Do internal audit reports contain a large volume of detailed information, running to unmanageable lengths, or do they follow normal 'exception' reporting practices, i.e. referring only to matters of immediate concern? (The danger is that reports which are produced regularly, mechanically following an established pattern, risk being equally regularly and mechanically ignored.)

4. *Routine testing role*:

    (a) Is the system which the internal auditors are testing clearly laid down in a procedures manual or series of flowcharts?

    (b) Do internal auditors normally report all deviations from established practice which they discover during testing?

    (c) What objective evidence of their testing routines exists?

    (d) Do they work strictly to an audit programme? In which case, how often is the programme reviewed?

    (e) Do they operate a system of rotation testing to ensure that the whole of the work under their purview is surveyed at reasonable (but irregular) intervals?

    (f) Does their programme include surprise cash counts, surprise visits to observe the wages distribution, unscheduled and unadvertised computer 'test pack' runs, and any other unscheduled checks of this nature?

The answers to these questions would normally be ascertained by including an internal audit section within the external auditor's standard internal control questionnaire. The questions should be put to the chief internal auditor, and the answers independently verified by the member of the board to whom he is responsible.

Other more general questions which are also important would concern the professional qualifications of the senior members of the internal audit department; their length of service with the company; whether they were required to work initially in other departments to familiarize themselves with the operating routines prior to joining the internal audit; and a realistic appraisal of the extent to which they are independent of the staff in other senior and junior management positions whose work they are required to check.

3.6.2 The APB Statement of Auditing Standards on internal audit

The APB has produced a Statement of Auditing Standards, no. 500 – 'Considering the work of internal audit', which provides guidance on the use of internal audit work by external auditors. Many of the precepts governing the external auditor's reliance on the internal audit function, as discussed above, are incorporated in the Statement of Auditing Standards.

3.7 Ascertaining and evaluating the system

As the system of internal control in force plays a large part in determining the nature, the range and the depth of audit tests executed, we now review the techniques by means of which the auditor may:

1. Record the system.
2. Ascertain where the respective strengths and weaknesses lie.
3. Assess and evaluate their importance in relation to the functioning of the system as a whole, and hence determine the reliability of the records which represent the system's natural product.

In reaching his conclusions under (2), we see that the auditor will have to give due consideration to the materiality of any weaknesses discovered, as well as to the possible existence of compensating controls which may offset their effect in practice. Our concern therefore falls within the scope of stages II, III and IV in the 'chronology' diagram (Figure 2.1); and will include the first audit tests referred to in 'the incidence of audit testing' (Figure 2.2).

It will be appreciated that the audit of smaller concerns will rarely require the use of sophisticated audit techniques, and a relatively brief period of intelligent observation of the system in operation, together with interviews on the nature of the business and its records, will normally suffice in such cases. It should nonetheless be understood that even where this task is uncomplicated, the client being a compact unit, with a simple organization employing a small number of staff whose designated functions are clearly laid down, the records and the final accounts are still derived from the system such as it is – and there is no question of being able to 'go straight into the audit'. Furthermore, in order to satisfy the Statements of Auditing Standards requirements on evidence, recording and working papers, notes should be taken and periodically updated ensuring that the audit files reflect the accounting system's workings, however straightforward it may appear to be.

The means and techniques of discovering and assessing the qualities and defects in a system will vary according to circumstances, but certain of these techniques have gained widespread application in recent years. Having stood the test of time, then, they are worth considering in some detail. Throughout this chapter the term 'substantive procedures' should be understood to convey the meaning given in the Statement of Auditing Standards on audit evidence. Compliance tests are referred to as 'tests of control' in this SAS and represent tests to provide evidence that internal control procedures are being applied as prescribed. Substantive tests are those tests of transactions and balances, and other procedures such as review, which seek to provide evidence as to the existence, completeness, accuracy, valuation and validity of information in the accounting records or in the financial statements.

3.8 Recording – the use of flow diagrams

3.8.1 Advantages of flow diagrams

We have already observed in this text how information presented in diagrammatic form can often be conveyed and assimilated far more effectively than when presented as a narrative. Earlier in this chapter, for example, a number of organizational structures were presented, demonstrating the two-way flow of authority (in a 'downward' direction through the hierarchical systems) and information (in the corresponding 'upward' direction which, in turn, enables management decisions to be reached and subsequently disseminated downwards as part of a continuous 'flow' cycle).

In the context of internal control systems, apart from the more subtle flows referred to above, there is the more obvious sequence of work activity, and the creation of documents and records which it inevitably entails. The auditor will, in establishing the nature of the system in operation, include flow diagrams of the system, supplemented by detailed systems notes, in the permanent audit files. These are updated on the basis of regular periodic reviews. The auditor's flow diagrams may be adapted from those already prepared by the client, or may, especially in the case of a new client, be produced from scratch by the auditor himself. The execution of this highly disciplined exercise will, of itself, usually teach the auditor a good deal more about the detailed functioning of the system at work in each department or division than any amount of study of the client's procedures manuals prepared in narrative form. For this reason, flowcharting is a highly effective method of achieving the objectives of stage II of the audit, as set out in the chronology diagram (Figure 2.1).

The auditor should refrain from committing the chart to his files until he is, as a result of questioning and observation, reasonably certain that it represents what actually takes place. The importance of this should be obvious: the nature of the audit tests subsequently carried out will, to a large degree, follow the pattern reflected in the chart and a good deal of time may be wasted (apart from the risks associated with reliance upon erroneous assumptions) if the charts are incomplete or lacking in accuracy.

Flowcharting has been used for this purpose for many years, and it has a number of additional advantages which may be summarized as follows:

1. The system or any part of it may be presented as a totality without any loss of detail.

2. The relationship between procedures in different areas can be depicted simply.

3. Control features (or their absence in cases where they might be expected) may be highlighted by the use of designated symbols.

4. References to the other related audit documents may be easily incorporated.

5. Diagrammatic representation facilitates subsequent reference to particular features in the system more readily than pure narrative.

6. New members of the audit team are enabled to participate in the audit work after a shorter induction period as a result of the advantages already mentioned, thus effecting a considerable saving of time.

Although most of the above advantages are largely applicable to all flowcharting systems, charting methods will vary according to the nature of the system portrayed, and what is required of the systems charts, once completed. A straightforward method, quite satisfactory for the depiction of less complicated procedures (and ideal for use in examinations) is the one-dimensional chart. This simply follows the time sequence of operations in a downward vertical flow until the concluding event, document or file is reached. An example is given in section 3.8.4.

3.8.2 The standardization of symbols

Although the British Standards Institution (BSI) has published a substantial list of flowchart symbols, relatively few are required for audit purposes, especially when the one-dimensional method is used. The following BSI symbols are those which the auditor will employ most commonly:

1. Manual or clerical operation

2. Document

3. Decision (yes or no)

4. Merging of documents

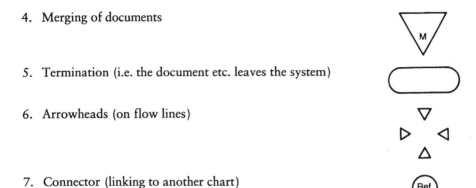

5. Termination (i.e. the document etc. leaves the system)

6. Arrowheads (on flow lines)

7. Connector (linking to another chart)

8. Additionally, the symbol ▽ may be used to indicate 'file', with a code letter in the bottom section of the triangle, thus:

P = permanent
T = temporary
D = date sequence
A = alphabetical sequence
N = numerical sequence

3.8.3 Rules of one-dimensional flowcharting

It is difficult to lay down hard-and-fast rules for a technique which has been independently developed by a number of firms working without any effective co-ordination. As a result, a wide variety of symbols proliferates at present; flow lines move in vertical, diagonal and horizontal directions; in fact there is little uniformity on matters of detail. Although the standard BSI flowcharting symbols have been adopted almost in their entirety by the computer industry, the auditing profession has not followed suit.

Despite the variety of techniques in operation it is possible to list the following rules, which are most generally observed in practice:

1. The direction of flow adopted should be followed consistently. Except in the case of a loop (usually called a subroutine where computers are involved), which depicts the continuous repetition of an operation until a specified occurrence takes place, the flow direction should never be reversed.

2. Unless BSI symbols are used, a key should always be provided.

3. A specially designed template should always be used – freehand flowcharting is rarely acceptable.

4. The chart should not be cramped – use a connector symbol and begin a new page rather than attempt to fit an inordinate amount of detail on one page.

5. If it is necessary to refer to a document a second (or third, etc.) time on the same chart, the outline on successive occasions should be broken ('ghosted') thus:

6. Remember what is being charted: the diagram represents a series of events etc. in *time* (as opposed to *space*). The *sequence* is therefore all-important.

7. The chart must reflect the system – weaknesses included. It is often tempting to assume that the sensible procedure is always adopted by the client's staff in practice, but it is the *actual* procedure that must be drawn.

8. Activities often involve the production of a *document* – always *separate* the symbols for the activity and the document respectively.

9. Avoid the crossing of flow lines if possible. If unavoidable, use this recognized device:

10. Marginal comment should be included in the chart where appropriate using a dotted flow line and a marginal bracket, thus:

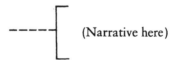 (Narrative here)

This avoids congestion in the body of the chart.

3.8.4 Examples of one-dimensional charts

Let us assume that the following is included in a client's procedures manual.

Example I

The Requisitions Section of the Purchases Department originates two copies of standard goods Requisition PRQ, upon receipt of Advice from Storekeeper. The first copy is filed in the Requisitions Section, together with the Advice from Storekeeper. Copy no. 2 is passed to the Purchases Manager for authorization. Requisitions rejected are noted by him and returned to the Requisitions Section, with the reason stated. Approved requisitions are then passed to the Orders Section for the typing of official orders in triplicate:

▶ Copy I is sent to supplier.

> ▶ Copy 2 is attached to the original requisition and both are filed in date order in the Orders Section.
>
> ▶ Copy 3 is passed back to the Requisition Section as evidence of the goods having been ordered, and it is filed temporarily until the goods and delivery note have arrived. It is then transferred to a permanent file and stamped 'goods received'.

The above procedures can be simply depicted as shown in Figure 3.4. The method used in the figure is very much of the ad hoc variety, not subject to rigorous 'do's and don'ts', but it succeeds in portraying the underlying events simply and concisely. The fundamental direction of flow is from top to bottom, very broadly following the time sequence in which the events allegedly take place. It may be useful in limited applications, for example where only one section of the recording process needs to be depicted.

It should be noted that the information given in the procedures manual is incomplete in the first place; for example, we are not informed of the criteria used by the Purchases Manager in deciding whether to approve the PRQ, nor of what ultimately happens to much of the documentation held on file. In practice, the auditor would attempt to fill in these gaps before finalizing the chart. Under no circumstances, however, should he make assumptions as to how the missing steps are filled, on the basis of common sense – an attribute all too rarely encountered in practice, especially at the clerical level.

Our second example has a number of similar features but also makes greater use of the 'decision' symbol, and at one point employs a 'loop' (the one instance in which the direction of flow may legitimately be reversed).

Example 2

Your client's internal audit staff frequently find it necessary to incur expenditure in the course of their duties, and claims for repayment are made monthly. The repayment system (portrayed in Figure 3.5) is as follows:

1. Expenditure is repayable only if incurred for one of the purposes listed in the company's Procedures Manual.

2. Claims will be considered only if entered on official repayment forms, which must be signed by the claimant.

3. Where no supporting vouchers are available, claims under £20 will be considered if covered by the additional signature of the head of section. In other cases, duplicate vouchers must be obtained, and attached to the repayment form.

4. If it is impossible to obtain duplicate vouchers, repayment by cheque is at the sole discretion of the Chief Accountant (after reference to the Chief Internal Auditor for clarification) to whom direct application is necessary.

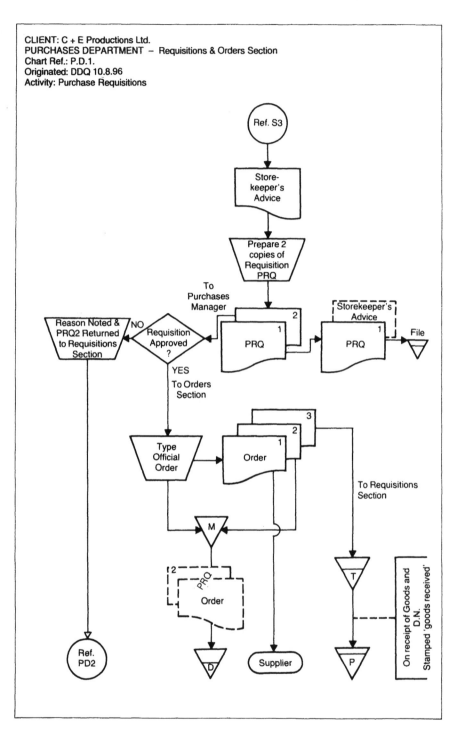

Figure 3.4 One-dimensional flowchart (1)

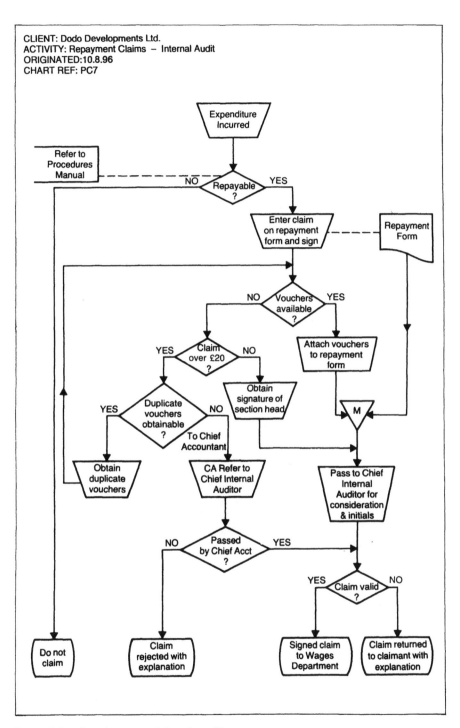

Expenditure Incurred

Refer to Procedures Manual

NO — Repayable ? — YES

Enter claim on repayment form and sign

Repayment Form

NO — Vouchers available ? — YES

YES — Claim over £20 ? — NO

Attach vouchers to repayment form

YES — Duplicate vouchers obtainable ? — NO

Obtain signature of section head

To Chief Accountant

M

Obtain duplicate vouchers

CA Refer to Chief Internal Auditor

Pass to Chief Internal Auditor for consideration & initials

NO — Passed by Chief Acct ? — YES

YES — Claim valid ? — NO

Do not claim

Claim rejected with explanation

Signed claim to Wages Department

Claim returned to claimant with explanation

Figure 3.5   One-dimensional flowchart (2)

> 5. Completed repayment forms, with appropriate attachments, should be passed to the Chief Internal Auditor who initials valid claims and passes them to the Wages Department for inclusion in the monthly salary cheque.
>
> 6. Invalid or rejected claims are passed, with explanation, back to claimant for amendment where appropriate.

3.8.5 Other one-dimensional applications

Flowcharting is an ideal medium for describing the steps in a computer program since it is based upon a series of logical steps. Most computer programs will comprise alternate 'activity' and 'decision' (yes/no) symbols. Although a detailed description and reproduction of such programs in diagrammatic form falls outside the scope of this text, algorithmic logic (as it is usually called) can be usefully employed in general systems, provided the sequence of operations depends upon a clearly defined series of 'logic' steps.

Many systems interface with data-processing departments by means of a computer, and in such cases a wider range of symbols is necessarily used. The IBM template (Figure 3.6) employs BSI symbols for use in a computer context.

The use of many of these symbols can be seen to good effect in the one-dimensional flow diagram (Figure 3.7) which condenses a remarkable amount of detailed information into a compact top-to-bottom flow. Although no previous narrative is supplied in this case, the reader of the chart will experience little difficulty in following procedures and records involved.

There is surprisingly little consistency in the flowcharting methods used in practice, both by companies preparing their own procedural manuals and by auditors in compiling their systems notes on the clerical procedures followed by client organizations. Yet whatever method is adopted, assuming the basic conventions are adhered to, a chart should prove to be of immense value in providing a 'ready reference' to each point of detail lying behind a veritable mountain of complexity. There are certainly no absolute rights and wrongs in the drawing of the charts – indeed, clearly labelled rectangles can in many cases be almost as effective as symbols. Any chart is right if it is neat, its meaning is clear and explicit, and it is accurate. There is, incidentally, only one way to become a flowcharting expert – practice.

3.8.6 The two-dimensional flowchart

In most of the charts illustrated above, the flow has been a function of time. Events such as decisions or the creation of documents were portrayed in the sequence in which they arose in reality. To the extent, therefore, that the charts were limited to the time sequence they have been referred to as one-dimensional; references within the charts to physical movement of documents, etc. (from a particular department or location to another) has had to be indicated on the flow lines themselves. Furthermore, the only

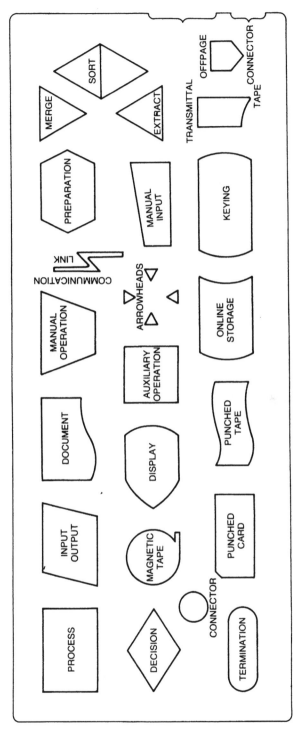

Figure 3.6 IBM template

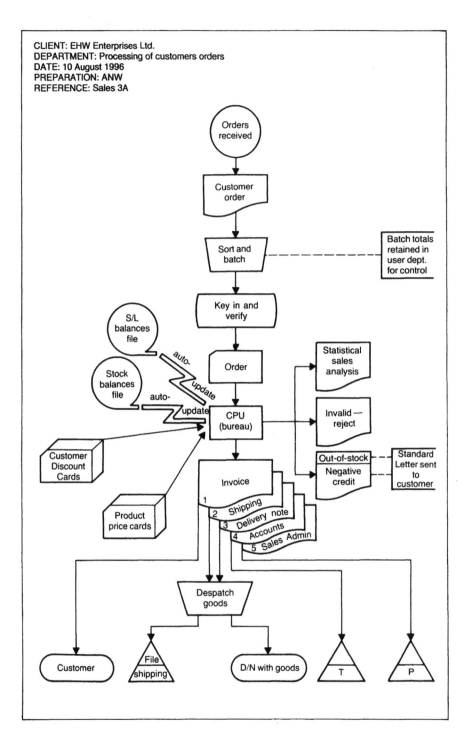

Figure 3.7 One-dimensional flowchart (3)

indication of where the activity commenced lay in the 'header' label at the top of the chart. The great advantages of the one-dimensional chart lie in its simplicity, the flexibility with which the method can be approached, and its relative ease of execution. Moreover, very little prior planning is required: it is possible to go straight in and simply chart the given narrative top to bottom. It is for these reasons that it is ideal for use in examinations, unless some other method is specified. The two-dimensional approach, the one normally adopted by professional auditors, retains the top-to-bottom time flow but uses lateral movement (usually within clearly labelled adjacent columns) to indicate movement in space. The considerable advantages achieved by this more sophisticated procedure are demonstrated in the examples shown in Figures 3.8 to 3.11 which are typical of the charts to be found within the files of many firms. These advantages will be seen to include:

1. The charts themselves are kept clear of all narrative and directional 'signposts'.

2. The section or department in which the activity is taking place, and to and from which documentation is passed, is clearly shown by the system of columnar labelling.

3. A concise summary of all activities, in the sequence in which they actually take place, is retained in narrative form.

4. Special features, indicated by the use of designated symbols, can easily be incorporated. For example, in the charts which follow, the small diamond-shaped symbol will be seen on each occasion it appears to represent the presence of some form of check, and therefore provides a quick guide to the control features within the system.

5. The division of the page into 'location columns' enables the chart to show that certain activities take place at the same time, albeit in different places.

   It will also be seen that these charts do not employ British Standards symbols. Despite this, they are readily understood and have in fact been widely adopted within the UK auditing profession. To the extent that they differ from the symbols explained above, the key below will assist the reading of the chart.

   Documents numerically pre-numbered

   Any clerical activity

   Presence of internal check

   File

	SEQ	STORES	BUYER
INFLEXIBLE PLASTICS LIMITED			PURCHASES — CHART 1 OF 4

	SEQ	STORES	BUYER
Requisition is raised when goods in stock are down to re-order level. A label with purchase requisition attached is removed from box representing re-order level. Order quantity is pre-determined. Requisition is a copy of previous purchase order omitting price details	1	Req'n	
Requisition signed by warehouse manager	2		Suppliers price list
Buyer checks authorization of requisition	3		
Purchase order prepared using supplier's latest price list	4		
	5		
	6		
	7		
	8		
	9		
	10		
File of outstanding purchase orders scanned weekly for overdue deliveries. If overdue follow up with supplier	11		
When goods arrive quantity is checked against the purchase order. Goods are in sealed cartons. If obviously damaged, delivery is refused. If they appear sound, the quantity of cartons is counted. No further inspection	12		
Raises goods received note. If goods are short-delivered a shortage memo is raised at the same time and cross-referenced to the GRN	13		
Filed in GRN numerical order	14		
Filed in shortage Memo numerical order	15		
	16		

Figure 3.8   Two-dimensional flowchart (1)

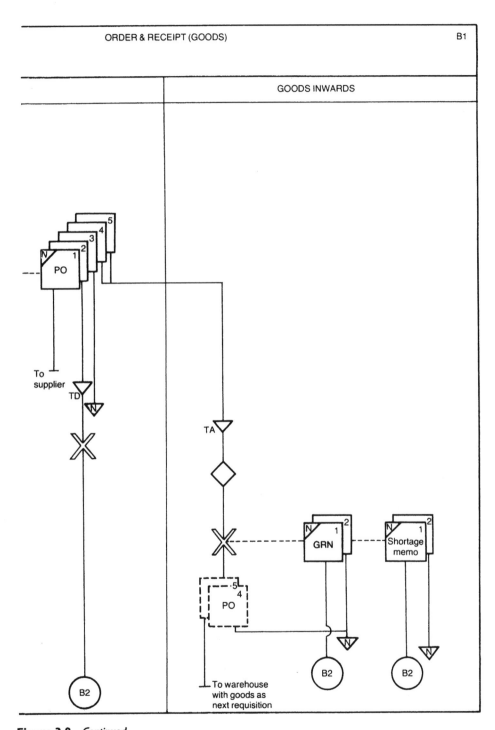

Figure 3.8   *Continued*

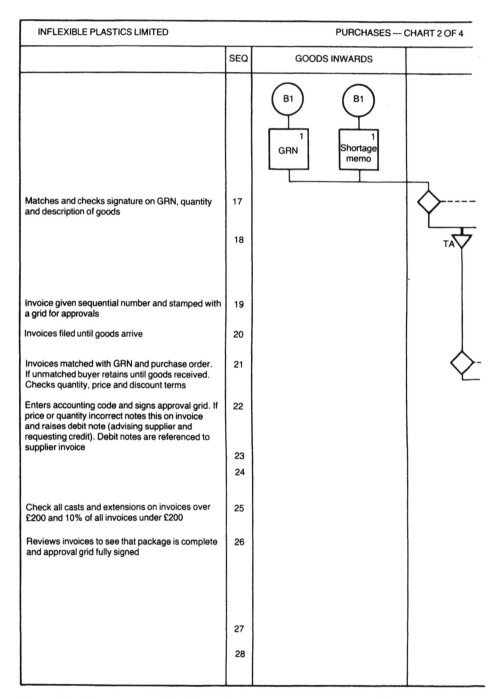

INFLEXIBLE PLASTICS LIMITED		PURCHASES — CHART 2 OF 4

Figure 3.9 Two-dimensional flowchart (2)

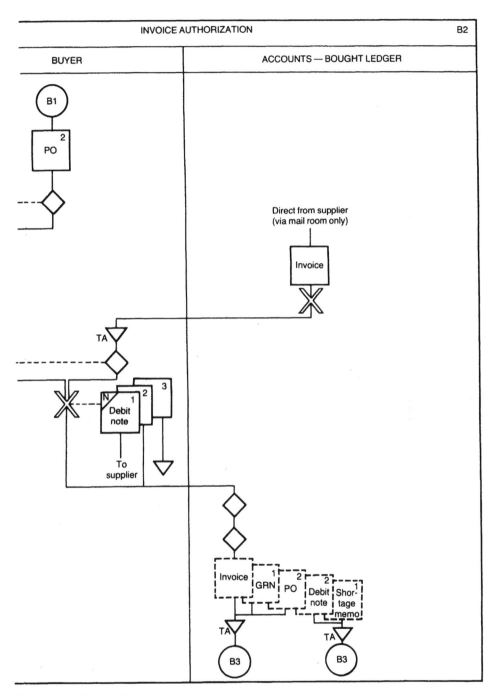

Figure 3.9   *Continued*

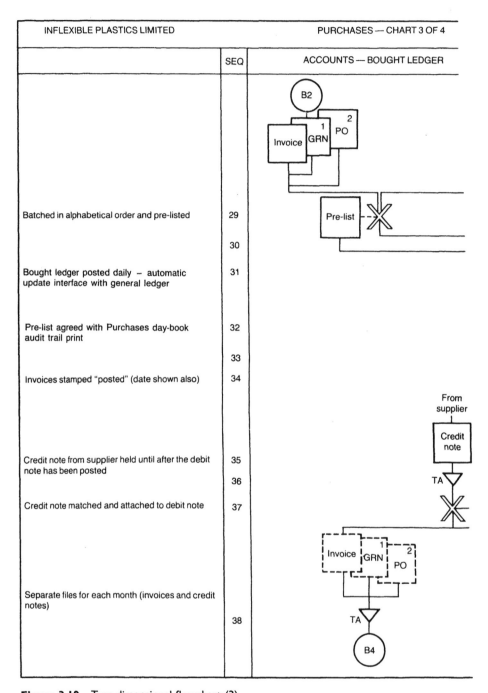

	SEQ	ACCOUNTS — BOUGHT LEDGER
Batched in alphabetical order and pre-listed	29	
	30	
Bought ledger posted daily – automatic update interface with general ledger	31	
Pre-list agreed with Purchases day-book audit trail print	32	
	33	
Invoices stamped "posted" (date shown also)	34	
Credit note from supplier held until after the debit note has been posted	35	
	36	
Credit note matched and attached to debit note	37	
Separate files for each month (invoices and credit notes)		
	38	

Figure 3.10   Two-dimensional flowchart (3)

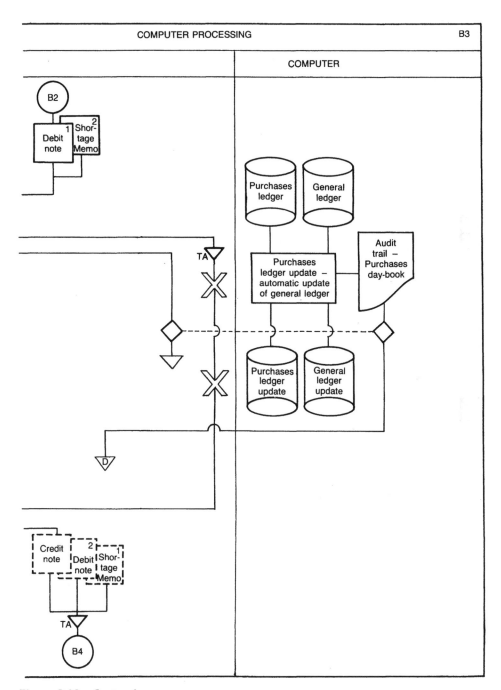

Figure 3.10 *Continued*

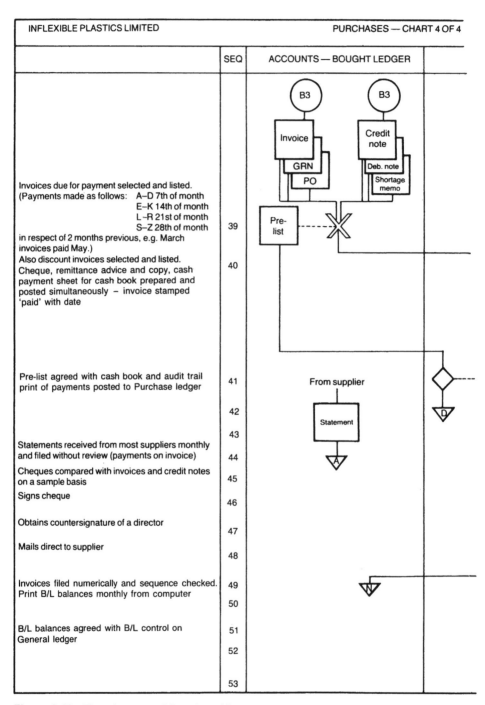

Figure 3.11   Two-dimensional flowchart (4)

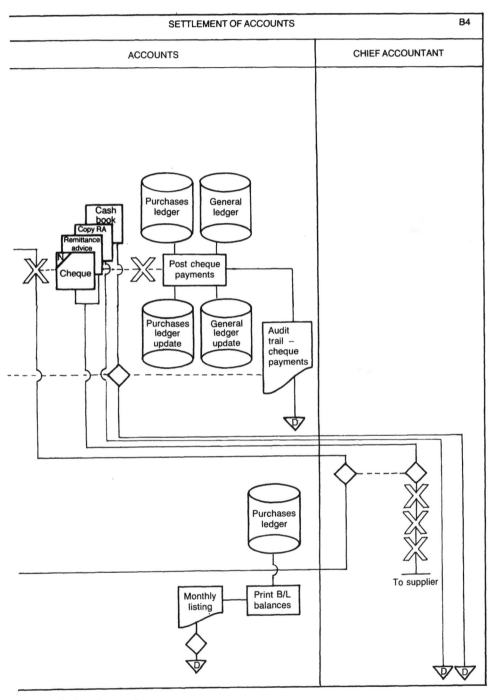

SETTLEMENT OF ACCOUNTS   B4

ACCOUNTS   CHIEF ACCOUNTANT

Figure 3.11   *Continued*

File in date order

 File in alphabetical order

 File in numerical order (Note that the additional presence of the letter 'T' indicates *temporary* file.)

The use of these few symbols is extremely economical of time and effort in relation to the wealth of information revealed, and the charts in Figures 3.8–3.11 will repay careful study.

3.9   Assessment – internal control questionnaires (ICQs)

Of all systems assessment techniques, ICQs have been operational for the longest period of time, which is testimony to their effectiveness. Although there are a number of variations in the way in which the technique is applied by different firms, its broad function and design have remained fairly consistent over the past three decades. Its function is to highlight precisely the areas of strength and weakness in internal control, and this process should once again be seen within the context of the overall audit chronology as set out in Figure 2.1.

3.9.1   Use of ICQs in practice

The questionnaire is a standardized pre-printed document designed by the audit firm using it, and comprises a series of questions on internal control. It is divided into sections which roughly correspond with the client organization's natural divisions, as set out in section 3.2. Those of its sections which are inapplicable (e.g. the Cash Receipts section in the case of a mail order company) are disregarded and marked N/A (not applicable). The following points concerning the use of an ICQ should be carefully noted:

1. An ICQ would normally be used only if the size and complexity of the client organization justified this. Internal control in smaller organizations can usually be assessed by:

   (a) raising relevant questions concerning procedures, documentation and records, and carefully noting the replies;

   (b) observation of the procedures while they are taking place;

   (c) recording the system by means of flow diagrams and/or systems notes.

2. A completed ICQ should have an effective life of approximately three years, during which time only updating would be necessary. It is sound policy, however, to appraise the system from scratch once the original ICQ is clearly out of date. The completion of a new ICQ would in any event be necessary if a radical change in the system had taken place (e.g. a transfer from manual to computerized accounting records).

3. The ICQ should be completed by a senior member of the audit staff after putting the questions to the client company officers responsible for each of the sections into which the ICQ is divided. This questioning should take place as a series of interviews specially arranged for the purpose. Some firms pass the blank ICQs to the client company officers for completion in their own time. This is not satisfactory since it deprives the auditor of the opportunity to observe instances where the officer responsible for a department clearly does not have important information at his fingertips; it also allows, in certain cases, an opportunity for the system to be changed purely in order to provide the 'right' answer on the ICQ.

4. Observation and selected tests will ensure that the ICQ accurately reflects the strengths and weaknesses within the procedures that operate from day to day. These audit tests are known by various titles, such as 'procedural' tests, or 'walk-through' tests. It is important to remember that they do not constitute part of the main audit programme, which can only be performed at a later stage, after the internal control system has been satisfactorily assessed and evaluated.

5. As was noted in the Statement of Auditing Standards on internal control (section 3.3), the auditor should not place reliance on controls on the basis of this preliminary evaluation. He should conduct further tests (compliance tests) designed to give a reasonable assurance that the controls are functioning properly, and were doing so throughout the accounting period.

6. A well-drafted ICQ will facilitate rapid assessment of the system. This is achieved by formulating questions in which the relevant internal control criteria are implicit, so that no more than a yes/no answer is required to indicate compliance or non-compliance (the former always being indicated by 'yes' and the latter by 'no'). This degree of simplicity is not possible for every question, for example in cases where it is necessary to know the names of executive officers authorized to sign cheques, or the upper monetary limit on the authority of a particular officer to authorize expenditure.

3.9.2 The form of the ICQ

The form of the ICQ may differ substantially between one audit firm and another, although the purpose in each case is the same. For the purposes of the illustration that follows, a genuine ICQ has been slightly modified, and only a selection of questions in two key areas of the ICQ are included. The subdivisions selected are Purchases and Trade Creditors, and Payments. Although the other major areas are not represented here (e.g. Sales and Trade Debtors, Stocks and Work in Progress, Wages, Receipts, and Acquisition and Disposal of Fixed Assets), the sections shown demonstrate the usefulness of ICQs in practice. Each of the sections includes up to nineteen questions of particular significance, specially selected from a much longer series in the original ICQ.

Important note

Throughout the ensuing pages a number of specimen documents are reproduced for illustrative purposes. It should be appreciated that their value is not confined to a demonstration of form, but that their content has also been carefully compiled to contain maximum instructional value on the internal controls appropriate to each area incorporated in the particular form. An effort should therefore be made to understand the reasoning which lies behind each question in the ICQs. This is more important than merely noting the appearance of the form which, in practice, will vary considerably from firm to firm.

Specimen internal control questionnaire

Notes:

(a) Answers should be based on replies given by senior client personnel as well as on your own tests and observations.

(b) Wherever the 'no' column is ticked an explanatory note should be added to the 'weakness' section of the current working paper file, and cross-reference made to the internal control (I/C) letter which follows the completion of this phase of the audit. The explanatory note should either confirm the presence of the weakness which the 'No' answer highlights, or give reasons why, in this particular instance, the potential weakness is not material, or is otherwise compensated for.

(c) At the completion of the final audit the ICQ should be carefully reviewed to ensure its continued accuracy in the light of the audit experience just gained.

(d) All controls indicated should be subjected to compliance tests to ensure their operation at all times.

| | ICQ Reviewed | Initials | |
| | | Date | |

| | Tick as Appropriate | | Not applicable | Ref. to I/C letter ('No' Answers) | Ref. to Flowchart/ Systems Notes | Date of Answer |
| | Yes | No | | | | |

Section (a) Purchases and Trade Creditors

(i) Are official orders issued showing names of suppliers, quantities ordered and prices?

| | ICQ Reviewed | Initials | |
| | | Date | |

	Tick as Appropriate			Ref. to I/C letter ('No' Answers)	Ref. to Flowchart/ Systems Notes	Date of Answer
	Yes	No	Not applicable			

Section (a) Purchases and Trade Creditors (cont'd)

(ii) Are copies of orders retained on file?

(iii) Who authorizes orders and what are their authority limits?

   Specify:
   Name   Position   Authority Limit
   .... £.......................

(iv) Are the above persons independent of those who issue requisitions?

(v) Is a record kept of orders placed but not executed?

(vi) If the answer to (v) is 'yes', how is this record compiled? *Specify:*

(vii) Are goods from suppliers inspected on arrival as to quantity and quality?

(viii) How is the receipt of supplies recorded (e.g. by means of goods inwards notes)? *Specify:*

(ix) Are these records prepared by a person independent of those responsible for:

   – ordering functions?

   – processing and recording of invoices?

(x) Are all invoices received:

   – compared with copy orders?

| | ICQ Reviewed | Initials | | | | | |
| | | Date | | | | | |

	Tick as Appropriate		Not applicable	Ref. to I/C letter ('No' Answers)	Ref. to Flowchart/ Systems Notes	Date of Answer
	Yes	No				

Section (a) Purchases and Trade Creditors (cont'd)

   – compared with goods inwards records?

   – checked for calculations, extensions and additions?

(xi) Are the above functions (see (x) above) carried out by a person independent of those responsible for:

   – ordering functions?

   – receipt and control of goods?

(xii) Are bought ledger personnel independent of those responsible for:

   – approving invoices and credit notes?

   – cheque payment functions?

(xiii) Is the control account function independent of bought ledger personnel?

Section (b) Payments

A. *By cheque*

(i) Is the signing of blank cheques prohibited?

(ii) Is the signing of cheques restricted to directors/secretary/other senior official (*Specify title.*)

	ICQ Reviewed	Initials	
		Date	

	Tick as Appropriate			Ref. to I/C letter ('No' Answers)	Ref. to Flowchart/ Systems Notes	Date of Answer
	Yes	No	Not applicable			

Section (b) Payments (cont'd)

(iii) Are authorities to sign cheques stratified on the basis of amount so as to require:

   – one signature?

   – two signatures?

   – more than two signatures?

   (*State number of signatures, names of signatories and authority levels.*)

(iv) Is a duly authorized invoice, statement or other voucher produced in respect of each payment for which a cheque is being signed?

(v) Excluding cash wages, travelling and petty cash expenses and other payments normally made by cash, are all payments made by cheque? (*State whether any exceptions.*)

(vi) Are all cheques (other than those for cash) suitably crossed?

(vii) Are 'paid' cheques returned by the bank monthly?

(viii) Are these cheques filed in the order in which they appear in the cash book?

(ix) Are creditors' statements, advices, invoices or other vouchers of payments:

   – attached to the 'paid' cheques

	ICQ Reviewed	Initials	
		Date	

	Tick as Appropriate			Ref. to I/C letter ('No' Answers)	Ref. to Flowchart/ Systems Notes	Date of Answer
	Yes	No	Not applicable			

Section (b) Payments (cont'd)

   – otherwise suitably filed to facilitate easy reference?

B. *By cash*

  (i) Apart from salaries and wages, are all cash payments made from an imprest?

  (ii) Are supporting vouchers required before making cash payments?

  (iii) Are supporting vouchers examined and authorized by a party other than the cashier or the claimant?

  (iv) Are these vouchers filed in the order of payment?

  (v) Is the expenditure appropriately analysed?

  (vi) Does the system disallow:

   – the cashing of cheques?

   – cash payments unsupported by vouchers?

   – IOUs?

  (vii) Is the amount of the claim entered on a specially designed petty cash or other voucher?

  (viii) Is the expenditure incurred during the period of the imprest independently checked before refunding the amount expended?

					Tick as Appropriate		Not applicable	Ref. to I/C letter ('No' Answers)	Ref. to Flowchart/ Systems Notes	Date of Answer

ICQ Reviewed	Initials	
	Date	

	Tick as Appropriate		Not applicable	Ref. to I/C letter ('No' Answers)	Ref. to Flowchart/ Systems Notes	Date of Answer
	Yes	No				
Section (b) Payments (cont'd)						
(ix) Are checks made on the balance of cash in hand at random intervals by an independent official?						
(x) How are such checks evidenced? *Specify.*						

It should be noted that a number of columns and spaces are included in the right-hand margin of each ICQ page, each of which has a specific function. Although most of these are self explanatory their significance should not be missed:

1. The yes/no technique highlights potential weakness instantly.

2. The review date indicates whether the time for a new ICQ to be completed may be approaching.

3. The requirement for initials to be inserted always has a salutary effect in that it 'pins' responsibility. Particular care (as opposed to mechanical response) usually precedes the insertion of one's own name or initials.

4. The date of answer indicates whether the answer was filled in before or after certain significant systems amendments may have been introduced.

5. The reference to the internal control (I/C) letter is designed to ensure that in cases where the weakness in question is adjudged to be material, its substance (together with appropriate recommendations for improvement) is communicated to the management in the letter (sometimes referred to as management letter, or weakness letter).

6. The reference to flowcharts/systems notes ensures that the correctness of the answer to the particular ICQ question can be verified by the evidence portrayed in the previously drafted flowcharts or, in cases where charts are not warranted (e.g. small companies), the systems notes on file.

3.10 Internal control evaluation

If reference is made once again to the chronology diagram (Figure 2.1), it will be seen that the wealth of detailed information gathered through interviews, tests and by observation, and as reflected in the auditor's systems notes, diagrams and ICQs, should be carefully evaluated by him before the full extent of tests on the client organization's underlying records are finally determined. It might be thought that reference to the completed ICQ, which automatically highlights strengths and weaknesses in the system through the yes/no answering technique is all that is needed for this purpose, but this would in fact be insufficiently reliable and would still depend upon a good deal of subjective judgement. It is therefore far better to think of the evaluation process as a distinct stage in the procedures leading to the drafting of the detailed audit programme itself. This is not to suggest that evaluation criteria cannot successfully be incorporated within the ICQ – indeed some firms have done so – but rather that (1) the gathering and recording of detailed control-oriented data and (2) the careful evaluation of the effect that those data may have upon the overall quality of control in the area in question (and hence upon the records and final accounts in turn) are indeed two separate auditing phases, and should be recognized as such.

As has been noted, the controls indicated by the ICQ must be subjected to carefully planned compliance tests – otherwise the auditor lacks the necessary assurance that the controls were operating effectively throughout the period. The Statement of Auditing Standards on internal control (see section 3.3) should be referred to.

3.10.1 Evaluation in practice

A quick reference to either of the specimen ICQ sections reproduced above will show that on completion the auditor will be faced with a substantial number of 'yes' answers and (it is hoped) a rather smaller number of 'no' answers. In the face of this somewhat overwhelming array, he may well ponder his appropriate response: it is in determining this response that the evaluation process assists, by asking two vital questions:

1. What is the materiality, to the section as a whole, of the weakness highlighted by each 'no' answer?
2. If it appears that the weakness revealed by a 'no' answer is in fact material, what compensating controls, if any, exist which might reduce or overcome the effect of the weakness?

In certain cases, these two questions may be thought of as just one, since the presence of a compensating control will immediately be seen to overcome what would otherwise be a material weakness.

Compensating controls, though, are not always readily apparent. For example, the internal check arrangements within a client company's Cash Received department may be shown by 'no' answers within the ICQ to leave a good deal to be desired – in particular, there would seem to be ample opportunity for the cashier to misappropriate remittances received from customers and to conceal this by allocating amounts from the next day's remittances to fill the gap left by the earlier misappropriation: in short, to perpetrate what is usually (and mysteriously) labelled 'teeming and lading'. We may assume that the defect in the system which facilitates this potential fraud is the usual one, discussed earlier in this chapter, of ignoring the authority/custody/recording 'barriers': in this case allowing the cashier to handle remittances received (custody), as well as to enter these sums against the accounts of individual customers (recording), and thereby ensuring that there is no obvious evidence of any sums having been misapplied.

(What would be still worse for the client – and correspondingly better for a dishonest cashier – would be a situation in which controls over (1) the granting of discounts to customers, and (2) the writing off of bad debts, were so ineffective as virtually to allow the cashier to employ either or both of these media to eliminate the disparities in customer accounts arising because of the missing funds.)

Despite the apparent gravity of lack of control over monies received, let us for the purposes of this illustration assume that on further enquiry the auditors discover:

1. That the cashier is not present when the mail is opened each day.

2. That the opening of the mail is closely supervised by a senior officer of the accounting department (say, assistant chief accountant).

3. That all remittances received, in every post, in whatever form, are independently listed in a memorandum 'cash diary', showing the total receipts and how it is made up, and retained by the assistant chief accountant.

4. That each morning the company's chief accountant checks the previous day's bankings as shown in the paying-in book, in total as well as by the analysis, against the counterpart details shown in his assistant's cash diary, to ensure that everything received has been paid in intact and at the earliest opportunity, and that he signs the cash diary to indicate correctness.

5. That the check described under (4) takes place in the chief accountant's office and is not included in the accounting section of the company's procedures manual, i.e. that the other employees (including the cashier) would not necessarily know of its existence or, at any rate, its details.

The above additional checks (possibly revealed in the ICQ – but not linked with the previously described weaknesses) may together be regarded as an effective compensating control and will largely offset the previously described weaknesses. There is, of course, always the possibility of collusion between the parties, but this is a lesser risk and is in any case unlikely to arise when it requires the involvement of the company's senior ranking officers. This is not to suggest that such a possibility should be ignored by the auditor: indeed he should always remain alert to the variety of ways in which a system may lend itself to manipulation for the personal gain of one or more of those participating in its operation, but in the present context the auditor's overall evaluation of the system's security will be more favourable than would have been the case without the compensating control described.

As far as determining the materiality of a particular weakness is concerned, the auditor must exercise his judgement on this matter. It cannot simply be said that certain ICQ questions are more material than others: it all depends on the circumstances. In one system a particular answer 'no' may be so material as to nullify the apparent value of many 'yes' answers, while in another system the same answer may be adjudged insignificant, due either to the different nature of the business or possibly to the presence of effective compensating controls. Each situation must be approached with a completely open mind (an essential attribute for the successful auditor) and judged on its own merits; the blank ICQ form is a pre-printed standard, but what it will indicate to the skilled eye at the evaluation stage is anything but standard.

3.10.2 Internal control evaluation (ICE) forms

We have seen how well-designed documentation can facilitate the execution of the audit procedures to which they relate. In the same way, a number of firms have designed internal control evaluation (ICE) forms (examples of which follow) which may be used at this stage of the audit. Whatever design is used, all evaluation work on a particular section (wages, sales, cash receipts, etc.) has one objective: a decision on the extent of further testing to be incorporated in the full audit programme, itself designed to assess the reliability of the company's records as the basis for the extraction of the final accounts to be issued to members.

As already pointed out, a valid decision can only be reached in relation to overall strengths and weaknesses: the subsequent audit tests may therefore be correctly seen as complementary to the system's own control features. Putting it another way, substantive tests carried out within the audit programme must be seen to relate as precisely as possible to the extent to which the internal control system (including internal audit) fails to 'audit itself'.

The highly skilled task of evaluating the likely effect of internal control weaknesses on the reliability of the records should therefore be viewed as the central pivot on which the effectiveness of the entire audit rests: it acts as the bridge between all preceding systems work, on the one hand, and all subsequent work on testing the reliability of the records – and hence of the accounts that are directly derived from those records – on the other hand.

The evaluation work is considerably facilitated by condensing the control criteria for each functional area of the organization down to just a few key questions whose chief characteristic is that they go straight to the heart of the matter. In this sense they may be contrasted with the questions included in an ICQ. Whereas the latter relate to points of fine detail within each functional area concerned, the key questions used for evaluation relate to the functional area as a whole. The nature of the key questions (sometimes referred to as control questions) may be best seen and understood by reference to the examples shown in Figure 3.12.

In relation to the ICE form, the following points should be noted:

1. The key questions within each section are not necessarily exhaustive. Additional questions may be considered appropriate but they should not be allowed to

SECTION	KEY QUESTIONS	ANSWER 'Yes' or 'No'	SUMMARIZE REASON FOR ANSWER
PURCHASES	(a) Can liabilities be recorded in respect of goods/services which are either unauthorized or not received? (b) Can liabilities for goods/services be incurred but remain unrecorded? (c) Can goods be returned to suppliers without being recorded?		
SALES & TRADE DEBTORS	(a) Can goods leave the premises without being invoiced? (b) Can invoices be created but remain unrecorded in the sales accounting records? (c) Can goods be despatched to a bad credit risk? (d) Can overdue accounts escape prompt follow-up?		
CASH	(a) Can sums be received but not banked at the earliest opportunity? (b) Can cash payments be made if not properly authorized? (c) Can cheque payments be made if not properly authorized? (d) Can cash or bank balances be misappropriated or improperly used?		
STOCKS	(a) Can stocks be lost, pilfered or wasted? (b) Can stocks be consumed/transferred without the movement being recorded? (c) Can incorrect quantities (under or over) be included in the stock count? (d) Can incorrect values (under or over) be attributed to the physical stocks included in the accounts?		
FIXED ASSETS	(a) Can fixed assets be acquired/disposed of without proper authorization? (b) Can the acquisition/disposal of fixed assets remain unrecorded in the fixed assets register or financial accounts?		
NOMINAL LEDGER	(a) Can unauthorized access to the journal/nominal ledger be obtained? (b) Can unauthorized journal entries be processed?		

Figure 3.12   Example of a simple internal control evaluation (ICE) form

proliferate (as could so easily happen), since their function as an evaluation aid may then be diluted.

2. Note that the yes/no pattern is reversed when compared with the ICQ: in the ICE it is the danger areas that are affirmed.

3. It would be possible to condense certain of the key questions still further: for example, the crucial question of Sales and Trade Debtors could be expressed thus: can goods be despatched without being paid for within the normal terms of credit? This effectively (and concisely) deals with everything in the four questions listed on the form. The 'short form' is not recommended, however, since the four questions have the advantage of enabling any broad area(s) of weakness to be more precisely located.

4. The section on Sales and Trade Debtors does not deal with remittances received. Functional delineation, even if apparently contrived, is important in the ICE, as it is in the ICQ, and the remittances are in fact dealt with in the section on Cash.

The form adopted in Figure 3.12 is rudimentary, and a variety of more sophisticated versions are now in use. That shown in Figure 3.13, relating to the payment of industrial wages, is far more comprehensive. There would be little point in extending our range of examples of ICE forms further, since they all have the same objective. Some variations on the theme provide the key question in its alternative form as a stated 'control objective', and in certain cases this is given at the head of each section subhead in the ICQ, no separate ICE being used. It is, of course, possible to combine the ICQ and ICE in one form, especially if space is allocated to the twin questions of materiality and compensating controls, and senior audit staff are directed to provide constructive comment thereon. Some firms attempt, still more ambitiously, to combine the functions of ICQ, ICE and audit programme (Figure 3.14 shows an extract). Although the format has the advantage of compactness, it has certain complementary disadvantages:

1. The form does not of itself make it clear that the programme on the right can be commenced only after a thorough evaluation of questions on the left, as reflected in the conclusions at the foot. This means that the programme can state only the nature of the audit tests in broad outline and cannot specify the depth of testing which is appropriate at each stage.

2. By linking the programme, somewhat artificially, with the ICQ sequence, it does not follow the more natural 'depth test' sequence, which would, in the case of the replacement of fixed assets, begin with an examination of asset retirement schedules and related board (or other appropriate) authorities, and conclude with physical inspection and examination of asset register entries.

3. The control objective declared at the head of the form is not clearly linked with the conclusion at the foot. The control objective is, in any case, far more effective if phrased as a question which the audit senior is obliged to answer in writing as shown in the ICE form.

INTERNAL CONTROL EVALUATION	FORM: ICE

Notes to Senior Audit Personnel on Use of Form ICE

(a) The 'checklist of control requirements', with the reference to the appropriate section of the ICQ where necessary, should be carefully studied and then ticked, as indicated, *before* answering the Key Question.

(b) Where the answer to the Key Question is 'Yes', the subsidiary question on the *materiality* of the weakness must also be answered, after giving due consideration to the presence of any effective *compensating controls*.

(c) The right-hand column should be completed with a brief summary of your reason(s) for providing the answers shown in the left hand column.

INTERNAL CONTROL EVALUATION	EVALUATION DATES	INITIALS
	on........................19..	....
SECTION: INDUSTRIAL WAGES	on........................19..	....
	on........................19..	....

KEY QUESTIONS	CHECKLIST OF CONTROL REQUIREMENTS	ICQ REF.	TICK WHEN REVIEWED	REASONS FOR ANSWERS GIVEN
(1) CAN EMPLOYEES BE PAID FOR WORK NOT DONE? ANSWER YES or NO: .... IF 'YES', MIGHT WEAKNESS BE MATERIAL? ANSWER YES or NO:	(1) Satisfactory time records. (2) Supervision of time clocks, preparation of time sheets, piece-work tickets or other source documents and, where appropriate, evidence of approval by foreman, etc. (3) Control over spoilt work. (4) Reconciliation of job time with rate time. (5) Correct recording and calculation of adjustments for lateness, sickness and absenteeism. (6) Correct treatment of sickness benefits. (7) Proper authorization and control of overtime. (8) Checking of calculations on source documents.			
(2) CAN BONUSES OR COMMIS-SIONS BE WRONGLY PAID? ANSWER YES or NO:	(1) Control over and checks on the validity of source documents upon which the payments are based. (2) Regular procedures to check the basis and calculations.			
IF 'YES', MIGHT WEAKNESS BE MATERIAL? ANSWER YES or NO:	(3) Independent check of sales commissions with sales recorded, and proper adjustment for bad debts and goods returned. (4) Effective supervision of bonus and commission claims.			

Figure 3.13   Example of a comprehensive internal control evaluation (ICE) form

ICQ	Answer Yes/No or N/A	AUDIT PROGRAMME	Initial when completed
SECTION: FIXED ASSETS AND DEPRECIATION **CONTROL OBJECTIVE:** The fixed assets are correctly classified, in existence and owned by the Company.			
1. Do company records adequately classify fixed assets under appropriate headings?		1. Obtain summary of movements.	
2. (a) Are registers of fixed assets maintained? (b) Do they show the date when each asset was acquired/first came into use? (c) Are they reconciled annually (at least) with the impersonal ledger control account(s)? (d) Are physical inventories taken out periodically by persons not concerned with custody of assets? (e) Are discrepancies arising under (d) above, between the physical and book records reported to the management? (f) Are the records subsequently adjusted to agree with the physical inventories? (g) Do assets which have been fully depreciated remain under accounting control?		2. Check fixed asset registers as follows: (a) additions and disposals are reflected (b) existence of assets with company's physical inventories (c) arithmetical accuracy of records (d) extracts of balances and agree with control accounts.	
3. Is there adequate control over fixed assets in hands of third parties?		3. Where fixed assets are in the hands of third parties, carry out a test circularization thereof. Summarize results.	
4. Is there adequate control over tools and other small equipment?		4. Test system for controlling tools and small equipment. Ensure that the company's policy is being followed in practice.	
5. (a) Are property title deeds in the safe-keeping of a suitable third party, e.g. bank vault, solicitor? (b) If held by the company, are they under proper control? (c) Are documents of title to all fixed assets in the name of the company?		5. (a) Unless the company keeps its own property register (in which case, take copy), record brief details of all properties on permanent file. (b) Inspect titles to properties or obtain certificates from authorized custodians. (c) Inspect/confirm titles to other registered assets (e.g. motor vehicles, ships, copyrights, patents etc.).	

CONCLUSIONS: (1) ARE WEAKNESSES ('No' answers) MATERIAL? ....
           (2) GIVE REASONS FOR ANSWER TO (1) ABOVE, INCLUDING REFERENCES TO
               COMPENSATING CONTROLS, IF ANY..
               ....

Date............................ Signed ....

Figure 3.14 Combining ICQ, ICE and the audit programme

Review questions

*1. Set out in a memorandum to your audit team the matters which statutory auditors should address before reliance is placed on the work of an internal auditor.

*2. You are the senior on a large plc audit and have been approached by one of your junior staff who has expressed the opinion that flowcharting is a waste of time and effort and that time would be better spent on other tasks.

   Indicate the principal advantages of flowcharting.

3. A client of your firm is concerned that there is not enough control over stocks within his organization. He states that they form a high proportion of the assets within the company's balance sheet and requires you to prepare a formal letter to his Production Director outlining the controls that are necessary in this area.

4. Draw up an Internal Control Questionnaire relating to the payment of trade creditors to be used on a new audit of a medium sized retailing company.

Exercises

1. You are the leader of an audit team which is preparing to visit a new client, a group of manufacturing companies having a high level of plant and equipment situated at sites around the United Kingdom. Your partner in charge has delegated to you the responsibility of preparing the matters to be addressed within the audit programme for plant and machinery.

   You have ascertained that there is a high level of internal audit control in this area and are currently writing a questionnaire for use by your team. What are the matters that should be addressed?

2. Your firm has been appointed the auditor for a small manufacturing company that has 50 staff in the production department and 15 administrative staff, of whom 8 are in the office.

   The recruitment is done by one of the original directors who has his own secretary. The wages department keep manual records and make up pay packets each week. The production staff work a standard $7\frac{1}{2}$ hour shift with overtime as necessary. All employees have clock cards. The foremen calculate the overtime payments and also the bonus which may or may not be payable to the production staff dependent on the production of their department – the workforce is divided into 5 teams of 10. The foremen are responsible for giving the wages department a standard form showing the level of bonus and overtime. Bonus is calculated at a standard rate. Wages are paid on the Wednesday of each week and the level of pay is based upon the production figures up to the previous Friday. The wages department is run by Betty, who has been with the firm for 40 years. She met her husband Bert, one of the foremen, at a function and the director responsible for recruitment is planning to hold a surprise party for her retirement. Betty knows PAYE and National Insurance inside out and also knows which employees are members of trade unions and which members of staff have savings plans with the local Co-operative Society. She also administers deductions for any loans which the company has given members of staff for such things as home improvements.

Required

(a) Design an Internal Control Questionnaire for the above system.

(b) Draft a letter to your audit partner outlining any possible weaknesses in the current system.

4

Auditing procedures – the underlying records

THIS CHAPTER DEALS WITH:

▷ techniques of testing an entity's records;

▷ identifying and testing the transaction audit trail;

▷ basic substantive depth tests in the key audit areas of sales and receipts, purchases and payments and payroll;

▷ reporting of accounting errors and weaknesses in the accounting and internal control system to directors and management.

4.1 The role of the audit programme

As with each new aspect of our subject dealt with thus far, we should refer to the master diagram (Figure 2.1). This provides the broad context within which specific topics may be studied in detail, just as a rambler refers to his map of the county before turning to the 1:50,000 map. This has always been the difficulty for students of auditing – particular audit procedures are usually viewed as ends in themselves, rather than a means towards a specific objective: with such an approach our rambler would undoubtedly get lost.

The fault lies not with the student but with the traditional way in which he is both taught and trained. Few texts adequately distinguish the stages of an audit in terms of their function and, although most describe the usual audit techniques, they rarely relate those techniques to the objectives which they are intended to serve. So far as training is concerned, again the situation that prevails leaves a good deal to be desired. The age-old system of indentured training – requiring the provision of care, guidance and practical instruction on the one side, in return for loyal service and diligent study on the other – has been replaced by an arrangement far more in keeping with the age in which we now live, i.e. an arrangement which is in essence impersonal, commercial and thus potentially inimical to the true aim of the respective parties involved. Indeed, it is hardly surprising that these aims are so often found to be in conflict today – whether on issues of remuneration, overtime and study leave, or on the quality of training and the cost of education.

Confusion between means and ends is nowhere more clearly in evidence than in relation to the subject matter of this chapter: the audit work performed on the underlying records of the client entity. A team of audit clerks may plough their way through an audit programme designed in the distant past – and hence bearing no more than an incidental relationship to present needs – with little thought for the real purpose of what they are supposed to be achieving. This unintelligent philosophy sees the programme as 'something to be done because it's there', and, not surprisingly, it is largely a waste of time.

The audit programme, as reference to the master diagram (Figure 2.1) shows, is itself no more than a technique, and its purpose is to assist us as efficiently as possible to determine the reliability of the underlying records as a basis for the preparation of final accounts. (Certain major portions of most audit programmes relate to the verification of balances in the final accounts themselves, and to this extent they go beyond the testing of basic records.)

Our concern in this chapter lies with those parts of the audit programme designed to test the entity's records, and with the associated techniques of so doing. Most of these techniques, as might be expected, are suitably labelled with terms which, in order to avoid confusion, it will be necessary to explain.

4.2 Vouching and verification

Once compliance tests on control features have been conducted so as to indicate the level of substantive tests necessary to authenticate the records and final accounts, vouching and verification procedures (both within the scope of substantive tests) may be performed. These two terms are initially singled out since they are fundamental to all audit procedures, yet, surprisingly often, they are used indiscriminately and hence incorrectly. Broadly speaking, an auditor vouches transactions and verifies assets and liabilities. Although this is an over-simplification, it nevertheless points the way. The definitions of compliance and substantive tests were given in section 3.7.

The aim of vouching is to ensure that the underlying records accurately reflect the nature of the transactions entered into. It may, for example in the case of year-end accruals and the transfer of nominal ledger balances to the final accounts, be necessary to adjust the entries already recorded in order to ensure that the final accounts give a true and fair view. These adjustments will in turn have to be carefully vouched.

The process of vouching invariably involves the examination of the documentary evidence necessary to authenticate and support the recorded transactions which are purported to have taken place during the period under review. In practical terms, such examination will primarily establish:

1. The correctness of the monetary amount at which the transaction is recorded: cost in case of purchases, and proceeds in the case of sales.
2. That the transaction was properly authorized in the first place.

In connection with (2) it should be remembered that 'authority' means a good deal more than a signature on a petty cash voucher. Authority, appropriate to the transaction in question, is necessary (or should be) at all levels, and it is obviously essential that the auditor is on familiar terms with the authority required at each of these.

At the lowest level, the signature of the officer responsible will suffice. When larger expenditures are involved, rules are laid down to require, say, two signatures on the cheque issued in payment. At the next level, the sanction of a director (or possibly the full board) may be needed, for example where commitment to a material contract involving capital expenditure is entered into.

Beyond board level, authority must reside in a company's own Articles and Memorandum of Association (specifying, for example, borrowing powers), and beyond that, the law itself. Neither the company nor its officers can execute transactions specifically prohibited by company law, such as making unrestricted loans to directors – prohibited by the *Companies Act 1985*.

The following subsidiary objectives would also be sought from inspecting the documentation in question:

1. The transaction took place within the period under review.
2. Goods and services acquired (or, in the case of sales, provided) appear to be compatible with the company's normal trading activities, i.e. in the context of the ordinary course of business.
3. All calculations of costs (or proceeds), extensions, discounts, etc., are arithmetically accurate.
4. The expenditure (income) has been correctly allocated, so that effect has been given to the distinction between capital, revenue and deferred revenue, i.e. the correct determination of write-offs as opposed to carry forwards.
5. There is evidence (e.g. rubber stamp, initials or signature) that the document in question has been authorized and checked internally as part of the company's own control procedures.
6. The transaction took place validly, i.e. on behalf of the company's business, rather than, say, of any individual officer or employee.

Vouching is, therefore, the bedrock of auditing procedures, and vouchers (i.e. any documents which may be used for this purpose) supporting all transactions at a given level of materiality, throughout the period, must stand an equal chance of being selected for inspection. This is necessary to ensure that the auditor arrives at an unbiased opinion about the reliability of the records in question. The matters of sample size, randomness and bias in connection with audit testing are dealt with in the next chapter.

Verification, in contrast to vouching, relates to assets, liabilities and other items in the balance sheet at the year end. The balance sheet may be described as a financial photograph, capturing the position of the company at one moment in time; and it is on that moment that verification procedures throw their spotlight. The variety of transactions which we have vouched may or may not result in assets or liabilities appearing in the balance sheet; the purchase and the sale of a machine within the accounting period represents two distinct transactions which are eligible to be vouched (if selected as part of our testing procedures), but there is no machine to be verified at the balance sheet date, its sale having already taken place. Verification procedures are considered in detail in Chapter 6.

4.2.1   Vouching returned cheques

A common fraud is the misappropriation of company funds by an employee who either forges the signature of an authorized cheque signatory, or alters the cheque payee details after the cheque has been signed, and then conceals the misappropriation in the accounting records.

This type of fraud would stand a chance of discovery by the auditor if he vouched a sample of returned cheques and one of the items selected represented one such cheque, i.e. he would notice that the signature appeared to be unlike the specimen signature shown on the bank mandate or that there was a difference between the payee written in the cash book and that shown on the cheque. In either case the auditor would be alerted to make further enquiries. The intelligent auditor would seek explanation from a company official independent from the day-to-day responsibilities of the payments function.

Nowadays companies tend not to receive returned cheques from the bank, especially as the bank will charge for supplying them on request. The auditor may therefore experience some reluctance when he notifies the company's officials of his intention to undertake vouching work. Nevertheless, the auditor should consider whether or not he should insist in carrying out this vouching test as part of his requirement to obtain sufficient audit evidence. Should a fraud subsequently be found to exist then, despite the fact that this had not been revealed in the audit testing, the fact that the auditor had reasonably selected and vouched a sample of returned cheques could be a major factor in the successful defence of a subsequent negligence claim for damages against the auditor. This is discussed further in a later chapter.

4.3   Depth testing

No business transaction takes place in isolation. Purchases of materials are made in anticipation of manufacture and eventual sale: a machine or vehicle is sold in anticipation of its replacement by another which is more efficient or cost effective. In the same way, once a transaction is initiated, a chain response is triggered which affects a number of different departments, individuals within those departments, and the records which reflect the latters' work. The vouching of purchase invoices relates to only a small part of the chain of responses, presumably by the warehouseman's initial observation that stocks of a particular commodity have reached their predetermined reorder point, and that more are therefore required.

Depth testing is the general term which describes the retracing, through the retained documentation, of all the links in that chain. It may thus be thought of as a re-enactment by the auditor of the transaction itself, as reflected in the company's records. The test follows the same sequence: it begins with the inception of the transaction, traces its threads through every department affected (observe the usefulness of the flow diagrams for this purpose) to its apparent conclusion.

I say 'apparent' conclusion since, for a going concern, there are no real conclusions to transactions, only convenient demarcation lines: the proceeds of a sale will not be idle for long, and will soon be reinvested in goods or other assets as part of the continuous flow cycle of business. However, since cash, once it enters the pool, can no longer be separately identified, we may treat its new application as the commencement of a new transaction. Alternatively, we may, in this context, see inception and conclusion in contractual terms – as the acceptance and satisfaction respectively of a contractual obligation.

The positioning of the 'demarcation zones' for depth testing purposes is unimportant. The main point is that the auditors executing the tests should be fully aware of the areas defined for the purpose in their programme of work. As an indication of the natural (as opposed to contractual) coverage of a depth test on, say, the purchase of raw materials required for manufacture, the following may be cited. It is a list of the documentary references through which the auditor should trace the evidence of the transaction under examination:

1. Stores record (e.g bin card) indicating the fact that reorder level had been reached.

2. Pre-printed and sequentially pre-numbered requisition, duly authorized by warehouse foreman, arising from (1).

3. Official company order, also sequentially pre-numbered, authorized by chief buyer, arising from (2).

4. List of authorized suppliers (i.e. testimony to their reliability in terms of quality of service and merchandise, price, delivery, etc.) against which the name on (3) may be checked.

5. Delivery note from supplier, accompanying goods.

6. Internal goods inwards or inspection note, duly signed or stamped, indicating:
   (a) satisfactory condition
   (b) correct quantity
   (c) detailed matching with original order.

7. Entries in stores records on date of receipt.

8. Amendment of bin card quantities, reflecting goods received.

Notes

(a) The list begins and ends with the bin cards (or other rudimentary quantity indicator) highlighting the cyclical nature of the transaction.

(b) The auditor would have to move his area of work interdepartmentally in order to follow the documentation listed. His examination of records referred to at stages (1) and (2) in the list would probably take place in the stores; (3) and (4) in the buying department; (5) and (6) in the goods inwards section (which may be an adjunct of stores); while for (7) and (8) he will have to return to the stores.

There is a parallel list, the tracing of which also forms an integral (although separate) part of the depth test, and for this the auditor will have to move into the accounts department. (It is, incidentally, worth referring to the columnar flow diagrams in Chapter 3 to see similar data presented in that form.) The documentary references making up this list are as follows:

1. Copy of official order (see (3) in previous list).
2. Copy of goods inwards note (see (6) in previous list).
3. Invoice received from supplier, with which (1) and (2) may be matched.
4. Entries in purchases day book or equivalent (e.g. invoice summary created by computer).
5. Postings from (4) to bought ledger or equivalent, and control account.
6. Supplier's statement, on which (3) should feature.
7. Counterfoil of cheque issued in settlement, after deduction of appropriate discounts.
8. Cash book entry recording (7).
9. Entry on bank statement and returned (receipted) cheque.
10. Postings from cash book to bought ledger and control account.

It will be observed that at point (7) in this list, cash enters the picture which, until that point (including the earlier list), had related only to goods purchased and trade creditors. Some auditors may prefer to treat the recording of cash payments and receipts as the subject of a totally separate depth test – an example of the flexibility in 'demarcation' already referred to.

From what has been written above it should be clear that:

1. Once the first step is taken (i.e. the filling-in of a requisition form for goods) the whole predetermined process is set in motion.
2. Relationships exist between all stages in the process.

It is this latter observation that the auditor should take into account when planning his audit of purchases transactions, and his audit tests are not necessarily confined to depth tests (i.e. tracing the steps in their chronological sequence). He may wish to vary his tests to highlight the relationship between steps which are not adjacent – for example, he may be concerned to know the time elapsed between the date of requisitioning goods and the date of their admission to store, and will therefore compare a series of requisition forms with the corresponding goods inwards, or inspection notes (see steps (2) and (6) in first list above).

This freedom to use as many permutations as an intelligent audit approach requires is facilitated in the first instance, of course, by:

1. Careful and accurate recording of the system by means of flow diagrams.
2. Establishing the reliability of the documentary links in a series of co-ordinated depth tests.

Such a link is often (usefully) termed an 'audit trail', which is of special relevance in the context of computer auditing, which we deal with in detail in due course.

One permutation which should always be included as a matter of course is the reverse-order depth test. To stay with our example of purchases: if we trace the steps from reorder and requisition through to entry in the stores records on arrival of goods, we may (that is, provided our sample size was valid and items were randomly selected) reach a measurable degree of assurance that validly executed requisitions result in goods on the shelf. This is rather different, however, from saying that all other goods on the shelf of the warehouse arrived there by equally valid and authorized means. If we require a corresponding assurance on this score we must reverse the sequence of the depth test and trace a sample of goods back to the ordering stage.

Assuming that the number of transactions selected for tracing is a valid sample size in the first instance, it is acceptable practice to check a slightly smaller number at each successive stage within the depth test, on the grounds (based on probability theory) that the optimum sample size decreases as the auditor's own confidence in the correct working of the system increases. If, on the other hand, the auditor finds that the system is being abused or is malfunctioning in a significant way at any stage in the test, he may have to extend the number of items he examines.

Traditionally, audit testing has suffered (and, sadly, still does in many quarters) from the following defects:

1. Sample sizes are determined haphazardly rather than rationally. It has already been pointed out that in the systems-based audit, the volume of audit testing is consciously related to the strengths and weaknesses in the system of internal control. Only rarely has audit practice followed this obvious approach, audit programmes often specifying rigidly predetermined testing volumes, unrelated to the particular situation in hand, such as 'Vouch 3 months' purchases invoices'.

2. Once the sample size is determined, items within the sample are selected for examination in a biased (as opposed to random) fashion. In the next chapter we observe the difference between these two more clearly.

3. Tests at any particular stage are unrelated to any other stage, i.e. the thinking behind the tests is horizontal, as opposed to the depth test, which may be thought of as vertical. For example, auditors may vouch a vast number of day-book entries

against suppliers' invoices (all tests being in the same 'plane', hence the term 'horizontal') without thinking to test at least some of these entries against, say, valid purchase orders, or any other documents related vertically.

4. The thoughtlessness of much audit testing usually results in the mechanical (and superficial) examination of a vastly inflated number of documents. Valid sample sizes, provided tests are correctly planned and executed, are surprisingly small.

A final point which should be made about depth testing is that it can be conducted beneficially at any stage of the audit. Our master diagram (Figure 2.1) highlighted the need for testing in three places:

1. At stage II, when discovering the functioning of the system in practice, objectively (walk-through tests).

2. At stage III, when identifying strengths and weaknesses within the system critically, and ensuring adherence to the system laid down (compliance tests).

3. At stage V, when executing the audit programme itself, i.e. the full-scale review of the reliability of the company's records (substantive tests).

It should be clear that depth testing may be employed to advantage at all three of these stages, since it will always reveal:

1. The actual procedures whereby transactions and decisions are initiated and recorded.

2. Bottlenecks and delays in processing data.

3. Ineffective checking of documentation.

4. Unauthorized transactions.

5. Non-processing or non-recording of authorized transactions.

6. Suppression of documentation in order to conceal irregular transactions or procedures.

7. Ineffective liaison or communication between departments (and individuals within departments), e.g. incorrect assumptions as to checks carried out by others.

We see, then, that the advantages of depth testing, and the disadvantages of the blind and misguided horizontal approach outlined above, are complementary. Depth testing has found an indispensable place in the practice of modern auditing and, if intelligently conducted, its reconstruction of the audit trail reveals more about the functioning (or malfunctioning) of the client's system and of the reliability of the recorded entries than the thoughtless pantomime which has for so many years passed as auditing but which has, in fact, succeeded only in blighting its effective practice.

For illustrative purposes a summary of basic substantive depth tests which might be undertaken on the accounting transactions under the following key audit areas are listed:

► Sales and receipts
► Purchases and payments
► Payroll

These tests cannot be considered as exhaustive but aim to provide a useful summary of some of the practical tests that feature in many audits.

Sales and receipts

Objectives

▶ To confirm the reliability, accuracy and completeness of the accounting.

▶ To confirm that all goods supplied were duly and properly invoiced and recorded.

1. Test numerical sequence of despatch notes.
2. Select a sample of transactions from the goods despatched notes/goods outward records (if no such records from sales day-book):
   (a) Check to sales invoice.
   (b) Check to sales day book.
   (c) Trace goods from stock records.
   (d) Trace to proof of delivery records
3. For each sales invoice selected:
   (a) Check with customer's order.
   (b) Check that credit control procedures have been applied.
   (c) Compare prices charged with price lists, quotations or correspondence.
   (d) Check calculations and additions of invoices (including VAT).
   (e) Check analysis in sales day book if applicable.
   (f) Post to sales ledger.
4. For each invoice tested:
   (a) Check that the invoice has been paid per the sales ledger (note: payments made after the year-end should be traced to the relevant records).
   (b) Check receipt to cash book.
   (c) Check to copy paying-in slip identifying individual amount and trace to bank statement.
5. Test numerical sequence of sales invoices.
6. Test the casts and cross-casts of the sales day-book and control accounts.
7. Test the postings of the sales day-book to the nominal ledger.
8. Review the sales day-book throughout the year for large or unusual items.
9. Select a sample of credit notes from the sales day book and vouch as follows:
   (a) Vouch with correspondence or other original documents.
   (b) See that copy credit notes have been signed as authorized by a director or other senior official.

(c) Trace goods back into stock where appropriate.

(d) Check postings to sales ledger.

(e) Check analysis in sales day-book (if appropriate).

(f) Where returns affect commissions, check that proper adjustments have been made.

10. Scrutinize credit notes throughout the year and verify that they have been signed as authorized by a director or other senior official. Vouch any large or unusual items.

11. Test the casts and cross-casts of the receipts cash book:

(a) Verify a sample of receipts to original receipts records (e.g. till rolls, cash sheets). Ensure that all items in the detailed records are recorded in the cash account.

(b) Confirm that discounts taken by credit customers are in accordance with the client's terms of trade.

12. Test the postings of the receipts cash book to the nominal ledger.

13. Test miscellaneous receipts with supporting evidence.

14. Scrutinize a sample of sales ledger accounts through the year and up to the date of the audit, noting any large or unusual items.

15. Scrutinize a sample of sales ledger accounts throughout the year and ensure that all credit items originate from books of prime entry that have been subjected to audit testing.

Purchases and payments

Objectives

▶ To confirm the reliability, accuracy and completeness of the accounting.

▶ To confirm that all incurred liabilities are recorded and that they represent goods or services actually received by the client.

1. Test numerical sequence of goods received notes.

2. Trace goods received notes to invoice or entry in day-book.

3. Select a sample of invoices from the purchase day-book (or payments from the cash book if no purchase day-book):

(a) Verify authorization.

(b) Confirm that cash discounts were correctly taken.

(c) Verify price with order or agreements.

(d) Confirm receipt of goods with delivery note.

(e) Check additions and calculations on invoices (including VAT).

(f) Check allocation in day-books.

(g) Check to stock records.

(h) Check to work in progress records.

(i) Post to purchase ledger.

4. For each invoice selected:

   (a) Ensure that payment has been made per purchase ledger (including payments after the balance sheet date if applicable).

   (b) Trace to cash book, ensuring correct allocation to purchase ledger column.

   (c) Trace to bank statement.

   (d) Vouch returned cheques.

5. Test numerical sequence of purchase invoices.

6. Test the cast and cross-casts of the purchase day-book and control account.

7. Test the postings of the purchase day-book to the nominal ledger.

8. Review the purchase day-book throughout the year for large or unusual items.

9. (a) Select a sample of goods returned to suppliers and ensure that credit notes have been received.

   (b) Check additions and calculations (including VAT) on credit notes.

   (c) Trace to purchase day-book to ensure credit taken.

10. Select a sample of miscellaneous payments from the cash book:

    (a) Verify authorization.

    (b) Check additions and calculations on invoices.

    (c) Check nominal ledger allocation.

    (d) Check to bank statement.

    (e) Vouch returned cheques.

11. Test the casts and cross-casts of the payments cash book.

12. Test the postings of the payments cash book to the nominal ledger.

13. Test the posting of payments to replenish petty cash to the petty cash book.

14. Scrutinize the payments cash book throughout the year and up to date and note any large or unusual items.

15. Select a sample of payments from the petty cash book and:

    (a) Vouch with supporting voucher and any independent evidence.

    (b) Verify authorization.

    (c) Check nominal ledger allocation.

16. Scrutinize petty cash receipts for miscellaneous receipts. Vouch with available evidence and ensure correct nominal ledger allocation.

17. Test the casts and cross-casts of the petty cash book.

18. Test the posting of the petty cash book to the nominal ledger.

19. Scrutinize the petty cash book throughout the year for large or unusual items. If there are any casual labour payments ensure that PAYE regulations have been complied with.

Payroll

Objectives

▶ To ensure that levels of pay are in order.

▶ To check validity and accuracy of deductions.

▶ To confirm proper payment.

▶ To test reasonableness of net pay figures.

▶ To confirm reliability, accuracy and completeness of the accounting.

▶ To ensure correct treatment of PAYE and NI.

1. Select a sample of employees from different periods in the year from both weekly payroll and monthly salaries and:

   (a) Ensure gross pay has been properly authorized by checking to:

      (i)   Lists of hourly rates.

      (ii) Lists of piece-work rates.

      (iii) Lists of overtime rates.

      (iv) Lists of annual salaries.

      (v)   Commission lists.

      (vi) Contracts of employment.

   (b) For hourly paid employees check the hours worked with the time records, and the authorization of overtime and bonus payments.

   (c) For piece workers check quantities with output returns of job slips initialled by a foreman.

   (d) Check that hours/quantities/gross pay (as appropriate) have been entered into cost records.

   (e) Check SSP calculations and ensure that there is supporting evidence of absence and that the SSP calculation rules have been correctly applied.

   (f) Check calculation of PAYE and NI and cross-cast to net pay.

   (g) For payments in cash inspect receipts given by employees.

   (h) Trace gross wages to income tax deduction cards and to holiday pay records.

   (i) Trace a sample of net wages to cash book and vouch returned cheques.

2. (a) Check to wages summaries.

   (b) Check casts and cross-casts of summaries.

   (c) Check postings from summaries to the nominal ledger.

3. Review monthly/weekly total payroll costs and investigate any unusual variations.

4. Inspect the copy P.35 and examine agreement with control accounts as at 5th April. Pay particular attention to recovery of SSP.

5. Check that authorization of payroll is evidenced.

6. Trace a sample of joiners and leavers to the payroll ensuring that payments commence and end in the correct periods.

7. Test payroll with contracts of employment to ensure that all employees with three months' service have a valid contract.

8. If there are significant amounts paid in cash, then consider attending to observe pay out procedures.

4.4   The terminology of audit testing

It is natural for every discipline to develop its own terminology and auditing is no exception. There is, however, a degree of confusion arising from differences in usage. Individual auditing firms develop new techniques or, more usually, variations of existing techniques, and these are then identified by descriptive jargon. As the use of the technique spreads to other firms, with or without further variation or adaptation to meet particular needs, so the jargon spreads too and eventually becomes entrenched as a part of auditing terminology.

In a number of cases, however, distinctly different meanings are attributed to particular terms by different users, and it is therefore important to clarify what one means when using such terms. It is not an area in which anyone is in a position to say which meaning is correct and which incorrect, and in this section the terms are described in accordance with their most widely held connotations. Terminology, of itself, is unimportant. It is merely a shorthand: a means of avoiding lengthy and explicit definition each time a particular method of work is referred to.

4.4.1   Terms relating to systems-based audits

Definitions of compliance and substantive tests have already been given – see section 3.7.

Walk-through tests

Walk-through, in its most usual sense, refers not to a technique but to the stage in the audit when the testing takes place. These tests take place at an early stage, when company procedures are still being ascertained, recorded and assessed by the auditor (stages II and III in the master diagram, Figure 2.1), and it is usual for the depth testing techniques described above to be used in this process.

The completion of an internal control questionnaire, for example, is largely based upon information supplied by the company's senior executives, and one purpose of the walk-through tests is to establish independently the accuracy of this information. The tests will therefore cover all typical situations (transactions, recorded entries, documents, etc.) so that the auditor obtains as broad a picture as possible; it is certainly not the intention at this stage to ensure that items selected for testing should be representative in the statistical sense – the selection of four or five items would be normal.

Weakness tests

Weakness tests is a term sometimes used for any additional tests which the auditor considers necessary in view of the number of errors or weaknesses which become apparent during the execution of the audit programme. The weakness tests thus amount to an extension of the work originally planned due to the discovery of a higher proportion of errors than was anticipated. If statistical sampling is used, this extension of testing is obviously necessary because the high proportion of errors discovered indicates that the auditor's initial assessment of the system (on which the sampling scheme was based) was unduly optimistic; a larger sample size is therefore necessary in order to support valid conclusions at the same level of confidence. This is examined in the next chapter. Strictly speaking, weakness tests fall within the scope of substantive tests.

Rotational tests

A variety of meanings has been attributed to the term 'rotational tests', but these fall into two basic types:

1. Where the system of internal control is known from past experience to be sound, and the sample of items tested is correspondingly small, it is considered useful to carry out a series of additional tests in one selected area (e.g. wages, sales, stores records, etc.), over and above those which are scheduled in the programme. The area to be probed in this way is not disclosed in advance, and this practice has the dual effect of:

    (a) acting as a moral check on staff working within a basically sound system, in which complacency can all too easily set in; and

    (b) making quite sure that the system is in fact operating as effectively in day-to-day practice as the auditor has been led to believe.

    This is known as 'rotation of audit emphasis'.

2. Where the client company has a large number of branches, depots, warehouses, etc., it will be impracticable if not impossible for the auditor to test procedures at all of these in the course of one cycle of audit duties; in such a case visits and tests may be devised on a 'rotational' basis, thus giving an acceptable spread of testing over a longer cycle than one financial year. Tests at the branch selected would be designed to ensure compliance with procedures laid down by head office, as well as

an acceptable level of accuracy in the recording of transactions locally for the purposes of branch returns.

With all forms of rotational tests it is important to select the object of the tests on a random basis (i.e. all departments or branches stand an equal chance of being selected on the occasion of each audit, irrespective of the time elapsed since last selected).

4.4.2 Other relevant terms

The 'vouching audit'

The term 'vouching audit' has been given to the audit situation in which there is a virtual absence of internal control, as a result of which it is necessary for the auditor to check in detail a substantial proportion of all documentary evidence before reaching his conclusions and compiling his report. This does not fall within the context of the systems-based audit since there is no system on which the auditor may rely.

It is not uncommon in such a situation for the checking of up to 50 per cent of all transactions to be considered necessary. The reason for this is usually that the organization is haphazard both in conception and execution. Terms like 'system' and 'organization' imply a discernible measure of order and regularity; where, for one reason or another, this is not present, the auditor has little option but to carry out a 'vouching audit' programme since each item examined can be assumed to represent only itself.

Judgement sampling

Unlike statistical sampling, described in Chapter 5, judgement sampling is based entirely upon the auditor's judgement of an audit situation. Clearly, he will bring to bear on his decision all he has gathered about the operation of the system of internal control as applied to the recording of day-to-day transactions, but no matter how skilful his assessment of appropriate sample sizes, this judgement is necessarily subjective and hence devoid of any mathematical basis. Its validity is correspondingly difficult to substantiate. In situations in which a relatively small number of transactions is under review, judgement sampling is largely unavoidable. The judgement in question relates to the determination of sample sizes and materiality criteria. It is advisable that the items selected for testing be chosen randomly.

The balance sheet audit

The balance sheet audit is usually considered appropriate in circumstances in which the following conditions are known by the auditor to exist:

1. The client company is a large and complex organization.
2. The auditor has acted for the client company for some years and has a detailed knowledge of its organization.

3. The client's system of internal control is known to be sound in every material regard, such an opinion being based upon:

   (a) experience gained on audits in previous years; and

   (b) recent reviews, involving compliance tests, of the system of internal control.

4. An interim audit has already covered basic tests of routine procedures in each department of the organization.

The balance sheet audit operates in the opposite direction to normal audit procedures in that it commences with a detailed examination of the draft balance sheet to be presented to the company's members and works back to the underlying records. In a sense it reverses the sequence of stages VI and VII of the master diagram (Figure 2.1).

The balance sheet approach is more common in the USA, where auditors generally concentrate far more heavily on the balance sheet (statement of financial position) than on the profit and loss account (revenue statement). It is interesting to note that the reverse has traditionally characterized UK audits, although to put it so glibly is obviously an over-simplification.

Since the programme for the full balance sheet audit is virtually identical with that which covers year-end verification and review work on the final accounts, it is more appropriate to deal with this in section 6.7. Its main burden is, however, clearly indicated in stage VII of Figure 2.1.

The term 'balance sheet audit' is also used to describe audits at the 'small end of the spectrum', in which the system of controls is unreliable, the records sparse and rudimentary, and hence undue reliance has to be placed on management assurances. In such circumstances it is not surprising that the burden of testing falls on the 'end results', i.e. the financial statements, with one question dominant: 'Do the figures make sense?' This will require resolution by reference to comparisons, ratios, etc., all in the light of knowledge of the trade, the ability of the proprietors/directors to support their lifestyle on the level of remuneration indicated by the records, and other related considerations.

4.5 The use of audit programmes

4.5.1 The dangers

The disadvantages implicit in the use of a standardized audit programme may be cited thus:

1. Being predetermined it takes no account of the particular circumstances of each client to whose records it is applied.

2. It does not encourage spontaneous responses on the part of the audit technicians engaged in its execution.

3. It requires little originality in approach and encourages mechanistic attitudes which inevitably lead to tedium and poor quality audit work.

4. It is possible for any member of the client's staff who gain sight of it to see, almost at a glance, what proportion of the total programme for the year is regarded by the auditors as having already been completed.

5. It enables each section of the work programme to be completed independently of other sections which may, in fact, be closely related. This is probably the most serious disadvantage of all. The use of a formal audit programme often leads to audit work being done at a particular time in order to suit the client's staff, for example because the records concerned happened to be 'free' at that moment – an absurd situation if considered objectively. This attitude leaves the audit firm highly vulnerable and, once entrenched, it is difficult to establish a different standard.

The lessons of the Equity Funding fraud, uncovered in 1973 in the USA, are salutary. The audit programme required the auditors of this life assurance company to examine the support files relating to a random selection of policy numbers. These files should have contained applications, proposals, acceptances, transmittal sheets, doctors' certificates, etc., all of which would have substantiated the genuine existence of the policies in question. So bound were the auditors by the idea of simply complying with the letter of the programme laid down that they failed to recognize the dangers of:

1. Accepting, for convenience, 'randomly' selected policy numbers from the client company's staff; and

2. Acceding to the staff's request that the files should be presented to the auditors the following day, 'in view of the fact that they were in different parts of the building, and would have to be discovered and collected together'.

The policies in question were fake, and support files were manufactured overnight. The audit work carried out, in total compliance with the programme laid down, was in fact totally useless – lethal might be a more apt epithet – and enabled the fraud to proceed undisturbed.

4.5.2 Avoiding the dangers

Despite the clear warnings, a surprising number of firms seem prepared to continue conducting audits on the basis of formal programmes which expose them to the risks implicit in the content of the foregoing paragraphs.

The disadvantages of standard audit programmes may be overcome in the following three ways:

1. Written audit programmes may be abandoned altogether. This may be acceptable, even advisable, in the case of small client entities, and will enable the audit staff to devise a programme of work that (a) is appropriate to the system and the records employed at the time, and (b) may be compared, for the purpose of corroboration, with work shown on the files as having been carried out in previous years. Abandonment is not to be recommended, however, in cases where the system under audit moves beyond a certain level of complexity, since this would place far too great a responsibility on the audit seniors in charge of the particular assignment. A

written programme would also be important in the case of large clients in that (a) it ensures completeness, no major part of the work being overlooked; and (b) it ensures continuity from one period to another. The idea of a financial year is, after all, a contrived imposition on the natural situation, which is that a business proceeds uninterrupted from day to day, month to month, and year to year. A well-designed programme of work simulates the continuous and cyclical nature of business by ensuring that suitable sections of work on the recording of routine transactions are completed at interim stages.

In the case of large entities, therefore, the standard programme may be replaced by one that is tailored to the specific requirements of the client. Although this avoids the depersonalized nature of the predetermined standard (referred to in disadvantage (1) at the start of section 4.5.1), it still suffers from the remaining disadvantages and is thus far from an ideal solution.

2. The programme may be personalized (i.e. designed to cater for the audit of a particular client entity) and its sections clearly cross-referenced to ensure that a planned sequence is imposed on the audit checks carried out. This is designed to overcome disadvantage (5) in section 4.5.1 by ensuring that the various parts of the programme are not completed in isolation from each other, thus enabling the natural depth test sequence to be observed.

    This suggestion is admirable in many ways, and is pursued by a number of firms today with a reasonable measure of success. It has the advantage of appealing to the good sense of the audit technicians, and this always ensures a higher degree of intelligent compliance with the underlying audit objectives, rather than with the mere letter of the programme, blindly. The method nevertheless has certain disadvantages, in that:

    (a) it requires the auditors to 'jump around' the programme to ensure the continuity sequence which the cross-referencing system is designed to achieve;

    (b) it does not appear to follow the flowcharting sequence already recorded on file;

    (c) it is difficult to gauge progress in the audit to date since at any one time most sections of the programme will be partially incomplete.

3. It will be seen from the above that perhaps the ideal form of programme governing the testing of routine transactions is one that is:

    (a) designed on a depth test basis throughout; and

    (b) based upon the actual system operated by the client entity, and as recorded in the auditor's systems notes and flowcharts.

The adoption of such a programme ensures, as far as possible, the intelligent appreciation by audit staff of the interdependence of the company's records, and the need to retrace and test the normal procedures by following the audit trail. This method exploits to the full the close correspondence between the flowcharts of the system (which follow the actual time sequence in which documentation is created, used and filed) and the successive stages in the depth test carried out, and this correspondence should be highlighted by a suitable method of cross-referencing.

4.5.3 Final observations

It is clear that no single method of auditing transactions has all the answers, and it is not surprising that research, experimentation and field testing are continuously carried out by audit firms of all sizes in their search for new approaches and techniques. Much of this research effort is duplicated and it is a pity that the competitive spirit which today ruthlessly pervades professional work precludes the possibility of operating a clearing house for documenting the nature of new projects and for recording observations on their usefulness in a co-ordinated series of field tests.

4.6 Weakness letters

At the conclusion of this stage of the audit it is normal for the firm to send to the client a letter of weakness (sometimes referred to as 'internal control letter' or 'management letter') detailing areas in which internal control weaknesses have been shown up as a result of the audit procedures carried out. Opinion varies considerably on:

1. The precise stage at which the letter should be sent.
2. How far the letter's contents should extend, bearing in mind that a 'management audit' as such has not been conducted.
3. What action the auditor should take if his observations on material systems weaknesses are ignored by the client.

Specimen letter of weakness

The Directors,
Rising Sunsets Ltd
Doomsday House
41 Clydesdale Avenue
Stanmore
Middlesex

29 April 1996

Gentlemen:

1995 FINAL AUDIT

Following the finalization of our audit work relating to the Company's accounts for the year ended 31 December 1995 we set out below certain points which we have discussed with the Company's officials but consider it appropriate to report formally thereon as we feel that these points should be drawn to your attention as a matter of priority. As you are aware these points emerged from our routine review of the Company's current accounting and internal control systems. We stress, however, that our audit testing was undertaken in accordance with the scope of our audit engagement and, therefore, will not necessarily identify all weaknesses that may exist. As you are aware, it is the responsibility of the directors to ensure that satisfactory internal controls are maintained at all times.

A.   Purchases

We have to reiterate our comments contained in our letter of 29 October 1994:

1. The procedure for receiving incoming goods is poor in that:

   (a) No goods received notes are raised in the store, or as an alternative, no formal goods inwards book is maintained on a regular basis linked with the appropriate records.

   (b) With the exception of 'small components' no records are kept on the production floor to record transfers of goods from stores.

   (c) Although some delivery notes are retained by way of being attached to supply invoices, the delivery notes, which are the only evidence of goods received, are not being retained as a matter of routine by the accounts department.

   (d) Steps are not taken by the purchasing department to achieve competitive prices from suppliers.

In addition to the above the following weaknesses were also revealed:

   (e) When orders are placed verbally, no record is made to indicate the prices quoted and quantity of goods ordered.

   (f) Delivery notes are not always signed.

   (g) Purchases invoices are rubber stamped but never fully completed. The arithmetic, in particular, is never checked or at least no indication is given.
   Data: An invoice from Alfred Archer & Co. was passed for payment. On our checking the corresponding delivery note it was noted that only two of the three invoiced items had in fact been received. The missing item of 3 sets of 8 mm piping @ £24.22 per set = £72.06 had, however, been passed for payment.

2. The purchase control for Burnham Cross was not agreed until the second week in February. We were informed that the reason for this delay was that the person in charge was sick and no standby was competent to deal with the situation.

B.   Sales and debtors

Again we have to reiterate our comments contained in our letter of 29 October 1994.

1. The present system of processing customers' orders is inadequate in that there is

insufficient evidence to indicate whether the following checks have been carried out:

(a) That the prices quoted to the customers are in agreement with the Company's current price list.

(b) That where the order is from a new customer, its creditworthiness has been established and approved.

(c) That where the order is from an existing customer, its present credit limit has not been exceeded.

(d) With the exception of bad debts, where the respective sales ledger cards indicate that no further goods are to be supplied, the credit limits are not noted on the relevant ledger card.

(e) Where established credit limits are revised, such revisions are not formally authorized in writing.

(f) There is insufficient evidence on either retained copies of sales invoices or other media to show that the following checks have been carried out:

(i) That they have been compared with customers' orders as regards quantities.

(ii) That the correctness of the prices used have been checked.

(iii) That the extensions and additions have been checked.

2. The method of issuing credit notes is weak in so far as:

(a) The goods received notes in respect of the returns made by customers are not retained by the accounts department.

(b) There is no evidence that the issue of credit notes is officially approved.

(c) There is insufficient evidence that the tests mentioned in (f) (ii) and (iii) above are carried out on credit notes issued.

The following additional weakness was also revealed:

(d) On our sample test it appears that credit notes can be issued without evidence of goods having in fact been returned and conversely, insufficient evidence exists to indicate that goods have in fact been returned in respect of credit notes issued.

3. *Returns*

(a) Faulty goods returned are entered in a book kept in the repairs department. If a customer requires a credit note, the invoicing department is informed as soon as the faulty goods are received. However, when the faulty goods are repaired and returned, invoices are not raised and hence the customer's account can be left with a fictitious credit balance where the account has previously, or in the meantime, been settled.

Data R. L. Matthews
        Credit note issued No. 1997
        Goods despatched after repairs on 1.12.95
        No invoice ever raised

(b) The validity of credit balances on customers' accounts is not regularly reviewed by the sales ledger department.

4. *Sales invoice department*

The system apparently in use is that delivery notes and invoices (together with other media) form a single pack. The assumption is that a customer's order will be despatched in full and the pack is typed at one stage on such basis. However, on certain occasions customers' orders are not despatched in full and although the quantity may be altered by hand on the delivery note on these occasions, due to inadequate liaison between the relevant departments the matching invoice is not always correspondingly altered. As a consequence certain customers are not invoiced on the basis of quantities actually despatched and when the additional goods are despatched so as to fulfil the customer's original order and thus correspond with the original invoice rendered, additional invoices are raised on a 'no charge basis'. However, there is an insufficiency of evidence to check the actual quantities short delivered.

5. *Sales ledger department*

Age analyses were not effected for large customers and such balances are not analysed over various months. Consequently it is not possible to readily ascertain the length of the credit period for these particular customers.

Data: Army & Navy Stores

	Total	Nov. & prior	Dec.
Our analysis	7,046.44	1,732.76	5,313.68
Your analysis	7,046.44	—	7,046.44

Other notable examples were British Oxygen and Cosmetics.

C. Fixed assets

Again we have to reiterate below our previous comments of 5 July 1995 and also of 29 October 1994 as follows:

1. *Plant & machinery*

(a) Although certain schedules for depreciation purposes are available no formal Plant Registers are maintained with the result that the location and identification of some items can become difficult.

(b) Modifications or alterations to plant and machinery are not scheduled and nor are such alterations authorized in writing.

(c) Authorization for the scrapping of plant and machinery is not in writing.

(d) Physical checks of fixed assets do not appear to be made on a frequent basis.

(e) No formal system as regards loose tools exists.

2. *Furniture & fittings*

The remarks made in the above connection with Plant and Machinery also apply in many respects to furniture, fittings, etc.

D. Wages

The following weaknesses were revealed:

1. *Employees' clock numbers*

We have been informed that the 'Employee Codes' on the computer configuration are based on their clock card numbers. However, no standing index is maintained.

2. *Van drivers' wages*

The van drivers do not as a matter of routine clock in at night or in the mornings. Our findings indicate that the average time paid to each van driver is in the region of 55 hours per week. Perhaps the matter can be investigated by your internal management and in future some controls should be instituted for recording the correct amount of time worked.

3. The computer application maintained at the outside bureau does not provide for exception reports and consequently when an unusual payment is made, which is not checked manually, it can be completely overlooked.

E. Inventories

In the course of our audit of the Company's inventories the following weaknesses were revealed:

1. *Stock control*

There is no perpetual inventory system in operation and as a consequence no adequate controls on raw materials or finished goods exist. From our overall quantity check it would appear that there is a shortfall of approximately 1.2% of annual production which could represent some 35 cases a week not being accounted for.

2. *Pricing*

(a) The raw materials are priced for internal costing purposes on a basis that could be construed as a form of replacement cost, which method of valuation is quite unacceptable for accounts purposes and some of the typical anomalies arising from this form of valuation are as follows:

(i) Prices are updated on the notification of a price increase which may not be effective for some months ahead.

(ii) Topping-up orders at a higher price effectively increases the value of the total stockholding.

(iii) No allowances are made for price reductions.

(b) The cost of certain goods was taken at invoice value which was subsequently found to be free issue.

(c) Poor description on the stock sheets led to wrong pricing and confusion existed between the price in relation to the quantity.

(d) There is no clear ageing on the stock sheets despite the fact that obsolete items were clearly marked as such. Neither were there any indications of non-current range of stock items.

3. *Work in progress*

The system of pricing work in progress was incorrect in that:

(a) No weighted average was used in respect of the overhead recovery on executive cases.

(b) Whilst the overhead was incurred over 52 weeks it was not appreciated that there were only 48 production weeks to recover such overhead.

(c) The actual annual overhead was taken as the recovery required whereas the overhead for the last three months to 31 December extrapolated to an annual rate is the appropriate figure for work in progress purposes.

4. *Finished goods*

Our comments in relation to work in progress apply to finished goods.

5. *Stock sheets*

Arithmetical errors were found on many sheets and indeed two stock sheets were not even cast thus clearly indicating that no overall check existed.

6. *Cut-off*

Credit notes in January were found to refer to the previous year indicating:

(a) that the cut-off was not properly carried out; and

(b) that there was no system to check that for each debit note issued a credit was subsequently received.

However, this has now been rectified.

F. Management accounts

It was not possible to check the accuracy of the management accounts as during our visit they were not prepared for the month of December.

G. General points

1. No daily cheque-received diary or other record is maintained and consequently there is no method of confirming whether all cheques received were in fact banked.

Data: Cheque received from Hamstrung Limited for £1353.87 on 3.12.95. Cheque banked on 11.2.96 as it had been inadvertently misplaced in one of the desks.

2. *Authority limits*

These are not clearly defined and it would be advisable to clarify these formally in writing.

3. *Private ledger*

The current system is insufficient in that there are still no posting references available for checking entries from the prime books to the Private Ledger.

Conclusion

It would appear from the foregoing that very few changes in the systems and procedures of internal control have been implemented since the 1994 Audit. Our letters of 5 July 1995 and 29 October 1994 refer.

We again reiterate that these matters are of significance and as we understand that certain changes and improvements are in the course of being effected and that such may be germane to our above comments, we should be obliged if in due course you would advise us in writing as to the steps you either propose to take or have taken on each of the foregoing points.

Yours faithfully,

Warrington Smith & Co.

In 1995, the APC issued Statement of Auditing Standards no. 610 – 'Reports to directors or management', which provides guidance on auditors' reports to directors (including any audit committee) of weaknesses in the accounting and internal control systems and other matters, including errors, identified during the audit. Its key points may be summarized as follows:

1. The auditor should report to the client matters of relevance arising from the audit, in particular accounting errors and weaknesses in the accounting and internal control systems.

2. Any points for management attention should ideally first be discussed with the client prior to the issue of a formal letter, in order to clear any misunderstandings on the part of the auditor and to avoid any impractical suggestions being made.

3. It is essential that, where matters are serious, these are brought to the attention of management at the earliest opportunity, preferably in written form. In so doing the auditor should carefully consider, especially in the case of suspected fraud, that the person to whom he is reporting is sufficiently senior and independent.

4. Even in the case of small companies, written communication is a requirement of the Standard since, in the absence of a formal letter or report, a file memorandum should be made which summarizes the subject matter of any discussion during

which the weaknesses and recommendations were raised. A copy of the file note should then be sent to the client.

5. Where a report is to be issued, it is usual to stress that the audit will not have necessarily identified each and every weakness.

6. It should be an audit procedure that matters reported are followed up at the next audit to determine what action has been taken as a result.

7. Such reports may be regarded by the client as a useful product of the necessary audit cost and this aspect should encourage the auditor to issue them.

8. It may be that the points raised are not of such significance that a formal report is needed. In such a case the auditor should make a file note to record that he has discussed the points with the client, together with his reason for not issuing a formal report.

9. The format of the report may be made such that the client has space to respond against each matter raised and return a copy of the report to the auditor with proposed action. For example:

Appendix to management letter

Audit Matters Arising   Client Comment
Cheque signatories
We note that A. Smith, accounts clerk, has bank
mandate authority to be sole signatory on company
cheques without restriction.

There is a risk that he could incur unauthorized
expenditure.

We recommend that the mandate should be altered
so that for all cheque payments a second signature
by a company director is required.

10. A copy of the management letter should be placed on the permanent file for future reference.

11. Evidence of negligence claims against auditors highlights the serious consequences for auditors of failing to report matters subsequently found to have involved fraudulent activity. Had the auditor made a report he might have been in a stronger position to defend any action against him.

4.6.1   Practical applications

1. Group companies

A particular consideration is whether it is necessary to prepare separate management letters for each group company. This can lead to the situation where a single individual (say, the group MD) receives six or seven letters in which many points are repeated.

There is no straight answer to this. If an auditor acts for groups in which each subsidiary operates autonomously with its own MD, board and management reporting structure, internal controls and accounting systems, management letters may be sent to each client company as an independent entity. Alternatively, the group structure may be one in which each subsidiary has no more effective autonomy than an operating division, and the group MD in effect serves as MD for every company. In those circumstances the auditor may be specifically asked to provide a single management letter to the MD embracing all the individual entities.

It should be remembered that the contractual relationship is between the auditor and each individual company, thus any report to management is a confidential matter between the auditor and the management of the company concerned. It is therefore necessary to obtain formal permission from the management of each subsidiary to disclose the contents to the holding company's management.

If the effective management is identically composed throughout the group, nevertheless, the auditor should retain in the permanent file a set of appropriate permissions which can be drafted to remain effective until specifically countermanded.

2. Is the letter necessary?

Some practitioners may take the view that at a time when fee resistance is high, it is tempting to cut down on any audit procedures that are not absolutely essential and decide not to write a management letter in future, i.e. consider that where no formal controls exist, the letter is a bit of a farce anyway. However, inessential audit procedures are always best avoided, not just because of fee pressures. SAS 610 makes it clear that if there are indeed no significant matters to report there is no point in reporting!

The letter should therefore never be a 'farce'. The auditor must always assess issues to be brought to management's attention and decide accordingly.

There is no general statutory obligation to write reports to management, except in certain specialized public sector and financial services contexts. But the professional duty to do so is quite clear.

The report to management should not only cover weaknesses in internal controls but additionally embrace:

► deficiencies in the operation of accounting systems;

► inappropriate accounting policies and practices;

► non-compliance with legislation, standards and other regulations.

No concession is made to the size of the client entity. Recommendations for improvement may, of course, be included at the auditor's discretion. But the obligation to issue the letter itself is not negotiable.

Even small companies with few controls welcome suggestions for improvement. These are usually discussed at a meeting followed by a summary in writing. If followed, these suggestions will often save on audit costs in subsequent years.

The report to management could be the one constructive by-product of a service otherwise thought of as a necessary evil – a by-product for which the client actually sees value for money.

3. To whom should it be sent?

With regard to litigation, the failure to report weaknesses to management undoubtedly increases the auditor's exposure to allegations of negligence, especially when (i) normal audit procedures have brought such weaknesses to light, and (ii) when those weaknesses are later found to have caused losses to the client entity. Indeed, it was held in the recent landmark *AWA* v *Deloittes* case in Australia that auditors have a responsibility to report weaknesses to the highest authority of the group – its main board of directors.

4.7   Microfilming – the audit problem

A substantial number of companies are turning to the use of microfilm for the purpose of storing their records. Such a development will cause auditors to consider whether the destruction of original records, once they have been microfilmed, presents any control or verification difficulties.

4.7.1   The distinction between internally and externally generated documents

Generally speaking, microfilm copies of internally generated documents, e.g. copy sales invoices, goods inwards notes, are satisfactory evidence for audit purposes. It is felt, however, that no matter how good are the control procedures relating to externally generated documents, e.g. purchase invoices, the possibility of their being altered does exist, and that it will be extremely difficult, if not impossible, to detect an alteration from an examination of a microfilm copy. Auditors should therefore give careful consideration to insisting that 'third party' documents be retained in their original form, at least until after the audit has been completed.

4.7.2   Essential microfilm controls

These are similar to controls instituted over computer input and processing, and would be expected to include the following additional matters:

1. A policy should be formally recorded and approved by senior management, setting out the documents which may be destroyed and the detailed control procedures governing the implementation of this policy. All destructions should be properly authorized in accordance with the policy laid down, and the authorization evidenced.

2. It is important for audit purposes that the company should arrange for the microfilming to be done under adequate supervision (for example, by the internal audit department or other official independent of the microfilming personnel), and the external auditors should carry out such tests of the destruction and microfilming procedures as they consider necessary.

3. Special microfilming registers should be maintained, using batch numbers to record and control the documents microfilmed and destroyed respectively.

4. Indexing and the retrieval controls should ensure that the company is able to refer quickly and easily to any microfilms of documents.

5. A complete set of back-up films should be maintained at a different location from that of the originals.

To enable the auditors to execute whatever tests they consider necessary, they will require complete access to the microfilm records, and a reader will have to be made constantly available to them during the audit.

It is essential that auditors liaise with their clients before any microfilm system is installed, otherwise they may find, too late, that essential records have been destroyed. It is, in any event, desirable that no records applicable to the year under review should be destroyed before the audit report is signed, but if, for any reason, the client considers such destruction necessary, it should take place only after discussion with the auditors, and this may therefore necessitate audit visits on a more frequent basis than would otherwise be the case.

Review questions

*1. What, in your opinion, are:

   (a) the principal aims of audit checking?

   (b) the main classifications into which the various methods of making such tests can be conveniently classified?

   (c) the most important matters that the auditor needs to consider when deciding which areas of the client's system to test and the extent of the testing to be carried out?

   (d) the transactions or records that are not suitable for the adoption of any form of test checking?

*2. In what audit areas would you consider that depth testing is most appropriate?

3. Standard audit programmes are said to have many dangers – but to let an inexperienced audit staff member carry out testing without a programme could be deemed to be equivalently fraught with danger. How do you consider that this situation may be simply resolved?

4. Letters of weakness are sent to the directors of the company being audited at the conclusion of the audit. Given that the letter is likely to be a confirmation of conversations which have already taken place between the auditor and the directors of the client

company, could it not be argued that they are a waste of time – especially if they are ignored?

Exercises

1.   Autocomputers plc is one of your largest clients. The year-end of the company is 30 September. In July the company announces that there is to be a relocation of the business to a specialist business park in the south of England. The move is scheduled to be completed by 23 December. News of this has been kept very quiet on a 'need-to-know basis,' and out of the workforce of 200 only 40 key personnel will be moving with the company.

   The managing director has indicated that he requires the audit of the financial accounts to be completed by the end of November so that the AGM of the company can be held early December – probably on or around the 10th of the month.

Required

   (a) Specify the additional audit work that you would incorporate into an audit programme in respect of the planned relocation.

   (b) Identify any additional work that is required in respect of post year-end events.

2.   You are the senior audit partner of your firm. One of your most experienced audit seniors, a non-qualified accountant, has approached you and enquired why, with the usage of pre-prepared audit programmes, it is necessary to include on file full sets of working papers since initialling of the programme plus notes would probably suffice.

Required

A memorandum to the senior outlining four reasons why audit working papers are prepared together with the elements which you consider to be essential in a set of audit working papers.

The use of sampling techniques for audit purposes

▷ the framework for audit sampling, as laid down by Statements of Auditing Standards;

▷ advantages and disadvantages of statistical sampling;

▷ conditions appropriate to the use of statistical sampling;

▷ different types of statistical sampling and their application in practice;

▷ interaction between statistical sampling and risk-based auditing;

▷ relationship between materiality and audit risk.

5.1 Statement of Auditing Standard (SAS) 430 – Audit sampling

In March 1995 the APB issued SAS 430 – 'Audit sampling'. This standard is suitably permissive, since undue prescription would deny the wide range of methods by which sampling objectives can be achieved.

The key points covered by this SAS are as follows:

1. Auditors are not expected to carry out a 100 per cent check on an entity's records and transactions – hence the sampling process.

2. Sampling excludes the testing of 100 per cent of items in a discrete population (e.g. all items over a certain monetary value or having a particular characteristic).

3. Various methods of sample selection are mentioned, which may apply to both statistical and non-statistical sampling methods. Sample items must be selected in such a way that all items in the population have an equal chance of being selected.

4. When determining sample sizes, auditors should consider sampling risk, tolerable

(or acceptable) error and the expected error. The Standard details the factors which influence sample sizes.

5. Any errors (as defined) found in the sample tested should be analysed and inferences drawn for the population as a whole. This may or may not require the auditor to extend the level of his testing to provide the required degree of assurance.

Whichever method of sampling is used, the auditor's working papers should clearly show:

(a) The population being sampled and how the auditor is satisfied as to the completeness of that population – for example, by sequence checks and tests on reciprocal populations. *Valid conclusions can be drawn only by sampling from complete populations.* If any items are missing they are clearly not available for testing. Where there have been material changes in the system operated during the period under review, separate populations exist on either side of the date of change, and separate tests must therefore be devised and executed.

(b) The method of sample selection. Initial sample sizes will normally be based on a combination of high value items (not strictly sampling, as all the items above the threshold will be tested) and a number of other representative items from the rest of the population. For valid conclusions to be reached, each item in the sample of representative items must stand an equal chance of being selected. Random number tables will generally be used to select these items. In addition to the high-value and representative items, other items carrying high inherent risk may also be selected for testing on a judgement basis, e.g. slow-moving stock or debtors; once again, the reasons for the selection of these items must be documented.

(c) The individual items tested. To enable the auditor to support the conclusions reached, he may be called upon to refer to the items he has tested. This will be achieved either by recording the details of the individual items in the audit working papers or by use of audit ticks, or an audit stamp, in the client's records, as appropriate for each type of test.

(d) The method of responding to any errors detected. In the case of an error found during substantive testing, the potential effect on the whole population from which the sample was drawn should be evaluated. If this exercise shows that the expected error rate exceeds the tolerable error (or materiality) level, additional substantive testing may be necessary to enable the auditor to be satisfied about the degree of mis-statement in the population as a whole. In all cases, the evaluation of the errors found, the subsequent action and the reasoning behind that action should be recorded.

5.2   Attitudes to statistical sampling

A number of references to statistical sampling have been made in earlier chapters, particularly in Chapter 4. Our primary concern thus far has related to the techniques whereby an auditor records, assesses and evaluates the system of internal control, and then proceeds to establish the reliability of the records which that system produces. In fulfilling the latter objective he will rarely find it necessary to examine the records relating to every single transaction; such an undertaking would, in any case, be virtually impossible in practical terms and would certainly extend beyond what is legally expected of him, i.e. to form an opinion – not to issue a guarantee or a certificate.

In certain enterprises (e.g. a merchanting house, bill broker, property agent or estates manager) the total number of transactions recorded each year may be relatively small, and number no more than, say, a few hundred. In such a case each transaction may well be material in relation to the business as a whole, and it is clear that the use of statistical sampling will be wholly inappropriate. Materiality is therefore an important factor to consider in relation to sampling in general. Even in the audit of major corporations there will be certain items which are actually or potentially so significant that the records relating to them should be scrutinized by the auditor on an item-by-item basis. The company's year-end closing entries in the main journal, for example, are potentially manipulative, and each must therefore be carefully examined and authenticated by the auditor.

In relation to the broad mass of entries, statistical sampling may have very definite application. It should nevertheless be pointed out that the experience of some firms which have sought to use such techniques is that their usefulness has turned out to be more limited than was first anticipated. Indeed, some firms have come full circle and now require their audit technicians to obtain the prior sanction of a manager or partner before spending time on statistical sampling. There are several reasons for this, in particular:

1. Auditing has never been a mathematical discipline, and a highly developed intuition has always been a more valuable audit attribute than the possession of scientific knowledge.

2. Properly designed (i.e. mathematically valid) sampling schemes often take an inordinate length of time to set up, during which time a good deal of representative random sampling could have been conducted, with the reasonable assurance that its conclusions would be valid for audit purposes.

3. Statistical sampling invariably results in the examination of sample sizes much smaller than those traditionally used by auditors, and the validity of the conclusions drawn therefore depends upon rigid adherence to the tenets of the discipline, and thus upon the technical grasp by all members of the audit team of the statistical principles involved.

4. Many of the decisions which have to be reached before a sampling scheme can be implemented are invariably based upon subjective views. Many auditors are therefore suspicious of the validity of the technique or, in the last analysis, of how a court of law might view audit conclusions arrived at in this way.

5.3 Conditions prerequisite to the use of statistical sampling

Having outlined the background to some of the scepticism concerning statistical sampling, let us consider some of the factors which must be present before its use should be contemplated:

1. The population, field or universe (i.e. the total number of items potentially subject to scrutiny within a defined area) must be sufficiently large. Statistics is the law of large numbers and is concerned with random behaviour patterns (entropy) within those numbers. Although the mathematical laws of probability on which statistical sampling is based would still apply, the potential margin of error in the conclusions drawn would, in the case of a small population, be too great to justify the use of the method. It is impossible to state in general terms what the minimum size of the population should be: this is a question which can only be answered in a particular context.

2. The system that produces the records to be tested must be sufficiently reliable. Although, once again, this level of reliability cannot be quantified objectively it should be clear that if there is no system worthy of the name, it will be dangerous for the auditor to believe that any transaction recorded within it is representative of anything but itself. The very word 'system' suggests a certain level of orderliness and regularity, and where this is absent (a situation not unfamiliar to auditors of smaller business entities) there may be little alternative but to conduct what is known as a 'vouching audit', involving the detailed examination of a high proportion of all recorded entries.

3. All items within a particular population must be homogeneous, i.e. they must fall within the same 'category'. In practice, for audit purposes, the category would be defined within the following two parameters:

    (a) Items must fall within the same 'materiality bands', thus ensuring that the significance which attaches to each is comparable. It may therefore be necessary to 'stratify' the population before it is possible to satisfy this condition, or to use 'monetary unit' sampling.

    (b) The recording of all items must be effected in the same manner and must be subject to the same internal checks and controls. If, for instance, a particular clerical task is shared between two members of staff, it would clearly be incorrect for the auditor to draw conclusions concerning the reliability of the work of one, based upon an examination of the work of the other. (He could, of course, ignore the clerical division altogether and draw conclusions as to the reliability of the work as a whole, but only if the sharing of work between the two clerks was both equal and random.)

4. Items within the population must be both identifiable and accessible. This is a purely practical requirement, but if it is not met the execution of the sampling exercise may prove to be impossible. To understand its importance one must appreciate that the validity of any sample depends upon the requirement that each

item within the population must stand an equal chance of being selected for examination. Such selection should therefore be entirely random, and for this purpose random number tables are often used. The difficulty often arises, however, that the items within the population are themselves not identifiable in a way which enables such random selection to take place. Petty cash vouchers, for example, are rarely pre-printed with a sequential numbering series and randomness will thus have to be ensured in some other way.

Even if suitably identifiable by means of unique pre-printed numbers, items within the population are sometimes found by the auditor to be inaccessible for all practical purposes. This situation could all too easily arise in the context of a computer system in which the large number of homogeneous items normally create conditions otherwise ideal for a statistical test. If, however, the auditor is not sufficiently aware of the company's processing routines he may well discover (too late) that the population in question has been reorganized for some other purpose. His examination of source documents for credit sales may be frustrated, for example, by the fact that they have been completely re-sorted for the purpose of creating marketing statistics based on the geographical location of the sales, or for the purpose of calculating the sales team's commission. It is precisely this type of eventuality which underlines, for the auditors of an (E)DP system, the need to be prepared to conduct a contemporary (as opposed to historical) audit.

5.4   The difference between statistical and other sampling methods

When deciding whether or not to use statistical sampling in a particular context, the auditor should remember that sampling is only a tool, an audit aid. The statistical tables will certainly not do this job for him, and will not in any way reduce the need for exercising judgement. In fact, the opposite is nearer the truth, since the disciplines of statistical sampling force the auditor to exercise his judgement in reaching decisions which the traditional 'guesswork' methods (ironically termed 'judgement sampling' in many quarters) simply avoid by sweeping the questions under the carpet.

The objective behind all audit testing, whether statistically or otherwise based, is to enable the auditor to reach valid conclusions as to the dispersion throughout the population of the key 'attributes' (usually errors), based upon the attributes which he discovers in the sample examined. Sampling for this purpose may therefore be conveniently divided into three aspects:

1. Determination of the sample size.

2. The process of randomly selecting the items within the population for examination.

3. Evaluation of the sample results.

The requirements of all these aspects have to be satisfactorily met if the final conclusions are to be valid.

It should be clear, even at the common sense level, that 100 per cent certainty concerning the population being tested is impossible (unless, of course, 100 per cent of items are examined – but that is not sampling).

The differences between statistical tests and other methods (which differences should be seen as the advantages of statistical sampling) therefore lie in:

1. The need for the auditor to predetermine the reliability that he requires that the sample size is representative of the population.

2. The need to predetermine this degree of certainty in the assumption that the number of errors in the sample applies proportionately to the unsampled portion of the population as well.

3. The need to define in advance exactly what constitutes an error.

4. The need to predetermine the level of errors which the auditor may regard as acceptable (or non-material) for his purposes.

5. Following from (3) and (4), the possibility that the sample evaluation may disclose an unsatisfactory result, thereby forcing upon the auditor the need to take appropriate additional action (rather than to discover some convenient, and totally subjective, reason for justifying his acceptance of the unacceptable).

6. The precision with which the result of a statistical sampling exercise may be evaluated, and applied to the whole population (rather than something like: 'Well, we are reasonably sure that everything is OK').

It is, in fact, not possible to use the tables specially designed for statistical sampling unless the criteria referred to in (1), (2) and (4) are predetermined.

5.5   Understanding the sampling criteria

Some elaboration of factors (1)–(6) above is now called for.

5.5.1   Confidence level

The 'reliability' referred to is usually termed the confidence level. Stated informally, this is the extent to which the auditor is justified in believing that this sample drawn at random reflects (within a stipulated range) the attributes of the population from which it has been taken. More precisely, in an auditing context it is the mathematical probability that the error rate in the sample will not differ from the error rate in the population by more than a stated amount ('precision' – see section 5.5.2 below). Confidence level is conveniently expressed as a percentage; thus, when we speak of a confidence level of 90 per cent we mean that there are 90 chances in 100 that the sample result will represent the true condition of the population, against 10 chances that it will not, which latter is the risk we take (once again, at a specified level of precision). Confidence level is therefore seen to be complementary to risk.

5.5.2 Precision

The degree of certainty in the assumption that the error rate in the sample applies proportionately to the population is known as the precision, precision range, precision limit or monetary precision (when related to monetary unit sampling – see section 5.9 below). It is ordinarily expressed as plus or minus a given number of percentage points within which the true error rate in the population will fall, at the particular confidence level being used. If, for example, on the basis of our audit tests, we conclude that the projected error rate in our population of, say, goods inwards notes, is 5% ±2%, we mean that the error rate in the sample examined was exactly 5%, and that the precision associated with the sample (at the specified confidence level) was ±2%. The potential error rate in the population may therefore be as low as 3%, or as high as 7%.

So we see that confidence level and precision are closely interrelated, and to cite one without the other is potentially misleading. The selection of a particular confidence level, and its associated precision, must depend upon the auditor's own assessment of the situation: in particular, he will have to bring the following two chief factors to bear on reaching his decision.

The first factor is his prior evaluation of the functioning of the system of internal control in the area under examination. It is obvious that the efficacy of control in one area, say authorization of credit sales, does not necessarily correlate with that in another area, say the checking of prices and extensions. The evaluation of each section's control strengths and weaknesses – as outlined in Chapter 3 – is thus an essential prerequisite. This evaluation will be based not only upon the most recent systems reviews but also upon the auditor's own experience, gained during previous audits of the particular client, of the extent to which the execution of day-to-day routines complies with the control procedures laid down. Many auditing firms have found that it is both convenient and valid to 'classify' the reliability of the controls operative in a particular client company by the use of what may be called a 'reliability factor'. A grading system along the following lines may be used:

Grade	Description
A	Major companies whose internal control leaves little to be desired.
B	Major companies with good internal control but certain areas in which controls do not operate effectively.
C	Major companies whose internal control system is inadequate in relation to their size and complexity.
D	Smaller companies whose controls, bearing in mind the constraints necessitated by their lack of size, are as sound as might reasonably be expected, and the auditor is involved, in varying degrees, in accounts preparation work.
E	Smaller companies in which there are virtually no controls upon which the auditor may rely.

The audit of client companies falling within grade E would clearly not fall within the scope of a system-based audit, and hence of a statistical sampling test, for reasons already given in this chapter. A vouching audit would be appropriate in such cases. Such companies may not satisfy the legal requirement for proper accounting records, and may therefore require an appropriate reference in the audit report anyway.

Where such a grading system is in force, a particular grade in the range A – E would be entered in a designated section of each client's permanent audit file, together with an explanatory memorandum on the reasons for the particular selection and the date of the last systems review and evaluation. It will be noticed, however, that the description of each grade given in the table inevitably suffers from the sort of vagueness and subjectivity which, in using statistical methods, we are attempting to get away from. Furthermore, the grade applies to the client organization as a whole, rather than to a particular area, such as wages. For these reasons some firms have taken the matter a stage further and created a useful matrix such as the following, the significance of the figures being explained in section 5.9.1 below:

Reliability (confidence) level required	Reliability factor
39 per cent	0.5
63 per cent	1.0
78 per cent	1.5
86 per cent	2.0
95 per cent	3.0
97 per cent	3.5

Once again it will be necessary for the audit files to disclose the basis for the attachment of a particular assessment grade to the section concerned, and regular reviews are clearly important. Although the use of this matrix does in some senses restrict the auditor's freedom to select from the full range of possible confidence levels, in practice it is found that this is easily outweighed by the convenience, and consequent time-saving, of using the classifications provided – as well as ensuring that well-intentioned audit personnel, untrained in the highways and byways of statistical probability, do not become ensnared in technicalities whose proper consideration lies outside their particular level of competence.

The second important factor that must be taken into consideration by the auditor is the materiality of the amounts involved. Petty cash transactions, for example, may be sufficiently material to warrant the expenditure of audit time and attention but, given that they operate according to a satisfactorily controlled imprest system, their relative lack of materiality in relation to the amounts as a whole may justify a confidence level for audit tests of as low as 63 per cent, with a wide precision range. Only if the sample results showed a level of control inferior to that previously believed (and a corresponding increase in the error rate) would the auditor be expected to alter the parameters to give a larger sample size.

In contrast to petty cash, the authorization and recording of the company's commitment to contracts involving capital expenditure may, according to the criteria established in section 5.3 above, also be amenable to statistical examination; yet their overall significance may be such as to require a confidence level of 97 per cent (or possibly 95 per cent given the likelihood of this important area being closely monitored at board level) accompanied by a narrow precision range.

A third important factor, often overlooked in auditing texts, should also be mentioned. No area of an organization acts in isolation: despite sectionalization, usually arranged for convenience or for control purposes, there is a surprising degree of interdependence, not only in the form of documentary flows, meetings or other verbal communication, but also in terms of the effect which the standard of conduct in one area has upon that in associated areas. This transmission of 'tone' is important to the auditor, in the sense that the discovery of a flagrant disregard for ordained procedure in one section should cause him to consider its possible consequences in other related sections.

To revert to our example of petty cash, which may in itself carry little significance: the auditor may discover that the imprest rarely balances; a number of IOUs and 'payments on account' are being allowed to members of staff against the rules laid down; reimbursements to staff are permitted despite the absence of supporting vouchers, and so on. He would be missing much of the point of his tests if his reaction to this situation were confined to an insistence that the oversights and omissions be remedied, and that the system be more effectively controlled in future.

Far more important from his point of view is the fact that the work of the petty cashier is nominally under the jurisdiction of the chief cashier, whose responsibility in turn extends into other areas of cash movement where the amounts involved are very much more significant. The question to which the auditor should therefore be addressing himself is: 'If this is the manifestation of so-called control in the petty cash section, what might be the effect of such evident lack of tone in related sections, under the same branch of the organization tree?'

Thus we see that the auditor's own assessment of significance, on which his sampling criteria will be based, may extend beyond the immediate confines of the population under view. There are few audit crimes greater than the planning and execution of audit tests 'in isolation'.

5.5.3 Defining an error

One of the subsidiary disciplines implicit in statistical sampling is that which compels the auditor to define in advance what constitutes an error, and for this purpose a distinction must be drawn between:

1. A departure from an internal control procedure which the auditor considers essential to the particular confidence level selected, such departure possibly having material consequences; and
2. A clerical error which affects the amount of any item in the client's annual accounts.

The first type of error is more serious from the auditor's point of view since, unlike those in type (2), its implications for the correctness of the accounts under audit are not immediately quantifiable. It is therefore important for the auditor to evaluate the effect of the non-compliance errors, which may require an adjustment of the confidence level selected (or of the reliability factor in the case of the matrix shown on page 154, before evaluating the clerical errors.

Since the materiality of clerical errors discovered is the auditor's chief concern, it is usually possible to 'build in' a weighting system whereby the £1 unit is regarded as a unit of population. When using this technique, sometimes known as cumulative monetary sampling (or monetary unit sampling – see section 5.9), the auditor adds the monetary amounts in the population progressively and makes his sample selection in monetary intervals. The effect of this method is to give the larger items within a population a proportionately greater chance of selection than the smaller items. It should be stressed that this is not always either possible or appropriate, and should not be thought of as a substitute for stratification (dealt with below) whereby the auditor should ensure that all items within the stratum (or sub-population) are homogeneous in terms of materiality.

It is not always practicable to use monetary sampling since certain accounting populations, such as despatch notes, or goods received notes, do not contain monetary amounts. In these cases the sample must be based upon the number of items in the population, and the sample can only be evaluated statistically in terms of the number of errors. This is known as numerical sampling.

5.5.4   Determining the acceptable level of error

Wherever human agency applies, some degree of error is inevitable; the question is, what level of error is acceptable? The answer will, in practice, take into account the following:

1. The auditor's own prior assessment and evaluation of the system of internal control, with or without the use of classification grades referred to above.

2. The auditor's previous experience of the quality of work and effectiveness of supervision in the department whose records are under scrutiny, and the adequacy of the training provided for new staff who have joined since the previous review.

3. The quality of overall control, as reflected in the organization chart, which is exerted outside the immediate area under review.

4. The materiality of the items within the population (and, indeed, the population as a whole) in relation to the accounts being audited.

Note that if the auditor should conclude from items 1–3 that the expected error rate is likely to exceed what is acceptable, i.e. that the system is inherently defective, it is unlikely that a statistical sampling scheme will yield any useful result. In such circumstances the sample size (for obvious reasons) would have to be particularly large, and would probably achieve no more than to confirm the unsatisfactory state of affairs. The auditor should rather use his own judgement in executing extended tests in the weak areas, obtaining as much co-operation as possible from the client in discovering and correcting errors, until he reaches his conclusion as to whether reliable accounts could in fact be extracted from the suspect area. In such cases, having to qualify his report on the accounts becomes a likely prospect.

5.5.5 Action following evaluation

The results of the sampling exercise must be evaluated in relation to the level of errors that the auditor was prepared to regard as acceptable, all relevant factors having been taken into account. Once successfully completed, therefore, the exercise provides the auditor with the information which he originally sought: a mathematical estimate, clearly expressed, of the likely condition of the population under review based upon the sample examined. The question then arises: what do we do about it?

If it is clear that the actual error rate is not significant, in terms of (1) the pattern of error it reveals, (2) the number of errors, and (3) the amounts involved, the auditor may regard the test as having been successfully completed. He should, of course, ensure that his audit files show full details of tests carried out and express the conclusions reached.

If, on the other hand, the error rate was unacceptable, thereby indicating that his original view of the quality of internal control – and hence of the confidence level and precision selected – was unduly optimistic, the auditor has four possible courses of action:

1. Enlarge the sample to a size which is compatible with the revised confidence level and precision range determined as a consequence of the earlier findings. This will also establish that the original test did not give rise to a 'freak' result.

2. Apply alternative auditing procedures in appropriate cases. If, for instance, the test related to the verification of debtor balances, the auditor may wish to carry out a more detailed review of sales recording and control procedures without further delay.

3. Request the client to follow up the sample test by:
   (a) scrutinizing the population for errors of the type discovered;
   (b) correcting them; and
   (c) ensuring that their cause, so far as possible, is eliminated.

4. The ultimate recourse – qualify the audit report on the accounts. This is an extreme measure and would only be appropriate after exhausting the possibilities of the other three. In certain cases, however, it may be unavoidable.

Before taking any action on the results of a sample test the auditor should double-check his original assumptions and calculations to discover whether his conclusions are based upon a false premise, or whether they suffer from any logical or mathematical defect arising at the stages of planning, execution or evaluation.

It need hardly be pointed out that there is a fifth option which, tempting though it may be, is totally unacceptable: to 'reconsider' the question of what is acceptable, and 'conclude' that the actual error rate discovered in the sample is acceptable after all.

5.5.6 Expressing the sample result

It is important that the conclusions based on an evaluated sample test, as well as a detailed description of the work which preceded and led to that conclusion, should be unequivocally stated in the current audit file. The following is an example of a correctly stated conclusion:

> The error rate in the matching of despatch notes with copy invoices is 3 per cent ±1 per cent, at a confidence level of 80 per cent.

This could, of course, be expressed more simply and equally correctly in laymen's terms. If we assume that the population was approximately 50,000 we could have said:

> We are four-fifths certain that out of the 50,000 copy sales invoices under examination, the number which are either unmatched or incorrectly matched with despatch notes is between 1,000 and 2,000.

This degree of precision in expressing conclusions is not possible with any form of audit testing other than statistical sampling. The form of expression must be adapted to the type of sampling used. For example, in sampling for variables (sometimes referred to as estimation sampling and described in section 5.6 below) in the course of verifying the value of inventories, we might conclude:

> The total value of the population (inventory) is £4,520,000 ± £240,000, at a confidence level of 90%.

Which expression, once again, may be simply restated thus:

> We are nine-tenths certain that the true value of the inventory lies between £4,280,000 and £4,760,000.

(It should be clear that the auditor is precluded from complaining subsequently that the full (±) precision range of £480,000 is too material: he, after all, selected the precision in the first place.)

5.6 Other forms of statistical sampling

Our chief concern so far has been with what is usually called attributes sampling, since so much of audit work is designed to highlight a particular attribute: errors. There are, however, other techniques that auditors may find useful in certain circumstances.

5.6.1 Stop-or-go sampling

This plan prevents over-sampling by conducting a progressive evaluation of test findings, by means of specially designed stop-or-go tables. These tables provide a ready means of determining the risk involved in accepting the results of reduced sample sizes.

5.6.2 Sampling for variables

This technique is often referred to as estimation sampling or survey sampling, and is used for answering the question 'how much?' It is therefore ideal for verification purposes when the population contains variable values expressed in the form of the monetary unit. It might, for example, be used to ascertain the estimated sterling value of an entire inventory from a sample taken therefrom. Special tables are available for this purpose.

5.6.3 Discovery sampling

Sometimes referred to as exploratory sampling, this technique is used in situations where evidence of a single error or irregularity would call for intensive investigation or other action. It would be useful where, for instance, the audit objectives included the discovery of fraud, serious evasion of control procedures, the deliberate circumvention of authority, or other critical departure. The special tables needed for discovery sampling will indicate the probability of finding at least one occurrence of the specific attribute sought in a sample of designated size, taken from a population having a specified occurrence rate.

5.7 Techniques for selecting the sample

It has already been pointed out that a valid statistical exercise demands that all items within a population must have an equal chance of being selected for examination, and for this reason random number tables are used wherever possible, which eliminates the entry of personal bias in the selection process. As an example of unwitting bias, if students in a classroom are asked to think of a number 'from 1 to 10', very few – and certainly far fewer than 20 per cent – will select either one or 10 (although 1 and 10 together make up 20 per cent of the total available numbers in the choice). One can only conclude that, unconsciously, most members of the class are biased against the numbers at the extremes of a numbered population.

The use of random number tables may in practice be unduly time-consuming, and some firms have found that one or other of the following selection techniques are more appropriate in the circumstances obtaining.

5.7.1 Interval (or systematic) sampling

In using interval sampling, items are selected from the population in such a way that there is a uniform interval between them. The population size is divided by the sample size to arrive at the fixed interval (n), and our first selection would be made by drawing an item at random from the range between the first item in the population and the nth item, inclusive. We add n to the number of the item selected to arrive at the next item, and so on.

Let us imagine, for example, that we are sampling from a file of 10,000 serially numbered goods inwards notes, and that our statistical tables indicate a sample size which works out at 1 per cent of the population (i.e. 100 goods inwards notes). Our fixed interval n will be $10,000 \div 100$, which is 100. We can select a random starting point by taking out a £5 note and observing the last two digits of its unique number, say, 36. (The first two digits will not do since this would preclude the chance of numbers 1 to 9 being selected, whereas the penultimate digit may well have been a zero.) Our first selection is thus goods inwards note number 36. The next selection is number $36 + n = 136$, then number $136 + n = 236$, and so on.

Systematic sampling eliminates bias by using a random start. This random start not only eliminates bias from our selection of the first item, but also from our selection of all subsequent items. There are, however, two dangers in its use:

1. The method of selecting the random start must itself be free of bias. If, for example, the numbering system on £5 notes were not purely sequential, the positioning of digits having some other significance, this might give rise, in turn, to a bias in favour of certain digits in a particular position. In case of doubt it may be preferable to use another method to arrive at the first selection, such as looking at the second hand of your watch (assuming that n is not greater than 60), or using the first number on a page of random number tables.

2. The items in the population may themselves not be arranged in a random manner, the fixed interval method therefore creating an inadvertent bias. Suppose, for example, that a company employs several team of employees, each team having a foreman and nine others; and that on the payroll the foreman's name always appears first. If our payroll sampling interval n turned out to be 10, our sample will contain the payroll records of either foremen or men – but there is no possibility of it containing both, and herein lies the bias.

5.7.2 Stratified sampling

Stratified sampling involves the division of the population into layers or strata, each stratum being subject to a separate test which could be conducted by random or interval sampling methods. This technique is appropriate where the population consists of a wide range of values among the items under examination. Under such circumstances the entire population would be split into a number of layers, each covering a specific range of values or prices, and each layer would then be subject to a separate test. The relative materiality of each stratum would determine the confidence level and precision range required. It may even be necessary for the top stratum to be examined in its entirety.

The debtors ledger, for example, will usually contain a large proportion of balances each of which is relatively small in amount, and a correspondingly small proportion of 'high value' accounts; the remaining accounts could also be arranged as a pyramid. In such circumstances it is clear that it would be incorrect for the auditor to treat all debtors as part of the same population for sampling purposes. Let us consider a situation in which the auditor wishes to carry out a selected circularization of debtors, requesting them to reply *only* if they disagree with the details shown (known, incidentally, as a negative circularization, and used only in conjunction with other tests in the context of a strong internal control system):

| Total number of accounts | 1,130 |
| Total value of ledger | £566,501 |

Analysis of account balances:

	Number	Value (£)
Over £5,000	14	192,612
£2,501–£5,000	28	88,002
£1,001–£2,500	43	60,892
£501–£1,000	262	199,382
£0–£500	783	25,613
	1,130	£566,501

This population may be stratified so that all debtors whose balances exceed £2,500, and a random sample of the remainder, are circularized. By this means, 50 per cent of debtors *by value* are verified through 42 circularization letters. The remaining 1,088 balances can be sampled by reference to the tables of attributes sampling, predeterming the following criteria:

Anticipated error rate 3 per cent
Precision limit ± 3 per cent
Confidence level 90 per cent

We are therefore prepared to accept that up to 6 per cent of the circulars in our lower stratum will be returned to us, indicating that the account balance is in dispute.

Reference to our tables shows that a sample size of 81 accounts (out of the population of 1,088) will have to be circularized to satisfy the above requirements. This represents a sample of (approximately) 1 in 14. Systematic sampling could be used for selection in these circumstances. By reference to, say, random number tables, a starting point between 1 and 14 would be fixed. The 81 balances would then be selected from the schedule of debtors by taking the balance corresponding with the random starting point, and every fourteenth balance thereafter. If any balance coincides with one already selected (in the 100 per cent check of balances over £2,500) the next following balance would be taken in its place.

5.7.3 Cluster sampling

Cluster sampling is suitable when data to be examined are stored in such a manner that the selection of a group, or cluster, would be an appropriate test, e.g. in filing cabinet drawers. In these circumstances each drawer could be allocated a number, the particular drawer to be tested being selected by the use of random tables. The contents of the drawer selected could in turn be tested completely, or by random number, or by interval sampling. The most precise results with this method will be obtained when:

1. Each cluster contains as varied a mixture as possible; and

2. Any one cluster is as nearly alike any other cluster as possible.

Cluster sampling is helpful when the population is so dispersed as to make other forms of selection either burdensome or excessively time-consuming.

5.7.4 Selection with the aid of a computer

The auditor may use a computer to render considerable assistance in the performance of statistical sampling tests, employing the following methods:

1. *Interval sampling.* The computer is programmed to select every nth item stored on a computer file, and the items so selected can be copied onto a separate computer file and printed out in the form required by the auditor.

2. *Random number selection.* The technique of random number selection can be computerized, the random numbers being generated by the computer separately for each application.

3. *Random interval selection.* The dangers of selecting a biased sample by the use of a uniform interval can be avoided by the use of random variation of the interval between successive items. Random intervals are selected from random number tables, or produced by means of a random number generator program.

5.8 Summary of practical steps (attributes sampling)

In practice, the following steps would have to be taken in order to test a population of entries, vouchers, etc. for errors:

1. The population category and the population unit should be clearly defined. All units within the population must be of the same type (e.g. cheques returned from the bank), and the population must be complete. It is clear that audit conclusions will only be derived from items present – hence the importance of ensuring that there are no missing items at the time of the test. Where there have been material changes in the system operated during the period under review, separate populations exist on either side of the date of change, and separate tests must therefore be devised and executed.

2. The approximate population size must be determined. This is simplified if all documents within the population are pre-numbered, but in other circumstances it may be difficult to estimate, in which event the largest estimate should be adopted. Many students are surprised at the minimal effect which the population size has on sample size, by comparison with the very great effect on sample size of altering the confidence level or the precision limits. At the same time it should be clear that once we have randomly tested a population (in which the attribute sought is equally

randomly dispersed) with a sample size of, say, 100 items, the examination of further and equally typical items will hardly produce a very different picture. In other words, once one samples beyond a certain optimum level (i.e. the size indicated in the tables, in practical terms) one's audit efforts are subject to rapidly diminishing returns, almost regardless of population size.

3. Examine the way in which the population is constituted and consider whether stratification is necessary. This step will be taken where the population is made up of items of varying materiality, or otherwise giving rise to different confidence levels. It is then suitably stratified and separate sampling tests are carried out on each stratum.

4. Define an 'error' so that there is no confusion once testing has begun. The anticipated error rate in the population should then be estimated.

5. The precision limits and the level of confidence required for the particular population being sampled should be determined. The 'plus' part of the precision range is added to the anticipated error rate to arrive at the maximum error rate which the auditor is prepared to accept.

6. Refer the data thus determined to the tables in order to discover the appropriate sample size, and a random selection method should then be used for drawing the individual items in the sample.

7. The test should now be evaluated comparing the number of errors discovered in the sample with the predetermined level regarded as acceptable, in order to discover whether or not the result is satisfactory from the audit viewpoint. If the result is unsatisfactory the next course of action must be positively decided. This will normally involve extended audit work, e.g. to ensure the sample result was not a freak, and to assess the effect of the errors and weaknesses on the accounts as a whole.

8. Ensure that the final expression of the conclusion of the test is valid, and that the details of the sampling tests (criteria adopted, numbers selected, description of errors found, etc.) as well as the conclusion, are clearly documented in the current audit file.

5.9 Monetary sampling in practice

Section 5.5 above features a table that translates the required level of confidence into a reliability factor, which in turn is used for determining the appropriate sample size. A little more elaboration of this method may prove useful. In essence, the sampling plan covers two types of sampling:

1. Monetary sampling (sometimes known as monetary unit sampling, MUS) – to be used when the auditor wishes to obtain conclusions expressed in monetary terms.

2. Numerical sampling – for use when the auditor wishes to obtain conclusions about the incidence of specified occurrences (e.g. mispostings, unauthorized despatches, etc).

In its instructions issued to audit staff, the firm stresses the importance of deciding the purpose of each test prior to its execution so that the most suitable population can be selected. For example, if a sample is to be selected from a list of debtors, the conclusions reached cannot be said validly to apply to any debtor balance omitted from that list. The list must therefore first be tested for completeness, which in turn entails the examination of an independent but related (or reciprocal) population. In this example, a possible approach would be to undertake tests which compare sales records with detailed ledger entries, in order to detect sales to customers which for one reason or another might have been omitted from the ledger balance. This testing of reciprocal populations, in order to establish completeness, is known as 'directional' testing.

We have already seen in this chapter that statistical assurance is a combination of reliability (i.e. confidence) and precision, and that these two factors are inseparably interrelated. If, when testing for understatement of sales, a sample of despatch notes is examined, the sample evaluation might indicate 95 per cent reliability that not more than 1 per cent of the despatch notes have been incorrectiy matched with sales documentation. If a precision narrower than 1 per cent is required, but without an increase in the sample size, a lower level of reliability would have to be accepted. Thus, the same sample size might achieve only 78 per cent reliability at a precision level of 2 per cent. Conversely, the same sample might give us 99 per cent reliability at a potential error rate of 12 per cent. Thus we see that it is totally misleading to cite the precision of a sample without, at the same time, citing the reliability level. In this example the potential error rate is the same as the upper precision limit.

5.9.1 Monetary unit sampling

The aim of the monetary sampling plan is to enable the auditor to achieve a measurable level of precision and reliability for the financial statements as a whole by predetermining the monetary precision (MP) required in forming an opinion on the financial statements, and then using this MP in sampling all audit areas. This has the advantage of causing the volume of audit tests to vary according to the monetary totals (and hence materiality) of each area. The MP is based on the auditor's judgement *of the maximum amount of monetary error considered to be not material in relation to the financial statements as a whole*, and it therefore becomes the threshold of 'high value' items which, because of their inherent individual materiality, must be examined and tested by the auditor on an individual basis.

To assist the appreciation of the concepts involved the table first shown in section 5.5 above is reproduced here as Table 5.1.

In practice, once MP and reliability (R) factors have been determined, the sampling interval is arrived at by the fraction MP/R-factor. If the population is then divided by the sampling interval, the sample size results. For example, let us suppose that the maximum monetary error which the auditor is prepared to accept may be £3,000 out of a total population of £100,000, and a confidence level of 95 per cent is required. Reference to the table above shows that the latter level of confidence indicates an R-factor of 3.0. Thus, £3,000/3.0 gives the sampling interval of £1,000. By dividing the

Table 5.1 Relationship between confidence levels and reliability factors

Required confidence level	R-factor
39%	0.5
63%	1.0
78%	1.5
86%	2.0
95%	3.0
97%	3.5

population of £100,000 by the sampling interval of £1,000 we arrive at the appropriate sample size of 100.

The *R-factor* is simply the *negative natural log* of the risk percentage associated with each of the six confidence levels used in the table. This facilitates calculation, without which hypergeometric progression would be needed in order to determine sample sizes. The MUS system is thus to be commended for its simplicity (while not in any way compromising the underlying precepts of probability theory, from which the validity of all sampling schemes is derived), and hence the ease with which, in appropriate circumstances, it may be applied.

This simplicity and ease of application are due to the ready translation of confidence levels into reliability factors. In the use of the table only six discrete confidence levels (from 39 per cent through to 97 per cent) are available, but this limitation hardly matters, especially since in practice the auditor will ensure that any rounding-up to the nearest confidence level will increase, rather than decrease, the sample size. The use of this method similarly obviates the need to refer to voluminous pages of statistical tables.

5.10 Risk-based auditing

Risk-based auditing is an application of MUS which is designed to avoid over-auditing in low risk areas and under-auditing in high risk areas, and is an approach now considered vital by many auditors.

What are the risks we are talking about? Audit risk is the possibility that financial statements contain material misstatements which escape detection both by the management controls (i.e. internal controls) on which the auditor relies, and by the auditor's own substantive tests of transactions and balances.

We have already seen in Chapter 3 the importance of judging the audit risk of an assignment and designing procedures to ensure it is reduced to an acceptably low level. Statement of Auditing Standard no. 300 – 'Accounting and internal control systems and audit risk assessments' is summarized in that chapter.

Audit risk is the risk that auditors may give an inappropriate opinion on the financial statements and has three components:

1. Inherent risk – the susceptibility of an account balance or class of transactions to material misstatement either individually or when aggregated with misstatements in other balances or classes, irrespective of related internal controls over the accounting system.

2. Control risk – the risk that material misstatement could occur in an account balance or class of transactions, either individually or when aggregated with misstatements in other balances or classes, and not be prevented, or detected and corrected, on a timely basis by the accounting and internal control systems.

3. Detection risk – the risk that the auditors' substantive procedures do not detect a material misstatement in the financial records.

A common approach to risk evaluation is to consider:

1. The adequacy of the client's accounting records and the control systems which ensure their accuracy and reliability.

2. The relevance of accumulated prior knowledge and reliability of evidence from past audit assignments.

As a guide, the following questions should be considered when assessing the overall level of risk that a material misstatement arising in the financial statements will not be detected:

▶ Do we have detailed prior knowledge of the client and his business?

▶ Are sufficient staff employed within the accounting function to achieve adequate separation of duties?

▶ Have client's management proved to be responsible, reliable and truthful in the past?

▶ Have previous analytical review tests supported the audit evidence obtained from other sources?

▶ Are the auditors also significantly involved in the preparation of accounting records and/or financial statements?

▶ Are shares held by parties not involved in the management of the business?

▶ Is there a going concern problem?

▶ Is there a prospect of the sale of all or part of the business?

▶ Have there been new branches or acquisitions or a change in the trading pattern?

▶ Have there been significant changes in the accounting systems?

A review of the above criteria will facilitate the formulation of an initial assessment of the level of risk into suitable categories such as:

1. *Negligible risk:* i.e. where there is only a remote possibility of the accounting records and financial statements containing material errors.

2. *Low risk.*

3. *Medium risk*: this risk evaluation factor might be appropriate when the nature of the company's activities and the systems of internal control generally present a low audit risk but there are identifiable areas which are more risky. For example, a company may have a large value of cash sales which by their nature are more susceptible to misstatement whether through innocent error or fraud.

   Another example is of a freight forwarding company which may be subject to claims from its clients for damage to property or for not fulfilling delivery times. The validity and value of claims made and whether a provision is required in the accounts is clearly subjective and as such increases the risk that the view given by the accounts will be distorted. In this case an overall risk assessment of 'medium risk' might be appropriate.

4. *High risk.*

The importance of evaluating the accounting systems and controls operating in individual functions of the business (e.g. purchases, sales) has already been discussed in Chapter 3. This is achieved through the completion of internal control questionnaires (ICQs) and internal control evaluation (ICE) forms. The evaluation of each function will enable an assessment of risk levels to be made in each case. The risk levels may vary between functions: for example, the controls over the completeness and accuracy of the recording of sales may be sound but the company may have a history of poor credit control and consequently bad debts, in which case the question of the value and recoverability of recorded debtors would attract a higher risk evaluation. Another example might be where the company undertakes a detailed, well-planned stock-take at the year-end except that the cut-off procedures have not been vigorously applied. The doubt over whether sales and purchases of stock are matched with the related stock movements in the same accounting periods means there is a greater risk that an error could occur, and therefore this area of the company's activities will be assigned a higher risk level at the planning stage.

Low-risk areas are those that require the application of routine 'nuts and bolts' audit procedures in the ordinary course of vouching, casting, checking, etc., at both compliance and substantive stages. *High-risk areas* are those which should be the primary concern of partners and senior managers, and will include such matters as:

► Adequacy of provisions.

► Full disclosure of liabilities, including contingent liabilities.

► Interpretation of SSAPs and FRSs and new companies legislation.

► Post-balance sheet review of subsequent events.

► Analytical reviews on draft financial statements.

► Implications of tax legislation.

► Detecting overstatement of assets, e.g. by capitalizing expenditure.

► Identifying high value items and 'error-prone' conditions.

► Drafting the audit report itself.

Full fee-recovery on an audit assignment which is completed to a high standard overall will therefore have the best chance of being achieved if routine work (low-risk) is performed efficiently, intelligently and economically by junior staff in accordance with sampling criteria which are validly related to the associated level of risk.

For this reason it is essential that all high-value items and error-prone conditions within the population to be sampled are identified as risk-prone, and individually verified or covered by a specific provision, as necessary. Sampling procedures will then be applied to the remaining items in the population.

Setting materiality limits

To meet the above objectives it is clearly essential that a materiality limit is set (referred to above as monetary precision), and this is unavoidably a matter for the audit partner's judgement, based an previous knowledge and assessment of the client's business and organizational structure.

In March 1995, the APB issued SAS no. 220, Materiality and the Audit, which provides guidance on the auditor's consideration of materiality and its relationship to audit risk. The key points covered by this SAS are as follows:

1. Materiality is a subjective issue and should be considered in the light of the possible influence on the reader of the financial statements.

2. Materiality should be assessed initially at the planning stage and reviewed during the course of the audit work. This may result in further audit work being carried out.

3. Prior to completing his report, the auditor should assess the materiality of the *total* of any uncorrected errors. This avoids the danger of a large number of immaterial errors being ignored, when, if taken together, the overall effect would be considered material.

4. In order to consider the effect of any uncorrected errors, the auditor may need to extrapolate the results of his sample tests to the population as a whole (as a result, additional checking by the client combined with additional audit tests may be necessary).

5. Materiality should be considered at both the overall financial statement level and in relation to individual account balances, classes of transactions and disclosures. Accordingly different levels of materiality may apply to different areas, depending on the auditor's perception of the risk involved.

Materiality is a relative factor, and any decision on materiality will require a 'base' to be selected, such as total revenue (in the case of companies with a turnover) or total assets (in the case of financial institutions such as banks, building societies, pension funds, investment trusts or insurance companies).

Some firms make use of a table of bases, to which a scale of materiality percentages may be applied – although it would clearly be highly dangerous to apply this mechanically, without appropriate exercise of judgement. Such a table is shown as Table 5.2.

Table 5.2 Table of bases and materiality scales

Range of chosen base (£)	Materiality limit (%)	Materiality range (£)
0 to 25,000	5.00	0 to 1,250
25,000 to 50,000	4.00	1,250 to 2000
50,000 to 100,000	3.00	2,000 to 3,000
100,000 to 500,000	2.00	3,000 to 10,000
500,000 to 2,000,000	1.50	10,000 to 30,000
2,000,000 to 5,000,000	1.00	30,000 to 50,000
5,000,000 to 10,000,000	0.75	50,000 to 75,000
Over 10,000,000	0.50	75,000 and over

Thus we see that the auditor of a company whose turnover is £200,000 may select 2 per cent, or £4,000, as the materiality limit. This means that all sales transactions in excess of £4,000 will be individually vouched as high value items. If one such high value transaction could not be vouched, the auditor would not be able to conclude that the accounts did not include a material misstatement within the parameters which he had set.

The most obvious base for trading company audits is turnover since:

1. Turnover is not usually susceptible to major inaccuracy due to error, and its amount in draft financial statements is generally reliable.
2. Turnover is a large item, against which relative materiality is easily judged.
3. The size of the turnover will have a direct relationship with the scale of the company's undertaking (e.g. number of personnel) and it is thus ideal for purposes of assessing overall materiality.

Some auditors, by contrast, believe that materiality should be related to the profit figure, since this is of such importance to users of financial statements, but this is rarely practical nor necessarily valid, for the following reasons:

1. The amount of profit is not finally known until all the accounting adjustments have been made, by which time the substantive tests have been completed.
2. The amount of profit will vary considerably from year to year, thus necessitating corresponding shifts in sample sizes despite the constancy of all other factors, such as internal control, business activity levels and turnover.
3. If the trading result is 'break-even', i.e. zero profit, the materiality reference point disappears.
4. Profit or loss is not a trading item in its own right, but purely a residual value based on an accumulation of transactions which are themselves subject to statistically determined audit tests. If those tests are valid, so then is our reliance on the resulting profit or loss balance. It is therefore preferable that materiality should be assessed in relation to a large item which, because of its size, is not susceptible to the vagaries of

smaller items. Turnover or gross assets are ideal for this purpose, and are normally adopted as the base figure for determining materiality. The profit figure is, of course, a valid reference point for considering materiality in relation to the disclosures required in published financial statements, and the drafting of the audit report itself.

MUS in practice

Since the aim of all sampling routines is to draw valid conclusions concerning a population from the attributes observed in the sample, it is important to eliminate from the population to be tested those items which are known to require individual attention, either because of their materiality (size) or because they possess significant features which otherwise distinguish them. (Amounts due from a debtor company known to be in financial difficulty would be an example of this.)

We could express this principle by saying that routine sampling procedures should be applied to the population under scrutiny only after all (1) high-value and (2) 'error-prone' items have been eliminated for individual examination, and (3) 'directional' tests have confirmed that these reciprocal populations are complete. In view of (1), it is necessary to set materiality limits, so that high value items can be easily identified. Until this is done, we are in no position to define the general (i.e. remaining) population to be tested on a statistical, as opposed to individual, basis.

Furthermore, stratification of the remaining population to be tested is important, so that the larger items (although not individually significant) stand a proportionately greater chance of being selected for examination than the smaller items. For this purpose we could treat a population of, say, debtors as consisting not of individual accounts, but rather of £1 units. Since every £1 unit of the monetary population must stand an equal chance of being selected, an account balance of £1,000 (i.e. comprising a 'cluster' of 1,000 units of £1 each) will therefore be twice as likely to be selected for scrutiny as an account balance of £500.

How are materiality limits to be set? All standard percentage yardsticks are suspect, and hence highly dangerous if used mechanically. In some situations, a range of ±10 per cent might be acceptable; in others a difference of as low as 2 per cent might be too great. As already explained, a materiality percentage based on the profit figure in the draft accounts is clearly useless since every adjustment alters the base, and if the company breaks even the base disappears altogether.

For these reasons, most major firms apply materiality percentages to the largest available base, which is normally turnover in the case of trading concerns, and gross assets in the case of financial institutions such as banks (see Table 5.2 above). Thus, against a low base of, say, £25,000 or less, 5% will be considered material, while a base in excess of, say, £10 million will require a materiality limit of 0.5 per cent to be set. Thus a factor of 10 operates between the top and bottom of the range and partners will construct a sliding scale of percentages applicable to bases in between – the percentage falling as the value of the base rises.

The materiality limit (i.e. the threshold of high-value items) thus determined is then used for the sampling of all subordinate populations of transactions and balances in the financial statements, even though their totals are less than the original base (i.e. turnover or gross assets). Once again, it is necessary to issue a warning against mechanical use of the method, and audit partners should always give prior specific approval to the percentage applied.

Adjusting materiality

The materiality thresholds shown in a table such as Table 5.2 on p. 169 are based on the assumption that (1) internal control is sound, and (2) the auditor's analytical tests on the draft financial statements show that these are reasonable, i.e. that the figures make sense. If, however, internal control cannot be relied upon (or it is not cost-effective to perform compliance tests due to the size and/or resources of the client); or the analytical review produces a conclusion that the accounts do not seem reasonable, materiality must be adjusted downwards, thus giving a higher sample size. This may be done in accordance with Table 5.3, which assumes (for purposes of illustration) a materiality threshold of £4,000.

The following is an explanation of these adjustments. Internal control, if sound, may provide the auditor with one-third of the assurance sought; another third may be obtained from analytical review, assuming these show the draft accounts to be reasonable. The remaining third, in all cases, must be sought from substantive testing of transactions and balances.

If the auditor's desired assurance level is, say, 95 per cent, this means he is prepared to accept a 5 per cent risk that the sample is unrepresentative and hence that material error may exist and remain undetected. The three sources of assurance, if relied upon, are hence equally sources of risk, and probability mathematics requires us to multiply the *component* risk levels in order to arrive at *total* risk. If the acceptable total risk is 5 per cent, the maximum acceptable *component* risk is 37 per cent, thus:

Reliance on internal control		Reliance on analytical review		Reliance on substantive tests		Acceptable risk
↓		↓		↓		↓
0.37	×	0.37	×	0.37	=	0.05

Table 5.3 Materiality adjustments

Audit findings	Adjustment	Revised materiality (£)
Internal control } satisfactory Analytical review	£4,000 ÷ 1	4,000
Only *one* of two above satisfactory	£4,000 ÷ 2	2,000
Neither of two above satisfactory	£4,000 ÷ 3	1,333

Another way of expressing this is that exclusive reliance on, say, internal control can never provide the auditor with a greater level of assurance than 63 per cent (the complement of a risk percentage of 37 per cent). Reliance on both internal control and analytical review can, on their own, never provide a greater level of assurance than 86 per cent (the complement of a risk percentage of 14 per cent, which is in turn the result of multiplying the two component risks: 37 per cent × 37 per cent).

The adjustments in Table 5.3 are obtained by using natural (negative) logarithms. The logarithm of 37 per cent is 1. The logarithm of 14 per cent is 2. If neither internal control nor analytical review are relied upon, substantive testing alone must give us our 95 per cent assurance, and the natural negative logarithm of the complement risk (5 per cent) is 3. The numbers 2 and 3 are therefore used for adjusting materiality in order to give a larger sample size. The same result can be obtained by using hypergeometric progressions, but logarithms are far simpler. The natural negative logarithm of 0.37 (the risk associated with substantive testing when both other sources of assurance are also available) being 1, there is no adjustment to the £4,000 threshold in this situation.

Reference to the earlier table of confidence levels and R-factors (Table 5.1) shows that the R-factors are simply natural negative logarithms of the risk factors which complement the confidence levels concerned. Against 63 per cent we find 1; against 86 per cent we find 2; and against 95 per cent we find 3. The other figures are merely intermediate steps.

Similarly, it may be considered appropriate to apply a variation of the materiality factor (as calculated) for audit areas deemed to be of a more risky nature. For example, the stock valuation may be assessed as presenting a greater audit risk in general than the other areas of fixed assets, debtors, creditors, etc. In these circumstances, to provide greater audit assurance on the valuation of stocks the materiality factor could be reduced by a factor of, say, 2, for the purposes of substantive testing. Accordingly, this would result in greater audit coverage of the stock valuation to compensate for the higher risk compared with other balance sheet areas.

The impressive advantage of the MUS methods outlined here, coupled with the risk-based approach and materiality thresholds, is their abiding simplicity, while retaining integrity. They can be used for audits of all sizes.

Review questions

*1.   Risk-based auditing is utilized by auditors in the performance of their duties. The term may however be misunderstood by the general public or indeed the shareholders. What exactly is 'risk-based auditing'?

*2.   As audit manager you have been approached by a junior member of staff who has enquired how the materiality on an assignment should be determined and exactly how materiality can be related to the overall sample size.
      Prepare a concise memorandum to clarify the points raised.

3. SAS 430.3 states that 'when determining the sample size the auditor should consider sampling risk, the tolerable error and the expected error'. Outline the meaning of each of the terms and indicate some of the factors which influence the sample size.

4. Should the auditor always act upon errors found within a sample irrespective of the nature of the error? Explain your answer.

Exercises

1. You have been put in charge of the audit of a division of a large multinational chemical company and have located a systematic error which occurs during inter-divisional sales, which form a substantial part of your sample of 'sales'. Individually the errors are not material but cumulatively they are significant. Your fellow managers, who have been on the assignment before, have indicated that they usually ignore these errors because they are inter-divisional and therefore do not affect the overall trading results. What should you do?

2. It can sometimes be stated that in selecting a sample for testing, unless a precise systematic method is used, there will be unwitting bias. Assuming that you are to have an open discussion with an advocate of 'systematic sampling', justify the use of techniques other than systematic sampling.

Auditing procedures – the final accounts

THIS CHAPTER DEALS WITH:

▷ the various methods of obtaining audit evidence including analytical review;

▷ specific verification procedures for the main balance sheet headings;

▷ the use of external confirmations;

▷ letters of representation;

▷ accounting for post-balance sheet events.

This chapter is the natural follow-up to Chapter 4, in which we examined the audit procedures which may be used in determining the reliability of the company's underlying records. Our review and assessment of the published accounts which are directly based upon those records form the subject matter of this chapter. The previous chapter, on the use of statistical sampling in auditing, was therefore something of a diversion – but was placed in that position in view of the volume of *representative* checking and testing which the auditor must execute when performing substantive tests on the client's records.

As mentioned in Chapter 4, which made extended references to the use of an 'audit programme', our work on the final accounts is also within the scope of most formally drafted audit programmes. However, reference to the chronology diagram (Figure 2.1) should make it clear that most of this work must await the preparation by the client's staff of the year-end accounts and supporting schedules, whereas audit work on the records is the natural occupation of the interim audit. It is possible during our interim audit to carry out certain routine work on the verification of, say, stocks and debtors – for example, to observe a test count of stores within the context of a system of continuous stocktaking – and although this will assist the auditor to form an opinion on the reliability of the system (and hence the accuracy of the stock records), there will always remain certain key procedures which must await the closing stages of the audit.

6.1 The bridge from records to final accounts

Before commencing to analyse these procedures in detail we should not overlook the 'bridge' stage of the audit, which represents the *transition* from the basic records to the published profit and loss account, balance sheet, cash flow statement, directors' report, and all their supporting notes. (This stage is represented in Figure 2.1, in our 'total view', by the contents of the column headed 'stage VI'.)

Since the preparation of these accounts for publication (i.e. on file at Companies House) and distribution to members is the statutory responsibility of the company's directors, it is usual for them also to prepare the supporting schedules which summarize the contents of the accounts, and to relate the summaries to the detailed records from which the information has been drawn. If this has been done, the auditor should check and enter the detailed cross-references and retain a copy on his own current file. If, however, the client has not prepared the supporting documentation to the auditor's satisfaction (it being incomplete, incorrect, or insufficiently detailed) he will have no alternative but to prepare his own schedules for this purpose. The *Companies Act* recognizes the importance of this stage; section 237 of the 1985 Act specifically requires the auditor to qualify his report if, in his opinion, the accounts issued to members are not in agreement with the records.

This process of checking accounts back to records is straightforward in practice. The profit and loss account schedules will simply summarize the make-up of each item in the published profit and loss account and its related 'notes to the accounts' and, in view of the considerable degree of 'grouping' whereby many expense headings are shown under global subheadings, subsidiary and sub-subsidiary, etc., schedules may well be needed. Finally, however, the auditor's schedules as a whole will prove that the global amounts in the published accounts are traceable back to the individual accounts in the company's nominal ledger.

So far as the balance sheet is concerned, there should be one schedule for each item it contains. The schedule will invariably commence with the figure which appeared for the item in question in the audited balance sheet of the *previous* year, and will end with its counterpart in *this* year's balance sheet. The two amounts are, of course, reconciled by means of detailed cross-references back to the underlying ledger accounts.

6.2 Formal and informal aspects of the final review

The audit work at this crucial stage has a direct bearing upon the content, with or without qualification, of the auditor's report to the members, and makes demands upon the auditor's skill, experience and judgement which are, in some ways, considerably heavier than at any prior stage of the audit. The nature of much of this work has in fact already been summarized in the diagrams shown in Figure 2.1 (stage VII), but it is now necessary to consider it in detail.

As clearly shown in Figure 2.2, the review of the final accounts may be seen to comprise two aspects which we may conveniently label 'formal' and 'informal' respectively. The formal aspect is largely concerned with the disclosure requirements which govern the presentation of the final accounts, and their formality lies in the fact that they are *externally* determined by:

1. The *Companies Act 1985*.
2. Statements of Standard Accounting Practice (SSAPs) and Financial Reporting Standards (FRSs).
3. Stock Exchange requirements for listed companies.
4. Requirements of other statutes and regulations, e.g. building societies, friendly societies, solicitors, investment businesses, pension funds, charities, etc.
5. Requirements of Securities and Exchange Commission (SEC) for UK subsidiaries of American parent companies.

The auditor's work in each case is, quite simply, to ensure compliance.

The 'informal' aspect, by contrast, relies heavily upon the auditor's own intuitive skills in appraising a set of final accounts after all underlying records have been set aside. In forming his audit opinion for reporting purposes, i.e. whether the accounts present a true and fair view, the results of both the formal and informal procedures must be carefully considered. Although it is possible to attempt to 'formalize' the informal through the usual media of programmes, checklists and other documentation (and, indeed, advisable to do so up to a point) none of these rigid frameworks can ever substitute for the sixth sense which the skilled auditor gains from many years of experience in analysing the accounts of a wide variety of business concerns. In this chapter we can therefore do no more than consider the ideal audit approach to the informal aspects of the final review.

6.3 Verification of assets and liabilities

We saw in Chapter 4 that there is a clear distinction between vouching and verification; the verification procedures in relation to the contents of the published accounts will rely heavily upon the vouching work having been properly executed – either in the current year's audit programme (in the case of assets and liabilities recently acquired), or in earlier years (assets and liabilities in existence at the commencement of the current period). This previously executed vouching work will have ensured that:

1. The original transactions were accurately recorded, distinguishing between expenditure of a capital and revenue nature respectively.
2. The transactions were properly authorized at the appropriate level in accordance with the company's stipulated regulations.

6.3.1 Audit evidence – specific verification objectives

The auditor's concern at the final review stage, therefore, is to complete the verification process. The APB has issued a Standard on 'Audit Evidence' (SAS 400) which provides guidance on the quality and reliability of evidence to be obtained by auditors, and the procedures for obtaining that evidence. Its key points may be summarized as follows:

1. The SAS gives guidance on what is meant by sufficient and appropriate audit evidence. This is, however, a matter for the auditors' judgement.

2. Auditors should consider obtaining audit evidence from different sources to support the same assertion. The obvious example of this is third party confirmations, e.g. bankers' confirmations or debtor circularizations.

3. The SAS refers to sampling as a technique for obtaining audit evidence (refer to SAS 430).

4. Audit evidence can be obtained by:
   (a) inspection (e.g. invoices and other documentary evidence),
   (b) observation (e.g. of stock-taking procedures),
   (c) enquiry and confirmation (e.g. current developments borne out by post-balance sheet tests),
   (d) computation (e.g. tax liabilities),
   (e) analytical procedures (refer to SAS 410).

   Each of these procedures is considered in the SAS.

   For each procedure the auditor should document the extent of his audit work in his working papers, which should also summarize the results and conclusions.

5. In practice, the use of audit stamps is commonly employed when inspecting accounting records and source documents to leave visible evidence of inspection, and also to prevent the risk of the same document being vouched for more than one transaction.

A few points of practical application of the above Standard arise as follows:

1. Examining statutory books, registers and minutes

One valuable but underrated source of information produced by the entity is the statutory books which are not part of the accounting records, but are examined at the same time and are sometimes seen as being of little relevance by auditors.

However, there are reasons why auditors will normally need to concern themselves with the statutory books, and a few examples may help to illustrate this.

Although there is no requirement to audit the directors' report and it does not fall within the pages referred to in the audit report there is certainly a professional duty to check that it is factually reliable, particularly when, as is the case with the majority of small companies, the auditor prepares the draft on the directors' behalf.

The note stating the identity of the company's ultimate parent undertaking, if applicable, may need to be checked against the statutory registers, and details of transactions involving changes in the company's issued share capital should be corroborated by reference to the share register.

It should be remembered that directors' and shareholders' minute books form an important part of the statutory books, and reference to these is usually essential – for example, to identify any contracts in which directors have a material (and hence disclosable) interest to confirm the shareholders' approval of dividend proposals.

2. Verifying title to investments

Another example is where an audit client holds substantial investments in Securities. The company uses the services of a broker to manage the portfolio and to hold the share certificates and other documents of title. The broker supplies regular reports indicating the securities held in the name of their mutual client. The auditor may wonder whether it would be insufficient to rely on the reports of the broker as evidence of existence and ownership.

In the specific context in question, there is unlikely to be any problem because we may assume that the broker is itself subject to regulation, including monitoring and compliance visits, with special reference to the custodianship of clients' documents of title, their periodic reconciliation with the client assets register and written certification to that effect. It is recommended that the auditor makes contact with the broker requesting direct confirmation of the custody of title certificates for the named securities and of their valuation at the reporting date.

The more specific verification objectives may be summarized as follows:

Valuation

The auditor must be satisfied that assets appear in the balance sheet at a fair value which may, of course, be rather different from their original cost. (He is also concerned that liabilities are fairly 'valued', i.e. stated at the amount at which they are likely to materialize for settlement.) It is therefore important, in relation to assets, for the auditor to ensure that, apart from the correct determination of cost, depreciation or any other fall in value due to, say, obsolescence, has been fully taken into account on an acceptable basis, consistent with that adopted in previous years. In the case of assets other than fixed assets, such as investments, or stock of goods, any fall in value must also be taken into account, (1) if it is material, and (2) if it is regarded as permanent.

Existence

The auditor should rely upon physical verification procedures wherever practicable and appropriate. This is specially relevant in cases where the physical assets may be directly compared by the auditor with the company's own records (see Table 6.1) for example.

Such physical tests should be carried out on a carefully planned random selection basis (which may, if appropriate, be part of a statistical sampling scheme) and a record

Table 6.1 Physical verification procedures

Asset	Record to be compared
Cash balances	Petty cash books, vouchers, etc.
Stocks of raw materials, finished goods and work in progress	Stores records, bin cards, work in progress schedules, costing schedules
Investments	Investments ledger
Vehicles, plant and machinery	Vehicle registers, plant registers

retained, describing the nature, extent and findings of each test executed. It is an obvious, but nonetheless often overlooked, fact that a great deal of information can be derived from physical observation by the auditor or his agents. A factory building included in the accounts on the basis 'that it is substantially complete' can be seen to be so (or not so) at an audit inspection arranged for the purpose.

Ownership

Existence is one thing, ownership quite another. It is impossible to lay down hard and fast rules on methods of establishing that the client is in fact the beneficial owner of the assets concerned (or that the liabilities concerned are in fact required to be met by the client), since much depends upon the circumstances prevailing. In simple cases it will be possible to verify ownership by reference to a document, such as deeds or leases in relation to property, but in other cases it may be necessary to rely upon corroborative evidence or the representations of outside parties.

If the use of the asset in question gives rise to either a *benefit* or an *expense* (or both), the vouching of the benefit/expense will probably provide sufficient corroborative evidence of both the ownership and the existence of the underlying asset in cases where it is impracticable to verify these features directly. For example, a hotel owned abroad should produce a verifiable income, regularly remitted, as well as identifiable outgoings on maintenance, repairs and general upkeep. From a close examination of those items the auditor might reasonably infer (1) that the hotel exists, and (2) that it is beneficially owned by the client company.

Circumspection is still needed, however, as many major frauds have depended not only upon the creation of fictitious documentation, but also upon the contrived appearance of income and expenditure. (The *McKesson and Robins* (1938) and *Equity Funding* (1973) cases are but two US classics in this particular genre.) On occasion, therefore, the auditor may well believe that there is no substitute for direct audit work to be carried out in the location in question, in which case the usual procedure would be to request his associate audit firm in the area to undertake the examination, details of which he will clearly specify in advance. It may, of course, be necessary for him specially to appoint an associate for the purpose. This has become a widespread audit practice today.

6.3.2   Audit evidence – specific verification procedures for the main balance sheet headings

It is impossible, within the confines of a theoretical text, to deal in detail with the application of these verification objectives to every balance sheet asset and liability. However, to give an appreciation of the basic approach to auditing the main balance sheet areas, there follows a summary of audit objectives and specific audit procedures which are by no means exhaustive, relating to each of the following main balance sheet items:

▶ Fixed assets.

▶ Investments.

▶ Stocks and work in progress. (This is considered in more detail at section 6.3.3.)

▶ Debtors.

▶ Cash and bank balances.

▶ Creditors.

Fixed assets

Objectives

▶ To determine whether fixed assets in the balance sheet are owned by the company, are recorded at cost or valuation and represent properly capitalized items.

▶ To verify that any assets built or manufactured by the client have been duly capitalized.

▶ To determine whether additions and disposals during the period are properly authorized and that related costs, gains and losses, have been properly recorded.

▶ To determine whether depreciation and amortization are reasonable and computed on a consistent basis and whether accumulated depreciation is reasonable in relation to continuing usefulness.

▶ To determine whether the amounts shown in the accounts are properly classified and adequately described.

▶ To verify physical existence and ownership.

▶ To ascertain commitments.

▶ To confirm that proper provision has been made for liabilities under leases.

Audit programme

1. Obtain a summary of fixed assets under categories showing how the figures in the balance sheet are made up and reconciling with the figures shown in the previous year's balance sheet. Cast and cross-cast.

2. Obtain schedules of additions during the year and for all classes of asset (including intangibles):

    (a) Test items with suppliers' invoices or other independent vouchers (i.e. architects' certificates, completion statements). Ensure revenue and capital are properly distinguished.

    (b) Test capital expenditure authorizations.

    (c) For fixed assets constructed using own labour test analysis of wages allocated with time sheets and materials with stores issues. Test basis of inclusion of overheads.

    (d) Check appropriateness of capitalization policy in light of accounting standards.

3. Obtain schedules of disposals and:

    (a) Test proceeds of sales with independent evidence (sale agreement or correspondence).

    (b) Enquire if any assets scrapped in year.

    (c) Test authority for disposals.

    (d) Verify that the original cost and accumulated depreciation have been eliminated from fixed assets accounts.

    (e) Check calculations of profits/losses on sales and agree with profit and loss account.

4. Inspect or obtain certificates for title deeds and leases of land or buildings and

    (a) Establish the reason for which those documents are held and the status of the third party.

    (b) If held by a bank for safekeeping, and if there are any doubts about the bank's status or independence, arrange to inspect the documents of title and suggest to the client that he considers removing them from the bank's custody. If satisfied with the bank's status and independence, request the bank to confirm direct to the auditor that it holds them free from any charge or lien. Periodically inspect the documents of title held by the bank.

    (c) If held by a solicitor who is working on the documents of title, request the client to write to the solicitor asking him to confirm direct to the auditor that he holds the documents of title free from any lien or charge.

    (d) If the client has a liability to a third party that is specifically secured upon the property or if the client holds a debenture that charges the company's assets and undertaking and requires deeds to be deposited even though the property is not specifically charged, request the client to write to the lender asking him to confirm direct to the auditor that he holds the documents of title and to give details of the charges on the property.

    Note particularly any registered charges.

5. If any assets have been revalued during the year obtain a copy of the valuation report and inform manager. If the revaluation is to be incorporated into the accounts then:
    (a) Verify that the basis of valuation is acceptable.
    (b) Verify the independence and qualifications of the valuers.
    (c) Confirm accounts disclosure.
6. In the case of leasehold properties verify that provision has been made for dilapidations in accordance with the terms of the lease.
7. Physically inspect samples of all types of assets.
8. Inspect motor vehicle registration documents.
9. Obtain or prepare a schedule of outstanding capital expenditure distinguishing between items contracted for but not provided and items authorized by directors but not contracted for. Check schedule with orders placed, minutes, etc.
10. Verify depreciation rates have been approved by the board and review reasonableness.
11. If rates of depreciation have been changed in the current year obtain explanation, test reasonableness and bring to partner's attention for possible accounts disclosure.
12. Check calculations of depreciation.
13. Reconcile plant register with accounts.
14. Scrutinize the repairs accounts for capital expenditure.
15. Verify grants received and vouch with available evidence, check treatment of receipts with accounting policy adopted by the client.
    Consider whether any grants may be available which have not been claimed.
16. Verify the adequacy of insurance cover on fixed assets.

Investments

Objectives

To determine whether:

▶ There is documentary evidence of the ownership of investments.
▶ Changes during the period represented bona fide transactions.
▶ Gains, losses and income from investments have been properly accounted for.
▶ The basis on which investments are stated is appropriate and the method employed in valuation has been consistently applied.
▶ Amounts shown in the balance sheet are properly classified and described.

Audit programme

1. Obtain or prepare an analysis of investments and:
    (a) Test the clerical accuracy of the analysis.
    (b) Trace the amounts to the records from which the analysis was prepared.

(c) Compare opening balances with last year's working papers.

(d) Review the nominal ledger accounts for the period and investigate any unusual entries.

(e) Obtain third party confirmation and/or make physical inspection of securities listed on analysis and investigate any items not covered.

2. Test transactions for the period:

(a) Examine contract notes and other data supporting transactions.

(b) Trace transactions to authorization including signed minutes.

(c) Review basis for taking profit/loss on part disposals.

(d) Review the treatment of capital distributions, bonus and rights issues.

(e) Test interest and dividend income received and accrued by reference to supporting documents and published data.

3. Verify quoted prices for listed investments at balance sheet date.

4. Determine whether unlisted investments are valued on a reasonable basis.

5. Check whether investments are properly described and classified as current assets or long-term investments.

6. Where the client has 'investment properties' ensure that the latest accounting standards have been complied with.

Stock and work in progress

Objectives

To confirm that:

► All stock and work in progress belonging to the client has been brought into accounts.

► All stock belonging to others in the possession of the client has been separately identified, counted, reconciled and excluded from the valuation.

► All obsolete, damaged or slow-moving stocks have been separately identified and stated at realizable value.

► The value at which stock and work in progress is stated in the balance sheet is correctly calculated on a basis consistent with previous years.

► Security arrangements for the safe custody of stock and work in progress are adequate.

Audit programme

QUANTITY

Observation

1. Before the stock count takes place, review the client's own stocktaking instructions to its staff and consider whether they are adequate. Ensure that the stocktaking procedures questionnaire has been completed.

Note any weakness in the system which would invalidate the reliability of the count and bring to the manager's attention immediately so that he may discuss the problem with the client.

2. Attend to observe the physical count and ensure that the client's stocktaking procedures are followed and in particular that:

    (a) All stores locations are covered by the count.

    (b) All slow-moving, obsolete or damaged stocks are segregated and counted separately and clearly marked on the stock sheets.

    (c) All stock belonging to third parties is counted and segregated on stock sheets.

    (d) All stock sheets issued are accounted for, completed properly, dated and signed by the persons carrying out the count.

3. Complete a stocktaking report.

4. Obtain details of the last few goods outward and goods inward/delivery notes for use in cut-off tests.

5. Audit procedures

    (a) Ensure that all rough stock sheets have been processed to make up the final stock sheets.

    (b) Check all quantities test checked at observation to final sheets.

    (c) Test the extensions and additions on the final stock sheets.

    (d) Check all final stock sheets to stock summary.

6. Scrutinize the stock sheets for obvious errors and compare with the comparative sheets for the previous years to ensure that no section of the stock has been excluded.

7. (a) Select a sample of goods outward notes pre- and post-year-end and check that the goods have been entered in the stock records in the correct year.

    (b) Carry out a similar test for goods inward/delivery notes.

    (c) Using the samples selected in (a) and (b) above ensure that the relevant sales and purchase invoices are included correctly in the accounts.

    (d) Where no goods notes exist carry out tests (a) and (b) using sales/purchase invoices.

8. (a) Compare final stock sheets with any perpetual inventory records maintained (e.g. bin cards or stock ledgers). Note any discrepancies and obtain adequate explanations for the differences. Ensure that all necessary adjustments are made to the inventory records.

    (b) Reconcile stock and work in progress figure in the final accounts with amounts shown in total by perpetual inventory records or management accounts. Prepare a schedule giving the reasons for any divergence, stating the evidence obtained to verify the explanations given.

9. Obtain certificates direct from third parties in respect of stock held by them. The certificates should identify the nature of the stock, the quantities held and the purpose for which it is held.

It should also confirm that the stock held is in good condition and not subject to any lien or charges. Confirm that all necessary deductions are made in respect of slow-moving, damaged or obsolete stocks.

VALUATION

Stock

10. Test the prices on the final stock sheets to purchase invoices.

11. (a) Scrutinize the bin cards or stock records to identify any apparently obsolete stock.

    (b) Review all slow-moving and obsolete stock with storekeepers and responsible officials.

    (c) Consider the value placed upon the items in the previous year, the prospect of sale in the immediate future and decide what reduction in value is appropriate.

    (d) Enter details on a schedule and bring to the manager's attention.

12. Work in progress: Test the reliability of work in progress prices by examining the costing system in force. Ensure that:

    (a) Methods of accounting and control over stores issues and labour usage are adequate;

    (b) Method of allocation of overhead is reasonable. Confirm by calculation that the amount added is in line with the actual rate incurred during the year under review unless the factory operated below normal capacity, in which case the normal activity rate should be used; and

    (c) Method of valuation of work in progress is consistent with previous years and has not been distorted by changes in the level of production.

13. Compare the price of the selected items of work in progress with selling price by adding an estimate of the cost required to complete.
    The projected/actual final cost should be compared with selling price and any anticipated losses provided for.

14. For long-term contracts consider SSAP 9 and determine whether the basis for the calculation of work in progress is permissible.

15. Finished goods:

    (a) Compare the values of finished goods with the work in progress calculations for those goods.

    (b) Test prices with purchase invoices/price lists where appropriate.

    (c) Compare with current selling prices to ensure that all finished goods in stock can be sold at a profit in current trading conditions. Ensure that provision is made to meet any losses.

16. General: Obtain or prepare a schedule summarizing the stock and work in progress by general category, showing the comparative figures for the previous year. Reconcile the total with the amount shown in the balance sheet and with the final stock sheets. State on the schedule the basis of valuation used and the nature of the evidence obtained to verify the quantity of stock at the valuation used. The schedule or detailed working papers should indicate the audit work carried out and identify the particular items of stock which have been tested. Ensure the basis of the valuation is consistent with previous years.

17. State on the schedule of stock and work in progress the amount and proportion of value which were subject to:

   (a) Observation at a stock count;

   (b) Other audit tests.

18. Compare the ratios of:

   (a) Stock and work in progress to sales;

   (b)   (i) raw materials to cost of sales

       (ii) work in progress to cost of sales

       (iii) finished goods to cost of sales

   with those for the previous period.
   Prepare a schedule stating reasons for significant changes in the above ratios and evidence obtained to verify the explanations given.

19. In conjunction with debtors' programme ensure all payments on account are deducted from stock and work in progress, to the extent that value is included therein. Balances in excess of the work in progress valuation should be transferred to advances from customers.

20. Review the stock valuation on a current cost basis. If materially different, discuss possible disclosure with the directors.

Debtors and prepayments

Objectives

► To confirm accuracy and collectability of trade debtors' balances.

► To confirm approval of bad debts write offs in the year.

► To confirm the provision for bad debts and its adequacy.

► To confirm the accuracy of sundry receivables and prepayments.

Audit programme

1. Trade debtors: Examine a sample of ledger accounts and all accounts with balances equal to or over the materiality factor and trace balances to summary lists. Note on lists whether since paid, or date of earliest unpaid items. If not paid,

ensure that balances are made up of specific items and make enquiries to ascertain whether the debt is genuine and recoverable in full.

2. Check the casts of the lists of balances and cross-cast if age-analysed. Trace totals to lead schedule.

3. (a) Check that the total balances agree with the balance on the control account.

    (b) Examine control account for the year and verify unusual items.

4. Select balances for direct confirmation if required by manager/partner.

    (a) Arrange for standard letters of request.

    (b) Prepare summary of balances on standard schedule, and summarize replies as received.

    (c) Investigate discrepancies and reconcile.

    (d) Carry out suitable alternate procedures (i.e. telephone confirmation or verification of cash received) on non-replies.

    (e) Complete summary and conclusion sheet and consider amount of testing to be done under 5 below.

5. If no circularization of debtors has been carried out select a sample of balances and check paid after date. Trace such receipts to the paying-in book and cash book.

6. Examine list of balances for credit balances and:

    (a) Ensure separated and shown under creditors (see also (c) below).

    (b) Enquire into reasons for credit balances.

    (c) Test payments on account to cash book and paying-in book. Ensure deducted from stock and work in progress if applicable.

    (d) Ensure that payments in respect of credit balances are authorized by the correct official.

7. (a) Verify that the provision for bad debts and discounts are both reasonable and adequate (having regard to any aged debtors reports). Discuss with management if appropriate.

    (b) Examine the credit control procedures and consider if any recommendations should be made.

8. Verify that bad debts written off during the period were correctly authorized and that all reasonable recovery procedures had been taken prior to writing off.

9. Examine ledger for transfers between accounts throughout the year. Verify reasons for these, and check authorization.

10. Examine the sales day-book pre- and post-year-end and verify that any large or exceptional items are genuine transactions.

11. Examine credit notes issued after the year-end to ascertain whether they relate to genuine sales, or whether any provision is required to be made at the balance sheet date.

12. Test despatches and returns for the period covering the year-end with goods despatched/returned records to ensure that sales or returns included were actually despatched or returned before the year-end and that credit notes or provisions have been made where appropriate.

13. In the case of sales under deferred credit terms ensure that:

    (a) Income has been properly apportioned between the accounting periods.

    (b) There is adequate provision for bad debts.

    (c) Treatment in the accounts is correct both:

        (i) where the client has provided finance;

        (ii) where an external company has provided finance.

14. Check the reasonableness of the total outstanding trade debtors by the ratio of debtors to net credit turnover.

15. Other debtors and prepayments: Obtain a schedule of loans to employees, including directors and test as follows:

    (a) Test authority for loans granted during the year.

    (b) Check interest calculations and trace postings to nominal ledger.

    (c) Test amounts repaid with cash book or salary records as appropriate.

    (d) Verify that the terms of repayment and interest are being complied with.

    (e) Inspect certificates from the borrowers confirming the balances at the year-end.

    (f) Confirm adequacy of security.

    (g) Confirm collectability of outstanding balances.

    (h) Examine board minutes confirming substantial loans.

    (i) Ensure proper disclosure in the accounts.

16. For telephone and other similar deposits, confirm that the amount is the same as the previous year. For new deposits, examine correspondence. If amounts are substantial obtain direct third party confirmations.

17. Obtain a schedule of bills receivable and test as follows:

    (a) Check with bills book.

    (b) Where due date has occurred since the balance sheet date, confirm that bill was duly paid.

    (c) Check the casts of the schedule.

    (d) Inspect bills held at the year-end.

    (e) Obtain certificates from agents where appropriate.

    (f) For bills still outstanding at the time of the audit make a note for them to be looked at on the next audit. Confirm collectability.

    (g) Verify that no discounted bills have been dishonoured since the balance sheet date.

    (h) Ascertain the contingent liability for bills discounted with recourse.

18. Test other prepayments, etc. with available documentation. Compare with previous year and obtain explanations of material variations.

Cash at bank and in hand

Objectives

▶ To confirm the existence and accuracy of year-end balances.
▶ To confirm the amounts shown in the balance sheet are properly classified and adequately described.

Audit programme

1. Obtain/prepare lead schedule. Transfer balances to other sections where appropriate (e.g. long-term loans, overdrafts, etc.)
2. Bank: Obtain a copy of the year-end bank reconciliation.
   (a) Compare cash book and statements in detail covering items in the reconciliation.
   (b) Trace outstanding cheques to subsequent bank statements and ensure that all cleared.
   (c) Verify by reference to paying in slips that lodgements outstanding were actually lodged with the bank prior to the end of the financial year.
   (d) Scrutinize bank statements of the new period for dishonoured cheques and investigate any such items.
   (e) Obtain direct from bankers a certificate of balance and check to reconciliation.
   (f) Note details of any security for an overdraft.
3. Cash: Obtain a statement setting out details of the cash in hand and test as follows:
   (a) Count the cash at the year-end or subsequent date in the presence of the cashier. Reconcile balance to year-end figure.
   (b) Verify that the monies received on the last day of the financial year were duly banked on that date or included in the cash in hand balance.
   (c) Examine the cash book pre- and post-year-end cash count and verify that all cheques drawn to replenish the cash fund have been entered in the records.

Creditors; amounts falling due within one year

Objectives

▶ To confirm that all liabilities existing or incurred at the balance sheet date are recorded at the correct amount.
▶ To confirm that amounts included in the balance sheet are stated on a consistent basis and are properly described and classified as amounts falling due within one year.

► To confirm that all items included as creditors have been tested during the audit.

► To ensure that amounts falling due after more than one year have been correctly classified.

Audit programme

1. Trade creditors: Test extraction of purchase ledger balances.

2. (a) For balances examined in 1 reconcile with suppliers' statements.

    (b) Where suppliers' statements are not available, verify the balance by alternative means, including where necessary circularization.

3. (a) Check casts of lists of balances, trace totals to lead schedule.

    (b) Test a sample of additions of ledger accounts selected in 1 above.

4. Verify that the list of balances agrees to the control account.

5. (a) Examine list of debit balances and ensure separated and shown under debtors.

    (b) Enquire into the reasons for debit balances and ensure that they are recoverable.

6. Establish whether the control account is regularly written up and agreed throughout the year. Test one such reconciliation. Review the year control accounts and verify unusual items.

7. Review the procedures adopted for ensuring that goods received up to the balance sheet date, but not invoiced by the supplier have been provided for and taken up as stock (if appropriate) and test by reference to delivery notes and goods inwards records, if any. Repeat for period immediately after year-end.

8. Reservation of title:

    (a) Review terms of sales of major suppliers to determine whether their terms of trade include a reservation of title.

    (b) Review and test procedures for quantifying liabilities to suppliers who have reserved title to goods.

9. Inter-company balances: Scrutinize the list of purchase ledger balances and separate any inter-company balances.

10. Other creditors and accruals:

    (a) Agree VAT control account with outstanding balance.

    (b) Verify payment to cash book after date.

11. (a) Agree outstanding PAYE/NI and SSP balance with control accounts.

    (b) Check balance to wages records and agree.

    (c) Verify payment to cash book after date.

12. (a) Verify schedule of directors' current accounts. Note any special repayment terms.

    (b) List confirmation of balances as a point for letter of representation or obtain certificate from director (if not signatory to letter of representation).

13. Ensure full provision for PAYE/NI on directors' remuneration paid/made available in the year has been made.

14. Bills payable:

    (a) Obtain a schedule of bills payable outstanding at the balance sheet date.

    (b) Check with bills book.

    (c) Check casts and agree with accounts.

    (d) Inspect cancelled bills for those paid after the balance sheet date.

15. Check calculations of accruals and vouch with available evidence.

16. Scrutinize after date cash book and petty cash book, day-books, invoices and previous years' schedules for unrecorded liabilities.

17. Ensure that all material creditors and accruals have been verified during the course of the audit.

18. Obtain a certificate relevant to each short-term loan confirming the amount outstanding at the balance sheet date and stating the nature of any security held.

19. Discuss any contingent liabilities with the client and write to the client's solicitor to verify any outstanding matters. Vouch with available evidence.

20. Ensure that long-term liabilities and provisions for charges are correctly identified.

6.3.3 The verification of stocks

The special problems

Of all the items that may appear in the balance sheets of trading and manufacturing companies, the one that must be singled out for special attention is stocks (or inventories). From the auditor's point of view, this has always been the asset that presents the greatest verification problems. Why is this? There are five interrelated reasons:

1. The amount at which the stocks are stated in the accounts is almost always material in relation to the accounts as a whole – indeed, surveys of published accounts have shown that for many companies the stock figure is the largest single item in the balance sheet. Materiality of this order is, of itself, bound to increase the dimension of the verification problem.

2. The amount at which it is stated has a direct 'one-to-one' effect on the company's financial results: any overstatement of the stock figure represents an overstatement by equal amount of the profit figure (or understatement of the loss). Let us assume, for example, that we believe the stock valuation of say, £500,000 to be accurate to within a margin of ±5 per cent, and that we regard this as sufficiently precise for our purposes (i.e. the true value of the inventory lies between £475,000 and £525,000). If, at the same time, the profit figure is stated at, say, £20,000 it is obvious that our £50,000 precision range on stocks renders any belief in the 'accuracy' of the profit figure somewhat speculative.

3. It is the only item in the published accounts which does not also feature in the closing trial balance, i.e. it does not arise from the double entry process itself. In certain accounting systems production costing and financial accounting will be integrated to give a book figure of work in progress, for example, but in the majority of cases the determination of stocks is largely dependent upon physical stocktaking procedures. This factor alone makes the stock figure the most susceptible to manipulation.

4. It is, in the case of manufacturing companies, not really one asset at all: it is at least *four*, i.e. raw materials, bought-out components, work in progress, and finished goods, and each of these (together with further subdivisions) creates its own valuation difficulties.

5. The verification process will often involve a special, even a highly technical, approach which lies far beyond the auditor's own expertise. One may think of a stocktaking as a relatively straightforward *counting* process, for example; but what is it that is being counted? In certain cases the answer will be apparent from simply looking at the assets concerned, but in many other cases careful *identification* may be vital before any counting can take place. The item being counted may indeed be a box of 50 mm screws – but what a difference if they are made of brass as opposed to an inferior alloy.

Auditors may therefore frequently find themselves out of their depth when attempting to identify the ingredients of an inventory. Obvious examples relate to precious substances such as metals or gems; technical specifications requiring chemical analysis for determination of content, such as specially graded sheet metal or cable alloys; different quality raw foodstuffs and fibres such as grain, fruit, cotton or wool; chemicals and powders in the pharmaceutical industry, and so on. Additionally, apart from pure identification of goods, there is also the question of their condition. Many companies create categories relating to the condition of their stocks, especially where perishable items are involved. Examples of such categories (each of which is quite distinct and will carry its own valuation basis) are:

► Sound (full value)
► Shop-soiled
► Defective (i.e. 'seconds')
► Slow-moving
► Obsolete
► Scrap

Such categorization may have a significant impact upon balance sheet values, yet the auditor will usually lack the competence so much as even to comment intelligently on the categories selected.

Another aspect of the identification problem is the fact that goods will often be held in a variety of locations, in all of which counting must proceed simultaneously to avoid omissions and/or double counting caused by the subsequent movement of goods between locations. At any point in time many items will be in transit and these too must obviously be included in the count. Certain goods may be held by outside parties, often overseas, as agents, consignees, or on a sale-or-return basis, in which event the auditor may be obliged to accept certificates, as described in section 6.4 below.

Further the 'location' may be a moving assembly line, or a construction site to and from which materials and plant are constantly being conveyed; and it is unlikely that work will be deliberately brought to a halt purely to facilitate the stocktaking.

Finally, certain types of goods create unique identification and measuring problems. How, for instance, does one 'count' large volumes of powder or liquid? Possibly by volume or by weight, in accordance with predetermined measuring disciplines which the auditor may observe. One of the problems that arose in connection with the giant Salad Oil swindle (USA, 1963) lay in the fact that the oil in the tanks solidified below a certain temperature and this rendered useless all the usual techniques for sampling the quality and grades of the oils in stock. The presence among the inventories of items which may be lethal (e.g. highly poisonous, dangerous to the touch, or radioactive) adds still further to the auditor's difficulties.

Official guidance on stock verification

The Council of the ICAEW has issued a Statement (no. 3.902) for the guidance of members, and the APC issued an auditing guideline in 1983 entitled 'Attendance at stocktaking'. These statements relate primarily to company audits, but the considerations outlined apply equally to other audits which involve the auditor in expressing an opinion on the truth and fairness of the view given by the accounts. The auditing guideline is primarily concerned with auditors' duties in relation to the physical stocktaking. The broader aspects of stock verification are dealt with in Statement no. 3.902. This guideline and statement are not reproduced but are recommended reading.

Valuation of stocks

The method selected for determining cost will depend upon whether the inventories concerned relate to raw materials, bought-out components, work in progress, or finished goods. If we were considering retailers rather than manufacturers we might determine the cost of goods by simply adjusting the selling prices downwards to eliminate the mark-up. One therefore cannot be dogmatic when discussing the valuation of stocks and work in progress, since ultimately the basis selected depends on the company's circumstances. Accounting Standards, however, are not so flexible, hence the number of 'authorized' (i.e. approved by the auditors) departures.

The word 'cost', like the word 'profit', therefore covers a multitude of concepts, each with its own designation or label. Hence we have a range of possible meanings of cost, such as average, actual, unit, batch, process, job, marginal, standard, FIFO, LIFO, NIFO (next in, first out), base stock, adjusted selling price, and many others. Company accounts which declare in their accounting policies that 'stocks are valued at the lower of cost and net realizable value' are therefore telling us nothing. They should be telling us which basis is employed for determining the 'cost' of each major category (e.g. raw materials, etc.) within the inventories.

Long-term work in progress presents altogether different problems, and it is interesting that SSAP 9 actually allows a notional departure from the strict definition of prudence given in SSAP 2, which declares that 'revenue and profits are not anticipated'. In SSAP 9, the inclusion of 'attributable' profit on uncompleted contracts is required (to be calculated on a 'prudent' basis, of course). Directors are required to value the turnover element in incomplete contracts, against which cost of sales are to be shown as a profit and loss account charge. Work certified can be included in debtors (rather than work in progress). Reference should be made to the standard itself for a complete grasp of the accounting requirements.

Returning to the determination of cost: the most usual basis adopted for determining the cost of raw materials is FIFO (first in, first out). Where the materials are of such a nature that individual purchases, once admitted to store, can no longer be separately identified (such as chemicals stored in central tanks), the precise determination of costs of raw materials passed to production is extremely difficult. The adoption of FIFO, however, is a convenience which (apart from foodstuffs and other perishables, which have in any case to be identified on the basis of age) *assumes* that goods admitted to store 'queue up' before being withdrawn and passed to production. Its effect is that goods in store at the balance sheet date (or any other date) are assumed to have been acquired during the latest period, all earlier purchases having since been passed to production. This in turn causes stocks to be valued at recent prices, assuming a fairly brisk stock/turnover.

The use of LIFO or base stock accounting, by contrast, automatically recognizes the need to determine trading results by reference to 'operating' gains rather than gains attributable simply to the holding of stocks whose price has increased during the accounting period.

The chief difficulty with LIFO is the maintenance of detailed stock records which would be required to show *separately* each purchase of a particular commodity which takes place at a different price, and to produce running balances *at each price level*, going back to the date on which the particular commodity was first acquired. By contrast, FIFO assumes that the closing stock was the most recently acquired, and in many cases a straightforward add-listing of the latest covering invoices will compute 'cost' under this basis. Only a computerized stock-recording system is capable of maintaining the necessarily intricate details of a LIFO system.

Due to the complexity of LIFO stock records and LIFO's lack of approximation to physical reality, LIFO has not been favoured by the accounting profession in the UK. Its consistent application, however, will not necessarily distort a company's trading profits. It is specifically permitted under the *Companies Act 1985*, and SSAP 9 (revised) includes LIFO as an acceptable method in appropriate circumstances, e.g. stocks of commodities with fluctuating prices.

For balance sheet purposes it may sometimes be necessary to reduce the value of raw materials from cost (however determined) to *replacement price*. This is permitted by

SSAP 9, although it warns that it may produce an unrealistically pessimistic view; after all, the fact that materials may now be replaced for less than they cost does not of itself mean that their original purchase price will not be recovered when the finished goods are sold – and a reduction may therefore be unwarranted. The qualified approval which such a reduction is given under SSAP 9 is therefore restricted to circumstances in which cost recovery is unlikely, such a view subsequently being confirmed by post-balance sheet transactions. A company may, for example, have misread the market indicators and indulged in substantial stockpiling before an unexpected fall in prices.

Replacement price thus provides a prudent alternative to raw materials cost in appropriate circumstances; and it is similarly necessary, in respect of work in progress and finished goods, to consider the need to reduce valuations from cost to net realizable value. Cost may, of course, have been calculated by any one of several methods, although in manufacturing industries some form of standard costing is almost certain to have been used. This method uses past experience together with forecast data as a guide to quantifying the cost of each element comprising the final product cost – from direct labour/materials/carriage, etc. through to the allocation of indirect overheads such as rent, rates, light, power, supervisory wages, and so on. All factory expenses have to be allocated, and, it is hoped, absorbed, if accurate cost determination is to be achieved. Standards must be compared regularly with actual results and the resulting variances adjusted in the light of inaccuracies and permanent changes.

Net realizable value has been described in a variety of ways, but the only real issue on which differences arise is that concerning *which* expenses should be deducted from the proceeds which, at the balance sheet date, it is estimated will be realized from sales in the ordinary course of business. One simple way of expressing net realizable value is to treat it as the amount which will yield neither profit nor loss in the year of sale – but that still leaves the question of which costs should be charged in arriving at that result.

SSAP 9 refers to costs of 'completion, selling, marketing and distribution' only; thus omitting estimated allocations in respect of central administrative overheads. This is sensible, since most attempts to allocate such items to individual products would be either inaccurate or futile, and it is probably more sensible either for the basic standard costings to carry a suitable loading to cover central overheads or, preferably, to write them off when incurred.

It should therefore be clear that the auditor cannot do his job without becoming involved in, and understanding, the costing system which results in the balance sheet values. If auditing the stocks is to have any real meaning there is more involved than counting a few items on the shelves, and totting up the year-end invoices.

A further point to be borne in mind is that the *Companies Act 1985* stipulates that 'proper accounting records' includes records of stocktakings and all supporting summary schedules. If the client company's records do not include these (assuming stocktakings had been held), an audit report qualification would be necessary, subject to the comments given in Chapter 8, section 8.2.9 below.

Reservation of title clauses

In the case *Aluminium Industrie Vaassen BV* v. *Romalpa Aluminium Ltd* (Court of Appeal, January 1976) it was decided that a seller of goods may validly reserve his title to the goods, to other goods produced from them, and even to the proceeds from resale of those goods, until they have been paid for by the immediate buyer. This case (which has come to be known as the Romalpa case) has considerable implications for auditors who must now give detailed attention to the precise wording of each contract when determining its significance to the ownership and title of related assets, especially as there is no standard form of wording for such contracts. The ICAEW has issued a guidance statement on this matter.

Banks and others who lend money secured by a floating charge are vitally concerned with the strength of the borrowers' balance sheet, and the inclusion in stock of an unrecognized value of goods purchased under Romalpa-type contracts could seriously undermine their security. Where both the company and its auditors fail to detect and indicate the amount included as that part of creditors protected by such clauses, they could be laying themselves open to serious consequences if the company fails, and its suppliers exercise their rights.

In view of the fact that the title of goods sold subject to such contract terms does not pass until full settlement, the Romalpa decision presents one of the classic 'substance against form' situations. Specifically, at what stage should the goods be treated as sold by the supplier, and as purchased by the buying company? In general it is considered that, so far as accounting treatment is concerned, the commercial substance of the transaction should take precedence over its legal form, unless there is evidence that either the buying or the selling company is unlikely to remain a going concern.

In other words, if the circumstances indicate that the reservation of title is regarded by the client company (the purchaser) as having no practical relevance (except in the event of the insolvency of the purchasing company) then it is recommended that, to give a true and fair view, goods should be treated as purchases in the accounts of the purchasing company, and as sales in the accounts of the supplier (i.e. on a commercial basis).

If, on the other hand, the financial position of the purchasing company throws doubt on its viability as a going concern, the accounting treatment of goods supplied on such terms will need particular consideration. In the rare circumstances that the accounts have been drawn up on some basis other than the going concern basis, it would be necessary to have regard to the strict legal position in relation to the transaction.

There are two matters that may require to be disclosed in the accounts.

1. *Accounting policy.* If the accounts are materially affected by the accounting treatment adopted in relation to sales or purchases, subject to reservation of title, the company's accounting policy should be disclosed.

2. *Secured liability.* Where, as would normally be the case, the commercial basis has been adopted, the accounts of the purchasing company should disclose that liabilities, subject to the reservation of title, are secured. The secured liability should be quantified in the accounts, usually as the subject of a separate note.

Clearly, therefore, the auditor has a responsibility to enquire whether the client purchases goods from suppliers on terms that include reservation of title by the suppliers, and, if the answer is the affirmative, to review the client's own procedures for accounting for and identifying such transactions. It may be appropriate to obtain formal written representation, included in the letter of representation from the directors (see section 6.5), either that there are no material liabilities of this nature to be disclosed, or that the amount is fully disclosed in the accounts.

6.3.4 Deferred taxation and the auditor

The effects of SSAP 15

Accounting for deferred taxation introduces new areas of judgement and assessment of probabilities for the auditor. The main requirements of SSAP 15 are that:

1. Tax deferred or accelerated (computed under the liability method) by the effect of timing differences should be accounted for to the extent that it is *probable that a liability or asset will crystallize.*

2. The assessment of whether deferred tax liabilities will or will not crystallize should be based on reasonable assumptions taking into account all relevant information available up to the date on which the financial statements are approved by the board of directors, and also the intentions of management.

3. The deferred tax element in the annual tax charge must be separately disclosed.

4. The deferred tax balance and the potential amount of deferred tax on all timing differences should be disclosed by way of a note to the accounts analysed into its major components.

Main audit considerations

The critical audit points that arise would appear to be as follows:

1. It is up to the company to demonstrate that a deferred tax provision is not required.

2. There must be a reasonable probability that tax reductions will continue.

3. The period for consideration is the foreseeable future (see below).

4. The existence of material unutilized capital allowances at the balance sheet date will usually mean that the company does not have to demonstrate to the auditor as much in the way of future expenditure intentions and availability of finance as will be the case where no backlog of unutilized allowances exists. In other instances, the pattern of past capital expenditure and stock investment may mean that the auditor will not need to rely solely on future projections.

5. If there is real doubt as to whether tax will or will not be payable, then full provision for deferred tax clearly should be made.

It should be noted that recent *Finance Acts* have removed some of the importance of deferred taxation. The policy of 'fiscal neutrality' has led to the gradual abolition of first year allowances for capital expenditure which has in turn removed much of the cause of timing differences, and hence of deferred taxation.

Examination of budgets

Differing circumstances will require companies to provide differing degrees of supporting documentation for auditors. However, it may be necessary (particularly where no backlog of unutilized allowances exists, or where no consistent pattern of expenditure can be shown from past experience) for a company to prepare, and for the auditor to examine, a series of forecasts and budgets in respect of:

1. The future trading position, showing estimated profit and the depreciation charges.
2. A cash flow budget.
3. A capital expenditure (and disposals) budget.

A company that does not provide these statements may well find it difficult to convince its auditor that a deferred tax provision is not required.

'Probable that a liability or asset will crystallize'

After examining all available evidence (including the company's past level of success in forecasting) the auditor must decide whether a deferred tax provision is required. Auditors will need to judge which types of timing difference in a company are likely to be most susceptible to variation from the forecast level.

The word 'probable' is subjective, and the standard does not include a definition. However, in order to provide some assurance that provisions for taxation, deferred or current, are not created and/or released at frequent intervals, and in the wrong accounting periods, it is necessary to forecast the relevant factors set out above over a substantial period, and it is thought that some three years would be suitable in this context.

Land and buildings

Deferred taxation on revaluation surpluses on land and buildings will generally no longer be necessary, but should the directors decide to dispose of the property and not to reinvest the proceeds (and thereby obtain rollover relief), the auditor should insist that a provision be made.

The practical questions

In order that auditors can form a view as to the general acceptability of the provisions of SSAP 15, they will need to consider, in the light of their everyday experience, the following questions:

1. How far ahead in time should the forecasts extend, be they documented or not?
2. To the extent that forecasts do need to be documented, what degree of supporting evidence will be needed, and is such information likely to be available?
3. What, in practical terms, constitutes 'reasonable probability'?

6.4 The auditor's use of external confirmations

As an important feature of the verification procedures outlined above, the auditor is obliged, in many situations, to make use of confirmations requested from outside parties who are in a position to certify particular information relevant to the accounts. These outside parties are sometimes referred to as 'third' parties, the client and the auditor being the first two parties (to their contract). For this purpose, therefore, even an employee of the client may be thought of as a third party. Such *outside* confirmations, or certificates, may be contrasted with those supplied from *within*, so to speak, i.e. from the officers of the client organization, usually embodied in what is known as the letter of representation. This is discussed in the next section.

One of the most influential legal cases on the question of the auditor's entitlement to rely upon certificates from third parties arose after the liquidation in 1924 of The City Equitable Fire Insurance Co. The auditors were charged with negligence in accepting, from the insurance company's stockbrokers, a certificate confirming the custody of a substantial portfolio of securities, representing the investment of premiums already received. The securities in question had, in fact, been fraudulently pledged by the stockbrokers (who were heavily indebted to City Equitable at all material times) to outsiders in order to cover losses on unauthorized dealings in the investments of other clients; as a result of which the insurance company suffered severe losses. Although it was usual for auditors to follow the practice of accepting certificates in appropriate circumstances, the City Equitable auditors were held to have acted negligently for two special reasons:

1. It is not normal for stockbrokers to act as the permanent repositories or custodians of clients' stocks and shares, a function for which they in any event generally lack the facilities. (This does not of course apply to the relatively brief period of time when the ownership of securities is transferred on behalf of the client.)
2. The senior partner in the stockbroking firm, who subsequently faced criminal charges, was, at the time of the audit, the chairman of City Equitable, a fact known to the auditors when they accepted his firm's (supposedly) external certificate.

Incidentally, it is interesting to note that despite their negligence the auditors suffered no personal liability. This was due to a clause within the City Equitable articles of association which indemnifed all officers and auditors of the company against liability consequent upon proven charges of negligence. Such 'indemnity clauses', which were quite common, were made null and void under section 310 of the *Companies Act 1985*, except that a company is permitted to pay the premiums on directors' and auditors' indemnity insurance policies.

The lessons of the City Equitable case may be summarized thus:

1. Whenever a material asset is concerned the auditor should, wherever possible, verify it directly. This would certainly have been possible in the case of City Equitable: had the auditors called for the securities for inspection purposes they would have discovered the fraud immediately.

2. Certificates should be requested only from third parties whose ordinary course of business includes the activities or custodianship being certified. In City Equitable's case the securities documents would be expected to be held either in the company's own secured\ vaults, or with its bankers – from whom a certificate would undoubtedly have been acceptable.

3. The involvement, in the person of the chairman, between the stockbrokers and the company was known to the auditors, and the certificate therefore lacked an independent source. It is vital that the suppliers of certificates upon which the auditor relies should be independent of the client organization. There are occasions when full independence is impossible – such as certificates from staff confirming their indebtedness to the company under a staff loan scheme. In such a case, however, the auditor's reliance upon the certificate *per se* is unlikely to be either excessive or material.

6.4.1 Circularization of debtors

Many audit firms use certain external confirmations so extensively that they have developed standardized formats for the purpose. The circularization (with the client's permission) of a sample of debtors requesting them to confirm the amounts outstanding is an obvious example, and is the subject of ICAEW Guidance Statement 3.901. Despite the low response rate often experienced (mainly due to computerization of records) this is still a common practice, and takes two forms:

1. The *negative* circular, which requires a reply only if the debtor disputes the balance shown on the form.

2. The *positive* circular, which requests in every case confirmation of details of sums shown as outstanding in the records of the debtor.

Although the negative method is simpler and requires no follow up, it should only be used in the following circumstances:

1. Where the auditor already has a good deal of faith in the internal control governing sales and debtors.

2. Where other verification work on the records of sales and debtors has already been executed and has shown a satisfactory result.

3. In conjunction with a large and carefully selected sample – otherwise the value of the test may be negated by the number of debtors who simply throw such requests into the wastepaper basket.

The usefulness of the positive method, by contrast, depends largely upon the auditor's tenacity in following up the non-replies, by telephone or even personal call if necessary. It is essential that replies be sent to the auditor directly at his own office, otherwise there is a risk of tampering or suppression by client staff. (In this context one calls to mind once again the lessons of Equity Funding, whose auditors on occasion attempted to verify with branch managers by telephone the amount of life insurance business undertaken at each branch. The calls were dialled in the Equity Funding offices, but the switchboard, acting under instruction from one of the senior 'conspirators', transferred all calls to the latter's office. He then proceeded to confirm every figure given by the auditors, call after call, even remembering to fake the accent appropriate to the location in question.)

Skill is also needed, of course, in *selecting* the debtor accounts for circularization. We have already seen in Chapter 5 that a suitably stratified ledger may be subjected to a statistical sampling test; but it is important for the auditor first to scrutinize the accounts individually to ensure that the sample includes the 'special cases' of accounts which may be significant, such as:

1. Accounts which show negative balances.
2. Accounts which have been written-off as bad, or against which specific provision for loss has been made.
3. Accounts in which debits and credits do not appear to relate, e.g. round sums 'on account' are constantly received – especially where this process results in an ever-enlarging balance.
4. Nil balances on active accounts.
5. Accounts which remain unpaid beyond the normal terms of credit.
6. Accounts showing balances which habitually exceed the designated credit limit.
7. Accounts showing balances which are materially smaller at the balance sheet date than the usual amount outstanding, i.e. where it appears that the balance has been specially reduced at the year-end to escape the auditor's attention.
8. Accounts of debtors known to have connections with the client company or its officers (i.e. accounts of 'related parties').
9. Accounts which reveal usually favourable (to the debtor) 'terms of trade' in terms of discounts, credit period and credit limits allowed.
10. Accounts which, when in arrears, do not appear (for any obvious reason) to be followed up by normal credit control procedures as rigorously as would be expected.

6.4.2 Bank confirmations

This is probably the external confirmation upon which auditors in general rely most heavily. For this reason the Auditing Practices Committee, after due consultation with the appropriate committees of clearing bankers, issued an auditing guideline on this subject in 1982, and this includes a comprehensive standard form of such a request. The specimen report included in the guideline is reproduced below.

Appendix: Standard letter of request for bank report for audit purposes

(a) The form of the letter is not to be amended by the auditor.

(b) Sufficient space should be left for the bank's replies (two-thirds of each page is recommended).

The Manager

.... *(bank)*

.... *(branch)*

Dear Sir,

.... *(Name of customer)*

Standard request for bank report for audit purposes for the year ended

....

In accordance with your above-named customer's instructions given

(1) hereon

(2) in the attached authority   *(delete as*

(3) in the authority dated .... already held by you   *appropriate)*

please send to us, as auditors of your customer for the purpose of our business, without entering into any contractual relationship with us, the following information relating to their affairs at your branch as at the close of business on .... and, in the case of items 2, 4 and 10, during the period since .... For each item, please state any factors which may limit the completeness of your reply; if there is nothing to report, state 'none'.

We enclose an additional copy of this letter, and it would be particularly helpful if your reply could be given on the copy letter in the space provided (supported by an additional schedule stamped and signed by the bank where space is insufficient). If you find it necessary to provide the information in another form, please return the copy letter with your reply.

It is understood that any replies given are in strict confidence.

Information requested

Bank accounts

1. Please give full titles of all accounts whether in sterling or in any other currency together with the account numbers and balances thereon, including nil balances:

    (a) where your customer's name is the sole name in the title;

(b) where your customer's name is joined with that of other parties;

(c) where the account is in a trade name.

Notes

(i) Where the account is subject to any restriction (e.g. a garnishee order or arrestment), this information should be stated.

(ii) Where the authority upon which you are providing this information does not cover any accounts held jointly with other parties, please refer to your customer in order to obtain the requisite authority of the other parties. If this authority is not forthcoming please indicate.

2. Full titles and dates of closure of all accounts closed during the period.

3. The separate amounts accrued but not charged or credited at the above date, of:

(a) provisional charges (including commitment fees); and

(b) interest.

4. The amount of interest charged during the period if not specified separately in the bank statement.

5. Particulars (i.e. date, type of document and accounts covered) of any written acknowledgment of set-off, either by specific letter of set-off, or incorporated in some other document or security.

6. Details of:

(a) overdrafts and loans repayable on demand, specifying dates of review and agreed facilities;

(b) other loans specifying dates of review and repayment;

(c) other facilities.

Customer's assets held as security

7. Please give details of any such assets whether or not formally charged to the bank.
If formally charged, give details of the security including the date and type of charge. If a security is limited in amount or to a specific borrowing, or if there is to your knowledge a prior, equal or subordinate charge, please indicate.
If informally charged, indicate nature of security interest therein claimed by the bank.
Whether or not a formal charge has been taken, give particulars of any undertaking given to the bank relating to any assets.

Customer's other assets held

8. Please give full details of the customer's other assets held, including share certificates, documents of title, deed boxes and any other items listed in your registers maintained for the purpose of recording assets held.

Contingent liabilities

9. All contingent liabilities, viz.;

   (a) total of bills discounted for your customer, with recourse;

   (b) date, name of beneficiary, amount and brief description of any guarantees, bonds or indemnities given to you by the customer for the benefit of third parties;

   (c) date, name of beneficiary, amount and brief description of any guarantees bonds or indemnities given by you, on your customer's behalf, stating where there is recourse to your customer and/or to its parent or any other company within the group;

   (d) total of acceptances;

   (e) total sterling equivalents of outstanding forward foreign exchange contracts;

   (f) total of outstanding liabilities under documentary credits;

   (g) others – please give details.

Other information

10. A list of other banks, or branches of your bank, or associated companies where you are aware that a relationship has been established during the period.

Yours faithfully

....

(official stamp of bank)

....

(authorized signatory)

....

(position)

Reply: Sufficient space should be left for the bank's replies (two-thirds of each page is recommended).

Notes to the standard letter

1. Bank accounts: The phrase 'all accounts' includes details of all current, deposit, loan and foreign currency accounts and other advances or facilities, money held on deposit receipt. The reply should indicate whether the balance is in favour of the bank or customer, and account numbers. Where a number of deposits have been made or uplifted during the year, it is not necessary to give details of each separate deposit transaction as would be required in the case of the opening and closing of accounts.

3. Accrued charges: These can be quoted only on a provisional basis; the rate of notional allowances will not be fixed until near the end of the charging period.

4. Analysis of charges: For the purposes of profit and loss disclosure requirements it is only necessary to ask for details of interest charged. (But see note (6)(b) below in respect of balance sheet disclosure requirements.) The details of the rate of interest applicable to any interest-bearing accounts, or the appropriate formula by which interest is calculated, should be required only exceptionally.

6. Loans and other facilities: The following details are not normally required:

   (a) the date term loans were granted if new or renewed during this period;

   (b) rate of interest charged or similar form of compensation (which information is required by the Companies Act to be disclosed only for facilities which are wholly or partly repayable in more than five years' time);

   (c) the purpose of the facility;

   (d) loan repayment arrangements, where these are included in a written agreement which is available for inspection by the auditor.

7. and 8. Customer's assets:

   (a) *Security* includes details of charge, mortgage or other claims or security registered (e.g. debenture, memorandum of deposit), assets charged and, where appropriate, cross reference to facility specifically secured.

   (b) *Assets* include bonds, stock and share certificates, investments, bearer or other securities; title deeds relating to freehold, leasehold or other property; certificates of tax deposit, bills of exchange or other negotiable instruments receivable (other than cheques); shipping and other commercial documents; deposit receipts (as distinct from any account represented by the deposit receipt). The names of persons who are able to obtain release of the assets should be ascertained from the customer and are usually covered by the bank mandate.

   (c) *Lien:* auditors should be aware that any assets held by the bank for safe custody may be subject to some form of banker's lien, although this may operate only under particular conditions. It should be necessary to enquire only in exceptional circumstances.

   (d) *Bearer securities:* detailed enquiries on bearer securities should be made of the bank only when evidence cannot be obtained from the customer or his banking records.

9. Contingent liabilities: The liabilities under indemnities given in respect of missing bills of lading do not have an expiry date. From time to time the banks take a view on old liabilities and remove some of them from their records. Certain of these old liabilities may not therefore be shown in the figure quoted by the bank, but it cannot be guaranteed that no claim will be incurred subsequently.

10. Other information: Banks are often asked for introductions to other branches or banks for the purpose of establishing new sources of finance. The provision of any available information relating to introduction of new accounts will assist auditors to satisfy themselves that they have information about all of their client's banking relationships.

Notes on matters excluded from the standard letter

Supplementary requests

The standard letter contains all items found to be regularly required for audit purposes. In case of doubt, or specific requirement, auditors may wish to make supplementary requests regarding other items which are not regularly required. These may include the following:

(a) copies of bank statements;

(b) copies of paying-in slips for specified lodgement on specified dates;

(c) details showing make-up of those lodgements;

(d) any list of securities or other documents of title which have been lodged by a bank with its customer as security for deposit with that bank (this particular matter would probably apply only between banking organizations);

(e) interest on any account paid to or by third parties, and the names of those third parties;

(f) receipts for fire and other insurances, and similar documents in the bank's possession;

(g) returned paid cheques;

(h) stopped cheques—these are normally presented through the banking system within the audit period, and therefore there should be no need to seek specific details;

(i) details of third party security, including directors' guarantees if this information is required, the request must be accompanied by a specific authority from the appropriate third parties;

(j) details of outstanding forward foreign exchange contracts, including the particulars of each contract, the dates of maturity and the currencies concerned.

Notes

1. The cost of providing audit information falls on the customer and supplementary requests should be kept to a reasonable minimum.

2. Depending on the terms of the authority which has been given, it may be necessary to seek specific authorization for the disclosure of supplementary information.

Bank mandates

Auditors may require supplementary information about bank mandates as independent verification that board resolutions concerning a company's banking affairs have been duly communicated to the bank so that they may ensure that only authorized persons are acting on behalf of the company. Auditors should ensure that they receive copies of all such resolutions from their clients.

6.4.3 Pending legal matters

Confirmation will often be required from a client company's solicitors regarding contingent liabilities arising from legal matters outstanding at the balance sheet date. From the audit viewpoint pending lawsuits and other actions and claims against the client company may present problems both of ascertainment and appraisal. For this purpose the ICAEW, after consultation with the Council of the Law Society, issued an auditing Statement (3.903) for the guidance of its members. The essential advice conveyed in the Statement is as follows.

The following audit procedures are suggested for the verification of the existence of such claims, though they will not necessarily provide the auditor with adequate information on the likely amounts for which the company may ultimately be responsible:

(a) Reviewing the client's system of recording claims and the procedure for bringing these to the attention of the management or board.

(b) Discussing the arrangements for instructing solicitors with the official(s) responsible for legal matters (for example the head of the legal department, if any, or the company secretary).

(c) Examining the minutes of the board of directors and/or executive or other relevant committee for references to, or indications of, possible claims.

(d) Examining bills rendered by solicitors and correspondence with them, in which connection the solicitors should be requested to furnish bills or estimates of charges to date, or to confirm that they have no unbilled charges.

(e) Obtaining a list of matters referred to solicitors from the appropriate director or official with estimates of the possible ultimate liabilities.

(f) Obtaining a written assurance from the appropriate director or official that he is not aware of any matters referred to solicitors other than those disclosed.

In appropriate circumstances auditors may decide to obtain written confirmations from third parties of certain representations made by directors; for example, the identification and appraisal of contingent liabilities. In the field of legal actions the normal and proper source of such confirmation is the company's legal advisers.

Requests for such confirmations should be kept within the solicitor–client relationship and should thus be issued by the client with a request that a copy of the reply should be sent direct to the auditors.

In order to ascertain whether the information provided by the directors is complete, auditors (especially in certain overseas countries) may decide to arrange for solicitors to be requested to advise whether they have matters in hand which are not listed in the letter of request, and to provide information as to the likely amounts involved. When considering such a non-specific enquiry, auditors should note that the Council of the Law Society has advised solicitors that it is unable to recommend them to comply with requests for information which are more widely drawn than the specimen form of wording sent out in the paragraph below.

Specimen form of request

In these circumstances, the enquiry should normally list matters identified as having been referred to the company's legal advisers in accordance with paragraph (e) above. The following form of wording, appropriate to specific enquiries, has been agreed between the Councils of the Law

Society and the ICAEW as one which may be properly addressed to, and answered by, solicitors:

> In connection with the preparation and audit of our accounts for the year ended ... the directors have made estimates of the amounts of the ultimate liabilities (including costs) which might be incurred, and are regarded as material, in relation to the following matters on which you have been consulted. We should be obliged if you would confirm that in your opinion these estimates are reasonable.

Matter	Estimated Liability, including Costs (£)

The Council of the ICAEW understands the reasons for the view of the Council of the Law Society regarding non-specific enquiries, but nevertheless believes that there may be circumstances in which it is necessary as an audit procedure for an enquiry of a general nature to be addressed to the solicitors in order to confirm that the information provided by the directors is complete in all material particulars.

If the outcome of the enquiries set out above appears satisfactory, auditors would not normally regard the absence of a corroboration of the completeness of a list of legal matters as a reason in itself for qualifying their report. If the enquiries lead to the discovery of significant matters not previously identified, the auditors will wish to extend their enquiries and to request their clients to address further enquiries to, or arrange a meeting with, the solicitors, at which the auditors will wish to be present. *If, however, having regard to all the circumstances, the auditors are unable to satisfy themselves that they have received all the information they require for the purpose of their audit, they must qualify their report.*

6.4.4 A table of typical examples

The instances in which auditors may regard requests for external confirmation as appropriate are too many and too varied to be dealt with exhaustively. Table 6.2 provides a few examples, however, of assets and liabilities whose verification may be facilitated by such confirmation.

6.4.5 APB guidance

In 1995, the APB issued a Standard on 'Using the work of an expert' (SAS 520). Its key points may be summarized as follows:

1. In certain circumstances, the auditor does not possess sufficient knowledge of a matter of material audit significance and he will therefore seek the advice of an expert prior to forming his audit opinion. Examples might include:

   (a) Solicitors – to provide legal opinion, e.g. on the legality of business transactions, or possible outcome of legal actions;

Table 6.2 Assets and liabilities verification by external confirmation

Assets	Liabilities	Confirming third party
Bank balances Securities	Overdrafts Loans Contingent liabilities Accrued interest	Bank (see 'bank letter' in section 6.4.2 for details)
Debtor balances	Creditor balances	Individual debtors/suppliers (see section 6.4.1)
Staff loans		Individual members of staff
	Mortgages Advances Secured loans Accrued interest	Finance house
Valuation of property Valuation of specialized stocks, e.g. gems		Acknowledged/qualified valuation experts
Assets held abroad	Liabilities repayable abroad	Overseas agents; Associate firms
Goods sent to agents on consignment and out on sale-or-return basis		Agents, consignees and sale-or-return holders
Information pertaining to investments in subsidiary companies		Auditors of subsidiaries
Goods held in bond or in warehouse		Harbour Board; Warehouse company
Leased premises – insurance of		Landlord of leased premises
	Pending litigation, possible damages, costs and legal fees outstanding	Solicitors (see section 6.4.3)

(b) Chartered surveyors – to provide property valuations;

(c) Other chartered accountants – to provide technical advice on accounting issues;

(d) Stock valuers – to provide estimates of the resale value of unusual stock items.

2. The auditor should be satisfied that the expert is both competent and objective, and that the terms of reference to the expert are consistent with the audit objectives in seeking the particular expertise.

3. The auditor should consider the form and clarity of the report provided by the expert and the effect of any disclaimers included.

4. Where the direct cost of the services of the expert is to be borne by the client this should be discussed and agreed in advance.

5. The expert's report should be retained on the current year audit working papers file.

6.5   Letters of representation

Having now considered the use by the auditor of confirmations received externally, we must turn to the confirmations received from the officers of the client company itself. These confirmations are usually contained in what used to be known as a directors' certificate, now called the letter of representation.

The broad purpose of such letters is to place on record the representations of management on significant matters directly affecting the accounts. The letter of representation also serves to remind directors that it is their statutory responsibility to ensure that a true and fair view is given by the accounts which they have prepared and placed before the members in general meeting (a matter about which they, regrettably, all too often need reminding). Such a letter will not, of course, relieve the auditor of any of his own responsibilities in connection with the audit.

Being signed by the directors, the letters represent audit evidence from the highest authority within the company on a range of important questions, particularly those that are in essence matters of opinion, e.g. obsolescence and wear and tear of plant, or contingent liabilities. These are questions which the auditors would discuss with the directors in any event: the letter of representation merely formalizes this. The letter therefore plays a part within the context of normal verification procedures, and should be requested just before the final approval of the accounts by the directors.

Unfortunately, many audit firms do not appreciate its significance and all too often request the letter of representation as an afterthought; perhaps they believe, quite erroneously, that it might in some way protect them in the event of subsequent litigation by shifting responsibility onto the shoulders of the management. Responsibility which is already on the shoulders of management hardly needs to be shifted there, and is in any case quite distinct from the auditor's own duty to express an opinion. It is not surprising that when the auditors are themselves unclear about the letter's true purpose and effect, the directors often resent (and even refuse) the request.

6.5.1   Recommended procedure and content

The letter of representation should normally be obtained from the client's principal executive. However, when in a large company the executive responsibilities are divided, a single all-inclusive letter may be inappropriate, and it might be preferable to obtain separate statements from the members of the executive in relation to the particular matters within their charge. It may be desirable, however, to obtain a general overriding letter covering all the relevant matters.

The client's headed notepaper should be used for the letter, which should be addressed to the auditors; the relevant representations may be incorporated either in full in the text of the letter itself, or set out in an annexed memorandum. If the audit firm uses a standard form of letter, it should be carefully adapted to meet the circumstances of each client and should concentrate on the matters which have a material effect on the accounts. It is most important to avoid giving the impression that the letter is a matter of form only, or that it is regarded by the auditor as being a mere 'routine'. In certain circumstances it will be desirable for the representation to be recorded in board minutes, to ensure that *all* directors are aware of what is being represented to the auditors in their name.

The following are examples (not exhaustive) of the areas where the directors' confirmation might be sought in the letter:

General

► Acknowledgement of the directors' responsibility to keep proper accounting records and to prepare true and fair accounts.
► Disclosure to the auditors of all accounts, books and records, including minute books.
► Consistency of application of accounting policies.
► Events occurring after balance sheet date.
► Compliance with certain specialized legislation.
► Outstanding litigation.
► Disclosure of all material capital commitments.
► Disclosure of related party transactions and of the party controlling the company.

Assets

► The company has a satisfactory title to all its assets.
► Adequacy of depreciation charged.
► Basis of valuing stocks of materials, work in progress and finished goods.
► Adequacy of provisions for obsolescence and other inventory losses.
► Realizability of certain assets (e.g. debtors).
► Amount of capital expenditure authorized by the board and amount contracted for at balance sheet date.

Liabilities

► All known liabilities have been fully provided for.
► The nature and amount of all contingent liabilities have been disclosed.
► Disclosure of all secured liabilities.

Profit and loss account

▶ Disclosure of all extraordinary, exceptional non-recurring and prior year items.

▶ Disclosure of details of any change in accounting policy.

6.5.2   APB guidance on representation by management

In 1995 the APB issued Statement of Auditing Standards no. 440 – 'Management representations'. The appendix to the Standard includes an example of a management representation letter which is reproduced below.

Example of a management representation letter

The following example of management representations from a company to its auditors is in the form a letter, but it is not intended to be a standard letter, nor to imply that management representations must necessarily be in the form of a letter. Representations by management vary from one entity to another and from one year to the next.

Although seeking representations from management on a variety of matters may serve to focus management's attention on those matters, and thus cause management specifically to address those matters in more detail than would otherwise be the case, auditors are cognisant of the limitations of management representations as audit evidence as set out in SAS 440.

(Company letterhead)

(To the auditors)   (Date)

We confirm to the best of our knowledge and belief, and having made appropriate enquiries of other directors and officials of the company, the following representations given to you in connection with your audit of the financial statements for the period ended 31 December 19...

(1)   We acknowledge as directors our responsibilities under the Companies Act 1985 for preparing financial statements which give a true and fair view and for making accurate representations to you. All the accounting records have been made available to you for the purpose of your audit and all the transactions undertaken by the company have been properly reflected and recorded in the accounting records. All other records and related information, including minutes of all management and shareholders' meetings, have been made available to you.

(2)   The legal claim by ABC Limited has been settled out of court by a payment of £258,000. No further amounts are expected to be paid, and no similar claims have been received or are expected to be received.

(3) In connection with deferred tax not provided, the following assumptions reflect the intentions and expectations of the company:

(a) capital investment of £450,000 is planned over the next three years;

(b) there are no plans to sell revalued properties; and

(c) we are not aware of any indications that the situation is likely to change so as to necessitate the inclusion of a provision for tax payable in the financial statements.

(4) The company has not had, or entered into, at any time during the period any arrangement, transaction or agreement to provide credit facilities (including loans, quasi loans or credit transactions) for directors or to guarantee or provide security for such matters.

(5) There have been no events since the balance sheet date which necessitate revision of the figures included in the financial statements or inclusion of a note thereto.

As minuted by the board of directors at its meeting on .... (date)

———————   ———————
Chairman   Secretary

Other signatories may include those with specific knowledge of the relevant matters, for example the chief financial officer.

The paragraphs included in the example above relate to a specific set of circumstances. Set out below are examples of other issues which, depending on the particular circumstances, the materiality of the amounts concerned to the financial statements and the extent of other audit evidence obtained regarding them, may be the subject of representations from management:

▶ *the extent of the purchase of goods on terms which include reservation of title by suppliers;*

▶ *the absence of knowledge of circumstances which could result in losses on long-term contracts;*

▶ *the reasons for concluding that an overdue debt from a related party is fully recoverable; and*

▶ *confirmation of the extent of guarantees, warranties or other financial commitments relating to subsidiary undertakings or related parties.*

The letter of representation should not normally include matters on which the auditors are able to obtain evidence from independent sources. Essentially, the letter should include reference to matters known only to the directors (by seeking 'negative assurance'), and technical or highly subjective judgemental issues.

A final point worth making is that the *Companies Act 1985* makes it a criminal offence for officers of a company to supply auditors with false information – whether orally or in writing, and whether knowingly or recklessly. It is therefore unnecessary for a prosecution to establish wilful intent to deceive; the establishment of recklessness (a high degree of carelessness) is all that is needed. This naturally increases the usefulness to the auditor of the letter of representation (but may in some cases correspondingly increase the reluctance of the management to give it).

6.6   Requests for 'comfort' letters

6.6.1   Requests from other auditors

These requests may arise when auditors of a holding company, other than the firm in question, have written requesting general statements about the accounts of a subsidiary which the firm have been auditing. It appears that these statements are intended to give the auditors of the holding company 'comfort' before they sign their report on the group. An example of the type of statement they have asked subsidiary auditors to make is as follows:

> We know of no reason why the enclosed statements or our report cannot be used by you in forming an opinion on the consolidated financial statements of XYZ Limited and we know of no inter-company transactions or other information, not fully disclosed in the financial statements, which should be considered by you in relation to such purpose except as set forth below:

It is unwise to make such a statement. It is not generally possible for auditors of a subsidiary company to know whether information which, for instance, auditors of the subsidiary do not consider relevant for their purposes might be relevant to the auditors of the holding company. It is considered that the request for such a representation should be put to the management of the holding company and to the management of the subsidiary, and not to the auditors.

Advice to auditors who receive such letters is that a reply along the following lines should be made:

> We refer to your request dated ... asking for certain general confirmations.
> We regret that it is not our practice to make such general statements on financial statements audited by us as we are not aware of what matters you should consider when forming your opinion, and we believe such information should be supplied to you by your client.
> Should you have any specific query which you would like us to consider, please do not hesitate to let us know.

Similarly, requests from auditors of subsidiaries are submitted to auditors of the parent company. This is a complementary situation to that described above. It is believed, here again, that a general statement of 'comfort' should not be made. Auditors of the parent company do not necessarily know whether information which (for instance) they as parent company auditors are aware of is relevant to the auditors of one, or some, of the subsidiaries. It is considered that the request for such a general statement should be made to the management of a subsidiary company for them to transmit it to the management of the parent company. It is not considered that the request should be made to parent company auditors. It is suggested that firms should reply to any such requests along the following lines:

> We refer to your request dated ... which requested certain information from us in connection with your audit of the above subsidiary companies of the XYZ Group for the year ended 31 December 19XX.
>
> We regret that it is not our practice to make such general statements in respect of matters which might affect the audit of subsidiary companies not audited by us, because we are not necessarily aware of what matters you should consider when forming your opinion. We believe such information should be supplied to you by your client.
>
> Should you have any specific query which you would like us to consider, please do not hesitate to let us know.

6.6.2 Requests to parent company

Auditors of a subsidiary company whose financial position is such that, taken by itself, its accounts should not be prepared on a going concern basis, should attempt to obtain confirmation from the holding company that it intends to continue supporting its subsidiary company.

If the auditors are satisfied that the holding company is in a position to give the required financial support, they should request their clients to obtain the confirmation in writing, addressed to the subsidiary company, along the following lines:

> It is the intention of AB Holding Company Ltd to continue for the foreseeable future our financial support of XY Limited, and to ensure that the company is in a position to meet its liabilities. This intention is subject of a board minute dated xxx.

The subsidiary auditors should ensure that they file a copy of such a letter on their audit file.

If, however, the subsidiary auditors are not satisfied that the holding company is in a position to give the required financial support or that it may be unwilling to provide such a letter of support to its subsidiary, the auditors should consider qualifying the accounts.

While it is unlikely that such letters are enforceable at law, they do provide appropriate audit evidence to corroborate the directors' contention that the accounts of the subsidiary should be prepared on a going concern basis. It is recommended that reference be made to the judgments in the High Court and Court of Appeal in the case of *Kleinwort Benson Ltd* v *Malaysia Mining Corporation* (*TLR* 14 January 1988 and 8 February 1989) in which the legal status of comfort letters was contested.

6.7 The auditor's use of analytical review

Audit work on the final accounts involves a good deal more than the direct or indirect verification of specific assets and liabilities. It is equally important that the accounts, in themselves, should be seen by the auditor to 'make sense'. This is a gradual process, and the auditor's confidence in the view conveyed by the accounts builds up steadily as his verification work proceeds. Towards the closing stages of the review of the accounts the auditor may find that the decision-type flow diagram shown in Figure 6.1 assists in determining the extent of further evidence of an analytical nature which may be needed in reaching the audit opinion to be embodied in the report. The importance of analytical review procedures in forming the audit opinion is stressed in the APB Standard on 'Analytical procedures' (no. 410).

The flowchart suggests that (1) the existence of available analytical evidence, and (2) the creation or procurement of evidence by the auditor himself may be viewed as

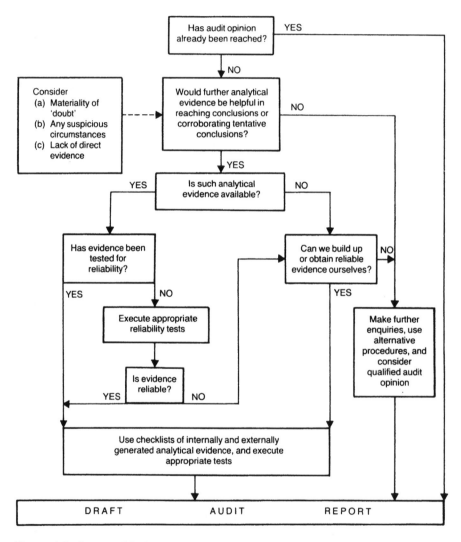

Figure 6.1   Review of final accounts – the use of analytical evidence

alternatives. In practice, where both appropriate and practicable, the auditor will make use of both sources of evidence.

The flowchart makes reference to 'checklists of internally and externally generated analytical evidence'. The terms 'internally' and 'externally' should be taken to relate respectively to evidence created *within* the client organization and that which has been independently generated (including evidence compiled by the auditor himself). The precise form and content of such checklists will vary considerably from one audit firm to another, but Table 6.1 provides a clear picture of the nature of evidence envisaged.

The auditor should assess the extent to which the internally generated data in the left hand column may be used for his purposes. The point is that data *exist* – is he justified in ignoring them simply because they do not form a part of the company's 'normal' accounting records? The statutes give the auditor the right to receive *all* information and explanations that he considers necessary for his purposes, as well as the right to examine *all* records, documents and vouchers. There is therefore no restriction other than that which he imposes upon himself.

Nevertheless, far too few auditors take the trouble to examine the management and costing records, either for the purpose of forming (or for corroborating) their opinion on the reliability of the financial and accounting records, and hence the draft published accounts. If, for example, divisional profit figures are produced internally each month, it is unlikely that they will agree with the figures in the published accounts – but some form of reconciliation, possibly within predictable margins, should certainly be possible.

Table 6.3 provides only a handful of examples of the use of analytical evidence. The full review of the final accounts would, so far as the auditor's own comparisons, etc., are concerned, include the following additional tests and examinations:

1. Consider whether increases or decreases in charges for wages, materials consumed and other variable expenses appear to be proportionate to the increase or decrease in turnover. Ascertain the quantities of turnover where the monetary value thereof has been inflated or deflated by price changes, alterations in rates of VAT or customs duties.

2. Obtain a satisfactory explanation for any material change in the rate of gross profit shown.

3. Scrutinize any exceptional transactions or items of a non-recurring nature which have resulted in charges or credits of a material amount to the revenue of the period under review.

4. Consider the changes in the position disclosed by the balance sheet; for example, does this reveal increased liquidity, a proportionate reduction in capital or long-term liabilities, or increases in fixed assets?

5. Compare the values of stocks with those adopted for insurance purposes.

6. Compare the total due by trade debtors to turnover and compare this ratio with the corresponding figures for the previous year. If it is found that longer credit appears to have been taken by customers, pay particular attention to the provision

Table 6.3 Examples of the auditors' use of analytical evidence

Examples of evidence generated within client organization (internal)	Examples of evidence generated independently (external)	
	By auditor	By outside organizations
Cash budgets/forecasts	Comparisons of material items	Returns to trade federations
Departmental expenditure budgets	▶ previous years ▶ other companies in same trade	Interfirm comparisons
Divisional/Company/Group profit forecasts	Trends in accounting ratios, e.g.	Published government statistics for the particular industry/trade
Divisional results (e.g. monthly)	▶ closing stock : cost of sales ▶ debtors : sales	
Internal management ratios, e.g.	▶ purchases : creditors ▶ gross profit : sales	Information supplied to insurance companies
▶ profitability	▶ net profit : sales	
▶ efficiency	▶ current assets : current liabilities	Returns to Customs and Excise and other government agencies
▶ liquidity	▶ fixed assets : shareholders' equity	
▶ other performance indicators		
▶ product/sales mix	Age analysis – Stocks	
▶ marketing expenditure and sales	– Debtors	
▶ sales and R&D expenditure		
Standard costing records		
▶ fixed cost recovery rates		
▶ variance analysis		
▶ adjustments to standards		
▶ pricing analysis		

for bad and doubtful debts, and the possibility that remittances have not been accounted for. If sales of an exceptional amount are recorded towards the end of the period, make certain that the cut-off procedure has been closely observed and that the sales in question are properly attributable to that period; examine the returns for the following period.

7. Scrutinize the directors' minutes books for references to matters affecting the accounts, e.g. capital commitments, pending litigation, sums payable under service agreements, capital and loan issues, etc.

8. Consider the reasonableness of provisions made for depreciation and the adequacy of any further sums set aside for the increased cost of replacing the assets concerned, whether or not part of an established system of current cost accounting.

9. Ascertain whether there have been any changes in the basis of accounting which have resulted in a material increase or decrease in recorded profit.

10. Determine the amounts and nature of any contingent liabilities and commitments for capital expenditure not provided for in the accounts, and ascertain the extent of any contracts for forward purchases or sales. In cases of forward contracts, consider whether any provision for anticipated losses is required at the balance sheet date.

Auditors will, in practice, design working papers or computerized schedules to assist them in performing this type of analytical review. It will be remembered (see the concluding pages of the previous chapter on risk-based auditing) that the results of analytical review may well contribute up to one-third of the total assurance sought by an auditor that the financial statements are free of material misstatement or distortion. An illustration of a working paper sheet which auditors might use in the course of implementing analytical review work is shown in Figure 6.2.

6.7.1 APB Statement of Auditing Standards

In 1995 the APB issued Statement of Auditing Standards no. 410 – 'Analytical procedures'. Its key points may be summarized as follows:

1. The SAS stresses the importance of applying analytical procedures at both the planning and overall review stages.

2. Analytical procedures in practice are:
   (a) Comparison of current year results to prior year;
   (b) Comparison of current year results to previously prepared budgets/forecasts;
   (c) Comparison of current year records to competitor or industry norm;
   (d) Reconciling amounts, ratios or statistics derived from current year results with other related features within the current year results, e.g. an increase in turnover being consistent with an increase in debtors and doubtful debt provision.

SIGNIFICANT ACCOUNTING RATIOS	PRIOR YEARS			CURRENT YEAR		Yardstick ratios
FINANCIAL STATEMENTS FIGURES	19..	19..	19..	Interim .../.../...	Final	
Credit sales	_____	_____	103,248	_____	204,791	
Total sales	_____	_____	103,248	_____	204,791	
Cost of sales	_____	_____	66,476	_____	137,943	
Gross profit	_____	_____	36,772	_____	66,848	
Net profit	_____	_____	4,565	_____	14,848	
Stocks and work in progress	_____	_____	9,556	_____	30,310	
Debtors	_____	_____	31,816	_____	65,217	
Liquid assets	_____	_____	100	_____	100	
Current assets	_____	_____	41,472	_____	95,627	
Current liabilities	_____	_____	41,795	_____	97,010	
Net current assets	_____	_____	(323)	_____	(1,383)	
Fixed assets	_____	_____	31,299	_____	80,838	
Total assets	_____	_____	72,711	_____	176,465	
Total liabilities	_____	_____	54,706	_____	141,752	
Capital employed	_____	_____	30,976	_____	79,455	
Shareholders' funds	_____	_____	18,065	_____	34,713	
PROFIT RATIOS						
Gross profit to total sales	_____	_____	36%	_____	33%	_____
Net profit to total sales	_____	_____	4.4%	_____	7.3%	_____
Net profit to capital employed	_____	_____	15%	_____	19%	_____
TRADING RATIOS						
Total sales to capital employed	_____	_____	3.3 : 1	_____	2.6:1	_____
Total sales to net current assets	_____	_____	_____	_____	_____	_____
Cost of sales to stocks and work in progress	_____	_____	7.0 : 1	_____	4.6:1	_____
SOLVENCY RATIOS						
Current assets to current liabilities	_____	_____	1:1	_____	1:1	_____
Liquid assets to current liabilities	_____	_____	_____	_____	_____	_____
Credit sales to debtors	_____	_____	3.2: 1	_____	3.1:1	_____
CAPITAL RATIOS						
Shareholders' funds to total assets	_____	_____	0.2:1	_____	0.2:1	_____
Current liabilities to shareholders' funds	_____	_____	2.3:1	_____	2.8:1	_____
Gearing/total liabilities to shareholders' funds	_____	_____	3.0:1	_____	4.1:1	_____
Other	_____	_____	_____	_____	_____	_____

Figure 6.2   Significant accounting ratios

In each case, explanation is sought for variations or, indeed, non-variations if a variation was expected.

3. The SAS states that analytical procedures may also be performed as substantive procedures. It is a matter of judgement by the auditor of the available procedures of reducing detection risk. It is recommended that auditors should use analytical procedures in conjunction with other substantive procedures so that all underlying accounting records are audited. It can be dangerous to employ analytical procedures as a substitute for other substantive tests without due regard to the detection risk.

4. The SAS stresses that the auditor should follow through any apparent distortions and inconsistencies and obtain appropriate corroborative evidence. Evidencing in the form of an audit file note should be encouraged. Such matters may also be included within the scope of the management representations letter.

5. Analytical procedures are often overlooked at the planning stage, especially where the auditor also prepares the financial statements, and left until later. However, in order to comply with SAS 410.2 the auditor should attempt to obtain some form of financial information e.g. budgets or interim management accounts in order to undertake analytical procedures that might identify areas of potential audit risk. This could be incorporated in an audit planning checklist.

6. As an example, if a payroll clerk has registered dummy employees to pay himself additional salaries fraudulently, and, say, there is no other formal evidence of authorization of the payroll by management, then his otherwise plausible explanation for the increase in total salary costs in the year cannot be regarded as reliable. Alternative substantive procedures should be carried out.

7. The auditor should consider how to evidence and record in his working papers the results of his analytical procedures. A typical schedule for the profit and loss account is shown on Table 6.4. Clearly any audit conclusions can only be based on a schedule that is properly prepared and contains sufficient detail.

8. It will rarely be sufficient simply to accept the explanations given by management without attempting to corroborate them, at least by inspection of the underlying records.

Table 6.4   Typical record of profit and loss account analytical review

	Current Year	Prior Year	Variance	% Change	Explanation/ Commentary
Sales	x	x	x	x	
Cost of sales	x	x	x	x	
Gross profit	x	x	x	x	
Overhead costs (as analysed)	x	x	x	x	
Net profit	x	x	x		

6.8 Related party transactions

Within the realm of questionable transactions are those whose terms and conditions are, or appear to be, unduly favourable to one of the parties. Depending upon the circumstances and materiality of the transactions concerned, the auditor may need to consider the adequacy of the disclosure of these transactions in the accounts. For example, the *Companies Act 1985* requires the specific disclosure of transactions, etc. in which directors have a material interest, but aside from such statutory provisions the auditor may take the view that the disclosure of what are usually called 'related party transactions' is required to enable the accounts to present a true and fair view.

The following might be included within a definition of related parties themselves:

1. Organizations under common control with the client company (regarding 'control' as the power to direct the financial and operating policies with a view to gaining economic benefits from its activities).
2. Shareholders with substantial holdings of voting shares (exceeding, say, 20 per cent).
3. The key management of the reporting entity and of its parent and their immediate families.
4. Associated companies, subsidiary and parent undertakings.
5. Any other party which has the ability to prevent the company from pursuing its own interests independently.

The following types of transaction may indicate to an auditor the existence of related parties:

1. Borrowing/lending at rates of interest substantially higher/lower than current market rates.
2. Sales/purchases of assets at prices substantially different from those currently ruling.
3. Straightforward exchanges of assets in a manner which masks the underlying value of the assets exchanged.
4. The granting of loans with no scheduled repayment terms specified at the time of granting the loans, against little or no security.

In order to ascertain the existence of any related parties the auditor should:

1. Evaluate the company's own procedures, if any, for identifying, and properly accounting for, related party transactions.
2. Enquire of appropriate management personnel for the names of all related parties and for details of any transactions between these parties and the company during the period.
3. Examine the company's annual return to ascertain in which other companies the directors hold directorships.

4. Ascertain the names of all pension funds connected with the company and the managers thereof.

5. Examine the register of substantial shareholders in order to identify shareholders holding more than 20 per cent of the voting shares in issue.

6. Review material investment transactions during the period to discover whether the nature and extent of these investments have created related parties.

Once related parties have been identified, all audit staff members should be supplied with their names so that they may become aware of transactions with the parties during their examination.

It should be remembered that related party transactions are not illegal – the questions which arise relate purely to disclosure in the accounts and/or the directors' report. Many related party situations result in one or more companies within a group incurring expenditure at a level which exceeds what would be incurred if they were dealing with outsiders on an arm's length basis. In such situations it is of paramount importance for the auditor to ensure the following:

1. That all directors of the companies adversely affected are fully aware of the situation and that the amounts have been quantified as far as possible.

2. That the position of minority interests has been considered. Where an auditor is responsible for the accounts of a subsidiary thus adversely affected, he has a primary duty to ensure that minority interests in that subsidiary are made aware of the position in the notes to the accounts or, if necessary, in the auditor's report.

Accounts which do no more than reflect the trading results in terms of accurate monetary amounts cannot be said to give a fair as well as a true view since they give no indication of profitability/net asset levels attainable in circumstances in which all transactions with outsiders are conducted at arm's length.

6.9 Events after the balance sheet date

6.9.1 The Accounting Standards SSAP 17 and SSAP18

The unavoidably contrived nature of the financial year, ending at close of business on a particular day, has long been recognized. For this reason it would be totally unreasonable deliberately to blind oneself to events which, though they may have a bearing on the results and financial position reported, fall outside of the strict confines of the period in question. The question of the extent to which account should be taken of such events, and how their effect may be reflected in the published accounts, has long been debated, and the ASC has published Accounting Standard SSAP 17 – 'Accounting for post-balance sheet events'. The appendix to SSAP 17 gives examples of items normally classified as adjusting and non-adjusting events. This appendix is reproduced below.

Appendix

This Appendix is for general guidance and does not form part of the statement of standard accounting practice. The examples are merely illustrative and the lists are not exhaustive.

The examples listed distinguish between those normally classified as adjusting events and as non-adjusting events. However, in exceptional circumstances, to accord with the prudence concept, an adverse event which would normally be classified as non-adjusting may need to be reclassified as adjusting. In such circumstances, full disclosure of the adjustment would be required.

Adjusting events

The following are examples of post-balance sheet events which normally should be classified as adjusting events:

(a) *Fixed assets.* The subsequent determination of the purchase price or of the proceeds of sale of assets purchased or sold before the year-end.

(b) *Property.* A valuation which provides evidence of a permanent diminution in value.

(c) *Investments.* The receipt of a copy of the financial statements or other information in respect of an unlisted company which provides evidence of a permanent diminution in the value of a long-term investment.

(d) *Stocks and works in progress*

 (i) The receipt of proceeds of sales after the balance sheet date or other evidence concerning the net realizable value of stocks.

 (ii) The receipt of evidence that the previous estimate of accrued profit on a long-term contract was materially inaccurate.

(e) *Debtors.* The renegotiation of amounts owing by debtors, or the insolvency of a debtor.

(f) *Dividends receivable.* The declaration of dividends by subsidiaries and associated companies relating to periods prior to the balance sheet date of the holding company.

(g) *Taxation.* The receipt of information regarding rates of taxation.

(h) *Claims.* Amounts received or receivable in respect of insurance claims which were in the course of negotiation at the balance sheet date.

(i) *Discoveries.* The discovery of errors or frauds which show that the financial statements were incorrect.

Non-adjusting events

The following are examples of post-balance sheet events which normally should be classified as non-adjusting events:

(a) Mergers and acquisitions.

(b) Reconstructions and proposed reconstructions.

(c) Issues of shares or debentures.

(d) Purchases and sales of fixed assets and investments.

(e) Losses of fixed assets or stocks as a result of a catastrophe such as fire or flood.

(f) Opening new trading activities or extending existing trading activities.

(g) Closing a significant part of the trading activities if this was not anticipated at the year-end.

(h) Decline in the value of property and investments held as fixed assets, if it can be demonstrated that the decline occurred after the year-end.

(i) Changes in rates of foreign exchange.

(j) Government actions, such as nationalization.

(k) Strikes and other labour disputes.

(l) Augmentation of pension benefits.

Following the publication of SSAP 17, the APC sought Counsel's opinion on its implications for auditors, with particular reference to the dating of the audit report. The APC published a summary of this in question and answer form, as follows.

Question 1
Should directors date their signature on annual accounts?

Answer
There is no statutory need for them to date their signatures, although they should be encouraged to do so, as an indication of the date on which they formally considered and approved the accounts. SSAP 17 (paragraph 26) now requires disclosure of the date on which directors have approved the accounts.

Question 2
If the directors decide to date their signature, what date should they use?

Answer
The date on which they met and approved the accounts. In some cases where they are unable to obtain up-to-date information from a subsidiary, it may be appropriate for them to make it clear that when approving the accounts they did not have information from the specified subsidiary regarding any subsequent events which may have occurred after a stated date.

Question 3
What date should the auditor use when he signs his report on the accounts?

Answer
The date on which he commits himself to expressing an opinion on accounts which the directors have approved. This may not be the same as the date on which he physically signs a final printed copy of his report, but if this date is substantially later (for

instance, where the auditor's final signature has been delayed by illness) then both dates should be given.

Question 4

Can the auditor date his report before the date on which the directors may wish to approve the accounts?

Answer

No. Until the directors have approved the accounts, accounts do not exist on which the auditor can report.

Question 5

Can the directors approve the accounts, subject to certain matters being resolved or certain figures adjusted?

Answer

If the directors approve the accounts subject to a specific, quantified adjustment, that is a valid approval (e.g. they may require a different amount of dividend payable, or an increase of £5,000 in the bad debt provision). However, it does not constitute valid approval of the accounts if there remains outstanding an unidentified or unquantified adjustment which requires further exercise of judgement or discretion (e.g. the directors cannot validly approve accounts 'subject to reviewing the adequacy of the bad debt provision').

Question 6

Does the auditor have responsibility for events which occur between the date of the balance sheet and the date of an annual general meeting?

Answer

Yes. From the end of the accounting year up to the time he finishes his fieldwork, the auditor has the responsibility to look actively for events which would materially affect the view given by the financial statements. During the whole of the period when the accounts are being finalized and approved by the board and by the auditor, the auditor should carry out procedures with respect to the period after the balance sheet date in order to discover any subsequent events that may require adjustment or disclosure (as defined in SSAP 17). From then on, until the date of the annual general meeting, the auditor should remain receptive to information which could affect his view of the financial statements. He need not actively look for evidence during this period, but he should take note of and evaluate any information that he comes upon.

Question 7

What should the auditor do if, after he has signed his report but before the annual general meeting, he obtains information which materially affects his view of the financial statements?

Answer

He should in the first instance draw the matter to the attention of the directors. In extreme circumstances (e.g. refusal of the directors to take any action) he may need to make a statement at the annual general meeting.

Question 8

Does the auditor have any responsibility in relation to the accounts laid before the annual general meeting for events occurring after that meeting?

Answer

No.

It is worth observing that Counsel's opinion was probably sought chiefly because SSAP 17 implies that once directors have approved the accounts no further adjustments to them can be made. Should post-balance sheet events, which indicate a need for revised accounts, occur *after* such approval has been given, the Standard blandly states that they do not fall within its scope, and that the onus is on the directors to consider publishing the relevant information so that readers are not misled. Where, one is compelled to ask, does this directorial discretion leave the auditor?

The problem stems from the notion that some final date must exist after which the accounts should no longer be subject to amendment – an idea which has no basis whatever in the law, whose ultimate and overriding requirement is the ephemeral 'true and fair view'. Even if it means publicly withdrawing accounts already issued, the discovery of a material misstatement at *any* time, even after the AGM, should surely not be suppressed. It is noteworthy that, in his answer to question 7, Counsel did not suggest any amendment to the audit report; this is a curious omission, in effect allowing a misleading opinion to go on permanent public record.

Of special interest is Counsel's view on the level of audit responsibility for considering the effect of events between the balance sheet date and the AGM (question 6), since this accords to a large degree with the American standard SAS 1 in suggesting that there is a logical distinction between periods of 'active' and 'passive' responsibility. Until the auditor's 'fieldwork' is completed he has an 'active' responsibility to look out for events which may materially affect the view presented by the accounts; during the ensuing period, when accounts are being finalized and approved, special 'procedures' should be employed to discover whether adjusting or non-adjusting events have occurred – although how these procedures differ from the earlier ones (prior to completing fieldwork) is not explained by Counsel. Between the date of approval of the accounts and the annual general meeting the auditor, according to Counsel, should 'remain receptive to information which could affect his view of the financial statements' – although the meaning of this suggestive attitude is open to a range of interpretations.

What of events occurring *after* the AGM? Does the auditor have any lingering responsibility? Counsel, as we have seen (question 8), gave an emphatic and un-equivocal 'no', but it is difficult to see any legal basis for so bald an assertion. In one well-publicized *cause célèbre* in 1977, it transpired that the accounts of a public company, having been approved at the AGM, published and filed, included a material debt due from an associate (which was in fact never received) of £4.3 million within the figure of 'cash at bank'.

Although the full details of the fiasco and its discovery were never fully revealed, it was believed that the error was discovered during the following interim audit. In such circumstances, especially in the case of a public company whose shares are traded every day on the basis of its latest publicly filed accounts, it is difficult to see how silence by the auditor can ever be justified on the grounds that the AGM has already passed the accounts. The question of the auditor's responsibility at different times is considered further in the following chapter.

In 1995 the APB issued Statement of Auditing Standards no. 150 – 'Subsequent events'. It key points may be summarised as follows:

1. Auditors should perform audit procedures which will identify subsequent events that occur between the balance sheet date and the date of the audit report.

2. Typical audit procedures include:

   (a) enquiry of management,

   (b) review of minutes,

   (c) review of post-year-end accounting records and management accounts.

3. The auditor may, as a matter of course, seek a written management representation that there are no subsequent events that should be reflected in the financial statements.

4. Subsequent events (favourable or unfavourable) are those that:

   (a) provide additional evidence relating to conditions existing at the balance sheet date; or

   (b) concern conditions which did not exist at the balance sheet date, but which may be of such materiality that their disclosure is required to ensure that the financial statements are not misleading.

5. Timing delays, for whatever reason, can arise between the completion of the on-site audit fieldwork and the finalization of the audit. In these circumstances the auditor may consider it necessary to make a further site visit prior to signing the audit report.

6. Where, however, more than, say, two months elapse following the completion of the fieldwork OR the auditor has been put on enquiry, he should consider and document his reasoning as to whether further representations from the client should be sought, combined where necessary with a review of management accounts or a site visit to look through the accounting records for large/unusual transactions. Such further representations might take the following form:

   We consider that since the balance sheet date:

   (a) we have not become aware of any material changes being required to estimates or assumptions used in preparing the financial statements, particularly in relation to stocks, debtors, creditors, provisions or litigation in progress;

(b) no additional or revised commitments, borrowings or guarantees have been entered into; nor has any notification been received of a review of these arrangements;

(c) there have been no major acquisitions, disposals, losses or changes in value of the fixed assets;

(d) no new issues of shares or debentures, or any agreement to merge or liquidate has been made or is planned;

(e) no assets have been destroyed, for example by fire or flood;

(f) no unusual accounting adjustments have been made to the financial statements or are contemplated;

(g) no events have occurred which might bring into question the appropriateness of the accounting policies used in the financial statements;

(h) no litigation has arisen which has not been previously disclosed;

(i) there has been no significant change in the structure or organisation of the business;

(j) minutes of all meetings of the shareholders and directors (including committees of the board) held during the year and up to date of this letter have been produced to you, and are complete and authentic records of proceedings at such meetings.

7. The logistics of dating of audit reports (refer to SAS 600 covered in a later chapter) may require that all letters to audit clients sending accounts for approval and return should include the following paragraph (or similar):

Professional rules require the date of our Auditors' Report to be the date on which we physically sign it. Since it is not possible for us to sign our Report before you have indicated by signature your own approval of the financial statements, it is essential that these, duly signed, should be returned to us promptly, preferably by return post. Any undue delay in returning the financial statements to us, say beyond five working days, may necessitate further audit enquiries to ensure that nothing has occurred that may affect our opinion.

8. In certain cases it may be acceptable to request a faxed copy of the signed balance sheet from clients, in order to allow the audit report to be dated on the same day.

9. If more than five working days elapse, or the auditor has been put on notice of a possible change in circumstances, further enquiries may be necessary to ensure the audit opinion remains unchanged. These further enquiries should be documented and signed by the audit partner.

Inevitably there are situations that cannot be resolved by reference to any formal advice. Before the advent of SSAP 17 the published accounts of Grand Metropolitan Hotels included a note explaining their treatment of post-balance sheet events. Two such events were described: the first related to the sale of Grandmet's interest in Carlsberg Breweries for £10 million; and the second was a substantial 'rights' issue of shares, of some £27 million. Both events were effected and concluded after the balance sheet date, but were treated as adjusting events on the 'grounds' that effective board decisions relating to them had been reached shortly before the balance sheet date.

No one would dispute the legitimacy of regarding such material post-balance sheet transactions as 'non-adjusting' events – indeed the 'true and fair view' surely demands that they be fully explained in the notes to the accounts. However, by treating them as 'adjusting' (the *nunc pro tunc* syndrome of pretending that what happened after, actually happened before) the consequences were:

1. To treat £37 million of cash, which came in some time after the year-end, as if it were in the bank on the balance sheet date, and show it as such (one wonders how the audit schedules for bank balances must have appeared).
2. To include some £3.5 million of profit of the Carlsberg deal in the results 'for the period' which, without this transaction, would have disclosed a £2.9 million loss.
3. To enable the funds statement (after the £37 million injection) to show that the year's activities were self-financing.

All of this was on the strength of pre-balance sheet board decisions. The audit report, incidentally, was presented without qualification.

Would the existence of SSAP 17 at that time have made any difference? The answer, I regret, is no. The Standard does, it is true, require disclosure of those post balance sheet events which represent the 'maturity ... of a transaction entered into before the year-end, the substance of which was primarily to alter the appearance of the company's balance sheet'. But this disclosure was, as we have seen, amply provided in the notes to the Grand Metropolitan accounts.

What is clearly missing from the Standard, however, is a requirement that the mere minuted intention of the board (e.g. to sell an asset or issue shares) is not of itself enough to fall within the definition of adjusting events, i.e. those 'which provide additional evidence of conditions existing at the balance sheet date'.

Accounting for contingencies

Accounting for contingencies presents difficulties which are obviously closely related to those dealt with above, and it is therefore worth referring to SSAP 18 on this subject.

The APC, in *True and Fair*, has provided some rule-of-thumb advice on how the standard should be interpreted by auditors. Although its expression is rudimentary, it nevertheless provides a useful starting point for such considerations. It is paraphrased in Table 6.5.

6.9.2   The 'subsequent events' programme

Although it is generally accepted that the earliest possible publication of the accounts materially enhances their value to all interested parties (and this view is reflected in the heavy penalties for late filing prescribed in the *Companies Act 1985*), there is a certain conflict which should not be overlooked: this lies in the extraordinary usefulness to the auditor of the period between the balance sheet date and the signing of the accounts. As we have seen, events which take place during this period may be highly instructive as to

Table 6.5 Summary of how SSAP 18 should be interpreted

| Likelihood of crystallization | Contingent | |
	Assets	Liabilities
1. Remote	Do not disclose	Do not disclose
2. Possible → Probable	Do not disclose	Disclose by way of note (CA 1985)
3. Highly probable	Disclose by way of note	Make specific provision
4. Virtually certain	Accrue	Make specific provision

Notes:
1. The Standard deals with contingent assets (gains) as well as liabilities (losses), whereas the Act refers only to the latter.
2. Examples of contingent assets are:
   (i) Insurance claims, the related losses having already been written-off or provision made.
   (ii) Pending litigation, client as plaintiff.
   (iii) Alteration of contract terms in client's favour.
   (iv) Compensation following nationalization or sequestration of company assets.
3. Examples of contingent liabilities:
   (i) Financial guarantees on behalf of others.
   (ii) Product warranties issued to customers, unexpired at balance sheet date and at date of audit completion.
   (iii) Pending litigation, client as defendant.
   (iv) Bills of exchange receivable, discounted with recourse.

the true position at the end of the financial period in question and a shortening of this period may therefore be correspondingly disadvantageous from the point of view of accuracy.

Therefore, in order to optimize the usefulness of the post-balance sheet period, most firms incorporate what is usually termed a *subsequent events programme* within the scope of their prescribed audit procedures, and its detailed content should be designed to implement as efficiently as possible the essentially simple message of SSAP 17, which may be summed up as follows. Events taking place after the financial period has ended should be disregarded unless (1) they relate to legislative change which requires reflection in the accounts retrospectively, such as new disclosure requirements, or a change in corporation tax rate affecting charges for future taxation; or (2) they tell us something about the company's *true* results and position which, on the balance sheet date, were not known either at all, or with any degree of certainty.

Examples of (2) will readily be appreciated in those events which either confirm or allay doubts concerning, say, bad debt provisions, pending litigation, and contingent liabilities. In every such case, an event *within* the period under review raises the doubts; the *subsequent* event merely informs us of the outcome or materially increases our knowledge of what the outcome is most likely to be.

SSAP 17 is not intended to provide a mechanical rule for all situations, and an assessment of the relevance of each individual post-balance sheet event remains of paramount importance. It does nonetheless suggest the basis on which that assessment should be exercised, and it sensibly concludes with the recommendation that material events or transactions which relate wholly to the subsequent period, and which therefore should not be reflected in the accounts under review (known as non-adjusting events), should be clearly and fully explained by way of note. Examples of this would be the expropriation of a foreign investment, the uninsured destruction of property, or the loss of a major customer.

Certain post-balance sheet happenings will require particular care, such as a fall in the realizable value of stocks of finished goods as a result of which incurred overheads (included in the balance sheet values of those goods) may not in fact be recovered. In such a case a thorough assessment of the circumstances and cause of the fall must be made to determine which of the two accounting periods should bear the likely loss.

To make optimum use of the post-balance sheet period it is preferable that the subsequent events programme should be both formal and flexible; a *written programme* should be used, rather than leaving matters to the 'intuition' of the audit clerks (an attribute for which, generally speaking, they are not famous). Such a standard programme should be divided into the following four stages:

1. *Tests of year-end cut-off arrangements.* These tests would ensure that balance sheet quantities had been determined on a valid basis, consistent with that used for arriving at purchases and sales respectively. Such confirmation would be based upon:

   (a) subsequent recorded book entries;

   (b) independently received documents (from customers and suppliers);

   (c) movements of goods in and out of stores.

2. *Comparison of business activity levels before and after the year-end.* Normally this comparison would focus on the monthly totals for sales, purchases, receipts and payments and, if available, would also include the results of operations. Any unexplained material discrepancies would be thoroughly investigated.

3. *Formal discussions.* These should take place with senior executives of the client company, during which full notes must be taken on a wide range of post-balance sheet matters, including:

   (a) current market conditions, the effect of new products and changes in competition;

   (b) changes in selling prices of company products;

   (c) significant variations in production and other costs;

   (d) subsequent bookings/cancellations of sales orders, and losses of major customers;

   (e) capital expenditure commitments;

   (f) new borrowings and share or loan issues;

   (g) liabilities (e.g. guarantees) in dispute and pending lawsuits;

   (h) changes in accounting and financial policy.

Minutes of all post-balance sheet board meetings should be carefully examined in the course of this stage.

4. *Review*. A thorough review should be undertaken of all the findings to date, so that decisions may be reached on any necessary adjustments which, in the light of subsequent events, appear to be required, and these should be discussed in detail with the directors.

Review questions

*1. In the course of an audit an auditor will sometimes have cause to seek independent verification from third parties of certain assets which appear in the balance sheet.

Identify three such assets and in each case describe the steps that the auditor needs to take in order to obtain the verification and the points which need to be addressed within the information when supplied.

*2. You are the auditor of Fire Limited, a company with share capital and reserves totalling £750,000. The annual profits are usually below £50,000.

Included within the assets of the latest balance sheet is an investment in Water Limited. This investment comprises a 10 per cent stake in the equity of that company. It is shown in the balance sheet of Fire Limited at its original cost of acquisition which was £300,000.

You have now finished the audit of all balance sheet areas except this item.

What enquiries would be required in respect of the value placed on this investment?

3. In a normal set of annual financial statements, a company states its accounting policies. What should an auditor look for in reviewing the client's accounting policies and how far might the review of the policies affect the audit and the final report?

4. Expanding plc is an international company with operating divisions in various locations in the UK. For the last two years it has received development grants from European funds in respect of some of its capital expenditure. What audit tests is it necessary to perform in order to verify the receipt of the grants and to ensure the correct treatment within the accounts of the company?

Exercises

1. You are the partner in charge of the audit of Compquick Limited, a new company in the area of computer retailing to accountants. During the course of your audit of the year ended 30 June your staff have discovered the following:

   (a) On 6 August one of the company's debtors, who owed £75,000, went into liquidation. The total debtor balances are £550,000. It is not anticipated that the liquidator will pay any amounts to unsecured creditors but Compquick Limited are considering utilizing a reservation of title clause to recover the goods.

(b) A lease for new offices was signed during the year. It is a 10-year lease. The totals of all due amounts have been capitalized.

Describe in detail the steps that you would take to audit the above points and also identify how they should be treated within the accounts.

2. As auditor of Deliverquick Limited you have always had special problems. The managing director – and major shareholder – attempts to interfere whenever possible and invariably does not know how to adjust accounts properly. The company exchanges vehicles frequently due to high mileages and usually has hire purchase agreements for each. These give rise to balancing charges from the hire purchase companies on sale. The accountant invariably posts these costs to 'new' accounts and frequently does not even realise when the managing director has changed vehicles.

   Outline the problems that are present on this assignment and how the balance sheet items, in particular fixed assets and liabilities may be best audited.

7

The audit report

7.1 The basic legal requirement

The words 'true and fair' represent the final objective of financial reporting. The *Companies Act* places upon the directors of every company the responsibility of ensuring that the balance sheet gives a true and fair view of the state of affairs of the company, and that the profit and loss account gives such a view of its profit or loss for the financial year. While this duty remains exclusively that of the directors, the auditor, in his report to the members, is required to state whether, in his opinion, the accounts meet the above requirement. If the company has subsidiaries the true and fair view requirement extends respectively to the state of affairs of the group and the results of the group so far as they affect members of the holding company. The auditor's report is also required to confirm that the accounts have been properly prepared in accordance with the *Companies Act*.

The only other specific statutory inclusions in the audit report arise in connection with certain information, relating especially to the emoluments of, and loans to, directors. Where this information is not given in the accounts as required it must be included in the auditor's report so far as is practicable.

The significance of the two words 'true' and 'fair' should be soberly appreciated. The inherent subjectivity with which 'fair' has to be assessed represents the auditor's most severe challenge, rather than a licence to authenticate any of a range of views. He must consider the impression created by the accounts as a whole; the fact that every individual figure may be justified does not automatically mean that the total picture is fair.

In this context it is still relevant to quote part of the 1980 APC guideline 'Review of financial statements':

> The auditor should consider the information in the financial statements in order to ensure that the conclusions which a reader might draw from it would be justified and consistent with the circumstances of the enterprise's business. In particular, he should bear in mind the need for the financial statements to reflect the substance of the underlying transactions and balances and not merely their form. He should consider also whether the presentation adopted in the financial statements may have been unduly influenced by management's desire to present facts in a favourable or unfavourable light.

7.2 Length versus significance

Until the issue of APB's 1993 SAS 600, the audit report, in most instances, was very brief and occupied no more than a few lines. It is therefore not surprising that its presence was often viewed as constituting little more than a necessary legal formality, somewhat lacking in substance. This is indeed a paradox, especially in view of the very great care which must be exercised before its formulation is agreed, and the final version signed. In the earlier chapters we have observed the auditor's work proceeding through its successive stages; we have noted the reasoning which underlies each stage, and the considerable care which has to be exercised throughout the systems enquiries and the detailed investigations into the records and into the final accounts themselves. Yet the report, which may correctly be seen as the consummation of the entire project, is sometimes regarded as lacking in any real significance. The rising level of corporate fraud and misconduct in recent years has, of course, provided the holders of this rather cynical view with plenty of ammunition. Even the extended APB version includes a good deal of material and serves as standard content for virtually all reports, and no doubt its paragraphs remain unread for that very reason. Yet the current trend on both sides of the Atlantic is to move away from 'exception reporting' towards a far more explicit, albeit standardized, form.

So far as the statutory requirements are concerned, apart from reporting on the truth and fairness of the financial statements and presentational compliance, auditors must report *only by exception* on whether:

▶ proper accounting records have been maintained;

▶ they have received all the information and explanations they required for audit purposes, including that in respect of subsidiaries;

- The accounts and the records are in agreement;
- returns, adequate for audit purposes, have been received from branches not visited;
- the directors' report is consistent with the accounts.

A study in the USA some years ago highlighted the irony of a vast quantity of audit work followed by a minuscule report, and speculated that some users of published accounts may in fact prefer the 'short form' report purely because of the reassurance which the impact of its brevity renders to the reader. Putting it another way, an anxious investor does not want to plough through a lengthy catalogue of work done and detailed findings if the final inference which he is expected to draw is that 'everything is okay'.

7.3   The timetable of responsibility

The drafting of the audit report, as we can see from Figure 2.1, features in the final column as the last major task to be accomplished. Yet the signing of his report does not necessarily signify the end of the auditor's responsibility. The diagram shown in Figure 7.1 provides a temporal perspective in which the audit report may be placed.

In many cases no interim audit is conducted, the auditor's appearance being confined to a solitary annual visit exclusively connected with the published accounts. The question remains unresolved, however, as to whether an audit responsibility exists at other times. Section 392A of the *Companies Act 1985* does imply an audit responsibility towards creditors. Suffice to say at this point that it is difficult to see how continuing care towards interested parties, whoever they may be, may be exercised without any interim attentions, especially in view of the rapidity with which the financial position of a client concern may be transformed from one of security to insecurity, and even disaster.

In view of the apparent distinction made between levels of audit responsibility during periods of 'active' and 'passive' attention to the client's affairs, it would seem to be practical to indicate in the audit report the date on which 'fieldwork' was completed and the current files put away, i.e. the date on which the auditors would, for their part, be ready to sign their report. This simple statement of audit completion would be unproven, but would be declared in good faith by professional men of integrity; it would run no risk of sounding like a disclaimer or a subtle warning – unless it were 'slotted' into the audit report thus: '... In our opinion, at the conclusion of our audit on 18 February 1996, the financial statements gave a true and fair view ...'

In view of the uncertainty on this question of continuing responsibility, the significance of the date on the audit report should be considered carefully. For obvious reasons it is never good policy to sign the audit report before the accounts themselves are signed by the directors. Nor is it advisable to sign the audit report before the directors' report is signed since its contents must be carefully considered to ensure

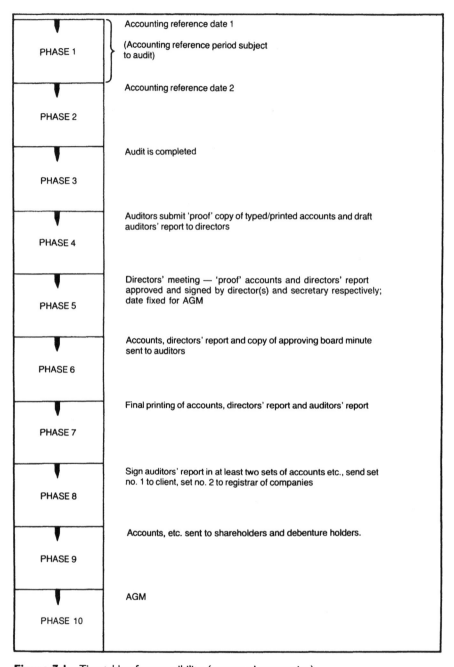

Figure 7.1   Timetable of responsibility (unquoted companies)

that it:

1. Contains no incorrect information.
2. Is not innocently or deliberately misleading.
3. Does not create an impression which is at variance with that conveyed by the audited accounts.

In the event of any of the above being the case it would be necessary for the auditor to seek a change to remedy the defect or else, *in extremis*, to qualify his own report, since it is a statutory duty of the auditor under the *Companies Act 1985* to ensure that the content of the directors' report is consistent with the information provided elsewhere in the financial statements and, if not, to report that fact.

Apart from placing the audit report in time as an authenticated document, what other significance attaches to the date on which it is signed? Whatever date appears, it cannot be taken as a point of cessation of responsibility. There is such a thing as 'after-acquired' information, and if this is material in relation to the accounts, the auditor cannot refuse to act on the grounds that his report, the contents of which were honestly believed at the time, has already been signed. After-acquired information may, of course, arrive even years later, but materiality in relation to current accounts tends to diminish with the passage of time and, in any event, prior-year adjustments can always be made explicitly in order to set the record straight. Nevertheless, the requirement to give a true and fair view represents a statutory obligation, and if the auditor becomes aware (even after the AGM) of a material error or omission in audited accounts, regardless of whether such omission is attributable in part to his own negligence, he can hardly claim that the lateness of the hour represents an excuse for continuing silence. The appropriate course of action will depend upon the circumstances, but he would at least have both a moral and professional (if not statutory) duty to write to the directors recommending that corrected accounts be submitted to the Registrar. If the directors fail to respond he should consider communicating with the Registrar directly.

All things considered, it would be an improvement on existing reporting methods if three dates appeared in the audit report:

1. The accounting date of the client company.
2. The date on which the audit fieldwork was concluded.
3. The date on which the audit report was signed.

Dates (1) and (3) now appear on reports as a matter of course, but the third date would surely offer the auditor a measure of protection from responsibility for post-audit events of which he was totally unaware – a responsibility which might otherwise be virtually open-ended.

SAS 600 insists that the date of the audit report should be the date on which it is physically signed. Back-dating is not permitted. If accounts sent to the directors for their signed approval are for any reason delayed before being returned to the auditors it may therefore be necessary for a further review of post-balance sheet events to take place prior to signing the audit report.

7.4   The influence of accounting standards on audit reports

At the outset of the 'standards' era in the early 1970s, the ICAEW made it clear to its members that they were expected to uphold standards regardless of the capacity in which they were employed – whether as professional auditors, directors or company accountants. Auditors, in particular, have had the implication spelt out for them since the issue of auditing standards in 1980. Like its predecessors, the new reporting standard (SAS 600) makes it clear that they must specifically ensure compliance with the accounting standards, except in those rare circumstances when such compliance might fail to give a true and fair view.

7.5   Qualifications in audit reports

7.5.1   Uncertainty as to purpose of qualifications

It is not surprising that qualifications in audit reports will, in general terms, to some degree reflect the prevailing economic climate. The response of auditors to the financial circumstances of their client companies over a span of time may be partly gauged by reference to the audit reports themselves; it will be an interesting exercise for someone one day to attempt to discern the nature of the dominant economic climate at any time during, say, the previous fifty years, from no source material other than the audit reports on the accounts of a cross-section of companies. Our distant researcher will have little hesitation in identifying the last three decades of the twentieth century as a distinctly troubled period, and the nature and form of the audit reports and their qualifications during this period have reflected the economic malaise.

Some of these difficulties have rendered a valuable service in highlighting, *inter alia*, the inherent subjectivity in conventional forms of accounting, as well as their potential use as vehicles of deception in a variety of forms and degrees. The glare of adverse publicity (usually associated with the inevitable 'what were the auditors doing?') has had a salutary effect on the conduct of auditing and, in particular, audit reporting. Whereas an audit qualification was a distinct rarity in earlier years, they now abound on an apparently escalating scale. Yet despite auditing standards there is, unfortunately, still a lack of consistency within the profession on:

1. What justifies a qualification.
2. The wording of qualifications.
3. The reference within a qualified report to notes in other parts of the accounts, as opposed to a full explanation of the contentious matter in the audit report itself.

In fact, it is by no means uncommon to find that different offices of the same firm will manifest entirely different positions in their reports, in relation to apparently analogous circumstances, e.g. uncertainty of property valuations.

In times of financial crisis there is also a great temptation for investors to seek a scapegoat on whom their company's ills may conveniently be blamed, and the auditor is unfortunately a rather obvious target. A further cause, therefore, of the increase in audit qualifications lies in the greater exposure to liability associated with this particular syndrome. It is incorrect to imagine that a carefully guarded audit report will always afford real protection from liability – at best it may reflect the auditor's own understandable uncertainty as to the company's true financial position – indeed, it may well have the opposite effect and render the auditor liable for failing to specify in unequivocal terms the true import of his findings.

7.5.2 The meaningful report versus the protective statement

The requirement for auditors to provide explicit expression of any reservation they may have is by no means a recent development. Exactly one hundred years ago a judge in the House of Lords found the auditors of London and General Bank guilty of negligence. In their report the auditors had stated that the value of assets in the balance sheet (no profit and loss account was required in those days) was 'subject to realization'. The judge pointed out that the statement was so obvious that it suggested the auditors were hinting at something important – and hints were no substitute for the explicit communication of information in the auditor's report, areas of doubt and uncertainty included.

One might have expected that a century later the auditing profession would have abandoned the 'hinting' in what is, after all, one of the few statutorily recognized media through which the auditor communicates with those to whom he owes responsibility; but this is regrettably far from being the case. In fact, it might be true to say that audit reports these days demand a greater than ever degree of expertise on the part of the reader than at any earlier time.

Despite the fact that the wording of the audit report, *per se*, will achieve little in terms of avoiding liability for negligence, far too many reports these days betray a lack of appreciation of this point in the minds of their authors. Indeed, many appear more akin to 'protective statements' than positive media for communicating with shareholders. Negligence, after all, will usually be decided on the basis of the quality of audit work executed before the issue of the report, and no report, no matter how tentatively (even inconclusively) drafted, will make up for deficient procedures. Indeed, as already suggested, such a report may even have the opposite effect and attract liability in circumstances where more explicit reporting is warranted.

Here, for example, is an extract from an audit report on the accounts of a public company:

> Shares in the subsidiary companies are included in the company's balance sheet at £13,734,000, and the consolidated balance sheet includes £1,411,000, representing the balance of the premium on the acquisition of those shares. In view of the group losses, we are unable to form an opinion concerning the value of such shares.

The auditors then go on to say that in view of the materiality of this matter 'we are unable to state whether the accounts give a true and fair view of the state of affairs of the company and of the group at 31 March 19XX and the loss of the group for the year ended on that date. In all other respects the accounts have been properly prepared in accordance with the Companies Act 1985'. The accounts show a group loss of £1,766,000 before taxation for the year.

Readers of this report may be justified in wondering whether they are getting value for money from the auditors, since the report surely raises more questions than it answers. The auditors' function is to express a professional opinion, not to catalogue the matters on which, for one reason or another, they have *failed* to form an opinion. In certain circumstances it may, of course, be impossible to form an opinion, e.g. where the directors claim to have incurred material expenditures for cash which are unsupported by any documentary evidence, or where no physical stocktaking has occurred and the directors refuse to arrange one, but these situations (which naturally justify a qualified opinion) are rather different from that cited in the audit report quoted above – which in fact seems to suggest, *inter alia*, that an opinion on the valuation of shares can be reached only when the companies concerned are making a profit.

Uncertainty on property valuations, even in circumstances where the company is using the premises and has no intention to dispose of them, sometimes attract vague 'caveats' from the auditors. The fact is that auditors have never been experts on property valuations, nor are they expected to be, and the spate of reservations on this matter which often feature in their reports displays a basic lack of appreciation of the realities involved. Does it matter, after all, that a company which owns the freehold site on which its factory stands would, on a forced sale, realize proceeds which are less than the original cost of the site? Even if the site were held on lease, which would be valueless at its termination, a hypothetical interim loss on a forced sale is of academic interest only, provided sums are set aside for its continuous amortization.

The converse situation is equally true: there is no need to set aside sums to deferred taxation which might become payable if the freehold were to be disposed of for a sizeable gain, provided that:

1. There is no intention to dispose of it in the foreseeable future, or
2. If disposed of, it would be replaced with another property, thus giving rise to full tax allowances.

If trivia are allowed to clutter up the audit report it is difficult for really major qualifications to be given the serious attention which they clearly deserve. A proliferation of extraneous comment, which is of academic interest only, merely serves to 'devalue the currency' of the auditors' report. This danger will, however, continue to exist as long as there are auditors who see their report as a protective, rather than an informative, statement.

7.5.3   Qualification by degrees

Broadly speaking, qualifications in audit reports may be seen as either major or minor, but there is also a variety of intervening shades which it is important to recognize.

Major qualifications

Major qualifications will generally contain a significantly adverse opinion on the accounts themselves or on the position of the company concerned.

There are three convenient subdivisions of major qualifications, the first of which concerns doubts as to the company's viability as a going concern. The following extract is from a report that does *not* fulfil the requirements of SAS 130 and SAS 600 but is typical of those encountered in recent recession years:

> We have examined the accounts on pages four to nine which have been prepared on the normal going concern basis. The applicability of the going concern basis is dependent on the continued availability of adequate finance either from within the group or from the group's bankers.

There is obviously doubt in the auditor's mind as to whether the client company will be able to continue as a going concern in the foreseeable future. The auditor's expression of doubt is not sufficiently explicit, however, and much depends upon the amount of detailed information available in the accounts, notes and directors' report, to which the audit report should have referred.

The auditor's reservations relate to the willingness of (1) the group, and (2) the group's bankers to provide further working capital. No attempt is made by the auditors to quantify the position for shareholders – another example of a qualification which raises more questions than it answers. What shareholders and other users of the accounts really need to know relates to:

1. The extent of finance needed, based on budgets examined by the auditors.
2. The purpose of such finance, i.e. immediate (for payment of wages and suppliers) or medium term (to repay borrowings), etc.
3. The extent to which the parent company board and the bankers, respectively, have indicated their intentions on this matter, or their silence in response to audit requests if that is the case.
4. The requirement under (1) in relation to the utilization of existing credit lines.
5. The date, if known, set by the bank for a review of facilities.
6. The timescale within which repayments are due and refinancing will be required.

One would reasonably expect information of this nature in the above circumstances, yet none is forthcoming. If it is included in the notes, reference to these should have been made.

The first sentence of the report tells us that the normal going concern basis has been used. 'Good!' the non-accountant reader might, justifiably, think. The second sentence, taken at its face value by a non-accountant shareholder, creditor or other reader of accounts, will be recognized as applicable to a vast majority of business enterprises; after all, the word 'continued' suggests that adequate finance is available now. Thus, 'subject to the foregoing' boils down to 'subject to the forenothing' in the innocent mind. More sophisticated readers might, however, realize that the reporting of 'non-data' is unusual and that the auditors are therefore trying to get some sort of message through to us – but even they would be at a loss to know exactly what the message is.

The second class of major qualification is that contained in a report which states categorically that, for reasons given, the accounts do not give a true and fair view. Such reports are understandably rare, and when they do appear they usually relate to a difference between auditors and directors on a matter of accounting treatment, possibly involving an infringement of an accounting standard.

Example

As described in Note ..., the company's reserves have been directly charged with £10 million representing goodwill previously acquired and now considered by the directors to be worthless. This accounting treatment conflicts with that prescribed in Financial Reporting Standard No. 3. The prescribed accounting treatment, which we believe to be correct, would have been to treat the goodwill written-off as an exceptional item and disclose it as such as a charge in the profit and loss account for the year. This treatment would have had the effect of converting the trading profit after taxation of £6 million, into a loss of £4 million.

In view of the materiality of the sums involved, in our opinion, the financial statements do not give a true and fair view...

Principles involved: The write-off of goodwill previously acquired represents an actual loss to the company of sums originally capitalized, and as such should be treated as a charge in the profit and loss account in the year in which such loss is recognized.

The third class of major qualification is that which states that, for reasons specified, the auditors are unable to form an opinion as to whether the accounts convey a true and fair view of the company's results and/or financial position. In such a case the specific area of doubt or uncertainty would have to be both of considerable significance in relation to the accounts as a whole and such that no further audit work could have resolved the matter conclusively.

Minor qualifications

Although there are considerable 'degrees of seriousness' within the 'minor league' of audit qualifications, they invariably have one feature in common: despite the auditor's expressed reservations the 'true and fair view' given by the accounts is not fundamentally impaired. Such qualifications may be recognized by the fact that the 'opinion' paragraph of the audit report usually reads 'except for the foregoing, the financial statements give a true and fair view'. The possible reasons for such a qualification are too various to be catalogued, but the following two examples are typical.

Example 1

Government cash grants of £13.5 million received during the year have been credited directly to profit and loss account. This treatment departs from Statement of Standard Accounting Practice no. 4 which requires such grants to be dealt with on an accruals basis over the full life of the assets to which the grants relate. Had this accounting treatment, which we believe to be correct, been adopted, the declared profit for the year before and after taxation would have been reduced by £12.1 million.

Except for the foregoing...

Principles involved: The purpose of cash grants is to provide a cash boost to eligible companies and this is achieved regardless of the accounting treatment adopted. If the grant relates to the purchase of specific assets, it is strictly in accordance with the accruals concept of accounting that it should be credited to profit and loss account over the life of the assets to which it relates.

Example 2

The purchase consideration for the acquisition of Spectre plc during the year included 100,000 shares of £1 each in the company. At the date of transfer, this class of shares was quoted on the London Stock Exchange at £6 per share, and, in our opinion, the correct accounting treatment would have been to record the issue of these shares at the value effectively attributed to them, thereby giving rise to a share premium of £500,000.

Except for the foregoing...

Principles involved: Although section 130 of the *Companies Act 1985* does not clearly specify the circumstances in which a share premium arises, it would seem that since the sale agreement does not appear to have computed the value of assets acquired, the auditors are reasonably entitled to look to the independent Stock Exchange valuation of the shares issued as an effective indication of the amount which the former shareholders of Spectre plc expected in return for the sale of their shares. The obvious outcome of this view is that £500,000 over and above the nominal value of the shares in question was paid and this should correctly have been shown as a share premium.

It will be observed that in both examples the matter at the root of the qualification is sufficiently material to justify its inclusion, but not so fundamental as to invalidate the view given by the accounts as a whole. This principle may be regarded as a feature of all (relatively) minor qualifications. SAS 600 seeks to establish uniformity, and a dozen illustrations are provided in it to cover the majority of audit reporting situations.

7.5.4   Guidance on qualified reports

Most auditing firms now recognize that current attitudes require their reports to be qualified more frequently than previously. The main reason for this is the ever-widening range of audit responsibilities, in particular due, albeit indirectly, to:

▶ A more volatile economic climate, and consequent 'going concern' doubts.

▶ The 'exposure' arising under quasi-regulations (e.g. Lloyds insurance rules, Stock Exchange rules, City Code on takeovers and mergers, Cadbury, etc).

▶ New case law.

▶ Greater exposure to professional liability, especially to third parties.

▶ New statute law, notably the *Financial Services Act 1986*, the *Building Societies Act 1987* and the *Banking Act 1986*, which together have completely overhauled investor protection legislation in the UK.

▶ The continuous stream of Financial Reporting Standards, each one of which opens up an area of potential audit qualifications.

▶ Developments in the audit role in relation to corporate governance and wider public interest expectations.

It is therefore incumbent upon every firm to ensure a responsible attitude towards the drafting of qualified opinions, and many have a technical partner to whom all suggested qualifications are automatically referred for approval. One factor which such a partner is bound to consider, quite apart from the particular circumstances prevailing, is the extent to which the draft formulation complies with best practice and, most especially, the requirements of SAS 600 and SAS 130.

7.5.5   References to 'notes to the accounts'

In practice one often encounters the discreditable policy of including, as a qualification, a bland reference to a note without any amplification whatever. For example, the accounts of one publicly quoted investment trust attracted the following (barely discernible) qualification in the report of its auditors: 'With the reservation concerning the accounting treatment referred to in Note 12, in our opinion the company's balance sheet and the group accounts have been properly prepared ... and give a true and fair view ...' The reference to Note 12 sounds almost incidental, yet in fact tells us:

> The consideration for the acquisition of ... Ltd included 94,598 shares in the company. In the opinion of the auditors, the correct accounting treatment would have been to record the issue of these shares at the value effectively attributed to them in the sale agreement, thereby increasing share premium account by £1,885,402 and increasing by the same amount:
>
> (a) the cost of shares in subsidiary companies (in the company's balance sheet), and
>
> (b) the excess of cost of shares over the book value of assets of subsidiary companies acquired, at date of acquisition (in the Group accounts).

However, the directors decided to adopt a more conservative basis of accounting by showing the shares issued at the nominal value of £1 each and by not increasing the accounts referred to in (a) and (b) above by the sum of £1,885,402.

The auditors obviously recognized that the nominal value (of £1) of the shares issued in exchange was totally irrelevant and that the real issues underlying the accounting treatment had nothing whatever to do with 'a more conservative basis of accounting'. It is obvious, for example, that on a subsequent sale of the shares in the subsidiary for, say, £2 million the distributable profit would be around £1.9 million (less tax), instead of a mere £20,000 on the basis of the auditors' view. Far from the directors' basis being 'more conservative', it is a device which would enable the company to repay by way of dividend what its auditors see as a share premium. The note quoted makes it abundantly clear that the sale agreement itself incorporated a valuation of £1.98 million (£1,885,402 + £94,598), and there can be little doubt that a share premium arose, since nominal values are irrelevant in this context, except as a means of calculating the share premium.

By leaving what is, in effect, a major audit qualification as a mere reference to a note to the accounts, the responsibility for framing it residing with the directors and not the auditors, the true significance is totally lost on the lay reader. The Note 12 referred to, incidentally, was but one of nineteen notes; and as to the materiality of the £1.885 million at issue, one need do no more than point out that the total capital employed in the group balance sheet was only £4.63 million. The creditors (whom the creation of a share premium account is designed to protect) and accrued charges amounted to £1.557 million; and the previously existing share premium account to a little under £743,000. One wonders how the accounts can possibly be said to give a true and fair view subject to 'reservations' of that magnitude. In general terms it is difficult to excuse any major relegation from the auditors' report to the notes. References to notes should always outline the nature of the subject matter in question, the notes providing the full explanation.

7.6   Reliance on the work of subsidiary auditors

7.6.1   Legislation under the *Companies Act 1985*

The detailed audited accounts of subsidiaries would on their own normally provide little more than a starting point for the audit of the group accounts. A breakdown of individual items is necessary for two main reasons:

1. To ensure that uniform accounting policies have been adopted by all companies within the group.

2. To ascertain the effect on the accounts of subsidiaries of transactions with other companies within the group, so that internally accrued profits and losses can be eliminated for all purposes other than that of reflecting minority interests.

Such considerations do not arise when the subsidiaries' accounts are themselves being prepared, but they are of obvious importance from the viewpoint of the group audit.

Nevertheless, the Acts made no provision for direct access by group auditors to this information. In practice, communication channels are established and much reliance is placed on the co-operation of all parties involved, including the subsidiary auditors; from a legal viewpoint the situation is covered by the statutory entitlement of group (i.e. parent company) auditors to such information and explanations as they consider necessary for the purposes of the audit of the group accounts.

It is not that the standards of the subsidiary auditors are necessarily in question especially when all concerned may well be members of the same professional body. It is also fully accepted that, within the framework of the highest professional standards, considerable margins exist in the way data may be interpreted and hence portrayed in the accounts. These points are not in question. At the same time, however, those who are risking professional liability should at the very least be entitled to risk it on the basis of their own, rather than someone else's, work, no matter how highly that work may be regarded. It is therefore necessary for parent company auditors to be resourceful in obtaining all the information to which, in law, they are entitled. Extensive use of inter-firm questionnaires is recommended.

Section 389A of the *Companies Act 1985* imposes a duty upon subsidiaries and their auditors in the UK to provide the parent company auditors with the information and explanations they require to enable them to perform their duties in relation to the group accounts; and, in the case of foreign subsidiaries, the directors of the UK parent have a duty to obtain the information, etc. required by their auditors. SAS 510 deals comprehensively with the relationship between principal auditors and other auditors, and reference to this should be made.

7.7 Small companies

7.7.1 Internal control

Special considerations arise when reporting on the accounts of small companies whose internal control system is effective to a limited degree only. The following points provide a useful reminder of the problems faced by auditors of small companies:

Internal control weaknesses

Problems invariably arise in the application of normal auditing principles and procedures to the audits of companies employing a small number of administrative staff. These problems derive from two basic causes:

1. substantial domination of the accounting and financial management functions by one person;
2. limitations in the effectiveness of internal control owing to the small number of employees.

The provision of a check whereby the work of one person is proved independently by (or is complementary to) the work of another may therefore be absent to a considerable extent. Whilst in such cases internal control, including internal check, may be effective for its primary purpose as a check for *management use*, it will usually be defective as a *check on management itself.*

These deficiencies may cause the auditors to extend their detailed testing procedures and to intensify procedures for verification of assets, including:

▶ attendance at stocktaking
▶ direct communication with debtors.

Reliance on representations of management

1. In the circumstances outlined above it will be necessary to rely on the representations of management to a more significant extent than is the case with audits of larger companies.

2. These representations may not be capable of direct confirmation by outside evidence or by other personnel.

3. Auditors must consider the surrounding evidence as a whole (primarily the records, their knowledge of the circumstances affecting the company, significant ratios, and the materiality of the items under examination) in order to decide whether it is consistent with these representations, and sufficient to support them. It does *not* necessarily follow that representations for which direct confirmatory evidence is not available may *not* be relied upon by the auditors.

Despite the foregoing considerations it will usually be possible for auditors to provide an unqualified report on the accounts of a small company if:

▶ they have gained a familiarity with the nature of the client company's business; its management's strengths and weaknesses; and the reliability and integrity of the directors;

▶ they have undertaken a direct involvement in the accounts preparation work;

▶ they have obtained satisfactory, comprehensive and plausible explanations in response to queries;

▶ they have undertaken audit tests and procedures that effectively compensate for the lack of internal control and proprietorial domination.

7.7.2 Reports on accounts compiled or prepared by accountants

Technical Release 1/95 issued by the ICAEW Audit Faculty updates previous guidance on reports on the accounts of partnerships, sole traders and other unincorporated entities, first issued in February 1973. It confirms that Chartered Accountants should not produce, or allow their names to be associated with, accounts which they believe to be misleading. The following are examples of the forms of report that may be suitable in many instances.

Accountants' report to the Directors on the unaudited accounts of Company Ltd

As described on the balance sheet you are responsible for the preparation of the accounts for the year ended ..., set out on pages ... to ..., and you consider that the company is exempt from an audit and from a report under section 249A(2) of the Companies Act 1985. As instructed, we have compiled these unaudited accounts in order to assist you to fulfil your statutory responsibilities from the accounting records, information and explanations supplied to us, and we report that they are in accordance therewith.

Accountants' report on the unaudited accounts of Mr Sole Trader

As described on page ..., you have approved the accounts for the year ended ... set out on pages ... to .... As instructed, we have compiled these unaudited accounts from the accounting records, information and explanations supplied to us, and we report that they are in accordance therewith.

Accountants' report including an explanatory paragraph (Misleading accounts): Accountants' report on the unaudited accounts of Mr Sole Trader

As described on page ..., you have approved the accounts for the year ended ... set out on pages ... to .... In accordance with your instructions, we have compiled these unaudited accounts from the accounting records and information and explanations supplied to us.

In preparing the accounts it has come to our attention that the balance sheet total of debtors includes a debt of £... which has been outstanding in excess of one year. Sole Trader has informed us that he has no security for this debt. No provision has been made against the debt being irrecoverable as Sole Trader has informed us that he is satisfied that it will be recovered in full.

Chartered Accountants   *Address*
Date

7.8   Is the client a going concern?

In view of the large number of limited companies which, in recent years, have been forced into insolvent liquidation due to financial difficulty, auditors should take positive steps to investigate the client company's post-balance sheet health before simply assuming that it is viable as an ongoing entity. This active search is stated as a requirement in SAS 130, in contrast to the passive approach that was previously adopted.

Many firms have given careful consideration to compiling checklists of danger symptoms, and the presence of any of these would indicate the need to instigate further, more specific and more detailed steps, before reaching a conclusion on this important question.

If, after pursuing all their enquiries, the auditors still find themselves uncertain as to whether the company will remain a going concern in the foreseeable future, they will obviously need to devise a suitable qualification in their report, ensuring that it is as explicit as their knowledge of the situation permits.

There are a number of symptoms that may be used to diagnose going concern difficulties, and most checklists drafted for this purpose will incorporate some or all of the following:

1. Loan repayments are falling due in the near future, and refinancing facilities are not immediately available.

2. High or increasing debt-to-equity ratios exist (high gearing).

3. The company is heavily or increasingly dependent upon short-term finance, particularly from trade creditors and overdrafts.

4. There is inability to take advantage of discounts, the time taken to pay creditors is increasing, and suppliers impose cash terms.

5. Normal purchases are being deferred, thereby reducing stocks to dangerously low levels.

6. Substantial losses are occurring, or the state of profitability is declining.

7. Normal capital expenditure is being switched to leasing agreements.

8. The company is in an exposed position in relation to future commitments, such as long-term assets being financed by short- or medium-term borrowings.

9. The company has a net deficiency of current assets, or its ratio of current assets to current liabilities is declining.

10. The company is near to its present borrowing limits, with no sign of a reduction in requirements.

11. Collection rate from debtors is slowing down.

12. Rapid development of business is in danger of creating an over-trading situation.

13. There is substantial investment in new products, ventures or research, none of which is so far successful.

14. There is dependence upon a limited number of products, customers or suppliers.

15. There is evidence of major reductions or cancellations of capital projects.

16. There is heavy dependence on an overseas holding company (for finance or trade).

Should the presence of one or more of such features cause the auditors concern, they should, at the very least:

1. Compare the client's cash flow forecasts with the overdraft or other loan facilities available for up to twelve months from the accounting date.
2. Obtain written confirmation from the board of the holding company (if any) that it intends its subsidiary to continue in business and will not withdraw existing finance facilities.
3. Enquire into and obtain written evidence of the steps (if any) the client is taking in order to correct its decline in fortunes.

If the auditor cannot satisfy himself that the client will remain in business in the foreseeable future, then he must consider the validity of the going concern basis, and the need to qualify his audit report in appropriate terms.

Small companies

Particular care should be taken in reviewing the accounts of small or proprietor-controlled companies, especially where there are substantial 'loans' from the directors/proprietors. In effect, such loans should be regarded as forming part of the longer-term capital of the company. For the purposes of the going concern assessment, they should be so treated only if they are legally subordinated to all other creditors, and there should be adequate disclosure of the position.

If the directors are not prepared to sign representations that they will not draw down the current account balances for at least twelve months, the account balances should be separately included in creditors due for settlement within twelve months, i.e. they should be treated as ordinary current liabilities. This will help to emphasize any deficiency of assets as regards unsecured creditors unless other financial support has been arranged, and will indicate whether or not the going concern basis of asset valuation is applicable. Any purported subordination of loans to directors to the other creditors' claims should ideally be supported by correctly drafted and legally binding documentation, but in practice its inclusion in a signed letter of representation will often have to suffice.

In summary, SAS 130:

1. Requires auditors to make active going concern enquiries in every instance.
2. Requires auditors to vet for reasonableness any statement of the directors that in the directors' opinion the company is a going concern, and their statement of circumstances that could render it otherwise.
3. Requires auditors to extend the time horizons of their going concern assessment, normally to twelve months beyond the date of the audit report.

The auditor's safest course of action, in reporting terms, is to ensure that the accounts give as much information as possible with regard to: (1) what is known (e.g. bank facilities extended and letters of support/subordination already received from parent company/directors, etc.), and (2) what is unknown (e.g. facilities still under negotiation, alternative funding sources being explored, merger discussions under way but not finalized, etc.).

According to research findings published by the ACCA in May 1995, going concern qualifications are at best only very short-term indicators of looming company failure. The City University Business School report says that 'results suggest that it is unsatisfactory for users to have to rely on the auditor's subjective evaluation of going concern uncertainty'.

The researchers base their conclusions on an examination of 125 listed and USM (unlisted securities market) non-financial companies that failed between 1987 and 1994. The last year-end accounts of only one in seven bore a going concern qualification. This was fewer than the 26 per cent of companies found to have received going concern qualifications in a comparable study covering 1977–86.

'While the difference in the going concern rates between the two periods is not statistically significant, the clear reduction in qualification rates is worrying,' say the authors who point out that economic conditions were less favourable when the second sample was examined. '*It indicates the concerns widely expressed in recent years, that auditors are not providing adequate warning of impending company failure, are not confined to the handful of usually cited highly publicised cases.*'

The key points of SAS 130 may be summarized as follows:

1. Going concern must be considered in the course of every audit.

2. SSAP 2 uses the term '*foreseeable future*' in relation to the going concern accounting concept. The SAS does not prescribe any particular time horizon on the auditor, but expects that in practice this will be at least a period of one year from the date of approval of the financial statements. Where a shorter period has been considered by the directors in forming their own view on the applicability of the going concern basis, this should be disclosed, and the auditors should consider whether the directors' reasons for so doing are justified. If not so justified the auditor may need to explain the scope limitation in his report.

3. In practice, discussion with the directors should be sufficient to establish that the directors have in fact paid particular attention to a period of one year from the date of approval of the accounts and, as a result, this type of reference in the audit report will be rare.

4. It may be helpful for a going concern checklist to be completed on each audit assignment.

5. In practice the key areas for review in assessing going concern include:
   - bank facilities and review dates;
   - cash flow forecasts;
   - profit forecasts;
   - continued support in the form of loans from directors or others;
   - the attitude of creditors;

- committed capital expenditure;
- material currency exchange rate changes and import price rises;
- dates for rent reviews, contract renewals, etc.

6. The auditor may consider obtaining written confirmations in respect of going concern in the management representation letter. In addition, third party confirmation of continued financial support may be sought from specific lenders.

7. The SAS requirements for auditors' reports may be summarized by way of the following examples:

   (a) Entity dependent on overdraft facility that can theoretically be called in at any time but there is no indication that this is likely in the foreseeable future:

   No need for note in financial statements. No need for comments in audit report.

   (b) Entity dependent on continuing financial support from bank, other creditors and/or directors, holding company, etc., particularly where there are periodic peaks and troughs in the cash flows:

   Explanatory narrative in creditors' note. This should be sufficiently detailed to explain, so far as possible, particular sources of finance, probable timescale before repayment is expected and other relevant factors, e.g. post-balance sheet events, current (unaudited) profitability, operating within existing facilities, etc. If auditor is satisfied with note, no need for any reference in audit report.

Example 1

Extract from notes to the financial statements

Note 12 *Creditors: amounts falling due within one year*	19X1	19X0
Current instalments due on debenture loans	x.x	x.x
Bank overdrafts	x.x	x.x
Obligations under finance leases	x.x	x.x

The company meets its day-to day-working capital requirements through an overdraft facility which, in common with all such facilities, is repayable on demand. The directors expect that the company will continue to operate within the facility currently agreed and within that which they believe will be agreed on (date), when the company's bankers are due to consider renewing the facility for a further year. The directors' views are based on their plans and on discussions with the company's bankers but, inherently, there can be no certainty in relation to these views.

   (c) Serious doubts regarding the entity's ability to continue as a going concern for the foreseeable future, despite which the directors have prepared the accounts on the going concern basis:

The accounting policy note should set out fully the nature of the entity's problems, the circumstances that could lead to a cessation of trading, the directors' reasons for believing that it is nevertheless appropriate to present the accounts on the going concern basis, and the fact that no adjustments have been made in respect of the consequences of the company not being able to continue to trade. In view of the seriousness of the doubts, the auditor should refer explicitly in his report to the content of the accounting policy note and state his concurrence that the going concern basis should have been adopted.

Example 2

Extract from notes to the financial statements

Note 1   Basis of preparing the financial statements

The company meets its day-to-day working capital requirements through an overdraft facility which, in common with all such facilities, is repayable on demand.

The nature of the company's business is such that there can be considerable unpredictable variation in the timing of cash inflows. The directors have prepared projected cash flow information covering the year ending 11 months from the date on which they approved the financial statements. On the basis of this cash flow information, other financial information covering the period thereafter and discussions with the company's bankers, the directors consider that the company will continue to operate within the facility currently agreed and within that which they believe will be agreed on (date), when the company's bankers are due to consider renewing the facility for a further year. However, inherently, it is impossible for there to be certainty regarding these matters. On this basis, the directors consider it appropriate to prepare the financial statements on the going concern basis. The financial statements do not include any adjustments that would result from a withdrawal of the overdraft facility by the company's bankers.

Example 3

Auditors' Report to the Shareholders of XYZ Limited

We have audited the financial statements on pages ... to ... which have been prepared under the historical cost convention and the accounting policies set out on page ....

Respective responsibilities of directors and auditors

As described on page ... the company's directors are responsible for the preparation of financial statements. It is our responsibility to form an independent opinion, based on our audit, on those statements and to report our opinion to you.

Basis of opinion

We conducted our audit in accordance with Auditing Standards issued by the Auditing Practices Board. An audit includes examination, on a test basis, of evidence relevant to the amounts and disclosures in the financial statements. It also includes an assessment of the significant estimates and judgements made by the directors in the preparation of the financial statements, and of whether the accounting policies are appropriate to the company's circumstances, consistently applied and adequately disclosed.

We planned and performed our audit so as to obtain all the information and explanations which we considered necessary in order to provide us with sufficient evidence to give reasonable assurance that the financial statements are free from material misstatement, whether caused by fraud or other irregularity or error. In forming our opinion we also evaluated the overall adequacy of the presentation of information in the financial statements.

Going concern

In forming our opinion, we have considered the adequacy of the disclosures made in the financial statements concerning the inherent uncertainty as to the continuation and renewal of the company's bank overdraft facility. The company meets its day-to-day working capital requirements through this overdraft facility which, in common with all such facilities, is repayable on demand. Since the last balance sheet date, the company has operated within the facility currently agreed with the company's bankers. However, the nature of the company's business is such that there can be considerable unpredictable variation in the timing of cash inflows.

In view of the circumstances relating to this inherent uncertainty, as described in Note 1, we consider that there is a significant level of concern about the ability of the company to continue as a going concern. The financial statements do not include any adjustments that would result from a withdrawal of the overdraft facility by the company's bankers. However, our opinion is not qualified in these respects.

Opinion

In our opinion the financial statements give a true and fair view of the state of the company's affairs as at 31 December 19 ... and of its profit for the year then ended and have been properly prepared in accordance with the Companies Act 1985.

Registered auditors   *Address*
Date

(d) The going concern basis has been adopted in circumstances that, in the auditor's opinion, required the adoption of an alternative basis, e.g. the valuation of assets at realizable amounts, regardless of the effect of the potential adjustments:

> *The notes should, as with (c), set out the circumstances and the directors' reasons for adopting the going concern basis. Even if the auditor accepts that the directors had no real alternative, the audit report should express fundamental disagreement and the opinion that the financial statements do not, for these reasons, give a true and fair view. (This could arise if, for example, the entity has gone into receivership or otherwise ceased to trade normally after the balance sheet date.)*

7.9 The APB's auditing standard on reports

7.9.1 The current form of extended reporting

In 1993 the APB issued SAS 600 on auditors' reports, effective in respect of audits of accounts for periods ending on or after 30 September 1993. The APB clearly made a prodigious effort to transform UK audit reports from four line rituals into informative opinions. Only time will measure its success. The risk is that the previous ritual is simply replaced by a wordier one.

Earlier practice permitted disclosure of the date on which audit work was concluded as the 'effective' date of the audit opinion. The drawback is that this date necessarily precedes that of the directors' approval of the accounts: clearly, auditors cannot legally express their opinion of accounts that are still in draft. SAS 600 sensibly requires the date of the audit report to be the date on which it is physically signed.

It is, nevertheless, unfortunate that auditors are precluded from recording the date on which fieldwork was completed, since this is often a crucial consideration when allocating responsibility for determining the impact on accounts of post-balance sheet events – particularly when, through no fault of the auditors, there is a long delay before the accounts are approved. American standards recognize a distinction between auditors' active and passive reponsibilities respectively, fieldwork completion representing the demarcation point.

Another anomaly is that company law requires prior period comparatives to be included within the statutory accounts. Yet the Act requires the true and fair view to be given by only the current set. Again, by contrast, US standards prescribe that the audit opinion should explicitly refer to results and financial position at *both* dates. UK auditors tacitly ignore the question of whether the prescribed comparatives also give a true and fair view, an issue which the SAS might have addressed.

More serious is the implication carried by Example 9 (p. 281) that a total disclaimer is required whenever auditors are appointed after the balance sheet date and therefore did not attend the year-end stocktake. In practice there are many ways in which the year-end stocks and work in progress can be authenticated retrospectively – yet this possibility appears to have been completely disregarded.

Finally, Example 8 (pp. 279–80) simply substitutes an 'except for' opinion for the existing 'subject to' opinion when there is uncertainty over the completeness of recorded cash sales. This appears to be in conflict with the SAS's new principle of issuing clean opinions when inherent uncertainties are satisfactorily explained in the notes to the accounts. If, despite the directors' controls over the recording of cash sales, the uncertainty remains, *and* the position is fully explained in the notes, would an unqualified opinion not be appropriate?

The APB still has some way to go before these and other anomalies are satisfactorily resolved.

Extracts from SAS 600 and its illustrative examples are reproduced below.

Statement of Auditing Standards 600 – Auditors' reports on financial statements

Statements of Auditing Standards (SASs) contain basic principles and essential procedures ('Auditing Standards'), indicated by paragraphs in bold type with which auditors are required to comply in the conduct of any audit. SASs also include explanatory and other material which is designed to assist auditors in interpreting and applying Auditing Standards.

Introduction

1. The purpose of this Statement of Auditing Standards is to establish standards and provide guidance on the form and content of auditors' reports issued as a result of an audit of the financial statements of an entity ('the reporting entity'). Much of the guidance provided can be adapted to auditors' reports on financial information other than financial statements.

2. **Auditors' reports on financial statements should contain a clear expression of opinion, based on review and assessment of the conclusions drawn from evidence obtained in the course of the audit (SAS 600.1).**

3. An appreciation of the interrelationship between the responsibilities of those who prepare financial statements and those who audit them is also necessary to achieve an understanding of the nature and context of the opinion expressed by the auditors. Readers need to be aware that it is the directors (or equivalent persons) of the reporting entity and not the auditors who determine the accounting policies followed. Auditors' reports therefore also set out the respective responsibilities of directors and auditors.

4. It will aid communication with the reader if the auditors' report is placed before the financial statements and, where the directors set out their responsibilities themselves, if this description is immediately before the auditors' report.

5. The requirements of the SAS are intended to achieve informative reporting by auditors within the reporting obligations current at its date of issue. Further developments may in the future alter the matters on which auditors are required to report or the manner in which they are required to report; such changes will be reflected in amendments to the requirements in this SAS when appropriate.

Nature of assurance provided

6. The view given in financial statements is derived from a combination of fact and judgement and consequently cannot be characterized as either 'absolute' or correct. When reporting on financial statements, therefore, auditors provide a level of assurance which is reasonable in that context but, equally, cannot be absolute. Consequently it is important that the reader of financial statements is made aware of the context in which the auditors' report is given.

Applicability

7. This SAS applies to all reports issued by auditors which express an opinion in terms of whether financial statements give a true and fair view, or where statutory or other specific requirements prescribe the use of a term such as 'presents fairly' or 'properly prepared in accordance with'.

Definitions

8. The following definitions apply in interpreting the requirements of this SAS.

9. *Financial statements*: the balance sheet, profit and loss account (or other form of income statement), statements of cash flows and total recognized gains and losses, notes and other statements and explanatory material, all of which are identified in the auditors' report as being the financial statements.

10. *Directors*: the directors of a company, the partners, proprietors or trustees of other forms of enterprise or equivalent persons responsible for the reporting entity's affairs, including the preparation of its financial statements.

11. *Material*: a matter is material if its omission or misstatement would reasonably influence the decisions of a user of the financial statements.

    Materiality may be considered in the context of the financial statements as a whole, any individual primary statement within the financial statements or individual items included in them.

12. *Inherent uncertainty*: an uncertainty whose resolution is dependent upon uncertain future events outside the control of the reporting entity's directors at the date the financial statements are approved.

13. *Fundamental uncertainty*: an inherent uncertainty is fundamental when the magnitude of its potential impact is so great that, without clear disclosure of the nature and implications of the uncertainty, the view given by the financial statements would be seriously misleading.

    The magnitude of an inherent uncertainty's potential impact is judged by reference to

    - the risk that the estimate included in financial statements may be subject to change
    - the range of possible outcomes, and
    - the consequences of those outcomes on the view shown in the financial statements.

Basic elements of the auditors' report

14. Auditors' reports on financial statements should include the following matters:

   (a) a title identifying the person or persons to whom the report is addressed;

   (b) an introductory paragraph identifying the financial statements audited;

   (c) separate sections, appropriately headed, dealing with:

      (i) respective responsibilities of directors (or equivalent persons) and auditors.

      (ii) the basis of the auditors' opinion,

      (iii) the auditors' opinion on the financial statements;

   (d) the manuscript or printed signature of the auditors and

   (e) the date of the auditors' report. (SAS 600.2)

15. The use of a standard format for auditors' reports on financial statements assists the reader to follow the report's contents. The section headings indicate to the reader the nature of the matters contained in the section concerned: for example, where a qualified opinion is expressed, the heading 'Qualified opinion' may be used.

16. Auditors draft each section of their report on financial statements to reflect the requirements which apply to the particular audit engagement. However, the use of common language in auditors' report assists the reader's understanding. Accordingly, Appendix 2 includes examples of auditors' reports on financial statements to illustrate wording which meets the Auditing Standards contained in this SAS.

Title and addressee

17. An appropriate title is used to distinguish clearly the auditors' report from other information relating to the reporting entity with which it may be published.

18. The auditors' report on the financial statements of a company is addressed to its members (normally the shareholders) because the audit is undertaken on their behalf. The auditors' report on financial statements of other types of reporting entity is addressed to the appropriate person or persons, as defined by statute or by the terms of the individual engagement.

Identification of financial statements

19. The purpose of the introductory section of the auditors' report identifying the financial statements that have been audited is to ensure that there is no ambiguity regarding the information to which the auditors' opinion relates. The introductory section may refer to the accounting convention and accounting policies which have been followed in preparing the financial statements.

Statements of responsibility and basis of opinion

20. (a) **Auditors should distinguish between their responsibilities and those of the directors by including in their report**

   (i) **a statement that the financial statements are the responsibility of the reporting entity's directors;**

   (ii) **a reference to a description of those responsibilities when set out elsewhere in the financial statements or accompanying information; and**

   (iii) **a statement that the auditors' responsibility is to express an opinion on the financial statements.**

   (b) **Where the financial statements or accompanying information (for example the directors' report) do not include an adequate description of directors' relevant responsibilities, the auditors' report should include a description of those responsibilities. (SAS 600.3)**

21. The matters to be included in the description of the directors' responsibilities reflect the specific requirements applicable to the reporting entity. A description of the responsibilities of a company's directors is normally considered adequate when it includes the following points:

   (a) company law requires directors to prepare financial statements for each financial year which give a true and fair view of the company's (or group's) state of affairs at the end of the year and profit or loss for the year then ended;

   (b) in preparing those financial statements, the directors are required to:

   ► select suitable accounting policies and then apply them on a consistent basis, making judgements and estimates that are prudent and reasonable;

   ► (*large companies only*[1]) state whether applicable accounting standards have been followed, subject to any material departures disclosed and explained in the financial statements;

   ► (*where no separate statement on going concern is made by the directors*) prepare the financial statements on the going concern basis unless it is not appropriate to presume that the company will continue in business.

   (c) the directors are responsible for keeping proper accounting records, for safeguarding the assets of the company (or group) and for taking reasonable steps for the prevention and detection of fraud and other irregularities.

   These points may be adapted for different requirements applicable to different categories of reporting entity, for example to reflect special legal requirements relating to small companies, insurance companies or banks, or specific requirements applicable to a non-corporate entity.

22. In the case of reporting entities other than companies, auditors assess the adequacy of the description by reference to statutory or any other specific requirements with which the reporting entity's directors are required to comply.

---

[1] 'Large' in this context means those companies which fall outside the categories of small and medium-sized companies as defined in the *Companies Act 1985*.

23. Illustrative wording of a description of the directors' responsibilities, which may be included in auditors' reports on company financial statements where the directors' statement is inadequate, is shown in Appendix 3. Auditors' reports on the financial statements of other reporting entities provide equivalent details, reflecting appropriate legal and regulatory requirements when necessary to do so.

24. **Auditors should explain the basis of their opinion by including in their report**

   (a) **a statement as to their compliance or otherwise with Auditing Standards, together with the reasons for any departure therefrom;**

   (b) **a statement that the audit process includes**

      (i) **examining, on a test basis, evidence relevant to the amounts and disclosure in the financial statements,**

      (ii) **assessing the significant estimates and judgements made by the reporting entity's directors in preparing the financial statements,**

      (iii) **considering whether the accounting policies are appropriate to the reporting entity's circumstances, consistently applied and adequately disclosed;**

   (c) **a statement that they planned and performed the audit so as to obtain reasonable assurance that the financial statements are free from material misstatement, whether caused by fraud or other irregularity or error, and that they have evaluated the overall presentation of the financial statements. (SAS 600.4).**

25. A reference to compliance with Auditing Standards is necessary in order to provide assurance that the audit has been carried out in accordance with established standards.

26. In some exceptional circumstances, a departure from Auditing Standards may be appropriate to fulfil the objectives of a specific audit more effectively. If this is the case, the auditors explain the reasons for that departure in their report. Other than in such exceptional and justifiable circumstances, a departure from an Auditing Standard is a limitation on the scope of work undertaken by the auditors. In such circumstances the auditors assess whether a qualified opinion or disclaimer of opinion is required, as set out in SAS 600.7.

27. In certain circumstances, auditors are required by statute to follow other comparable standards, such as the Code of Audit Practice for Local Authorities and the National Health Service in England and Wales or the requirements of the Scottish Accounts Commission. Where this is the case, auditors refer to these standards.

28. In some circumstances, auditors may be required to report whether the financial statements have been properly prepared in accordance with regulations or other requirements, but are not required to report on whether they give a true and fair view. Where the special circumstances of the reporting entity require or permit the adoption of policies or accounting bases which would not normally permit a true and fair view to be given, auditors would refer to those circumstances in the paragraphs dealing with the respective responsibilities of directors and auditors (unless the matter is included in a separate

statement given by the directors) and may draw attention to them in the basis of opinion section of the report.

29. Auditors may wish to include additional comment in this part of their report to highlight matters which they regard as relevant to a proper understanding of the basis of their opinion.

Expression of opinion

30. **An auditors' report should contain a clear expression of opinion on the financial statements and on any further matters required by statute or other requirements applicable to the particular engagement. (SAS 600.5).**

31. An auditors' report may include an unqualified opinion or qualified opinion. The circumstances giving rise to each type of opinion are set out below and example reports illustrating each form of opinion are contained in Appendix 2.

Unqualified opinions

32. An unqualified opinion on financial statements is expressed when in the auditors' judgement they give a true and fair view (where relevant) and have been prepared in accordance with relevant accounting or other requirements. This judgement entails concluding whether *inter alia*:

▶ the financial statements have been prepared using appropriate accounting policies, which have been consistently applied;

▶ the financial statements have been prepared in accordance with relevant legislation, regulations or applicable accounting standards (and that any departures are justified and adequately explained in the financial statements); and

▶ there is adequate disclosure of all information relevant to the proper understanding of the financial statements.

Qualified opinions

33. A qualified opinion is issued when either of the following circumstances exist:

(a) there is a limitation on the scope of the auditors' examination (see SAS 600.7); or

(b) the auditors disagree with the treatment or disclosure of a matter in the financial statements (see SAS 600.8);

and, in the auditors' judgement, the effect of the matter is or may be material to the financial statements and therefore those statements may not or do not give a true and fair view of the matters on which the auditors are required to report or do not comply with relevant accounting or other requirements.

Adverse opinions

34. An adverse opinion is issued when the effect of a disagreement is so material or pervasive that the auditors conclude that the financial statements are seriously misleading (see SAS

600.8). An adverse opinion is expressed by stating that the financial statements do not give a true and fair view.

35.   When the auditors conclude that the effect of a disagreement is not so significant as to require an adverse opinion, they express an opinion that is qualified by stating that the financial statements give a true and fair view except for the effects of the matter giving rise to the disagreement.

Disclaimers of opinion

36.   A disclaimer of opinion is expressed when the possible effect of a limitation on scope is so material or pervasive that the auditors have not been able to obtain sufficient evidence to support, and accordingly are unable to express, an opinion on the financial statements (see SAS 600.7).

37.   Where the auditors conclude that the possible effect of the limitation is not so significant as to require a disclaimer, they issue an opinion that is qualified by stating that the financial statements give a true and fair view except for the effects of any adjustments that might have been found necessary had the limitation not affected the evidence available to them.

Compliance with relevant accounting requirements

38.   The auditors' opinion is expressed in the context of the particular accounting requirements applicable to the financial statements concerned and normally includes, in addition to an opinion on the view given by the financial statements, an opinion on whether or not those requirements have been followed. For example, an auditors' report on the financial statements of a company incorporated in Great Britain includes the words '... and have been properly prepared in accordance with the *Companies Act 1985*'.

39.   Save in exceptional circumstances, compliance with accounting standards is necessary to give a true and fair view.

40.   Financial statements are normally required to contain particulars of any material departure from an accounting standard which applies to the reporting entity, together with the financial effects of the departure unless this would be impracticable or misleading in the context of giving a true and fair view.

Requirements of company law

41.   In the context of financial reporting by companies, directors are required by law to prepare annual accounts which consist of a balance sheet and profit and loss account together with accompanying notes and which give a true and fair view of the state of affairs of the company (or group) at the end of the financial year and of the profit or loss of the company (or group) for that year. Company law requires the auditors to state whether in their opinion the company's annual accounts give such a view.

42.   There is no specific legal requirement that companies should comply with accounting standards. However, legislation in the UK gives specific recognition to accounting standards

and requires large companies to state in their financial statements whether those statements have been prepared in accordance with such standards and to give particulars of any material departure and the reasons for it — paragraph 36A of Schedule 4 to the *Companies Act 1985*.

43. It is likely that a Court would infer from this requirement, taken together with other changes introduced into UK company law by the *Companies Act 1989*, that financial statements which meet the Act's requirements will follow rather than depart from accounting standards, and that any departure would be regarded as sufficiently abnormal to require justification. Therefore, in general, compliance with accounting standards is necessary to meet the requirement of company law that the directors prepare annual accounts which give a true and fair view of a company's (or group's) state of affairs and profit or loss.

Primary statements

44. Accounting standards contained in Financial Reporting Standards require, in certain circumstances, further 'primary statements' in addition to the balance sheet and profit and loss account. It follows from the principle stated in the last paragraph that, where required by an accounting standard, these further primary statements are normally necessary in order that the annual accounts give a true and fair view, as required in the United Kingdom by the *Companies Act 1985* or the *Companies (Northern Ireland) Order 1986* and, in the Republic of Ireland, the *Companies Acts 1963 to 1990*. The annual accounts, including the additional primary statements required by accounting standards, are referred to by the term 'financial statements'.

45. Accordingly, reference in an auditors' opinion on a company's financial statements to the primary statements required by accounting standards is unnecessary. It may also be misleading to the reader of the auditors' report, in that it may appear to detract from the role of the additional primary statements in supporting the information contained in company's balance sheet and profit or loss account so as to give a true and fair view as required by the law.

46. Auditors may be requested to report separately on one or more primary statements. When making such a separate report, they need to ensure that in doing so no impression is given that the primary statement(s) referred to is other than integral to the financial statements as a whole and that it is clear to a reader that the primary statement is necessary to give a true and fair view of the state of affairs and profit or loss for statutory purposes.

Non-compliance with accounting standards

47. When the auditors conclude that the financial statements of a company do not comply with accounting standards, they assess:

(a) whether there are sound reasons for the departure;

(b) whether adequate disclosure has been made concerning the departure from accounting standards;

(c) whether the departure is such that the financial statements do not give a true and fair view of the state of affairs and profit or loss.

In normal cases, a departure from accounting standards will result in the issue of a qualified or adverse opinion on the view given by the financial statements.

48. Where no explanation is given for a departure from accounting standards, its absence may of itself impair the ability of the financial statements to give a true and fair view of the company's state of affairs and profit or loss. When auditors conclude that this is so, a qualified or adverse opinion on the view given by the financial statements is appropriate, in addition to a reference (where appropriate) to the non-compliance with the specific requirement of company law referred to in paragraph 42 above.

Small companies – Great Britain and Northern Ireland

49. Directors of companies which fall within the category of small companies as defined by company legislation in the UK may draw up financial statements taking advantage of a number of exemptions from the full requirements of company law.[2] Financial statements prepared using these exemptions are nevertheless required to give a true and fair view, and the legislation further specifically provides that they shall not be deemed not to do so by reason only of the fact that advantage has been taken of the exemptions.

50. Auditors reporting on the financial statements of a small company prepared using these exemptions are permitted (but not required) to report in terms which omit reference to whether a true and fair view is given, referring only to the proper preparation of those statements in accordance with the requirements of company law applicable to small companies. However, their legal obligation to consider whether the financial statements give a true and fair view as required by company law remains unchanged. The requirement for a clear expression of opinion (contained in SAS 600.5) is therefore best met by referring to the true and fair view, except for particular circumstances in which the auditors consider it impossible to do so.

51. Illustrative wording for an auditors' report on financial statements of a small company taking advantage of the exemptions is given in Example 5 of Appendix 2.

Further matters required by statute or other regulations

52. Further opinions or information to be included in the auditors' report may be determined by specific statutory requirements applicable to the reporting entity, or, in some circumstances, by the terms of the auditors' engagement. Such matters may be required to be dealt with by a positive statement in the auditors' report or only by exception. For example, in the Republic of Ireland auditors are required to state whether, in their opinion, proper books of account have been kept, whereas company legislation in the United Kingdom requires auditors to report only when a company has not maintained proper accounting records.

53. Where further opinions are required by statute or other regulation, matters which result in qualification of such an opinion may also result in a qualification of the auditors' opinion on the financial statements: for example, if proper accounting records have not been maintained and as a result it proves impracticable for the auditors to obtain sufficient evidence concerning material matters in the financial statements, their report indicates that the scope of their examination was limited and includes a qualified opinion or disclaimer of opinion on the financial statements arising from that limitation, as required by SAS 600.7.

[2] Set out in Schedule 8 to the *Companies Act 1985*, as inserted by SI 1992 No. 2452.

Fundamental uncertainty

54. (a) **In forming their opinion on financial statements, auditors should consider whether the view given by the financial statements could be affected by inherent uncertainties which, in their opinion, are fundamental.**

    (b) **When an inherent uncertainty exists which:**

      (i) **in the auditors' opinion is fundamental, and**

      (ii) **is adequately accounted for and disclosed in the financial statements,**

      the auditors should include an explanatory paragraph referring to the fundamental uncertainty in the section of their report setting out the basis of their opinion.

    (c) **When adding an explanatory paragraph, auditors should use words which clearly indicate that their opinion on the financial statements is not qualified in respect of its contents. (SAS 600.6)**

Inherent uncertainties

55. Inherent uncertainties about the outcome of future events frequently affect, to some degree, a wide range of components of the financial statements at the date they are approved. It is not possible for the directors to remove the uncertainties by obtaining more information at the date they approve the financial statements: the statements can reflect only the working assumptions of directors as to their financial outcome and, where material, describe the circumstances giving rise to the uncertainties and their potential financial effect.

56. In forming an opinion, auditors take into account the adequacy of the accounting treatment, estimates and disclosures of inherent uncertainties in the light of evidence available at the date they express that opinion.

57. Auditors recognize that, in preparing financial statements, directors are required to analyse relevant existing conditions, including uncertainties about future events and their effect on financial statements. An audit includes assessment of whether there is sufficient evidence to support the directors' analysis and resulting estimates and disclosures given in the financial statements. Usually auditors are able to obtain sufficient evidence concerning the directors' assessment of the outcome of inherent uncertainties by considering various types of evidence, including the historical experience of the reporting entity.

58. Forming an opinion on the adequacy of the accounting treatment of inherent uncertainties involves consideration of:

    ► the appropriateness of accounting policies dealing with uncertain matters;
    ► the reasonableness of the estimates included in the financial statements in respect of inherent uncertainties; and
    ► the adequacy of disclosure.

59. Auditors distinguish between circumstances in which an unqualified opinion is appropriate and those in which a qualification or disclaimer of opinion is required due to a limitation on the scope of their work. An inherent uncertainty can be expected to be resolved at a future

date, at which time sufficient evidence concerning its outcome would be expected to become available. When evidence does or did exist (or reasonably could be expected to exist) but that evidence is not available to the auditors, the scope of their work is limited and a qualification or disclaimer of opinion is appropriate.

60. Where auditors conclude that the accounting policies followed lead to material misstatements in the financial statements, or that the estimates included in the financial statements are materially misstated, or that disclosures relating to the uncertainty are inadequate, a qualified or adverse opinion is required by SAS 600.8.

Fundamental uncertainties

61. In some circumstances, the degree of uncertainty about the outcome of a future event and its potential impact on the view given by the financial statements may be very great. Where resolution of an inherent uncertainty could affect the view given by the financial statements to the degree that the auditors conclude that it is to be regarded as fundamental, they include an explanatory paragraph when setting out the basis of their opinion describing the matter giving rise to the fundamental uncertainty and its possible effects on the financial statements, including (where practicable) quantification. Where it is not possible to quantify the potential effects of the resolution of the uncertainty, the auditors include a statement to that effect. Reference may be made to notes in the financial statements but such a reference is not a substitute for sufficient description of the fundamental uncertainty so that a reader can appreciate the principal points at issue and their implications.

62. Communication with the reader is enhanced by the use of an appropriate sub-heading differentiating the explanatory paragraph from other matters included in the section describing the basis of the auditors' opinion.

63. In determining whether an inherent uncertainty is fundamental auditors consider

    (a) the risk that the estimate included in financial statements may be subject to change;

    (b) the range of possible outcomes; and

    (c) the consequences of those outcomes on the view shown in the financial statements.

64. Inherent uncertainties are regarded as fundamental when they involve a significant level of concern about the validity of the going concern basis or other matters whose potential effect on the financial statements is unusually great. A common example of a fundamental uncertainty is the outcome of major litigation.

Opinions expressed

65. An unqualified opinion indicates that the auditors consider that appropriate estimates and disclosures relating to fundamental uncertainties are made in the financial statements. It remains unqualified notwithstanding the inclusion of an explanatory paragraph describing a fundamental uncertainty. The explanatory paragraph is included as part of the basis for the auditors' opinion so as to make clear that it describes a matter which the auditors have taken into account in forming their opinion, but that it does not qualify that opinion.

66. When the auditors conclude that the estimate of the outcome of a fundamental uncertainty is materially misstated or that the disclosure relating to it is inadequate, they issue a qualified opinion.

67. A disclaimer of opinion is issued by auditors as a result of an inherent uncertainty which in their opinion is fundamental only when a limitation of the scope of their work directly affects their assessment of the adequacy of its accounting treatment and disclosure.

Limitation of audit scope

68. **When there has been a limitation on the scope of the auditors' work that prevents them from obtaining sufficient evidence to express an unqualified opinion,**

    (a) **the auditors' report should include a description of the factors leading to the limitation in the opinion section of their report;**

    (b) **the auditors should issue a disclaimer of opinion when the possible effect of a limitation on scope is so material or pervasive that they are unable to express an opinion on the financial statements;**

    (c) **a qualified opinion should be issued when the effect of the limitations is not so material or pervasive as to require a disclaimer, and the wording of the opinion should indicate that it is qualified as to the possible adjustments to the financial statements that might have been determined to be necessary had the limitation not existed. (SAS 600.7)**

69. In considering whether a limitation results in a lack of evidence necessary to form an opinion, auditors assess

    (a) the quantity and type of evidence which may reasonably be expected to be available to support the particular figure or disclosure in the financial statements; and

    (b) the possible effect on the financial statements of the matter for which insufficient evidence is available. When the possible effect is, in the opinion of the auditors, material to the financial statements, there will be insufficient evidence to support an unqualified opinion.

70. Inherent uncertainties do not arise from, or give rise to, a limitation on the auditors' work and are considered under SAS 600.6.

71. A description of the factors leading to a limitation enables the reader to understand the reasons for the limitation and to distinguish between:

    (a) limitations imposed on the auditors (for example, where not all the accounting records are made available to the auditors or where the directors prevent a particular procedure considered necessary by the auditors from being carried out); and

    (b) limitations outside the control of the auditors or the directors (for example, when the timing of the auditors' appointment is such that attendance at the entity's stock-take is not possible and there is no alternative form of evidence regarding the existence of stock).

72. When the proposed terms of an audit engagement include a limitation on the scope of the auditors' work such that they believe the need to issue a disclaimer exists, they would normally not accept such a limited engagement as an audit engagement, unless required by statute to do so.

73. Where a scope limitation is imposed by circumstances, auditors would normally attempt to carry out reasonable alternative procedures to obtain sufficient audit evidence to support an unqualified opinion.

Disagreement on accounting treatment or disclosure

74. **Where the auditors disagree with the accounting treatment or disclosure of a matter in the financial statements, and in the auditors' opinion the effect of that disagreement is material to the financial statements**

    (a) the auditors should include in the opinion section of their report

         (i) a description of all substantive factors giving rise to the disagreement;

         (ii) their implications for the financial statements;

         (iii) whenever practicable, a quantification of the effect on the financial statements;

    (b) when the auditors conclude that the effect of the matter giving rise to disagreement is so material or pervasive that the financial statements are seriously misleading, they should issue an adverse opinion;

    (c) in the case of other material disagreements, the auditors should issue a qualified opinion indicating that it is expressed except for the effects of the matter giving rise to the disagreement. (SAS 600.8)

75. An auditors' report including a qualified opinion arising from disagreement includes a description of the reasons for qualification and the effects on the financial statements. Whilst reference may be made to relevant notes in the financial statements, such reference is not a substitute for sufficient description of the circumstances in the auditors' report so that a reader can appreciate the principal points at issue and their implications for an understanding of the financial statements.

Date and signature of the auditors' report

76. **(a) Auditors should not express an opinion on financial statements until those statements and all other financial information contained in a report of which the audited financial statements form a part have been approved by the directors, and the auditors have considered all necessary available evidence.**

    (b) The date of an auditors' report on a reporting entity's financial statements is the date on which the auditors signed their report expressing an opinion on those statements. (SAS 600.9)

77. The report may be signed in the name of the auditors' firm, the personal name of auditor, or both, as appropriate. The signature is normally that of the firm because the firm as a whole

assumes responsibility for the audit. To assist identification, the report normally includes the location of the auditors' office. Where appropriate, their status as registered auditors is also stated.

Date of the auditors' report

78. Dating the auditors' report informs the reader that the auditors have considered the effect on the financial statements of events or transactions of which they are aware which occurred up to that date.

79. The auditors are not in a position to form their opinion until the financial statements (and any other financial information contained in a report of which the audited financial statements form a part) have been approved by the directors and the auditors have completed their assessment of all the evidence they consider necessary for the opinion or opinions to be given in their report. This assessment includes events occurring up to the date the opinion is expressed. Auditors therefore plan the conduct of audits to take account of the need to ensure, before expressing an opinion on financial statements, that the directors have approved the financial statements and any accompanying financial information and that the auditors have completed a sufficient review of post-balance sheet events.

80. The date of the auditors' report is therefore, the date on which, following

    (a) receipt of the financial statements and accompanying documents in the form approved by the directors for release;

    (b) review of all documents which they are required to consider in addition to the financial statements (for example the directors' report, chairman's statement or other review of an entity's affairs which will accompany the financial statements); and

    (c) completion of all procedures necessary to form an opinion on the financial statements (and any other opinions required by law or regulation) including a review of post-balance sheet events

    the auditors sign (in manuscript) their report expressing an opinion on the financial statements for distribution with those statements.

81. The form of the financial statements and other financial information approved by the directors, and considered by the auditors when signing a report expressing their opinion, may be in the form of final drafts from which printed documents will be prepared. Subsequent production of printed copies of the financial statements and auditors' report does not constitute the creation of a new document. Copies of the report produced for circulation to shareholders or others may therefore reproduce a printed version of the auditors' signature showing the date of actual signature.

82. Before signing a report expressing their opinion after consideration of final drafts of the financial statements and other accompanying documents, auditors will need to consider whether the form of draft documents is sufficiently clear for them to assess the overall financial statement presentation. When the auditors conclude that this is not the case, it will be necessary for them to defer signing their report until it is possible for them to do so.

83. If the date on which the auditors sign their report is later than that on which the directors approved the financial statements, the auditors take such steps as are appropriate

   (a) to obtain assurance that the directors would have approved the financial statements on that later date (for example, by obtaining confirmation from specified individual members of the board to whom authority has been delegated for this purpose); and

   (b) to ensure that their procedures for reviewing subsequent events cover the period up to that date.

Registrar of companies

84. The copy of the auditors' report which is delivered to the registrar of companies is required to state the name of the auditors and be signed by them. Where the auditors sign their report in a form from which a final printed version is produced, they may sign copies for identification purposes in order to provide the registrar with appropriately signed copies. No further active procedures need be followed at that later date.

Compliance with International Standards on Auditing

85. Compliance with the auditing standards contained in this SAS will ensure compliance in all material respects with the basic principles and essential procedures proposed in the exposure draft of International Standard on Auditing 'Auditors' report on financial statements'.

Effective date

86. Auditors are required to comply with the requirements of this SAS in respect of audits of financial statements for financial periods ending on or after 30 September 1993. Adoption of the requirements when reporting on financial statements for accounting periods ending before that date is encouraged.

Appendix 1: Forming an opinion on financial statements

1. This appendix sets out in the form of a flowchart (Figure 7.2) the steps involved in forming an opinion as to whether a set of financial statements presents a true and fair view of the reporting entity's state of affairs and profit or loss. The flowchart is intended to provide guidance to readers in understanding the Statement of Auditing Standards. It does not form part of the Standards themselves.

2. The flowchart is drawn up on the basis that the directors make no further amendments to the financial statements following the audit. In practice, directors may make amendments in response to comments by the auditors: any amendment of the financial statements (for example, to provide additional disclosure in order to give a true and fair view) would require auditors to begin the sequence of questions afresh.

3. In applying the logic in the flowchart, auditors may find it necessary to address the questions for discrete sections of the financial statements as well as for the financial statements as a whole.

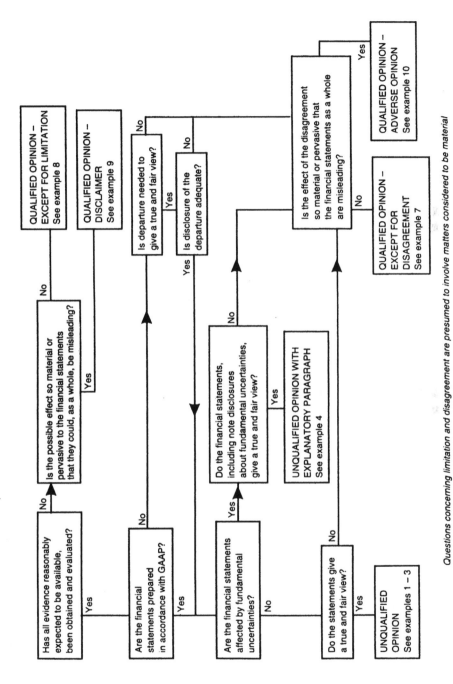

Figure 7.2 Forming an opinion on financial statements

Questions concerning limitation and disagreement are presumed to involve matters considered to be material

4. The principal matters which auditors consider in forming an opinion may be expressed in three questions:

    (1) *Have they completed all procedures necessary to meet Auditing Standards and to obtain all the information and explanations necessary for their audit?* This question is considered in paragraphs 68 to 73 of the SAS.

    (2) *Have the financial statements been prepared in accordance with the applicable accounting requirements?* This question is considered in paragraphs 38 to 51 of the SAS.

    The flowchart refers to these requirements as GAAP (generally accepted accounting practice) as a convenient shorthand to indicate those accounting requirements which apply in the case of the particular financial statements concerned. In the case of a company subject to company legislation in Great Britain, this will normally mean that the financial statements have been prepared in accordance with Schedule 4 and (if appropriate) 4A to the *Companies Act 1985* – sections 226(3) and 227(4) – and with applicable accounting standards.

    As a starting point, compliance with applicable accounting requirements is likely to result in financial statements giving a true and fair view. However, compliance alone may be insufficient in a particular instance. Section 226(4) and (5) and section 227(5) and (6) therefore <u>require</u> directors of a company to provide additional information or even depart from the rules in order to give a true and fair view.

    Similarly, a breach of the rules, whether by omission or substitution of an alternative accounting treatment, may mean that a true and fair view is not given, but departures from the rules are needed in some specific cases so that a true and fair view can be given.

    Hence the third question:

    (3) *Do the financial statements, as prepared by the directors, give a true and fair view?* The following are extracts from Appendix 2.

Example 1 – Unqualified opinion: company incorporated in Great Britain

Auditors' report to the shareholders of XYZ plc

We have audited the financial statements on pages ... to ... which have been prepared under the historical cost convention[3] [as modified by the revaluation of certain fixed assets] and the accounting policies set out on page ... .

Respective responsibilities of directors and auditors

As described on page ... the company's directors are responsible for the preparation of financial statements. It is our responsibility to form an independent opinion, based on our audit, on those statements and to report our opinion to you.

[3] A reference to the convention draws attention to the fact that the values reflected in the financial statements are not current but historical and, where appropriate, to the fact that there is a mixture of past and recent values.

Basis of opinion

We conducted our audit in accordance with Auditing Standards issued by the Auditing Practices Board. An audit includes examination, on a test basis, of evidence relevant to the amounts and disclosures in the financial statements. It also includes an assessment of the significant estimates and judgements made by the directors in the preparation of the financial statements, and of whether the accounting policies are appropriate to the company's circumstances, consistently applied and adequately disclosed.

We planned and performed our audit so as to obtain all the information and explanations which we considered necessary in order to provide us with sufficient evidence to give reasonable assurance that the financial statements are free from material misstatement, whether caused by fraud or other irregularity or error. In forming our opinion we also evaluated the overall adequacy of the presentation of information in the financial statements.

Opinion

In our opinion the financial statements give a true and fair view of the state of the company's affairs as at 31 December 19... and of its profit [loss] for the year then ended and have been properly prepared in accordance with the *Companies Act 1985*.

Registered auditors   *Address*
Date

Example 4 – Unqualified opinion with explanatory paragraph describing a fundamental uncertainty

Auditors' report to the shareholders of XYZ plc

We have audited the financial statements on pages ... to ... which have been prepared under the historical cost convention [as modified by the revaluation of certain fixed assets] and the accounting policies set out on page ... .

Respective responsibilities of directors and auditors

As described on page ... the company's directors are responsible for the preparation of financial statements. It is our responsibility to form an independent opinion, based on our audit on those statements and to report our opinion to you.

Basis of opinion

We conducted our audit in accordance with Auditing Standards issued by the Auditing Practices Board. An audit includes examination, on a test basis, of evidence relevant to the amounts and disclosures in the financial statements. It also includes an assessment of the significant estimates and judgements made by the directors in the preparation of the

→

financial statements, and of whether the accounting policies are appropriate to the company's circumstances, consistently applied and adequately disclosed.

We planned and performed our audit so as to obtain all the information and explanations which we considered necessary in order to provide us with sufficient evidence to give reasonable assurance that the financial statements are free from material misstatement, whether caused by fraud or other irregularity or error. In forming our opinion we also evaluated the overall adequacy of the presentation of information in the financial statements.

Fundamental uncertainty

In forming our opinion, we have considered the adequacy of the disclosure made in the financial statements concerning the possible outcome to litigation against B Limited, a subsidiary undertaking of the company, for an alleged breach of environmental regulations. The future settlement of this litigation could result in additional liabilities and the closure of B Limited's business, whose net assets included in the consolidated balance sheet total £... and whose profit before tax for the year is £.... . Details of the circumstances relating to this fundamental uncertainty are described in note ... . Our opinion is not qualified in this respect.

Opinion

In our opinion the financial statements give a true and fair view of the state of affairs of the company and of the group as a 31 December 19... and of the group's profit [loss] for the year then ended and have been properly prepared in accordance with the *Companies Act 1985*.

Registered auditors   *Address*
Date

Example 5 – Company incorporated in Great Britain, using accounting exemptions available for small companies

Auditors' report to the shareholders of XYZ Limited

We have audited the financial statements on pages ... to ... which have been prepared under the historical cost convention [as modified by the revaluation of certain fixed assets] and the accounting policies set out on page ... .

Respective responsibilities of directors and auditors

As described on page ... the company's directors are responsible for the preparation of financial statements. It is our responsibility to form an independent opinion, based on our audit, on those statements and to report our opinion to you.

Basis of opinion

We conducted our audit in accordance with Auditing Standards issued by the Auditing Practices Board. An audit includes examination, on a test basis, of evidence relevant to the amounts and disclosures in the financial statements. It also includes an assessment of the significant estimates and judgements made by the directors in the preparation of the financial statements, and of whether the accounting policies are appropriate to the company's circumstances, consistently applied and adequately disclosed.

We planned and performed our audit so as to obtain all the information and explanations which we considered necessary in order to provide us with sufficient evidence to give reasonable assurance that the financial statements are free from material misstatement, whether caused by fraud or other irregularity or error. In forming our opinion we also evaluated the overall adequacy of the presentation of information in the financial statements.

Opinion

In our opinion the financial statements give a true and fair view of the state of the company's affairs as at 31 December 19 ... and of its profit [loss] for the year then ended[4] and have been properly prepared in accordance with the provisions of the *Companies Act 1985* applicable to small companies.

Registered auditors   *Address*
Date

[4] When reporting on the financial statements of a small company which takes advantage of the exemptions available under Schedule 8 of the *Companies Act 1985* (as inserted by SI 1992 No. 2452), auditors may consider that, were it not for paragraph 14(1) of the schedule, a true and fair view is not given because of the use of some or all of these exemptions. In such circumstances, they may give the form of report allowed by paragraph 14(3) of Schedule 8, as follows:

'In our opinion, the financial statements have been properly prepared in accordance with the provisions of the *Companies Act 1985* applicable to small companies'.

When the auditors consider that a true and fair view is not given for other reasons, they should qualify their opinion as required by the Auditing Standards contained in this SAS.

Example 6 – Auditors' statement on a summary financial statement

Auditors' statement to the shareholders of XYZ plc

We have audited the summary financial statements set out above/on page ... .

Respective responsibilities of directors and auditors

The summary financial statement is the responsibility of the directors. Our responsibility is to report to you our opinion as to whether the statement is consistent with the full financial statements and directors' report.

Basis of opinion

We conducted our audit in accordance with Auditing Standards issued by the Auditing Practices Board. The audit of a summary financial statement comprises an assessment of whether the statement contains all information necessary to ensure consistency with the full financial statements and directors' report and of whether the detailed information required by law has been properly extracted from those documents and included in the summary statements.

Our report on the company's full financial statements includes information on the responsibilities of directors and auditors relating to the preparation and audit of financial statements and on the basis of our opinion on the financial statements.

Opinion

In our opinion the summary financial statement above/on page ... is consistent with the full financial statements and directors' report of XYZ plc for the year ended ... and complies with the requirements of the *Companies Act 1985*, and regulations made thereunder, applicable to summary financial statements.

Registered auditors   *Address*
Date

Example paragraphs for inclusion in the basis of opinion section where applicable:

(1) *Referring to a fundamental uncertainty:* Our report on the group's full financial statements included an explanatory paragraph concerning a fundamental uncertainty arising from the outcome of possible litigation against B Ltd., a subsidiary undertaking of the company, for an alleged breach of environmental regulations. Details of the circumstances relating to this fundamental uncertainty are described in note ... of the summary financial statement. Our opinion on the full financial statements is not qualified in this respect.

(2) *Referring to a qualified opinion:* Our opinion on the company's full financial statements was qualified as a result of a disagreement with the accounting treatment of the company's leased assets. Details of the circumstances giving rise to that opinion are set out in note ... of the summary financial statement.

Example 7 – Qualified opinion: disagreement

Auditors' report to the shareholders of XYZ plc

We have audited the financial statements on pages ... to ... which have been prepared under the historical cost convention [as modified by the revaluation of certain fixed assets] and the accounting policies set out on page ... .

Respective responsibilities of directors and auditors

As described on pages ... the company's directors are responsible for the preparation of financial statements. It is our responsibility to form an independent opinion, based on our audit, on those statements and to report our opinion to you.

Basis of opinion

We conducted our audit in accordance with Auditing Standards issued by the Auditing Practices Board. An audit includes examination, on a test basis, of evidence relevant to the amounts and disclosures in the financial statements. It also includes an assessment of the significant estimates and judgements made by the directors in the preparation of the financial statements, and of whether the accounting policies are appropriate to the company's circumstances, consistently applied and adequately disclosed.

We planned and performed our audit so as to obtain all the information and explanations which we considered necessary in order to provide us with sufficient evidence to give reasonable assurance as to whether the financial statements are free from material misstatement, whether caused by fraud or other irregularity or error. In forming our opinion we also evaluated the overall adequacy of the presentation of information in the financial statements.

Qualified opinion arising from disagreement about accounting treatment

Included in the debtors shown on the balance sheet is an amount of £Y due from a company which has ceased trading. XYZ plc has no security for this debt. In our opinion the company is unlikely to receive any payment and full provision of £Y should have been made, reducing profit before tax and net assets by that amount.

Except for the absence of this provision, in our opinion the financial statements give a true and fair view of the state of the company's affairs as at 31 December 19... and of its profit [loss] for the year then ended and have been properly prepared in accordance with the *Companies Act 1985*.

Registered auditors   *Address*
Date

Example 8 – Qualified opinion: limitation on the auditors' work

Auditors' report to the shareholders of XYZ plc

We have audited the financial statements on pages ... to ... which have been prepared under the historical cost convention [as modified by the revaluation of certain fixed assets] and the accounting policies set out on page ... .

Respective responsibility of directors and auditors

As described on page ... the company's directors are responsible for the preparation of financial statements. It is our responsibility to form an independent opinion, based on our audit, on those statements and to report our opinion to you.

Basis of opinion

We conducted our audit in accordance with Auditing Standards issued by the Auditing Practices Board, except that the scope of our work was limited as explained below.

An audit includes examination, on a test basis, of evidence relevant to the amounts and disclosures in the financial statements. It also includes an assessment of the significant estimates and judgements made by the directors in the preparation of the financial statements, and of whether the accounting policies are appropriate to the company's circumstances, consistently applied and adequately disclosed.

We planned our audit so as to obtain all the information and explanations which we considered necessary in order to provide us with sufficient evidence to give reasonable assurance that the financial statements are free from material misstatement, whether caused by fraud or other irregularity or error. However, the evidence available to us was limited because £... of the company's recorded turnover comprises cash sales, over which there was no system of control on which we could rely for the purpose of our audit. There were no other satisfactory audit procedures that we could adopt to confirm that cash sales were properly recorded.

In forming our opinion we also evaluated the overall adequacy of the presentation of information in the financial statements.

Qualified opinion arising from limitation in audit scope

Except for any adjustments that might have been found to be necessary had we been able to obtain sufficient evidence concerning cash sales, in our opinion the financial statements give a true and fair view of the state of the company's affairs as at 31 December 19... and of its profit [loss] for the year then ended and have been properly prepared in accordance with the *Companies Act 1985*.

In respect alone of the limitation on our work relating to cash sales:

▶ we have not obtained all the information and explanations that we considered necessary for the purpose of our audit; and

▶ we were unable to determine whether proper accounting records had been maintained.

Registered auditors   *Address*
Date

Example 9 – Disclaimer of opinion

Auditors' report to the shareholders of XYZ plc

We have audited the financial statements on pages ... to ... which have been prepared under the historical cost convention [as modified by the revaluation of certain fixed assets] and the accounting policies set out on page ... .

Respective responsibilities of directors and auditors

As described on page ... the company's directors are responsible for the preparation of financial statements. It is our responsibility to form an independent opinion, based on our audit, on those statements and to report our opinion to you.

Basis of opinion

We conducted our audit in accordance with Auditing Standards issued by the Auditing Practices Board, except that the scope of our work was limited as explained below.

An audit includes examination, on a test basis, of evidence relevant to the amounts and disclosures in the financial statements. It also includes an assessment of the significant estimates and judgements made by the directors in the preparation of the financial statements, and of whether the accounting policies are appropriate to the company's circumstances, consistently applied and adequately disclosed.

We planned our audit so as to obtain all the information and explanations which we considered necessary in order to provide us with sufficient evidence to give reasonable assurance that the financial statements are free from material misstatement, whether caused by fraud or other irregularity or error. However, the evidence available to us was limited because we were appointed auditors on (date) and in consequence we were unable to carry out auditing procedures necessary to obtain adequate assurance regarding the quantities and condition of stock and work in progress, appearing in the balance sheet at £... . Any adjustment to this figure would have a consequential significant effect on the profit for the year.

In forming our opinion we also evaluated the overall adequacy of the presentation of information in the financial statements.

Opinion: disclaimer on view given by financial statements

Because of the possible effect of the limitation in evidence available to us, we are unable to form an opinion as to whether the financial statements give a true and fair view of the state of the company's affairs as at 31 December 19... or of its profit [loss] for the year then ended. In all other respects, in our opinion the financial statements have been properly prepared in accordance with the *Companies Act 1985.*

In respect alone of the limitation on our work relating to stock and work-in-progress:

▶ we have not obtained all the information and explanations that we considered necessary for the purpose of our audit; and

▶ we were unable to determine whether proper accounting records had been maintained.

Registered auditors   *Address*
Date

Example 10 – Adverse opinion

Auditors' statement to the shareholders of XYZ plc

We have audited the financial statements on pages ... to ... which have been prepared under the historical cost convention [as modified by the revaluation of certain fixed assets] and the accounting policies set out on page ... .

Respective responsibilities of directors and auditors

As described on page ... the company's directors are responsible for the preparation of financial statements. It is our responsibility to form an independent opinion, based on our audit, on those statements and to report our opinion to you.

Basis of opinion

We conducted our audit in accordance with Auditing Standards issued by the Auditing Practices Board. An audit includes examination, on a test basis, of evidence relevant to the amounts and disclosures in the financial statements. It also includes an assessment of the significant estimates and judgements made by the directors in the preparation of the financial statements, and of whether the accounting policies are appropriate to the company's circumstances, consistently applied and adequately disclosed.

We planned and performed our audit so as to obtain all the information and explanations which we considered necessary in order to provide us with sufficient evidence to give reasonable assurance as to whether the financial statements are free from material misstatement, whether caused by fraud or other irregularity or error.

In forming our opinion we also evaluated the overall adequacy of the presentation of information in the financial statements.

Adverse opinion

As more fully explained in note ... no provision has been made for losses expected to arise on certain long-term contracts currently in progress, as the directors consider that such losses should be off-set against amounts recoverable on other long-term contracts. In our opinion, provision should be made for foreseeable losses on individual contracts as required by Statement of Standard Accounting Practice 9. If losses had been so recognized the effect would have been to reduce the profit before and after tax for the year and the contract work in progress at 31 December 19... by £... .

In view of the effect of the failure to provide for the losses referred to above, in our opinion the financial statements do not give a true and fair view of the state of the company's affairs as at 31 December 19... and of its profit [loss] for the year then ended. In all other respects, in our opinion the financial statements have been properly prepared in accordance with the *Companies Act 1985*.

Registered auditors   *Address*
Date

Example 12 – Qualified opinion: disagreement arising from omission of a primary statement required by Financial Reporting Standards

Auditors' report to the shareholders of XYZ plc

We have audited the financial statements on pages ... to ... which have been prepared under the historical cost convention [as modified by the revaluation of certain fixed assets] and the accounting policies set out on page ... .

Respective responsibilities of directors and auditors

As described on page ... the company's directors are responsible for the preparation of financial statements. It is our responsibility to form an independent opinion, based on our audit, on those statements and to report our opinion to you.

Basis of opinion

We conducted our audit in accordance with Auditing Standards issued by the Auditing Practices Board. An audit includes examination, on a test basis, of evidence relevant to the amounts and disclosures in the financial statements. It also includes an assessment of the significant estimates and judgements made by the directors in the preparation of the financial statements, and of whether the accounting policies are appropriate to the company's circumstances, consistently applied and adequately disclosed.

We planned and performed our audit so as to obtain all the information and explanations which we considered necessary in order to provide us with sufficient evidence to give reasonable assurance as to whether the financial statements are free from material misstatement, whether caused by fraud or other irregularity or error.

In forming our opinion we also evaluated the overall adequacy of the presentation of information in the financial statements.

Qualified opinion arising from omission of cash flow statement

As explained in note ... the financial statements do not contain a statement of cash flows as required by Financial Reporting Standard 1. Net cash flows for the year ended 19... amounted to £... and in our opinion information about the company's cash flows is necessary for a proper understanding of the company's state of affairs and profit [loss].

Except for the failure to provide information about the company's cash flows, in our opinion the financial statements give a true and fair view of the state of the company's affairs as at 31 December 19... and of its profit [loss] for the year then ended and have been properly prepared in accordance with the *Companies Act 1985*.[5]

Registered auditors   *Address*
Date

---

[5] Omission of a primary statement normally results in the issue of an opinion qualified as to the effect on the view given by the financial statements and the compliance with the Companies Act's other specific requirements, because the Act requires additional information to be included in financial statements when necessary to give a true and fair view.

Appendix 3: Statement of directors' responsibilities

Example wording of a description of the directors' responsibilities for inclusion in a company's financial statements

Company law requires the directors to prepare financial statements for each financial year which give a true and fair view of the state of affairs of the company and of the profit or loss of the company for that period. In preparing those financial statements the directors are required to

▶ select suitable accounting policies and then apply them consistently;

▶ make judgements and estimates that are reasonable and prudent;

▶ state whether applicable accounting standards have been followed, subject to any material departures disclosed and explained in the financial statements;[6]

▶ prepare the financial statements on the going concern basis unless it is inappropriate to presume that the company will continue in business.[7]

The directors are responsible for keeping proper accounting records which disclose with reasonable accuracy at any time the financial position of the company and to enable them to ensure that the financial statements comply with the *Companies Act 1985*. They are also responsible for safeguarding the assets of the company and hence for taking reasonable steps for the prevention and detection of fraud and other irregularities.

---

[6] Large companies only.

[7] If no separate statement on going concern is made by the directors.

7.9.2 Reporting substance versus form

One major area on which APB pronouncements have so far been conspicuously silent relates to audits of small companies, despite the fact that an auditing guideline on this subject, having undergone due process, was handed to them on a plate by APC on 1 April 1991. SAS 600 is no exception in that it provides no guidance whatsoever on the problems faced by auditors of such companies, particularly in relation to reliance on management representations or the extent to which audit assurance is derived from accounts preparation work.

It is worth noting that the significant feature usually attributed to small business managements, i.e. domination by a managing director of all primary financial and administrative functions, and which constitutes for such businesses the chief form of control, exists just as pervasively in many major public companies.

Although those managements which over the past thirty years have had to endure the indignities of Department of Trade and Industry (formerly Department of Trade) investigations are not necessarily typical, they were all at one time highly successful market front-runners, whose exceptional performance, by any measure, established the reputation of their chief executives' leadership qualities and business acumen. They operated in diverse fields, some specialized, some conglomerate in character, but they shared one distinguishing feature: the irrepressible determination of their chief executives to brook no opposition to their sway on policy matters – as if all their decisions had been divinely inspired and hence required no explanation, still less justification.

Yet all of these companies had, so far as appearances go, large boards of well-qualified directors, and many had audit committees too – as if to prove that responsibility, and hence control, at the highest level was truly shared. So much for the form; the substance that unfailingly emerged from one DTI Report after another was that the entire directorial superstructure, audit committees included, amounted in the event to no more than an ill-informed, rarely consulted, highly expensive, and utterly impotent rubber-stamping contrivance. The revelations of these investigators' reports undoubtedly relate to no more than the tip of the iceberg, since it is an observable fact that many successful enterprises owe a great deal to the charismatic flair of one dominating personality: one who is prepared from time to time to risk his reputation and position on a venture which, for those whose inclination is to await the boardroom vote, would represent yet another lost opportunity.

While all proceeds in accordance with the higher and higher expectations placed by shareholders (particularly the institutional class) upon the performance of these talented entrepreneurs, few problems manifest; but since the downturn, whether due to a misread market situation, an unwarranted speculation, or any other cause, is almost always unexpected, it is clear that the unfettered judgement of auditors is just about the only safeguard against the concealment of true circumstances.

That clear-eyed judgement is particularly needed during the closing phases of the audit examination when (to quote the 1980 operational guideline) 'skill and imagination are required to recognize the matters to be examined in carrying out an overall review ...'. On the questions of presentation and disclosure, the guideline expected an auditor to 'bear in mind the need for the financial statements to reflect the substance of the underlying transactions and balances and not merely their form. He should consider also whether the presentation adopted ... may have been unduly influenced by management's desire to present facts in a favourable or unfavourable light.' If we live up to this guideline the lessons of the past will have been learnt. If we do not, all the detailed audit procedures which precede the final review are virtually a waste of time.

Yet in practice the information and explanations required by auditors from those at the top of the corporate tree are by no means always fully and freely forthcoming, nor is it always feasible to obtain satisfactory corroborative evidence from independent sources.

Observing the spirit of the standards

Any attempt, no matter how well intentioned, to improve standards (in any sphere) from without is destined to fail unless it is met with a corresponding inner willingness to observe them (in both letter and spirit) on the part of those to whom they apply. Without this essential willingness, a way will always be found to justify the expression of an opinion which falls short of the real message. The standard drafting of most reports – whether clean or qualified – inclines too far towards the unspoken motive of self-protection, at the expense of being truly informative to those who depend upon their content. It is a telling comment on the development of reporting standards, applicable in both the UK and USA, that when Price Waterhouse published their 'certificate of chartered accountants' on, for example, the first annual report of US Steel over a century ago, its content was conspicuously more informative than today's stereotyped formality!

One of the chief impediments to progress in reporting these days, and it cannot be dismissed just because it is unpalatable, is that the public practice of auditing is highly competitive, and no auditors can afford unnecessarily to incur the displeasure of those who, in effect, have the power to remove them.

So we see that it may be from their own clients that auditors require protection, and on any objective view it is difficult to see how members of a professional body should be expected to operate while under permanent threat of removal – and for the worst of all possible reasons: for doing their job a little too well.

We may indeed regard our responsibilities as being owed to 'the client', and continue to address our reports accordingly (as the standard requires); but the truth is that auditors owe a moral duty to the public, and virtually the whole of our society benefits from the code of corporate and financial conduct and integrity which our efforts, directly or indirectly, seek to sustain.

We as auditors tend to automatically regard the *management* of X Ltd as the client only because it is they who, in effect, wield the authority to replace us. If that authority, so easily abused, were removed, auditors would soon respond to meet the demands imposed by their wider duty, their public duty: the duty which they have, after all, always had but have lately sought to shun, even deny.

There is thus much to be said for a change in law which would give auditors the right to appeal against any overt or covert attempt to remove them from office for reasons which are, in their opinion, totally unwarranted by the circumstances.

Lack of independence is sometimes said to 'compromise' the auditor's position; it is in fact far worse – it actually destroys the audit function. It provides those who depend on the audit with a false sense of comfort, and thus lends credibility to deception. It transforms the auditor into a dissembler.

Opening balances and comparatives

In the light of the UK profession's difficulties in determining its responsibilities for establishing the reliability of comparative figures, which are included by law in financial statements, APB has produced an auditing standard (SAS 450) on this important subject. It also deals with the audit problems that arise when a firm conducts an audit of a company's accounts for the first time, either because they have just been appointed or because the entity, for whatever reason, was previously exempt from audit.

Its key points are summarized as follows:

1. The extent of audit evidence required by this Standard varies according to whether the auditors are continuing or incoming. The major impact relates to the position of

incoming auditors. The SAS lists suggested procedures in both cases; these would not normally include consultations with predecessor auditors.

2. An important issue in SAS 450 is the consistency of accounting policies adopted over subsequent accounting periods. The auditor should identify any changes and the disclosure given in the financial statements. It may be appropriate to make reference to this in the audit report itself. The auditor may wish to obtain specific confirmation from the client in the management representations letter that accounting policies have been consistently applied.

3. Additional procedures are likely to be necessary where the previous period's financial statements were unaudited, which is particularly relevant to the audit exemption regime under sections 249A to 249E *Companies Act 1985*.

4. SAS 450 provides some useful specimen audit reports appropriate to differing circumstances, including a qualified opinion on the profit and loss account due to uncertainty regarding the opening stock valuation.

5. Prior to accepting new appointments the auditor may wish to carry out a company search. This will provide a conclusive record of what audit reports have been issued in previous years and which may have relevance for him. (A company search is also relevant to the identification procedures in relation to money laundering and the *Criminal Justice Act 1993*.)

6. Where an incoming auditor has been appointed he will already have contacted the previous auditor in accordance with the *Guide to Professional Ethics*, para. 1.206 of the ICAEW Members' Handbook, to ascertain information that his predecessor may consider relevant to his decision whether or not to accept nomination. This may, but not necessarily, highlight matters for his consideration in respect of the opening balances and comparatives.

7. In the case of comparatives, where these have been changed as the result of a prior year adjustment, the auditors will need to consider whether the disclosures are in accordance with *FRS 3 – Reporting Financial Performance*.

A particular problem that arises in practice may be the audit of the first accounts of a company following the purchase of an unincorporated business. In particular, the business required may not have maintained adequate accounting records to attribute values to the assets purchased, especially stock.

However, the purchase of an unincorporated business by a limited company is normally undertaken in an orderly fashion. Realistic values are agreed and ascribed to the assets acquired on the purchase date, when a proper stocktaking would normally be carried out. Presumably the business submitted accounts including stock values to the Inland Revenue, and these were accepted as the basis of tax computations in successive years.

A reasonable approximation of the opening values of assets other than stock could be made by reference to account movements during the year, the closing position being the subject of normal verification procedures. This might be straightforward enough for fixed assets but could be complex in the case of debtors, and the client would have to be prepared to pay for the time costs involved; if not, the auditor's report would need to be qualified due to the scope limitation, setting out the circumstances.

The real stumbling block is the determination of the value of opening stock, and an audit report qualification would need to be expressed in relation to both the profit and loss account and the balance sheet. It may be possible to verify the year-end asset and liability position, but the balance sheet includes the closing profit and loss account balance. Opening inaccuracies may well have affected the sums respectively included in the directors' current accounts, reserves and the profit and loss account.

As already explained, APB issued SAS 600 in 1993, which had the effect of transforming the standard style and presentation of audit reports on financial statements in the UK. The earlier APC guideline reproduced below is, however, concerned with the *Companies Act 1985* requirements for reports by auditors in a much wider context than the annual stewardship accounts filed at Companies House. Any passage or examples that have, however, been superseded by SAS 600 have been deleted.

Reports by auditors under company legislation in the United Kingdom (issued June 1989)

Annual financial statements

Addressee and scope of report

1. The auditor of a company has a duty under the Act to make a report to the members of the company on the financial statements examined by him. Specifically, he is required to report on every balance sheet and profit and loss account and on all group financial statements laid before the company in general meeting during his tenure of office.

Standards followed

2. The audit of the annual financial statements of a company should always be carried out in accordance with Auditing Standards and the auditor should confirm that he has done so in his report.

The audit opinion

3. The Act requires the auditor to state in his report whether, in his opinion, a true and fair view is given:
    (a) in the balance sheet, of the state of the company's affairs at the end of the financial year;
    (b) in the profit and loss account (if not framed as a consolidated account), of the company's profit or loss for the financial year; and
    (c) in the case of group financial statements, of the state of affairs and profit or loss of the company and its subsidiaries dealt with by those financial statements.

4.   The auditor is also required to state whether, in his opinion, the financial statements have been properly prepared in accordance with the Act.

   (a)   In this context, the expression 'properly prepared' includes compliance with the requirements of the Act with respect to the form and content of the balance sheet and profit and loss account and any additional information to be provided by way of notes to the accounts, subject to an overriding requirement that the financial statements should give a true and fair view.

   (b)   The auditor of a company incorporated in Great Britain refers in his report to the *Companies Act 1985*.

Other information required by the Companies Act 1985

6.   Other statutory requirements give the auditor additional reporting responsibilities which may or may not affect the wording of his report. These are as follows:

   (a)   *Section 237(1)*
       The auditor is required to carry out such investigations as are necessary to enable him to form an opinion as to:

       (i)   whether proper accounting records have been kept by the company and proper returns adequate for his audit have been received from branches not visited by him; and

       (ii)   whether the company's balance sheet and (if not consolidated) its profit and loss account are in agreement with the accounting records and returns.

       If the auditor reaches a satisfactory opinion as to (i) and (ii) above he does not need to state this in his report. However, if he is of the opinion that either of these requirements has not been met, he is required to state this fact in his report.

   (b)   *Section 237(3)*
       If the auditor fails to obtain all the information and explanations he considers necessary for the purposes of his audit he is required by Section 237(3) to state the fact in his report. For example, the auditor should consider whether such a statement is required when there has been a limitation of the scope of the audit, leading to a qualification of the audit report.

   (c)   *Section 237(4)*
       If the financial statements do not comply with the requirements of Schedule 6, which deals with 'Chairman's and directors' emoluments, pensions and compensation for loss of office and loans, quasi-loans and other dealings in favour of directors', then the auditor must set out the required particulars in his report so far as he is reasonably able to do so.

   (d)   *Section 235(3)*
       The auditor is required to consider whether the information given in the directors' report is consistent with the financial statements and, if he is of the opinion that it is not, he must state that fact in his report. The Auditing Guideline 'Financial information issued with audited financial statements' gives detailed guidance on this area.

Modified accounts (Schedule 8)*

9. The Act entitles certain companies to exemption from filing their audited financial
    statements if instead 'modified accounts' are filed with the Registrar of Companies. Legal
    advice has indicated that, although they must be properly prepared in accordance with
    Schedule 8 to the Act, the modified accounts are not required to give a true and fair view.

10. Whether companies may file modified accounts depends upon their qualifying in particular
    financial years as small or medium-sized. The modified* accounts must contain a statement
    by the directors that:

    (a) they rely on sections 246 to 248 as entitling them to deliver modified* accounts; and

    (b) they do so on the ground that the company is entitled to the benefit of those sections
         as a small/medium-sized company.

    If the directors propose to rely on sections 246 to 248 it is the auditor's duty to provide
    them with a special report. This report will incorporate the following elements:

    (a) Addressee − the report should be addressed to the directors.

    (b) Scope of report − the report covers only the modified* accounts (as defined by
         Schedule 8) even though there must be reproduced in it the full text of the auditor's
         report on the full financial statements.

    (c) Standards followed − the auditor should indicate that his work is limited to determining
         whether the company is entitled to the benefit of sections 246 to 248 and to an
         examination of the modified* accounts and the annual financial statements on which
         they are based to confirm compliance with Schedule 8.

    (d) Opinion − the auditor should state whether in his opinion:

         (i) the directors are entitled to deliver modified* accounts as claimed in the directors'
              statement; and

         (ii) the modified* accounts have been properly prepared in accordance with Schedule 8
              to the Act.

    The statutory requirement for the modified accounts to be properly prepared can be
    taken in this context to mean only that the modified accounts accurately reproduce
    from the full financial statements the items and information required by Schedule 8.

    (e) Other information required − the report should include the full text of the auditor's
         report under section 235 on the full financial statements.

    (f) Date − the report should be dated on or as soon as possible after the date of the
         report on the full financial statements. The impression should not be given that this
         report in any way 'updates' the audit report on the full financial statements.

    If the auditor cannot make the positive statements indicated at (i) and (ii) of (d) above, he
    should report to the directors stating this, and the company should not proceed with filing
    modified* accounts with the Registrar of Companies.

11. If the report on the full financial statements is qualified, modified* accounts can nevertheless
    be deemed to be properly prepared so long as they are an accurate extract. If, however, the

---

* Since the *Companies Act 1989* these have become known as 'abbreviated accounts'.

qualification relates to one of the determinants for exemption, the auditor should consider whether the maximum effect of the matter giving rise to the qualification would cause the turnover, employee or balance sheet totals to exceed the exemption limits. If the qualification is in the form of an adverse opinion or a disclaimer of opinion, the auditor should consider whether he can properly assess the determinants for exemption on the basis of financial statements which in his opinion are, or could be, misleading as a whole.

12. If the report on the full financial statements is qualified, the auditor should ensure that a reader of the report on the modified* accounts will be able to understand the circumstances giving rise to that qualification. Usually this will be achieved satisfactorily by reproducing the qualified report, as required by the Act (see paragraph 10(e)). But where the qualification includes a reference to a note to the full financial statements, without stating explicitly all the relevant information contained in that note, the auditor should also reproduce the full text of the note in his report on the modified* accounts, immediately following the text of his qualified report on the full financial statements.

13. Where there is to be a change of auditor, it is desirable to plan for the auditor who reported on the audited full financial statements to report on the modified* accounts. If this is not possible the new auditor performing the latter function can accept the audited full financial statements as a basis for his work unless he has grounds to doubt the accuracy of the determinants for exemption, for example because of a qualified opinion. The new auditor should indicate in his report by whom the audit of the full financial statements was carried out.

Distributions (section 271(4))

14. The Act prohibits all companies from making a distribution otherwise than out of profits available for the purpose. Where a qualified audit report has been given on the last annual financial statements the company's ability to make a distribution, by reference to those financial statements, could be in doubt and the company may not proceed to do so unless the auditor has made a statement under section 271(4) concerning the company's ability to make the distribution. For the purpose of this additional statement a qualified audit report is specified by section 271(3) as a report which is not without qualification to the effect that in the auditor's opinion the accounts have been properly prepared in accordance with the Act.

15. The auditor's statement under section 271(4) will incorporate the following elements:

   (a) Addressee – the statement required of the auditor can be included as a separate paragraph in the audit report to the members on the financial statements. If, instead, a separate statement is made then it would be appropriate for it to be addressed to the members and sent to the company secretary.

   (b) Scope of report – the statement is restricted to an evaluation of the auditor's qualified report on the last annual financial statements in the context of distributable profits.

   (c) Standards followed – the auditor should refer to his audit which will have been carried out in accordance with Auditing Standards and state that his opinion was qualified.

(d) Opinion – the auditor must state whether in his opinion the subject matter of the qualification is material for determining whether proposed distributions, and those which have not yet been proposed, are permitted. A qualification is not material for this purpose if the financial effect of the matters giving rise to qualification could not be such as to reduce the distributable profits below the levels required for the purpose of such distributions. The level of the proposed or potential distribution should always be quantified in the opinion.

Where the maximum effect of a qualification is unquantifiable, it would normally be material for distribution purposes unless the auditor can conclude that the effect of the qualification on the distributable profits could only be favourable. A disclaimer of opinion on the financial statements as a whole would be material as the auditor would be unable to form an opinion on the amount at which the company's distributable profits are stated.

(e) Date – if a separate statement is made, the date used should be that on which the statement is completed. In any case the statement must be available to be laid before the company in general meeting before the distribution in question is made, and so the report will have to be completed by that date.

16. On a change of auditors, the report under section 271(4) can only be made by the auditor who reported on the last annual financial statement.

Re-registration of a private company as a public company (section 43(3)(b))

17. A private company applying to re-register as a public company is required to deliver certain documents to the Registrar of Companies including a copy of a balance sheet of the company prepared as at a date not more than seven months before the application, together with an audit report thereon without material qualification, and a further written statement by the company's auditor in respect of that balance sheet.

18. This written statement should take the form of a report incorporating the following elements:

(a) Addressee – the Act does not state to whom the report should be addressed; in the absence of any other requirement it may be addressed to the directors.

(b) Scope of report – the report is restricted to the relevant audited balance sheet of the company.

(c) Standards followed – the auditor should indicate that his work is linked to an examination of the relationship of amounts stated in the balance sheet already audited, so that it is clear that no further audit work has been carried out.

(d) Opinion – the auditor should express an opinion that as at the balance sheet date the balance sheet shows that the amount of the company's net assets was not less than the aggregate of its called-up share capital and undistributable reserves.

(e) Other information required – the Act requires that the audit report on the relevant balance sheet should not have any material qualification. For a qualified report to be acceptable, the auditor is required to state in that report that the matter giving rise to the qualification is not material for determining whether at the balance sheet date the net assets of the company were not less than the aggregate of its called-up share capital and undistributable reserves. In determining whether a qualification is not material for the above purpose, the considerations are similar to those outlined in paragraph 15 above.

(f) Date – the report should be dated when it is completed which cannot be earlier than the date of the audit report on the relevant balance sheet.

If there is a change of auditors, the new auditor can accept the balance sheet audited by his predecessor as a basis for the work referred to at (c) above unless the audit report thereon has been qualified. The new auditor should indicate in his report by whom the audit of the relevant balance sheet was carried out.

Other reports required

19. Other special statutory reports may be required of the auditor or a reporting accountant that do not arise from the audit report given on the annual financial statements. Some of these are summarized in paragraphs 20–32 below.

Allotment of shares by a public company otherwise than for cash (section 103(1))

20. Companies may allot shares and receive payment for them in a form other than cash. Where a public company proposes to allot shares for such non-cash consideration it must, subject to certain exceptions, obtain during the six months before the date of the allotment a report on the value of the assets to be received in payment for the shares.

21. The report should be made by an independent accountant who either is the auditor, or is qualified to act as auditor, of the allotting company. He is entitled, however, to rely on another person, a specialist, who appears to him to have the requisite knowledge and experience and who is not, *inter alia*, an officer or a servant of the company, to make the valuation of all or part of the assets. The report will incorporate the following elements:

(a) Addressee – the report should be made to the company itself and sent to the company secretary for circulation to the proposed allottees.

(b) Scope of report – as well as expressing the opinion set out in (d) below, the report must include the following information:

(i) the nominal value of the shares in question;

(ii) any premium payable on them;

(iii) a description of the consideration;

(iv) a description of the part of the consideration valued by the independent accountant, the method used and the date of the valuation; and

(v) the extent to which the nominal value of the shares and any premium are to be treated as paid up by the consideration and in cash.

(c) Standards followed – the report should indicate the basis of valuation of the consideration for the allotment of shares.

(d) Opinion – the independent accountant must state that in his opinion:

    (i) if the valuation has been made by another person, it appears to be reasonable to accept such a valuation. In this case, the report should also state the specialist's name and what knowledge and experience he has to carry out the valuation, and describe the part of the consideration valued by him, the method used to value it and the date of the valuation.

    (ii) the method of valuation was reasonable in all the circumstances;

    (iii) there appears to have been no material change in the value of the consideration since the valuation; and

    (iv) on the basis of the valuation, the value of the consideration including any cash to be paid, is not less than the total amount to be treated as paid up on the shares together with the whole of any premium.

(e) Date – the date used should be that on which the report is completed. There is no provision for the report to be qualified. The independent accountant should not issue any report unless his opinion is unqualified.

22. In certain circumstances the allotment of shares may represent only a part of the consideration for the transfer of a non-cash asset to the allotting company (e.g. cash may also be paid). In such cases, the independent accountant's report must apply to so much of the value of the non-cash asset as is attributable to paying up the nominal value of the shares (and any premium) and the report must also state:

(a) what valuations have been made in order to determine that proportion of the consideration;

(b) the reason for those valuations;

(c) the method and date of any such valuation; and

(d) any other relevant matters.

23. Before the independent accountant can make a statement that there appears to have been no material change in the value of the asset since the valuation, he may have to perform additional work. If the period of time between the making of the valuation and the date of the report is such that there may have been a change in the value, the independent accountant will need to reconsider the valuation. If he made arrangements for someone else to perform the valuation he should obtain written confirmation from that person as to whether there has been a change in value.

Transfer of non-cash assets to a public company by a member of the company (section 104(4)(b))

24. During the first two years following its registration (or re-registration if it was previously a private company) a public company may not lawfully purchase from certain of its members a non-cash asset for a consideration worth one tenth or more of the nominal value of the

company's issued share capital unless the terms of the transfer have been approved by an ordinary resolution. Similar restrictions apply where a third party acquires a non-cash asset for which the company pays.

25. In addition to approval by an ordinary resolution, a valuation report (similar to that described in paragraphs 20–3 above) on the asset purchased by the company (and on any asset given by the company in payment) must have been made to the company during the six months preceding the transfer. The report must be made by an independent accountant qualified to act as the company's auditor and will incorporate the following elements:

(a) Addressee – the report should be made to the company itself and sent to the company secretary for circulation to the members of the company and to the person selling the asset.

(b) Scope of report – as well as expressing the opinion set out in (d) below, the report must include the following information:

(i) the consideration to be received by the company, describing the asset in question, and the consideration to be given by the company and specifying any amounts to be received or given in cash; and

(ii) the method and date of valuation.

(c) Standards followed – the report should indicate the basis of valuation of the consideration.

(d) Opinion – the independent accountant must state that in his opinion:

(i) if the valuation has been made by another person, it appears to be reasonable to accept such a valuation. In this case, the report should also state the specialist's name and what knowledge and experience he has to carry out the valuation, and describe the part of the consideration valued by him, the method used to value it and the date of the valuation.

(ii) the method of valuation was reasonable in all the circumstances;

(iii) there appears to have been no material change in the value of the asset in question since the valuation (see paragraph 23 above); and

(iv) on the basis of the valuation used, the value of the consideration to be received by the company is not less than the value of the consideration to be given by it.

(e) Date – the date used should be that on which the report is completed. Circulation of the report must not be later than the notice calling the meeting at which the resolution to approve the transfer is proposed.

There is no provision for the report to be qualified. The independent accountant should not issue any report unless his opinion is unqualified.

Redemption or purchase by a private company of its own shares out of capital (section 173(5))

26. Where a private company redeems or purchases its own shares wholly or partly out of capital this must be approved by a special resolution of the company to which special voting

rules apply. In addition, the Act requires the directors to make a statutory declaration in the prescribed form specifying the capital payment permitted by section 171 (3). A factor in computing the capital payment permitted by the Act must be the amount of the company's distributable profits, determined by the directors by reference to accounts prepared as at any date within the three months prior to the date of their statutory declaration. The relevant accounts for this purpose are such as to enable a reasonable judgement to be made as to the amounts of profits, losses, assets and liabilities, provisions, share capital and reserves. In the statutory declaration the directors must also state that, having made full inquiry into the affairs and prospects of the company, they have formed the opinion:

(a) that there will be no ground on which the company could be found to be unable to pay its debts immediately after the date on which the payment out of capital is proposed to be made (for this purpose the directors must take account of all the company's prospective and contingent liabilities); and

(b) that, having regard to their intentions with respect to the management of the company's business during the year immediately following that date and to the amount and character of the financial resources which will in their view be available to the company during that year, the company will be able to continue to carry on business as a going concern throughout the year; and that accordingly the company will be able to pay its debts as they fall due throughout that year.

The declaration must be delivered to the Registrar of Companies, and must be available at the meeting at which any special resolution is to be proposed approving the payment out of capital.

27. The auditor is required to make a report regarding the directors' declaration to be attached to the declaration. It will incorporate the following elements:

(a) Addressee – the report should be addressed to the directors.

(b) Scope of report – the report concerns the directors' declaration.

(c) Standards followed – the Act requires that the report shall state that the auditor has inquired into the state of the company's affairs. The Act does not prescribe the scope of the work to be carried out by the auditor, but it will involve, as a minimum, a review of the bases for the statutory declaration by the directors.

(d) Opinion – the auditor is required to state that:

(i) the amount specified in the directors' declaration as the permissible capital payment for the shares in question is, in his opinion, properly determined in accordance with sections 171 and 172 of the Act; and

(ii) he is not aware of anything to indicate that the opinion expressed by the directors in their declaration as to any of the matters mentioned in section 173 (3) is unreasonable in all the circumstances.

(e) Date – the directors' declaration and therefore the attached auditor's report are required to be made in the week before the resolution is passed specifying the amount of the permissible capital payment for the shares in question. The auditor's report should not be dated earlier than the date of the directors' declaration to which it relates.

There is no provision for the report to be qualified. The auditor should not issue any report unless his opinion is unqualified.

Financial assistance for acquisition of a private company's own shares (section 156(4))

28. In general a company may only give financial assistance for the purchase of shares or those of its holding company if it meets certain conditions set out in section 153 of the Act. These conditions are relaxed in the case of a private company where the acquisition concerns shares in the company itself or, in the case of a subsidiary, shares in its holding company (if the holding company is a private company). Where a private company wishes to make use of the relaxation, the giving of assistance must normally be approved by a special resolution of the company.

29. Before the financial assistance is given, the directors must make a statutory declaration stating:

    (a) the prescribed particulars of the financial assistance to be given, the person to whom the assistance is to be given and the business of the company of which they are directors; and

    (b) that they have formed the opinion that there will be no ground on which the company could be found to be unable to pay its debts immediately following the giving of the financial assistance (for this purpose the directors must take account of all the company's prospective and contingent liabilities); and

    (c) (i)   if it is intended to commence the winding-up of the company within twelve months of the giving of the financial assistance, that the company will be able to pay its debts in full within twelve months of the commencement of the winding up; or

         (ii) in any other case, that the company will be able to pay its debts as they fall due during the year immediately following the giving of the assistance.

    The declaration must be delivered to the Registrar of Companies, and must be available at the meeting at which any special resolution is to be proposed approving the financial assistance.

30. An auditor's report regarding the directors' declaration is required to be attached to the declaration. The report will incorporate the following elements:

    (a) Addressee – the report is required to be addressed to the directors.

    (b) Scope of report – the report concerns the directors' declaration.

    (c) Standards followed – the Act requires that the report shall state that the auditor has inquired into the state of the company's affairs (see paragraph 27(c)).

    (d) Opinion – the auditor must state that he is not aware of anything to indicate that the opinion expressed by the directors in their declaration as to any of the matters mentioned in Section 156(2) is unreasonable in all the circumstances.

(e) Date – the directors' declaration and hence the attached auditor's report are required to be made in the week before the passing of the resolution normally required for approval of the giving of financial assistance. The auditor's report should not be dated earlier than the date of the directors' declaration to which it relates.

There is no provision for the report to be qualified. The auditor should not issue any report unless his opinion is unqualified.

Distributions by public companies; the use of initial accounts (section 273(4))

31. Paragraphs 14 to 16 of this guideline describe the statement required where a company wishes to make a distribution and a qualified audit report has been given on the annual financial statements. A company may wish to make a distribution during its first accounting reference period or after the end of that period but before the accounts for that period have been laid before a general meeting or delivered to the Registrar of Companies. 'Initial accounts' must be prepared for this purpose which, in the case of a public company, are required to comply with section 226 of, and Schedule 4 to, the Act with respect to the form and content of the balance sheet and profit and loss account and any additional information to be provided by way of notes to the accounts. Group accounts are not required. The initial accounts must be signed by the directors in the same manner as annual financial statements, and must be delivered to the Registrar of Companies.

32. In the case of a public company, the auditor is required to make an audit report on the initial accounts. The report will incorporate the following elements:

(a) Addressee – the Act does not state to whom the report should be addressed: in the absence of any other requirement it may be addressed to the directors.

(b) Scope of report – the report is concerned with the initial accounts. The period covered by the initial accounts should be identified.

(c) Standards followed – the audit of the initial accounts should be carried out in accordance with Auditing Standards, and the auditor should refer to this fact in his report.

(d) Audit opinion – the auditor must state whether, in his opinion, the accounts have been properly prepared within the meaning of section 273(2). For these purposes, the term 'properly prepared' means that the accounts must give a true and fair view of the state of the company's affairs as at the balance sheet date and of its profit or loss for the relevant period, and must comply with the provisions of section 226 of, and Schedule 4 to, the Act subject to such modifications as are necessary because the accounts do not relate to an accounting reference period.

If the opinion above is qualified, the auditor must state whether the matter giving rise to the qualification is material for determining whether the distribution is permitted (see paragraph 15).

(e) Date – the same principles apply for initial accounts as for annual financial statements (see paragraph 7 – not reproduced here).

Appendix 4 – Example of a statement required on a company's ability to make a distribution

Auditors' statement to the members of XYZ Limited pursuant to section 271(4) of the *Companies Act 1985*

We have audited the financial statements of XYZ Limited for the year ended 31 December 19... in accordance with Auditing Standards and have expressed a qualified opinion thereon.

In our opinion the subject matter of that qualification is not material for determining, by reference to those financial statements, whether the distribution (interim dividend for the year ended ... .) of £... proposed by the company is permitted under section 270 of the *Companies Act 1985*.

Notes: 1. Where the amount of the dividend has not yet been determined, the auditor's statement should be expressed in terms of the company's ability to make potential distributions up to a specific level. The opinion paragraph will be worded as follows:

> In our opinion the subject matter of that qualification is not material for determining, by reference to those financial statements, whether a distribution of not more than £... by the company would be permitted under section 270 of the *Companies Act 1985*.

2. This example assumes that a separate report is given regarding the company's ability to make a distribution. This matter is sometimes referred to in the statutory audit report by adding a separate paragraph. That paragraph might be worded as follows:

> In our opinion the subject matter of the foregoing qualification is not material for determining whether the distribution of £... proposed by the company is permitted under section 270 of the Act.

Appendix 5 – Example of a statement required when a private company wishes to re-register as a public company

Auditors' statement to the Directors of XYZ Limited pursuant to section 43(3)(B) of the *Companies Act 1985*

We have examined the balance sheet of XYZ Limited as at 31 December 19... which formed part of the financial statements for the year then ended audited by us/ABC and Co. The scope of our work for the purpose of this statement was limited to an examination of the relationship of amounts stated in the audited balance sheet in connection with the company's proposed re-registration as a public company.

In our opinion the balance sheet shows that at 31 December 19... the amount of the company's net assets was not less than the aggregate of its called-up share capital and undistributable reserves.

*We audited the financial statements of XYZ Limited for the year ended 31 December 19... in accordance with Auditing Standards and expressed a qualified opinion thereon. The matter giving rise to our qualification is not material for determining by reference to the balance sheet at 31 December 19... whether at that date the net assets of the company were not less than the aggregate of its called-up share capital and undistributable reserves.

*for inclusion as necessary.

Appendix 6 – Example of a report required when a public company wishes to allot shares otherwise than for cash

Independent accountants' report to XYZ Limited Company for the purposes of section 103(1) of the *Companies Act 1985*

We report on the value of the consideration for the allotment to ... (name of allottee) of ... (number) shares, having a nominal value of £1 each, to be issued at a premium of ... pence per share. The shares and share premium are to be treated as fully paid up.

The consideration for the allotment to ... (name of allottee) is the freehold building situated at ... (address) and X,000 (number) of shares, having a nominal value of £1 each, in ABC Public Limited Company.

The freehold building was valued on the basis of its open market value by ... (name of specialist), a Fellow of the Royal Institution of Chartered Surveyors, on ... (date) and in our opinion it is reasonable to accept such a valuation.

The shares in ABC Public Limited Company were valued by us on ... (date) on the basis of the price shown in The Stock Exchange Daily Official List at ... (date).

In our opinion, the methods of valuation of the freehold building and of the shares in ABC Public Limited Company were reasonable in all the circumstances. There appears to have been no material change in the value of either part of the consideration since the valuations were made. On the basis of the valuations, in our opinion, the value of the total consideration is not less than £... (being the total amount to be treated as paid up on the shares allotted together with the share premium).

Note: A similar form of report is required pursuant to section 104(4)(b) of the *Companies Act 1985* when a public company purchases non-cash assets from certain of its members.

Appendix 7 – Example of a report required when a private company wishes to redeem or purchase its own shares out of capital

Auditors' report to the Directors of XYZ Limited pursuant to section 173(5) of the *Companies Act 1985*

We have examined the attached statutory declaration of the directors dated ... in connection with the company's proposed purchase of ... (number) ordinary shares by a payment out of capital and reserves. We have enquired into the state of the company's affairs so far as necessary for us to review the bases for the statutory declaration.

In our opinion the amount of £... specified in the statutory declaration of the directors as the permissible capital payment for the shares to be purchased is properly determined in accordance with sections 171 and 172 of the *Companies Act 1985*.

We are not aware of anything to indicate that the opinion expressed by the directors in their declaration as to any of the matters mentioned in section 173(3) of the *Companies Act 1985* is unreasonable in all the circumstances.

Appendix 8 – Example of a report required when a private company wishes to provide financial assistance for the purchase of its own shares or those of its holding company

Auditors' report to the Directors of XYZ Limited pursuant to section 156(4) of the *Companies Act 1985*

We have examined the attached statutory declaration of the directors dated ... in connection with the proposal that the company should give financial assistance for the purchase of (number) of the company's ordinary shares. We have enquired into the state of the company's affairs so far as necessary for us to review the bases for the statutory declaration.

We are not aware of anything to indicate that the opinion expressed by the directors in their declaration as to any of the matters mentioned in section 156(2) of the *Companies Act 1985* is unreasonable in all the circumstances.

Appendix 9 – Example of a report required on initial accounts when a public company wishes to make a distribution

Auditors' report to the Directors of XYZ Public Limited Company pursuant to section 273(4) of the *Companies Act 1985*

We have audited the initial accounts of XYZ Public Limited Company on pages ... to ... in accordance with Auditing Standards.

In our opinion the initial accounts for the period from ... to ... have been properly prepared within the meaning of section 273 of the *Companies Act 1985*.

Review questions

*1.   Audit reports follow a predetermined format and the presentation has very little flexibility. Suggestions have been made that this should be abandoned and the auditor should have the ability to provide his own wording. Discuss the advantages and disadvantages of non-standardized reports.

*2.   As the new partner taking over an audit assignment in your firm, you are concerned over the preceding year's financial statements of one of your firm's biggest audit clients. The previous year's accounts were qualified and the reason for the qualification may extend to the current year.
      Identify the procedures that must be followed in order to be able to give an appropriate report in the current year.

3.   SAS 600 makes reference to 'fundamental uncertainty' within financial statements. Give examples of what might constitute such an uncertainty.

4.   'The majority of audit reports are unqualified so why do we need to have them? Surely a report only need be given if there is anything to report'.
      Critically discuss the above statement.

Exercises

1.   It is sometimes stated that the use of checklists within an audit file does little more than to enable seniors within an audit to delegate responsibility to more junior members who can then just tick the relevant boxes. There exist 'Review Checklists' for audit reports so it can be argued that this amounts to the same thing only with the partner delegating to audit senior.
      Discuss critically the above statement.

2.   SAS 130 relates to the 'Going Concern' aspect of auditing. It is expected that the auditor should look at a period of one year after the date on which the accounts are approved.
      State, giving reasons, whether this is reasonable given the rapid changes that may occur in business.

8

Auditors and the law

8.1   The backlog of company law reform

The role of the auditor exists within a legal framework. His appointment, removal, remuneration, powers, duties, etc., are all determined by the process of law. No study of auditing is therefore complete without considering the effect of the law – both statute and common – on his position. Statute law, primarily the *Companies Acts* in this context, is updated from time to time, but pressures on parliamentary time render it permanently out of date.

Until July 1985 there were five operative *Companies Acts* in the UK: the *Companies Act 1948, 1967, 1976, 1980* and *1981*. The consolidating Act, the *Companies Act 1985* received Royal Assent in July 1985. Like most consolidating Acts of the past (e.g. 1948), the 1985 Act introduced little new legislation. Its purpose was simply to house the existing body of companies legislation under one statutory umbrella, taking the opportunity to rationalize its sequence of subject matter and iron out certain anomalies. It was in turn amended by the *Companies Act 1989*.

Quite apart from statutory change, the auditor's position is also affected by developments in the common law, through cases decided in the courts on a whole range of proceedings, both civil and criminal. It should, however, be stressed at the outset that these pages are written from the viewpoint of the auditor, not the lawyer, and the use of legal terminology is eschewed in the interests of readability and of establishing in the mind of the reader a coherent picture of the legal framework in which the audit function takes its place. Any reader who requires to know the full and exact position on any matter, down to the fine details, is therefore advised to make reference to the legislation and law reports themselves.

The process of implementing European company law Directives began when our Acts of 1980 and 1981 respectively introduced the Second and Fourth Directives to our statute book. Both are therefore reflected in the 1985 Act. The *Companies Act 1989* implements the Seventh and Eighth Directives, the former on consolidated accounts and the latter on the regulation of auditors.

8.2   The auditor and the *Companies Act 1985*

8.2.1 Consolidation of company law

This section gives an overall picture of the relevant statutory provisions under the Act; a summary of its main provisions is given in a later section. Consolidating effectively brings all extant legislation together, and this was the main purpose of the Act of 1985, which has 747 sections and 25 schedules. All sections referred to below are those of the 1985 Act (as amended by the *Companies Act 1989*) unless otherwise stated.

8.2.2 Appointment of auditors (section 384)

The basic rule is that every company (unless eligible for audit exemption) shall at each annual general meeting (AGM) appoint an auditor (or auditors) to hold office until the conclusion of the next AGM. Private companies may, however, elect for automatic reappointment of auditors (section 386). There are two exceptions to this basic rule:

1. The directors may appoint:

   (a) the first auditors, to hold office until the conclusion of the first AGM;

   (b) auditors to fill a casual vacancy.

2. The Secretary of State may appoint auditors if neither members nor directors have done so. The company has a duty to inform the Secretary within one week of this power becoming exercisable.

8.2.3 Removal of auditors (section 391)

A company may by ordinary resolution remove an auditor before the expiry of his term of office. Where such a resolution is passed the company shall notify the registrar of companies within fourteen days.

8.2.4 Resolutions requiring special notice

Note the resolutions at a general meeting for which *special notice* (twenty-eight days) is required:

1. Appointing an auditor other than the retiring auditor (section 391A(1)).
2. Removing an auditor before expiry of his term of office (section 391A(1)).
3. Filling a casual vacancy (section 388(3)).
4. Reappointing a retiring auditor originally appointed by directors to fill a casual vacancy (section 388(3)).

8.2.5 Steps designed to protect the auditor from dismissal without recourse (section 391)

1. On receipt of notice of any resolutions listed under 1 or 2 of section 8.2.4 above, the company shall send a copy to the existing auditor.
2. The existing auditor has the right to make representations in writing, not exceeding a reasonable length, and may request that these shall be notified to the members.
3. Upon receipt of such representations the company has a duty:
   (a) in any notice of resolution given to members of the company, to state the fact that the representations have been made;
   (b) to circulate copies of the representations to every person entitled to receive notice of the meeting.
4. If the representations are not circulated as prescribed (either because they were received too late or due to the company's default) the auditor may have them read out at the meeting, without prejudice to his right to be heard orally on any matter which affects him as auditor.

[*Comment:* This is not a satisfactory substitute for circulation since only those attending the meeting will normally vote on the resolution.]

5. The representations need neither be circulated nor read out at the meeting if, on the application of any person who claims to be aggrieved, the court is satisfied that the auditor is abusing the rights conferred under this provision to secure needless publicity for defamatory matter. The court may order the costs of such an application to be borne (wholly or in part) by the auditor.

The procedures required on the resignation of auditors (see section 8.2.10 below) were extended by the *Companies Act 1989* to cover *all* changes of auditor, for whatever reason.

8.2.6   Rights of ex-auditor (section 391(4))

An auditor who has been removed may:

1. Attend the general meeting at which his term of office would have expired.
2. Attend any general meeting at which it is proposed to fill the vacancy caused by his removal. He is also entitled to receive all notices and communications relating to such meetings, and to be heard at any such meeting on any business which concerns him as former auditor.

8.2.7   Remuneration of auditors (sections 390A and 390B)

The basic rule here is that the auditor's remuneration shall be fixed by whoever makes the appointment, and remuneration, for this purpose, includes sums paid in respect of expenses.

[*Comment:* In practice a resolution appears on the agenda for the AGM authorizing the directors to fix the auditors' remuneration. This is not necessarily fixed in advance, the auditor simply making clear (usually in the letter of engagement) the basis of arriving at the audit fee. The remuneration, including expenses, must be disclosed in the company's published accounts regardless of how the fees are determined. There is a disclosure requirement covering fees paid to the auditor in other capacities, introduced by the *Companies Act 1989*, for companies which do not qualify as small or medium-sized under the Act's definition.]

8.2.8   Rights (or powers) of auditors (sections 389A and 390)

The following is a summary of the rights which constitute the counterpart to the auditor's duties. Duties without the corresponding rights needed to make them effective would clearly be unacceptable.

1. Right to receive notice of all general meetings of the company, and to attend such meetings.
2. Right to be heard at all general meetings of the company on any matter which concerns him in his capacity as auditor.
3. Rights associated with a proposal to replace him or to remove him from office (see sections 8.2.5 and 8.2.6 above).
4. Right of access at all times to records, documents and vouchers of the company.
5. Right to require from the officers of the company such information and explanations as are considered necessary for the purposes of the audit.

6. Right to require UK subsidiaries and their auditors to provide the primary auditors with 'such information and explanations as those auditors may reasonably require for the purposes of their duties as auditors of the holding company'.

[*Comment*: Does the latter provision go far enough? Two questions that arise are: what is 'reasonably require' for this purpose, and by whose standards? The auditor of every company has the right to the information and explanation which he, at his own discretion, may consider necessary for the performance of his duties.

Should primary auditors also be entitled to examine the records of the subsidiaries, if they consider it necessary, or even have the right to examine the audit programmes and other working papers on the subsidiary auditors' files? Auditors have no hesitation, after all, in examining the working papers of a client company's internal auditors in order to assess the scope and quality of their work, on the legitimate grounds that the ultimate responsibility for the opinion on the accounts is theirs alone. By exactly the same token, the primary auditors should not be barred access to whatever documentary evidence they feel inclined to examine if they believe it will assist them to fulfil their statutory obligations. Yet, as we see, the 1985 Act's powers fall short of this.]

8.2.9 Duties

The report to members (section 235)

The most important duty of the statutory auditor is to report to the members as required under section 235 of the Act. Every audit report on the accounts of a limited company must state whether in the auditor's opinion:

1. The balance sheet gives a true and fair view of the state of the company's affairs at the balance sheet date.
2. The profit and loss account gives a true and fair view of the profit (or loss) for the period ended on that date.
3. The accounts have been properly prepared in accordance with the provisions of the *Companies Act*. (In the case of group accounts submitted by the holding company, the auditor's opinion must refer to the state of affairs and profit or loss of the company and its subsidiaries dealt with thereby, so far as concerns members of the holding company.)

Under section 236, the auditors' report must state the names of the auditors (including the words 'registered auditor(s)') and be signed by them.

The matters which the auditor must consider, and report on 'by exception' only, are as follows (section 237):

1. Whether, in the auditor's opinion, proper accounting records (as defined in sections 221–2) have been kept by the company. These records must contain:
   (a) record of purchases and sales of goods in sufficient detail to identify the goods and their buyers and sellers (except in case of normal retail sales);
   (b) day-to-day details of receipts and payments of cash;

(c) details of assets and liabilities;

(d) statements of stock held and any supporting stocktaking schedules.

[*Comment:* Section 722 also refers to the records and specifies that where these are not kept in the form of bound books, adequate precautions shall be taken for guarding against falsification and for facilitating its discovery.]

2. Whether proper returns, adequate for audit purposes, have been received from branches not visited by the auditors.

3. Whether the balance sheet and profit and loss account are in agreement with the records.

4. Whether the auditor has received all information and explanations which were required for the purposes of the audit.

5. Whether the information given in the directors' report is consistent with the accounts (section 235(3)).

What are 'accounting records'? Section 221 requires that the records shall be such as to: (1) disclose with reasonable accuracy, at any time, the financial position of the company at that time, and (2) enable the directors to ensure that any balance sheet and profit and loss account prepared by them complies with the requirements of the Act as to form and content of company accounts. It is not entirely clear what the legislators have in mind in drafting this requirement, and its practical implications are worth exploring a little further. Does this, for example, affect the company whose 'accounting records' are unceremoniously handed over to the auditor once a year in a plastic shopping bag? If so, the Act does not make this clear. What, after all, is 'reasonable accuracy'? There can be few records more accurate than the original source documents. What of the requirement that the records must *disclose the company's financial position at any time*?

If the law assumes an understanding of accounting records on the part of the reader, then the bag full of scruffy documents, once converted into an orderly set of schedules, will disclose all. But what of the phrase *at any time*? Here the problem of complying with the law – if it is to be taken literally – affects the large public company far more acutely than the corner store, since the most efficiently organized, even computerized, accounts department cannot disclose the company's financial position *upon the instant*. Are *all* companies therefore in breach? Perhaps section 221 really means 'within a *reasonable* time'? In which event, what is 'reasonable'? Suffice it to observe that a competent trainee could produce a complete set of accounts from the contents of the plastic bag in a good deal less time than it takes the computerized might of multi-national conglomerates plc's accounting division to do likewise.

A more probable interpretation, and one which would invalidate the 'plastic bag brigade' is that the accounting records must be such that 'true and fair' financial statements can be *retrospectively prepared as at an earlier point in time*. We should, in May for example, be capable of producing accurate accounts (including stock valuations based on the records) as at 31 December, or *any* date earlier than May. The Act's actual requirements remain far too unspecifc, however.

Section 221 of the Act also requires that accounting records shall contain: (1) statements of stock held by the company at the end of each financial year of the company, and (2) all statements of stocktakings from which any such statement as is mentioned in 1 above has been or is to be prepared. What, exactly, does this requirement amount to? Is it designed to ensure that all companies should determine their stock quantities at formal stocktakings held at least once a year? Possibly, but this is not what it actually says. Compliance with (1) above is no problem, since a mere note of what the directors believe the stock figure to be is clearly a 'statement of stock held by the company' at its financial year-end.

Item (2) declares in effect that all statements of stocktakings from which the previous statement has been (or is to be) prepared are also deemed part of the accounting records. It is obvious, however, that if there is no physical stocktaking, there can be no records thereof. By analogy, accounting records must include a record of purchases; but if no purchases have taken place (the company having stockpiled in the previous year) it cannot be held in breach of section 221 for having no purchases records.

So we see that when the requirement is stripped of all legalistic pretension, it is in fact simply saying that if the final stock figure is supported by stocktaking schedules, they must be preserved, together with the other records, for the requisite three-year retention period (six years for a public company). Companies should nevertheless have the means of identifying stock values at every date if they are to satisfy the overriding requirement that the records must be able to disclose the financial position as at any date.

Inclusion of further information (section 232 and Sch. 6)

The following five requirements on disclosure of certain information in published accounts all extend the responsibility for the information specified to be given in the auditor's report, so far as it is practicable to do so, if it is *not* given as required in the accounts themselves or in the notes thereto:

1. Director's emoluments, distinguishing those received in the capacity as director from other emoluments, and also distinguishing payments as compensation for loss of office, and sums paid to directors, former directors or their dependants by way of pensions.

2. Loans and quasi-loans (see section 8.3.10, below) to officers, under which sums outstanding at the beginning and end of the year respectively, as well as advances and repayments during the year, must be disclosed.

3. Emoluments of the chairman, highest paid director, and the number of directors whose total UK emoluments fall within each of the specified bands.

4. Total directors' emoluments waived.

5. Details of transactions, arrangements and agreements involving directors and officers of the company required under Parts II and III of Sch. 6.

Reports in prospectuses (3rd Schedule)

If a company makes an issue of shares or debentures to the public a report must be placed in the prospectus by the company's auditors, giving details of:

1. Profits and losses arising in each of the previous five years.
2. Rates of dividend declared in each of the previous five years in respect of each class of shares for the time being paid up.
3. Assets and liabilities as at the latest balance sheet date.

[*Comments*:

1. The amounts of past profits and losses disclosed should be adjusted by the reporting auditors as they consider necessary, bearing in mind the purpose of the report.
2. If the company seeks a Stock Exchange quotation for its shares it will be necessary to comply with the requirements of the Stock Exchange, as set out in the yellow book entitled *Admission of Securities to Listing*. These requirements are far more extensive than those of the 3rd Schedule.]

8.2.10   Resignation (sections 392, 392A and 394)

A resignation notice is effective only if it contains either:

1. A statement to the effect that there are no circumstances connected with the resignation which the auditor considers should be brought to the notice of members or creditors, or
2. A statement of such circumstances.

Where the latter is appropriate, the auditor may also requisition the directors to call an extraordinary general meeting for the purpose of considering the resignation circumstances.

As with the *Financial Services Act 1986*, the *Companies Act 1985* requires auditors to serve a notice of circumstances (or a statement that there are none) on every occasion involving a change of auditors, not just on resignation. Furthermore, if there are circumstances to report, the onus is now on the auditor to file his statement at Companies House. It is the company's duty to file the resignation notice with the Registrar.

Application to the court may be made by the company or any aggrieved party to prevent the auditor's statement being circulated, which injunction the court will grant only if it is satisfied that the auditor is using the resignation notice to secure needless publicity for defamatory matter. As already stated, these provisions now apply on every change of auditor, no matter how it occurs.

8.2.11   False statements to auditors (section 389A)

It is an offence for any officer of a company to make a materially false, misleading or deceptive statement (either orally or in writing) to the auditor, whether knowingly or recklessly. Penalties of imprisonment and/or fines are specified.

[*Comments:*

1. A prosecution under this section would be concerned with whether the false statement was made recklessly. There is no need to establish a 'state of moral turpitude' in order to secure a successful prosecution.

2. In view of this responsibility of the directors to take particular caution over the information that they give the auditors, the latter should ensure that detailed notes are taken during all important meetings with the directors at which matters affecting the accounts are discussed. A letter summarizing the information supplied and matters agreed should then be sent to the directors with a minimum of delay, requesting that they should reply if there is anything in the letter with which they are not in agreement.

3. Similar considerations apply to the letter of representation which, as a result of this section, takes on far greater significance than previously, and much greater audit reliance may consequently be placed upon it as a source of internal evidence.]

8.2.12   The status of the auditor

The question of the auditor's precise status has been raised from time to time. It is fairly safe to regard him as the agent of the members to whom he is responsible. In the House of Lords' case *Spackman* v. *Evans* [1868] 3 HL 236, Lord Cranworth said 'the auditors may be agents of the shareholders as far as relates to the audit of the accounts. For the purposes of the audit, the auditors will bind the shareholders.'

The question of whether the auditor is an *officer* of the company is more problematic. The term 'officer' does not, as defined in the Act, include the auditor. Yet it is possible that, for certain purposes anyway, the auditor is to be regarded as an officer:

1. Section 385A speaks of the auditors as holding *office*.

2. Section 27 of the *Companies Act 1989* itself states (rather obviously) that for the purposes of the provision that an officer is not qualified to act as auditor, the references to 'officer' are not to be construed as including the auditor. *This nevertheless suggests that the term 'officer' may include the auditor in some other context.*

The question of how far the auditor may be considered an officer is of particular concern in connection with the winding-up penalty provisions in sections 206–13 *Insolvency Act 1986*. The last two of these sections concern civil offences, but all the others involve criminal offences. All the sections, however, refer to 'any *officer* of a company', or 'any person' and the following case law is relevant.

Civil offences (sections 212 and 213 Insolvency Act 1986)

Sections 212 and 213 are part of the general winding-up provisions and are concerned with the civil offences entitled *misfeasance, breach of trust* and *fraudulent trading*. Broadly speaking, these terms relate to the misuse of a position of authority with the object of personal gain. For example, the directors of a company may bind the company in a contract with an outside party with whom they have an existing financial relationship, i.e. a transaction which is not at arm's length. If a similar contract could have been entered into by the company on more favourable terms, it could be argued that the directors have abused their power and position in order to achieve a personal benefit, at the expense of the company for whom they are acting as stewards. In the event of such an offence being proved, the appropriate remedy would be financial damages, making up the loss. Similar considerations apply where it appears that the business of a company has been carried on with intent to defraud creditors.

It was decided in the two famous legal cases of *Kingston Cotton Mill* (1896, 2 Ch. 279) and *London and General Bank* (1895, 2 Ch. 682) at the end of the last century that, for the purposes of the above provisions, the auditor was to be regarded as an officer of the company.

Criminal offences (sections 206–11 Insolvency Act 1986)

Sections 206–11 all involve criminal offences, and in each case reference is made to 'officers' of the company. The question has therefore arisen as to how far, if at all, the auditor may be regarded as being an officer of the company for the purposes of these sections, bearing in mind that the two cases referred to in the previous section related only to civil liability.

It was held, however, in the case of *R. v. Shacter* (1960, 1 All ER 61) that the term 'officer' must be taken to include the auditor. In 1953 the appellant was appointed auditor of a company and his appointment was continued from year to year thereafter. He was convicted as a 'public officer' of a public company for falsifying the company's books and publishing fraudulent statements contrary to sections 83 and 84 of the *Larceny Act 1861* (now repealed and re-enacted in the *Theft Act 1968*) and for making false entries, fraud and defaults contrary to the relevant sections of the 1948 Act as they are now re-enacted in the *Companies Act 1985*.

8.3   Accounting and other statute law affecting auditors

8.3.1   Accounting reference

Accounting reference is the technical term for the financial year, and it terminates on the accounting reference date. Unless companies have notified otherwise, this date is deemed to be the last day of the month in which the anniversary of incorporation falls (section 224). The directors are permitted to alter the accounting reference date by up to seven days forwards or back, presumably for the purposes of convenience in the case of businesses that operate on a weekly trading cycle.

Section 225 permits the alteration of a company's accounting reference date subject to certain conditions.

8.3.2 Filing rules

1. *Filing:* Audited accounts of public companies must be filed with the Registrar no later than seven months after the accounting reference date (ten months for private companies).

2. *Penalties for late filing:* There are penalties on the company and on every director in office if accounts are not filed by the expiry of the deadline. A notice demanding compliance with filing regulations may be served on directors by the Registrar, a member or a creditor.

8.3.3 Provisions governing capital maintenance, directors' transactions and insider dealings

These provisions were first introduced by the *Companies Act 1980* and fall into three categories:

1. Provisions based on the Second Directive of the EEC. The primary purpose of these sections is to bring into English law the provisions of the Second Directive on Company Law of the European Economic Community. This Directive concerns the formation of public companies, the allotment of their share capital, and the maintenance of their share capital.

2. Provisions relating to directors. The main effect of these provisions is:

    (a) to introduce a written statement of the duties with regard to employees;

    (b) to place restrictions upon certain transactions by a company in which either its directors or persons with whom they are connected are interested (for example, certain service agreements, transactions for sale or the purchase of property and loans);

    (c) to provide for greater disclosure of matters relating to directors in the published financial statements of companies or groups.

3. Provisions prohibiting insider dealing (incorporated in Part V of the *Criminal Justice Act 1993*). These provisions make insider dealing a criminal offence in certain circumstances. In addition, the Act contains several other miscellaneous provisions, some of which are of considerable importance: for example, section 459 (power of court to grant relief where any members are unfairly prejudiced by the acts or omissions of the directors) and section 286 (qualifications of company secretaries).

Certain provisions of the Act concerning the status of public and private companies have already been described above.

8.3.4 The Second EC Directive

The principal changes in UK legislation introduced in consequence of the Second Directive were as follows:

1. Newly incorporated public companies must not commence business without having a certificate to do so from the Registrar. To obtain this, the company must

demonstrate (*inter alia*) that it has allotted the minimum share capital (currently £50,000).

2. Directors must normally have specific authority from the company in general meeting to allot securities. Although this authority may be expressed in general terms, it must be renewed not later than every five years.

3. A private company commits a criminal offence if it offers its shares or its debentures to the public.

4. Shares that it is proposed to allot for cash must generally be offered first to existing members on a pre-emptive basis.

5. A public company may not allot shares in consideration of an undertaking:

    (a) to do work or to perform services, or

    (b) to provide non-cash consideration, unless the consideration is to be provided within five years.

6. A public company may allot shares only when at least 25 per cent of the nominal value and 100 per cent of any premium have been paid up.

7. Shares must not, in certain limited cases, be paid up otherwise than in cash, unless an expert's report that complies with the Act has first been made.

8. Directors of a public company must convene an extraordinary general meeting if they become aware that the company's net assets are less than 50 per cent of its paid up capital.

9. A company is expressly prohibited from acquiring its own shares, except in certain circumstances.

10. A company may not make a distribution except out of profits that are available for the purpose. This excludes unrealized capital profits. A public company is also precluded from making a distribution if the distribution would reduce its net assets below the total of its paid up capital and its undistributable reserves. (There are special provisions relating to investment companies and insurance companies.)

8.3.5 The position and responsibilities of directors

There are two sections which were first introduced in the *Companies Act 1980* relating to employees. These are now included in the *Companies Act 1985*. The first, section 309, states that directors are to have regard to the interests of the company's employees in general. The second, now section 187 *Insolvency Act 1986* reverses the celebrated decision in *Parke* v. *Daily News Limited* (1962) Ch. 927. In that case, it was held that a company was not empowered to make *ex gratia* payments to its employees when it closed down its business. The reasoning behind this decision was that there was no benefit to the company. Under the current provisions, a company may make payments to employees in connection with the cessation or transfer of its business even if those payments will not benefit the company. In many cases, this power will be exercisable by the directors only with the sanction of a resolution of the company in general meeting.

Directors' service contracts are generally not capable of lasting for a period that exceeds five years unless the company has the right to terminate the contract during that period. This does not apply where the relevant term has first been approved by the company in general meeting.

Unless a non-cash asset is immaterial in the context of the company, an ordinary resolution is also necessary for:

1. The transfer of a non-cash asset by the company to a director or a person connected with him.

2. The transfer of a non-cash asset to the company by a director or by a person who is connected with him.

A company that is either a public company or a member of a group that includes a public company is subject to considerable additional prohibitions on making loans and quasi-loans to directors and on entering into 'credit transactions' with them.

There are extensive provisions relating to the disclosure in the financial statements of transactions with directors and others, and directors have a duty to declare interests in transactions to co-directors. Full details of the matters summarized here are given at section 8.3.10 below.

8.3.6 Prohibition of insider dealing

Insider dealing means dealing in securities on the basis of confidential information likely to affect their value. The restrictions on insider dealing are very narrowly drawn. They apply only to transactions on a recognized stock exchange and to dealings in advertised securities. They do not, for obvious reasons, apply to transactions in the shares of a private unlisted company. The provisions create criminal offences, but give no civil remedies.

The provisions which prohibit insider trading first came into effect in June 1980 amid much speculation as to whether their bark would prove to be worse than their bite. These provisions seek to outlaw the use of price-sensitive information which is not generally available to outside shareholders, and add an effective criminal edge to the Stock Exchange's own disciplinary powers. Dealers appreciate that direct sharedealing is covered by the rules, but the Department of Trade and Industry has made it clear that the law now extends to dealings in 'any right to subscribe for, call for, or make delivery of a share of debenture' – which includes all dealings in the highly volatile options market. Even relatively minor market raids (in relation to the size of the issue) have become increasingly risky.

8.3.7 Responsibility of auditors – directors' transactions and dividends

The chief responsibilities for auditors arise under: (1) the disclosure in the audit report of loans and quasi-loans to directors, and details of contracts with directors, if the information is not given as required under section 232, and (2) the question of whether a company is entitled to pay a dividend or not (sections 263–81). These audit duties are set out and explained in section 8.3.10 and following sections.

8.3.8 Converting 'private' to 'public'

Other audit responsibilities include the re-registration of a private company as a public company. One of the documents to be submitted to the Registrar in such cases is a *written statement by the auditors* that in their opinion the amount of net assets at the latest balance sheet date was not less than the company's called-up share capital and its undistributable reserves. The accompanying balance sheet must, moreover, be supported by an audit report which contains no 'material' qualification; and it is necessary for the auditor himself to decide whether the qualification is material in relation to the company's net assets position, as stated above.

In certain circumstances, it may be extremely difficult to quantify the precise effect of a qualified opinion on, say, asset values, and the risk to which the Act thus subjects the auditor – particularly as the client company is about to 'go public' – is obvious, to say the least.

8.3.9 Valuation reports by auditors

Auditors are likely to be called upon as experts to provide valuation reports on any non-cash assets taken as consideration for shares to be issued by a public company (sections 108–11). Such a report is essential prior to the issue of the shares, and it must state *inter alia*: the nominal value and premium attributable to the shares to be paid for by the non-cash consideration, a description of that consideration, the method of valuation and a statement that it is reasonable in the circumstances, and that the value of the consideration (together with any cash payable on the shares) is not less than the amount to be treated as paid up.

The auditor (acting as valuer) is entitled to receive from the officers of the company all information and explanations required for the purpose of the valuation, and this is supported by penalties of fines and imprisonment for anyone giving him false or misleading information, knowingly or recklessly, orally or in writing. This provision is therefore analogous to that in section 389A which deals with false statements by officers made to auditors in the context of their general audit duties (see section 8.2.11 above).

These rules are presumably intended to remedy the abuses whereby the directors of public companies and other connected parties acquired shares in those companies by providing non-cash consideration in the form of 'services to be rendered' (now specifically prohibited) or the sale to the company of assets at a valuation which bears little relation to their true underlying worth.

The Act, however, specifically excludes from its scope the issue of shares for non-cash consideration in the context of acquisitions and mergers, thus leaving unresolved the perennial problem of whether the consideration received (i.e. shares in another company) should be recorded in the books of the acquiring company at the nominal value of the shares issued or at a valuation attributable to the consideration acquired (identified, one hopes, in the sale agreement), which will invariably give rise to a significant share premium. The Act does, however, include provisions intended to give relief from the need to create a share premium in cases of merger where a new holding company is created to acquire the shares in the merging companies, purchase consideration being satisfied by an exchange of shares (sections 130 and 131).

8.3.10   Directors' loans and other transactions

The provisions on directors' loans were designed to overcome the abuses revealed in successive Department of Trade reports through the 1970s in which several major companies adopted 'banking articles', as a result of which loans were made to directors, ostensibly 'within the ordinary course of the company's business'. By this means, the company exploited the available exemptions, a practice to which auditors appeared rarely to take exception. It is worth noting that most auditors are now obliged to apply more rigorous criteria to this question, as follows:

1. The amount of the loan should not exceed the amount of a loan typically made to unconnected individuals. Also, if a bank's policy is to lend money only to corporate customers, a loan to a director could hardly be said to be in the ordinary course of its business.

2. The security required should be equivalent to that required for similar loans made to unconnected individuals.

3. The interest charged should be at least the lowest rate offered on loans made to unconnected individuals, and should not be 'rolled up' unless it is the company's practice to do so with similar external loans.

In practice, audit clients whose business includes the lending of money may still be found making loans to directors which fail to meet the above conditions. Where it is known that a client has made such loans to directors, the partner responsible for the audit should discuss the situation with the client as a *matter of urgency*, and should advise the clients' directors that this does not fall within the firm's interpretation of 'in the ordinary course of business', and remind them of the legal requirement to make disclosure in the accounts of the loans which, at the balance sheet date, do not fall within the restricted definition (specified in 1–3 above and now largely implemented by sections 335 and 338). Client directors should be strongly urged to correct the terms of the loans to bring them within this interpretation and to make the necessary disclosures.

A further abuse commonly found in the past relates to loans made by companies to apparently unconnected outside parties who, in the event, simply 'recycled' the loan to a director otherwise precluded from borrowing in this way. These loans are included within the definition of 'quasi-loan', as given in section 331. Further abuses, whereby loans are made to members of directors' families, are also covered by the existing provisions.

Section 335 also subjects transactions 'in the *ordinary* course of business' between a public company and its directors (and their families and other 'connected' persons) to a rigorous and objective test – since it became palpably clear that auditors had failed to do so in so many of the *causes célèbres* of the 1970s. Specifically, such a transaction is now permitted provided that its value 'is not greater, and the terms on which it is entered into are no more favourable ... than that or those which it is reasonable to expect the company to have offered to ... a person of the same financial standing ... but unconnected with the company.'

Auditors are given a specific watchdog duty in relation to all these onerous (yet incredibly garbled) provisions, in that they are now required to include in their report the disclosure of loans, quasi-loans and other transactions involving directors, as required by the Act, so far as the accounts themselves fail to do so.

In view of the complexity of the regulations concerning loans and other transactions affecting directors, the following tables are provided in order to clarify the situation as far as possible.

Permitted transactions concerning directors

N.B. Many transactions which are permitted are nevertheless subject to disclosure requirements.

Transactions, agreements, arrangements and guarantees between a company (or its subsidiary) and a director of the company (or a person connected with the director) in relation to loans, quasi-loans and credit transactions are generally prohibited, except as noted below. Other transactions etc. are generally permitted, except that special rules apply to directors' service contracts and substantial transfers of non-cash assets between companies and directors. Loans, quasi-loans and credit transactions which are permitted are:

Permitted for

1. Any company	A company may provide a director with funds (up to £20,000 in the case of a public company or the subsidiary of a public company) to meet expenditure for the purposes of the company or to enable him to perform his duties. Approval of the company in general meeting is required, failing which the loan etc. must be repayable within six months.		
	Loans	*Quasi-loans*	*Credit transactions*
2. Public company or subsidiary of a public company	Allowed up to £5,000. Otherwise prohibited to directors and other associated persons	Only if reimbursible within 2 months and the total for the director does not exceed £5,000	Either (i) where transaction is under normal commercial terms; or (ii) where the total for the director does not exceed £10,000

(continued)

Permitted for	Loans	Quasi-loans	Credit transactions
3. Private company not the subsidiary of a public company	Restricted to £5,000 in case of directors. No restriction for connected persons	Permitted	Permitted
4. Moneylending company	Either (i) where loan etc. is under normal company commercial terms, with upper limit of £100,000 per director (no upper limit for a recognized bank or for a private company not the subsidiary of a public company), or (ii) where loan, etc. is on terms available to other employees and is in connection with the purchase or improvement of the director's main residence, with an upper limit of £100,000 per director		No special rules

Disclosure of transactions concerning directors

The particulars indicated below should be disclosed in relation to each transaction, agreement, arrangement or guarantee, whether permitted or not, between a company (or its subsidiary) and a director of the company (or a person connected with the director) in respect of loans, quasi-loans, credit transactions and other transactions.

If the accounts do not give this information, the auditors must give it in their report.

Particulars to be disclosed	Loans	Quasi-loans	Credit transactions	Other transactions
1. A statement that the transaction, etc. was made or subsisted during the year 2. The name of the director (and, where applicable, the connected person) 3. The principal terms of the transaction, etc.	Yes	Yes	Yes, except where the aggregate outstanding sum for a director did not exceed £10,000 during the financial year	Only where the director's interest is material in the opinion of the majority of the other directors. Excludes service contracts

(continued)

Particulars to be disclosed	Loans	Quasi-loans	Credit transactions	Other transactions
4. The amounts due (including interest) at the beginning and end of the financial year				
5. The maximum amount due during the financial year	Yes	No	No	No
6. The amount of unpaid interest				
7. The amount of any provision				
8. The amounts guaranteed at the beginning and end of the financial year				
9. The maximum liability guaranteed	Yes	Yes	Yes, except as above	No
10. Any amounts paid or incurred since the inception of the guarantee				
11. The value of the transactions, etc.	No	Yes	Yes, except as above	No
12. The name of any director with direct or indirect material interest in a transaction (other than a service contract) and the nature of his interest. If no such transaction exists a statement of that fact should be disclosed in the directors' report (listed companies only)	No	No	No	Yes, except where the aggregate interest for a director did not exceed either: (i) the lower of £5,000 and 1 per cent of the net asset value or (ii) £1,000 during the financial year

8.3.11 Auditors as insiders

Part V of the *Criminal Justice Act 1993*, which prohibits insider dealings, makes no specific reference to the auditor although it is abundantly clear that auditors themselves fall within its scope. To some extent our own professional and ethical rules already cover the injunctions against acting on price-sensitive information to which we, in our capacities as auditors and advisers, have privileged access. Indeed, most firms have for many years categorically forbidden all dealings in client company securities by partners and staff, irrespective of whether the individuals concerned are personally involved with the assignment.

Nonetheless, the profession has a good deal of important research to conduct on these sections, since auditors may, quite innocently and unwittingly, find themselves in situations in which it appears that whichever way they turn they may fall foul of the new legal rules. Auditors may, for example, have a large number of public company clients, and investment relationships (not necessarily in a subsidiary or associated company context) may subsist between two of those companies without the respective audit partners being conscious at *all* material times that their own firm is acting for both the companies involved, even though both audits are conducted simultaneously.

The danger arises, of course, when company A has a significant (in relation to its own net assets position) holding in company B at a time when the latter has suffered a sudden and unheralded downturn in its trading fortunes as a result of which a 'going concern' audit qualification appears to be unavoidable. Such information is clearly of crucial concern to the directors and members of company A, but their auditors, also auditors of company B, dare not make this known (i.e. assuming the audit staff know about it). Yet they face the problem of having to form an opinion on the value of A's investment in B. Can they ignore for this purpose what they (much to their regret, no doubt) actually do know? Even if the respective partners and audit teams are operating quite independently, should it appear that price-sensitive information has been used to effect a well-timed disinvestment in B, will the law not *assume* 'perfect knowledge' to subsist between partners in the same firm?

This type of potential conflict of interest between public responsibility and the duty of confidence to one's client is by no means new, and individual firms have undoubtedly established highly professional and ethically irreproachable methods of coping with it; but the legislation on insiders now places a spotlight on matters which we would rather have left to professional integrity, and in respect of which auditors must tread warily.

8.3.12 Distributable profits

Sections 263 to 281, which seek to restrict dividend payments to such amounts as do not erode the paying company's capital base, place an onerous duty on its auditors while providing an interesting insight into the European approach to matters which we had been content to leave within the province of case law. Against a background of varied and somewhat confusing case law, the *Companies Act 1985* has gone a long way towards clarifying the meaning of 'distributable profits'. Section 263, applicable to all companies, states that for dividend purposes, available profits are those which are both *accumulated* and *realized* after charging any accumulated, realized losses (specific provisions being treated as realized losses for this purpose – apart from a provision in respect of a diminution in value of a fixed asset, as reflected in a revaluation of *all* fixed assets). Unless the directors can substantiate special reasons (which would have to be disclosed) to the contrary, capitalized development expenditure is also to be treated as a realized loss for purposes of determining distributable profits.

A feature of this legislation is its specific proviso (section 275(2)) that any depreciation charged over and above that computed on the historic cost of assets (e.g. if revalued by reference to replacement costs) may be disregarded for dividend purposes, and treated as part of the company's realized profits. The main reason for the provision is that the depreciation on the revaluation surplus element represents the extent to which that surplus has in fact become realized – by consumption rather than by sale.

Section 264, applicable to public companies, tackles the same problem of determining divisible profits, but this time from the standpoint of the balance sheet. It declares that a public company may make a distribution only if the amount of its net assets both before and after such distribution is not less than the aggregate of its called-up share capital and its undistributable reserves (defined so as to include (1) share premiums; (2) capital redemption reserve; (3) accumulated unrealized revaluation surpluses, less accumulated unrealized deficits, and (4) any reserve prohibited from distribution by law or the company's memorandum or articles). In simple graphic terms, the dividend can be paid only from the unshaded area of Figure 8.1.

One may well ask how, apart from its approach, this restriction differs in effect from that set out in section 263. The answer is that a private company is permitted under that section, for purposes of determining legitimate distributions, to ignore any *unrealized* losses, whether of a capital or revenue nature, since the section makes no reference thereto. Provisions, as we have seen, are regarded as realized losses in this context. Section 264, on the other hand, makes it clear that unrealized losses must be brought into the reckoning.

In the case of depreciable assets, revaluation deficits would normally be dealt with by adjusting depreciation provisions in accordance with SSAP 12, thus increasing

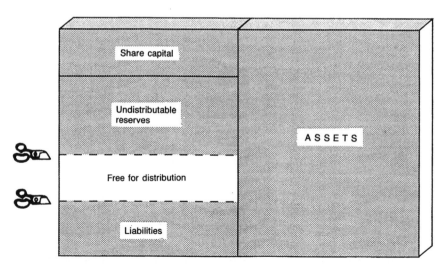

Figure 8.1 Distributable reserves

the sums to be treated as *realized* losses. The significant difference between the provisions applicable to private and public companies respectively therefore relates to unrealized losses on *non*-depreciable assets, such as freehold land. Private companies may ignore such losses, but public companies must reduce their distributable profits by them.

These somewhat complex rules are of particular concern to auditors, since section 271 imposes upon them a specific duty should a company make a distribution based upon a set of accounts on which the auditors have issued a qualified opinion. In such circumstances the auditors' duty is to state in writing whether, in their opinion, the subject matter of the qualification in their report is material for the purpose of determining whether the distribution is in contravention of the restrictions explained above. If such an unlawful distribution is made, section 277 requires any member who had reasonable grounds for believing it to be so (e.g. as a result of the statement by auditors) to repay it to the company.

Interim accounts (on which auditors are not required to report) may be used if necessary to form a proper judgement on the validity of a proposed distribution in circumstances where such distribution would not be permissible by reference solely to the last annual accounts, but in the case of a public company a strict 'true and fair' requirement is nevertheless imposed upon their preparation, which must also conform with all the usual disclosure rules applicable to published accounts (section 272). Section 273 requires the auditors of a public company, making a distribution based upon its initial accounts, to report whether in their opinion the accounts have been properly prepared.

The duty imposed in relation to qualified audit reports is more onerous and problematic than might at first seem to be the case. For example, prior to the *Companies Act 1985*, two of the leading cases on this subject – *Lee* v. *Neuchatel Asphalte Co. Ltd* (1889) and *Stapley* v. *Read Bros Ltd* (1924) – concerned depreciation not charged, and goodwill written up. Such circumstances would today almost certainly result in qualified audit opinions – especially when the particular aberration was deliberately contrived to facilitate the payment of a dividend.

However, auditing standards require auditors to quantify the monetary effect of their qualifications only in those circumstances when to do so would be reasonable and practicable. A qualified report following an SSAP 12 (depreciation) departure, for example, would not normally include the auditor's assessment of the actual amount by which profits had been overstated as consequence of, say, failing to depreciate freehold buildings in current use.

Under section 271 the auditors of a company proposing to pay a dividend and whose latest set of accounts were qualified must consider whether the measure of their reservations is material in relation to the dividend restrictions.

There are clearly many further examples of situations in which such an assessment by the auditor would seem arbitrary, even speculative. The law is, in effect, resorting to the audit function as the ultimate safeguard with respect to the dividend restrictions, and only time will tell whether this is a role which auditors can effectively fulfil.

Examples of the calculation of distributable profits

Table 8.1, which sets out extracts from the balance sheets of four companies, gives examples of the calculation of distributable profits as outlined above.

8.3.13 Qualified audit reports and distributions

As already stated, section 271 requires the auditors, if they have qualified their opinion on the financial statements, to state in writing whether the subject matter of their qualification is material in determining the legality of the proposed distribution. Consequently, where auditors qualify their report on the financial statements of a company that is proposing to pay a dividend, they will need to make an additional statement to the members of the company. Set out below are some of the matters to be considered when determining the content of this additional statement.

Where the audit report qualification arises from a disagreement

Where an audit report qualification arises from a disagreement between auditors and directors as to the amount at which an item should appear in the financial statements, it will generally be fairly easy to decide whether the qualification is material in determining the legality of the proposed distribution.

Table 8.1 Extracts from the balance sheets of four companies—calculation of distributable reserves

	Company (1) £	£	Company (2) £	£	Company (3) £	£	Company (4) £	£
A Share capital		1,000		1,000		1,000		1,000
B Unrealized profits	150		150		150		–	
C Unrealized losses	–		(200)		(200)		(200)	
		150		(50)		(50)		(200)
D Realized profits	300		300		300		300	
E Realized losses	–		–		(120)		(120)	
		300		300		180		180
F Share capital and reserves		£1,450		£1,250		£1,130		£980
Distributable profit: if a private company (D & E)		£300		£300		£180		£180
if a public company (lower of D – E and (D + B) – (C + E))		£300		£250		£130		Nil

The following is an extract from an audit report qualified on the grounds of disagreement. It is from the APB's Statement of Auditing Standards 600 – 'Auditors' reports on financial statements' issued in May 1993:

> Included in the debtors shown on the balance sheet is an amount of £Y due from a company which has ceased trading. XYZ plc has no security for this debt. In our opinion the company is unlikely to receive any payment and full provision of £Y should have been made, reducing profit before tax and net assets by that amount.
>
> Except for the absence of this provision, in our opinion the financial statements give a true and fair view of the state of the company's affairs as at 31 December 19... and of its profit [loss] for the year then ended and have been properly prepared in accordance with the Companies Act 1985.

In these circumstances, the proposed distribution would be legal if, by deducting from distributable reserves the amount of the required provision against the debt, the net figure is adequate for the purposes of the distribution.

Where the audit report qualification results from a scope limitation

Where an audit report qualification arises from an uncertainty as to the amount at which an item appears in the financial statements, it will be possible to decide whether the qualification is material in determining the legality of the proposed distribution only if the auditors can place an upper limit on the liabilities affected, and a lower limit on the assets affected. The following extract illustrates this point.

> However, the evidence available to us was limited because a physical stocktaking was not carried out on 30 September 19XX. There were no practicable alternative procedures which we could carry out to confirm the value determined by the directors of £XXX at which stocks are stated in the balance sheet.
>
> In forming our opinion we also evaluated the overall adequacy of the presentation of information in the financial statements.
>
> *Qualified opinion arising from limitation in audit scope*
>
> Except for any adjustments that might have been found to be necessary had a physical stocktaking been carried out, in our opinion the financial statements give a true and fair view of the state of the company's affairs as at 30 September 19XX and of its profit for the year then ended and have been properly prepared in accordance with the Companies Act 1985.
>
> In respect alone of the limitations on our work relating to stocks, we have not obtained all the information and explanations that we considered necessary for the purpose of our audit.

In these circumstances, the proposed distribution would be legal if, by deducting from distributable reserves the amount of stock affected (for example, by valuing that stock either at nil or at a reduced amount that depends on the nature of the qualification), the net figure is adequate for the purposes of the distribution.

If they cannot quantify the financial effect of an uncertainty, auditors should regard the effect as infinite in respect of a possible understatement of liabilities. In respect of a possible overstatement of assets, auditors will obviously regard the effect as being limited to the amount at which the asset is stated.

Where the audit report qualification results in a disclaimer of opinion

In circumstances where auditors disclaim an opinion on the financial statements as a whole, they will not be in a position to confirm the amount at which the company's net assets are stated. Accordingly, they will not be able to state that the qualification is 'not material' in determining the legality of the proposed distribution.

The wording of the additional statement

Where the audit qualification is not material (or is material but favourable) in determining the legality of the proposed distribution, the following statement, added as the final paragraph to the audit report, is suggested:

> In our opinion the qualification is not material for the purpose of determining, by reference to these financial statements, whether the final dividend for the year ended 31 March 19XX proposed by the company is permitted under the *Companies Act 1985*.

Where the audit qualification is material in determining the legality of the proposed distribution, the word 'not' before the word 'material' should be deleted. In addition, the auditors should, if practicable, add a brief explanation of the effect of the qualification on the company's ability to make the distribution.

8.3.14 Surpluses on revaluation of fixed assets and the disclosure of non-distributable reserves

All developments in the realm of accounting and law are of direct concern to auditors, and this is especially true in respect of the legislation on divisible profits. The requirement of the *Companies Act* to separate realized profits from unrealized in order to determine the amount of profits that are legally distributable has reopened the debate on the appropriate accounting treatment of surpluses that arise on the revaluation of fixed assets. It has also reinforced the need to keep realized reserves separate from unrealized reserves, and to distinguish them in that way.

The treatment of surpluses on the revaluation of fixed assets

Where a depreciable asset, such as a building, is revalued, the surplus comprises two elements. The first is the depreciation that the company provided on the building in the past years (assuming it has done so, in accordance with SSAP 12). The second is the difference between the revaluation amount and the original cost (or the previous valuation of the building). When reserves were divided between capital and revenue (as opposed to realized and unrealized) one method of accounting was to take the total of these two elements to capital reserve, because the revalued building was regarded as being stated at 'new cost' (which was its current purchase value). The other method was to take the first element to revenue reserves and the second to capital reserves.

In the absence of an accounting standard on the treatment of revaluation surpluses, it is considered that the most appropriate accounting treatment is to follow the latter alternative and split the revaluation surplus into the above two elements, and to deal with those elements by:

► Taking directly to *realized* reserves (in the balance sheet) the element that relates to the depreciation the company has previously provided on the asset.

► Taking directly to *unrealized* reserves (in accordance with FRS 3 para. 56) the other element, which is the difference between the new valuation and the original cost (or the previous valuation).

The treatment of depreciation on revalued fixed assets

A revalued fixed asset will be subject to an annual depreciation charge based on the new and, usually, higher figure. This new annual charge (the whole of which must be debited to profit and loss account) can notionally be divided between the part that relates to original cost, and the part that relates to the uplift on revaluation. The latter is, in effect, a reversal over a long period of time of the surplus taken to unrealized reserves. Accordingly, as we have seen, the *Companies Act 1985* (sections 263 and 275) allows a company which has revalued a depreciable fixed asset to treat as a realized profit the depreciation charged on the 'uplift'. Each year, therefore, the unrealized reserves will be reduced by, and the realized reserves will be increased by, an amount equivalent to the additional depreciation charge which results from the revaluation.

If the two reserves are shown separately in the balance sheet, it will be necessary to show this transfer in the notes to the accounts.

The treatment of surpluses on the disposal of revalued fixed assets

Prior to the publication of FRS 3 in October 1992, in the year in which a company sells a revalued fixed asset, the surplus it realizes on the sale could have been calculated in one of the following two ways:

► The difference between the sale proceeds and the net book value at the date of the sale.

► The difference between the sale proceeds and the net book value at the date of the sale, *together with the previously unrealized surplus on revaluation*. This unrealized surplus will be the original surplus on revaluation, less the amount subsequently transferred to realized reserves when the asset is depreciated.

Under para. 21 of FRS 3, the first method above is the prescribed treatment, whether the asset is carried at historical cost or at a valuation, in which case the amount that relates to the realization of a prior year revaluation surplus will need to be transferred from unrealized reserves to realized reserves.

Disclosure of non-distributable reserves in the financial statements of companies

Although the *Companies Act* does not require companies to disclose separately realized and unrealized reserves, it is preferable to disclose in a note the amount of the reserves that is not legally distributable. This is because the amount of the total dividend could be an important factor to some users of the financial statements. The wording of the note should not suggest, however, that the balance is distributable, since there may well be other restrictions, such as cash limitations. A suggested wording is as follows:

> The amount of the above reserves that may not be legally distributed under section ... of the *Companies Act* 1985 is £X (19XX–£Y).

The revised formats under the *Companies Act 1989* allow for the distinction between distributable and non-distributable reserves to be disclosed.

8.3.15   Implementation of the EC Fourth Directive

The EC Fourth Directive was introduced into the UK statute book in the form of the *Companies Act 1981*, and the subsections that follow explain the effect of its provisions (as included in the *Companies Act 1985* and subsequently amended by the *Companies Act 1989*) with special reference to auditors.

Auditors' report

Small and medium-sized companies

Small and medium-sized companies (as defined by the Act) are allowed to submit abbreviated accounts to the Registrar. Table 8.2 sets out the format for an abbreviated balance sheet. In this connection the auditors must:

1. provide a report to the directors stating whether in their opinion the accounts qualify for the filing exemption;
2. provide a special report to accompany the accounts lodged with the Registrar stating that in their opinion the exemption requirements are satisfied, and reproducing the full text of the report sent to the members: if the auditors do not confirm that the exemption requirements are satisfied, full statements must be filed.

In practice these two requirements are usually combined in one 'special' report.

A company qualifies as a small company if it satisfies (for both the financial year in question and the preceding year) any two of the following three conditions:

1. The amount of its turnover does not exceed £2,800,000.
2. The balance sheet total (basically, fixed assets plus investments plus current assets) does not exceed £1,400,000.
3. The average number of employees employed by the company does not exceed fifty.

A medium-sized company, if it fails to satisfy the criteria for a small company, must satisfy for both the year in question and the preceding year, any two of the following three conditions:

1. The amount of its turnover does not exceed £11,200,000.
2. The balance sheet total does not exceed £5,600,000.
3. The average number of employees employed by the company in the financial year did not exceed 250.

These thresholds are subject to amendment by statutory instrument from time to time.

A company is not eligible to submit abbreviated accounts if it is, or was during the financial year:

1. A public company.
2. A banking or insurance company.
3. An authorized person under the *Financial Services Act 1986*.
4. A member of an ineligible group.

Publication of accounts

All companies except unlimited companies are required to provide full accounts for their members, and small or medium-sized companies may file abbreviated accounts with the Registrar.

Section 240 is designed to prevent anyone being misled by accounts published in any other way. Its provisions are:

1. Any accounts, full or abbreviated, which are published must be accompanied by the 'relevant' auditors' report. This means that published full accounts must be accompanied by the full auditors' report and that published abbreviated accounts must be accompanied by the special auditors' report required by the Act.
2. If a company required to produce group accounts publishes its own accounts it must also publish the group accounts, which may be in abbreviated form if the company is small or medium-sized.
3. Any company publishing an abridged form of its accounts must include a statement that they are not full accounts, indicating also whether full accounts have been delivered to the Registrar and whether the auditors' report on those accounts was qualified. The auditors' report itself must *not* be published with abridged accounts.

Although it is obviously the directors' responsibility to comply with these requirements, auditors should be alert to ensure that their clients do not infringe them.

Application of auditors' report to directors' report (section 235(3))

It has always been good auditing practice for the auditor to confirm that the directors' report is consistent with the accounts on which the auditor is reporting. This is now a statutory requirement – the auditors must qualify their report if they are of the opinion

Table 8.2 Abbreviated balance sheet – small company

	£	£
Fixed assets		
Intangible assets		x
Tangible assets		x
Investments		x
Current assets		
Stocks	x	
Debtors	x	
Investments	x	
Cash	x	
	x	
Creditors due within one year	x	
Net current assets		x
Total assets less current liabilities		x
Creditors (due after more than 1 year)		(x)
Provisions for liabilities and charges		(x)
Net assets		x
Capital and reserves		
Share capital		x
Reserves		x
Profit and loss account		x
		x

that the information given in the directors' report is not consistent with the company's accounts.

Dormant companies (section 250)

Section 250 exempts dormant companies from the obligation to appoint auditors. A company qualifies as dormant for this purpose if it is a 'small' company as defined in sections 246–7, is not a holding company and has had no 'significant accounting transactions' since the end of the previous financial year.

The procedure is for the company to pass a special resolution that auditors are not to be appointed. The company is still required to lodge accounts with the Registrar, but instead of an auditors' report, a statement from the directors that the company was dormant must be filed.

Redemption of redeemable shares – private companies (section 173)

If a private company redeems shares out of capital, as they are allowed to (subject to certain safeguards), the directors must make a statutory declaration of the solvency of the company, accompanied by a report addressed to the directors by the auditors stating that:

1. They have enquired into the company's state of affairs.
2. The amount to be paid out of capital has been properly determined.
3. The opinion expressed by the directors is reasonable.

The statutory declaration and the auditors' report on it must be open for inspection by the members at the meeting to pass the special resolution approving the payment. Under this onerous requirement the auditors are virtually being asked to ensure that the company is solvent.

Private company purchasing its own shares

An auditors' report identical with that described above is required to accompany the directors' declaration when a private company purchases its own shares out of capital.

Private company providing financial assistance for the purchase of its own shares

Before such assistance can legally be provided the directors must file a statutory declaration of solvency which must again be accompanied by auditors' report to the directors similar to that indicated above.

Profits available for distribution – treatment of capitalized development costs (section 269)

The Act provides that any capitalized development cost is to be treated as a realized loss for the purpose of determining distributable profits under the Act, unless the directors are of the opinion that there are special circumstances making it reasonable not to treat that development cost as a realized loss. If the directors are of this opinion they must state so in the note to the accounts.

The provision applies also for the purpose of determining the distributable profit of an investment company.

Distributions in kind (section 276)

The Act provides that where a company makes a distribution in kind and the value of the asset distributed includes an unrealized profit, that profit is to be treated as a realized profit for the purpose of determining the legality of the distribution.

Other matters of importance to auditors

Formats (Sch. 4)

The Act sets out *two* alternative formats for the balance sheet, and *four* alternative formats for the profit and loss account. The directors may select which formats to use, but if they are subsequently changed, then the notes to the financial statements must disclose this fact, with the directors' reasons for the change. The auditor must ensure that the formats are followed, and that prescribed information disclosing and explaining a change is given.

Accounting principles (Sch. 4 (10)–(14))

The Act includes as *accounting principles* the four fundamental accounting concepts explained in SSAP 2 'Disclosure of accounting policies'. It adds a fifth principle (the aggregation principle) which states that the amount of each individual asset or liability within the aggregate amount shall be determined separately: the Act does not permit assets or liabilities to be 'set off' against each other.

The following summarizes and explains the five familiar accounting principles (concepts) as included in the Act.

1. *Going concern.* The company shall be presumed to be a going concern. This means that at the date on which the audit report to the members is signed it is believed that the company will continue to be financially viable for the foreseeable future. Such belief therefore justifies, for example, the carry forward of the value of assets not yet written off.

2. *Consistency.* The company's accounting policies shall be applied consistently from one financial period to the next. This ensures that the financial statements of successive periods may be used for the purpose of making valid comparisons. An unwarranted change of accounting policy, or a change whose effect is not adequately disclosed, will render such comparison misleading. The *Companies Act 1985* requires the consistency principle to be applied within the accounts for each accounting reference period as well as from year to year.

3. *Prudence.* Items included in financial statements shall be determined on a prudent basis. In particular:
   (a) only profits realized at the balance sheet date shall be included in the profit and loss account;
   (b) all liabilities and losses which have arisen or are likely to arise in respect of the period reported on shall be reflected in the financial statements, including those that become apparent after the balance sheet date but before the financial statements are approved.

4. *Accruals.* All income and charges which relate to the financial period in question shall be reflected in the financial statements without regard to the time of receipt or payment. Without this concept, financial statements would be prepared on a receipts and payments basis, which would be misleading since accrued income and accrued charges, due for settlement after the balance sheet date, would consequently be disregarded.

5. *Realized profits.* It should be noted that the prudence principle refers to realized profits. To explain what is meant by realized profits the Act states, 'in relation to a company's accounts realized profits are references to such profits of the company as fall to be treated as realized profits, for the purposes of those accounts, in

accordance with principles generally accepted with respect to the determination for accounting purposes of realized profits at the time when these accounts are prepared'. This means that, in general, we may assume that profits which have been determined in accordance with SSAPs and FRSs may be assumed to be realized profits for this purpose. Even attributable profits arising during the progress of a long-term contract, provided the rules of SSAP 9 are observed, may thus be regarded as realized profits.

The Act does not define the *true and fair* requirement, but it is clear from the above that SSAPs and FRSs should be taken into account by the auditor in reaching a decision on whether financial statements give a true and fair view.

The Act states that if the directors of a company depart from the five basic accounting principles they must give the particulars of the departure; the reason for it; and its effect, in a note to the accounts. Again, the auditor will have to ensure that if there is such a departure from the basic principles, he is satisfied with such a departure and that the note to the accounts is satisfactory.

Rules are given for *historical cost accounting* which largely implement many of the SSAPs and FRSs, but the *Companies Act* also takes account of current cost accounting. Intangible assets except goodwill may be valued at their *current* cost. Tangible fixed assets may be stated either at their market value on the date when they were last valued, or at their current cost. Stocks may be stated at their current cost. The effect of these provisions is to permit financial statements to be prepared in any of the following ways:

1. According to the historical cost convention.
2. According to the historical cost convention modified to take account of selective revaluation.
3. According to current cost principles.

8.3.16 Implementation of the EC Seventh Directive and miscellaneous changes – the *Companies Act 1989*

As with the implementation of earlier directives, the UK government took the opportunity in the *Companies Act 1989* to introduce statutory changes additional to those necessary to meet the EC requirements.

Under the Seventh Directive the UK was required to adopt provisions laid down governing the preparation and presentation of consolidated accounts. In consultative documents on implementation the Department of Trade and Industry announced that it intended to propose the minimum changes to allow maximum flexibility. Within this framework it was resolved to *exempt small and medium-sized companies from the obligation to prepare group accounts*. In laying down which companies must be included in group accounts, the opportunity was taken to tackle the use of non-subsidiary controlled companies for special-purpose transactions.

In addition to these matters the Act contains a number of other provisions:

1. To strengthen the range of investigation powers.
2. To reform various procedures for companies and for the Registrar of Companies.
3. To make various amendments to merger control procedures.
4. To modify the general law of insolvency in relation to settlement and clearing systems on financial markets.

In particular, the government introduced important provisions in the following areas:

1. Deregulation of private companies under an elective regime, which permits private companies to elect not to comply with certain provisions of the *Companies Act* governing their internal affairs.
2. Changes to the *ultra vires* law to enable companies to adopt more general objects clauses, and to render insignificant to third parties the fact that a company is contracting beyond its capacity. The directors of a company will still remain responsible to the shareholders for any breach of the objects or of their powers.
3. Implementation of certain of the recommendations of the Dearing Committee to reform the procedure for setting and applying accounting standards.

The deregulation of private companies

Whilst the changes are chiefly of benefit to proprietary or owner-managed companies, certain of the reforms are also of benefit to private company subsidiaries of public limited companies. The major changes introduced by the 1989 Act were:

1. Exemption of small and medium-sized groups from the obligation to prepare group accounts.
2. Provision for private companies to pass written resolutions, thereby avoiding the need for general meetings of members.
3. Provision for private companies to pass an elective resolution under which they may:
    (a) authorize the directors to allot shares without limit of time;
    (b) dispense with the need to lay accounts before a general meeting;
    (c) dispense with holding an annual general meeting;
    (d) dispense with the annual appointment of auditors; and
    (e) reduce the majority required to hold meetings at short notice.

Written resolutions

The Act provides for private companies to pass written resolutions covering all but two matters. These resolutions have an identical effect to those passed in the conventional way at a general meeting, and are subject to the usual rules regarding the necessary majority. The provisions are as follows:

1. Anything which may be done by a private company by resolution in general meeting or class meeting may be done, without a meeting and without any previous notice being required, by resolution in writing signed by or on behalf of all the members entitled to vote at that date.

2. The signatures must be on a document, or series of documents, each of which accurately states the time of the resolution. These shall be entered in the minutes.

3. The provisions may be applied to matters which must be passed by special, extraordinary, and elective resolution.

4. Written resolutions may not be applied to remove a director or auditor from office before expiry of the period of office.

5. Special rules apply to the use of a written resolution in the following cases:

    (a) disapplication of pre-emption rights;

    (b) financial assistance for the purchase of a company's own shares, or those of the holding company;

    (c) purchase of own shares (off-market);

    (d) approval for payment out of capital;

    (e) approval of director's service contract;

    (f) funding of director's expenditure in performing his duties.

6. Copies of written resolutions must be sent to the auditors, who may within seven days on matters concerning them as auditors state that in their opinion the resolution should be considered by a class or general meeting.

7. A written resolution will not have effect unless the auditors notify the company that the matter does not concern them as auditors, or does so concern them, but need not be considered by a meeting, or the period for giving notice expires.

8. Written resolutions have effect notwithstanding any provision of the company's memorandum or articles.

Election to dispense with the laying of accounts at a general meeting

As we have seen, a private company may elect to dispense with the laying of accounts at a general meeting. Such election must be made unanimously by the members, who may call for the accounts to be laid, and must be informed of this right when the accounts are sent to them.

Where the members of a company elect to dispense with the laying of accounts at a general meeting, copies of the accounts must be sent to them not less than twenty-eight days before the end of the period allowed for laying and delivering.

Within the next twenty-eight days any member may requisition a general meeting for the purpose by giving notice in writing at the registered office. If the directors do not call a meeting within twenty-one days, the member may do so himself; the meeting is to be held within three months and the costs borne out of directors' remuneration.

Where a company elects to dispense with the laying of accounts before the company in general meeting, it will be necessary to hold an annual general meeting to appoint auditors. The meeting must be held in the period twenty-eight days before the accounts are sent to members. However, the company may deal with the matter by written resolution, and in practice most companies which dispense with the AGM will elect to dispense with the annual appointment of auditors as well.

Election to dispense with annual appointment of auditors

A private company may elect to dispense with the obligation to appoint auditors annually. When such an election is in force the auditors will be reappointed automatically, except where a resolution is passed to end the appointment, and where an unlimited company passes a resolution to exempt the company from having an auditor.

Elective resolutions

Each of the elections for a private company must be authorized by elective resolution. These are:

1. Duration of authority to allot shares.
2. Dispensation from laying accounts before a general meeting.
3. Dispensation from holding AGM.
4. Majority required to authorize short notice of meeting.
5. Dispensation from appointment of auditors annually.

An elective resolution will not be effective without:

1. Twenty-one days' notice, stating terms, given in writing.
2. Agreement in person or by proxy of all persons entitled to attend and vote.

An elective resolution may be revoked by ordinary resolution, becomes ineffective upon re-registration as a public company, and has effect whatever the provisions contained in the articles of association.

The Secretary of State will be empowered to add to the matters on which private companies may pass an elective resolution to become exempt for certain compliance provisions, provided they relate primarily to internal administration and procedures.

Remedies for defective accounts

The Act introduces provisions under which directors may revise accounts which it appears to them did not comply with the requirements of the 1985 Act, for example an uncorrected mistake or error.

Where the accounts have already been laid and filed the revisions must be confined to corrections and consequential alterations. Subsequent regulations have been issued by statutory instrument concerning the application of this provision, covering circulation to members, audit, approval and filing.

The Secretary of State may give notice to a company where there is, or may be, a question as to whether the accounts comply with the requirements of the Act. The notice must indicate the respects in which it appears that such a question arises. The directors must give an explanation or prepare revised accounts within one month.

Where the Secretary of State is not satisfied, he may apply to the courts for a declaration that the accounts do not comply with the Act, and for an order requiring the preparation of revised accounts. The court may make appropriate orders concerning audit, revision of directors' report and summary statements and notification to interested parties. The costs of this procedure may fall upon the directors who approved the defective accounts, although it is a defence for an individual director to show that he took all reasonable steps to prevent their being approved.

The Secretary of State may authorize other persons to make applications to the courts under this section. The persons concerned must appear to him to have an interest in, and satisfactory procedures directed to securing, compliance with the accounting requirements of the Act. They must have proper procedures for receiving complaints about the annual accounts of companies and otherwise be a fit and proper person to be authorized.

Recognition of the Financial Reporting Council and Accounting Standards Board

The Act empowered the Secretary of State to make grants to or for the purposes of bodies concerned with issuing accounting standards, overseeing and directing the issuing of such standards and investigating departures from such standards or from the accounting requirements of the Act, and taking steps to secure compliance with them.

The Act made provision for delegation of certain functions to the Financial Reporting Council.

Group accounts

The Act requires parent companies to prepare group accounts. The current provisions differ from the previous arrangements in the following respects:

1. Group accounts must be consolidated accounts: it is no longer possible for the directors of a company to prepare accounts in some other form. However, the 1989 Act extended the exemptions from the obligation to prepare group accounts, and revised the provisions under which a subsidiary may be excluded from the consolidation.

2. Group accounts must include all subsidiary undertakings whether companies, partnerships, or unincorporated associations. Previously, the law required only subsidiary companies to be included in group accounts.

3. The obligation to prepare group accounts falls on parent companies rather than holding companies.

It is worth noting that the Act removed the prohibition on incorporated bodies acting as company auditors. Thus firms of accountants are able to take advantage of the options of corporate status and limited liability and a small number of firms have already done so. However, only those firms which incorporate will be obliged to lay and file group accounts. These must include all subsidiary undertakings, whether companies or partnerships. Those firms which do not incorporate may qualify as parent undertakings but will not be required to prepare group accounts.

8.3.17 Small companies – relaxation of mandatory audit

The Chancellor of the Exchequer's Budget Speech on 30 November 1993 first heralded the relaxation of the audit requirement for certain small companies. Much speculation on the subject followed and draft regulations were promulgated by the Department of Trade and Industry. The legislation was provided in the *Companies Act 1985 (Audit Exemption) Regulations 1994* (SI 1994/1935) which came into force on 11 August 1994.

The regulations inserted new section 249A–249E to the *Companies Act 1985* and substituted section 388A. They also contained transitional provisions which, when the transition was spent, were amended by the *Companies Act 1985 (Audit Exemption) (Amendment) Regulations 1994* (SI 1994/2879) as from 12 November 1994.

Features of the legislation

Readers are advised to study the legislation in detail rather than rely on synopses. The key features of the legislation can, however, be summarized as follows:

1. Eligibility for exemption

A company is *totally exempt* from an audit requirement in respect of a financial year if:

- ▶ it qualifies as a small company under section 246 of the *Companies Act 1985*;
- ▶ its turnover does not exceed £90,000; and
- ▶ its balance sheet total does not exceed £1.4 million.

A company is exempt from the audit requirement, but must have an 'accountant's report' in respect of a financial year, if:

- ▶ it qualifies as a small company under section 246 of the *Companies Act 1985*;
- ▶ its turnover exceeds £90,000 but does not exceed £350,000 (£250,000 gross income if it is a charity); and
- ▶ its balance sheet total does not exceed £1.4 million.

A company *is not eligible for exemption* if, at any time during the financial year, it was:

▶ a plc;
▶ a banking or insurance company;
▶ enrolled with the Insurance Brokers Registration Council;
▶ authorized under the *Financial Services Act 1986*;
▶ an entity governed by trade union and labour relations legislation; or
▶ a parent or subsidiary undertaking (unless dormant).

2. Members' right to require audit

Members of a company holding not less than 10 per cent in nominal value of its issued share capital (or any class of it) can insist on having an audit of its accounts by depositing written notice to that effect at its registered office no later than one month before its year end. (If the company does not have a share capital, ten per cent by number of its members may deposit such notice.)

3. Directors' statement

A company is not entitled to audit exemption unless its balance sheet contains a statement by its directors, to be shown above the signature(s), that:

(a) for the year in question the company was entitled to such exemption;
(b) no valid notice requiring an audit has been deposited by members in relation to its accounts; and
(c) the directors acknowledge their responsibilities for
   (i) ensuring that proper accounting records are kept as required by section 221 of the *Companies Act 1985*; and
   (ii) preparing accounts that give a true and fair view and otherwise comply with the accounting requirements of the *Companies Act* so far as applicable to the company.

4. Eligibility of reporting accountant

The accountant's report required by the companies referred to in (1) above must be prepared by a 'reporting accountant'. To be eligible to act as reporting accountant a person must be a member of one of the three Institutes of Chartered Accountants, the Chartered Association of Certified Accountants or the Association of Authorised Public Accountants and either entitled to engage in public practice, or eligible for appointment as company auditor.

5. Independence

The statutory provisions requiring the independence of auditors contained in section 27 of the *Companies Act 1989* apply fully to reporting accountants.

6. Report contents

The accountant's report must state whether in the opinion of the reporting accountant:

▶ the company's accounts for the financial year are in agreement with the records it keeps under section 221 of the *Companies Act 1985*;

▶ *having regard only to, and on the basis of, the information in those records* the accounts have been drawn up in a manner consistent with the accounting provisions specified in section 249C(6) of the Act, so far as applicable to the company (including Sch. 4 formats, Sch. 5 disclosures on related undertakings and Sch. 6 disclosures on directors' emoluments, benefits and transactions); and

▶ *having regard only to, and on the basis of, the information in those records* the company satisfied the requirements for exemption for the whole of the financial year in question.

7. Signature

The report shall state the name of the reporting accountant and shall be signed by him or, in the case of the reporting accountant being a partnership or body corporate, by a person authorized to sign on its behalf.

8. Companies Act 1985 audit report references

Where the directors have taken advantage of the exemption:

▶ references in the *Companies Act 1985* to the right of shareholders and debenture holders to receive or demand copies of accounts and reports shall apply with the omission of references to the auditors' report; and

▶ references to qualification(s) in the auditors' report (for the purpose of determining the lawfulness of distributions under section 271) shall not apply.

9. Right to information and explanations

References in the *Companies Act 1985* to the auditor's right to receive all information and explanations he requires shall apply equally to information and explanations required by the reporting accountant. Company officers will commit an offence if they knowingly or recklessly mislead the reporting accountant. There are, however, no provisions for giving the reporting accountant the other statutory rights and duties of auditors (receiving notices, attending meetings, rights on removal, duties on resignation, etc.).

10. Cessation of exemption

If a company that is exempt from the audit requirement subsequently, for any reason, ceases to be exempt, it will be subject to the statutory provisions governing appointment by the directors of the 'first' auditors of a company.

Practical implications of audit exemption

1. Directors' responsibilities

Directors' responsibilities for producing and issuing true and fair accounts are unaffected by audit exemption. However, the fact that they will not enjoy the comfort of an audit to support those accounts has the effect of increasing their own risks and they should consider the advantages of purchasing insurance cover with this in mind.

2. Position of banks

Banks and other lenders may well impose an audit requirement as a condition of lending to companies that would otherwise be eligible for exemption.

3. Amending the articles

It may be necessary to amend articles of association of eligible companies if these specify an audit requirement.

4. Resignation

When a company first becomes eligible there is no obligation for its auditors to resign. This is a matter for them and the client company's directors to determine.

5. Misleading accounts

Accountants remain subject to the abiding professional duty that they should never allow their names to be associated with accounts that they have reason to suspect may be misleading. This effectively imposes, at the very least, the need for an analytical exercise designed to test the plausibility of the accounts before giving an accountant's report.

It is important that all information supplied by the directors should be reduced to writing. While formal 'letters of representation' provide *audit* evidence, and are therefore not required by reporting accountants, it is sound practice always to have a written record of the information on which conclusions are based. Correspondence with client company directors encompassing any issues represented orally, is usually the most convenient medium for recording such information.

If there is any information provided by the directors (stocks and work-in-progress valuations are obvious examples) that immediately strikes the accountant as implausible, or if the view presented is generally irreconcilable with past performance or current expectations, accountants should not allow their names, in any capacity, to add credibility to such potentially misleading accounts.

6. Filing of accountant's report

The accountant's report, when required, must be included with the full statutory accounts issued to shareholders. It will also be filed at Companies House together with either the full accounts or the abbreviated accounts. The legislation requires no work to be carried out on the abbreviated accounts, and the accountant's report, when filed with abbreviated accounts, will refer to the full accounts to which it relates.

7. No authentication needed

The requirement that the accountant's report must report on whether the accounts have been drawn up in a manner consistent with the Act's accounting provisions does not of itself impose any duty to authenticate the figures. In practice, UK accountants will use their standard company accounting software for compiling the unaudited accounts and the foregoing reporting requirement should therefore create no special difficulties – *provided that up-to-date disclosure checklists are also being used.*

8. Turnover

The reporting accountant has no obligation to verify the accuracy of the turnover and balance sheet totals on which the directors have based the company's entitlement to exemption. This is made clear by the words in section 249C(3) of the *Companies Act 1985*:

> ... having regard only to, and on the basis of, the information contained in the accounting records kept by the company under section 221, the company satisfied the requirements ...

9. Going concern

It is advisable to use a standard 'going concern' checklist where appropriate, if only to be in a position to identify circumstances when the reporting accountant's firm should be warning directors of the consequences of wrongful trading. Going concern assessment is, however, an audit procedure, and does not fall within the scope of the reporting accountant's assignment.

10. Reports for very small companies (turnover below £90,000)

All professional services, without exception, entail negligence risks. Nevertheless, by definition the 'accounting' work carries less risk than auditing. Companies with turnover below £90,000 are subject to no statutory requirements for authenticating their accounts. Any accounts issued to the directors should therefore be accompanied by a report or letter that reflects the accountant's instructions, as well as a disclaimer that makes the position completely clear.

11. Examples of work required of reporting accountant

Listed below are examples of the work required to be done by a reporting accountant.

(a) Confirmation that the permanent file contains details of the client's accounting records and procedures.

(b) Confirmation of the company's eligibility for exemption from a statutory audit (without attempting to verify or substantiate turnover or balance sheet total).

(c) Checking that the trial balance has been correctly extracted from the accounting records and that the financial statements have been correctly prepared from the trial balance, taking account of journals, debtor and creditor adjustments (unless the reporting accountant has already completed the financial statements from these records on the client's behalf).

(d) Checking a sample of postings from the client's books of prime entry (e.g. cash book) to the ledgers or spreadsheets. (This is obviously unnecessary if the reporting accountant has written up these books and prepared the accounts.)

(e) Checking that the format of the financial statements complies with the relevant *Companies Act* provisions, i.e. ensuring that the amounts extracted from the records are correctly summarized under the appropriate *Companies Act* headings and properly described. For this purpose a company accounts checklist should be completed for every assignment.

(f) Checking disclosure of related undertakings and directors' transactions, emoluments and benefits, as covered by the company accounts checklist.

12. Examples of work not required

Listed below are examples of work of an auditing nature which is therefore *not* required to be done by a reporting accountant.

(a) Third party confirmations from banks, debtors, creditors, solicitors, warehouses, repositories, agents, etc.

(b) Observation of stock-taking.

(c) Verification of stock values and net realisable value assessments.

(d) Inspection of physical assets.

(e) Counting of cash or securities.

(f) Compliance testing of systems.

(g) Substantive testing of transactions and balances.

(h) Inspection of supporting source documents other than for accounts preparation purposes.

(i) Post-balance sheet events testing.

(j) Inspection of statutory books and minutes.

(k) Assessment of appropriateness of the going concern basis of accounting.

(l) Checking of appropriateness of accounting treatments.

Where the reporting accountant has been engaged to prepare the statutory accounts on behalf of the directors (which, is of course, the usual situation), it may be necessary to examine documentation to ensure the correct accounts treatment and disclosure, e.g. documentary evidence in respect of contingent liabilities or post-balance sheet events, assessment of stock net realisable values, VAT account reconciliations where this exercise has not been carried out by the directors.

13. Example of statement by the directors

A company is not entitled to the exemption, whether total (under the *Companies Act 1985*, section 249A(1)) or exemption subject to an accountant's report (under section 249A(2)), unless the balance sheet contains a statement to the following effect.

For the year ending ... the company was entitled to exemption under subsection (1) or (2) [delete as appropriate] of section 249A of the *Companies Act 1985*.

No notice has been deposited under section 249B(2) of the Act in relation to the accounts for the financial year.

The directors acknowledge their responsibilities for:

(1) ensuring that the company keeps accounting records which comply with section 221 of the *Companies Act 1985*; and

(2) preparing accounts which give a true and fair view of the state of affairs of the company as at the end of the financial year and of its profit or loss for the financial year in accordance with the requirements of section 226 of the Act, and which otherwise comply with the requirements of the Act relating to accounts, so far as applicable to the company.

[If applicable:
The directors have taken advantage of the exemptions conferred by Pt. III of Sch. 8 to the *Companies Act 1985* and have done so on the grounds that, in their opinion, the company is entitled to those exemptions as a small company

or

In the preparation of the company's annual accounts, the directors have taken advantage of special exemptions applicable to small companies and have done so on the grounds that, in their opinion, the company is entitled to those exemptions as a small company.]

Approved by the Board on ... and signed on its behalf by ....

This statement must appear on the balance sheet immediately above the signature required by section 233 (signing of annual accounts) or, as illustrated, above any statement required by section 246(1A) (advantage of small company exemptions under Sch. 8, Pt. 1) or by para.23 of Sch. 8 (advantage taken of exemptions under Sch. 8, Pt. III).

Reporting Accountants' Standard

In 1994 the APB published a standard titled *Statement of Standards for Reporting Accountants: Audit Exemption Reports*. This includes prescribed procedures and explanatory material governing most of the matters dealt with above as well as:

▶ engagement letters

▶ planning the work,

▶ working papers,

▶ signing and dating reports,

▶ permissible opinions.

Review questions

*1.   Recent case law has placed emphasis on the concept of insider dealing in shares. This is where an individual deals in shares having obtained information which is not generally available. Identify the implications of this for an auditor drafting an audit report on a group of companies, one of whom is in trouble with potential 'going concern' implications.

*2.   It would seem to be possible for the directors of a company to dismiss an auditor who is likely to form an opinion on the financial statements which is not to their liking. This is possible where the qualification could cause 'problems' for the directors. Given a situation in which the directors and shareholders are different, how do the provisions of the *Companies Acts* protect the auditor?

3   The finance director of a client company has prepared a full set of statutory accounts complete with all relevant notes. Due to the impending holiday of the managing director, the accounts have been sent to print and proofs have been made available and approved by the board of directors.

You are nearing completion of the audit and have found that there are significant errors within the accounts as prepared. There is also a possibility of a qualification being necessary. The finance director, with the backing of the managing director, has refused to amend the accounts. What course of action is open to the auditor and how may the *Companies Acts* assist?

4.   A company does not wish to publish a full set of accounts due to low turnover and low balance sheet total. They have told you, as auditor, that they are taking advantage of

Schedule 8 of the *Companies Act 1985*. Write a formal letter to the company outlining the effects of their decision.

Exercises

1. Tick & Bash are the auditors of Suspect Limited. During the audit of the financial statements for the year ended 30 June matters have come to light which have caused Tick to conclude that the auditors' report requires qualification. This has been discussed and the directors have indicated that unless the qualification is removed they will have no alternative but to remove Tick & Bash as auditors. Bash is not happy over the state of affairs and has called Tick in to discuss the reasons behind his decision.

    The main reason for the qualification is under the 'going concern' principle. Many of Suspect Limited's key customers have left following the opening of a rival firm. The cash flow has diminished to virtually nil.

    Bash has had an idea. He has suggested that they will remove the qualification only if Suspect Limited will pay the audit fee immediately instead of waiting the normal three months.

    Discuss the matters arising from the above scenario.

2. Longloan plc, a carpet distributor, is a large client of your firm. It is well known that the managing director likes to ensure that his fellow directors are well looked after by the company and in this respect it has been suggested in the past that loans be made to such directors for a variety of purposes at a low rate of interest.

    A review of the audit file has revealed that not only has this practice started, but various directors have apparently recarpeted their houses and not been invoiced. Your audit senior has seen 'evidence' but after discussion with the directors concerned has been told that the events have not happened.

    What further action should you take given the statutory duty of the auditor and what effect does this have on the audit report?

Framework for the regulation of auditors – the Eighth Directive and the *Companies Act 1989*

THIS CHAPTER DEALS WITH:

▷ legislation governing the regulation of auditors;

▷ independence of auditors in practice;

▷ regulations imposed by recognized supervisory and qualifying bodies;

▷ activities of the Audit Registration Committee and Joint Monitoring Unit;

▷ quality control procedures.

9.1 | Self-regulation

Until very recently the continuation of self-regulation in the accountancy profession appeared virtually unassailable. There have, of course, been rumblings, even threats, from government sources about the profession's need to 'get its house in order', and similar, but equally glib, expressions of dissatisfaction over the seeming disparity, in the public perception, between the profession's performance and the expectations laid upon it.

These murmurings can be traced back to the late 1960s when Department of Trade inspectors' reports first began to raise serious criticisms of the performance of company auditors. This became an unrelenting stream of *causes célèbres* variously involving corporate fraud, mismanagement, deception and other subtle forms of daylight robbery, incurring losses to investors, creditors and, often, the Exchequer, all on a fairly grand scale.

While UK auditing practice has been a major influence in raising professional standards all over the world, the public perception as expressed by the courts, Department of Trade and Industry inspectors and the media has often linked corporate scandal and collapse with audit failure. The government, therefore, seized the opportunity presented by the EC Eighth Directive to enforce a completely new regulatory regime on the profession, and its novel features, such as formal practice inspections, have created understandable anxiety amongst practitioners.

Under the Eighth Directive, member states of the European Union must adopt minimum requirements regarding the educational qualifications of persons wishing to train as auditors, and the form, length and content of their theoretical training. The provisions did not introduce any great changes in the qualification process, but resulted in government involvement in an area previously regarded as best left to the professional bodies. The *Companies Act 1989 (CA 1989)* contains arrangements for the recognition of professional qualifications.

Secondly, the Directive puts an obligation on member states to ensure that statutory audits are carried out with professional integrity and that there are appropriate safeguards in national law to protect the independence of auditors. The *Companies Act 1989* provides for the recognition of supervisory bodies, and for the establishment of a statutory regulatory body at some point in the future, if it proves to be necessary. (Presumably this will only come about if the government is dissatisfied with the efforts at self-regulation by the recognized supervisory bodies.) The majority of these provisions came into force under Part II of the *Companies Act 1989* with effect from 1 October 1991.

9.1.1 Eligibility to be appointed a company auditor

The *Companies Act 1989* contains provisions designed to ensure that only persons who are properly supervised and appropriately qualified are appointed as company auditors, and that audits are carried out properly, with integrity and with a proper degree of independence. This is achieved by the recognition of supervisory bodies and professional qualifications. Professional bodies may apply for both or either level of recognition.

A person is not eligible for appointment as a company auditor unless:

1. He is a member of a recognized supervisory body; and
2. He is eligible for appointment under the rules of that body.

A supervisory body is able to authorize as auditors only those who hold a recognized professional qualification. An individual or firm may be appointed a company auditor. In this context the word 'firm' applies to partnerships and bodies corporate.

Those unqualified persons previously allowed to act as company auditors under the provisions of the 1967 Act were able to apply for continued recognition but allowed to audit unquoted companies only. If application had not been made by 30 September 1992, such persons lost their entitlement to audit.

9.1.2 Provisions to secure the independence of auditors

The *Companies Act 1989* contains provisions designed to ensure that auditors have a proper degree of independence. An auditor may not be:

1. An officer or employee of the company, or a partner or employee of such a person, or a partnership of which such a person is a partner; or

2. A person who is ineligible for appointment of any associated undertaking by virtue of the foregoing.

An associated undertaking means a parent or subsidiary, or any other subsidiary of the parent.

9.1.3 The crucial question of independence

Questions relating to the effective (as opposed to notional) independence of the auditor came strongly to the fore during the difficult economic period of the 1970s. Any disinterested study of this matter must necessarily begin with the question of exactly what we mean by independent – and the very simplicity of the question makes it exceedingly difficult to find a completely satisfactory answer. One thing, however, is clear: the essential attribute of what we mean when we use this word is independence of mind. Those who would argue that financial independence is what matters should look further back – the danger of financial involvement lies only in the risk of clouded judgement, which is certainly a mental state.

Then there is also the question of the 'public eye' in which independence must be seen to exist. Many members of the profession might indignantly disclaim any taint of compromise (especially in situations which can only be described as 'compromising'), maintaining that they, in exercising their judgement, are totally free of any consideration other than that of servicing in a proper manner the needs of the interested parties to whom they are professionally responsible. Such a claim, in most instances, would probably be true yet it misses the point for two important reasons:

1. The claim would be impossible to prove, especially under a harsh and critical spotlight, and it is therefore preferable that the circumstances themselves should be avoided.
2. The individual is usually a poor judge of his own motivation: personal bias is dangerous precisely because, by definition, the person is oblivious of the bias itself.

Some may ask whether the issue is worth all the fuss; whether independence is really so essential. To that question there is a simple answer: the concept of audit and the concept of independence are the twin sides of the same coin. The auditor who has lost his independence has lost his *raison d'être*; he has become 'dependent', and a dependent auditor is a contradiction in terms.

Those situations which have the effect of undermining the auditor's independence are many and various. Most, however, have one distinguishing feature in common: they are situations in which there exists an implicit temptation on the part of the auditor to avoid incurring the displeasure of those in a position to remove him from office.

Impediments to the independent exercise of audit duties will persist while the widening sphere of responsibility remains unmatched by corresponding protection in the exercise of that responsibility. The remedy to this aspect of the problem lies in the realm of company law, which clearly should be amended to give the auditor protection from groundless removal by directors with controlling interests. It is difficult to see how, in the absence of any recourse or right of appeal against unwarranted dismissal, the auditor's facility for truly independent judgement can be allowed the free rein which it now, more than ever, requires.

One small measure exists in the *Companies Act 1985* which, whenever there is a change of auditor, imposes upon the auditor an obligation to make known to shareholders and creditors the circumstances of the change if, in the auditor's opinion, this in the interests of those parties. Unfortunately, it does not go so far as to permit them, at their discretion, to communicate matters of concern at all times. It is important to consider the circumstances which have the effect of undermining the auditors' independence. The most important of these may be summarized as follows:

1. *Fees are receivable for a wide range of professional work which has nothing to do with the audit function.* This may cause special problems when the client concerned is in severe financial difficulties: the auditors, in their other capacity as financial advisers, are searching for ways of keeping the company afloat (e.g. negotiating extended credit lines with banks and finance houses), yet they are aware that the heavily qualified audit report which would be appropriate in the circumstances may well render all salvage attempts useless.

    Even in ordinary circumstances the fees for conducting the audit may be considerably less than those receivable for performing all or some of the other services frequently provided by an organization's auditors. The 1989 Act, however, requires disclosure by plcs and large private companies of fees for services other than auditing. Where the 'other' work involves pure book-keeping, and possibly even the preparation of the final accounts, it is in any event very difficult to envisage the independent audit of those accounts by the person who prepared them.

2. *The fees receivable from one client (or one group of associated clients) make up an unduly heavy proportion of the firm's gross fees.* This problem is specifically dealt with in the Institute Statement: Integrity, Objectivity and Independence, which forms part of the *New Guide* referred to in Chapter 1, which recommends that, in general terms, fees from any source should not exceed 15 per cent of the gross recurring professional fees. For this purpose a group of companies or businesses under common control are to be regarded as a single source of fees. In the case of listed and other public-interest companies, the appropriate figure should be 10 per cent of the gross practice income.

3. *The auditor is a shareholder or debenture holder in a client company.* The Ethics Statement referred to above makes it clear that this particular form of entanglement is not permitted, and that a holder of shares in a company should divest himself of the holding before accepting engagement as auditor. Similar considerations apply to situations in which the auditor has loaned money to a client, and this form of involvement is also precluded. The rule on shareholdings makes a distinction in respect of non-beneficial holdings in which the auditor is acting in, say, the capacity of trustee: the holding is permitted in such instances provided the shares in question (a) do not exceed 10 per cent of the class of shares issued; and (b) do not have a value greater than 10 per cent of the trust's investments.

4. *The auditor has a personal relationship with an officer or senior official of the client company.* This is a frequent cause of potential conflict of interest. Members are advised in the Ethics Statement that they should play no part in the reporting function in respect of a client company of which they have been an officer at any time during the two years before the reporting date. Similarly, he or she should not exercise the reporting function if wife, husband, child, parent, brother, sister (in-laws included) is an officer.

The above, and other, potential causes of a loss of independence are covered in the Ethics Statement, and its emphasis throughout is that the spirit, as well as the letter, should be observed. If, for example, the member acts as personal financial adviser to a director of a company as well as to the company itself, in the event of a dispute between the company and that director, it may be necessary for him to elect the client for which he is prepared to act.

Most firms of auditors extend the application of these ethical rules to all members of the audit staff in their employment, and it is clear that this is a matter of considerable importance. Apart from the obvious prohibition on dealing in client company shares, even through nominees, some firms extend the rules further. Members of the audit staff may, for example, be prevented under the terms of their employment from joining a client company's staff for a minimum prescribed period after leaving the audit firm's employment: this avoids the conflict of interest whereby the clerk may be involved in the audit of his future employer. Furthermore, audit staff who are blood relations of client company personnel, or are known to be involved or associated with them in any other way, are never employed on the particular audit in question.

In order to enhance the independence of auditors the Act requires that disclosure should be made of fees paid to auditors in respect of non-audit work. The disclosure may be made within the audit reports for which the auditor is responsible, rather than the accounts, for which he is not. (This obligation does not apply to auditors of smaller companies.)

9.1.4 Registration and authorization of auditors

Under the *Companies Act 1989*, company audits must be undertaken by registered auditors only. These are:

1. Persons and firms who are authorized by a recognized supervisory body.
2. Individuals authorized under the *Companies Act 1967*.

Recognized supervisory bodies must authorize only persons:

1. Holding recognized professional qualifications; or
2. Holding approved overseas qualifications; or
3. Qualified for appointment as auditor of a company by virtue of membership of one of the bodies recognized immediately before 1 October 1991.

The Secretary of State is empowered to recognize overseas qualifications, and, where appropriate, to specify that additional qualifications must be obtained. In exercising this power, regard will be had to the eligibility of UK qualified auditors to practise in the country in question.

The *Companies Act 1989* provides that the regulatory supervisory bodies and their officers and employees are exempt from liability for damages for anything done or omitted in the discharge of their functions unless the act or omissions are shown to have been in bad faith.

The cost of implementing this regime has been borne by the supervisory bodies, offset by fees from those applying for registered status. None of the rules introduced by the supervisory bodies should constitute unacceptable restrictive practices.

9.1.5   Recognized supervisory bodies

The Secretary of State has issued regulations requiring the keeping of a register showing:

1. The individuals and firms eligible for appointment as company auditors.
2. The individuals holding an appropriate qualification who are responsible for company audit work on behalf of such firms.

This register shows names, addresses and the relevant supervisory body of those eligible for appointment as company auditors.

In addition to the register of auditors, each recognized supervisory body is required to keep a register showing the following details of firms eligible under its rules for appointment as company auditors:

▶ Body corporate: name and address of directors and members.

▶ Partnership: name and address of each partner.

Recognition

The body must have rules to the effect that a person is not eligible for appointment as a company auditor unless:

1. In the case of an individual, he holds an appropriate qualification.
2. In the case of a firm:
   (a) the individuals responsible for company audit work on behalf of the firm hold an appropriate qualification; and
   (b) the firm is controlled by qualified persons.

A firm is treated as controlled by qualified persons if and only if both the following hold:

1. A majority of the members of the firm are qualified persons.
2. Where the firm's affairs are managed by a board of directors, committee or other management body, a majority of the members of that body are qualified (for appointment as a company auditor).

The body must have adequate rules and practices to ensure that those eligible for appointment as company auditors are fit and proper persons, taking into account any matters relating to:

1. Employees and associates engaged in audit work.
2. Directors and controllers of corporate bodies and their related undertakings.
3. Partners and associates of the partners of a partnership.

Controllers are defined as those who alone or in association with others are able to control the exercise of 15 per cent or more of the voting rights of the body or its parent.

The body must have adequate rules and practices designed to ensure all of the following:

1. That audit work is conducted properly and with integrity.
2. That conflicts of interest are not likely to arise.
3. That individuals who do not hold an appropriate qualification and persons who are not members of the firm are prevented from exerting any influence over the way in which the audit is conducted which would affect its independence or integrity.

The body must have adequate and appropriate procedures governing the following:

1. The control and application of technical standards.
2. The maintenance of an appropriate level of technical competence.
3. Effective monitoring and enforcement of its rules.
4. Investigation of complaints against members.
5. The ability of members to meet claims arising out of their work as company auditors, which may include professional indemnity insurance.

The rules of the body relating to membership, eligibility and discipline must be fair and reasonable and include adequate provision for appeals. The body must be able and willing to promote and maintain high standards of integrity in the conduct of company audit work and to co-operate, by the sharing of information and otherwise, with the Secretary of State and any other authority, body or person having responsibility in the UK for the qualification, supervision or regulation of auditors.

Recognition of professional qualifications

A qualifying body may apply to the Secretary of State for an order recognizing its professional qualification. The basic requirements are:

1. The qualification must only be open to those with university entrance level, or a sufficient period of professional experience.
2. The qualification must only be given to those who have passed an examination testing theoretical knowledge and the ability to apply that knowledge in practice.

The standard must be equivalent to that required to obtain a degree from a university or similar establishment. Exemptions may be given to those with suitable equivalent qualifications.

3. Three years' practical training must be given, of which a substantial part is spent being trained in company audit work, or other audit work of a description approved by the Secretary of State as being similar to company audit work.

4. The training must be given by persons approved by the qualifying body, and at least two-thirds must be given by a fully qualified auditor.

9.1.6 Reporting as 'registered auditors'

Auditors must report on all annual accounts sent to members during their tenure of office. The report must state the names of the auditors, and be signed by them. They must also sign the copy sent to the Registrar of Companies. Every copy of the auditor's report which is laid before the company in general meeting, or which is otherwise circulated, published or issued, must state the names of the auditors. Failure to show the auditor's name on accounts sent to members and to sign the copy sent to the Registrar will render the company and every officer who is in default liable to a fine.

Registered auditors must use that title when signing the audit report. The *Companies Act 1989* requires a registered auditor, 'when signing any company audit report, in his own right or on behalf of a firm, [to] add after his name the words "registered auditor"'. Whilst there is no objection to continuing to use the term 'chartered' or 'certified accountant' this must be in addition to the title 'registered auditor'. Where the auditor is a body corporate or a partnership the signature is that in the name of the firm by a person authorized to sign on its behalf.

Failure to use the title 'registered auditor' is a matter for the disciplinary procedures of the supervisory bodies. (It was originally proposed that such a failure would be a criminal offence carrying a maximum penalty of six months' imprisonment.) There are severe penalties for using the title 'registered auditor' illegally. There are also severe penalties where a person furnishes information in connection with the regulation of audits which he knows to be false or misleading in a material particular, or recklessly furnishes such information. It is a defence to show that the person charged took all reasonable precautions and exercised all due diligence to avoid the commission of the offence. Parallel provisions apply to the officers of firms.

9.1.7 New terms and regulatory features

The following terms and regulatory features should be properly understood by registered auditors, although the brief explanations given here are not formal definitions. For the latter it is necessary to refer to the 'Blue Book' – the revised version of the Audit Regulations and Guidance issued by the Chartered Institutes in December 1995, and distributed to all firms that applied for registered auditor status.

Recognized supervisory body (RSB)

An RSB is a professional body recognized by the Department of Trade and Industry under the *Companies Act 1989* as competent to establish audit regulations to which registered auditors (see below) are subject. Firms granted registration are entitled to record such status on their writing paper and letterhead.

Recognized qualifying body (RQB)

An RQB is a professional body recognized by the DTI under the *Companies Act 1989* as competent to establish regulations for entry requirements, training of unqualified staff, setting examinations and other qualifying criteria for those undergoing training to become qualified persons (see below).

Registered auditor

A firm that has been granted registration by its RSB as satisfying the conditions in that RSB's audit regulations. The RSB's register will include details of the firm and its principals who have been nominated as responsible individuals (see below). Each RSB holds its own register as well as those of all the other RSBs. These are open to inspection by the public. (Unlike the Chartered Institutes, the Chartered Association of Certified Accountants has granted registered auditor status to individuals rather than firms.)

Qualified person

A member of one of the three Chartered Institutes or a certified accountant who has a practising certificate. A qualified person is an accountant who holds an 'appropriate qualification' obtained in the UK or an equivalent overseas qualification.

Responsible individual

A qualified person who is a principal within a firm and is responsible for audit work and hence for signing audit reports.

Affiliate

A principal of a firm who is not a chartered or certified accountant but who has agreed to be bound by the relevant RSB's regulations and ethical guidelines, has agreed to provide any necessary information and has satisfied the 'fit and proper' criteria (see below) for conducting audit work.

'Fit and proper'

All registered auditors must satisfy these criteria in deference to the statutory requirement for integrity in audit work. Such criteria will cover financial propriety, any former convictions, civil liabilities, refusals of authorization, professional censure and investigations into misconduct. Before a firm can satisfy these conditions it must apply a similar 'fit and proper' test to all principals and staff that provide any input to the firm's audit work, including new recruits, subcontract staff and agency personnel. This assessment will normally be based on a form to be completed by each person affected by the regulations.

The integrity requirement is not susceptible to external scrutiny in the same manner as technical competence, or even independence. In practice, therefore, a firm that demonstrates a serious approach to training and competence and abides by both the letter and the spirit of the independence rules will have gone a long way towards establishing its integrity.

Control

At least 75 per cent of voting power in the registered auditor firm must be held by qualified persons, and every principal must be a qualified person or an affiliate. Although the *Companies Act 1989* requires only a simple majority, the Chartered Institutes persuaded the DTI to raise the control threshold to 75 per cent, thereby enhancing the ability of those bodies to achieve and enforce the independence and integrity criteria more effectively.

Audit

Under the revised Audit Regulations (December 1995), the term 'audit' has been restricted to the expression of an opinion on financial statements, in the following circumstances:

1. Under the 1985 Companies Act, opinions on:
    - annual financial statements, section 235;
    - revised annual financial statements and directors' reports, sections 245, 245A and 245B;
    - abbreviated accounts, Schedule 8, Part III;
    - summary financial statements, section 251;
    - exemptions from preparing group financial statements, section 248;
    - distributions, section 271(4) and section 273(4);
    - re-registration of a private company as a public company, section 43(3)(b);
    - redemption or purchase by a private company of its own shares out of capital, section 173(5);
    - financial assistance for acquisition of a private company's own shares, section 156(4).
2. Under legislation governing:
    - building societies;
    - credit unions;

- registered charities;
- friendly and provident societies; and
- persons authorized under legislation relating to the conduct of investment business.

Other acts, including the *Companies Act 1985*, require reports to be given by a registered auditor but the reports are not an expression of an opinion on all or part of the accounts. One such example is the report under section 104 of the *Companies Act 1985* on the transfer of non-cash assets to a public company. This is not a report on the accounts so would not fall within the scope of these regulations. However, a report on the initial accounts of a company wishing to make a distribution (section 273(4) of the *Companies Act 1985*) would be within these regulations because it is a report on financial statements.

The definition of 'audit' does not include an independent accountant's report required by section 249C of the *Companies Act 1985*. Nor does it include a report required as part of a public offer of securities (prospectus) required by investment business legislation.

Some unincorporated entities, such as clubs, charities and social societies, require their accounts to be audited under their own constitutions. Where such entities do not fall within the definition above, the phrase 'registered auditor' should be avoided when signing the audit report, especially since the informal nature of most such organizations' activities, including controls and accounting methods, renders a full-scale audit somewhat impracticable, not to mention uneconomic, and beyond the real requirements of their members.

In such instances it is preferable to sign the report as 'chartered accountants', but it is nevertheless always advisable to ensure that the form of words used adequately reflects the audit work (and, in most instances, accounting work) that preceded the issue of the report. The 'audit' report is often associated with a level of authentication that is not warranted by the scope and extent of fieldwork actually carried out, especially in circumstances where activities are poorly controlled, where many transactions are for cash and most administrative work is performed by voluntary committee members.

It should be remembered that any report which the firm signs in its registered auditor capacity will be deemed by the regulators to have been issued following a full audit in which auditing standards and guidelines have been applied. Although work done under the Solicitors' Accounts Rules does not culminate in an auditors' report as such, only persons or firms qualified to act as company auditors may accept appointments to act for solicitors in this context. Investment business audits (regardless of whether the business is incorporated) must, if required, be undertaken by registered auditors.

Audit reports

Following the enforcement of the audit regulations, firms are obliged to add 'registered auditor' after the signature on their audit reports. Under transitional provisions, this applied to reports issued in respect of all new appointments and reappointments that took place after 1 October 1991. Failure to comply with these provisions will cause the accounts to be rejected by Companies House and may lead to disciplinary action against the firm. Use of the term 'registered auditor' by a firm that is not so registered is a criminal offence.

Audit Registration Committee (ARC)

This Institute Committee has responsibility for granting registration to firms after careful assessment of their applications and ensuring that they fulfil the necessary criteria. The Committee also has power to requisition monitoring visits, and to withdraw or suspend registration, or to grant it subject to special conditions.

The membership of the ARC comprises accountants drawn from firms of all sizes and geographical locations, and independent members drawn from the legal profession, banking and general business backgrounds. Registered auditor status is subject to annual renewal, for which purpose an annual return must be submitted by every registered auditor. The ARC has identified several areas of particular concern on the basis of its work to date. These are, not surprisingly, issues affecting independence; 'fit and proper' criteria (all disciplinary referrals and complaints being automatically notified to the ARC); subcontracting arrangements between firms, and arrangements for training and maintaining competence in auditing.

Joint monitoring unit (JMU)

The JMU acts as an agent of the ARC, and its function is to carry out regular monitoring visits to a selection of firms, as it has already been doing for some years for the purposes of the *Financial Services Act 1986*. Indeed, registered auditors who are also authorized by the Institute to undertake investment business will find that the JMU will usually choose to monitor both activities in the course of a single inspection visit.

The scale of audit registration in the UK does not allow for more than a small sample of firms being randomly selected for monitoring purposes. However, in addition to these routine sample visits, the ARC also requests the JMU to visit any firm whose original application or annual return highlights potential problems, or if it has been the subject of a complaint that casts doubt on its auditing competence. A visit may also be required if the firm is involved in an issue in which there is a strong public interest.

The JMU is not in a position to take action against a firm on its own initiative; it may make recommendations to that effect, but its reports are passed to the ARC for review and consideration, and it is the ARC alone that takes any appropriate action.

9.2   Audit regulation – the experience so far

The impact of the *Companies Act 1989* on UK auditing firms has been far more dramatic than the equivalent legislation in other EC countries. There are two reasons for this:

1. There are far more incorporated businesses in the UK than elsewhere in the EC.

2. In October 1991, all UK companies were required to have their annual accounts audited by professionally qualified auditors, although this legislation has subsequently been varied by the audit exemption regime introduced in August 1994, whereas most other EC members insist on an audit for listed (or large private) companies only, with various options for shareholders in smaller, private companies.

The result is that over 12,000 firms of auditors fell within the regulatory net, thus creating a logistical problem of some magnitude for the monitors of practising standards. Firms themselves are, of course, highly experienced in audit work – a very different situation from that imposed at the onset of investment business regulation, which created a novel set of rules that are still being adjusted to accord with operational practicalities while still affording a reasonable measure of public protection. In theory, therefore, audit regulation should have posed no real problem. All that was required was to formalize on a legal footing what has become standard procedure for many years past (perhaps upgrading ethical guidelines here and there, and re-emphasizing the importance of independence).

In reality the legislative process amounted to far more than adding a modicum of judicial gloss to pre-regulation practice. The act of formalization means that much of what auditors have hitherto taken for granted must now be made evident. For example, while most auditors are able competently to review a set of financial statements to assess their plausibility in the context of known business and economic developments, they are not always very good at recording the process of assessment itself. Naturally, for firms to succeed in complying with the new regime, the partners as a whole must have the will to persevere with an overhaul of attitudes to training, technical improvement and enhancement of methods, despite the loss in chargeable time.

Each of the four professional bodies named in the *Companies Act 1985* as bodies whose members may undertake company audits in the UK was accepted to act as an RSB and RQB, and their detailed audit regulations and guidance became enforceable with effect from 1 October 1991.

The following extract has been taken from the executive summary of the report to the DTI on audit regulation from the three Chartered Institutes for the year ended 31 December 1995.

> 1995 has seen the satisfactory continuing implementation of the changes and improvements developed over the previous two years, including the issue of the revised Audit Regulations in December 1995.
>
> All firms have now received at least one of the new style annual returns. This means that all firms of registered auditors have been subject to a comprehensive review. Those with perceived deficiencies or variations from normal are followed up, either by verbal or written communication with the firm or by a focused monitoring visit.
>
> In addition, the substantially increased target for numbers of monitoring visits has been achieved. Inevitably these have concentrated on firms where the annual return indicated

that there were potential difficulties. In spite of the bias towards firms where problems could exist the results of such visits are continuing to be satisfactory and demonstrate the continuing improvement in firms' performance.

1996 will be a year of consolidation. While an objective is to continue to improve the regulatory process it is also, and particularly important, one of continuing to raise professional standards through training, education and technical developments.

The report also identified the 'commonly encountered concerns' arising from the work of the Audit Registration Committee. These are reproduced here:

---

1. Firm's procedures

These are the procedures a firm has in place to control its overall audit practice, as opposed to individual audits. The more common problems are:

(a) lack of, or insufficient, quality control procedures to prevent poor work leaving the firm;

(b) failure to consider fully and record the firm's consideration of matters that may affect its appointment or reappointment;

(c) sole practitioners often do not have written consultation agreements or if consultation takes place, it is often not recorded;

(d) declarations covering independence, confidentiality and fit and proper status are often not signed and subcontractors are not always included.

2. Individual competence

Most firms are achieving satisfactory levels of 'continuing professional education'. The more common problem is that audit related CPE cannot be identified from records maintained and also a lack of appropriate training for specialized audits.

3. Quality assurance

Compliance with this aspect will have been assisted by the publication of details on how to conduct an audit compliance review, both in *Audit News* and the annual return. Guidance is also contained in the revised audit regulations, so it expected that further improvements will be seen in this area.

In a number of cases firms simply need to refine the procedures so they are appropriate to the individual firm.

The most common problems associated with quality assurance are not covering both 'whole firm' procedures and 'cold file' reviews. Also, the results of the review are not fed back to other partners and staff to make improvements.

Although not required, it is useful if firms use one of the available pre-printed checklists so the quality assurance review covers all relevant areas.

4. *Proper performance*

This aspect relates to the work on individual audits. Again, it is encouraging to see an increase in the level of firms doing well in this area.

The more common problems are:

(a) *Lack of planning, controlling and recording*

▶ The planning does not take account of changes that have occurred in client's business environment or the regulations it is subject to.

▶ Standard audit programmes are not adapted for individual clients.

▶ Audit work is sometimes poorly recorded, particularly when a firm also prepares the accounts and there is insufficient distinction from the audit work.

(b) *Lack of audit evidence*

Common areas where audit evidence is not always sufficient include:

(i) stock – stock-takes are not always attended and, if not, there is often little evidence of other work conducted to confirm the existence and condition of stock. Work on pricing and to confirm the allocation of sales and purchases to the correct accounting period also needs to be evidenced more fully.

(ii) Trade debtors and creditors – there is sometimes little evidence to prove the work done on, for example, the existence and recoverability of trade debtors. Trade creditor balances are often not agreed to supplier statements and any other work which could prove their existence and valuation is not clearly evidenced.

(iii) Bank balances – a certificate or other third party evidence is not always obtained.

(iv) Fixed assets – work done on existence, ownership and valuation is not always evidenced. For example, fixed asset additions and the continued existence of assets are not always verified. Title to property is not always ascertained and valuations not checked to ensure that they are still valid.

(v) There is a tendency to assume that a computer-produced document is correct, without further work on the underlying records.

(c) *Incorrect or inadequate disclosure in the financial statements*

Incorrect or incomplete disclosure is usually caused by not using a disclosure checklist, or by using a checklist (computerized or manual) which is out of date.

(d) *Errors within audit reports*

The Statement of Auditing Standards, 'Auditors' reports on financial statements', is not always followed and 'subject to' qualifications are still used, although this is no longer allowed under the standard.

(e) Reliance on the work of assistants

Even if an audit is properly planned and communicated to staff, that plan will not be achieved if staff do not have the necessary skills. These extend beyond technical auditing and accounting knowledge. Auditors at all levels of seniority need:

► the skill to ask open questions;

► knowledge of the industry and the client to understand the answer and put any necessary extra questions; and

► the skill to summarize and record the information gained together with a conclusion in terms of the particular audit objective.

(f) Adequacy of the final review

This is the final quality control within the audit process. It is essential that the final review:

► deals with all outstanding matters;

► reviews both the original and the supervisory work performed by the person presenting the work for review;

► confirms that the planned work, or an appropriate alternative, has happened and been recorded;

► pays particular attention to the more complex technical matters (for example, the many disclosure requirements);

► checks that any key judgemental decisions have been audited;

► records the link from the detailed work to the final opinion (including why those key judgemental decisions were accepted as presenting a true and fair view); and

► provides feedback to those contributing to the audit and acts as the basis for planning the next year's audit.

Even the most well-organized and technically up-to-date firms are likely to find something on the above list that warrants improvement.

Most firms on the initial list of registered auditors were granted their status on the strength of little more than an application form. Annual renewals are another matter entirely. The experience of practice monitoring so far will enable the regulators' annual returns to focus on the serious failings commonly encountered and to insist on firm evidence of remedial steps before renewing registration.

9.3 Quality control

All firms have been well advised for many years to institute internal programmes of quality control enhancement with a view to: (1) improving their services to clients,

(2) improving practice efficiency and profitability, and (3) minimizing their exposure to liability risks. SAS 240 – Quality Control for Audit Work – lays down minimum standards to assist in this process.

The key points covered by this SAS are as follows:

1. Auditors should have in place, and be in a position to demonstrate, their quality control procedures both for the firm as a whole and for individual audit assignments.

2. Auditors should monitor the effectiveness of their quality control procedures.

3. Engagement partners should exercise proper control over the direction, supervision and review of work delegated to assistants.

4. The quality control policies to be adopted by auditors usually incorporate the following:

   (a) professional requirements – personnel adhere to the principles of independence, integrity, objectivity, confidentiality and professional behaviour;

   (b) skills and competence – personnel have attained and maintained the technical standards and professional competence required to enable them to fulfil their responsibilities with due care;

   (c) acceptance and retention of clients – prospective clients are evaluated and existing clients are reviewed on an ongoing basis. In making a decision to accept or retain a client, the auditors' independence and ability to serve the client properly and the integrity of the client's management are considered;

   (d) assignment – audit work is assigned to personnel who have the degree of technical training and proficiency required in the circumstances;

   (e) delegation (direction, supervision and review) – sufficient direction, supervision and review of work at all levels is carried out in order to provide confidence that the work performed meets appropriate standards of quality;

   (f) consultation – consultation, whenever necessary, within or outside the audit firm occurs with those who have appropriate expertise; and

   (g) monitoring – the continued adequacy and operational effectiveness of quality control policies and procedures are monitored.

Reference should also be made to the author's text, *Risk Management for Auditors*, published in 1989 by APC as an audit brief. This makes extensive reference to the relationship between audit risk and quality control attitudes and procedures. The following extract highlights, in questionnaire form, the quality control features which firms should currently be enforcing as a matter of routine. This questionnaire has been updated to reflect considerations required in the light of audit regulation.

Sample questionnaire

1. New clients

Before accepting appointment to act for new clients in any capacity specific enquiries are made:

(a) Of the prospective clients/previous appointee/other sources as applicable:

    (i) Seeking relevant background information.

    (ii) Reason for approach/change in adviser/auditor.

    (iii) Usual ethical clearance.

    (iv) Disputes.

(b) Within the firm:

    (i) Consideration of matters arising from any of the above.

    (ii) Capability of handling the assignment:

        ► technically

        ► adequate staffing?

    (iii) Are appropriate steps taken to identify whether such clients have the potential for generating claims of a size out of proportion to the fee they are likely to generate?

    (iv) Independence of partners and staff.

(Most of the issues listed above should also be considered before accepting reappointment each year for on-going audit clients.)

2. Engagement letters

(a) Are these issued to *all* new clients irrespective of the nature of the assignment?

(b) Are these issued to all existing clients whenever:

    (i) The nature of the assignment alters?

    (ii) Additional work, different from that hitherto undertaken, is requested?

(c) Do the form and content of the engagement letter comply with the auditing standard in all respects?

(d) Does the letter used for audit engagements make specific reference to *material* irregularity or fraud and the firm's responsibility in relation thereto?

3. Structure and supervision

(a) Is there a formalized management structure within the firm in which responsibilities are delegated hierarchically?

(b) Does this structure ensure adequate supervision and monitoring of the quality of work of managers/seniors/juniors, etc?

(c) Is work on each assignment preceded by briefing/planning meetings of all members of the team, convened for this purpose?

(d) (i) Are meetings of partners/managers held periodically on a regular basis?

    (ii) Are these formally convened, preceded by agenda, and followed by minutes of agreed action?

    (iii) Is there a system for communicating and implementing resolutions agreed?

4. Assignment reviews – past

(a) Are completed assignment files subjected to independent review on a regular basis? (These are often referred to as 'peer reviews'.)

(b) Does the method of file sampling ensure that all have a reasonable chance of being selected, and that no assignments/categories could escape inspection for an indefinite period?

(c) Are files selected for review subjected to systematic scrutiny designed to ensure that:

    (i) Firm's procedures have been complied with?

    (ii) Operative accounting/auditing standards and guidelines have been complied with?

(d) Are reviews followed by written conclusions? If so, do these indicate the nature of any remedial steps needed? Is there a procedure in place to ensure any remedial action is taken?

5. Assignment reviews – current

(a) Is independent partner review/consultation sought whenever warranted by sensitive/complex circumstances?

(b) Is independent opinion sought before reporting on/concluding assignment for client known to be:

    (i) Seeking substantial external finance?

    (ii) Seeking/negotiating sale of the undertaking or material part of it?

    (iii) Dissatisfied or otherwise considering a change of adviser/auditor?

    (iv) 'High risk', in the public arena, or subject to regulation elsewhere?

6. Procedures

(a) Is a standardized staff manual used?

(b) If so, does it include sections on:

    (i) Auditing procedures?

    (ii) Accounting standards, conventions and legal requirements?

    (iii) Taxation?

    (iv) Office administration?

(c) Is the manual periodically reviewed, revised and updated in light of:

    (i) The firm's experience?

    (ii) Externally imposed standards/guidelines?

(d) Does the section on auditing give advice on:

    (i) Testing/sampling methods?

    (ii) Materiality assessment?

    (iii) Analytical review procedures?

    (iv) Audit files/documentation/recording of evidence generally?

(e) Is compliance with prescribed procedures properly evidenced?

7. Communication

(a) Does the firm have a system for ensuring that messages/communications are received and logged;

    (i) Within the firm (including inter-office)?

    (ii) To and from clients?

(b) Wherever appropriate, are all clients specifically informed of external developments affecting them directly or indirectly, and which may require action on their part (e.g. changes in legislation, such as VAT regulations, *Finance Acts, Insolvency Act, Financial Services Act*, etc.)?

8. Training and competence

(a) Does the firm issue periodic technical bulletins on current professional/legal developments affecting assignment work to all members of the professional staff?

(b) Are all qualified personnel obliged to comply with formal guidelines on continuing professional education (CPE) requirements?

(c) Are CPE records completed by all qualified personnel and retained on file?

(d) Does the firm arrange/provide structured training for all professional staff either in-house or as part of a consortium with other firms?

(e) Does the range of subject matter covered by such training encompass:

    (i) Auditing standards and guidelines?

    (ii) Accounting standards?

    (iii) New legislation?

    (iv) Taxation/*Finance Acts*/post-budget guidance?

    (v) Wills/pensions/trusts/executorships?

    (vi) Investment advice?

    (vii) Topics specially elected for current or ongoing relevance?

    (viii) Personal development skills?

(f) Are there procedures to ensure that partners and staff involved in specialist or non-routine assignments have received appropriate training?

(g) Does the firm maintain an accessible technical library with a reasonable annual budget for up-to-date texts on mainstream professional work and official publications?

(h) Is the library list kept up to date and its contents notified within the firm?

(i) Does the library retain a satisfactory range of professional journals after circulation amongst partners and staff?

(j) Does the firm's recruitment policy operate to ensure that audit staff of appropriate skills and experience are recruited?

9. General

(a) Does the firm have a procedure to ensure that all persons engaged in audit work are fit and proper persons?

(b) Does the firm have any specific means of identifying signs of stress in partners/staff for any reason, which are likely to create problems/adversely affect performance?

(c) Are new/recently opened offices of the firm:

    (i) Adequately staffed?

    (ii) Adequately supervised and monitored?

    (iii) Brought into conformity with the criteria implicit in this questionnaire as rapidly as possible?

(d) Before entering into a practice merger, is every reasonable enquiry and assessment made concerning:

    (i) The quality control in force in the other firm involved?

    (ii) The competence of its partners and staff?

    (iii) Any outstanding claims or notification of circumstances of any latent claim?

(e) Do the terms of any practice mergers, demergers and retirements require the other parties to maintain professional indemnity (PI) run-off cover for claims by any clients brought in/taken over by them?

(f) When a partner retires from practice are anticipatory arrangements made for the handing over of all client work for which that partner has been responsible to other partners in such a way that staffing and supervision of assignments remains satisfactory?

(g) Are any arrangements for using the services of third party experts/specialists:

(i) Formally approved by and notified to partners?

(ii) Periodically reviewed and assessed?

(h) In any circumstances in which the firm's work may be relied upon by third parties without the firm's knowledge or approval, are appropriately worded restrictive written disclaimers always used?

Partners in smaller practices may feel that the questions are pitched at much larger firms, but there are few questions that cannot be intelligently adapted to reflect the standards to which firms of all sizes should now aspire, especially since so many small firms now have arrangements of mutual cooperation which provide a forum in which discussion of problems and exchange of information and experience can take place openly but confidentially. Many go further and have systems of file reviews and back-up arrangements during periods when practitioners are away from the office.

Indeed, the broad framework for quality control procedures within firms that are registered auditors has now been codified in the audit regulations issued by the recognized supervisory bodies. The relevant extracts from the ICAEW regulations are given below; the original paragraph numbers have been preserved.

Quality control

3.11 A Registered Auditor must make arrangements so that all principals and employees doing audit work are, and continue to be, competent to carry out the audits for which they are responsible or employed. In doing so, the Registered Auditor should follow all relevant material issued by the Council of the registering Institute.

3.12 A Registered Auditor must maintain an appropriate level of competence in the conduct of audits.

3.13 A Registered Auditor must make sure all principals and employees involved in audit work are aware of and follow these regulations, the Act, any relevant rules and regulations issued under the Act and any procedures established by the firm.

3.14 A Registered Auditor must monitor, at least once a year, how effectively it is complying with these regulations.

Review questions

*1. One of your audit managers recently left your employment, obtained registered audit status and has set up a small audit and accounting practice. He has approached you for advice particularly in the area of audit independence. Prepare a list of items to be considered in evaluating 'independence'.

*2. An auditor is always required to have control procedures in place over internal operations. In the case of small partnerships or sole practitioner auditors this has caused numerous problems. Highlight areas in which you consider that these may occur and suggest possible solutions.

3. With the introduction of Limited Liability Audit Companies there exists even more potential for non-qualified individuals being present within the firm and, with the necessity only of a simple majority of qualified individuals, there is an erosion of the current majority requirements. Given the Chartered Institute's amendment to the statutory rule, discuss the relative advantages and disadvantages of incorporation together with the possible control diminution to qualified individuals if the exception to statutory provisions is not maintained.

4. The JMU is not authorized to take action against a firm which is failing in its audit function – it merely submits a report to the firm's regulatory body. Discuss the advantages which may be obtained if the JMU were to be capable of taking action.

10

Statute and case law affecting auditors' liability

THIS CHAPTER DEALS WITH:

▷ liability of auditors under statute and the common law;

▷ third party liability;

▷ case law developments affecting proximity;

▷ auditors' responsibility for detection of fraud;

▷ paid cheques as audit evidence;

▷ responsibility of auditors for statutory and regulatory breaches of clients.

10.1 Auditors' liability – the branches of law

The liability of auditors may be divided into the following broad areas:

1. Negligence under the common law:

   (a) under contract;

   (b) third parties.

2. Liability under statute:

   (a) civil liability under the *Companies Act 1985*;

   (b) criminal liability under the *Companies Act 1985*; and the *Theft Act 1968*.

It should be borne in mind that legal cases affecting auditors have played an important role in creating a body of law to which current cases, notably concerning professional liability, will be referred by the courts. In cases involving disputes over the interpretation of statute law, the courts will decide how the particular provision is to be interpreted in the circumstances in question. Nevertheless, despite the importance of precedent, one should never adopt a dogmatic attitude on questions relating to liability, since the weight of contemporary conditions will often be regarded as more significant than a legal decision arrived at many years earlier. Moreover, no two cases contain identical circumstances – at most, the circumstances will be similar.

10.1.1 Negligence under the common law

Liability under contract

This liability springs from the general principle of law that when a person is under a legal duty to take care, whether imposed by specific contract or otherwise, the failure to exercise a reasonable standard of care will make that person responsible for any resultant damage or loss to those to whom the duty is owed.

What conduct satisfies the standard of care required will, in any particular case, depend entirely upon the circumstances. The general degree of skill and diligence demanded of (and generally attained by) auditors today is unprecedented, and the question as to whether an auditor is or is not guilty of negligence in any particular case is necessarily determined by reference to the standard to which contemporary members of the profession conform.

It will readily be appreciated that contemporary standards provide an ever-shifting criterion, and this has never been more true than at the present time, when judges are likely to place far less reliance than in previous years upon legal decisions reached when the standards and skills demanded of an auditor were, from both the statutory and the general professional viewpoint, far less exacting. The establishment of auditing standards for the profession has undoubtedly made an important contribution towards formulating criteria by which performance may be more objectively judged.

Liability to third parties

Liability to third parties in respect of physical injury has a long and well-established legal history. Most students of law will be aware of the famous case of *Donoghue* v. *Stevenson* (1932, AC 562) in which damages were awarded in favour of the young lady who consumed the contents of a gingerbeer bottle in a seaside cafe only to be made aware, too late, that the contents included the decomposed remains of a snail. Although the contractual relationship was between her and the vendor of the bottle, damages were awarded against the manufacturers, with whom there was no such relationship.

Similarly, in *Grant* v. *Australian Knitting Mills*, the plaintiff was awarded damages in respect of a skin irritation suffered due to a defect in the underwear which he had acquired from a retailer. The damages were awarded against the manufacturer as well as the retailer.

However, legal cases relating to third party liability for financial (as opposed to physical) injury is by no means as consistent. In the Court of Appeal in 1951, in *Candler* v. *Crane Christmas & Co.* (LT 96), a majority (Lord Denning dissenting) decided that there could be no liability in the absence of a contractual relationship. The decision was reached despite the fact that Mr Candler had been induced to invest sums in a company on the strength of a set of accounts negligently prepared by the company's auditors. The auditors knew that this was the purpose of the accounts which they had been asked to prepare (in their capacity as accountants) and did not deny that they had been negligent in executing this assignment.

The key paragraph in Denning's dissenting judgment, subsequently vindicated in the Hedley Byrne case (see below) and cited with approval in Caparo (see below), was as follows:

> I think the law would fail to serve the best interests of the community if it should hold that accountants and auditors owe a duty to no one but their client. There is a great difference between the lawyer and the accountant. The lawyer is never called on to express his personal belief in the truth of his client's case, whereas the accountant, who certifies the accounts of his client, is always called on to express his personal opinion whether the accounts exhibit a true and correct view of his client's affairs, and he is required to do this not so much for the satisfaction of his own client, but more for the guidance of shareholders, investors, revenue authorities and others who may have to rely on the accounts in serious matters of business. In my opinion, accountants owe a duty of care not only to their own clients, but also to all those whom they know will rely on their accounts in the transactions for which those accounts are prepared.

The Lords took a totally different view in the 1963 case of *Hedley Byrne & Co. Ltd v. Heller & Partners Ltd*, in which they held that the Candler case had been wrongly decided. In the 1963 case, a certificate of creditworthiness had been negligently issued by a firm of merchant bankers in response to a request from a third party; the certificate related to the financial standing of one of the bank's customers.

The Lords decided that since it was quite clear that such a certificate, issued in the ordinary course of the bank's business, would be relied upon by the party to whom it was issued, the absence of contract did not constitute a valid defence in a negligence claim against the bank. Heller & Partners Ltd nevertheless escaped without having to pay any damages, but purely on the grounds that they had included a clause with the certificate specifically disclaiming any liability consequent upon reliance on such statement. It was clear that they escaped liability by virtue of this disclaimer, rather than the absence of contractual relationship.

The Institute of Chartered Accountants in England and Wales in 1967, following the Hedley Byrne decision, sought Counsel's opinion as to how far such liability might extend, and in reaching a decision, Counsel paid particular attention to cases decided abroad, notably *Ultramares Corporation v. Touche & Co.* (New York, 1932). In this case, Mr Justice Cardozo sought to establish a rational limitation to otherwise open-ended potential liability of auditors in the following oft-quoted words:

> If liability for negligence exists, a thoughtless slip or blunder, the failure to detect a theft or forgery beneath the cover of deceptive entries, may expose accountants to a liability in an indeterminate amount for an indeterminate time to an indeterminate class. The hazards of a business conducted on those terms are so extreme as to enkindle doubt whether a flaw may not exist in the implication of a duty that exposes to these consequences.

Counsel's opinion may be summarized in the following way. Duty of care, and hence liability, towards a third party in respect of a document or statement would arise only if both the following criteria are fulfilled, assuming there is negligence, and financial loss has occurred:

1. It is clear that the financial loss is attributable to reliance upon the negligently prepared document, etc., and to no other cause.

2. The party issuing the document, etc., knew the purpose for which it was being prepared, and knew (or ought to have known) that it was to be relied upon in that particular context.

As a consequence, Counsel put forward the view that liability to shareholders would not extend to the consequences of their reliance upon the audit report, etc., in the context of an investment decision, since it is not the purpose of accounts prepared under statute (nor of the auditor's report attached thereto) to assist existing or potential shareholders in exercising an investment decision. Such accounts are prepared for stewardship purposes only, within the confines of companies legislation, and these accounts, together with the auditor's report, are therefore addressed to existing shareholders. This view has been firmly upheld in the more recent Caparo case (see below). This view continues to create controversy, however, since it is difficult to see what a potential investor (or an existing shareholder contemplating disinvestment) would rely upon to assist such a decision, if not the published accounts and auditor's report, particularly when shares in listed companies are involved. No separate accounts are ordinarily prepared for the purposes of making such investment decisions, and auditors are fully aware of the fact that stewardship accounts are in fact commonly used for this purpose, although not exclusively so.

The Hedley Byrne decision has been followed in a number of subsequent cases. In the Canadian case of *Myers* v. *Thompson & London Life Insurance Co.* (1967), an insurance agent failed to see that the insurance company carried out the instructions of the plaintiff's solicitor for surrender of the plaintiff's term policy and issue of a new one to his wife. Thus, when the plaintiff died shortly after, a part of the insurance proceeds was taxed in his estate. Following Hedley Byrne, the agent was held personally responsible, for he knew that reliance was being placed on him and his negligence caused the loss to the estate through his failure to exercise the implied duty of care.

In 1971, in an Australian case, *Evatt* v. *Mutual and Citizens Life Assurance Co. Ltd*, the Hedley Byrne principle was restricted to situations in which the issue of the negligent opinion, etc., arose in the ordinary course of the issuing party's business. In the Evatt case, the parent company of an insurance group negligently gave Mr Evatt an opinion on the financial standing of one of its subsidiaries, and Mr Evatt lost heavily as a result of such reliance. The Privy Council of the House of Lords held, on appeal, that the opinion had been issued honestly, the company believing it to be true and, since there was no contractual relationship between the litigating parties, there was no cause for action as the statement was made outside of the ordinary course of the parent company's business.

Late in 1975 the House of Lords held, in *Arenson v. Casson, Beckman Rutley & Co.*, that an accountant or auditor of a private company who, on request, values shares in the company in the knowledge that his valuation is to determine the price to be paid for them under a contract for their sale, may be liable to be sued if he makes his valuation negligently.

In April 1970, Mr Arenson's employment in his uncle's company was terminated. He and his uncle asked the company's auditors, Cassons, acting as experts and not as arbitrators, to determine the 'fair value' of his shares in the company as at 4 April. The value given was £4,916. On 11 June, Mr Arenson, relying on that valuation, transferred his shares to his uncle at £4,916.

In September 1970, a holding company, A. Arenson (Holdings) Ltd, was incorporated to acquire the company's issued share capital; and in 1971 the shares of the holding company were offered to the public on the basis of a valuation jointly prepared by Cassons and another firm of accountants which, if applied *pro rata*, would allegedly have given Mr Arenson's shares a value of almost six times what he had received for them.

He issued a writ claiming, among other things, that Cassons's valuation was not binding on him; that a fresh valuation should be made; and that his uncle should pay him the true worth of the shares; and, alternatively, that Cassons were 'negligent in making the valuation'.

This case was of particular importance since it dealt with an unusual aspect of third party liability, i.e. where the defendant has acted in a quasi-judicial capacity, holding the scales of equity between two disputing parties (who had failed to agree on a valuation on their own). The House of Lords decided that, despite appearances that Cassons had acted in a quasi-judicial capacity, and might thus expect to be entitled to a qualified privilege or immunity from action, they were fully answerable to the plaintiff for the valuation originally determined by them. Such immunity would have been available if, for example, Cassons had been acting as arbitrators. As a consequence, the case was returned to the lower court for the purpose of determining whether or not negligence had taken place, and if so, the extent of the appropriate damages. The case was then settled between the parties.

An important side-effect of this decision for auditors is the obvious advisability of maintaining secrecy as to their method of arriving at share valuations, and of the computations supporting the valuation; only the final figure should be supplied. This is known as a 'non-speaking' valuation. In this way it would be difficult for any party validly to contest a valuation of shares (which, in any event, are notoriously difficult to value, even within a range of amounts). Once a valuation basis and supporting computation is supplied, however, it is always possible for another 'expert' to provide evidence as to why such value is 'defective'. It should be obvious that shares in companies can have no 'intrinsic' or 'objective' value other than the price that another party is prepared to pay for them.

Third party liability – through the post

Auditors sometimes receive letters from potential investors about to acquire substantial interests in companies whose accounts had been audited by those to whom the letters were addressed. These letters usually contain statements along the following lines:

▶ 'We are writing to advise you that we are contemplating making a substantial investment in XYZ Limited, of which we understand you are the auditor.'

▶ 'We have not commissioned an independent report relating to the financial position of XYZ Limited.'

▶ 'We shall place material reliance upon the audited accounts of XYZ Limited when making a decision as to whether or not to proceed with such an investment.'

The import of such letters obviously suggests a wider accountability on the part of the auditor than is currently envisaged under the statutes and as determined by the courts, and is designed to exploit the uncertain nature of the common law in the direction of third party liability. A formal reply to such letters should always be made, in which it is clearly pointed out that accounts prepared and audited under the *Companies Act* are not designed for use in an investment context, and that while they will undoubtedly contain useful information for such a purpose, they are not an effective substitute for a specially commissioned acquisition or investigation report. This is always essential in the case of shares in private companies. Reference should also be made to the fact that published accounts do not convey the company's current financial situation, and they will, in any case, have incorporated management estimates acceptable to the auditor in the context of the company's overall financial position, but which may turn out subsequently to be significantly different.

Counsel's opinion (1967) following the famous Hedley Byrne decision (1963) maintained that no third party liability would attach to auditors if the accounts they have audited under the *Companies Act* are used, without their knowledge or consent, by outsiders in an investment context.

It is likely that a reply on the lines suggested above will prove legally effective simply because it would clearly be unwise and grossly incautious for anyone to rely exclusively upon conventional audited accounts in reaching an investment decision. What is always risky, of course, is the possibility that any reliance on the audited statements may be regarded as reasonable if it has featured within the context of a wider investigation, orientated towards investment. In such a case, any loss traceable to the negligence of the auditor could not easily be defended on the grounds suggested by Counsel since statutory accounts contain much information of use to a potential investor.

The Jeb Fasteners case

The very risk envisaged above crystallized in the case of *Jeb Fasteners Limited* v. *Marks Bloom & Co.* (1981, 3 All ER 110.4). As has already been indicated, the general view of potential liability to outside parties depends upon certain key ingredients being present, including the fundamental requirement that the defendant ought to have known that the negligently prepared statement etc. was to be relied upon by the plaintiff in the context for which the statement was prepared, and in the context which actually gave rise to the loss. The absence of this crucial ingredient did not, however, deter the judge in this case.

The plaintiff acquired the entire share capital of a company called B.G. Fasteners in June 1975. In so doing, he claimed to have relied on the audited accounts of that company for the year ended 31 October 1974, prepared by the defendant auditors, a firm of chartered accountants. The plaintiff alleged that such accounts, on which an unqualified report had been given by the defendants, did not give a true and fair view of the state of the company, and consequently the plaintiff had suffered substantial loss and damage as a result of the purchase of the company.

The court accepted as fact – indeed it was common ground between the parties – that at the time the accounts were audited, the defendants did not know of the plaintiff, or his purpose, or that a takeover of the company from any source was contemplated. At the outset of his judgment Mr Justice Woolf acknowledged that there was no direct English authority on the question of whether a defendant can owe a duty of care to a plaintiff in these circumstances. It was nevertheless held that:

1. A duty of care was owed by the defendant auditors to the plaintiff.

2. The plaintiff, in reaching his decision as to the takeover, had relied on the financial statements and unqualified report of the defendants.

3. These accounts did not show a true and fair view of the company, and were negligently prepared in that some sales and purchases had been omitted; there had been a failure to make provision for interest due on the company's overdrawn account; and there was a valuation of stock at a figure in excess of cost of approximately £13,500. Consequently, whereas the audited trading and profit and loss account had shown a net profit of £11, the reality was a loss in excess of £13,000;

4. Judgment would be given for the defendant auditors, but by reason only of the fact that on the evidence before the court the plaintiff would have acted no differently and would still have gone ahead with the takeover even had the true position of the accounts been known to him. Thus, on the facts, the defendants' negligence was not the direct cause of the plaintiff's loss.

From this we see that the auditors, Marks Bloom & Co., were not required to pay damages – but the grounds for this finding lay in the court's view that the plaintiff would have acquired the shares in question in any event, irrespective of the content of the negligently prepared accounts. The court would not permit the plaintiff merely to use the auditors as a scapegoat following a disappointing investment decision. The important point to note, however, is the finding of the existence of a legal duty of care owed by auditors to a complete stranger (at the time of the audit).

In considering the liability of auditors the judge, Mr Justice Woolf, stated that the appropriate test for establishing whether a duty of care exists is whether the defendant auditors knew, or reasonably should have foreseen at the time the accounts were audited, that a person might rely on those accounts for the purpose of deciding whether or not to take over the company, and therefore could suffer loss if the accounts were inaccurate.

The position now seems to be that auditors' liability depends upon a qualified test of 'reasonable foresight', i.e. on a principle whereby negligent accountants owe a duty of care to those who can be foreseen as likely to sustain damage if carelessness exists. Any prospective plaintiff must, however, first establish that it was reasonable in the circumstances for him to rely on the audited accounts.

The case went to appeal in July 1982, and the verdict of Mr Justice Woolf was upheld in all material particulars.

The Jeb Fasteners decision was further strengthened in the Scottish decision of *Twomax Ltd & Goode* v. *Dickson, McFarlane & Robinson* (1982) in a case also involving the decision to acquire shares, based on negligently audited financial statements. Lord Stewart cited and quoted with evident enthusiasm the Jeb Fasteners judgment, and awarded damages of some £65,000, plus costs, against the auditors.

It should be noted in passing that the majority of cases are settled out of court, leaving the amounts involved to the insurance companies to provide under professional indemnity policies.

The legal status of standards

In 1985 in the unreported case of *Lloyd Cheyham & Co Ltd* v. *Littlejohn Co.* (QBD) the auditors successfully defended the third party plaintiff's allegation of negligently audited accounts on which he claimed to have relied in deciding to purchase a company. Of a range of possible defences (including lack of proximity between the parties), the auditors opted for the most direct defence of all: that they had not in fact been negligent in issuing an unqualified report on accounts which failed to include any specific provision for the wear and tear of tyres on the company's trailers. (The company hired out trailers, and shortly after the acquisition went into insolvent liquidation, allegedly because of the cost of essential tyre replacement, which made the business uneconomic.)

The importance of the case lies in the vindication of adherence to accounting standards. The auditors had, in fact, carefully considered the need for a provision and had rejected it on the criteria set out in SSAP 2, which states that costs and revenues should be matched only 'so far as their relationship can be established or justifiably assumed', and only 'so far as these are material and identifiable'. No clear relationship could be found between the tyre wear and the amount of any meaningful provision, and so it was decided to charge depreciation on the trailers as a whole, including the tyres.

The judge declared, in effect, that a firm adhering to accounting (and, by inference, auditing) standards could not be guilty of negligence. On the subject of standards, Mr Justice Woolf said: 'While they are not conclusive, so that a departure from their terms necessarily involves a breach of duty; and while they are not clear, rigid rules they are very strong evidence as to what is the proper standard which should be adopted, and unless there is some justification, a departure from this will be regarded as constituting a breach of duty.'

The Caparo case

In what was clearly a seminal judgment on the question of auditors' duty of care to third parties, five Law Lords unanimously concluded that such a duty does not extend to investors and individual shareholders acting on stewardship accounts for investment purposes (*Caparo Industries plc* v. *Dickman & Others, The Times*, 12 February 1990).

Caparo already held a small number of shares in Fidelity plc prior to its purchase, on the strength of Fidelity's audited accounts for the year ended 31 March 1984, of the whole of the remaining shares. It was alleged that: (1) the accounts, which showed a profit of £1.3 million, were misleading in that a loss of £400,000 should have been shown; and hence that (2) the directors and auditors had been negligent. Criminal charges were subsequently brought against two directors.

The House of Lords, reversing the judgement of the Court of Appeal, distinguished cases where the defendant gave advice which he *knew* would be relied upon by the plaintiff in contemplation of a specific purpose, in contrast with situations where information was put into general circulation and might therefore conceivably be used by strangers for purposes that the defendant auditor had no reason to anticipate.

In the context in question, the purpose of the audit report was to conform with the requirements of the *Companies Act 1985*, rather than to serve the interests of investors – notwithstanding that the investor, Caparo, happened also to be a shareholder. The report's purpose was to enable shareholders, as a class, to exercise the rights of stewardship that their shareholding conferred, and these did not extend to individual speculation with a view to profit. Accordingly, any duty of care was owed to shareholders as a class rather than to individuals.

It should be remembered, of course, that all three Caparo judgments were concerned only with the proximity question, i.e. whether auditors owed Caparo a duty of care and therefore had a case to answer; not with the question of negligence. Only if the Lords had supported the Appeal Court's majority view would the auditors have been required to defend the charge of negligence.

Proximity following Caparo

The present position on proximity in such circumstances was clearly laid out by Lord Bridge, and may be summarized thus: an auditor owes a duty to a third party if, and only if, he

1. is aware of the nature of the transaction that the third party is contemplating;

2. knows that the report or statement will be communicated to that party directly or indirectly;

3. knows that the third party is likely to rely on his or her report in deciding whether or not to engage in the transaction in contemplation.

Ironically, this resounding affirmation of the restricted view on proximity produced a mixed reception in the auditing profession, some commentators almost suggesting that the Caparo judgment had suddenly rendered all accounts useless because it was no longer possible for any party to sue if they later proved to be misleading.

The mistake was to equate information that is useful with that which is legally actionable. A great deal of information is disseminated throughout the public domain that is valuable for a variety of purposes, but in which a negligible slip cannot sustain a successful lawsuit. The published accounts of a public company are in such a category. The problem with Caparo's situation was that its bid for the target company, itself listed, was rejected by the Fidelity board, and there was therefore no possibility of obtaining information relevant to the bid decision other than what was already in public circulation.

The judgments delivered in respect of third party reliance on accounts of private companies must therefore be carefully distinguished, since they referred to steps which purchasers could and should have taken to protect themselves – steps simply not available to a prospective purchaser making a hostile bid. Such a purchaser's inability to sue, following Caparo, adds to the considerable risks he or she is already taking when pursuing an unwelcome bid semi-blind. But the solution, if there is one, lies elsewhere than being able simply to blame the target company's auditors.

A notable exception to the restricted principles of legal proximity now formulated may be discovered in the findings of the Court of Appeal in *Morgan Crucible plc* v. *Hill Samuel & Others* (1991): the advisers and auditors of a target company may well be liable to a known bidder in respect of misleading forecasts and other representations made in the course of rejecting the unwelcome bid. This case was settled, however, before proceeding to a full trial.

The Al-Saudi Banque case

A High Court judge ruled (*Al-Saudi Banque* v. *Clark Pixley* [1990] Z WLR 344) that auditors are not liable for losses suffered by banks which lend money on the strength of accounts on which the auditors have given an unqualified report. Ten plaintiff banks had brought a negligence suit against the auditors of a company, Gallic Credit (GC), to which they had lent money over the period 1980 to 1982.

The business operations of GC consisted of providing import/export trade finance to its overseas customers. Advances by the company were secured by bills of exchange accepted by customers and drawn in the company's favour. They were negotiated to the banks to secure their advances to the company. These bills of exchange were shown in the company's audited accounts and represented virtually all the assets on the balance sheet. Following allegations that a large part of GC's business was fraudulent and the bills of exchange were worthless, GC was compulsorily wound up. The banks' advances were unsecured and they then sued the auditors for negligence in examining the company's accounts and in making reports which were stated to be 'true and fair'.

The Court held that the auditors were not liable in negligence to the banks and did not owe them a duty of care in respect to the preparation of reports on which the banks claimed to have relied. To establish a duty of care in relation to a negligent misstatement three conditions must be satisfied: (1) it must be reasonably foreseeable that the statement will be relied on by the plaintiff; (2) proximity must exist between the parties, and (3) it must be reasonable to impose this duty of care. Although it may be foreseeable that prospective lenders would take the accounts into consideration, there is no relationship between the auditors and the banks which would give rise to the creation of a duty of care.

The McNaughton case

In *McNaughton* v. *Hicks Anderson* the accountants were again found to owe no duty of care to the plaintiff, a purchaser of their client's business – although the judge's rationale included the *reasonableness* of reliance on statements made by the accountants in the context of the acquisition, and on the company's latest (although unaudited) accounts. After the draft accounts were prepared, a meeting took place between the purchasers and the accountants, at which the latter confirmed, in response to a specific question, that following rationalization the company was now 'breaking even or doing marginally worse', when it was in fact already insolvent. The three Appeal Court judges concurred in applying the principles formulated in the Caparo judgement (see above) requiring a more restrictive approach to liability in tort to be applied. They held that no duty of care was owed by the accountants for the following reasons:

1. The accounts in question were in draft and should not have been regarded as final.
2. The accountants' role in the negotiations had been limited to the meeting.
3. The purchasers were experienced businessmen and it would be anticipated that they would consult independent accountants.
4. The reply given at the meeting was far too general and it could not have been foreseen that it would be relied on without further pre-takeover investigation.

The judgment, in effect, reinstated the old adage *caveat emptor*, reaffirming the view of Mr Justice Woolf in *Lloyd Cheyham Ltd* v. *Littlejohn Frazer* (see above):

> While the purchaser no doubt believed in the merits of the claim in fact he was placing a wholly unjustified responsibility on the auditors. He failed to obtain the usual warranties or make the usual enquiries before investing and then sought to blame his loss on the failure of the auditors to provide him with the protection which he did not provide for himself. While it is right that auditors should exercise a duty of care to those who they appreciate will rely on their audited accounts this duty does not mean that a purchaser need not exercise any care to protect himself.

The Berg case

The judgment in the case of *Berg Sons & Co. Ltd* v. *Adams* (1992) further consolidated the principles of restricted proximity. The Berg company was a commodity trader that went into insolvent liquidation in 1983 due to the actions of its principal shareholder and *de facto* proprietor.

The third party joint-plaintiff was a finance house that discounted Berg's bills receivable and provided finance on bills that Berg itself had discounted for third parties. It claimed that it was owed a duty of care by the auditors, since they were aware that it was extending credit to Berg and it was foreseeable that the plaintiff would rely on the audited accounts when deciding whether or not to continue to extend credit on the bills of exchange which subsequently proved to be irrecoverable.

When auditing Berg's 1982 accounts, the auditors had received assurances from the acceptor of certain bills, and from Berg's director and principal shareholder, that these bills would be honoured on their due dates. In the judge's view, this evidence was unsatisfactory and should have led to an audit report qualified on grounds of uncertainty. Yet on the proximity question, the judge cited *Al-Saudi Banque* v. *Clark Pixley* (1989) (also approved by the Caparo judges), stating that foreseeability that a lender might rely on audited accounts was not enough to establish a duty. There had to be a specific relationship between the auditor's function – in this case, to meet statutory requirements – and the transaction for which the plaintiff claimed to have relied on his work. The discount house's transactions were too remote from reporting on the accounts for stewardship purposes and the claim therefore failed.

The Galoo case

The 1993 case of *Galoo & Others* v *Bright Grahame & Murray* is particularly significant in that it concerned causation rather than proximity *per se*. The plaintiffs supported the Galoo company, a subsidiary, with very substantial funding on the basis of its audited financial statements. They claimed that had the accounts been properly prepared and audited, they would have known much earlier that the subsidiary was in fact insolvent and huge losses would have been avoided. The Court held, however, that the company's continuation provided merely the *opportunity to incur losses*, and that the risk of making losses was implicit in trading generally.

In English law causation requires proof of a more direct connection, and in this case the Court was satisfied that the trading losses of Galoo were not caused by any negligence (which was never proved) on the part of its auditors.

Anthony v Wright

It was held in the case of *Anthony* v *Wright* that investors who lost money in a collective investment vehicle due to the frauds of the directors of its operating company, Garston Amhurst Associates Ltd, were owed no duty by the company's auditors, Sieff Davidson & Co, arising from the latter's failure to expose those frauds.

The investors, conceding that they had not relied on the audited accounts of GAA before making their investments, based their unsuccessful proximity claim on the fact that the auditors would have foreseen the possibility of loss if the invested funds were misappropriated by the directors. The trial judge, however, concluded that an action by the liquidators against the directors would be the appropriate remedy in such circumstances.

ADT v Binder Hamlyn

In the 1995 case of *ADT plc* v *BDO Binder Hamlyn* in the High Court Mr Justice May held that Binder Hamlyn, as auditors of Britannia Securities Group prior to its acquisition by ADT in 1990, were liable to ADT for losses allegedly suffered as a result of the takeover. It was held that Britannia's true worth was some £65 million less than the consideration paid, and interest and costs over the past six years had swollen this to £105 million, against which the firm's insurance cover of £71 million left individual partners with uninsured personal liability.

An ADT director told the Court that, at a crucial pre-takeover meeting, Binder's audit partner confirmed, in response to a specific question, that he stood by Britannia's audited 1989 financial statements as giving a true and fair view of the state of the company's affairs, and that ADT had relied on this reaffirmation in deciding to proceed with the proposed acquisition.

The judge held that the audit partner, in standing by the accounts, '*assumed responsibility to ADT for the professional competence with which they had been prepared*' and that ADT placed reliance on his statement.

> So far as Binders admit that they were in certain respects negligent in the auditing and certification of those accounts, it follows that they were in breach of the responsibility which I have held that they assumed.

At the time of preparing this edition the defendants were appealing the High Court's decision.

Some commentators proclaimed the ruling to be an implied reversal of the judgment in *Caparo*, and that on this basis Binder's appeal had a good chance of being allowed. It should, however, be remembered that the Caparo judges laid down the proximity criteria for a successful third-party action against auditors in tort to be:

1. the auditor is aware of the transaction that the third party is contemplating;
2. the auditor knows that the statement in contention will be communicated to that party; and
3. the auditor knows that the third party is likely to rely on his statement in deciding whether to engage in the transaction.

On this basis the Caparo action failed, as described above. The *ADT* v *Binder Hamlyn* circumstances, however, appear to be distinguishable, and the appeal is awaited with considerable interest by the whole profession. It should also be noted that Caparo had little to assist them beyond the audited accounts of the target company, whereas ADT enjoyed the possibility of full due diligence work by their own advisers. Such extensive reliance on Britannia's accounts and audit, as alleged by ADT, is therefore surprising. It is, however, also to be noted that there was no admission of negligence by the auditors of Fidelity in the Caparo action.

The overwhelming case for reform

The imbalance between risk and reward in auditing has become so pronounced on the side of risk that the profession has made a concerted effort to alert government to the need for statutory change. The major firms, despite their size and resources, are naturally the most vulnerable, since they audit all the largest enterprises, and collapse of one of these invariably leads to litigation against all potential targets, among which auditors feature prominently, irrespective of fault. One consequence is that insurance cover is virtually unobtainable for the largest practices, who therefore see a major claim as prospective extinction.

Possible reforms currently under consideration include:

▶ repeal of section 310, *Companies Act 1985*, which would have the effect of allowing auditors to agree contractual liability limits with their clients, just as any other professionals (including accountants acting in that capacity) are able to do;

▶ setting a statutory 'cap' – either as an absolute amount (as in Germany) or by means of a formula – which would serve as the measure of auditors' maximum liability for negligence;

▶ introducing a system of proportional liability to replace joint and several liability, which at present gives plaintiffs a choice of defendants from whom to attempt to recover the full extent of their losses, irrespective of any rational measure of proportional fault;

▶ admitting the principle of contributory negligence to actions brought in contract, which would allow the Court to recognise the extent to which directors of defrauded companies had failed to safeguard their companies' assets;

▶ introducing the legal concept of limited liability partnerships on the US model that will serve to combine the benefits of incorporation with the advantages of partnership status.

Despite the overwhelming case for significant reform, it remains to be seen whether parliamentary time will be found for its enactment.

10.1.2 Liability under statute

Civil liability – officers of companies

The civil liability of the officers of a company arises in connection with the civil offences of misfeasance and breach of trust. It was decided in both the Kingston Cotton Mill and the London and General Bank cases at the end of the last century that, for the purposes of the above provisions the auditor was to be regarded as an officer of the company.

There is a 'safety clause' under section 727, however, that where, in any proceedings for negligence, default, breach of duty, or breach of trust against an officer or an auditor, it appears to the court hearing the case:

1. that he is or may be liable; but
2. that he has acted honestly and reasonably; and
3. that, having regard to all the circumstances of the case, including those connected with his appointment, he ought fairly to be excused for the negligence,

the court may relieve him wholly or partly on such terms as it may see fit. (Section 727 applies equally to civil and criminal liability.)

Criminal liability – the Insolvency Act 1986

Sections 206–15, the winding-up sections, all involve criminal offences, and in each case reference is made to 'officers' of the company. The question has therefore arisen as to how far, if at all, the auditor may be regarded as an officer of the company for the purposes of these sections. The section on fraudulent trading (*CA 1985*, section 458) imposes criminal penalties irrespective of whether the company is wound up.

Criminal liability – the Theft Act 1968

The *Theft Act 1968* repealed the *Larceny Acts 1861* and *1916* and *Falsification of Accounts Act 1875*, and re-enacted many provisions contained in the earlier statutes. Under sections 17 and 18, an officer of a company may be imprisoned for up to seven years if he destroys, defaces, conceals or falsifies any account, record or document required for any accounting purpose; or, in furnishing information, produces or uses any account, record, etc., which to his knowledge is or may be materially misleading, false or deceptive. In view of the decision in R. v *Shacter* (1960) it is to be assumed that the term 'officer' includes the auditor.

Section 15(i) of the *Theft Act* provides: 'A person who by any deception dishonestly obtains property belonging to another, with the intention of permanently depriving the other of it, shall on conviction or indictment be liable to imprisonment for a term not exceeding ten years.'

Section 16(i) states: 'A person who by any deception dishonestly obtains for himself or another any pecuniary advantage shall on conviction or indictment be liable to imprisonment for a term not exceeding five years.' Cases of pecuniary advantage arise where debts or charges are reduced, evaded or deferred; or overdrafts and insurance policies are negotiated on improved terms; or opportunity is given to earn greater remuneration or win money by betting (section 16). (Note that offences under sections 15, 16 and 17 are extended to 'officers' of companies and members.)

Under section 19 an officer may be imprisoned for up to seven years if shown to have published or concurred in publishing a written statement or account which to his knowledge is or may be materially misleading, false or deceptive, with intent to deceive members or creditors about the company's affairs. This section is very similar to section 84 of the *Larceny Act 1861*, which it replaced.

It was under the latter section of the *Larceny Act 1861* that Lord Kylsant was convicted in the case of R. v *Kylsant & Morland* (1931). In this case, criminal proceedings were taken against the chairman and the auditor of the Royal Mail Steam Packet Co. Ltd, the allegation being that the chairman had issued false annual reports to the shareholders with intent to deceive, and that the auditor had been guilty of aiding and abetting the issue of such false reports. Both the chairman and the auditor were acquitted of this charge, but the chairman, on a further charge, was found guilty of publishing a prospectus which he knew to be false in a material particular.

For some years the Royal Mail Co. had incurred actual trading losses, but its published accounts revealed considerable profits available for dividend. This position was largely brought about by the utilization of taxation and other reserves created in past years and no longer required for the purposes for which they were made. It was alleged by the prosecution that the result of such adjustments was to cause shareholders to believe that the company was trading profitably, whereas it was in fact making losses. The specific charge against the defendants concerned the issue of false reports to shareholders with intent to deceive, in that the profit and loss account showed a profit of £440,000 'including adjustment of taxation reserves'. In fact, the company had traded at a loss of some £300,000, but this was concealed by the transfer of £740,000 from taxation reserves no longer required.

Despite the obvious inadequacy of the form of disclosure employed, Mr Morland (the auditor) was acquitted following a superbly assembled defence by Sir Patrick Hastings, based entirely on the extraordinary observation that all accountants appeared to be doing exactly the same thing. To quote from Sir Patrick's own story of the case: 'Whether or not the accountancy practice was to be commended was in our view, wholly immaterial. The charge we had to meet was a charge of dishonesty, and if it could be shown that Mr Morland had merely adopted the customary practice, it would be very difficult for anyone to accuse him of dishonesty.'

The section of the *Larceny Act 1861*, under which this prosecution against the auditor was brought, referred to 'officers', and it may reasonably be assumed that its counterpart section in the *Theft Act 1968* (section 19) similarly includes auditors as officers.

10.2 Auditors and fraud detection

The subject of fraud detection has arisen in a number of contexts throughout this volume. Nevertheless, it is of sufficient importance to justify a separate section in this chapter, particularly since there would appear to be a considerable divergence of views, especially when contrasting the profession's own attitudes with a general public expectation of the auditor's role.

10.2.1 Contrasting attitudes to fraud detection – is the auditor responsible?

Some auditors persist in adopting the attitude that no liability in this direction exists. Evidence of this may still be found in engagement letters that attempt to establish a total disclaimer of responsibility for fraud detection: a position both unrealistic and without legal basis.

It should be remembered that the engagement letter is the document in which the essential contractual relationship is encapsulated, and that the auditor invariably asks the client to acknowledge its status by signing a copy and returning it. The stance adopted in SAS 140 quite reasonably relates the auditor's responsibility to frauds which are material in relation to the financial statements, and hence directly affect the auditor's reporting responsibilities on the truth and fairness of the financial statements.

There are two reasons for seriously questioning the validity of a disclaimer on fraud responsibility. First, after declaring such a stance in the engagement letter, most auditors then ignore the sanctuary it ostensibly affords by the manner in which they conduct the audit – as if they never quite believed it anyway. Secondly, the high incidence of out-of-court settlements of negligence claims under this very heading reveals a considerable divergence of the proclaimed 'disclaimer' and the reality of public expectation.

As far as the first of these factors is concerned, procedures often include an intensive examination and evaluation of internal control systems, often employing specially designed questionnaires. Even a superficial glance at a typical ICQ reveals an obsession with 'who does what' in the organization of each department. The vast majority of questions are drafted so as to highlight strongly any overlap of functions relating respectively to (1) authorization of transactions, (2) custody and handling of assets, and (3) recording of transactions; and any potential overlapping thus revealed leads automatically to weightier substantive checking in the suspect areas. Why such concern over this particular form of delineation? The answer must include potential fraud.

It could be argued that fraud, if it exists, may well affect the view presented by the accounts – on which it is undoubtedly the auditor's primary responsibility to report – and some audit work in this style is therefore necessary. This does not explain, though, the heavy emphasis of work which is directly or indirectly orientated towards the detection of irregularity, both potential and real. Perhaps those who first formulated the 'systems-based' approach some thirty-five years ago did not think of this. If the spread of procedures applied in practice were to reflect accurately the relative importance of stated audit objectives, far more time would be spent on checking the accuracy of the records and their translation into final accounts, and correspondingly less time spent on appraising and evaluating control systems – although the two are obviously connected.

If, as it appears, auditors' actions tend to belie their words, so too does the level of negligence claims for failure to detect fraud. Recently published statistics clearly demonstrate that a high proportion of out-of-court settlements relate to this very matter. It seems that the basis of many negligence claims is not that the audited accounts fail to give a true and fair view, but are rather contested on the age-old criterion of 'reasonableness' or, more crudely, 'what does the man on the Clapham omnibus expect of his auditor?' Fraud detection would undoubtedly feature high on his expectations list.

It is fair to state that the auditor's degree of responsibility for fraud detection cannot at this moment be quantified; further, that tendencies to cover claims with insurance, to settle at any price, and to adopt untenable postures in letters, do not help matters.

SAS 110 on the auditor's responsibility for fraud detection gives further support to the principles indicated in SAS 140 on engagement letters, particularly that those irregularities which are sufficiently material to affect the truth and fairness of the financial statements should be discovered in the course of normal audit procedures.

10.2.2 Auditors and paid cheques

The majority of cases brought against auditors under contract law relate to failure to detect and report employee or management fraud, the company being the plaintiff.

In many instances of employee fraud in which company funds have been misappropriated, auditors have found it difficult to marshal an adequate defence due to their failure to examine paid cheques held by the client company's bank. Such a test would have revealed the true identity of payees paid fraudulently.

The examination by auditors of paid cheques forms part of their compliance and substantive testing programmes. In the former case, auditors will wish to ensure that the signatories are authorized by current mandates, perhaps requiring reference to monetary size criteria. Substantive tests will focus on consistency of detail between accounting records and cheques, including dates of payment (differences possibly indicating a window-dressed cut-off point at the year-end); and, most important, names of payees.

Auditors will also wish to note any endorsements, ostensibly made over by the scheduled payee to unknown (or known) third parties. The possibilities in this area for deception by management and fraud by employees are both wide and various, and need not be fully explored here. What is clear, however, is that in many cases auditors require access to paid cheques if they are to do their work properly.

Developments in computerization of banking operations have caused some banks to cease their practice of automatically returning paid cheques to customers, and branch managers sometimes display reluctance, no doubt for reasons of containing administrative costs, to provide paid cheques in cases where these were required for audit purposes only.

The ICAEW discussed the problem with the Committee of London Clearing Bankers (CLCB) and a joint guidance note (TR 472) was issued in April 1982. This gave auditors the assurances they sought – in particular, that the service of returning paid cheques will continue to be provided, and that the cheques will otherwise be retained for a minimum of three years.

In an APC published guidance statement, auditors were in effect warned against the consequences of disregarding the objective need to inspect paid cheques in the ordinary course of their work especially when required by circumstances. Despite this, auditors sometimes fail to examine cheques in circumstances when it would be appropriate to do so, the usual reason being the banks' apparent reluctance to co-operate, despite the above policy agreed with the CLCB.

In some cases, a bank's attitude may be reflected in a relatively high level of charges for the service, rather than outright decline. These charges are obviously unpopular with client companies and tend to isolate the auditors, making it more difficult for them to insist on the cheques being returned. The entire issue was re-examined by the ICAEW and the British Bankers Association in 1993, following which a fully revised policy statement, superseding the 1982 version, was issued.

Banks' charges – the inconsistency

Part of the difficulty was the lack of a consistent policy on the service itself and the levying of charges. The 1982 joint guidance note made it perfectly clear that the question of charges was entirely a matter for each individual customer and his bank. It added, however, that auditors should consider whether they really require the routine return of all paid cheques or whether their needs could be met at less cost in some other way, for example, by requesting selected cheques for particular audit purposes.

Unfortunately, however, it seemed that some banks charged more for returning specially selected cheques than for the routine return of all cheques or samples thereof. Variations of policy persist even between different branches of the same clearing bank, and it is clearly sensible for auditors to encourage client companies to come to a firm arrangement with bank managers, including the basis of any charges, well before any requests are formally issued. In this way few surprises should be caused when requests are received by the bank.

In the majority of cases, auditors will wish to examine only a small sample of paid cheques, but they are solely responsible for determining the size and construction of that sample. The great advantage of having all cheques returned is that the auditors can then perform their tests without anyone else (including even bank personnel) being aware of which cheques have been included in the sample.

The importance of this feature is illustrated by a recent case in which, ironically, it was the auditors' very insistence on inspecting cheques that facilitated a fraud of considerable proportions. The bank branch concerned offered to reduce the charges for its service if the return of cheques could be confined to a sample of one month to be specified by the auditors. The month of September was selected and duly notified – but not confidentially – to the bank, the company secretary becoming aware of the request.

Knowing that the auditors would see only the September cheques, during October and for two months thereafter (when he departed without trace) the secretary made out several cheques to 'ABA' (a regular supplier's approved abbreviation), easily converted after signature into 'A.B. Arthur' – the name of an account specially opened by him in another town.

Another case demonstrated an unexpected feature of audit work on returned cheques. A life assurance underwriting agency's auditors noticed a sudden and sharp drop in the incidence of death claims following the departure of the company's managing clerk. He had forewarned his successor that this would be the case 'because I decided to clear up all the old outstanding claims before leaving, to give you a clean start'.

The auditors decided, sensibly, to pay particular attention to the settlement of death claims for the period prior to the clerk's departure, including an examination of returned cheques and related documentation. The supporting hospital letters and death certificates (always copies anyway) looked authentic enough, and the returned cheques, all signed by the directors as per mandates, were correctly made out to the estates of deceased policyholders, or other properly authorized agents on behalf of beneficiaries.

One eagle-eyed audit junior, blessedly free of any preconceptions of 'what auditors are supposed to look for', noticed that every cheque in the sample, regardless of the geographical location of the ostensible payee, was either rubberstamped as presented for clearing at a major building society in Gloucester, or at Gloucester branches of the clearing banks.

The death claims and all supporting papers were in fact very clever forgeries, and accounts had been opened at the building society in the names of the authentic sounding payees. A few cheques had been endorsed over to Gloucester publicans or shopkeepers, but were nevertheless paid in for clearing in the same city.

The police were called in and the perpetrator was duly apprehended. The method used for establishing the extent of the fraud was to telephone life assurance policy-holders in respect of whom death claims had been submitted in the previous five years – clearly a task of some delicacy. The majority were alive and well and did not take kindly to being asked whether they had recently died. (What the clerk had done with the post-demise premiums was, of course, another mysterious aspect of this unusual fraud.)

It would be a mistake to infer from the foregoing examples that the lessons are primarily relevant to auditors of small companies. There are lessons for internal auditors and even for audit committees of major enterprises. In all cases, however, the auditors' facility for inspecting paid cheques, if considered necessary, is surely beyond question.

The 1993 joint statement of the ICAEW's Auditing Committee and the British Bankers' Association on paid cheques is reproduced below.

Introduction

1. Traditionally, clearing banks returned paid cheques to their customers with their statements. In recent years, however, this practice has diminished as banks have sought to reduce their costs. The provision of paid cheques to auditors was previously addressed in a guidance note issued in 1982 (TR472) by the Consultative Committee of Accountancy Bodies, following consultations with the then Committee of London Clearing Bankers.

2. This guidance note, which replaces TR472, returns to the subject of paid cheques in the light of recent changes in auditing and banking practice, and the additional security afforded by the *Cheques Act 1992*. Its principal objectives are as follows:

    (a) to encourage auditors to consider using alternative, more cost-effective ways of obtaining audit evidence (where possible) rather than examining paid cheques;

    (b) to encourage auditors to advise clients to adopt rigorous controls over cheque payments; and

    (c) where it is considered necessary to examine paid cheques, to encourage auditors to do so in a cost-effective manner that accords, as far as possible, with the banks' preferred methods for providing paid cheques.

    However, this guidance note does not seek to give detailed procedural guidance.

3. The contents of this guidance note have been agreed between the Institute of Chartered Accountants in England and Wales and the British Bankers' Association. Banks which have issued guidelines to their branches based on this guidance note are listed in an appendix,

which also indicates their preferred methods for providing paid cheques. However, this listing is merely indicative of what is available; it is not prescriptive, and the facilities offered by individual branches of the same bank may vary. Nevertheless, auditors should normally be able to obtain paid cheques even where they cannot use the preferred method.

4. The charges levied by a bank are the subject of a contractual agreement between the bank and the customer. Where an auditor does require to examine a paid cheque for audit purposes the resulting charge must be borne by the bank's customer and not the auditor.

Audit evidence

5. In many circumstances, such as when controls over purchasing and payments are adequate, it is not necessary to examine paid cheques. However, where, for example, controls are weak or there are concerns about the authorization of cheque payments or the identity of payees, auditors may want to examine paid cheques in order to obtain assurance that business funds have been disbursed as accounted for, and that liabilities are not understated or expenses overstated. Particular risks are fraudulent endorsement (but see paragraphs 9 and 10 below on the *Cheques Act 1992*), and falsification of the cheque payee and cash book. The auditor may seek to examine a paid cheque for the following purposes:

    (a) to identify unusual circumstances, such as alterations or endorsements, or cheques made payable to cash or bearer: in such circumstances, the auditor will need to examine supporting documentation;

    (b) to confirm that the payee and amount match the details in the client's accounting records;

    (c) to confirm that it has been signed by an authorized signatory; and

    (d) when the auditor judges it to be necessary, to check other details such as the date, and the name and location of the bank which cleared the cheque.

6. With regard to purchase ledger items, it will often be possible to perform substantive tests on balances (such as examining third party evidence of receipt and reconciling suppliers' statements) which will make a physical examination of paid cheques unnecessary. Nominal ledger items may be more problematical, and in the absence of other evidence it may be desirable to examine the relevant paid cheques. Other evidence may be obtained from an analytical review of the profit and loss account, examination of supporting evidence or from a review of internal controls.

7. In deciding whether to make a physical examination of paid cheques, an auditor should consider the potential cost to his client of such an exercise and whether other, more cost-effective, audit techniques could be employed.

Internal controls

8. Good internal controls over cheque payments are designed to prevent the fraudulent or irregular diversion of funds and to ensure that creditors and expenses are not materially under- or overstated. An adequate system of internal controls is likely to include the

following procedures:

(a) rigorous controls over the custody of cheque books, and the issue and completion of cheques;

(b) the listing of authorized signatories, together with details of their authorization limits. Such records should also clearly set out where a payment needs to be authorized by more than one person;

(c) a requirement for independent documentation to support all cheque payments. Once a payment has been made, this should be clearly shown on the related documents in order to ensure that no payment is duplicated;

(d) segregation of duties to ensure that responsibilities (for authorizing cheque payments, preparing cheques, recording and signing) do not overlap; and

(e) regular bank reconciliations and independent review.

The implications for auditors of the *Cheques Act 1992*

9. Further control is afforded by the *Cheques Act 1992*. The Act gives statutory recognition to the 'account payee' crossing, in that a cheque so crossed is not transferable, and is only valid as between the drawer of a cheque and the payee. By definition, therefore, such cheques cannot be transferred by way of endorsement.

10. Most banks are now pre-printing their cheques 'account payee' since this will protect their customers from the danger of fraudulent endorsements. Where a client's cheques are pre-printed 'account payee', this should greatly reduce the risk of fraudulent endorsement, and auditors may wish to take this into account in deciding whether there is a need to examine paid cheques. If such an examination is considered necessary, photo-copies (if available – see paragraph 17(c) below) may well be sufficient. Equally, if a client does not use 'account payee' cheques, auditors may wish to consider recommending a change of policy.

Use of other payment methods

11. Auditors may also wish to consider whether a particular client could curtail the use of cheques through adopting other methods of payment. Alternatives include CHAPS, BACS, standing orders and direct debits. Other electronic methods of payment may also be available, and details should be available from the account-holding branch. The audit implications of alternative methods of payment will need to be taken into account when planning and carrying out an audit.

Means of obtaining paid cheques

12. Banks keep paid cheques – where they have not already been returned to the customer or his agent – for varying periods. However, the Money Laundering Regulations 1993 require that supporting evidence and records of transactions (which include paid cheques) must be retained for a period of at least five years after the date on which the relevant transaction or

series of transactions is completed. Such records must be the original documents or copies admissible in court proceedings. Where paid cheques are not returned to the customer or his agent they should be kept, in their original form, for at least one year. Thereafter, paid cheques will be available – if not in their original form then in the form of legally admissible copies – for the remainder of the five-year period mentioned above. The banks appreciate that original paid cheques may be required for audit purposes for up to 10 months (or longer in exceptional circumstances) after the end of the relevant accounting period. Many banks retain paid cheques in their original form for more than the one year provided for in the Money Laundering Guidance Notes (which supplement the Money Laundering Regulations 1993), and banks have agreed to take account of audit requirements in any future review of their retention policy for original paid cheques.

13. While a bank can normally provide paid cheques if a customer asks for them, finding the cheques may well take time. Typically, paid cheques are stored at bank branches, and are filed in batches according to their date of payment. Within each batch, the cheques may be sorted into account number order, although not all banks do this.

14. Alternatively, some banks operate centralized clearing systems, in which case paid cheques are unlikely to be returned to an account holding branch, but will probably be stored centrally.

15. Even in a medium-sized branch, a single day's batch of paid cheques may number up to 2,000 items. Retrieving paid cheques will almost certainly involve a significant amount of manual work, and this will increase in proportion to the number of batches examined. A bank will usually charge its customer for providing him – or his auditor – with paid cheques, and the charge is likely to increase significantly as the number of items to be retrieved increases.

16. If it is decided that an examination of paid cheques is to be carried out, the auditor's client (that is, the account holder) should consult the account-holding branch to determine how the auditor's needs may best be met. Alternatively, the auditor may approach the branch direct if the account holder has given appropriate authority.

17. The account-holding bank may have a preference for one of the following options:

    (a) To return all paid cheques to the customer concerned.
        Although most banks no longer return all paid cheques to their customers, in some cases this may be the most cost-effective way of providing paid cheques. Auditors will need to consider whether they are content for the paid cheques to be made available in this way, and the possible cost to their client.

    (b) To provide an agreed number of paid cheques direct to the auditor, the selection to be left to the account-holding branch.
        Where the auditor only needs to see a random selection of his client's paid cheques, this may be the most cost-effective method. The auditor will need to obtain an appropriate form of authority from the customer (see Appendix 2) in order that the bank can send the paid cheques direct to the auditor. He may wish to consider obtaining such an authority before an audit is undertaken, particularly if such a measure is seen as acting as a deterrent to fraud.

The number of cheques so provided will need to be agreed between the auditor and the account-holding branch (unless the auditor is content to leave this to the discretion of the branch concerned). The selection process should make due allowance for the need to guard against fraud; for example, it would normally be inadvisable to make the selection from cheques paid during the course of a few days only.

(c) To provide photocopies of paid cheques.

In some cases, it may be easier for the account-holding bank – and therefore less costly for the customer – to provide photocopies of paid cheques (or copies of comparable authenticity created by other image-retrieval procedures). Such copies should nevertheless permit an auditor to check payee names, payment authorizations, the date of a cheque, and the cheque amount. It would not normally be feasible for a photocopy of the reverse of a cheque to be provided, but this is only relevant where it is considered that checks should be made for possible fraudulent endorsements (and see paragraphs 9 and 10 above).

(d) To extract cheques before they are stored, for despatch to the auditor direct.

It may be possible for a bank to extract paid cheques, and send them direct to the auditor, as part of the sorting process and before they are stored. In this case, the account-holding branch will need adequate prior notification from its customer – not less than, say, one month. In addition, the branch will need an appropriate form of authority from its customer before paid cheques can be despatched to the auditor (see Appendix 2).

(e) Provide specific paid cheques at the auditor's request.

An auditor may, from time time, need to examine a particular cheque or cheques. As already indicated (see paragraphs 12 to 15 above), this may be expensive, and such requests should not be made lightly. If such a request is to be made, the following details should be provided to the account-holding branch:

► the date the cheque was paid;

► the amount;

► the cheque number; and

► the payee name.

It should be possible to obtain this information either from the customer's own records or from his statements.

18. The methods set out above will generally be useful when selecting a sample of paid cheques throughout an audit period. However, if the audit approach only requires examining cheques in unusual circumstances, these methods may not always be appropriate.

Truncation

19. Truncation (the use of money transmission systems that restrict the movement of paper between bank branches) does not preclude the provision of documentary evidence such as cheques.

20. It is understood that, for technical and legal reasons, full truncation will probably not be introduced for some years. At present, truncation is generally limited to cheques drawn for cash, normally (but not invariably) under a pre-arranged cashing facility at a bank branch other than the branch at which the customer's account is held. In the meantime, cheques can still be provided in the manner outlined in paragraphs 12 to 17 above.

Appendix 1

Preferred methods for providing paid cheques

	Option				
	a	b	c	d	e
Name of bank	Customer return	Bank select for auditor	Photocopy	Intercept for auditor	Single items
Abbey National (1)	[not applicable]		✓(single items)	[not applicable]	
Bank of Scotland	✓		✓		✓
Barclays (4)		✓			
Clydesdale		✓			
Girobank	✓(2)	N/A	✓(3)	N/A	
Lloyds		✓(4)			
Midland (4)				✓(5)	
National Westminster (4)		✓		✓(5)	
Royal Bank of Scotland (6)		✓			
Standard Chartered	✓(7)		✓		
TSB (8)		✓			

The methods listed above correspond (reading from left to right) to the methods described in paragraphs 17(a) to 17(e) respectively.

The preferred methods indicated above will normally represent the least expensive option for the customer. Where an option is definitely not available this is shown as N/A.

Notes to table

(1) Current accounts are for personal customers only. In this case of Abbey National, therefore, it is not expected that there will normally be any need for auditors to obtain paid cheques.

(2) All paid cheques are returned to major corporate customers.

(3) For small business customers, upon request.

(4) Other listed options may also be available. Refer to the account-holding branch for further details.

(5) Prior notification required for this option (see paragraph 17 (d)).

(6) Other listed options are available in the following order of preference: (d), (e), (c) and (a).

(7) If requested by the customer.

(8) Options (a), (c) and (d) are also possible: option (e) is likely to be expensive.

Appendix 2: Suggested form of authority where paid cheques are to be sent to an auditor direct

To: [name and address of account-holding   date
    bank branch]

Dear Sirs

[NAME OF CUSTOMER AND ACCOUNT NUMBER(S)]

I should be grateful if you would provide our auditors (name and address given below) with such paid cheques or other vouchers as they may request in respect of the above account(s).

It is understood that a charge may be made for providing these items.

This authority is to remain in force until (date)/further notice.*

The name and address of our auditors are as follows:

Messrs A B & C
1 XYZ Street
Anytown
AB1 2CD

Yours faithfully

Authorized signatory**

*Delete as appropriate
**This form of authority must be signed in accordance with the current mandate held by the bank

---

10.2.3   The 'fraudulent' checklist

For as long as auditors are expected to be concerned with fraud detection, it is important that they recognize the most obvious features of this form of irregularity. The possibility of fraud occurring is always real, but in times of economic depression, when company profits are squeezed and interest rates or inflation rates are high, fraud becomes even more likely, even involving the state sector. One recent example was the fraud publicized in the press in which contractors employed by a major public authority falsely claimed sums totalling £250,000 for power station maintenance work that was never carried out. In that particular case both the contractors and their employees directly benefited from the additional false claims.

The two main areas of fraud to which auditors should always be alert are:

1. The manipulation of the financial statements by members of management, either to meet business and financial expectations, or to obtain indirect personal gain (including keeping a job).

2. The abstracting of assets (primarily cash) by either members of management or employees for personal gain.

When auditors fulfil audit and other engagements, they should consider the possibility that fraud may have been perpetrated for either or both of the reasons stated above. To help with this task, they should ask certain key questions. A list of appropriate (but not exhaustive) questions is set out below.

Manipulation of the financial statements

A 'yes' answer to any of the following indicates an increased risk that the financial statements may have been manipulated:

1. Have the company's operations deteriorated recently?
2. Do present business conditions indicate potential future difficulties for the company?
3. Is the company likely to have difficulty in meeting its financial obligations as they become due?
4. Is there any intention either to liquidate or to curtail significantly the scale of operations?
5. Does the company propose to raise substantial additional finance in the near future?
6. Is there likely to be a contest for control of the company in the near future?
7. Is there likely to be a change of control of the company in the near future?
8. Is more than the usual significance likely to be attached to financial statements?

Abstraction of assets

1. Are excessive discretionary powers granted either to new employees or to employees of comparatively low calibre?
2. Are wage levels below the average for either the locality or the industry?
3. Is there unexplained extravagance by any employees (especially those who are in key positions and have custody of assets)?
4. Does any employee refuse to take his due holiday (which may be because he wishes to avoid having his duties subjected to the independent scrutiny of a relief employee)?
5. Are any employees either excessively uncooperative or antagonistic towards the auditors or are they excessively co-operative?
6. Does a single individual unaccountably dominate the activities of any department, branch or activity?
7 Are accounting records consistently written up a long time after the transactions they record have taken place?
8. Are filing systems such that, for no apparent reason, documents are difficult to retrieve?

A positive answer to any of these questions does not necessarily mean that fraud is taking place. However, it does indicate that auditors need to consider carrying out *further* audit tests to overcome the obvious inherent risks. The decision to extend tests will depend upon the examination of various factors and will require consultation among the partner, manager and senior responsible for the engagement.

No matter how sophisticated auditing techniques become, there can never be any effective substitute for verification by means of direct inspection, and it is worth noting that many notorious frauds might have come to light much earlier had the auditors concerned paid more attention to this rather obvious point. Two instances, now firmly established in twentieth-century auditing history, are briefly described below.

Although these notorious cases occurred many years ago, their circumstances remain relevant today, and they serve as timeless warnings to auditors everywhere of the importance of remaining alert to suspicious symptoms encountered in the course of audit work, including analytical review anomalies that require thorough investigation prior to signing off, and of direct physical verification.

McKesson and Robbins Inc.

The famous McKesson and Robbins swindle in the United States during the 1930s arose from a conspiracy among the four brothers who headed this pharmaceutical company to make the company appear far more profitable and financially more substantial than it really was. This was achieved by fabricating documentation which purported to reflect transactions that had, in fact, never taken place. The illusion was created of a vast amount of trading activity, which the auditors meticulously authenticated via the forged documentation. They were regarded by the Securities and Exchange Commission (SEC) as negligent in the execution of their duties in view of their failure (1) to confirm the stock levels by direct inspection, and (2) to confirm the level of debtors by direct circularization. These assets were overstated by no less than $25 million. These two vital procedures became mandatory for auditors of listed companies in the USA immediately following this celebrated case.

Giant Stores Corporation

The Giant Stores Corporation went public in 1969. Between 1969 and 1973 the corporation expanded the number of its outlets from six to forty-three. To finance this expansion, it made three public stock offerings and took out substantial loans. In order to obtain finance for further expansion, management considered it imperative that Giant's results for the year ended 29 January 1972 met market expectations. The management of the corporation suppressed an anticipated loss for the year of $2.5 million and the corporation published a profit of $1.2 million on a turnover of $64 million. The major part of the loss was concealed by creating false credits from suppliers totalling $1 million (which were deducted from trade creditors), and by suppressing $1.4 million of suppliers' invoices at the end of the year.

The deficiencies in the audit procedures which were identified in the SEC report are summarized below:

1. *Inadequate third party confirmation procedures.* The majority of the false credits arose in respect of a few major suppliers and were supported only by the internal documentation of the client. The explanations offered by the client's management were often incomplete and were the subject of frequent change. In one instance, three different irreconcilable explanations were offered to support an amount of $257,000.

   The auditors did not insist on sending written confirmations to third parties, but with the permission of the client, agreed a number of balances by telephone. In each instance, the client telephoned the supplier and passed the telephone to the auditor. In at least one case it since became apparent that the person with whom the balance was 'confirmed' was an impostor.

2. *Acceptance of unreliable representations from management.* The audit was conducted under considerable duress. Giant asked for a removal of the partner, and senior management physically and orally threatened the audit staff. Management offered inconsistent explanations of major adjusting items. Despite these circumstances, considerable audit reliance was placed on management representations in preference to, and almost to the exclusion of, third party confirmations.

3. *Failure to recognize an accumulation of irregularities.* The auditors accepted inconclusive audit evidence for a series of accounting adjustments. Several of the adjustments were material to the appreciation of the financial statements, and others were material in total. The auditors failed to appreciate the cumulative significance of the contentious items, and consequently they applied neither sufficient nor adequate verification procedures to ensure that no material misstatement was present in the financial statements.

4. *Inadequate adjustment of errors.* The work conducted on accruals by the auditors indicated a substantial understatement of trade liabilities at the year-end. The test on suppliers' statements at the year-end produced an estimated understatement of liability of $290,000, and an examination of invoices received after the year-end indicated an understatement of liability of $500,000. Both these amounts were recorded in the working papers. The adjustment subsequently agreed with the client was $260,000. The auditors considered this figure was adequate because, in their opinion, the client had valued stock conservatively, and thus the 'net effect' was acceptable. The SEC heavily criticized the practice of 'trading off' adjustments to the financial statements. The report stated that each accounting area must be considered in isolation and stated in the financial statements at a figure consistent with that indicated by the evidence obtained.

5. *Structure of the audit team.* The responsibilities of the audit team were ill-defined. The initial audit team did not have the specialized experience to test adequately all the accounting areas, primarily stock and creditors.

   With the existing staff under pressure from the client, two additional partners were called in to provide specialized assistance but this caused conflict and confusion. Eventually, when the client pressed strongly for the finalization of the financial statements, a supervising partner was brought in. He was not fully informed of the facts of the situation by his colleagues, notably the serious doubts over the attitude and the integrity of the management. The report states that, at a final meeting with the client, he acted more as an arbitrator than an auditor, and he expected and obtained compromises on various contentious adjustments.

The matters set out above are relevant to a number of audit procedures. Auditors should ensure that the planning and conduct of audit work includes:

1. The provision of personnel of sufficient seniority and experience to staff the engagement adequately.
2. The identification of contentious areas and adjustments that may interact to produce material misstatements in the financial statements, and the adequate verification of the adjusting items.
3. The requirement to obtain reliable audit evidence in each accounting area. Auditors should consider carefully the reliance that they are able to place on management representations to provide audit evidence. Where they have reason to doubt the integrity of management they must obtain increased assurance from alternative audit procedures, and these should incorporate independent verification. Where they apply third party confirmation procedures, they should ensure that they control the conduct of these procedures.

While major frauds appear to have certain common features, a clear distinction must be drawn between, on the one hand, those that appear on the staff level (i.e. within the confines of a legitimate organizational structure), and, on the other hand, management frauds, in which the company itself has been set up as the vehicle for the intended misdemeanours.

In the former case, advantage is taken by staff of defective internal control and management will often seek redress from the auditor in cases where it is believed that more effective audit scrutiny might have revealed defalcations. From the audit point of view, although such instances are troublesome, they are not frequently encountered on a scale which involves very substantial sums.

Management frauds, however, are altogether more dangerous in that they invariably involve window-dressed accounts and, since these are publicly filed, outside investors, suppliers and creditors generally may depend upon their veracity as a primary means of assessing trading and investment risks. It is clear that the potential liability of auditors in such situations is very great indeed.

The APB issued a Standard on 'Fraud and error' (SAS 110) in 1995, and this reinforces the position that auditors' responsibilities in this area are to be related to the materiality of the effect that any fraud or error may have on the financial statements of the entity in question. Its key points may be summarized as follows:

1. Audit procedures should be designed so as to have a reasonable expectation of detecting material misstatements arising from fraud or error.

2. It is not the auditors' function to prevent fraud and error.

3. The SAS gives a definition of fraud and the extent to which the detection of fraud or error may reasonably be expected.

4. Appendix 1 to the SAS gives examples of conditions or events which may increase the risk of fraud or error. These should be assessed at the planning stage.

5. The SAS sets out the criteria to assist the auditor to determine whether he has a duty in the public interest to report his suspicions or findings to a proper authority.

6. In the last resort, particularly if fraud is suspected to pervade senior management, the auditor may consider resignation, and seek legal advice.

7. It is often the case that when frauds are discovered, ignoring those involving collusion, they were found to have been committed by trusted members of staff over whom authorization controls have been relaxed. There are also numerous instances of fraud being committed by persons with known financial difficulties or a past history of dishonesty. The planning stage should at least include some assessment of character and potential motive, even if this is limited to a brief enquiry of management as to whether they have any grounds for suspicion.

8. When fraud or error is suspected, the auditor has a responsibility to investigate further to assess materiality, but also to discuss and report his findings to management, subject to any requirement to report to a third party. It is clearly advisable not to communicate with the implicated person (or others under suspicion) in the first instance.

9. The audit report should be carefully considered. The audit engagement partner may wish to seek a second opinion from a colleague.

10. Post-fraud audit reports may need to reflect the impact on prior-year comparatives, depending on how long it was going on prior to discovery, and the possible recovery of losses from other parties.

Clients' breaches of law or regulations

Auditors are also bound to retain a reasonable responsibility for assessing the possible impact on financial statements of any breaches by audit clients of legislation or regulations governing their activities and operations, such as environmental transgressions. APB issued SAS 120 on this subject in 1995, 'Consideration of law and regulations'; its key points are summarized below:

1. The auditor should perform procedures to help identify possible or actual instances of non-compliance with those laws and regulations which provide a legal framework within which the entity conducts its business and which are central to the entity's ability to conduct its business and hence to its financial statements.

2. Suggested procedures include:
   (a) obtaining an understanding of the legal and regulatory framework applicable to the entity and industry and the procedure adopted by the entity to ensure compliance;
   (b) inspecting correspondence with relevant authorities;
   (c) enquiring of the directors;
   (d) obtaining written confirmation from the directors.

3. The auditor must be aware of the requirement under the *Criminal Justice Act 1993* to report suspected money laundering.

4. The auditor should have due regard to the requirements of the *Companies Act 1985* which relate to the financial statements, and as detailed in paragraph 23 of the SAS.

5. The SAS gives guidance regarding compliance with the *Taxes Acts*.

6. The appendix includes examples of matters which, if identified, may indicate non-compliance. Where potential non-compliance has been identified, subject to any requirement the auditor should discuss his findings with management. Where the auditor no longer has confidence in the integrity of the directors, he should report to a third party in the public interest. He should also consider reference to the matter in the audit report.

7. Controversially, the SAS requires auditors to familiarize themselves with the legal framework in which the client entity operates and to examine correspondence between the entity and any relevant regulatory authorities. This onerous duty goes further than merely seeking representations from directors regarding known or suspected regulatory transgressions.

8. In the last resort the auditor may consider resignation, and seek legal advice on any matters arising.

9. Of particular concern to auditors, including those acting for clients in a wider capacity, are:
   (a) pollution and environmental transgressions by the client;
   (b) maintaining proper accounting records;
   (c) VAT legislation breaches;
   (d) PAYE and NI liability of subcontractors or freelance workers.

Review questions

*1. One of your plc company audit clients, Little plc, with a year end of 30 June, was taken over by Growquick plc over two years ago. Growquick plc had purchased a number of the shares from a shareholder/director some years previously but did not hold a seat on the board of directors. After the audit of the last accounts, which showed a healthy profit, the takeover offer was made and, although the board of directors recommended rejection, accepted. All of the original shareholders/directors have now been replaced.

Following the AGM of two years ago you were replaced as auditor and the incoming auditor was the group auditor of Growquick plc. You raised no objection to the replacement and submitted a letter to that effect to the company.

The new auditors have now caused Growquick plc to consider taking legal action against you and the former directors of Little plc. The reason is that the profit shown within the accounts was totally incorrect and indeed should have been a loss and hence those who were responsible for the preparation of the accounts had been negligent. As the accounts had also been audited, it is alleged that the auditor must also have been negligent in the non-detection of the errors.

What should you do in this case? Do you have a case to answer and what are your possible defences?

*2. There has been a great deal of discussion relating to the detection of fraud by auditors. Before 1984 there was evidence that disclaimers were being included in letters of engagement in order to exclude responsibility in relation to fraud. Why were such disclaimers without legal foundation?

3. One of your audit clients has refused to pay the charges which are going to be levied by the bank in respect of the bank letter and the associated paid cheques which you have requested and has told the bank that since you have asked for them you will have to pay.

Draft a formal letter to your client, using fictitious names and addresses, to explain the position precisely.

4. In certain legal circumstances the auditor is referred to as an officer of the company – yet clearly this is not the case as the auditor must be independent. Outline the legal situations when the auditor is referred to as an officer and indicate why it is in no way inconsistent with the normal perception of the auditor.

The audit approach to computer systems

THIS CHAPTER DEALS WITH:

▷ interaction between computers, internal control systems and the audit approach;

▷ use of computers for audit purposes;

▷ problems associated with the use of computer bureaux and remote terminals;

▷ audit approach to accounting systems using personal computers;

▷ computer security issues.

[Comment: Certain texts which deal with this subject assume no computer knowledge whatever on the part of the reader. This is no longer a realistic assumption for a large section of the population, let alone students of accounting and auditing; for the purposes of this chapter, therefore, a passing familiarity with certain basic computer concepts is assumed, reasonably I trust. Throughout this chapter the terminology employed by the APC in its guideline 'Auditing in a computer environment' (1984) has been used.]

11.1 What difference do computers make?

Such is the magnitude of the transformation which electronic technology has wrought in data processing methods, the implications of which we consider in this chapter, that the profession has had to acknowledge that computers radically alter:

1. The way in which accounting data are recorded.
2. The way in which such recording must be controlled and authenticated.
3. The training needs and attitudes of the staff responsible, at both management and technical levels.
4. The way in which the process and its results must be audited.

A computer's capacity for producing information, in terms both of volume and speed, is vast – but it is important to recognize that every benefit has its price: for its potential as a vehicle of manipulation and fraud is equally great. Even if we leave aside questions of fraud, it is generally true that when the production of vital data is dependent on a computer, if things go wrong, they go wrong on a truly grand scale.

There are several excellent texts devoted exclusively to the audit of DP (data processing) systems, and a bibliography of these is included at the end of the chapter. Within the constraints of space it is hoped in this chapter simply to alert readers to the fact that there are implicit in all DP systems genuine security hazards related to: (1) hardware functions; (2) software deficiency, malfunction and manipulation; and (3) data loss and reconstruction, and that the auditor has a certain responsibility for testing the adequacy of the controls designed to overcome these hazards. It will be shown that these hazards do not exist, either in that form or on that scale in the conventional recording systems.

Although a certain number of technical references are unavoidable it is not my intention to suggest a need for auditing students to become computer experts in their own right; auditing skills and electronics respectively are, and will remain, very different disciplines. This is not to suggest that computer experts have no role to play in the conduct of the audit – on the contrary, both internal and external auditors now employ, in appropriate contexts, the services of technical computer staff. I stress the far-reaching effects of computers upon internal control systems and the records they produce – and hence upon the manner of executing the audit. Later sections of the chapter deal with the use of the computer itself for audit purposes, and with the problems associated with the use of computer bureaux, remote terminals and microcomputers.

The APC guideline 'Auditing in a Computer Environment' (1984)

The following notes summarize this guideline regarding internal controls:

The main control headings in computer-based systems and their relationships

The location of controls, distinguishing between those which are user-based and DP-based respectively, is illustrated in Figure 11.1.

Application controls

These are controls within a computer application which ensure the completeness and accuracy of input and processing and the validity of the resulting accounting entries. They are a combination of manual and computer-programmed procedures.

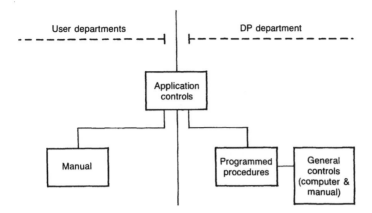

Figure 11.1   Computer-based systems – location of controls

Application controls performed by computer are not controls themselves, but parts of computer programs which allow controls to be exercised. They aid the provision of controls over completeness and accuracy of input and processing and the validity of accounting entries in the same way as the manual controls. In addition they provide control over the calculations, summarization and categorization carried out by the computer.

General controls

These are controls covering the environment within which such applications are developed, maintained and operated and they ensure the effective operation of programmed procedures.

The effects of the interrelationship between application controls and general controls on the balance between compliance and substantive testing

Evaluating and testing application controls are likely to be more cost-effective than evaluating and testing general controls. But where the satisfactory operation of programmed procedures is not assured by user controls, reliance will have to be placed on general controls, provided they have been evaluated and tested. In practice, the assurance that the auditor may draw from general controls will be limited, particularly in small installations, and consequently the auditor will be able to limit his substantive test levels only by placing reliance on manual application controls. The bias towards substantive testing is not such a disadvantage as it might be in a manual system, since vast amounts of data can be validated using a computer audit program.

The initial stages of a computer audit

There are two initial steps in the audit procedures in relation to internal controls:

(a) initial review;

(b) evaluation of internal controls.

The purpose of the initial review is to obtain a general understanding and not a detailed knowledge of the system of internal control. The aim is to identify the existence of internal controls on which the auditor may choose to place reliance.

The evaluation of internal controls (preliminary evaluation) involves evaluation of controls by means of internal control questionnaires. The internal control system will be more extensive than a manual accounting system due to the existence of programmed procedures and general controls in the data processing department.

The purposes and techniques of control

The guidelines are much more specific about the control techniques used to ensure completeness and accuracy of input and processing. They also specify additional techniques to ensure the validity of master files and standing data.

In designing a system of internal control for a computer application the whole system of processing must be considered, both manual and computer, from when the initial event occurs to the final output document review and follow-up by the user.

Within the framework of application controls the controls are divided under the following headings:

(a) completeness of input;

(b) completeness of processing;

(c) accuracy of input;

(d) accuracy of processing;

(e) validity of data processed;

(f) maintenance of data on files.

In practice some of these controls may be linked (for example, controls over completeness of input may ensure completeness of processing).

Some data require a higher degree of accuracy than others, and therefore it follows that higher standards of control should be established. Standing data, for example, require a higher degree of control than transaction data, since standing data are used in processing large numbers of transactions. Likewise data which are converted into financial terms can be of much greater importance than reference data. Of course, reference data themselves have varying degrees of importance.

Table 11.1 Application controls

	Completeness		Accuracy		Master files and standing data	
	Input	Processing	Input	Processing	Validity	Maintenance
Purpose	All transactions are recorded, input and accepted by the computer. (Control over the number of documents.) Each document is processed only once.	All input and accepted data update the master file. Output reports are complete.	Control over the data fields to ensure the accuracy of data transcribed from source to input document (where applicable) and the data are accurately converted to machine-readable form.	Accurate data are carried through processing to the master file. Computer-generated data are accurate. Output reports are accurate.	Only authorized data updates the master files. No changes to the data are made after authorization.	Data on master files cannot be changed without authority and there are no long-outstanding or unusual items on file.
Some control techniques which may be applied by the computer (programmed procedures) or by the user (manual). All rejected data must be investigated and corrected.	Control totals Matching sequence One for one Summary processing	Control total } after update Matching sequence One for one Summary processing	Control totals Matching One for one Programmed checks (e.g. reasonableness)	Control (after update) One for one Summary processing Manual reconciliation of accepted item totals with file totals	Programmed checks (e.g. authority limits) Manual authorization and review	Manual reconciliation of file totals with manual control account Exception reports

General controls

The general controls incorporated into the data processing system will cover two major aspects:

Administrative controls

These arise chiefly from the risks implicit in:

(a) concentration of power in the DP department;

(b) carrying a large number of files of important data centrally stored; and

(c) storing data in a form which is highly inflammable, concentrated, sensitive to temperature and atmospheric conditions, and dependent for processing on machinery which is susceptible to breakdown.

Systems development controls

These are intended to ensure a valid system of processing whenever new applications are devised, meeting the requirements of management and user departments. These aims are achieved by:

(a) the use of standard documentation;

(b) the use of standard procedures, wherever possible;

(c) specifying rigid authorization procedures whenever new applications are envisaged, or existing programs amended or extended;

(d) the adoption of adequate testing routines prior to implementation;

(e) instituting a comprehensive system of program and document security.

Application controls

Application controls modify the operating routines to be followed by the DP and the user departments in their relations with each other. As shown in Table 11.1, application controls cover:

(a) the preparation of input, and its transfer to the computer;

(b) the processing of data within the computer;

(c) the preparation of output and its distribution;

(d) the maintenance of master files and the standing data contained therein.

11.2   General controls 1 – administration and physical security

Since computer security is a matter of genuine concern, only carefully planned control over every aspect of the DP function can overcome the hazards involved, many of them being natural by-products of the physical nature of the hardware. The concentration of power within the DP section and the centralization of job functions also raise problems concerning the division of responsibility among staff.

Computer security must therefore be seen as a dynamic concept, a discipline in its own right which adapts to changes and developments in electronics as and when they arise. A cynic might say that the computer security industry is rather like the doctor who informs his patient that although he cannot find a cure for the ailment, he can administer a remedy which will guarantee a change of side-effects.

11.2.1 Hardware vulnerability

Although modern machines are less susceptible to environmental hazards than their earlier versions, it is still generally true that incorrect processing and data loss can easily result if temperature, humidity, dust and other similar factors are not carefully controlled. Much of the equipment is highly inflammable and fire regulations covering the computer room are quite stringent. Moreover, magnetic or electric fields anywhere near the machine or the stored data represent a danger of potentially calamitous proportions.

Many of us will have heard of the case in which a computer manager travelled to a bureau on a London Underground train, with two of his company's reels of magnetic tape in his briefcase. Unfortunately, he unwittingly chose to sit in the carriage which housed the train's magneto system, placed immediately below the floor on which his case rested. When he reached the bureau he found that the data held on tape had been totally wiped out.

Another configuration was housed on the ground floor of a four-storey building in which the ground-floor walls and ceiling were lined with asbestos as protection against fire in other parts of the building. A fire did in fact break out on the third floor, but it was some time before the fire brigade arrived; by the time the fire was eventually extinguished the ground-floor ceiling had totally collapsed onto the computer section, and little could be salvaged from the waterlogged rubble remaining.

A nationally known pharmaceutical company had great difficulty with its disk packs after a new system was installed; the experts could find no reason for the loss of data which occurred when reading from the disks. It was eventually discovered that a dust extractor, housed next to the disks, had been incorrectly wired so that its fans revolved in the wrong direction. The effect of this was to extract dust from the corridor and blast it in the general direction of the disks. Dust on the disk surfaces interfered with the reading and writing processes and was thus responsible for the data loss.

Such are the hazards. Other, similar, stories are legion, but they all point to:

1. The need for carefully planned and meticulously executed administrative controls over protection of physical DP assets.

2. The fact that no matter how rigorously the above is heeded, no system is absolutely secure, and equal thought must be given to such matters as file reconstruction procedures, standby facilities and insurance cover in a 'worst loss' situation.

Providing for these matters is by no means straightforward. Disinterested and expert advice should be taken on the question of insurance cover before entering into a contract; and standby facilities may turn out to be ineffective if they are not regularly reviewed and tested. Such facilities are normally arranged with the hardware manufacturers; or on a mutual basis with another user of similar equipment, on which essential programs can be run in the event of machine failure or breakdown. Unless regularly tested, however, it may be found that the other user's own DP needs are so extensive as to allow insufficient processing time for any meaningful standby facility. Ideally, such arrangements should be the subject of a legal agreement, guaranteeing the parties a minimum amount of machine time in the event of either of them suffering breakdown.

One may well ask to what extent the auditor is concerned with such matters. In DP, as in all other systems, the records (in terms of format, accuracy and completeness) are a product of the working of the system itself, and the auditor is necessarily concerned with the reliability of the process by which the client's records are created. Other considerations apart, there are strict legal requirements (detailed in Chapter 8) governing both the form and content of every company's accounting records. In particular, section 722 of the *Companies Act 1985* specifies that where such records are not kept in the form of bound books, adequate precautions should be taken for guarding against falsification and for facilitating its discovery. In essence, although it is the final accounts which represent the 'interface' with the audit function, the auditor can by no means ignore the processes of which these accounts are a product.

11.2.2 The basic DP configuration

Before proceeding to explain the other aspects of administrative security, it may be helpful to consider the basic diagram shown in Figure 11.2, which establishes the usual functions within a DP department using a disk/tape-based third-generation mainframe computer, with no terminal access. Although most modern systems incorporate the use of terminals, the illustration is useful as an introductory position, enabling us to understand the principles involved and dealing later in the chapter with problems relating to terminals and microcomputers.

Apart from identifying the job titles and functions of personnel in the DP section, which occupies the central area, the diagram also symbolizes the relationship between external ('user') departments and the DP section. This has significant internal control, and hence audit, implications which we shall consider later in the chapter. Many modern systems, unlike that portrayed in Figure 11.2, would now employ terminals in each department so that centralized data preparation is avoided, each department having access to the central processing unit at specified times. Although this reduces the dependence of user areas on the DP department, it creates security problems of its own, to which we return later in the chapter.

Most readers will be reasonably familiar with the responsibilities of those labelled in the diagram, and to set these out in detail would be outside the scope of this book; brief explanations will, however, be provided wherever this is warranted.

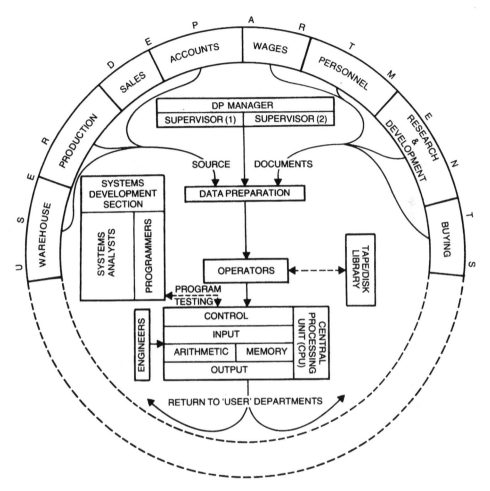

Figure 11.2 The basic DP configuration

11.2.3 Security of the files

Reference has already been made to the need for file reconstruction arrangements no matter how carefully the magnetically encoded data are stored. Information held on magnetic tape or disk is usually referred to as 'off-line' storage, as opposed to that which is held in the computer's own memory ('on-line'), and is retained for as long as necessary in the tape/disk library, all movement of files to and from the library being carefully controlled. (Data held on disk may, of course, become 'on-line' for the time that the disk is linked to the central processor.)

The files (a general term for stored data) in question will hold a wide variety of information, but may be broadly classified as:

- Programs, comprising the sets of instructions which govern all sequential functions to be performed inside the central processor.

- Transaction data, i.e. the machine-readable data describing the current period's transactions: cash received, goods and services charged, hours worked, warehouse movements, etc. These are the data which have to be fed into the computer, which (by following the programmed instructions) will then use them to bring master files (see below) up to date.

- Standing data, i.e. data of a permanent or more lasting nature such as price lists, employee codes, rates of standard and overtime pay, standard deductions, customer names and addresses, standard forms used for circulars, stock or part part codes, etc.

- Master files, being all files of lasting or continuous importance; these will also include certain files whose content is subject to frequent change, e.g. sales and bought ledgers, stores ledgers and plant registers.

In view of the susceptibility of computerized data to corruption and even destruction (e.g. through erroneous deletion) it is essential that each item of off-line magnetic storage is supported by a back-up copy adequate for reconstruction purposes in the event of errors, accidents or sabotage. The form that such reconstruction reserves will take will differ according to the nature of the storage base (i.e. magnetic tape or disk).

Information stored on magnetic tape (which is still used for economic reasons in many mainframe installations) is organized *serially* and cannot be *directly* accessed, either for reading or for writing purposes. Such a process is extremely slow when compared with direct-access files, such as disks. Furthermore, it is not practicable to update an existing magnetic tape file by 'writing' onto it directly. This is because each address to be updated will first have to be found by reading, and the reading and writing processes on tape units cannot be performed simultaneously. In order to update the file it will therefore be necessary for the computer to:

1. Read the present contents into the computer's core storage (memory).
2. Apply programme instructions to the transaction data being fed in as input.
3. Finally write the up-to-date information, still held in memory, onto a 'scratch' (i.e. clean, or available for use) tape, which will then represent the updated version of the original tape read in.

Since the updating process involves new tapes, and both are likely to be in the computer environment at the same time, security requires that a third tape be retained elsewhere, such as in the library, should reconstruction become necessary. This arrangement is usually known as grandfather/father/son. When tape 1 is updated, as described above, tape 2 is created as its 'son'. In the next updating process tape 2 becomes the 'father' of tape 3, and tape 1 is renamed the 'grandfather'. Should the current ('son') tape become mislaid, inadvertently destroyed or found to be defective, its contents can be reconstructed by rerunning the source data against the 'father' tape; if that too has been destroyed, the 'grandfather' tape is still available and, by means of two series of retained transaction data, can be used for reconstructing the 'son' tape. Even if the computer files containing transaction data have been lost or irretrievably re-sorted, it will still be possible to reconstruct from the source documents filed in the user departments concerned. (The *Companies Act 1985* lays down retention periods for such data – see Chapter 8.)

Although three 'generations' of tape are regarded as standard for security purposes, this is a matter for individual judgement; in some cases it will be considered necessary, depending upon the degree of security warranted, to hold a 'great-grandfather' tape at an entirely different (secret) location. The diagram shown in Figure 11.3 demonstrates the three-generation arrangement.

In contrast to data stored serially on magnetic tape, disk storage allows for direct, or random access. This means that there is no need to read through all preceding records before arriving at the address sought. Moreover, disks allow for virtually simultaneous

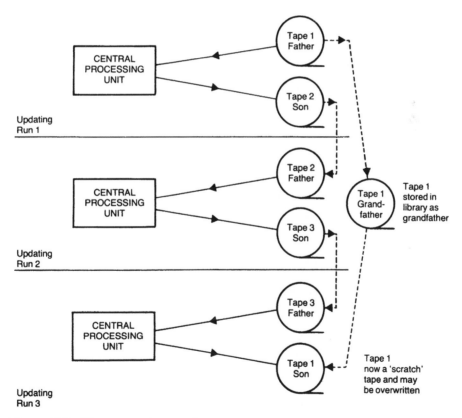

Figure 11.3   Three-generation security

reading and writing so that once the disk pack is 'on-line' to the processor immediate and direct updating is possible, there being no need for the out-of-date file first to be read into the core memory. An additional advantage is that only those addresses affected by the current transactions need to be accessed and overwritten, other addresses remaining unaltered. (With magnetic tape, as we have seen, the entire file may have to be read and, ultimately, written back to tape.)

Since the current magnetic disk file is updated directly, no additional files being created in the process, security requires that a duplicate be created (known as 'dumping') after every updating process. This duplicate may then act as the security copy should one become necessary. The security copy of the file can be created on disk or on tape.

11.2.4 Computer personnel – client's and auditor's

In conventional DP systems the prime concern of those responsible for staff recruitment will relate to:

1. Possession of requisite qualifications.
2. Possession of requisite experience, skills and proven ability.
3. Possession of appropriate personality attributes, such as co-operation, interest, loyalty, honesty.

In the case of computer staff, the above criteria are equally applicable, but an additional problem is created by the fact that, in general, staff orientation, identity and job affiliation will relate primarily to the computer itself rather than to the company: corporate objectives, in the minds of DP staff, are often of secondary consideration in terms of job satisfaction when compared with the opportunities for advancement, usually in a technical sense, afforded by the particular computer configuration in question.

As systems become more complex and data processing increasingly subject to the products of advanced technology, so does it become more important for the external auditor's own appreciation of the processes involved to match that of the client's computer staff. For this reason those firms that take seriously their responsibilities to clients whose records are processed in this way have established computer audit groups. Members of these specialized groups will, ideally, be qualified in the dual disciplines which their position makes requisite. In some cases, firms have recruited highly trained computer personnel for this purpose – presumably it has been found to be simpler to train such persons in the essentials of auditing than the other way round.

The simple fact is that the knowledge now needed to cope with the audit of a company whose recording systems are computerized cannot be acquired by reading books. Books and technical manuals are good as a starting point, but it is dangerous to pretend that there can ever be a substitute for proper training, and I do not exclude instruction in computer programming, followed by sound and comprehensive practical experience.

11.2.5   Division of responsibilities

The presence of a computer does not dispense with the need to observe that fundamental aspect of internal control, i.e. the division of responsibilities, in such a way as to ensure that:

1. Those in a position of responsibility do not themselves become involved in executing the mechanics of the procedures they have authorized.

2. Those occupied with recording functions do not have control over or access to the assets whose movement they are recording.

3. The work of one person is automatically checked for authority, accuracy, completeness and procedural adherence by an independent member of staff, preferably in another department.

In most mainframe systems recording is performed centrally, in the DP department itself. Consequently the auditor's usual approach to division of responsibility requires some adaptation. In effect, since the actual records are created in the computer area, clerical responsibilities in the many user departments will need to be allocated only in relation to:

1. Collection and sorting of input documentation.

2. Creation of batches and batch totals.

3. Retention of control data for comparison with output.

4. Authorization of input to be transmitted to DP department.

5. Collection and distribution of output.

6. Comparison of output with input control data, and reporting and acting on any discrepancies revealed.

7. Acting on output received, e.g. schedules, statistical analyses, exception reports, error reports, reprocessing requirements, etc.

The above breakdown presupposes that the user departments are not responsible for data preparation in machine-sensible form, or for keying-in the data directly via terminals, in which event job definition and allocation of responsibility would have to extend to these areas too.

Within the computer area itself, however, the principles of this aspect of internal control require to be appropriately observed, and these may be set out as follows:

1. Systems development staff, and programmers in particular, should play no part in actual processing and, ideally, should have no access to the computer room. Having written the programs, they will be aware of the controls which have been written into those programs, and would therefore be capable of by-passing any of them by appropriate intervention via the keyboard or control panel of the machine while processing is taking place.

This rigid separation of duties should apply even to the matter of program testing, when development staff will be anxious to know how the computer is going to react to any new program that has just been written. They should not be permitted to test the programs themselves, but should be required to observe the formal channels laid down. Once exceptions to this rule are permitted, even during a sleepy night shift, the overall security is eroded. After all, one tape looks much the same as any other, and who really knows what is being processed at that moment?

2. The DP manager and his supervisors, who between them are responsible for all activity in the DP area, should maintain their independence of all detailed procedures, and should therefore play no active part in day-to-day routine processing, otherwise it is all too easy for supervisory staff to become convenient operator substitutes, and generally to perform the tasks which they are supposed to be overseeing.

3. Responsibility for:

▶ recording, in a suitable log, the movements of all files;

▶ their safe custody when not in use;

▶ their clear identification at all times, distinguishing files in use from 'scratch' tapes and disks;

is that of the librarian who should have no routine duties in the DP section.

4. The console log (produced from the keyboard input) can, in many systems, perform an important security function by making a permanent record of every operator intervention. From time to time such intervention is necessary (apart from normal start and stop routines) in order to deal with rejections, say, due to an invalid input, or other special situations. However, since the risk of unauthorized interference is ever present, the printed log relating to each and every 'run' should be taken from the machine, read, filed and retained by the DP manager. However, this use of the log for security purposes becomes impractical with multi-programming, when using an operating system, or with multi-access through terminals; consequently the log should not be relied on for audit purposes in these circumstances.

11.2.6   Technology versus control

All the controls referred to above are of an administrative nature, and a well-devised system will cater for each of them. However, the usual caveat remains: the planning of controls is one thing, their continuous implementation by all members of staff, quite another.

The auditor will often find that his is a lone voice when it comes to respect for, and adherence to, the sensible precautionary measures originally laid down. Others will readily agree that they are sound in theory, but will produce a catalogue of cogent arguments why, in the particular circumstances, they should be relaxed or circumscribed. Although the auditor should always remain open to consultation on the question of adapting controls to meet a changed situation – after all, the 'audit ability' of records (and hence his own work) may be directly affected thereby – he should never allow himself to be persuaded, against his better judgement, that genuine risks can be disregarded in the interests of expediency, no matter how plausible it is all made to sound.

There will always be those, especially among computer personnel, to whom controls of any sort are a bore; the auditor should never be deterred by such an attitude. There is, after all, one argument which cannot be gainsaid: computers have proved to be the most significant aid to corporate crime in all its forms since the days of the South Sea Bubble. Many texts still naively declare that computers, of themselves, neither increase nor decrease the possibility of fraud. Where their authors got hold of such an idea is a mystery, quite apart from the fact that the claim is unprovable anyway – the only computer crimes of which we are aware being those that have been discovered.

What we *do* know is that many major frauds, such as Equity Funding and Penn Central, could not have been staged on their scale without the assistance of computers. In the case of Penn Central, for example, substantial quantities of brand new rolling stock were sold off at scrap value after false instructions were fed into the computer to write them off as worn out. The perpetrators, who bought the carriages at scrap value, were then able to resell at a vast profit. Equity Funding was the first widely publicized case of computer crime which demonstrated the manipulative possibilities of computers, when under the control of the criminal mind and subject to a totally ineffective audit.

The truth of the matter, by any reasonable assessment, is that with each technological advance the stages of data conversion, input, processing and output become both simpler and faster, and this places increasing pressure on the removal of constraining control procedures; computer security, as a consequence, is today a problem of unprecedented dimensions. The search for practical and effective solutions is rapidly becoming one of the major growth industries of the age.

11.3 General controls 2 – systems development

11.3.1 Standard applications

A number of computer applications may be standardized since their user requirements will be consistently uniform. These are usually referred to as 'packages'. Examples of these would include:

▶ Payroll applications;

▶ Stores ledgers (movement of goods);

▶ Sales and bought ledgers;

▶ Plant registers;

▶ Information retrieval, capable of interrogating the contents of any file.

Such programs may require a little modification to meet specific needs, and this is usually accomplished without difficulty. It is important, however, that package programs should be carefully tested before acceptance, especially to ensure that the controls built into their instructions are functioning as intended.

11.3.2   Specialist programs

Certain programs have to be tailor-made to meet user requirements, and these may be written by the company's own programmers or by a specialist software house. The complete development of new applications has to pass through several major phases, and the real control over systems development (and hence over the usefulness and reliability of its end-product) lies in the effectiveness with which each of these phases is individually monitored and authorized before staff are permitted to proceed further. The external auditor who knows what he wants from the system (in terms both of safeguards and documentation) will have much to do and to say, in a positive sense, during the sequential stages of the development: notably during systems analysis, when the details of the new system are being finalized, and during the later parallel running and file conversion stages, when the new system must be seen to have taken over from the old, and to meet all user expectations. (In this context the auditor should never forget that he, too, is a user.)

The stages of systems development may be briefly summarized as follows:

1. Feasibility study;
2. Systems analysis;
3. Programming;
4. Program testing – desk checking, test packs, pilot running;
5. Parallel run;
6. File conversion.

For a more detailed treatment of each of these stages, please refer to one of the specialist texts in computer auditing.

11.4   Application controls 1 – controls over input

11.4.1   The role of the user department

Effective input control begins 'at home', in the originating department. Although certain controls operate in the DP section, and in the programs themselves, there is no substitute for the imposition of clerical controls over the accuracy and the completeness of the data transmitted for processing: the importance of the GIGO (garbage in, garbage out) principle cannot be emphasized too strongly.

Clerical controls over input can be established in a variety of ways, according to the materiality, secrecy and nature of the data concerned, as well as the form of documentation in use. The extent to which the user department is itself involved with data conversion or able to transmit input directly via user-based terminals will also have a significant effect on the form of input controls in operation. Almost all controls will seek to ensure that the input:

1. Represents a valid record of actual transactions.
2. Is authorized by the appropriate official.

3. Is correctly classified (coded) for the purposes of the accounting or statistical exercise whose results are sought.

4. Is accurately translated into computer-acceptable form.

The source, or originating, documents which form the basis of most computer input will have been either raised by persons authorized to do so within the organization (e.g. goods requisitions), or received from outside organizations (e.g. suppliers' invoices), and these documents should be subjected to the same control procedures as in any manual system before being coded, batched and pre-listed for quantity, value, etc. The number of documents (or transactions) involved (a 'record count') should also be determined and retained for control purposes before the input is released.

Those responsible for data preparation will translate the prime documentation into machine-sensible form, where required, and in order to prove accurate translation the computer will create totals to be agreed with the original pre-list. In addition, a hash total can be created at this point, being a total of all the code numbers in the batch, for comparison with computer generated totals at later stages of the processing (as fully explained in section 11.5.2).

11.4.2 Other input controls

As we have seen, it is difficult to lay down demarcation lines as to exactly where user department responsibility for quality of input begins and ends, since this will differ from one situation to another. Broadly speaking, however, it may be assumed that user departments will take responsibility for the following:

► Collection of data;

► Batching.

► Establishing unique numbering systems for all classes of documentation, usually in sequence, to provide effective control against invalid suppression, duplication or substitution of documents.

► Pre-listing to create batch totals in terms of quantities and sterling values.

► Creating record counts.

► Entering the codes.

A variety of other input controls may be employed, of which the following are representative.

Printout

Some types of input preparation equipment provide printed lists of all items included in the input, thus providing a visible record against which the original documents may be checked by the DP manager, auditors or others responsible.

Check digits

The validity of account and other code numbers can be checked during input preparation by adding a 'check digit' as an integral part of each code number, to make each such number comply with a simple formula. The input machinery will then subject each code in turn to a simple compliance test, thereby preventing incorrect data being fed into the computer. These checks can also be carried out during processing, thus detecting any transcription and transcription errors in the code numbers fed into the machine.

Parity checks

The computer may also be built to operate on an odd or even 'parity' code. When the input machinery is preparing data it will insert an extra bit (binary digit) if this is needed to make the number of bits in each character odd or even, as the case may be. When the computer is reading data in, it will reject any character that does not conform to the parity codes, thus signalling errors. This check is useful in ensuring that dust or atmospheric conditions have not caused a digit to be obscured.

Tape labelling

The input tapes will include an identifying 'label' which will contain details of the application, the date the tape was made, its sequence, and possible 'scratch' date. The computer will check each tape to ensure that it belongs to the application being processed and is the next in sequence. This prevents irrelevant data being processed and destroying other records. These labels (header and tailer at the beginning and end of the magnetic record respectively) are encoded on the tape itself, and are read by the program.

Mechanical checks

In addition to the above controls, mechanical checks may also be incorporated. For example, a write-permit ring or a file-protection ring may be required to be attached to the output tapes on the 'writing' tape drive, without which they will not fit, as a safeguard against inadvertent deletion of current files by overwriting.

Record counts

A further record count may be included as part of each input tape to ensure that all the items on the tape are, in fact, processed. The computer program will contain instructions to add the number of items processed and agree with the record count on the tape. Should any omission or duplication have occurred, the computer will signify this and either stop or go into an error routine, depending on its programmed instructions, or special action taken by the operators. The computer may repeat this test at various control points during the processing to ascertain that all items are being properly processed.

11.5   Application controls 2 – controls over processing

11.5.1   Mechanical checks

Certain control features are usually built into the construction of the computer's own circuitry, which will improve the reliability of input, output and arithmetic functions within the machine. The following is a brief summary of these features:

1. The circuitry may have controls designed to ensure correct reading of input. The reading equipment will read the data twice and compare the result, ensuring that data are transferred to the storage section of the computer only when they have been proved accurate.

2. Controls built into central processors include the duplication of certain circuits in order to repeat calculations separately and compare the result, thus proving the accuracy of the calculation. Some processors are designed so that the complements of the true figures are used in repeating the calculation, which is then compared with the original calculation. This method has the advantage of allowing a different combination of machine components to be used in arriving at the same result.

3. The computer engineers will also test the computer regularly by using test programs on specially prepared data. Most failures are preceded by a loss of efficiency, and by running the machine at low voltage the engineers are able to locate faulty circuits and replace them before they fail. The computer will also conduct automatic parity checks on data as they are moved from one location to another inside the computer.

4. The computer may be designed so that as it produces output, either as printout or magnetic files, electrical impulses are created and compared with those produced by the computer to ensure that the output section is functioning correctly. Magnetic tape output equipment will be equipped with reading and writing heads. As the data are written onto the tape they will be read simultaneously by the reading head and compared by the computer with the data that have been written, thus ensuring accurate output.

11.5.2   Programmed controls

The controls described above are largely dependent upon mechanical checks built into circuitry. Invariably, controls of a totally different nature will be written into the programs themselves. Reference to this was made in section 11.3.2 on systems analysis, and it was pointed out that the auditor has an important role in ensuring (by both advising and testing), at the preliminary stages of systems development, that a suitable range of control procedures are included. The most straightforward of these controls, common to most systems, will ensure the following:

1. That only data relating to the particular application are processed, and reading the header labels will ensure that out-of-date input tapes, or those relating to other applications, are not read in accidentally.
2. Completeness and accuracy of processing, i.e. that all input is dealt with. The use of intermediate printouts of subtotals created for control purposes against which control totals created at the input stage may be checked, is one method of achieving this.

Three other forms of control designed to ensure accuracy and completeness are given below.

Reasonableness checks

These checks require the setting of parameters for totals of calculations, or data fed into the computer. The computer then checks to see that all data read in fall within the pre-set limits, and tests results of calculations to see that they too are reasonable, e.g. if no items of data read in should exceed, say, £20, the computer will reject any item in excess of this; similarly, if the results of any particular calculation should fall within the range £30 to £45, the computer will signal apparent errors for checking.

Reasonableness checks are normally built into programs for the additional purpose of providing exception reports upon which special action may be needed. This has obvious application in wages routines (overtime limits), debtor balances (age limits, credit limits), capital expenditure (authority limits), etc., and has powerful audit implications.

Sequence checks

Where data are recorded serially, as on magnetic tape, input data must be sorted into the correct sequence, usually by the computer, before processing begins. Sequence checks may be built into the program which ensure that the input data are processed in the same sequence as on the master file being updated. This would not be necessary, however, if disks were in use, since their direct access facility obviates the need for detailed pre-sorting. The disk 'address' system enables a particular item of information to be located, e.g. the number of items of a specific spare part in stock.

Hash totals and check digits

These have already been referred to in relation to their use as controls over input. It is appropriate to mention them again in this context since they do perform important checks while processing continues. All data read into the computer will be added to make a grand (hash) total which is checked against that encoded into the tape by the input preparation equipment. This control ensures that no item has been omitted, and that all descriptive figures, account numbers, etc, have been correctly read into the machine. This test can be effectively performed at intermediate stages of processing.

The appending of a check digit to descriptive codes, such as account numbers, will make them conform to a simple formula. The computer may then test the validity of the codes during processing.

11.6 Application controls 3 – controls over output

11.6.1 Comparing output with input

All the controls so far explained, i.e. those which relate to both input and processing itself, have, as their final objective, the assurance of output which:

1. Relates precisely to the original input.
2. Represents the outcome of a valid and thoroughly tested program of instructions.
3. Meets fully the requirements of the management in all user departments and at all levels.

If the controls are effective, users need normally have little concern for the accuracy and completeness of the data issued to them on the printed reports; nevertheless, it is always advisable for certain obvious checks to be executed, such as a comparison between the control data printed out (e.g. record accounts, batch totals, numerical sequence checks) and those that were originally passed for processing.

11.6.2 Other output controls

Distribution

Only those entitled to receive output reports should do so, and the distribution list in the custody of the DP manager should specify names of personnel rather than simply the recipient user department. In the case of classified output the recipient should be required to signify receipt by initialling a copy of the list. Apart from eliminating breaches in security, carefully controlled distribution acts as a safeguard against the following:

1. Proliferation of unwanted output documentation which is religiously filed ('in case someone finds it useful someday') but never read and still less acted upon.
2. A situation in which important information does not reach its appropriate destination, either at all or in sufficient time to enable the necessary action to be taken.

Acting on exception reports

Some output (usually preliminary or intermediate) will reveal errors in code allocation at the input stage, or other errors which have made processing impossible. Details of these 'rejections' will be passed back to those responsible, and reprocessing necessitated. Wherever appropriate, enquiry into the cause of the difficulty should be pursued.

Much output these days takes the form of exception reports, a product of the 'management by exception' philosophy which forms an inseparable consequence of the development of computer technology. Since, in many cases, the exception reports will be all that the user department receives, it is vital that the appropriate action should be taken on each of them by the officers responsible. These exception reports also represent the object of much audit scrutiny, especially where full printouts of master files and transaction data are not available.

11.7   Summary of internal control in a DP system

Before moving on to audit procedures relevant to DP systems it is worth reminding ourselves why we have spent so much of this chapter in gaining an appreciation of the controls that we would expect to find in operation, i.e. as an integral part of the internal controls laid down. Auditors are bound to investigate the system of internal control in any client organization as a prelude to the execution of detailed audit tests; quite simply, the system produces the records, and the records produce the final accounts on which the auditor is obliged to report. In DP systems, however, the nature of internal control, as we have already seen, is strikingly different and it therefore behoves the auditor of any company using DP to open his mind to the changes which this necessitates.

In a conventional system, a visual scrutiny of all clerical functions is possible at every stage of recording, and the allocation of tasks (so as to optimize control effectiveness) is relatively straightforward, as shown in Figure 11.4.

The counterpart controls in a DP system are difficult to portray, but Figure 11.5 provides some sort of comparison with Figure 11.4. Again, it assumes that input data are batched in user departments and passed to the DP department for processing, rather than (as is becoming increasingly common) having direct input from terminals in user departments.

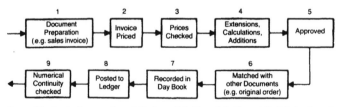

The execution of tasks in boxes 1 and 5, 2 and 3, 6 and 9, 7 and 8, *inter alia*, should normally be separated.

Figure 11.4   Sequence in a conventional system

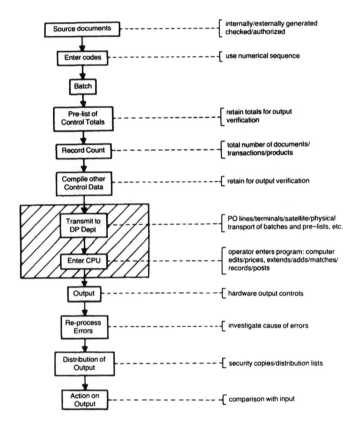

Notes
(a) The left-hand sequence represents a rough approximation of the processes which begin with the creation (or receipt of) original documents, and end with the final record. This should be contrasted with a machine accounting system, in which this entire operation takes place in *one* step: the authorized, checked and coded input documents are entered *directly* on to, say, suppliers' ledger cards by the machine operator, and an invoice register (suitably provided with columnar analysis) and control account are automatically created as by-products. Furthermore, *visual scrutiny* operates throughout the process.
(b) The right-hand marginal notes indicate something of the processes which may be involved, and some of the control factors which would be introduced.
(c) The shaded rectangular area marked in the left-hand sequence indicates the steps in the sequence which cannot be followed *visually*, and in which the audit trail is effectively lost.

Figure 11.5   Sequence in a DP system

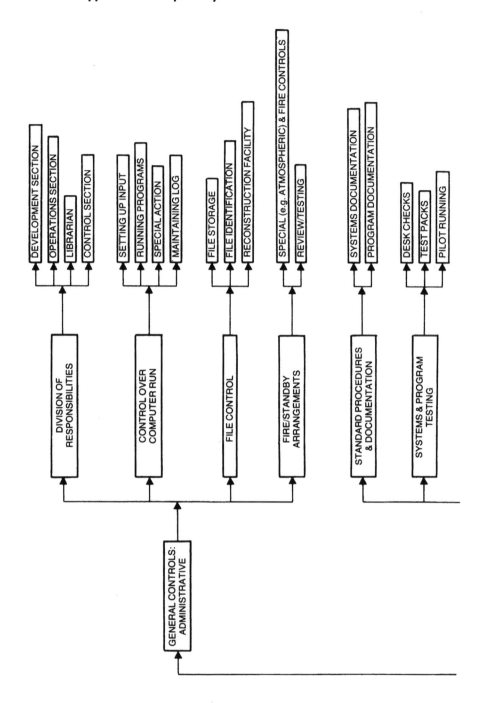

INTERNAL CONTROL

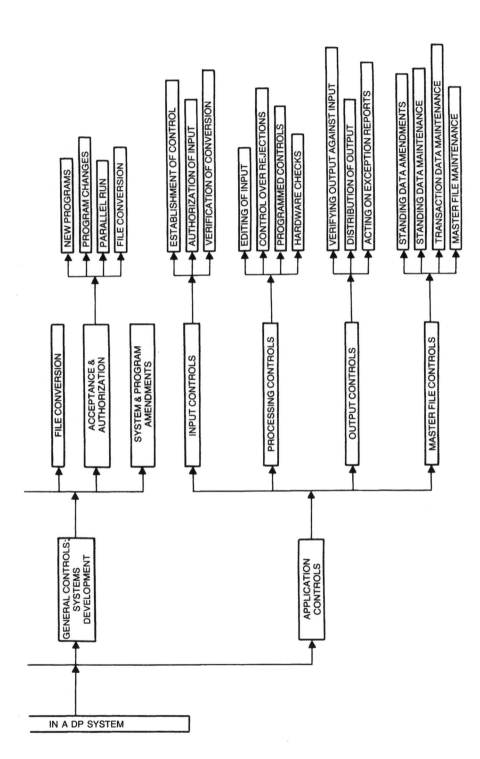

Figure 11.6 Internal control in a DP system (no direct terminal input)

Figure 11.6 provides a diagrammatic summary of internal controls in a computer-based system, and also acts as a useful reminder of the controls discussed in this chapter so far.

11.8 The auditor's approach

11.8.1 The control file

When auditing DP systems, it will be found that much reliance is placed within the system upon standard forms and documentation in general, as well as upon strict adherence to procedures laid down. This is no surprise since the ultimate constraining factor in the system is the computer's own capability, and all users are competitors for its time. It is therefore important that an audit control file be built up as part of the working papers, and the auditor should ensure that he is on the distribution list for notifications of all new procedures, documents and systems changes in general. The following should be included in the audit control file.

1. Copies of all the forms which source documents might take, and details of the checks that have been carried out to ensure their accuracy.

2. Details of physical control over source documents, as well as of the nature of any control totals of numbers, quantities or values, including the names of the persons keeping these controls.

3. Full description of how the source documents are to be converted into input media, and the checking and control procedures.

4. A detailed account of the clerical, procedural and systems development controls contained in the system (e.g. separation of programmers from operators; separation of control of assets from records relating thereto).

5. The arrangements for retaining source documents and input media for suitable periods. This is of great importance, as they may be required for reconstructing files in the event of error or mishap.

6. A detailed flow diagram of what takes place during each routine processing run.

7. Details of all tapes and disks in use, including their layout, labelling, storage and retention arrangements.

8. Copies of all the forms which output documents might take, and details of their subsequent sorting and checking.

9. The auditor's own comments on the effectiveness of the controls.

11.8.2 The ICQ for computer audits

Systems evaluation in DP systems, just as in other systems, may be enhanced by the judicious use of internal control questionnaires (ICQ). It will come as no surprise to see that the control features on which the ICQ elicits information largely coincide with those which we have already examined in some detail. In the example that follows, it is assumed that source documents require to be converted into machine-readable format.

The internal control problems associated with direct input via terminal or personal computers are dealt with in later sections.

Specimen questionnaire for evaluating the system of internal control in a computer-based accounting system

The specimen which follows deals with some of the principal questions that the auditor will wish to ask in evaluating the system of internal control in a computer-based accounting system.

Most questionnaires include questions relating to the make, type and size of the computer and ancillary equipment. These questions do not normally affect the assessment of internal control and have been ignored in this specimen.

	Tick as appropriate			
	Yes	No	N/A	Comments
I General controls – administrative				
Division of responsibilities				
1. Is the head of the computer department responsible to an appropriate senior official in the company?				
2. Is the following work carried out by separate sections or departments:				
(a) development?				
(b) data preparation?				
(c) computer operating?				
(d) file library?				
(e) control?				
3. Have organization charts and job descriptions been prepared?				
4. Do the following basic restrictions apply:				
(a) access to documents containing original data is limited to the control section and data preparation staff?				
(b) computer department staff do not have access to any of the company's clerically maintained financial records?				

	Tick as appropriate			
	Yes	No	N/A	Comments
(c) access to the computer during production runs is limited to computer operators?				
(d) access to files and current programs is limited to computer operators and file librarian?				
(e) computer operators and programmers do not amend input data?				
(f) control section staff and the librarian do not have other duties within the computer department?				
(g) computer department staff do not initiate transactions and changes to master files?				
(h) unauthorized access to the computer room is forbidden? (State how this is achieved.)				
5. Do the restrictions in question 4 apply at all times?				
Control over computer operators				
6. Is the work of computer operators controlled by the use of:				
(a) administrative procedure manuals?				
(b) work schedules?				
(c) operating instructions for each program?				
(d) computer usage reports (e.g. operating logs and console printouts)?				
(e) minimum of two operators per shift?				
(f) rotation of duties?				
(g) any other method? (Describe)				
7. Is all operator intervention recorded on the console printout?				
8. Are computer usage reports, including console printouts, reviewed by a responsible official?				

	Tick as appropriate			
	Yes	No	N/A	Comments
File control				
9. Is a permanent record of files maintained? (Describe)				
10. Are movements of files recorded? (Describe)				
11. On what authority are files issued?				
12. Are master copies of important files (e.g. programs and documentation) kept at outside locations?				
File identification procedures				
13. Are there adequate file identification procedures by use of:				
(a) visible reference numbers?				
(b) protection rings?				
(c) header label checks on set up?				
(d) any other method? (Describe)				
File reconstruction procedures				
14. Are there adequate reconstruction procedures by use of:				
(a) the establishment of retention periods for files, input media and documents?				
(b) file generation systems?				
(c) copying of disk files at appropriate intervals?				
(d) any other method? (Describe)				
Fire precautions and standby arrangements				
15. (a) Are there adequate fire precautions? (Describe)				
(b) Are there adequate standby arrangements for processing in case of equipment failure? (Describe)				
(c) If so, have these arrangements been tested?				

	Tick as appropriate			
	Yes	No	N/A	Comments
II General controls – systems development				
Standard procedures and documentation				
16. Does the documentation produced for an application include the following:				
(a) narrative description of the system?				
(b) flowcharts and block diagrams?				
(c) input and output data descriptions?				
(d) file record layouts?				
(e) control procedures?				
(f) program listing?				
(g) test data and results of testing?				
(h) output distribution instructions?				
(i) operating instructions?				
(j) procedure manuals?				
17. How does the system ensure that the documentation in question 16 is:				
(a) properly prepared?				
(b) properly altered for system and program changes? (Describe)				
Systems and program testing				
18. Are programs adequately tested by means of:				
(a) desk checking?				
(b) processing with test data?				
(c) use of operating instructions without programmers being present?				
(d) any other method? (Describe)				
19. Are systems adequately tested by means of:				
(a) processing test data?				
(b) pilot running?				
(c) parallel running?				

	Tick as appropriate			
	Yes	No	N/A	Comments
(d) involving the clerical and control procedures in all user departments concerned with the system?				
(e) any other method? (Describe)				
20. Who evaluates the results of testing and what report is prepared?				
File conversion				
21. Are the contents of master files checked before a system becomes operational? (Describe the safeguards)				
Acceptance and authorization procedures				
22. Is completed work reviewed and approved and further progress authorized by responsible officials in both user and computer departments at the following stages in development:				
(a) completion of outline systems specification?				
(b) completion of systems specification?				
(c) completion of program and systems testing?				
(d) accepting new systems into operational use?				
Systems and program amendments				
23. Do all changes to operational systems and programs require to be authorized?				
24. Are all changes:				
(a) documented;				
(b) tested;				
in the same manner as new systems and programs?				
25. How does the system ensure that all changes are notified to all concerned, including user departments? (Describe)				

	Tick as appropriate			
	Yes	No	N/A	Comments
III Application controls				
A. Input controls				
Establishment of control				
26. Is control for complete and accurate processing first established:				
(a) before the documents are batched by use of:				
(i) controls from prior procedures? (Describe)				
(ii) clerical sequence checks?				
(iii) retention of copies?				
(iv) any other method? (Describe)				
(b) clerically after batching by use of:				
(i) control totals? (Describe)				
(ii) any other method? (Describe)				
(c) by computer by use of:				
(i) control totals? (Describe)				
(ii) sequence checks?				
(iii) any other method? (Describe)				
27. What controls are established over data fields that contain significant reference data (e.g. check digit verification and matching with master file records)? (Describe)				
Verification of conversion				
28. (a) Is the conversion of data independently verified?				
(b) How does the system ensure that all errors are corrected? (Describe)				
Authorization of input				
29. Are all input data adequately authorized?				
30. If the documents are authorized before control is established, is the authorization				

	Tick as appropriate			
	Yes	No	N/A	Comments
checked after control is established (i.e. to guard against the introduction of unauthorized documents)?				
31. Is the computer programmed to carry out significant authorizing functions (e.g. limit and reasonableness checks)?				

B. Processing controls

Rejections

32. Is there a list of the reasons for which data can be rejected?

33. What are the procedures for investigating, correcting and resubmitting the rejected data and recording the action taken? (Describe)

34. How does the system ensure that all rejections are promptly reprocessed (e.g. maintaining suspense control records, independent scrutiny of rejection listings)? (Describe)

Intermediate printouts of control data during processing

35. **(a)** If control is established prior to processing is this control used to verify all (or some) accounting data on final output? (Describe)

    (b) If not, is it used to verify processing to certain stage by checking intermediate output (e.g. input totals printed and checked on edit list)? (Describe)

36. If the control used to verify final output is established by the computer either on input or during processing:

    (a) is it first printed out on intermediate output for subsequent clerical verification with final output (e.g.

	Tick as appropriate			
	Yes	No	N/A	Comments
computer totals printed on edit list)? (Describe)				
(b) if so, are there adequate program controls to ensure the completeness and accuracy of the data at each stage of processing until printed out? (Describe)				

C.   Output controls

General

37. What is the printout used for (e.g. to originate or support entries in the books for control purposes)? (Describe)

38. Does the printout contain sufficient information to:

(a) trace source documents to it?

(b) verify computer generated calculations and totals?

Output directly related to input

39. (a) Are the totals and details checked clerically with controls established prior to processing? – or obtained from intermediate printout?

(b) If not, are there adequate program controls to ensure the completeness and accuracy of the data printed out? (Describe)

Output indirectly related to input

40. (a) Are the totals and details checked clerically to external information? (Describe)

(b) If not, are there adequate program controls to ensure the completeness and accuracy of the data printed out? (Describe)

	Tick as appropriate			
	Yes	No	N/A	Comments
Exception reports				
41. Is the completeness of the report verified clerically? If so, give details.				
42. Are there adequate program controls to ensure the completeness (if applicable) and accuracy of the data printed out? (Describe)				
43. What are the procedures for investigating and taking action on exception reports and recording the action taken? (Describe)				
Distribution of output				
44. If receipt of output is not controlled by the user department how does the system ensure it receives all printouts intact? (Describe)				
D. Master file controls				
Amendments to standing data				
45. (a) How are amendments authorized? (Describe)				
(b) Is this authorization adequate?				
46. Are processed amendments checked in detail? (Describe)				
47. How does the system ensure that all amendments are controlled:				
(a) by controls total? (Describe)				
(b) by retention of copies?				
(c) by any other method? (Describe)				
Maintenance of standing data				
48. How, and how often, are standing data verified:				
(a) by printouts of individual items for checking with external information?				
(b) by printouts of totals for reconciliation				

	Tick as appropriate			
	Yes	No	N/A	Comments
with an independently or computer established record of totals?				
(c) by establishment and reconciliation of totals by the computer?				
(d) by any other method? (Describe)				
Maintenance of transaction data				
49. How, and how often, are transaction data on the file verified on a total basis:				
(a) by printouts of totals for reconciliation with a record of independently or computer established totals?				
(b) by establishment and reconciliation of totals by the computer?				
(c) by any other method? (Describe)				
50. Are individual balances printed out and externally verified? (Describe)				

11.8.3 'Round' the machine and 'through' the machine

Despite the very significant changes in recording systems brought about by computers, their effect upon the auditor's work would be minimal if it were still possible to relate, on a 'one-to-one' basis, the original input with the final output; or, putting it another way, if the audit trail were always preserved intact. Figure 11.7 is a simplified representation of the documentation in a manually created audit trail.

From Figure 11.7 we see that particular credit notes may be located by the auditor at any time he may wish to examine them, even months after the balance sheet date. He also has the means, should he so wish, of directly verifying the accuracy of the totals and subtotals that feature in the control listing, by reference to individual credit notes. He can, of course, check all detailed calculations, casts and postings in the accounting records, at any time.

In first- and early second-generation computer systems, such a complete audit trail was generally available, due, no doubt, to management's own healthy scepticism of what the new machine could be relied upon to achieve – an attitude obviously shared by the auditor. The documentation in such a trail might again be portrayed as shown, in an over-simplified way, in Figure 11.8.

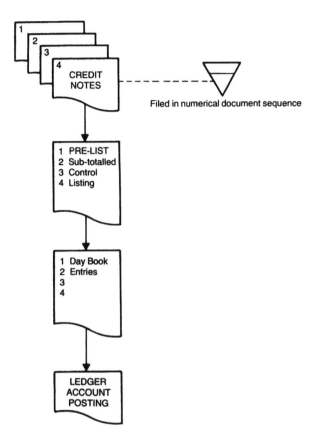

Figure 11.7   Manually created audit trail

It is once again clear from the diagram that there is an abundance of documentation upon which the auditor can lavish his traditional symbols of scrutiny, in the form of coloured ticks and rubber stamps. Specifically:

1. The output itself is as complete and as detailed as in any manual system.
2. The trail, from beginning to end, is complete, so that all documents may be identified and located for purposes of vouching, totalling and cross-referencing.

Any form of audit checking is possible, including depth testing in either direction.

The execution of *normal* audit tests on records which are produced by computer, but which are nevertheless as complete as indicated above, is usually described as audit testing *round the machine* – a good title, since in such circumstances the machine itself may be viewed by the auditor as the mere instrument through which conventional records, susceptible to audit, are produced.

The hardware improvements over the past ten years, however, have resulted in such rapid processing speeds and run times that it now tends to be vastly uneconomic to

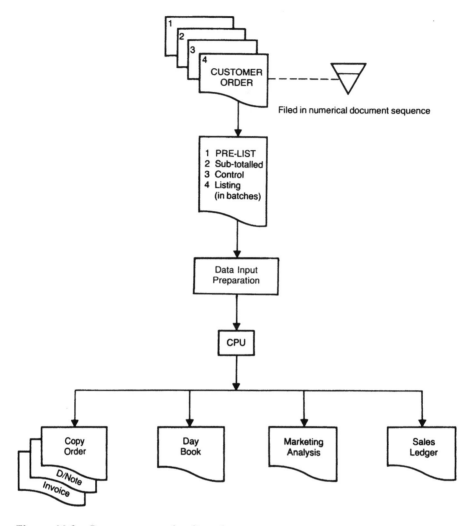

Figure 11.8   Computer-created audit trail

produce such a plethora of printout, the printer being the slowest link in the processing chain. It is this situation together with considerations such as storage requirements and stationery costs, which have led to such extensive dependence by management upon the 'exception reporting' principle.

This principle, in view of the reliability of modern machines, is eminently reasonable, since the exception reports give the selected information which the users at all management levels would, in any event, have had to extract had complete printouts been produced. Examples are debtors whose credit limit has been exceeded; debtor balances unsettled after lapse of period of credit; balances in excess of, say, £5,000 (or split into 'value strata'); stock quantities of different reorder levels; slow-moving or obsolete lines; overtime claims which exceed normal hours; net pay which exceeds specified parameters; expenditures in excess of budget, etc.

From the auditor's point of view, it must also be conceded, the exception reports which isolate the above data provide him with the very material that he requires for most of his verification work. The only problem which it raises, and it is a serious one, is that he cannot simply assume (or hope) that the programs which produce the exception reports

1. are doing so *accurately*;
2. are printing out *all* the exceptions which exist;
3. are the *authorized* programs, as opposed to dummy programs specially created for a fraudulent purpose, or out-of-date programs accidentally taken from the library;
4. contain programmed control parameters which do in fact meet the company's genuine internal control requirements.

In short, whereas it may be reasonable for management to have implicit faith in the system and the programs, such ingenuousness on the auditor's part would represent a dereliction of his duty of care.

So we see that wherever reliance by the management upon exception reports has effectively eliminated the audit trail between input and output, the auditor is forced to test the invisible processes which purport to embody the controls, and produce the output such as it is. These tests, which invariably involve the use by the auditor of the computer itself, are known as tests *through the machine*. Such measures represent a daunting prospect to the auditor, who is not equipped for the task in terms of knowledge and experience, in which event it will be tempting to persevere with tests round the computer. The consequences of such a fearful approach are exemplified in the Equity Funding computer fraud in which the auditors were totally deceived by the computer staff.

In the 'through the machine' approach the auditor starts by proving the accuracy of the input data, and then thoroughly examines (by applying tests) the processing procedures with a view to establishing the following:

1. That all input is actually introduced into the computer.
2. That unusual conditions in the input do not cause misprocessing.
3. That neither the computer nor the operators can cause undetected irregularities in the final reports.
4. That the programs appear, on the evidence of rejection and exception routines, to be functioning correctly.
5. That all operator intervention during processing is logged and scrutinized by the DP manager.

The application of tests of this nature calls for a rather wide knowledge of data processing routines in general, and also of the characteristics of the particular client's type of equipment and programs under audit.

Some auditors hold the rather naive view that the audit trail should be preserved for their exclusive benefit, i.e. so that the traditional audit tests which feature in their pre-DP standard audit programs can be applied to complete 'hard copy' (printout). The only situation in which the auditor's voice may be influential in securing additional hard copy as a regular product of processing would be when he justifiably believes that:

1. *Companies Act 1985* requirements (particularly section 722 as to form, and the retention regulation in section 222) are not being met.
2. The management of the company is not receiving the information which the auditor believes is necessary in order to control the company's operations effectively.
3. The internal audit is ineffective in overcoming the control weakness which is clearly due to an excessive reliance upon the 'management by exception' approach.
4. The company's security is significantly and continuously at risk due to the dependence of management upon exception reporting for the purposes of making decisions, and instituting corrective action. Such vulnerability is most likely to apply when there are known weaknesses in the systems development governing the creation and maintenance of programs and/or in the administrative controls (see section 11.2 above) in the DP section as a whole.

In any of the above circumstances the auditor should insist on the production of sufficient printout to overcome the weaknesses concerned, if necessary pointing out that failure to comply may result in an audit report qualification. Obviously, however, he will endeavour to persuade the management concerned that the changes recommended are entirely in their own best interests.

It should be understood that the loss of audit trail is not in most cases a total loss, since it is usually physically possible, given unlimited manpower and time, to reconstruct the trail. This would necessitate returning to source documents, possibly having to re-sort them into their original batches, and thenceforth simulate the DP trail manually until a result was reached equivalent to complete output documentation. However, the dimensions of such a task virtually rule it out as a practical proposition.

The auditor may, of course, reasonably request additional printout for audit purposes while present on a particular occasion, but this will not enable him to draw conclusions on the records in relation to other dates in the period under audit nor will he be certain that the 'correct' printout was not 'contrived' for the purposes of his tests. The positive approach on the part of the auditor, where it is clear to him that 'through the machine' tests are a necessity, requires a tacit acceptance that the nature of the audit will have to be adapted to the nature of the circumstances, and not the other way round. Inevitably, auditors are being forced to work in parallel with current processing, as opposed to 'historical' auditing; apart from a dearth of visible printout, source documents are often retained for a limited period only, after which they may be re-sorted for an entirely different purpose, or, in some cases, even destroyed.

The following brief quotation from a paper by the Chief Organizing Accountant of the National Coal Board, published some years ago, admirably assesses the position in which the auditor finds himself:

> It should be borne in mind that a data-processing centre is not, in popular terms, an 'electronic office', but is more akin to a factory. There is a planned production cycle, a flow-line of successive operations, and any idea of these processes being interrupted or halted for audit purposes cannot be entertained. The continuous, and in some cases automatic, inspection and control processes in a factory with a production belt must be simulated by the auditor in applying his own techniques. Indeed, it may well be that the auditor, while preserving his independence, will nevertheless have to subjugate his methods to the needs of the process, and may have to accept some disciplines in operation.

11.8.4   Audit advantages of DP systems

Once the auditor accepts the importance of auditing through the computer, and acquires the skills commensurate with the task, he will find that the computer's presence entails a number of distinct advantages from his point of view.

The amount of detailed audit work is, as always, governed by the degree of confidence which the auditor has in the controls operated by his client, and in many ways DP systems help to expedite the audit work on the final accounts through their ability to provide far more immediate and effective recording control over company assets and liabilities. For example, reconciliation between individual debtor and creditor account balances and total accounts may be effected monthly, weekly or even daily, if desired and necessary. By the use of exception reporting, debts of doubtful value are highlighted without delay, and any necessary action taken immediately to recover the sums due. Under these circumstances much of the auditor's verification work may be executed at the interim stage.

Similar controls may be exercised over slow-moving and obsolete stocks and regular reconciliations between physical and book stocks facilitated. With most manual systems it is found that these controls and tests are only applied half-yearly, or even annually, if at all.

Computers also assist in the preparation of monthly or other interim accounts by the use of files of standing data, such as price lists and depreciation charges, allowances for taxation purposes, etc., in respect of each item of plant, all held on one such file.

11.8.5   Computer-assisted audit techniques (CAATs)

As the phrase 'auditing through the computer' suggests, the tests applied will necessitate the use of the client's computer, as well as of the programs and master files under scrutiny. The close co-operation of the DP manager should therefore be enlisted and, once again, the auditor's position is immeasurably enhanced if it is clear to the DP manager that the auditor both understands the purpose and the underlying technical implications of the tests he wishes to conduct, as well as appreciates the existing pressures on computer time, which the audit tests may well increase.

Most audit tests on the computer are rendered more effective if neither operators nor programmers are aware of the fact that they are taking place; secrecy is therefore important. 'Test packs' and computer audit programs, described below, are the most commonly used CAATs.

The use of test packs

The auditor may use 'test packs' for the purpose of ascertaining whether the controls residing in the hardware and in the programs are operating correctly. For example, 'reasonableness' controls, which result in an exception report containing all items falling outside of programmed parameters (e.g. overtime claims in excess of 20 hours in a week), can be tested by a series of dummy inputs, and subsequent comparison between the output and a manually created schedule of expected results.

The transactions devised in a test pack should attempt to cover every type of entry, including deliberate errors, which are then processed through the computer, and the results obtained then compared with pre-calculated answers to determine whether or not the programs do in fact contain the necessary controls.

The devised test pack is converted into machine-readable form, if necessary, and then processed by normal means, using existing programs, and it is therefore important that the master file changes brought about as a result should subsequently be eliminated. Since this processing is executed by the operators, according to their standing instructions, it is necessary for the auditor to be reasonably familiar with the operating routines. He should be capable of ascertaining whether the 'edit' checks are operating as intended, and of interpreting the error reports arising from the deliberate input of invalid data. After processing, the printed result will be compared with his expected solutions, already determined and scheduled as part of the working papers on his file.

There are, of course, distinct limitations on the usefulness of test packs. For example, their results are valid only in respect of the actual run tested. The auditor cannot be certain that a similar result would have been obtained at any other date during the accounting period under audit. Nor can he be certain (unless no one else was aware that the tests were being conducted) that the usual program was used for the purposes of the test – it may have been specially taken out of cold storage in the auditor's honour.

Here are a couple of fraudulent program alterations, which provide an idea of but one aspect of what the auditor seeks to discover via a test pack. They relate to the suppression of exception reports on fictitious claims for overtime (OT). (The > and < are 'greater than' and 'less than' respectively.)

In the case shown in Figure 11.9 a programmer has inserted an extra program parameter which ensures that any claim carrying his own wages code (EX 4829) will not be subjected to the 20-hour reasonableness test and can therefore never be included in a printout.

In the case shown in Figure 11.10 our fraudulent programmer has simply extended the requirements of the logic test to include 'and < 40'. The effect of this is that only those overtime claims which fall between 20 and 40 hours (which will cover virtually every valid claim in excess of the 20-hour reasonableness limit) will be printed out. Claims of 40 hours and above will therefore not feature at all.

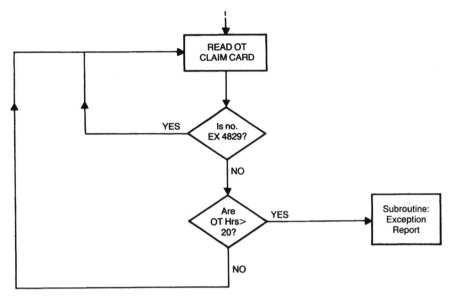

Figure 11.9   Fraudulent program alteration (1)

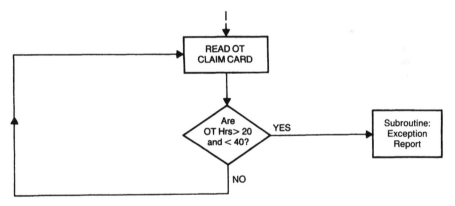

Figure 11.10   Fraudulent program alteration (2)

The use of computer audit programs

Whereas the test packs are suitable for monitoring day-to-day routine processing, computer audit software (CAS) will prove invaluable in a wider variety of ways, for example where there is a loss of audit trail, where there are large volumes of data to be audited, or where there is extended substantive or re-performance work on balances. CAS may be written by the auditor for use on a particular client's system, but this is time consuming and therefore expensive, and will also require an extensive knowledge of high-level programming languages. It is therefore usually preferable for the auditor to use generalized CAS which is applicable to a wide range of hardware, and a number of these are available as packages marketed by the manufacturers. They are used extensively in industry and commerce by internal auditors, and a number of external audit firms have produced their own versions.

Broadly speaking, CAS is a file interrogation program, with a facility for extracting any information selectively from the client's master files, and comparing it or merging it with any other data held in store, or simply printing it out in any array or format desired. Versatile CAS will be able to subject the data selected to a wide range of audit tests, in many cases in accordance with statistical sampling criteria, having also generated the necessary random numbers internally.

In relation to balance sheet work, CAS may be used for stratifying all major company assets (stocks, debtors, plant, etc) according to age and value, with a view to concentrating verification tests on high value, or otherwise material, items. This information can be merged to strike 80:20 ratios on any range of assets selected (e.g. 80 per cent of stocks of spares, in value, involve no more than 20 per cent of stock movements in a year, giving a guide to possible obsolescence; or 80 per cent, in value, of debtors is contained in only 20 per cent, in number, of accounts; and so on).

CAS will also extract the information of an exceptional nature described in section 11.8.3. In short, CAS provides an ideal medium for singling out any exceptional items (the auditor himself having decreed what is exceptional for this purpose) on all master files.

Since the use of CAS will expend valuable computer time, the auditor will not infrequently encounter a reluctance on the part of the management and the DP department to co-operate with him in implementing them. Furthermore, the insertion of additional programs into an already 'tight' schedule may cause normal processing runs to be delayed. To overcome this problem it is sometimes possible for comparable interrogation facilities to be built into the normal programs, preferably when the latter are being written. The current trend, however, is towards PC-based interrogative packages. Some of the advantages are:

1. The cost is usually less than the equivalent mainframe/mini packages.

2. A PC-based menu-driven package is easier for non computer-literate staff to learn and use.

3. The interrogation is run on the auditor's own PC, thus preserving independence and removing the possibility of corruption by outside sources.

4. The auditor is much less dependent on the client's DP staff and systems – the interrogation can be run when convenient for the auditor.

5. Any errors made by the auditor in running the interrogation are not noticed by the client.

Not surprisingly, there are also disadvantages to the PC-based file interrogation software. These include:

1. Downloading the clients's data onto the auditor's PC can be technically complex.

2. Large volumes of data may be difficult to accommodate within the storage capacity of the auditor's PC.

One of the most versatile packages currently available is IDEA, developed in Canada and marketed by the Canadian Institute of Chartered Accountants. The interrogation facilities of IDEA include totalling, ageing, stratification and summarization, sampling using various methods, extraction using any defined criteria, statistical information, file comparison and linking files together. Mindful of the difficulties of transferring data files to PCs (downloading), the developers of IDEA have incorporated a menu-driven data transfer method for certain common accounting packages such as Pegasus, Tetraplan and Sage. Other packages may require an understanding of file layouts before the data can be downloaded satisfactorily.

Clients expect their auditors to perform efficient and effective audits at a reasonable price, and they also expect the auditors' use of computers to increase audit efficiency and to keep pace with the computerization of their own accounting systems.

11.9   Personal computers – the audit problems

11.9.1   Personal computers – a greater risk?

Some may imagine that the relevance of many of the above remarks is confined to the few large audit firms who, for many years now, have been faced with the difficulties of computer auditing. On the contrary, the majority (but by no means all) of these already employ staff whose abilities are commensurate with the task in hand. It is in fact the vast majority of smaller audit firms who are most likely to feel the repercussions of their ignorance of modern methods of data processing. I say this advisedly, particularly in view of personal computers (PCs) which are now commonplace for all but the smallest of business entities. Many auditors erroneously regard these streamlined objects as little more than advanced forms of book-keeping machines, but nothing could be further from the truth; they are in every sense computers. Indeed, it could almost be said that their particular attributes render them potentially far more dangerous, from the security viewpoint, than their large mainframe counterparts. These attributes and resultant audit difficulties, include:

1. The system is often geared to a software package, not the reverse. The software is not tailor-made, e.g. bills of exchange received may have to be recorded as cash in a sales ledger package.

2. Packages are written by DP experts, not accountants. Accounting conventions, even double-entry and not setting-off income and expenses, are not necessarily followed, for example posting sales to general ledger may include VAT, or trade discounts incorrectly treated as if cash discounts.

3. Printouts may not accord with regulatory requirements, e.g. VAT returns and supporting schedules, PAYE/NIC reports.

4. Audit costs vary with the complexity of the system, not with hardware cost, which puts auditors under fee pressure as they must find a cost-effective method of doing their work.

5. Decentralization of large companies. Large companies have departmental budgets which easily include PCs. The resulting decentralization increases complexity, security risks and audit costs since economies of scale are lost; the audit process is akin to that required for a series of small independent applications.

6. PC users may be proprietor-dominated. If the owner becomes a DP expert, then records can be made to show anything and he can write his own programs and 'adapt' purchased software. The biggest problem is failure to retain copies of non-current files, and back-up copies of current files in use. File security is often non-existent. Errors may occur which are not discovered until much later.

7. The separation of functions is often impractical. Procedures for processing and reporting are informal; and staff have easy access to machines and records. It is essential to have back-up of data files and programs to ensure recovery from data loss and errors.

8. Controls over completeness and accuracy are difficult to achieve by conventional methods in real-time systems. Data are often processed singly, as and when needed, rather than in batches on a regular basis.

9. Hardware and file protection. Data are frequently lost, files corrupted or data distorted. Two reasons for these are:

   (a) some disks are of poor quality when purchased, but this is discovered too late;

   (b) there is insufficient care by staff when working with hardware, storing files, etc. In addition, insurance is inadequate and maintenance work, including machine hygiene and cleanliness, infrequent.

These same attributes, and the resultant audit difficulties, apply equally to stand-alone PCs, mini-computers or simple networks where a central 'file-server' holds the accounting data.

As a result, the installation of a cheap computer is often viewed by staff as being an 'open house' arrangement, and all and sundry have easy access to the machine in an unregulated and undisciplined manner. So simple is its operation that it could, for an entire processing run, remain under sole control of one person – an obvious security hazard. Such matters as controlled access, physical precautions, secrecy of output, authorization of program changes, logging of use, care of files, and the innumerable other security measures become secondary considerations and eventually fade entirely. That is, of course, until such neglect results in the inadvertent destruction of unsupported master files, or a power failure reveals the deficiency in standby facilities, to mention but two of a range of untoward consequences of varying degrees of seriousness for the entity concerned.

In such a case it may prove difficult for the auditor, having continuously acquiesced in what amounts to a flagrant disregard for basic internal control criteria, to establish his own freedom from culpability in the matter, especially if outside losses result. In short, if this section sounds like a warning, it is meant to. As we have seen in Chapter 10, liability can no longer be regarded purely in the light of the basic statutory reporting duty, and data processing methods do not alter principles of law or established standards of professional competence.

The use of PCs continues to spread rapidly in industry and commerce. The significant reductions in the cost of electronic equipment mean that there is no longer any economy of scale in using a large computer, and many organizations are decentralizing their computer operations or moving away from computer bureaux in order to obtain the advantages of flexibility and local control by using small computers in their own offices.

11.9.2 Audit approach to the small computer environment

The overall audit approach remains unchanged, having the following typical stages:

Recording the accounting and internal control systems

Simple overview flowcharts may be used, showing, *inter alia*, inputs, processes, reports and interfaces (if any) with other software also being run.

Assessing the risk of misstatement in the financial statements

The potential risks of misstatement are greatly reduced by the use of well tried-and-tested accounting packages, from which any major 'bugs' will already have been eliminated; conversely the risks of misstatement are increased where an in-house spreadsheet is used for accounting purposes. The most important source of information is likely to be from within the auditor's own organization i.e. his experience with packages used by other clients. As in a manual system, the environment surrounding the accounting routines is a factor which influences the assessment of risk, e.g. the quality of the accounting staff and training they receive, password protection, back-up procedures. The auditor should document his assessment of risk and the reasons for that assessment, just as he would in a manual system – perhaps using a checklist of some kind.

Determining the overall approach, particularly as to whether controls are to be relied upon

As there will be limited division of duties and limited formal controls, it is most unlikely that the auditor will be able to rely on controls for audit purposes; an audit approach using detailed substantive testing is likely to be the only realistic option.

Determining the nature and extent of substantive testing

The auditor should vary the levels of substantive testing applied to computer operations, depending on his assessment of the risks involved. Provided that the overall environment in which the computer operates is satisfactory it is likely that substantive test levels may be reduced in comparison to a manual system.

Executing the audit tests

The use of personal computers in carrying out audit tests is considered in more detailed below (11.9.3).

Concluding and reporting

Errors found in any computerized accounting system may well be systematic in nature and are therefore far more likely to affect a large number of transactions. This should be taken into account by the auditor in assessing the potential impact on the financial statements.

11.9.3   The use of PCs for audit purposes

The benefits

As the use of PCs spreads throughout the business community, it is appropriate that they should become instrumental in the performance of audit work on the records and accounts which arise as a product of those machines. Auditors who have a facility with the use of PCs will be capable of adapting them to meet the needs of specific client circumstances, with immediate benefits in terms of cost effectiveness.

The use of PCs by auditors can be subdivided into cases where the clients' own machines are used by the auditors, and cases where the auditor uses his own PC as an audit aid. In the former category the auditor can, with the client's permission (but not necessarily with the knowledge of the staff), perform 'test packs' and similar test runs on the client's system using the client's software and files – except, of course, that the test data will be contrived for audit purposes.

The former category is susceptible to investigation by file interrogation software. The benefit is that features of the client files (e.g. undepreciated assets, overdue debtors, obsolete stock, unmatched suppliers' invoices) can be extracted for audit purposes by means of specific questions put to the computer when loaded with the relevant data files.

Use by auditors of their own PCs (including portable computers) can be immensely beneficial in the context of analytical review procedures, which by their very nature involve calculations, comparisons and analyses, for which computers are ideally suited, providing the speedy processing of relevant data in a more advanced manner, using arrays extending over several years, and screen displays. Adjustments based on knowledge of specific conditions can be keyed in, giving almost instantaneous adjustment to the screen display, facilitating comparison by the auditor, and reference to anticipated results.

The projection and extrapolation facilities of computers allow for efficient 'what if' calculations to be prepared by auditors when considering the validity of the going concern assumption for any client in precarious circumstances.

Where smaller clients use their PCs to prepare accounts subject to audit, the post-audit journal entries can be very efficiently checked by the auditor if he uses the client's system for this purpose. (Great care, however, must be exercised in retaining on file all the supporting printouts of journal adjustments; there is a corresponding risk that the journal entry, which will not automatically update the nominal ledger, will not create any actual adjustment to the accounts.)

Risks

Use by auditors of PCs for creating and processing test data can easily lead to wrong conclusions. These tests can support an opinion only in relation to the processing on the particular day: it may be dangerous to assume that the system operates correctly at all other times.

Similarly, the use of interrogation software is highly selective in its application, and there is always the risk that skilled DP staff will have tampered with the files to avoid relevant data being selected for printout. The audit software can yield results no better than are facilitated by the questions asked, and the limitations of the system itself in the recording of transactions.

Tests designed to establish the effectiveness of programmed controls are successful only if independent completeness tests are undertaken. The system tests will be limited to data on file – what is not there (but should be) cannot be specifically tested. Tests which highlight the correct use of programmed reasonableness controls can lead to fallacious conclusions, since they are usually based on 'exception' reporting – again giving little confidence that *every* exception has been reported. These risks demonstrate the need for supplementary tests, e.g. on reciprocal populations for completeness.

Not all auditors have the same expertise in the use of PCs for audit work. They can be dangerous in the hands of less skilled staff and lead to invalid conclusions. There is also a risk that audit testing becomes geared to the needs of the PC being used, rather than the system being audited. The correct perspective can easily be lost. The best auditors recognize and remember that, in a sense, it is the client (not just the accounting system) that is being audited, and this entails an assessment of the environment in which the computer is operating. This includes management attitudes, which no PC can effectively audit. There is a risk that the orientation of audit parameters could become too narrow.

Other uses of PCs for auditors

1. Documentary
    (a) Drafting memos and reports.

(b) Documenting systems and flowcharts supported by systems notes.

(c) Preparation of financial statements for clients, with options to input journals and other adjustments.

(d) Audit planning, risk analysis and audit program preparation (there are a number of packaged software programs now available to assist the auditor).

2. Audit executions

(a) Sample selection and random number generation.

(b) Control accounts preparation.

(c) Testing calculations, e.g. reperformance of interest computations.

(d) Interrogating clients' own data files.

3. Access to information

(a) Use of internal and external databases and general accounting/tax information.

(b) Reference to comparative client data, library list references and searches based on keywords.

4. Training

(a) Use of PC in computer-based training (CBT) and interactive video.

(b) Ability to monitor progress and prepare reports in friendly conversational mode.

11.10   The client's use of a computer service bureau

11.10.1   The case for a third-party reviewer

Concern for security is sometimes caused where the client is using the facilities of a computer service bureau, particularly in those cases where most of the controls are at the bureau and therefore not under the client's direct supervision. It is most important that this is given due consideration at the time the system is being designed, preferably in consultation with the internal and external auditors so that the minimum reliance has to be placed upon the controls in operation at the bureau.

In many ways, however, audit problems are lessened when processing is executed by a bureau. Management often wishes to reduce the 'gap' between the bureau and themselves by requesting more detailed printout than would be the case with their own in-house installations, and input data are frequently retained for longer periods. If the auditor is able to demonstrate to the management that the evidence required for audit purposes coincides with that which is necessary for the purposes of effective management control and general security, little difficulty will be experienced in obtaining the necessary information. Hence in practice it is rare for bureau-oriented systems to be exclusively computer-controlled.

Before accepting the adequacy and effectiveness of controls supposedly operated by the bureau, the auditor should investigate these as directly as circumstances will permit; but the question of how far the auditor of a user company should (or is able to) transfer his attention to the bureau organization itself cannot be answered in abstract, nor is it a matter which any of the standard texts deal with. The pages which follow therefore examine this important question in some detail.

Third-party reviewers

The controls at computer bureaux, in which the auditor will be interested, are likely to be those relating to the computer installation ('general controls') but may include specific controls over individual applications ('application controls') such as controls built into the computer programs (e.g. feasibility or limit checks) and controls over transactions applied by bureau staff (e.g. control of cheque stationery).

Where the auditor wishes to evaluate and test the controls at a bureau and permission is obtained, there appear to be two options available:

1. A separate examination of controls by the auditors of each of the bureau's clients.
2. An examination of controls by a third-party reviewer (probably another firm of auditors) and issue of a report which can be made available to the auditors of each of the bureau's clients.

The first option may meet with some opposition from the bureau since it may understandably be alarmed at the prospect of each of its client's auditors performing separate examinations of its controls. The second option also has some problems:

1. A particular auditor may be unwilling to place reliance on an examination of controls commissioned by the computer bureau.
2. The interaction between the general controls exercised by the bureau and the application controls exercised by the client may be unclear.
3. It is often the case that different users place varying degrees of reliance on certain controls and hence their auditors need to gain different levels of knowledge about these controls.

The auditor may conclude that he can rely on examination by a third-party reviewer if he is satisfied that all the procedures which he himself would have wished to perform have indeed been carried out and with the same level of expertise as he would have applied. This is likely to involve consultations with the third-party reviewer, where the evidence provided by him is, in the auditor's opinion, insufficient for his particular purpose. Remember that the bureau is the client of the third-party reviewer and as such must give permission before a consultation can take place.

Finally, it is important in all cases for the auditor to consider the circumstances of the use of the computer bureau's services and the extent to which the control procedures within the computer bureau and at the client's workplace are comprehensive. Where the auditor is unable to rely on an examination by a third-party reviewer and is not granted permission to perform his own examination of the controls of the bureau, he may seek to rely on the application controls exercised by his client. Alternatively, he may seek to carry out additional substantive testing.

11.10.2 Matters for enquiry

Quite apart from the auditor's natural concern with security at the bureau, the client's own management would normally be equally anxious to establish that bureau employees were acting responsibly in relation to the client's data, and that all purported controls were in fact operational. In practice, the bureau will take full responsibility for hiring, training and supervising the personnel who program and operate the system. The user seldom has any voice in such matters; he is usually uninformed about the qualifications of bureau staff and has contact only with designated liaison personnel.

Users who are particularly sensitive about security measures are at liberty to furnish the bureau with code numbers instead of names for, say, customers or employees. Most users, however, are content to satisfy themselves as to the reliability of the bureau selected by pursuing appropriate investigations within the trade, and by ensuring its adherence to recognized codes of conduct, such as operate for all members of the CSA (Computer Services Association). If the security of the data is sufficiently critical, however, the bureau will normally appreciate the point and will co-operate by special arrangement, allowing the user to:

1. Deliver input data in person.
2. Observe all processing.
3. At completion, withdraw all transaction and master-file data from the bureau.

This would operate in extreme cases only. In normal situations, client and auditor would be more concerned with arrangements at the bureau for master-file reconstruction in the event of loss or destruction. The usual questions would relate to the use of fireproof vaults, off-premises storage, temperature and observance of the other appropriate environmental constraints. At the same time, queries should be raised in connection with back-up facilities, especially in cases where the bureau may itself be using the off-shift computer time of other organizations.

These, rather than problems of loss of trail, arise when bureaux are used since, as we have seen, visible data are generally more abundant than in the case of in-house computer processing. It is, after all, the legal responsibility of the client's management to retain adequate records for reconstruction in the event of a failure at the bureau. It is worthwhile for the auditor to look carefully at the contract between his client and the bureau with special reference to legal liability. If, for instance, a member of the user staff (albeit unwittingly) causes a service disruption at the bureau, as a result of which other bureau users suffer loss, the contract should indemnify the first user against all claims arising. Conversely, it should be seen that the agreed upper limit of the bureau's liability to the user in respect of service or security failures will provide commensurate compensation.

Despite their independent attitude, most bureaux, especially in these competitive times, will go a long way to meet user control requirements, even where the bureau regards them as mildly neurotic. In general terms, no exception could be taken to enquiries from the user on:

▶ Security provisions over the client's data and files, and the effectiveness of supervision.

▶ Provisions for back-up and reconstruction.

▶ Bureau procedures for handling special conditions such as 'unmatched' transactions (i.e. no record on the master file), control total (or count) inconsistencies, and error correction at the bureau.

Two final reminders about bureau processing situations:

1. The client will be one of many companies using the bureau, and a number of others will be larger, and hence more important to the bureau; it could therefore prove to be a formidable task to gain maximum co-operation from the bureau staff.

2. The client's end of the data processing system may appear straightforward enough – but it is worth remembering that operations at the bureau may be exceedingly complex.

The audit approach described in this section is consistent with contemporary standards of investigation, and a less conscientious attitude is fraught with risk.

11.11 Problems arising from the use of remote terminals

Technical innovations have increased the use of remote terminals, usually based upon VDU and keyboard input, and these have widespread application in commercial organizations. We see examples of the use of remote terminals in airline booking terminals, bank cash point (ATM) terminals, and information from branches which can be keyed in on a daily or weekly basis through remote terminals. Such data may relate to current purchases, sales or stock movements.

Examples abound, but in each case the chief audit problem arises from the fact that master files held in the central computer store (on disks or drums because of access speed and storage capacity) may be read and updated by remote terminal without an adequate audit trail or, in some cases, any record remaining. Necessary precautions should therefore be made to ensure that these terminals are used in a controlled way, by authorized personnel only.

11.11.1 Security techniques

In view of the risks outlined above, a number of recognized techniques have come into general operation in order to control the use of terminals for input purposes. The most important of these techniques include the following:

1. Hardware constraints, e.g. necessitating the use of a key or magnetic-strip badge or card to engage the terminal, or placing the terminal in a location to which access is carefully restricted, and which is constantly monitored by closed-circuit television surveillance systems.

2. The allocation of identification numbers to authorized terminal operators, with or without the use of passwords. These are checked by the mainframe computer against stored tables of authorized numbers and passwords.

3. Using operator characteristics such as voice prints, hand geometry (finger length ratios) and thumb prints as a means of identification by the mainframe computer.

4. Restricting the access to particular programs or master files in the mainframe computer to designated terminals. This arrangement may be combined with those indicated above.

5. In top-security systems, the authority to allocate authorities such as those indicated above (i.e. determination of passwords, nominating selected terminals) will *itself* be restricted to senior personnel, other than intended users.

6. A special file may be maintained in the central processor which records every occasion on which access is made by particular terminals and operators to central programs and files. This log will be printed out at regular intervals, e.g. the end of each day, or on request by personnel with appropriate authority.

11.11.2 Real-time systems

In some computer applications a buffer store of input data will be held by the central processor before accessing the master files; in such cases input from remote terminals may be checked by special scanning programs before main processing commences. However, in 'real-time' systems action at the terminal causes an immediate response in the central processor, whenever the terminal is on-line. Security against unauthorized input and access outlined above is therefore even more important in real-time systems because:

1. The effect of the input instantaneously updates the files held in the central processor.

2. Edit checks on the input are likely to be under the control of the terminal operators themselves.

In view of these control problems, most real-time systems incorporate additional controls over the security of the master files, for example by logging the contents of the files 'before look' and 'after look' respectively. Readers wishing to learn more about real-time systems should consult the reading list in the final section in this chapter.

11.12 Computer security – the wider problems

The following is a schedule of current computer security problems, and corresponding recommendations auditors can suggest to their clients with a view to overcoming these.

Password security

If intended to restrict access, staff should be required to be more disciplined. Password codes are often attached to terminals; sometimes complete password lists are left in unlocked drawers. Recommendations to clients would be:

▶ Change password periodically but not predictably.

▶ Instil stricter discipline.

▶ Use easily memorable phrases (e.g. 'time flies') to avoid the need to write down password codes.

▶ Change system to voice or fingerprint recognition, and abolish passwords altogether.

Control over input

Excessive reliance on manually created batch or other user-based input controls results in delays if performed properly, or in high input error rates if corners are cut. Recommendations to clients would be:

▶ Write adaptable application software for checking input at entry stage against:
  - normal parameter values;
  - user-produced control data.

▶ Query unusual data with originating department as soon as it is highlighted by the program.

▶ Produce exception reports for subsequent comparison with those normally produced at processing stage.

Scrambling of sensitive data during processing

Encryption of sensitive data takes place too close to processing, by which time it may have been seen or copied by unauthorized personnel. Recommendations to clients would be:

▶ Encryption should feature as early as possible, especially when highly sensitive data relate to very material sums, e.g. electronic funds transfer internationally, when destination is featured in original input.

▶ Encryption should be preceded by a message authentication device operated independently of the data source and destination.

▶ Unscrambling at output destination should again be preceded by a message authentication device, and should take place after output has left DP centre.

Software integrity

Sofware is used to authenticate messages, perform key accounting calculations, authorize asset movements, etc. The consequences of fraudulent or corrupted codes in programs used for such purposes could be disastrous. Recommendations to clients would be:

▶ Identify those source programs which, if manipulated, could cause substantial losses through fraud or other irregularity.

▶ Arrange for codes in programs to be checked regularly, without warning, by personnel independent of operators, programmers and analysts.

▶ Use test packs specially created for this purpose and record results for subsequent reference.

Data security

Highly confidential information is held on both current and non-current files. Tapes can easily be removed. Security guards do not search employees. Recommendations to clients would be:

▶ Identify data on file which could be exploited if in the wrong hands.

▶ Classify it according to a security hierarchy, which incorporates codes indicating data held on behalf of others (banks, computer bureaux, finance companies, stockbrokers).

▶ Apply appropriate encryption routines to sensitive data to ensure it is non-recognizable.

▶ Ensure compliance with *Data Protection Act 1984.*

Database security

In database systems only a small proportion of stored data is accessed daily or weekly. Some customer records may not be accessed for months. In the meanwhile, stored data may have inadvertently or deliberately been corrupted, and this may even have reached back-up files. Recommendations to clients would be:

▶ Remind staff to check the accuracy of standing data accessed from database.

▶ Institute a system of routine checking of database accuracy on sample basis, performed regularly.

▶ At prescribed (but longer) intervals, perform database dump and delete obsolete data, checking right through for accuracy.

▶ Investigate unauthorized changes.

11.13   Implications of computers for auditors – a summary

11.13.1   The DP problems summarized

The chief internal control problems likely to be encountered by the auditor of DP (as opposed to conventional) systems, as dealt with in this chapter, may be summarized as follows:

1. The user departments lose their recording autonomy; under conventional systems production records are in the production department; sales records in the sales

department; accounting records in the accounts department; stock records in the stores; and so on. In DP systems all these records are in the DP department. Furthermore, the staff in the DP department tend to be far more identified with the computer than with the company.

2. Computer hardware and records are vulnerable to atmospheric/environmental conditions, electrical and magnetic interference, accidental damage or destruction, and human manipulation. The files are also in the form of densely packed magnetic media and so their contents cannot be identified visually.

3. The visible processing trail, which is taken for granted in conventional recording systems, is lost in the course of computer processing, which is itself governed by programs whose reliability can be inferred only indirectly, as opposed to being capable of direct observation while functioning.

11.13.2 Implications for the auditor

The consequences for the auditor of the three major control problems highlighted above may, in turn, be summarized as follows:

1. *Knowledge and experience*: Technical knowledge and practical experience on the part of audit staff are an essential accompaniment to the planning and execution of all audit procedures. This may be gained from books, by attending courses, on-the-job training, and by appointing computer technicians to join the audit complement. (Reading this chapter, for example, would, on its own, provide a totally insufficient basis for conducting the audit; it does, however, provide an eminently sound foundation.)

2. *Audit documentation*: The documentation on the audit files must reflect the nature of the audit. Standard questionnaires and checklists must be redrafted accordingly, and the current files contain a record of all of the client's DP documentation, details of major controls included in the programs, flow diagrams of systems, and the other items listed in section 11.8.1 above.

3. *Timing of tests*: The auditor requires a totally revised approach to the timing of audit tests. When a complete and permanent record of all transactions, assets and liabilities is available at all times, audit tests on the records may be carried out at any convenient stage, by mutual agreement between client and auditor. In DP systems, however, contemporary, as opposed to historical, testing is often an inescapable imposition. We have already discussed examples of this in relation to the following:

   (a) Requests for special printouts for audit purposes. These indicate reliability only in relation to the specific tests conducted, and it would be dangerous to rely upon them as valid for processing which takes place at any other time; hence the need for periodic visits, often on an ad hoc basis, for purposes of making tests.

(b) Test packs which, like tests on special printouts, should be conducted intermittently throughout the period under audit, otherwise it will be impossible for the auditor to draw valid conclusions concerning the functioning of programs and programmed controls during the period as a whole.

(c) The loss of audit trail due to creation of, say, batch totals which give no breakdowns for checking purposes or for cross-referencing to original documents. The original documents may themselves, in some cases, have been re-sorted for another purpose, as a result of which the locating of specific items is rendered impracticable. Once again, therefore, it is essential for the auditor to be present while processing is taking place if he wishes effectively to audit the procedures in question.

4. *The incidence of audit tests*: Conventional records may be audited by vouching and checking the visible entries made at the very interface between the authorized and valid originating documents, on the one hand, and the books of account, on the other. In DP systems the recording counterpart takes place within the machine, and no equivalent record is left for subsequent individual verification. For this reason the auditor is forced to shift the target of his tests, and to concentrate his efforts on the following:

(a) Quality control over every stage in the creation of the input.

(b) The systems development controls responsible for ensuring that the programs function correctly.

(c) The administrative controls which are designed to ensure that the correct programs are always used; that staff observe designated job divisions; that hardware and files are physically secure and adequately supported by reconstruction and standby facilities.

(d) The use made by management of output reports, particularly exception reports, and the control procedures governing rejection of invalid data.

(e) The need for this shift of incidence is understood when one realizes that all tests 'through' the machine can, at best, provide indirect affirmation on program functioning; and although clearly better than nothing, such tests are always inferior, from the audit viewpoint, to tests in which the accounting entries may be scrutinized in their totality (albeit historically) at the very point of their creation.

11.14 Recommended reading

The following titles (all available at the time of writing) are recommended to those who seek a more detailed appreciation of computers and computer auditing:

An Audit Approach to Computers, B. Jenkins, R. Perry and P. Cooke (Accountancy Books)

Computer Control Guidelines and Computer Audit Guidelines (Canadian Institute of Chartered Accountants)

An Approach to the Audit of Less Complex Computerized Accounting Systems (Audit Faculty, ICAEW)

Information Technology Statements (Faculty of Information Technology, ICAEW):

'Security and Confidentiality of Data'

'Good Accounting Software'

'Control and Management of Information'

'Costs and Benefits of Information Technology Projects'

'Controlling Small Computers'

'Systems Development and Acquisition'

'Quality Assurance'

'Acquisition of Computer Systems'

'Control and Management of Small Computer Networks'

Review questions

*1. The managing director of one of your audit clients has approached you and announced that because he now has a computer system, and it does not make mistakes, he is dispensing with the services of 50% of his accounting staff. He has stated that one person can now do more jobs and that he does not need to segregate duties to the same degree.

Outline the contents of a formal letter to your client to inform him of the errors in his assumptions.

*2. Draw up a checklist which could be used to assess the risks present in a computerized environment.

3. Computer technology is advancing at a fast rate. With the advances come faster and apparently more efficient ways of performing tasks. However, there is also the problem that security and control measures devised to counteract fraud and other hazards are, by the time management have implemented them, effectively out of date.

Identify a minimum of five such areas of risk and the advice that you would give a client to counteract the perceived problems.

4. Personal computers are being used frequently by both auditors and other professionals. Outline, in a memorandum to your senior partner, the advantages and risks involved in widespread usage.

Exercises

1. When considering whether or not to rely on computer controls the auditor is not assessing impregnability and infallibility. Given that this is the case, exactly what *is* the auditor trying to assess?

2. Given current advances in technology, outline the controls and security measures that can prevent infiltration of a networked computer system for remote terminals.

12

Investigations

THIS CHAPTER DEALS WITH:

▷ specialized investigation assignments;

▷ auditor's reports in prospectuses and profit forecasts.

Although auditing has become a specialized discipline in its own right, there are a number of assignments which, although of a similar nature, differ significantly in certain important respects. Auditing, as dealt with in this text so far, is chiefly governed by UK companies legislation in which the rights, duties and responsibilities of auditors are clearly laid down by statute; but more specialized assignments, such as investigations undertaken for a particular purpose, are governed only by the terms of reference mutually agreed between the parties to the contract. Since work of this nature may form a significant part of the practising auditor's range of services, it is appropriate to deal with investigations in some detail.

12.1 Classes of investigation

Although there are no two investigations which are identical, they may nevertheless be classified for convenience under the following groups and subgroups:

Agreed investigations

1. Investigations related to investment decisions:
   ▶ prospectus reports (public company issues),
   ▶ profit forecasts.

Hostile investigations

2. Fraud.

12.2 The golden rules

Although in each of the above categories the auditor will have to bring to bear upon his work a variety of constraining factors (e.g. any governing legislation), there are a few golden rules which, in almost all cases, should be carefully observed.

First, the terms of reference under which the investigation is being conducted should be clearly set out in a letter of engagement before starting detailed enquiries. For example, the reason for the investigation should be known; the cost of the investigation should be discussed and agreed; it should be known, in the case of a business acquisition, whether it is the client's intention to participate in its management, or whether the acquisition is viewed purely as an external investment. Clarification of these and like matters will minimize the risk of subsequent disagreement as to precisely what the investigation was designed to accomplish.

Secondly, during the course of any investigation a substantial amount of detailed information will inevitably come to light, and it is all too easy to become side-tracked into non-essential issues. This danger should be carefully guarded against at all times by bearing in mind the main objective of the assignment, and by agreeing in advance the period which should retrospectively be included within its scope, unless this is laid down by law (as in the case of prospectus reports) or other external authority (as in the case of back duty investigations).

Thirdly, all detailed working schedules and notes, including those taken in the course of interviews, should be indefinitely preserved since the conclusions reached may subsequently be contested, possibly in the course of litigation, and in such circumstances it will obviously be highly dangerous to rely upon memory.

Fourthly, the language in which the final report is expressed should take into consideration the level of financial and accounting knowledge of the parties to whom it is addressed. An unduly sophisticated report, for example, might run the risk of being misunderstood, possibly leading to incorrect conclusions being drawn, and hence incorrect action being taken.

The fifth golden rule is that the form in which the final report is presented (unless formally governed by statute) should be carefully planned. In general:

1. Its subject matter should be immediately apparent from the main heading and the subsequent subheadings.

2. An index to the report and its appendices should be provided by means of which cross-references may be inserted and sections on matters of special interest readily referred to.

3. The introduction to the report should summarize the terms of reference and the object of the investigation.

4. The second section should summarize the work which has been undertaken, and should specify details of books and documents examined and persons interviewed.

5. The concluding section should set out, clearly and unequivocally, the results of the investigation so as to leave no room for doubt as to the action recommended.

6. All detailed workings, containing the key calculations and statistics used in arriving at (and in support of) the final recommendations, may be referred to in the body of the report where appropriate but should be included in full in attached appendices. In this way they will not interrupt the flow of the report nor interfere with a sound appreciation of its main contents.

12.3 Reports in prospectuses

The legal requirements governing reports in prospectuses are contained in the 3rd Schedule to the *Companies Act 1985*. Part II of the 3rd Schedule requires the inclusion in the prospectus of a report by the issuing company's auditors, disclosing:

1. The profits and/or losses of the company for the previous five years.

2. The rates of dividend paid on each class of share capital for the time being in issue for each of those five years.

3. The assets and liabilities of the company as at the last balance sheet date.

The requirements of the Stock Exchange, as issued from time to time in the Yellow Book (entitled *Admission of Securities to Listing*), have for many years proved to be far more demanding than the *Companies Act* requirements set out above. Companies seeking a full Stock Exchange listing for new issues of their securities are required to supply information with respect to the profits and losses, assets and liabilities, financial record and position of the company covering a period of three complete years preceding the application for listing.

Other Stock Exchange rules, as set out in the Yellow Book, include the following:

1. A period of more than nine months between date of final accounts reported on and the date of prospectus would normally be unacceptable, and an interim financial statement covering at least the first six months of the current financial year must be included.

2. Significant departures from the UK Accounting Standards, US Accounting Standards or International Accounting Standards, as applicable, must be disclosed and explained and the financial effects of such departures quantified.

3. The report should state that the profits or losses have been arrived at on defined bases in accordance with approved standards, and after making such adjustments as are considered appropriate.

4. Reports containing significant qualifications are normally unacceptable. Any reservations expressed must also indicate the extent and materiality of such

reservations. Similar considerations apply if the auditors' reports on any of the accounts dealt with in the prospectus have been qualified.

5. Reference in the report to reports, confirmations or valuations of other experts (e.g. valuers) which are not reproduced in the prospectus, should include their names, addresses and professional qualifications.

6. The rules make provision for a statement in standard form of all adjustments made in arriving at the figures of profits or losses (giving reasons) signed by the reporting accountants, to be available for inspection by the public.

7. The accounting policies followed in determining the profits and losses must be disclosed, as well as any other matters which appear to be relevant for the purpose of the report.

Points to note

First, it will be observed that provision is made for disclosure in standard form of the adjustments made by reporting accountants in arriving at the information included in the report. The purpose of these adjustments is to reflect *past results in contemporaneous conditions* (so far as these are known), a reasonable principle which is acceptable under both Stock Exchange rules and 3rd Schedule provisions. As a consequence of these adjustments it may be difficult to reconcile the reported figures with those in the past published financial statements of the company for the years in question.

The published stewardship accounts are prepared by a company's directors for presentation to *committed* investors, i.e. shareholders, in order to acquaint them with the results of the company's activities during the last complete year of stewardship. Information included in prospectus reports, on the other hand, is addressed to *potential* investors in such a way as to enable them to form an opinion on the likely prospects of the company in question under future trading conditions, so far as the latter may be assessed.

It is therefore necessary for the information in published accounts to be represented so as to facilitate this purpose. As far as possible, therefore, the adjustments to the published accounts should take future conditions into consideration. Examples of situations in which adjustments would be appropriate are:

▶ Income and/or expenditure which has arisen in the past, but which it is known will not arise in the future, may be eliminated (e.g. results of discontinued operations, nationalized overseas subsidiaries, uninsured losses, extraordinary items, interest paid on debentures or loan stock to be redeemed out of proceeds of issue, dividends on preference shares to be redeemed, etc.).

▶ Revaluation of assets (upon which the Stock Exchange may well insist) causing a change in depreciation charges. This should be adjusted only if revised figures can be produced with reasonable certainty – it may be preferable to explain the position in a note to the accounts.

► A significant change in the accounting policies at any point during the period reported on, in which event the accounts for all affected periods should be adjusted to reflect the accounting policies which are known to be applicable in the future.

Secondly, prospectus reports are signed sometimes by 'auditors', and sometimes by 'reporting accountants'. The latter title would be appropriate where it is known that part of the proceeds of the issue are to be applied in acquiring another undertaking. In such circumstances the *Companies Act* and Stock Exchange regulations require counterpart information to that outlined above to be supplied in respect of that other undertaking, such information to be set out in a report by 'accountants who shall be named in the prospectus' (i.e. not necessarily the auditors of that undertaking).

Sometimes, however, even when no other undertaking is involved, reports are signed by 'reporting accountants'; this usually arises when the Council of the Stock Exchange or the issuing company's financial advisers recommend that a major firm of accountants be invited to add its name to that of the company's auditors in a *joint report*, in order to add prestige and prominence to the new issue. This may indeed be welcomed by the company's auditors in view of the onerous nature of the disclosure requirements and the severe penalties for misstatement prescribed in various Acts of Parliament, in particular the *Companies Act 1985, Theft Act 1968* and *Protection of Depositors Act 1963*. In much of this legislation, penalties are prescribed for misstatements in prospectus reports irrespective of any fraudulent intent.

Thirdly, section 61 of the *Companies Act 1985* requires a statement (known as a consent) to be included in the published prospectus in relation to any expert (e.g. valuer, accountant, banker, or any person whose qualifications, skill and experience lend authority to their pronouncements) whose report is included in the prospectus. This statement declares that the experts concerned have given and have not withdrawn their written consent to the issue of the prospectus with the inclusion of their reports, etc., in the form and context in which they are included. It is difficult to express an opinion on the extent to which, before permitting publication of their consent, the reporting accountants should institute *fresh* investigations into the issuing company's financial position in circumstances where there has been a considerable delay (say, three months) between the completion of their report and the registration of the prospectus document.

Transatlantic indications are that the reporting accountants may well be liable in damages to any investor suffering loss through reliance upon a report which failed to take into account the company's position at the date of registration itself. In the case of *Escott* v *BarChris Construction Corporation* (US Southern District Court, NY 1968), the company's auditors were found guilty of negligence for having failed to report a material worsening of the company's position which took place *after* the time of signing their prospectus report, but *before* the date when the prospectus registration actually became effective. Under US law, the burden of proof in such cases alleging negligence is on the auditors, who must show that they had been neither negligent nor fraudulent by proving that they had reasonable grounds to believe, and did believe, that the statements were true not only as at the date when they signed the statements, but at the time the statements became effective, which in the above case was almost three months later.

12.4 Reports on profit forecasts

During the late 1960s, the Panel on Takeovers and Mergers was set up in order to regulate procedures in the City in connection with bid situations. This was partly due to a measure of adverse publicity surrounding instances of totally inaccurate forecasting, as a result of which bid prices were unrealistic.

One of the first major tasks of the Panel was the establishment of the City Code on Takeovers and Mergers ('the Code'), which was updated in October 1990.

The accountant's role

Under the rules of the Code, profit forecasts made by directors in any bid situation form part of the public documents available for inspection, and these must be examined by the company's auditors and confirmed by them as fulfilling certain basic criteria. In this way the accounting profession, traditionally concerned with the preparation and audit of historical data, has become involved with commenting on predicted results. *There is no question of the forecasts being 'audited', however, and this should be made clear at the commencement of the assignment and in the report itself.*

The Code requires the accounting bases and calculations of forecasts to be examined and reported on, and any document containing such forecasts must also include the accountant's report, together with a statement that the accountant has given and has not withdrawn his consent to publication. Forecasts are subject to substantial and inherent uncertainties, and therefore cannot be confirmed or verified in the same way as the results of completed accounting periods. The assumptions upon which the directors have based their forecasts must be clearly stated, and the reporting accountants (auditors) must examine and report upon the accounting bases and calculations of those forecasts. The paragraphs which follow are based upon the ICAEW guidance statement 3.908 entitled 'Accountant's reports on profit forecasts'.

Preliminary considerations

Before accepting instructions to report in connection with profit forecasts, the reporting accountant is advised to reach agreement with the directors on the following preliminary points:

1. The time available to the accountant for the preparation of his report should not be so limited that, having regard to the company's circumstances, it would be impossible for sufficient information to be obtained to enable the accountant properly to exercise such professional judgement as may be required.

2. It must be clearly established that the accountant's responsibility is confined to the accounting bases and calculations for the forecasts and does not extend to the assumptions upon which the directors have based their forecasts.

3. Since forecasts are subject to increasing uncertainty the further forward they extend, accountants should not normally undertake to review and report on forecasts which relate to more than the current accounting period and (provided a sufficiently significant part of the current year has elapsed) the next accounting period.

4. It must be established that the reporting accountant cannot relieve the directors of their own responsibility for profit forecasts which may be disclosed to, and relied upon by, outside parties.

Detailed work on profit forecasts

In the course of his review of profit forecasts, the reporting accountant should consider the following:

1. The general character and recent history of the company's business with particular reference to its main products, markets, customers, suppliers, labour force, and trend of results.

2. The major accounting policies (particularly on depreciation, deferred taxation, calculation of value of stocks and work in progress, etc.) normally adopted in preparing the company's annual accounts and the fact that these have been consistently applied in the preparation of the profit forecasts.

3. The accountant must satisfy himself that the preparation of the forecasts is consistent with the economic, commercial, marketing and financial assumptions which the directors have stated to be the underlying bases.

4. The company's general procedures in the preparation of forecasts; in particular the accountant will wish to ascertain whether forecasts are regularly prepared for management purposes and if so, the degree of accuracy and reliability normally achieved. He will also wish to discover the extent to which the forecast results of expired periods are supported by reliable interim accounts, and how the forecasts take account of any material exceptional items.

5. Matters of general concern include the adequacy of provisions made for foreseeable losses and contingencies, and the adequacy of working capital as indicated by properly prepared cash flow forecasts.

Main matters to be stated in accountant's report

The report should be addressed to the directors, and should:

1. Indicate in general terms the work carried out, i.e. review of accounting bases and calculations on which profit forecasts are based.

2. Ensure specific identification of the forecasts and the documents to which the report refers.

3. If an audit of estimated results for expired periods has not been carried out, include a statement to that effect.

4. Express an opinion as to whether forecasts are properly compiled on the basis of assumptions made by the board, and the figures presented on a basis consistent with normal practices.

5. Qualify the report if appropriate (qualifications may be necessary on grounds of substantial restrictions of time).

Restrictions of time

Before accepting instructions to report on the accounting bases and calculations for profit forecasts, reporting accountants should be satisfied that the time within which their report is required should not be so severely restricted that it would be plainly impossible for them to obtain the information they require to enable them properly to exercise their professional judgement for the purpose of reporting.

If for any reason, including unduly restrictive time limits, the reporting accountants have not obtained all the information they consider necessary, they should qualify their report accordingly. If they consider they have insufficient information to enable them properly to exercise their professional judgement for the purpose of giving a meaningful report, they should say so.

Specimen report

An accountant's report on the accounting bases and calculations for profit forecasts might, in appropriate circumstances, where there are no grounds for qualification, read as follows:

> To the Directors of X plc
>
> We have reviewed the accounting bases and calculations used for the profit forecasts of X plc (for which the directors are solely responsible) for the periods set out on pages ... of this circular. The forecasts include results shown by unaudited interim accounts for the period ... In our opinion the forecasts, so far as the accounting bases and calculations are concerned, have been properly compiled on the basis of the assumptions made by the Board set out on page ... of this circular, and are presented on a basis consistent with the accounting practices normally adopted by the company.

Letter of consent

Rule 28.3 of the Code requires that, other than in respect of a forecast made by an offeror offering solely for cash, the accounting policies and calculations for the forecasts must be examined and reported by the auditors or consultant accountants. Any financial adviser mentioned in the document must also report on the forecasts.

Rule 28.4 of the Code requires the reports to be accompanied by a statement that those making them have given and not withdrawn their consent to publication.

Before giving their consent to publication (which should be in writing), the reporting accountants should require to see the whole text of the circular and should be satisfied that it is appropriate, and not misleading, for their report on the accounting bases and calculations for profit forecasts to appear in the form and context in which it is included.

Rule 28.1 of the Code, which governs most of the above considerations, reads as follows:

Standards of care
There are obvious hazards attached to the forecasting of profits; this should in no way detract from the necessity of maintaining the highest standards of accuracy and fair presentation in all communications to shareholders in an offer. A profit forecast must be compiled with scrupulous care and objectivity by the directors, whose sole responsibility it is; the financial advisers must satisfy themselves that the forecast has been prepared in this manner by the directors.

12.4.1 Forecasting – under statute

Recent *Companies Acts* have brought forecasting responsibilities within the routine scope of statutory auditing procedures, and in respect of which no form of disclaimer is likely to be upheld by the courts. This refers most particularly to those sections of the *Companies Act 1985* which outline the methods whereby private companies may:

► Provide finance for the purchase of their own shares.

► Redeem shares issued as redeemable shares.

► Purchase their own shares.

In each of the above three instances, the duties and responsibilities of the auditors of the companies are the same, and essentially require them to report on the reasonableness of the opinions expressed by the directors on the continued solvency of the company, and on its ability to continue as a going concern for the ensuing year.

For companies to purchase and cancel virtually the whole of their share capital otherwise than out of the proceeds of a fresh issue of shares or from profits otherwise available for distribution is a serious matter indeed, and would appear to fly in the face of other statutory provisions governing the preservation and maintenance of capital as the fund of last resort for unsecured creditors: a continuous feature of UK company law for over a century.

To avoid such licence descending into a recipe for disaster on an undreamed-of scale, the safeguards against abuse must be seen, both conceptually and practically, to be virtually watertight. For this role the auditor has been appointed, thus giving *de facto* statutory recognition to the forecasting aspect of audit work.

Auditors are expected to respond to the challenge of this onerous responsibility, and such response should not include protective warnings similar to those still familiar in the context of profit forecasts, such as:

> The forecast of solvency and the assumptions on which it is based, as incorporated in the directors' statutory declaration, are the sole and exclusive responsibility of the directors, and we have consequently confined our own work to (i) ensuring that the methods used by the directors for projecting the continued solvency of the company are consistent with the forecasting methods used by them in preparing their normal management budgets; and (ii) checking the accuracy of their calculations.

Such ploys do not work for the simple reason that the Act requires auditors to do something which Rule 28 of the City Code does not: to state in writing that, having enquired into the state of the company's affairs, they are unaware of anything to indicate that the opinion of the directors (i.e. with regard to solvency and future viability as a going concern for at least twelve months) is unreasonable in all the circumstances.

If company law manifests a belief in the ability of auditors to perform such a task, will the time not come when those who rely on profit forecasts in bid situations expect a comparable degree of assurance from the auditors who examine the forecasts? The more so, I would venture to suggest, when the forecasting period is considerably less than twelve months.

The City Takeover Panel, unlike authorities in the USA, has never sought to discourage forecasts, only to curb the temptation of directors to indulge in extravagant flights of fancy whenever they feel threatened by sounds of a prospective takeover. Sir Alexander Johnstone, former deputy chairman of the Panel, in his book *The City Takeover Code*, declared that the Panel believes that ...

> directors' opinions on the immediate future profitability of the company are the most important single element in the formation of the decision whether to invest in the company or to disinvest. If forecasts were forbidden, uncorroborated statements for which no one would be answerable might pass by word of mouth to selected shareholders.

The Panel is, naturally enough, concerned that forecasts are 'prepared with care and a due sense of responsibility', and the strict rules embodied in the Code and its Practice Notes are drafted with this end in mind. In this process, the auditor is clearly allocated a key role. Yet in the performance of that role, auditors ...

> appear to be preoccupied more with what they cannot do than with what they can do and more concerned about raising false expectations in consequence of 'their special status and authority' than providing the reassurance which that status and authority puts them in a unique position to provide ...

to quote from a paper presented by Professor Robert Jack to the University of Glasgow Symposium on Auditing Research in 1982. Professor Jack continues:

> I am left with the doubt whether the shareholder who takes a decision whether to accept or reject a takeover offer is really aware of the limited scope of the 'comfort' or reassurance which the auditor's report is giving him on a part (which the Code regarded as crucial) of the information and advice which shareholders must be given so that they can arrive at 'a properly informed decision as to the merits and demerits of an offer' [Rule 23 of the

Code]. And in a context of law (which has found expression in the *Unfair Contract Terms Act 1977*) where attempts by providers of services to limit or exclude their 'liability ... for negligence or other breach of duty by means of contract terms or otherwise' (to use the words of the long title of the Act) can be ineffectual or at least rendered ineffectual by the application of a 'reasonableness test', I would think that if a failed forecast became the subject of legal proceedings the courts might not be too sympathetic to an explanation that the auditors' attestation was restricted to the extent and in the manner stated in the guidance statement.

Professor Jack's paper concludes its section on forecasts by citing this as a classical instance of the situation in which auditors so often find that they have been thrust – a situation in which:

1. The degree of reliance which others may reasonably place upon their work remains undefined.

2. Subjective judgement and inherent uncertainties are numerous and substantial.

In short, the mere act of becoming involved gives rise to the 'misunderstanding of the extent of assurance with respect to the credibility of financial statements which could be provided by independent examination', to quote the paper by R. K. Mautz, 'The role of auditing in our society' (1975), where he observes that this misunderstanding has existed from 'the very beginning' of auditing, and it persists and reemerges every time auditors become involved, either from choice or in response to outside instigation, in fields of responsibility outside their traditional area of reporting on the view presented by financial statements.

12.5 Fraud

A good deal on fraud, in a variety of manifestations, has already been written in this text (notably in connection with computers and auditors' responsibility for fraud detection in the context of their normal professional work). The question of the auditor's responsibility for its prevention and discovery is highly contentious these days, especially since the past few years have seen a dramatic increase in both the incidence and scale of corporate fraud; nor does the uncertain state of case law on the question of third party liability help to clarify the position. This aspect of fraud detection has already been dealt with extensively in Chapter 10 above. Most investigations into fraud are conducted at the behest of the client to discover whether in fact fraud has occurred, and if so, its magnitude. In 1995 the APB issued a Statement of Auditing Standards (110) on the auditor's responsibility in relation to fraud detection.

The majority of such investigations will relate to fraud in its 'petty' variety, usually perpetrated by one or two individuals who find themselves able to exploit for their own benefit specific internal control weaknesses. In relatively few of such instances does the fraud lead to the collapse of the company, and discovery is usually due to the neglect and carelessness of the perpetrator(s) in continuing to cover over the traces, e.g.

when another employee takes over their duties while they are ill or on holiday. Sometimes discovery is attributable to their personal greed in attempting to expand the area or scale of their criminal activity; and sometimes (unfortunately relatively rarely) to the efforts of the company's auditors.

It is impossible, within the confines of this text, to classify and examine every type of corporate crime, except to point out that there are two broad categories:

1. Frauds involving the manipulation of the records and the accounts, usually by the company's senior officers, with a view to benefiting in some way from the false picture which they convey (e.g. obtaining finance under false pretences, or concealing a material worsening of the company's true position).
2. Frauds, usually by employees, involving the theft, misappropriation or embezzlement of the company's funds, usually in the form of cash, or of its other assets (such as goods held in a warehouse).

It is probable that cash (or bank balances), the most readily and immediately useful of all corporate assets, provides the most frequent target for fraud in category 2 above; the following list is a useful summary of the procedures which, in most instances, the investigating accountant will be required to perform in arriving at estimates of losses from this cause, assuming it is already known that a defaulting employee has been 'at work':

1. Ascertain the level of authority and nature of duties of the defaulting employee.
2. Cast and vouch cash book, and obtain certificates of opening and closing balances from the bank.
3. Check cash book against bank statements, paying particular attention to dates of lodgements to ascertain whether receipts were banked without delay.
4. Examine original pay-in slips at the bank and compare with counterfoils, since this may reveal the practice known as teeming and lading.
5. Circularize debtors positively.
6. Note any apparently irregular cash payments.
7. Examine cancelled cheques and compare names of payees with details in cash book and invoices.
8. Obtain duplicates of missing expenditure vouchers.
9. Vouch all amounts shown as partners' or directors' drawings or loans.
10. Vouch and cast petty cash book.
11. Confirm names of all employees shown on wages lists with chief accountant or other senior official, and amounts payable to them.
12. Perform computer comparison of employee bank details and investigate duplicate payee details.
13. If defaulter had access to all books, all postings should be checked and a trial balance extracted.

14. Confirm all bad debts written off, discount allowances and returns.

15. Check order book against sales day book or copy-sales invoices to detect any sales which have been wholly unrecorded.

16. Cash sales should be verified against whatever evidence may be available.

17. Vouch purchase invoices with purchases day book, and see that none has been passed through twice.

18. Obtain duplicates of all missing purchases vouchers.

19. Compare creditors' statements against purchase ledger balances.

20. Check goods inwards book or order book against invoices to ensure that the latter relate to bona fide purchases.

21. Check contracts with third parties.

22. Perform computer comparison of supplier details, e.g. address or telephone numbers.

13

Special classes of audit

THIS CHAPTER DEALS WITH:

▷ the special work of the reporting accountant in cases where solicitors handle clients' monies;

▷ specific audit difficulties relating to the audit of insurance companies;

▷ guidance on the audit of pension schemes;

▷ joint audits.

13.1 Solicitors' Accounts Rules

13.1.1 Statutory provisions

The statutory provisions for regulating the handling of clients' money (and accounting therefore) and trust money are contained in the following:

Solicitors Act 1974

Solicitors' Accounts Rules 1991

Accountant's Report Rules 1991

In addition, the Law Society is a 'Professional Body' which is recognized as able to regulate the practice of its profession in the conduct of carrying out investment business under the *Financial Services Act 1986*. The Law Society adopted the *Solicitors' Investment Business Rules 1990 (SIBR 1990)* which came into force on 15 March 1990.

13.1.2 Purposes of the rules

1. To require a solicitor to keep clients' money and trust money separate from his own.

2. To ensure that a solicitor keeps adequate records of his transactions so that his books show money received and paid and the balance held on account of each client.

3. To ensure that the money of each client is clearly distinguished from that of other clients and from other money passing through the solicitor's accounts.

4. To require a solicitor to state annually on his application for a practising certificate where he has held or received client money.

5. To require the solicitor to submit an accountant's report if he has held or received clients' money.

6. To ensure that individual client accounts are never in debit since this would mean that the other clients' monies had been used for the client in question.

Rule 27(1) gives the Council of the Law Society power to order the inspection of individual solicitors' accounts to ascertain whether the rules have been complied with.

13.1.3 Broad effect of the rules

Money received by a solicitor which does not belong to him must be dealt with:

1. Through his client account if he receives it in connection with his practice.

2. Either through his client account or through a separate trust bank account opened for the particular trust if it is money subject to a controlled trust, i.e. one of which the solicitor is sole trustee or co-trustee only with a partner or employee.

3. Through his client account if it is subject to any other trust of which he is a trustee.

Points to note

1. Cheques on a client bank account should be signed by the solicitor. Only in exceptional circumstances, e.g. illness or unavoidable absence on business or holiday, should this procedure be departed from. The practice of signing cheques in blank and leaving them with an employee is clearly unwise and to be deprecated.

2. A solicitor must not treat himself as a client, nor may he finance a client out of his (the solicitor's) money held in a client account.

3. Money received by a solicitor as trustee may be paid into a client bank account.

4. A solicitor can withdraw his own money from a client bank account only by transfer to his office bank account or a cheque drawn up in his own favour.

5. A cheque or draft received on behalf of a client and endorsed over in the ordinary course of business would not pass through the solicitor's client bank account but it should nevertheless be recorded in his books as a transaction on behalf of the client.

6. Drawing against a cheque before it is cleared could result in the amount held for a particular client going negative, i.e. in other clients' money being used to make the payment. If this occurs, the solicitor will have committed a breach of the rules

(see 13.1.2 above). Even if the solicitor, on discovery of the breach, immediately pays the appropriate amount from his own resources into client account, the accountant may still need to qualify his report.

7.   Where money is received on account of costs:

(a)   it must be paid into the solicitor's office account if the costs have been incurred and a bill of costs has been delivered to the client;

(b)   it must otherwise be paid into client account.

13.1.4   *Accountant's Report Rules 1991*

General principles

Every solicitor who handles clients' money shall produce annually a report by a qualified accountant that the solicitor has complied with Parts I and II of the *Solicitors' Accounts Rules* and Rule 13 of the *Solicitors' Investment Business Rules 1990*. The report is required once in every practice year, and is a separate matter from the issue to a solicitor of his annual practising certificate. The report must be submitted to the Law Society within six months of the end of the solicitor's financial year.

Neither the *Solicitors Act* nor the *Accountant's Report Rules* requires a complete audit of the solicitor's account, nor do they require the preparation of profit and loss account or balance sheet.

Qualification of accountant

To be qualified to give a report the accountant must be an English, Scottish or Irish chartered accountant or a certified accountant. He must not be a partner or employee of the solicitor and he must not have been disqualified by the Council of the Law Society.

Examination of books and accounts

The reporting accountant's work is prescribed by the *Accountant's Report Rules 1991*, and although it is not referred to as an audit, the requirements have many audit characteristics. The accountant is not normally required to check and vouch each and every item in the books or bank statements, but if the general examination and detailed tests disclose evidence that the Rules have not been complied with, the accountant must pursue a more comprehensive investigation. For the purpose of giving an accountant's report an accountant must:

1.   Ascertain from the solicitor particulars of all bank accounts (including controlled trust bank accounts) kept, maintained or operated by the solicitor in connection with his practice.

2. Examine the book-keeping system in every office of the solicitor to see that the system complies with Rule 11 of the *Solicitors' Accounts Rules 1991*, and

   (a) that there is an appropriate ledger account for each client;

   (b) that the ledger accounts show, separately from other information, particulars of all clients' money received, held or paid on account of each client;

   (c) that transactions relating to clients' money and any other money dealt with through a client account are recorded in the solicitor's books so as to distinguish such transactions from transactions relating to any other monies;

   (d) make test checks of postings to clients' ledger accounts from records of receipts and payments of clients' money;

   (e) make test checks of the casts of such accounts;

   (f) compare a sample of lodgements and payments from the client account as shown in the bank and building society statements with the solicitor's records of receipts and payments of clients' money;

   (g) enquire into and test check the system of recording costs and of making withdrawals in respect of costs from the client account;

   (h) satisfy himself by test examination of documents that the financial transactions (including those giving rise to transfers between ledger accounts) are in accordance with the *Solicitor's Accounts Rules 1991*, and that entries in the clients' ledger accounts reflect the transactions in a manner which complies with those rules;

   (i) extract (or check the extraction of) all clients' ledger balances at not fewer than two dates selected by the accountant and at each date compare the total shown by the ledger accounts, including those for whom trust money is held, with the cash book balance on client account, and reconcile the cash book balance with that confirmed direct to the accountant by the bank. (The Law Society regards it as essential that the accountant should extract or check the extraction of all the balances, irrespective of the existence of an efficient system of internal control);

   (j) satisfy himself that reconciliations of clients' ledger with cash book and cash book with bank statements have been performed at least once every five weeks;

   (k) make a test examination to ascertain whether payments from client account have been made on any individual account in excess of the money held on behalf of that client;

   (l) peruse the office ledger, cash accounts, and bank and building society statements to see whether clients' money has not been paid into a client account;

(m) peruse the books of account containing details of clients' money which, with client's consent, is not held in a client account, to ascertain what transactions have been effected in respect of such an account;

(n) request such information and explanations as may be required arising out of the above tests and enquiries.

3. To ensure compliance with Rule 13 of the *Solicitors' Investment Business Rules 1990*, the accountant must:

   (a) check a sample of bills of cost to ensure that amounts attributable to discrete investment business are separately recorded and that they are maintained in a separate file or bills delivered book;

   (b) ensure the records are sufficient to produce the analysis required by the Law Society.

'The accountant is not required...'

The accountant is not required:

1. To extend his enquiries beyond the information contained in the relevant documents, supplemented by such information and explanations as he may obtain from the solicitor.

2. To enquire into stocks, shares, other securities or documents of title held by the solicitor on behalf of clients.

3. To consider whether the books of account of the solicitor were properly written up in accordance with the rules at any other time than that at which his examination took place.

13.1.5   Treatment of interest earned on client money

Where a solicitor holds or receives an amount of client money which, having regard to the circumstances (including the amount and length of time held), ought in fairness to the client to have earned him interest, the solicitor must either deposit the money in a separate account and account to the client for interest earned, or pass over to the client any interest that would have been earned if the money had been separately deposited. In general, interest is based on the amount and time held using the following table:

Number of weeks	Minimum balance
8	£1,000
4	£2,000
2	£10,000
1	£20,000

The Law Society will adjudicate in disputes if so requested.

13.1.6   Specimen form

ACCOUNTANT'S REPORT
Section 34. Solicitors Act 1974
Section 9 Administration of Justice Act 1985 and
Schedule 15, paragraph 6 of the Financial Services Act 1986
The Accountant's Report Rules 1991

NOTE.— *This form may be used for a report in respect of:—*

1.	*a solicitor;*
1 (a).	*a registered foreign lawyer ('RFL');*
2.	*a firm of solicitors provided the names of all the partners in the firm appear in section A1 below;*
2 (a).	*a multi-national partnership, provided the names of all the partners appear in section A1 below;*
3.	*a recognized body.*

SECTION A—DO NOT COMPLETE IF REPORT IS SUBMITTED ON BEHALF OF A RECOGNISED BODY

PLEASE INDICATE WHETHER THIS REPORT COVERS ALL THE PARTNERS WITHIN THE FIRM WHO HAVE HELD CLIENTS' MONIES (OR MONEY SUBJECT TO A CONTROLLED TRUST) DURING THE PERIOD UNDER REVIEW OR WHETHER INDIVIDUAL REPORTS ARE BEING SUBMITTED

*Tick box as appropriate.

* covers all partners/sole principal ☐   * individual reports submitted ☐

(a) Please complete in BLOCK CAPITALS; the letters 'RFL' must be entered against the surname of any RFL.

   1. Full name of solicitor(s) and/or RFL(s) *(a)* FORENAME(S)   SURNAME

(b) NOTE.—*All addresses at which the solicitor(s)/ RFL(s) practise(s) must be covered by an Accountant's Report or Reports. If an address is not so covered the reason must be stated.*

(In the case of an 'RFL', this report only refers to his or her practice(s) as a partner of a solicitor(s) or as a director of a recognized body.)

(c) NOTE.—*The period must comply with Section 34(3) of the Solicitors Act 1974, and the Accountant's Report Rules 1991.*

(d) NOTE.— *Delete (a) or (b) as appropriate.*

(e) NOTE.— *This name must comply with Rule 22 of the Solicitors' Incorporated Practice Rules 1988.*

(f) NOTE.— *The registered office must comply with Rule 8 of Solicitors' Incorporated Practice Rules 1988.*

2. Firm(s) Name(s) and Address(es) *(b)*

(Continue on a separate sheet as necessary)

3. Accounting period *(c)*

Beginning .... Ending ....

4. *(a)* I/we confirm that a copy of this Report has been sent to each of the solicitors and/or RFL(s) to whom this Report relates *(d)*.

or

(b) I/we confirm that one copy of this Report has been sent to the following partner of the firm, on behalf of the partners of the firm *(d)*.

SECTION B—TO BE COMPLETED ONLY IF REPORT IS SUBMITTED ON BEHALF OF A RECOGNIZED BODY.

1. Name of recognized body *(e)*.

2. Registered office *(f)*.

3. Principal office, if different from registered office.

4. Places of business other than those specified in (2) and (3).

(g) NOTE.—
Please complete in
BLOCK CAPITALS;
the letters 'RFL'
must be entered
against the
surname of any
RFL.

5.   *Name(s) of officers of recognized body (g).*

SURNAMES(S)   **FORENAME(S)**   **OFFICE HELD**

(Continue on a separate sheet as necessary)

(h) NOTE.—*The*
period must comply
with Section 34(3)
of the Solicitors Act
1974, and the
Accountant's Report
Rules 1991.

6.   Accounting period *(h)*.

Beginning .... Ending ....

7. *(a)*   I/we confirm that a copy of this Report has been sent to each of the directors of the recognized body to which this Report relates *(i)*.

or

(i) NOTE.—
Delete (a) or (b)
as appropriate.

(b)   I/we confirm that one copy of this Report has been sent to the following officer of the recognized body, on behalf of all the officers of the recognized body *(i)*.

SECTION C

1.   In compliance with Section 34 of the Solicitors Act 1974, and the Accountant's Report Rules 1991, made thereunder and under Section 9 of the Administration of Justice Act 1985 and Schedule 15, paragraph 6 of the Financial Services Act 1986, I/we have examined to the extent required by Rule 4 of the said Rules the books, accounts and documents produced to me/us in respect of the above practice(s) of the above-named solicitor/RFL(s) named in Section A1/the recognized body named in Section B1.

2.   In so far as an opinion can be based on this limited examination I/we are satisfied that during the above-mentioned period he/she/it has/they have complied with the provisions of Parts I and II of the Solicitors' Accounts Rules 1991 and, where he/she/it is/they are authorized in the conduct of investment business by the Law Society, Rule 13 of the Solicitors' Investment Business Rules 1990 except so far as concerns:—

(j) Delete the sub-
paragraph(s) not
applicable.

(a)   certain trivial breaches due to clerical errors or mistakes in book-keeping, all of which were rectified on discovery and none of which, I am/we are satisfied, resulted in any loss to any client *(j)*.

(b) the matters set out in Section E in respect of which I/we have not been able to satisfy myself/ourselves for the reasons therein stated (j).

(c) the matters set out in Section F, in respect of which it appears to me/us that the solicitor(s)/RFL(s)/recognized body has/have not complied with the provisions of Parts I and II of the Solicitors' Account Rules 1991 and, where he/she/it is/they are authorized in the conduct of investment business by the Law Society, Rule 13 of the Solicitors' Investment Business Rules 1990 (j).

(k) NOTE.—The figure to be shown in 3(i)(a) and 3(ii)(a) is the total of credit balances, without adjustment for debit balances (unless capable of proper set off i.e. being in respect of the same client) or receipts and payments not capable of allocation to individual ledger accounts.

3.   The results of the comparisons required under Rule 4(1)(A)(f) of the Accountant's Report Rules 1991, at the dates as selected by me/us were as follows (k):—

(i) at ....

(a) Liabilities to clients as shown by clients' ledger accounts ....

(b) Cash held in client account and client's money held elsewhere than in a client account after allowances for outstanding cheques and lodgments cleared after date ....

(c) Difference between 3(i)(a) and 3(i)(b) (if any) ....   £ _____

(ii) at ....

(a) Liabilities to clients as shown by clients' ledger accounts ....

(b) Cash held in client account and client's money held elsewhere than in a client account after allowances for outstanding cheques and lodgments cleared after date ....

(c) Difference between 3(ii)(a) and 3(ii)(b) (if any) ....   £ _____

SECTION D—DO NOT COMPLETE IF REPORT IS SUBMITTED
ON BEHALF OF A RECOGNIZED BODY

1. The following solicitor(s)/[RFL(s)] having retired from active practice as solicitor(s) [practice in partnership with solicitor(s) or as director(s) of a recognized body] ceased to hold clients' money (or money subject to a controlled trust) on the date indicated and in respect of this solicitor/these solicitors [this RFL/these RFL(s)] the report covers the period up to the date of cessation:

FULL NAME   DATE CEASED TO HOLD CLIENTS' MONEY
                         (OR MONEY SUBJECT TO A
                         CONTROLLED TRUST)

2. The following solicitor(s)/[RFL(s)], having left the firm and ceased to practise under this style, ceased to hold clients' money under this style (or money subject to a controlled trust in connection with the practice) on the date indicated and in respect of this solicitor/these solicitors [this RFL/these RFLs] the report covers the period up to the date of cessation:

FULL NAME   DATE CEASED TO HOLD CLIENTS'
                         MONEY UNDER THIS STYLE
                         (OR MONEY SUBJECT TO A
                         CONTROLLED TRUST IN
                         CONNECTION WITH THIS
                         PRACTICE)

3.   The following solicitor(s)/[RFL(s)] has/have joined the firm during the period under review on the date indicated and in respect of this solicitor/ these solicitors [this RFL/these RFLs] the report covers the period from the date on which clients' money was held under this style (or money subject to a controlled trust was held in connection with this practice):

FULL NAME

DATE FROM WHICH CLIENTS' MONEY HELD UNDER THIS STYLE (OR MONEY SUBJECT TO A CONTROLLED TRUST HELD IN CONNECTION WITH THIS PRACTICE)

SECTION E

Matters in respect of which the accountant has been unable to satisfy himself or herself and the reasons for that inability:—

SECTION F

Matters (other than trivial breaches) in respect of which it appears to the accountant that the solicitor(s)/[RFL(s)]/recognized body has/have not complied with the provisions of Parts I and II of the Solicitors' Accounts Rules 1991 and, where he/she/it is/they are authorized in the conduct of investment business, Rule 13 of the Solicitors' Investment Business Rules 1990:—

SECTION G

(l) NOTE.— *Please complete in block capitals.*	Particulars of the accountant *(l)*:—
	Full Name ....
	Qualifications ....
(m) NOTE.—*This Report may be signed in the name of the firm of accountants of which the accountant is a partner or employee provided that the particulars of the accountant signing the Report are also specified.*	Firm Name ....
	Address ....
	....
	Date .... Signature *(m)* ....
	To
	The Law Society,
	Accountants' Reports,
	Ipsley Court,
	Redditch,
	Worcs. B98 OTD.
	(DX 19114 Redditch)

The reporting accountant must state in the report the actual amount of the liabilities to clients and cash held for clients in client accounts or elsewhere at the two comparison dates, even if there is no difference between the figures.

The report may be signed in the name of the firm of which the accountant is a partner, but the name of the accountant who signed the report must also be specified.

The standard form of the accountant's report can also be used by a solicitor's incorporated practice.

13.2   Insurance companies – special audit difficulties

A definite distinction can be made between the preparation of a set of financial statements of a manufacturing enterprise and those of an insurance company. The most significant difference is in the use of estimates in the financial statements of an insurance company. This is necessary as a typical insurance contract will have a fixed 'sales' value but the cost of sales (i.e. claims) will not be known for a period of time after the 'sale' has taken place. It is therefore necessary to calculate by means of estimation the anticipated cost of claims before the results of the insurance company can be determined for any year. The specific audit problems that arise broadly relate to four main areas:

1. The treatment of premium income.
2. The allocation of expenses.

3. Unexpired risks.

4. The quantification of outstanding claims.

It must be recognized that there are different types of insurance company, namely those that write general business, those that write long-term business, and those that write both.

Long-term business is that primarily concerned with survival of individuals to a stipulated age or payment on death only. The types of risk involved are death, disability, annuity and pension business, permanent health and pension fund management business. Any form of insurance which is not long-term business is classified as general business.

As well as the statutory audit, it is normally a requirement of an insurance company's authorization to write business that an audited return is made each year to the Department of Trade and Industry. These returns are subject to audit under specific regulations introduced by and subsequent to the various *Insurance Companies Acts*.

It is beyond the scope of this publication to cover all the detailed knowledge required to be able adequately to perform an insurance company audit. What follows is therefore an outline of the major audit areas.

The treatment of premium income

The precise treatment of premium income will depend on whether the financial statements are being prepared on an annual, deferred annual or a fund basis. However, the auditor should ensure that the insurance company's accounting system enables:

1. Premium income to be shown gross of commission, even if notified net of commission.

2. Instalment premiums to be accounted for in total at inception.

3. Premium income to be identified gross of any reinsurance premiums ceded, as these should be disclosed separately.

In addition, the auditor will need to be satisfied that unearned premiums are accurately stated. An unearned premium represents the appropriate proportion of a premium received during the year under review which is applicable to a later accounting period. Once again it is important that a consistent approach is adopted and that the accounts declare the bases selected by the insurance company, under the heading of accounting policies, since a number of variations are possible although a time apportionment basis would normally be appropriate.

The allocation of expenses

The auditor will need to be satisfied that the enterprise's accounting system accurately records expenses which would normally be grouped under the following headings:

- Underwriting
- Claims handling

▶ Investment
▶ Corporate
▶ Capital

In particular, the auditor should be satisfied that an accurate method of calculating deferred acquisition expenses (i.e. those expenses which vary with and are primarily related to the acquisition of new insurance contracts and the renewal of existing insurance contracts which are carried forward from one accounting period to the next) has been used.

Unexpired risks

This amount represents the 'carry forward' to the next accounting period in circumstances where it appears that insurance business undertaken in the period under review is unprofitable; it is thus similar to the provision for future losses on long-term contracts in the construction industry. The chief audit difficulty is that a considerable element of adjustment enters the computation of such unexpired risks and the auditor will be required to form an opinion on the need for such a provision and, if one exists, whether the sum provided is adequate.

The quantification of outstanding claims

Outstanding claims may be classified as those which:

1. Have been notified and agreed, but are still outstanding at the balance sheet date.
2. Have been notified before, but not yet agreed at, the balance sheet date.
3. Have arisen but which have not yet been notified to the company by the balance sheet date (i.e. claims incurred but not reported or IBNR).

A good deal of estimation is needed with regard to claims in categories 2 and 3 above, and audit procedures will therefore include a review of the claims files in order to appraise the company's estimates, which should include related claims handling expenses.

It will also be necessary to compare the average cost of outstanding claims for each class of business with current experience. Finally, the auditor should examine statistical elements comparing past estimates with actual results, and should employ the use of 'market intelligence' wherever available. It is frequently the case that an actuarial exercise needs to be carried out to establish the adequacy of a company's claims provision.

Claims reserves should be shown gross of reinsurance recoveries which should then be separately disclosed. The auditor will therefore need to be satisfied that adequate provision has been made for any defaulting insurers in the calculation of reinsurance recoveries receivable.

13.3 The audit of insurance brokers

13.3.1 Background

For an insurance intermediary to call itself an insurance broker it has to be registered with the Insurance Brokers Registration Council (IBRC). The size and activities of insurance brokers are varied, ranging from sole traders to large public companies. Their activities may vary from specializing in one particular type of insurance (e.g. motor) to dealing with many different classes of insurance business.

The *Insurance Brokers Registration Council (Accounts and Business Requirements) Rules 1979* (SI 1979, no. 489) set out the rules to which an insurance broker must adhere. There are several accounting matters in these regulations which the auditor of an insurance broker must ensure his audit tests cover as he is required, within a period of six months from the balance sheet date, to lodge a set of audited accounts and an accountant's report in the form set out below.

PART IV

ACCOUNTANT'S REPORT

to the Insurance Brokers Registration Council in respect of this Statement of Particulars

This report must be given by an accountant qualified in accordance with the provisions of subsections (4), (5) and (6) of section 11 of the Insurance Brokers (Registration) Act 1977.

The accountant shall report in the following terms (setting out any qualifications or reservations in a separate letter to be attached):

1. We have examined the accounting records of ....
    ....
    for the period ended ..., being the period referred to in paragraph 1 of Part 1 of this Statement of Particulars.

2. In my/our opinion:

    (a) there were no material breaches of rules 6 and 7 of the Insurance Brokers Registration Council (Accounts and Business Requirements) Rules 1979 during the period referred to in paragraph 1 of this report;

    (b) the amounts shown in column 1 of paragraph 2 of Part 1 of this Statement of Particulars have been extracted from the audited balance sheet and have been analysed in accordance with the definitions and instructions applying to the said paragraph 2 of Part 1;

    (c) the amounts shown in column 2 of the said paragraph 2 of Part 1 have been stated in accordance with the said definitions and instructions;

    (d) the information set out in paragraphs 3, 4 and 5 of Part 1 and paragraphs 1 and 2 of Part II of this Statement of Particulars has been fairly stated.

---

3. I/We have inspected, in respect of each Insurance Broking Account maintained at any time during the period referred to in paragraph 1 of this report and each approved short-term asset defined in paragraph (9)(i) of rule 6 of the Insurance Brokers Registration Council (Accounts and Business Requirements) Rules 1979 and held at any time during the period referred to in paragraph 1 of this report, a written acknowledgement from approved bankers or licensed institutions in accordance with the provisions of paragraph (2) or (6) (v) of rule 6 of the Insurance Brokers Registration Council (Accounts and Business Requirements) Rules 1979 and have received confirmation from such approved bankers or licensed institutions that the terms of such acknowledgement were in respect of each Insurance Broking Account in force during the period referred to in paragraph 1 of this report or in respect of such approved short-term assets in force during that part of the period referred to in paragraph 1 of this report in which such approved short-term assets were held.

Signed .... Date ....
Name and address of practice (in block letters):
....

Note: It is the Council's policy to issue an acknowledgement of the Statement of Particulars to the accountant signing the above.

In addition, Lloyds Brokers must comply with the requirements of the Committee of Lloyds.

13.3.2 Accountant's report

The accountant's report makes specific reference to Rules 6 and 7 of the 1979 Rules, and in particular the accountant is required either to confirm that there were no material breaches of these rules or to provide qualification in respect of any material breaches that have occurred.

Rule 6 deals with the status of bank accounts held by the insurance broker and, in particular, gives detail on the transactions that should be carried out through the designated 'insurance broking account'. The accounting records which are required to be kept are dealt with in Rule 7.

The auditor should always consult the detailed rules but, in summary, will need to satisfy himself on the following matters in relation to all bank accounts designated as an insurance broking account (IBA):

1. That written acknowledgement for the following has been obtained from the brokers in respect of each IBA account that has been operated at any time during the year:
   (a) the account is designated 'insurance broking account' and that it contains the name of the practising broker;

(b) the IBA account is opened to comply with the rules;

(c) that the bank is not entitled to any charge, encumbrance, lien, right of set-off, compensation or retention against money standing to the credit of the IBA.

2. That all monies received by the broker in connection with their insurance broking business have been paid into an IBA account. This will include any brokerage received.

3. That all monies paid to insurance companies and assureds in respect of insurance broking business have been paid from an IBA account.

4. That the only other transactions for which the IBA account has been used are permitted under Rule 6. (These are limited, the most frequent being the withdrawal of brokerage.)

5. That at all times the aggregate value of insurance transaction assets is at least equal to the aggregate value of insurance transaction liabilities. (The assets referred to are IBA accounts plus recoverable insurance debtors; the liabilities are IBA account advances plus insurance creditors.)

Among the detailed requirements of Rule 7 is one which states that 'the accounting records shall be such as to enable compliance with the relevant provisions of these Rules to be demonstrated at any time'. Clearly, the auditor will need to establish that the records kept do enable such compliance, particularly with regard to item 5 above. Therefore, when planning his work, the auditor will need to ensure that his tests on the broker's systems will enable him to form an opinion on each of the matters detailed above.

13.4   Pension scheme audits

13.4.1   Pension law reform

In October 1993, the government published *Pension Law Reform*, the report of the Pension Law Review Committee, chaired by Professor Roy Goode. The Committee was appointed in June 1992 'to review the framework of the law and regulations within which occupational pension schemes operate...' following massive defalcations from pension funds associated with the late Robert Maxwell and a related report of the House of Commons Select Committee on Social Security.

The Goode Report made 218 recommendations, of which the following are a few of those relating to the regulation and reporting on pension funds.

▶ An *Occupational Pension Scheme Act* should be enacted to lay out a properly structured framework of rights and duties.

▶ A Pensions Regulator should be appointed, with overall responsibility for the regulation of occupational pension schemes.

▶ The trustees should be free to appoint the auditor acting for the employer provided that the terms of engagement are clearly set out, the roles and responsibilities of employer, trustees and auditor are clearly defined, and areas of conflict are made known.

▶ Auditors of occupational pension schemes should be statutorily required to report serious or persistent irregularities to the Regulator, and if they do so in good faith, should be exempt from legal liability.

The *Pensions Act 1995* makes the changes in pensions law that have been under discussion since the formation of the Goode Committee, although not all of the Goode recommendations have been adopted. Two of the key changes in the Act are:

▶ *Pensions regulator.* A new regulatory body – the Occupational Pensions Regulatory Authority (OPRA) – to be created. It will have wide-ranging powers to monitor and intervene in the running of occupational pension schemes. The scheme actuary and auditor must report immediately to OPRA if they believe the employer or the trustees are not performing their proper duties.

▶ *Member trustees.* The provisions of the Act allow for a third of the trustees to be members of the scheme, with a view to ensuring that members' interests are properly represented.

13.4.2 Audit requirement

Statutory Instrument no. 1046 *Pensions: The Occupational Pension Schemes (Disclosure of Information) Regulations 1986* as amended by subsequent regulations introduced a compulsory audit requirement for most types of pension scheme. The only exceptions are:

1. Schemes with fewer than two members.
2. Unfunded schemes (i.e. where monies are not accumulated to meet future pension liabilities).
3. Unapproved schemes, provided the scheme is not the subject of an application for approval which has not been determined.
4. Schemes providing benefits only on death of a member.

Only auditors eligible to act as company auditors under section 25, *Companies Act 1989* may accept appointments. The auditor must also be independent, and the regulations specify that the auditor must not be:

1. A member of the scheme.
2. A trustee of the scheme.
3. An employee of the scheme.
4. The employer of any member of the scheme.

13.4.3   Accounting and audit requirements

Form and content of accounts

Statement of Accounting Practice no. 1 (SORP 1) issued by the ASC in May 1986 sets out recommendations on the form and content of pension scheme accounts.

In September 1995, the Pensions Research Accountants Group (PRAG) issued an exposure draft of the Financial Statements of Pension Schemes – a revised SORP 1.

The objectives of the revision are:

▶ To update the SORP for developments in legislation and accounting practice.

▶ To give guidance on problem areas that have emerged since the issue of the SORP having regard to the recommendations of the Pension Law Reform Committee and government proposals for pensions reform.

The exposure draft of revised SORP 1 refers to the accounts as a stewardship report designed to give a true and fair view of the financial transactions of the scheme during the accounting period and of the disposition of its net assets at the period end.

This means that obligations to pay future pensions are not taken into account in drawing up pension scheme accounts. However, for defined benefit schemes, the actuaries will prepare triennial valuations to assess the long-term liabilities of the scheme and the funding rate required to meet those liabilities.

The regulations also require the accounts to include a statement as to whether the accounts have been prepared in accordance with Parts 2 to 4 of SORP 1 and, if not, an indication of where there are any material departures from the guidelines.

Audit report

The regulations set out the reporting requirements of the auditor, which are to confirm whether or not in his opinion:

1. The accounts show a true and fair view of the financial transactions of the scheme during the scheme year and the disposition at the end of the scheme year of the assets and liabilities, other than liabilities to pay pensions and benefits after the end of the scheme year.

2. The accounts contain the information specified in Schedule 3 to the regulations referred to in section 13.4.1 above.

3. Contributions payable to the scheme during the scheme year have been paid in accordance with the scheme rules or contracts under which they are payable, and with the recommendations of the actuary, if appropriate.

13.4.4   Auditing guideline

In November 1988 the APC issued auditing guideline 'Pension schemes in the United Kingdom' which sets out the important administrative procedures and controls that would be expected in a well-organized pension scheme. It is likely that the ASB will, eventually, issue a Practice Note to replace this guideline. The following reproduces the relevant extracts from the guideline and the original paragraph numbers have been preserved.

Procedures and controls

42. Paragraphs 43 to 52 below illustrate important administrative procedures and controls which the auditor would normally expect to find in a well organised pension scheme. Other types of controls that may exist are set out in the Auditing Guideline 'Internal controls'. The auditor will generally wish to structure his audit to identify and record important procedures and controls and to test them where appropriate as part of his overall audit approach.

Contributions receivable

43. Procedures and controls for contributions receivable include:

   (a) checking that contributions are received on a timely basis from the employer, on behalf of both the employer and employees, in accordance with the scheme rules or at rates based on actuarial recommendations;

   (b) prompt investment of contributions received; and

   (c) identification of the element of contributions which are AVCs or relate to life assurance premiums.

Benefits payable

44. Procedures and controls for benefits payable include:

   (a) checking calculations of benefits and taxation deducted (if any) for compliance with the scheme's rules, membership records, actuarial advice and relevant legislation;

   (b) checking changes in pension payments (amount and payee) to supporting evidence; and

   (c) periodic confirmation of the continued existence of pensioners and others in receipt of benefits.

   The pension payroll system may actually form part of the employer's payroll system. In any case, pension payments are often made using normal payroll systems, and the controls applicable to payroll systems used by employers should also be applied to pension schemes.

Transfers in and out

45. Procedures and control for transfers in and out include:

   (a) checking amounts payable in respect of pension obligations transferred out of the scheme or of refunds with scheme rules, membership records, actuarial tables or advice and other supporting documentary evidence;

(b) checking amounts receivable on the transfer of members to the scheme with supporting documentary evidence, actuarial advice and the scheme rules;

(c) checking amounts of state scheme premiums (if any) due to the Department of Health and Social Security with documentary evidence; and

(d) checking that all payments from the trustees to the sponsoring employer have been reported to the Inland Revenue and the correct tax deducted and accounted for.

AVCs

46. Procedures and controls for AVCs include:

(a) procedures to ensure that AVC arrangements are within Inland Revenue rules;

(b) checks over contributions and benefits as for the main scheme; and

(c) procedures to ensure that AVCs are paid promptly to the trust for the benefit of the individual and are subject to the appropriate degree of segregation, if any, from general funds.

Administration expenses

47. Procedures and control for administration expenses include an examination to ensure that administration expenditure and the costs of investment transactions are incurred only in accordance with the scheme's trust deed and rules. In general, the trustees will be entitled to recover from the trust fund expenses incurred in the carrying out of the trusts. However, the *trust documents* may provide that the employer will bear some or all of these expenses.

Investment transactions

48. Procedures and controls for investment transactions include:

(a) recording investment policy and approval by trustees of specific investments;

(b) periodic review by trustees of investment performance;

(c) reconciliation of investment transaction records to asset and cash records; and

(d) checks on the completeness of investment income, including tax refunds.

Where investment transactions are delegated to an investment manager, the trustees will need to ensure that they have adequate records to exercise proper control (e.g. by retaining transaction and valuation listings supplied by the investment manager).

Assets

49. Procedures and controls for assets include:

(a) agreement of asset records maintained by the trustees to those of custodians;

(b) holding of assets in safe custody under the control of persons other than those responsible for the keeping of records;

(c) holding of fidelity insurance against misdeeds of staff concerned with investment transactions and the holding of assets, whether employed by the trustee or another party, such as the investment manager;

(d) prompt banking of receipts to appropriate bank accounts; and

(e) adequate arrangements for control and communication of signatories to banks and investment institutions.

Membership records

50. The trustees of the pension scheme will need to ensure that reliable membership records are maintained which are adequate to enable them to fulfil their responsibilities to the scheme. In some cases the records may be kept by the employer or an administrator on behalf of the trustees.

51. Procedures and controls for membership records include periodic checks of the continued accuracy of membership records, and of the information used to update them, to appropriate authorities or directly with the members (e.g. by use of direct confirmation of the continuing existence of individual members). This applies to employees, pensioners and *deferred pensioners*.

52. Such checks are necessary because the membership records will be used by the actuary in determining the present and future liabilities of the scheme and thus the appropriate level of contributions, and by those responsible for administering the scheme in calculating the amount of benefit to be paid in the event of the member dying, leaving service or becoming entitled to other benefits. Inaccurate membership records may therefore lead to incorrect transactions in the future and to the scheme not discharging its responsibilities to deferred pensioners.

13.5 Joint audits

This is a specialized situation, although not infrequently encountered in practice and concerning which there is a surprising amount of confusion, especially with regard to the respective responsibilities and duties of the audit firms involved. The situation is often complicated by the fact that one of the firms of joint auditors acts for the client company in an accountancy capacity. Over the past few years Department of Trade inspectors' reports have heavily criticized joint auditors in one or two specific instances in which it was clear that the mutual interdependence, never properly codified, of the two firms involved resulted in gross neglect of the needs of the client.

Auditors accepting an appointment to act jointly with another firm should therefore be cognisant of the following factors:

1. Responsibility, which could lead to liability, is in no way reduced in such an arrangement, although damages would be apportioned in relation to the incidence of any negligence proved. Apportionment of blame in such circumstances is extremely difficult and it would be unwise to rely upon this form of protection.

2. It is essential that there should be a full and mutual exchange of information between the two firms acting jointly, and a planned co-ordination of the duties which each respectively agrees to undertake. Otherwise, the risk is that the client company, far from having the assurance of extra protection given by the overlapping of certain procedures, may find that lack of co-ordination between the auditors leads to a number of important areas not being adequately covered.

3. It is prudent that on the occasion of each audit the duties and responsibilities undertaken by each firm should be set out in writing and mutually exchanged.

4. Although the other firm is already undertaking extensive accountancy work for the client, this should not in any way minimize that firm's audit responsibilities, despite the difficulty in maintaining an independent view of work which they themselves have carried out. The circumstances thus place an additional burden on the firm invited to act jointly and the latter should therefore elicit assurances that the execution of accounting functions will not be regarded as a substitute for pure auditing.

14

Epilogue

THIS CHAPTER DEALS WITH:

▷ to whom the auditor is responsible;

▷ the relationship between auditors and directors.

14.1 The unspoken conflict

There is a question which, although not specifically formulated anywhere in this text, nonetheless lies behind every aspect of auditing practice and reporting. The question is: to whom is the auditor responsible? An impulsive answer would suggest that there *may* be a responsibility to 'outsiders' but that there is undoubtedly a prime responsibility towards shareholders, and the essence of this responsibility is to report whether the financial statements laid before those shareholders give, in the auditor's opinion, a true and fair view.

It has to be recognized, unfortunately, that in practice this is not as straightforward a matter as it may seem, since cases may well arise where the view considered by auditors to be true and fair may conflict with what the directors would like the accounts to show and, in such circumstances, it would by no means be certain whether the general body of shareholders would support the directors or the auditors (who, ironically, were appointed specifically by law to protect the shareholders' interests) in any such dispute.

In essence, it is conceivable that what the auditors hold to be the true and fair view may be the last thing in the world the shareholders would wish the accounts to disclose – especially where the outcome of the conflict may have a direct bearing on the company's share price. Can it be that, paradoxically, those to whom no statutory duty of care is owed – trade creditors in particular – are those who most depend (albeit passively) on the comfort indirectly provided by the audit function, while the shareholders to whom the audit report is addressed may be less eager to know its contents, if adverse?

The more rational view, of course, is that in periods of relatively low inflation investors, both institutional and private, are primarily concerned with yield rather than growth, since a secure, adequate and perennial yield will usually provide satisfactory growth as a by-product for a desirable and marketable stock. Subject, therefore, to safeguards against insider dealing, investors will depend on the accounts and, if made necessary by default, the audit report to communicate *all* the relevant news – both good and bad.

14.2 Learning the hard way

There has been a genuine sea-change since the publication of the previous edition of *Auditing Today*. As far back as I can remember (the early 1960s at least), auditors have, in number of instances, had to withstand accusations of complicity with client company management in furthering the latter's nefarious ends. This complicity may have occurred in any of a variety of guises from at worst, actually volunteering suggestions for creative accounting treatments, to merely legitimizing management's own accounting objectives by bringing them spuriously within the prevailing legal or professional frameworks. Hence the old joke about the chief executive doing the rounds to select a suitable auditor by asking successive candidates to answer the question: what would you get by adding two and two? He knew he had found the right firm when he eventually got the response, 'What sort of figure did you have in mind?' (Laws of libel preclude me from mentioning the name of the firm that reputedly provided him with this amenable reply.)

When giving evidence to official committees on law reform pertaining to the role and responsibilities of auditors I was repeatedly told by DTI representatives that 'the trouble with auditors is that they always confuse the client and the client's management'. This was a legitimate reminder that the precise relationships are easily overlooked when the auditor has a commercial interest in not biting the hand that feeds him. Company law does not help: auditors are, nominally anyway, hired and fired by the *shareholders* to whom they report, but they retain a contractual relationship with the *company*. Both management and shareholders (as a body and individually) stand in a third party relationship to the auditor, whose report to members is publicly filed and relied upon by a wide range of interest groups for a variety of purposes.

In practice, the members' role is passive, and decisions of executive management, including audit appointments and removals, are usually passed without a tremor. In the case of the substantial majority of private companies, the directors control the voting interests in their capacity as shareholders. Amid this curious amalgam of often conflicting relationships there is also something fondly referred to as 'the public interest'.

In the circumstances it is no surprise that volumes of case law, reflecting centuries of judicial wrangling, stand as testimony to this impossibly confusing web. Only recently have the courts, notably in the Caparo, Al-Saudi Banque and Berg judgments, succeeded in laying down intelligible criteria for auditors' accountability to third parties. Despite this, the escalation of litigation against auditors, much of it inspired by North American attitudes, continues unabated.

Wherein the change referred to at the beginning of this section? Quite simply this: the stakes have been raised to a level at which auditors are at last recognizing, and openly acknowledging, that – putting it in its simplest terms – they would now far rather lose the client than bend the rules.

The raising of the stakes has taken forms other than just litigation exposure. Endowing accounting standards with statutory force – backed by statutory sanctions – has played a notable part, not least of which is the facility of the Review Panel to bring transgressors to book on a mere suspicion of wayward accounting. The effects of audit regulation and more stringent ethical enforcement have been equally threatening. *Causes célèbres* of recent vintage – Guinness, BCCI, Barlow Clowes, Maxwell, Polly Peck, British & Commonwealth, Ferranti, *et al.* – have also contributed to the sea-change referred to by quite simply making life terribly unpleasant, one way or another, for the audit firms implicated.

Latest on the retribution scene is the enactment in 1993 of the Bingham Committee recommendations, following enquiry into the BCCI failure, which include the proposal that auditors' rights to report compliance failures directly to regulators under the *Financial Services Act 1986* should be accompanied by a positive duty so to do, in ill-defined circumstances.

This is how the cards are stacked, and no relief is in prospect. No wonder, then, despite unprecedented competitiveness in pitching for new work, and the gross wider commercialization of the profession, that auditors now know where to draw the line. Bitter experience has amply demonstrated that adherence to the straight and narrow, whatever the short-term cost, is preferable to long-term misery. It has been a strange means of achieving long-sought progress – but progress it is, nonetheless.

14.3 What price limited liability?

Although this question may appear to have special application to public companies, it in fact relates to the auditing profession as a whole, especially since company law relaxed the audit requirement for small companies in 1994.

It is therefore important at this point to emphasize the arguments in favour of retaining a meaningful form of professional input that endows financial statements with a degree of credibility that they would otherwise lack. This goes back to the very birth of the limited liability concept and the fact that those conducting business under the protection of limited liability are in effect given the right to put their companies into liquidation should they encounter difficult trading times or be made to face the consequences of bad management decisions. This means, quite frankly, that they are able to determine the point at which they will declare themselves free of the obligation to settle their debts, often bankrupting other businesses in the process – particularly their totally unprotected trade creditors. We have seen a great deal of this during the last few years, especially in marginal industries such as textiles, catering, building and construction. In such cases it is extremely difficult to establish any fraudulent intent on the part of the directors or shareholders concerned, and successful criminal prosecutions are rare. It may therefore be cogently argued that part of the price that has to be paid for conducting commercial activity in this extraordinarily privileged way should be to retain in some form the imposition of an independent scrutiny of the accounts that are publicly filed.

The fact that statute law recognizes responsibility by auditors to shareholders alone cannot be used as an argument against this view – rather, it highlights the inadequacy of statute law as it currently stands. It would indeed be more realistic if the audit report were not addressed to anyone in particular, but rather 'to all whom it may concern'. This would serve to remind us that at the inception of our system of limited liability (and hence the inception of modern auditing), the parties whom the audit was designed to protect included many who were not necessarily shareholders; and there is much to be said for re-establishing responsibility at this level.

Many will instinctively fear that this would dramatically extend the potential liability of the auditor to any third parties who have come to rely upon the financial statements which he audits. I do not believe that this is the case since recent legal decisions have made it abundantly clear that any plaintiff would have to establish beyond all reasonable doubt that (1) there had been negligence on the part of the auditor; (2) any financial loss suffered is attributable to that negligence, and to no other cause; and (3) the auditor knew (or ought to have known) that his report might reasonably be relied upon by the person or class of persons who suffered the loss. This eminently sensible set of legal guidelines would therefore continue to apply, and acknowledgement of the auditor's real responsibilities would not necessarily imply their further extension. Many of the profession's current problems are attributable to a general lack of readiness to face up to such responsibilities.

After all, the legal interpretation of 'proximity' in tort already extends potential liability to those who should be within the auditor's 'reasonable contemplation', irrespective of any specific knowledge of their existence, let alone of their reliance on the negligent statement or report. It is therefore difficult to see how it could be taken much further.

14.4 The relationship between auditors and directors

The difficulties in achieving effective communication through the medium of an audit report cannot be isolated from the crucial relationship between auditors and directors. Auditors report on the financial results of stewardship, but does their independence (or lack of it) permit them to go further and report on the effectiveness of that stewardship itself? To what extent should auditors make known to shareholders the substance of their communications with the directors? Clearly it would be inappropriate for every single exchange, either written or verbal, between auditors and directors to be passed on to members; the directors, after all, are the custodians of the company's affairs and as such are bound to be persons with whom the auditors will, in the ordinary course of their work, have to deal extensively. However, in the course of these dealings the auditors will form many impressions, ultimately crystallizing into firm opinions, concerning the quality of controls in force, the reliability and adequacy of the recording systems for the purposes of both financial and management accounts, and the strengths and weaknesses within the management structure at all levels – board level included.

The real question, therefore, is whether the traditional confines of the report to members (even in the extended form laid down by SAS 600) on the accounts as presented – which is all that the statutes require – can ever convey the full extent of the audit opinion. In answering this it has to be recognized that everything affects the accounts in one way or another.

Take the problems of control deficiencies, recording delays and bottlenecks, lack of evidence to support material transactions, the effects of supreme control residing with a single dominant personality, or simply a general ineptitude pervading the key management functions: these and other attributes inevitably have an effect on the accounts – even if only in that the accounts fail to reflect results which would have been obtained had such deficiencies been absent or swiftly remedied. Putting the question another way, is it possible to report on the accounts in isolation, ignoring the crucial internal factors which, individually and collectively, are instrumental in creating the results reflected in those very accounts? Would the shareholders not be especially eager to learn of such factors? Is it not entirely reasonable that they should be thus informed? The Cadbury initiatives have undoubtedly set this particular ball rolling, and I suspect it still has a good deal further to go.

This is not to suggest that auditors expressing an opinion on the accounts of a badly managed business should go so far as to attempt to quantify the effect on those accounts of such poor management – but it is to suggest that information contained in management letters, which they have privately addressed to the directors may, in regard to certain key matters, require to be made known to the shareholders. It cannot be reasonable to expect shareholders to reach an informed view on the abilities of the directors whom they have the right to appoint and dismiss, without possession of this type of information – information which the auditors are ideally placed to provide.

In the 1936 case of *Pendlebury's Ltd* v *Ellis Green & Co.* it was held that the auditor of a company whose directors are the sole shareholders will have discharged his duty by reporting to the directors separately on inadequacies in the system of internal control, even though his report to the members is silent on the subject. With the further development of case law on the auditor's responsibility to third parties, one cannot imagine such a view having much validity today, especially since the accounts and audit reports of all companies must be placed on file as a matter of public record, i.e. for all to see and take note of, presumably for any reasonable purpose.

The relationship between auditors and directors is at last being examined in a more critical light, chiefly as a result of the scandalous disclosures of the past thirty years. During this period there have been very few frauds or DTI investigations after which it has not become apparent that, quite aside from any questions of right and wrong, the auditors knew far more than their reports actually disclosed.

The truth is that the relationship between auditors and directors has been altogether too cosy, and in such circumstances it is very difficult, if not impossible, for auditors effectively to divide their loyalties and fulfil their real obligations. In the view of the DTI, auditors often confuse the client with the client's management. Is it possible to reach any conclusion on this matter other than that the manifest lack of independence repeatedly displayed by auditors is attributable to the power, in reality wielded by the directors and not the shareholders, to remove them from office? While it is true that there have been changes for the better in the wake of the *Cadbury Report* and audit regulation, all the ethical guides and disciplinary threats in the world will have little effect while the law remains blind to the impossibility of the auditor's situation, and neglects the need to protect auditors, possibly via an appeal procedure, who are sacked for doing the job, impartially and conscientiously, for which they were appointed in the first place.

14.5 Auditing – the wide view

What makes a good auditor? The acquisition of technical knowledge, skill and experience, no matter how extensive, will take one so far and no further. The best auditors are those who have developed their intuitive skills to the point at which these can be 'summoned' to deal with almost any situation. The best auditors, in short, are those who have developed 'a nose for the truth'. In writing this book I have therefore attempted to project auditing requirements beyond the purely technical level, and hope that my readers, as a result, will find themselves better equipped at both levels in the practice of auditing both as science and as art.

In preparing successive editions of this text I have endeavoured to capture the auditing scene at that particular point in time. Although I have, as it were, used a wide-angle lens, it must be acknowledged that the saga is a continuing one, and it is accepted that periodic revision is required. In the three years between the publication of the fifth and sixth editions, for example, changes and developments have taken place which have completely transformed the professional accounting and auditing landscape.

There is still a powerful view that suggests that an entity's annual report and accounts should be seen as a collective item for examination by all interested parties, and that a single section should no longer be selected for reference in the audit report to the exclusion of all other sections. The development of this mode of thinking will bear close observation in future years.

Investors are no longer the only sector interested in the contents of company reports, and in the context of auditors' legal liability we have considered some of the possible effects of this development: a development which recognizes that employees, trade unions, government, consumer groups, creditors, the financial press – not to mention the public at large – now examine these reports with a degree of interest never previously displayed.

As the horizons of accountability extend, so will they require to be accompanied and supported by independent authority, without which they will lack all credibility. It may therefore be argued that the real coming of age of the auditing profession is only now beginning to dawn. Whether the profession, with its entrenched insistence upon historical reporting and its reluctance to commit itself to comment on uncertainties, will rise to meet that dawn, only the years to come will reveal. Facing up to contemporary reality has never been its most striking attribute, however, and a measure of doubt persists. What is certain is that if the profession is to resist the calls for further state intervention than that already imposed by the *Companies Act 1989* it will have to consolidate and perhaps extend its existing requirements for continuing (post-qualification) education; materially enhance, in scope and in depth, the pre-qualifying examination syllabus in auditing; come to far more serious grips with the independence question that has cast its shadow over every critical event of the past four decades; and recognize that every new challenge or development represents an opportunity as well as a potential risk.

The auditing profession will also have to acknowledge that the public has now come to expect more of the auditor than mechanically drafted reports on financial statements. Minority shareholders now have unprecedented powers to pursue directors who breach their fiduciary duties, most notably under *CA 1985*, section 459; but they will require the auditor's skills to alert them to these breaches in the first place. Any failure of this aspect of the audit function will be construed as complicity.

As the content of company reports expands to provide more information on corporate and stewardship performance, we shall witness a demand for all published comment – even contents of the directors' report and the chairman's statement – to be authenticated, within reasonable bounds, by auditors.

The first line of this book reads: *Audit* is a Latin word, meaning 'he hears'; it is clear that in forming our attitude to auditing today we need to couple that with another Latin word: *Respondet* – he responds.

Review questions

*1. SAS 610 'Reports to directors or management' became effective in respect of the audit of accounts for years ended on or after 23 December 1995. Outline the content of this standard and evaluate whether it improves the relationship between auditors and directors. State also how it is likely to be applied by auditors of small companies.

*2. In view of the exemptions available to small companies relating to audit, professional firms have sometimes been accused of 'lowballing' to maintain their number of audit clients. Discuss critically, using examples where appropriate, which sector of the audit profession could suffer the most and whether the term 'lowballing' is appropriate.

3. The expectation gap is talked about on many occasions and in different contexts. What is it and how do you consider that it may be eliminated or at least reduced?

4. Critically discuss the advantages and disadvantages of limited liability auditing firms.

Table of cases

Table of statutes

Outline answers to review questions

Chapter 1

1. This is an interesting question in that it requires the relationships involved in an audit to be precisely identified. The limited company has a separate legal identity to its officers and shareholders. Therefore, the company is able to enter into contracts in its own right. The relationship between the company and the auditor is governed by the law of contract and it is essential to note that the contract is between the *company* and the *auditor*.

    It will be noted that this means that it is not between the directors or shareholders or any other officers and the auditor. The shareholders are effectively third parties to the agreement despite the fact that the audit report is specifically directed at them. However, the shareholders ultimately appoint the auditor in General Meeting (except in specific circumstances) and this is where an element of confusion arises. The contractual relationship must be considered when the question of the liability of auditors is addressed.

2. It is not only the large multinational companies that require an audit. In the United Kingdom there are many small limited liability companies that are required under statutory provisions to have an audit. The essential point to be made is that any organization can have an audit whether required by law or not. This usually arises if, for example, a club or organization has the requirement embodied within its constitution. Alternatively, a partnership or sole trader may request an audit. This is a private audit. The reasons for such a request may include the following:

    (a) A club or organization may wish to show to its members that there are no problems present in the running of the club.

    (b) A partnership may have a complicated set-up which could potentially cause disputes if there is not an independent viewpoint taken on the accounts.

    (c) If the partnership changes then again an independent viewpoint is taken.

    (d) Submissions to third parties such as banks (for raising finance perhaps) or even the

Inland Revenue tend to carry a greater degree of 'believability' if they have been audited.

(e) A qualified auditor has other areas of expertise such as:

(i) Accountancy

(ii) Taxation

(iii) Consultancy

(iv) Report preparation

(v) Profit forecasts or cash flow forecast preparation

Chapter 2

1. There is a difference between certifying that a set of figures are correct and expressing an opinion on the figures. In the United Kingdom an accountant would only use the word 'certificate' in the following circumstances:

   (a) He has drawn up a set of financial statements for an entity which does not require, nor has requested, an audit. In this respect the accountant knows all the underlying details from the books and records and therefore can certify the correctness.

   (b) He has physically checked all the figures being used within a document which is perhaps being used to underlie a submission to an authority – perhaps claiming a grant.

   The auditor is restricted to expressing an opinion as to the 'truth and fairness' of the accounts and uses the terminology 'in his opinion'. It is obvious that if an organization has thousands of transactions in a financial period then the auditor could not hope to check every one of them, nor is he required to.

   The above should not serve to indicate that the auditor does any less work in providing the report than he would at audit. The inherent risks to providing the report are extensive – the duty of care is paramount and the auditor must always be aware of it.

2. The acceptability of the certificate as audit evidence is dependent on two fundamental factors:

   (a) The materiality of the item being tested. If the value of the item is relatively small (and it could be argued that the term 'relatively small' is questionable) then the auditor may accept the certificate. In this respect a certificate confirming a petty cash balance which the auditor did not verify by another means would be acceptable.

   (b) The status of the person giving the certificate and the reason for holding it. This is more risky – the auditor may accept a certificate from a clearing bank which sought to confirm the securities held by the bank for safekeeping on behalf of the company. This is because the bank would hold such items for safekeeping in the normal course of business. However a similar certificate received from a stockbroker, however reputable the broker may be, would be unacceptable since it can easily be argued that it is not in the normal course of events that the broker would hold the asset.

   It should be emphasized that the auditor should not accept the certificate blindly. It would be a potential cause of negligence if the auditor did not confirm its existence by physical inspection on a regular basis.

Chapter 3

1. There are five main areas that the auditor should address when assessing the effectiveness of the internal auditor:

   (a) Independence – the internal auditor is an employee of the company but may well be able to organize his own work and report the findings to a high level of management. The internal auditor must be able to communicate freely with the external auditor.

   (b) The scope and objectives must be clearly defined. For example the internal auditor may well be responsible for reviewing the accounting systems and internal control as well as checking the financial and operating reports to management. This may be useful to the external auditor.

   (c) There must be professionalism. The internal auditor should plan, control and record his work and produce reports to a high standard.

   (d) The internal auditor must be suitably qualified – membership of a professional body assists as well since this serves to illustrate a commitment to standards.

   (e) The internal auditor must have adequate resources in order to be able to carry out his duties.

2. Flow charting has been in use both in computer programming and auditing for many years. In programming its primary function is to show the flow of information or data through a section of code. In this way it is possible to track the variables in use and check that the program code is correct.

   In auditing its usage is not dissimilar. It can be readily appreciated that in a large organization there are many systems which must be documented so that a future auditor does not need to ask the same questions over and over again. Information of this nature can be far more easily understood if it is in a pictorial form rather than purely narrative. The practical advantages are as follows:

   (a) Pictures can be more easily understood by the human brain;

   (b) The whole of a system under review can be documented in one picture without any loss of detail. It is also possible to split a system into sub-systems and document each in turn without any loss of detail or flow;

   (c) Links between sub-systems can be easily shown;

   (d) Control features can be easily shown by the use of designated symbols;

   (e) Cross references to the ICQ/ICE/audit program may be easily added;

   (f) New audit team members can easily understand a flow chart and commence work faster, thus saving precious chargeable audit time.

   It should be appreciated that considerable time is spent undertaking such work – hence on small company audits it is rarely necessary and is most certainly not cost effective.

Chapter 4

1. Audit test checking is the method adopted by the auditor to satisfy himself that the accounting records form a reliable basis for preparing the company accounts and whether or not the accounts so prepared form a true and fair representation of the state of affairs of the company. The auditor could not reasonably check every transaction of the company – if he were to do so then it could be argued that he may himself fail to observe an irregularity due to close proximity to the transactions.

    The two types of testing are:

    (a) Compliance testing – the auditor checks the operation of client controls and procedures;

    (b) Substantive tests – the auditor actually tests the final figures to be included within the accounts.

    In deciding whether or not to perform compliance testing the auditor must determine the following:

    (i) The system of internal controls which are present;

    (ii) the reliability of the controls.

    (iii) If the company has a good system of internal controls then clearly the auditor will be able to rely on those controls and will have a greater level of confidence in the results of his tests than if the company does not have a high level of internal controls.

    (iv) Test checking can be done in almost any area of the company's operations except where the matters being tested are so significant as to render full testing necessary. Such areas would include directors' minutes and statutory books, contingent liability reviews and testing taxation computations (although reviews of certain aspects of this may be done by sampling) and also possibly review of contracts/agreements.

2. It will be readily appreciated that depth testing can be applied to almost any area of audit testing. Business transactions do not exist in isolation. Purchases of goods and services ultimately work their way through a transaction cycle and provide added value at a final sale. Depth testing is also sometimes known as 'Walk-through testing' and this is exactly what the auditor is doing. The retracing of all links in the chain of a transaction is time consuming and the auditor may well perform the test in order to confirm his understanding of the client systems after a flowcharting exercise.

Chapter 5

1. Risk-based auditing is, to paraphrase, the usage of audit resources in the areas of a client business which are most prone to risk. The application of this approach is essential if the audit is to be cost effective. The intelligent application of the correct and appropriate techniques will enable the firm to perform the audit and not expose themselves to any increase in

potential liability risks. The methodology is such that it ensures that low risk areas are not overaudited and high risk areas are not underaudited.

In this respect more junior staff would undertake the bulk of the routine audit testing. This would include vouching and checking. High grade staff – partners and managers – would undertake the more risky areas such as:

- adequacy of provisions;
- liability/contingent liability disclosure;
- SSAP and Company Law compliance;
- analytical review;
- overall accounts review;
- creative accounting techniques in possible use;
- taxation;
- audit report.

Using the approach in risk-based auditing, the high value and error prone items are identified and the remainder of the population is sampled using an appropriate technique. This would effectively minimize the audit risk, that is to say the *inherent risk* (susceptibility to misstatement), *control risk* (lack of detection by internal controls) and *detection risk* (the risk that the auditor's substantive tests do not detect a material misstatement).

2. Materiality is a concept which has an undisputable underlying base which is understood by all users of accounts. In practice, what one auditor may deem to be material may well be immaterial to another. The judgement would be based on the knowledge that the partner has of the client business and the risk involved. Materiality is a relative factor and as such requires a 'starting point'. This may be, for instance, the total of the assets of the business or, perhaps, the turnover of the business.

Having decided on the materiality to be used, it is then necessary to select the items to be tested. The full testing of 'material items' means that a sample of the remainder requires selection. There are many different ways of selecting this sample and these are available to the auditor in any circumstances. The precise choice is dependent on the preference of the auditor and the nature of the client business and may include monetary unit sampling, attributes sampling etc.

Chapter 6

1. At the Balance Sheet date there may be certain assets in the hands of third parties. This will mean that the auditor may be unable to physically inspect the assets or may not be sure that all the assets that should be included actually have been included.

He may therefore supplement the normal audit tests by obtaining certificates from the third parties. This should obviously be done after all normal audit tests have been performed.

Three items for which this could be done are:

(a)   stock at an external location;

(b)   investment certificates held at a bank;

(c)   bank balances.

2.   When considering the value placed on the shares it is necessary to:

(a)   Inspect the share certificates. Enquiries should be made to ensure that there are no charges on the shares.

(b)   The original purchase price should be substantiated.

(c)   The latest final accounts of Water Limited should be obtained. Once obtained, the accounts should be reviewed and calculations performed to determine the price at which the shares should be valued. (Some idea of the valuation may be obtained by computation of dividend/earnings yield and comparing with companies in similar industries.)

If possible, communication should be made with the secretary of Water Limited to try to establish the price at which recent share transfers have been made. This should be compared with the calculated price.

Chapter 7

1.   The current audit report under Statements of Auditing Standard 600 represents a far longer version than was previously the case. It was, quite rightly, stated that the report was becoming ritualistic and was losing its value. It could not be disputed that any student of audititing could recite the short form audit report word for word.

The replacement however is still a 'ritual'. The contents are still predetermined and it could be argued that the report will not really be read by non-professionals because of its terminology and length. The report is, however, an integral part of the audit. The auditor must always satisfy the Statements of Auditing Standards and the end result is an expression of the 'truth and fairness' of the financial statements. As the conduct of the audit changes from assignment to assignment so too might a report change. Surely this would be more representative?

There is no real conclusion to the discussion. The APB needs to consider the uses to which the report is put and the fact that a standardized format is far easier to interpret and understand for non-professionals and professionals alike. Is the purpose of the report to impart information in a quick and sample manner or is it to force the reader to analyse in detail to ensure that there are no hidden meanings?

2.   If the previous report *had not been qualified* then there would be no real problem. Providing that the audit of the current period does not reveal any matters which cast doubt on the previous period then the checking need only be that the opening balances have been correctly brought forward and the accounting policies have not changed. If the policies have changed then appropriateness, accounting and disclosure need to be considered.

Given that the previous year had a qualified report then in addition to carrying out the above procedures there must be checks to see if the matter giving rise to the qualification has been resolved and dealt with in a correct manner in the current period. If the matter still affects the current period then it may well be that the report may still need to be qualified.

Chapter 8

1. It cannot be disputed that auditors come under the jurisdiction of the *Criminal Justice Act 1993*. Under Part V 57(2) a person has information from an inside source if and only if:

   (a)   He has it through

       (i)   being a director, employee or shareholder of an issuer of securities; or

       (ii)   having access to the information by virtue of his employment, office or profession; or

   (b)   The direct or indirect source is a person within (a) above.

   Professional ethics preclude the auditor from acting on information gained from the normal activities undertaken in the capacity of being an auditor. In its simplest sense this means that the auditor cannot trade or cause others to trade in the shares of the entity being audited. However the new legal framework could cause the auditor unwittingly to contravene the legislation.

   The simplest reason for this may arise from an audit report needing to have a qualification on the valuation of perhaps an associated shareholding. That is to say the holding company has to show in the accounts a value of the shares and currently it is overstated. If the company in which the investment is held is 'in trouble' but it is not generally known then the production of the report would effectively be the release of insider information. The problem is made worse if perhaps other employees of the audit firm hold shares — the law will always assume that a situation of 'perfect knowledge' is in existence.

2. The wording of the question is deliberately vague. It may well be the case that every time an audit report is required to be qualified the directors and auditor may disagree. The protection of the auditor is covered by section 391 of the *Companies Act 1985* — and this section was enhanced by the *1989 Act*. It could be argued that there is no real way to protect the auditor since the relationship between the auditor and the directors of the company must have, as a basis, trust and respect — if either is not present then the position of the auditor becomes untenable.

   The auditor is entitled to receive a copy of the resolution which is to remove him. This is really too late but presumably the auditor has become aware of the situation before this. Once this is received the auditor has the right to make written representation to the members of the company. This must not be too long (reasonable length). The company must circulate copies of the auditor's representations to all persons entitled to receive copies of the notice of meeting.

   If it transpires that the company does not circulate these representations then the auditor has the right to be heard at the meeting. On the face of it this sounds like an acceptable substitute but it must be remembered that this will only reach those who physically attend the meeting – and this is usually only a small percentage of the shareholders.

Chapter 9

1. The concept of independence is extremely important in the area of auditing. Professional and legal rules are necessary to ensure that there is no contravention of the concept. The following represent a brief outline of the main points:

   (a) The *Companies Act* states that officers and employees of a company, or a partner or employee of such a person, or a partnership of which such a person is a partner may not be auditors of that company. This effectively ensures that there is no conflict of interest to cloud judgement. There are also other criteria which must be considered.

   (b) Fees receivable from the audit client may be of such significance to the auditor that there may be a significant loss of revenue if the accounts were qualified and the client changed auditors. Note that in the case of an expanding or reducing client levels there may be a relaxation of these criteria. The maximum level is set at 15 per cent of gross fees.

   (c) There may be other fees which are far more than the audit level which would be lost from the client.

   (d) The auditor may have a relationship with an officer or senior official of the client company. This could obviously cause an unwitting problem and the only way of avoiding this would be to cease having any part of the reporting function. This could not occur in the case of a sole practitioner.

   In the case of a new partnership the previous employee would have to exercise extreme care in being seen not to be enticing any of the existing clients to follow him. This is a case of professionalism.

2. It is well known that all audit firms have to be seen to have internal controls to achieve the following objectives:

   (a) Improve the quality of client services;

   (b) Improve efficiency and profitability;

   (c) Minimize exposure to risk.

   It is very often thought that such objectives are merely the prerogative of the larger firms but this is not the case. The APC Audit Brief 'Risk Management for Auditors' serves to enforce the view that even the smallest practice must seek to raise standards in order to survive. It is in this area that improvements have been made. 'Hot' and 'cold' file reviews may be performed in even the smallest firm and groups of practitioners may form to enable confidential exchanges of views to take place. Such groups may also review files to suggest improvements that can be made. Attendance at courses to keep up-to-date is also essential. It is sometimes stated that the administration burden placed on the small practitioner is becoming too large. To a certain degree this is true – but in view of the litigious climate ever present in the business it is necessary for high standards to be maintained over all sizes of audit practitioner.

Chapter 10

1. This question is really reflecting the position as set out in the Caparao case. There have been many decided cases in the area of auditor liability and it must be stated that the case law is not always consistent. The essential element to be considered is proximity to the third party. *If* the auditor is aware of the transaction that the third party is contemplating *and* that the report is to be communicated either directly or indirectly to the third party *and* that the third party will use the report in deciding on a course of action then a duty of care is owed to the third party.

   It can be seen that in the above case there is information available to the third party but there is no way that the auditor can be deemed to be aware that the accounts were to be used in this way. This effectively means that a third party cannot really sue even if the accounts were misleading.

   Hence the evidence would appear to suggest that there is no case to answer.

2. It is the responsibility of directors to put in place controls and systems that are sufficient to prevent and deter fraud. This is part of the duties of the directors as defined under the *Companies Act*. The auditor has no part in these controls although the testing of them may well be part of the audit procedure anyway.

   One of the key factors is that part of the audit involves an examination and evaluation of internal controls and organisation. Use of internal control questionnaires which ask '*who does what and when*' serves to indicate that the auditor does, and indeed should, be concerned with the breakdown of such controls which would encourage fraud to occur. If the fraud does occur then it will undeniably affect the accounts – and in this respect the auditor, in the normal course of his work, should detect the discrepancy. There is of course the major element of materiality. An auditor cannot reasonably expect to find immaterial items except by chance – but if the fraud is material then there may be a finding of negligence if it is not detected.

   As a final note it is interesting that most claims for negligence are settled out of court due to cost considerations and the ensuing bad publicity.

Chapter 11

1. Note that this answer has omitted the letter format.

   The presence of a computer system does not in any way eliminate the necessity for common sense and segregation of duties. This segregation is a fundamental aspect of internal control. The division of responsibilities ensures that:

   (a) Those who supervise are not in any way involved in the mechanics of the procedures that they have authorized.

   (b) Those who are involved in the recording functions do not have any control over the assets over which they are recording.

   (c) Independent checks are performed over all work.

   In the past most computer systems were centralized, with a 'Computer Department' of some description. This scenario is no longer really the case . The old system would have had data preparation as a key element of controls and the following would represent the typical clerical controls:

(d) collection and sorting of input documentation;

(e) generation of batches with all associated controls;

(f) checking of control data with output;

There would obviously be other administrative controls but these are not included here.

Many systems are now networked. This provides increased risks. Security over access to the system and physical security over computer terminals is important – even so far as routers and bridges on the network. It is essential that software security is addressed.

Essential points to note in this respect is that the security precautions taken are only as good as the staff that operate them and if the number of staff has reduced to such a degree that there is no real segregation or checking then those controls, even with the best will in the world, will not succeed.

2. This question could have almost an infinite number of answers. Below are a selection of possible questions to be included on the checklist.

Software evaluation

(a) What versions of the software are in use?

(b) Are they the most up-to-date?

(c) Have any 'bugs' been identified?

(d) Is the application in its standard form or have modifications been performed?

(e) Does the client possess documentation to show how to use the software?

(f) As auditors, do we have other clients who use the same software?

(g) Are there any known problems?

(h) Has the client experienced any significant problems using this software – if so how were they resolved?

(i) Are current legal requirements automatically updated on the software (PAYE/VAT) or does the client have to request such updates ? Has the client actually done so?

Implementation

(a) Who installed the software?

(b) How qualified were they?

(c) Are there any technical back-up facilities present?

(d) Who converted the old filing system (manual or computerised) to the new system?

(e) What checks were performed?

Security

(a) Can the client staff access or amend the source code of the software?

(b) Have any of the client staff the known ability to amend the software?

(c) Is the network organized in such a way that access to data and software is limited only to those people who need to access the software or data?

(d) Is access to software and data controlled by appropriate means (password etc.)?

(e) Is virus protection in place?

(f) Are staff allowed to run software off the removable drives on the computer workstations or is the facility removed?

(g) Are backups regularly taken, stored away from the workplace, and tested on a regular basis to ensure that the restoration procedures work?

Chapter 14

1. SAS 610 comprises two brief sections:

(a) SAS 610.1 – auditors must assess the matters that they have discovered during the course of their audit and decide whether or not they should be communicated to management.

(b) SAS 610.2 – when a material weakness in the accounting or system of internal control is discovered during the audit, then the auditor should report them in writing to the directors, audit committee or an appropriate level of management on a timely basis.

This latter section includes such areas as errors (both adjusted and unadjusted) and inappropriate accounting policies or practices. The interesting point to note is that the standard says 'timely basis'. This means that the report does not have to be a formal letter (management letter) but may be raised orally and later communicated by way of a note for discussion at, say, a directors' or management meeting.

If fraud is discovered or suspected – either material or immaterial – the auditors should report as soon as possible. If non-compliance with the law or regulations is discovered it is essential that the management is informed and, if the non-compliance is intentional, then a report should be made to a higher level of authority who is not involved. This is termed a 'report direct' to a proper authority 'in the public interest'.

It is this last section that could cause the greatest problem in the relationship between the directors/management and the auditor. If there is non-compliance with the law, the auditor finds it and then finds that it is deliberate then he is obliged to report. This 'whistleblowing' action is surely going to cause the level of trust to diminish.

In practice, however, it could be said that SAS 610 will simply enhance the value of the normal 'letter of weakness' or 'management letter'. This has long been the normal method of providing post-audit observations to the client. Directors are accustomed to this and it is a medium where the auditor can report both the material matters and those matters that he considers will enhance the 'value' of the audit. There can only be an improvement in the director/management/auditor relationship.

2. There are many points at issue here. One of the first is whether it can be argued that 'lowballing' is a valid issue. If the competition is from firms of similar size and structure and one offers the services for half of the price of the other – or offers discounts and add-on services free of charge – then there can be little doubt that lowballing has occurred. However, if the two firms are totally different in size, then it is a different matter since the costs incurred and charge-out rates used for professional staff are totally different. Hence costing differs and so will the final charge.

   Overall competitive pricing is a bigger threat to the smaller firms. It is they who cannot reallocate the costs to other areas of business. Clients however tend to be guided not only by the price. They appreciate a job well done. Predatory pricing is often linked with poor quality work at the smaller end of the market. The lowest price is no longer a guarantee of winning the audit tender at the higher end of the market and in the future the same may well apply at the lower end of the market.

Index